HOLINESS

&

Selected Sermons

by

J. C. Ryle

Printed on acid free ANSI archival quality paper.
ISBN: 978-1-78139-541-7

Contents

HOLINESS

FOREWORD

ONE of the most encouraging and hopeful signs I have observed for many a long day in evangelical circles has been a renewed and increasing interest in the writings of Bishop J. C. Ryle.

In his day he was famous, outstanding and beloved as a champion and exponent of the evangelical and reformed faith. For some reason or other, however, his name and his works are not familiar to modern evangelicals. His books are, I believe, all out of print in this country and very difficult to obtain secondhand.

The differing fates suffered in this respect by Bishop Ryle and his near contemporary, Bishop Moule, have always been to me a matter of great interest. But Bishop Ryle is being rediscovered, and there is a new call for the re-publication of his works.

All who have ever read him will be grateful for this new edition of his great book on Holiness'. I shall never forget the satisfaction--spiritual and mental--with which I read it some twenty years ago after having stumbled across it in a second-hand book shop.

It really needs no preface or word of introduction. All I will do is to urge all readers to read the Bishop's own Introduction. It is invaluable as it provides the setting in which he felt impelled to write the book.

The characteristics of Bishop Ryle's method and style are obvious. He is pre-eminently and always scriptural and expository. He never starts with a theory into which he tries to fit various scriptures. He always starts with the Word and expounds it. It is exposition at its very best and highest. It is always clear and logical and invariably leads to a clear enunciation of doctrine. It is strong and virile and entirely free from the sentimentality that is often described as "devotional."

The Bishop had drunk deeply from the wells of the great classical Puritan writers of the seventeenth century. Indeed, it would be but accurate to say that his books are a distillation of true Puritan theology presented in a highly readable and modern form.

Ryle, like his great masters, has no easy way to holiness to offer us, and no "patent" method by which it can be attained; but he invariably produces that "hunger and thirst after righteousness" which is the only indispensable condition to being "filled."

May this book be widely read, that God's name be increasingly honoured and glorified.

D. M. Lloyd-Jones.
Westminster Chapel.

INTRODUCTION

The twenty papers contained in this volume are a humble contribution to a cause which is exciting much interest in the present day,--I mean the cause of Scriptural holiness. It is a cause which everyone who loves Christ, and desires to advance His kingdom in the world, should endeavour to help forward. Everyone can do something, and I wish to add my mite.

The reader will find little that is directly controversial in these papers. I have carefully abstained from naming modern teachers and modern books. I have been content to give the result of my own study of the Bible, my own private meditations, my own prayers for light, and my own reading of old divines. If in anything I am still in error, I hope I shall be shown it before I leave the world. We all see in part, and have a treasure in earthen vessels. I trust I am willing to learn.

I have had a deep conviction for many years that practical holiness and entire self-consecration to God are not sufficiently attended to by modern Christians in this country. Politics, or controversy, or party-spirit, or worldliness, have eaten out the heart of lively piety in too many of us. The subject of personal godliness has fallen sadly into the background. The standard of living has become painfully low in many quarters. The immense importance of "adorning the doctrine of God our Saviour" (Titus ii. 10), and making it lovely and beautiful by our daily habits and tempers, has been far too much overlooked. Worldly people sometimes complain with reason that "religious" persons, so-called, are not so amiable and unselfish and good-natured as others who make no profession of religion. Yet sanctification, in its place and proportion, is quite as important as justification. Sound Protestant and Evangelical doctrine is useless if it is not accompanied by a holy life. It is worse than useless: it does positive harm. It is despised by keen-sighted and shrewd men of the world, as an unreal and hollow thing, and brings religion into contempt. It is my firm impression that we want a thorough revival about Scriptural holiness, and I am deeply thankful that attention is being directed to the point.

It is, however, of great importance that the whole subject should be placed on right foundations, and that the movement about it should not be damaged by crude, disproportioned, and one-sided statements. If such statements abound, we must not be surprised. Satan knows well the power of true holiness, and the immense injury which increased attention to it will do to his kingdom. It is his interest, therefore, to promote strife and controversy about this part of God's truth. Just as in time past he has succeeded in mystifying and confusing men's minds about justification, so he is labouring in the present day to make men "darken counsel by words without knowledge" about sanctification. May the Lord rebuke him! I cannot however give up the hope that good will be brought out of evil, that discussion will elicit truth, and that variety of opinion will lead us all to search the Scriptures more, to pray more, and to become more diligent in trying to find out what is "the mind of the Spirit."

I now feel it a duty, in sending forth this volume, to offer a few introductory hints to those whose attention is specially directed to the subject of sanctification in the present day. I know that I do so at the risk of seeming presumptuous, and possibly of giving offence. But something must be ventured in the interests of God's truth. I shall therefore put my hints into the form of questions, and I shall request my readers to take them as "Cautions for the Times on the subject of holiness."

(1) I ask, in the first place, whether it is wise to speak of faith as the one thing needful, and the only thing required, as many seem to do now-a-days in handling the doctrine of sanctification?--Is it wise to proclaim in so bald, naked, and unqualified a way as many do, that the holiness of converted people is by faith only, and not at all by personal exertion? Is it according to the proportion of God's Word? I doubt it.

That faith in Christ is the root of all holiness--that the first step towards a holy life is to believe on Christ--that until we believe we have not a jot of holiness--that union with Christ by faith is the secret of both beginning to be holy and continuing holy--that the life that we live in the flesh we must live by the faith of the Son of God--that faith purifies the heart--that faith is the victory which overcomes the world--that by faith the elders obtained a good report--all these are truths which no well-instructed Christian will ever think of denying. But surely the Scriptures teach us that in following holiness the true Christian needs personal exertion and work as well as faith. The very same Apostle who says in one place, "The life that I live in the flesh I live by the faith of the Son of God," says in another place, "I fight--I run--I keep under my body;" and in other places, "Let us cleanse ourselves--let us labour, let us lay aside every weight." (Gal. ii. 20; 1 Cor. ix. 26; 2 Cor. vii. 1; Heb. iv. 11; xii. 1 .) Moreover, the Scriptures nowhere teach us that faith sanctifies us in the same sense, and in the same manner, that faith justifies us! Justifying faith is a grace that "worketh not," but simply trusts, rests, and leans on Christ. (Rom. iv. 5.) Sanctifying faith is a grace of which the very life is action: it "worketh by love," and, like a main-spring, moves the whole inward man. (Gal. v. 6.) After all, the precise phrase "sanctified by faith" is only found once in the New Testament. The Lord Jesus said to Saul, "I send thee, that they may receive forgiveness of sins and inheritance among them which are sanctified by faith that is in Me." Yet even there I agree with Alford, that "by faith" belongs to the whole sentence, and must not be tied to the word "sanctified." The true sense is, "that by faith in Me they may receive forgiveness of sins and inheritance among them that are sanctified." (Compare Acts xxvi. 18 with Acts xx. 32.)

As to the phrase "holiness by faith," I find it nowhere in the New Testament. Without controversy, in the matter of our justification before God, faith in Christ is the one thing needful. All that simply believe are justified. Righteousness is imputed "to him that worketh not but believeth." (Rom. iv. 5.) It is thoroughly Scriptural and right to say "faith alone justifies." But it is not equally Scriptural and right so say "faith alone sanctifies." The saying requires very large qualification. Let one fact suffice. We are frequently told that a man is "justified by faith without the deeds of the law," by St. Paul. But not once are we told that we are "sanctified by faith without the deeds of the law." On the contrary, we are expressly told by St. James that the faith whereby we are visibly and demonstratively justified before man, is a faith which "if it hath not works is dead, being alone."[1] (James ii. 17.) I may be told, in reply, that no one of course means to disparage "works" as an essential part of a holy life. It would be well, however, to make this more plain than many seem to make it in these days.

(2) I ask, in the second place, whether it is wise to make so little as some appear to do, comparatively, of the many practical exhortations to holiness in daily life which are to be

found in the Sermon on the Mount, and in the latter part of most of St. Paul's epistles? Is it according to the proportion of God's Word? I doubt it.

That a life of daily self-consecration and daily communion with God should be aimed at by everyone who professes to be a believer--that we should strive to attain the habit of going to the Lord Jesus Christ with everything we find a burden, whether great or small, and casting it upon Him--all this, I repeat, no well-taught child of God will dream of disputing. But surely the New Testament teaches us that we want something more than generalities about holy living, which often prick no conscience and give no offence. The details and particular ingredients of which holiness is composed in daily life, ought to be fully set forth and pressed on believers by all who profess to handle the subject. True holiness does not consist merely of believing and feeling, but of doing and bearing, and a practical exhibition of active and passive grace. Our tongues, our tempers, our natural passions and inclinations--our conduct as parents and children, masters and servants, husbands and wives, rulers and subjects--our dress, our employment of time, our behaviour in business, our demeanour in sickness and health, in riches and in poverty--all, all these are matters which are fully treated by inspired writers. They are not content with a general statement of what we should believe and feel, and how we are to have the roots of holiness planted in our hearts. They dig down lower. They go into particulars. They specify minutely what a holy man ought to do and be in his own family, and by his own fireside, if he abides in Christ. I doubt whether this sort of teaching is sufficiently attended to in the movement of the present day. When people talk of having received "such a blessing," and of having found "the higher life," after hearing some earnest advocate of "holiness by faith and self-consecration," while their families and friends see no improvement and no increased sanctity in their daily tempers and behaviour, immense harm is done to the cause of Christ. True holiness, we surely ought to remember, does not consist merely of inward sensations and impressions. It is much more than tears, and sighs, and bodily excitement, and a quickened pulse, and a passionate feeling of attachment to our own favourite preachers and our own religious party, and a readiness to quarrel with everyone who does not agree with us. It is something of "the image of Christ," which can be seen and observed by others in our private life, and habits, and character, and doings. (Rom. viii. 29.)

(3) I ask, in the third place, whether it is wise to use vague language about perfection, and to press on Christians a standard of holiness, as attainable in this world for which there is no warrant to be shown either in Scripture or experience? I doubt it.

That believers are exhorted to "perfect holiness in the fear of God"--to "go on to perfection"--to "be perfect," no careful reader of his Bible will ever think of denying. (2 Cor. vii. 1 ; Heb. vi. 1 ; 2 Cor. xiii. 11.) But I have yet to learn that there is a single passage in Scripture which teaches that a literal perfection, a complete and entire freedom from sin, in thought, or word, or deed, is attainable, or ever has been attained, by any child of Adam in this world. A comparative perfection, a perfection in knowledge, an all-round consistency in every relation of life, a thorough soundness in every point of doctrine--this may be seen occasionally in some of God's believing people. But as to an absolute literal perfection, the most eminent saints of God in every age have always been the very last to lay claim to it! On the contrary, they have always had the deepest sense of their own utter unworthiness and imperfection. The more spiritual light they have enjoyed the more they have seen their own countless defects and shortcomings. The more grace they have had the more they have been "clothed with humility." (1 Peter v. 5.)

What saint can be named in God's Word, of whose life many details are recorded, who was literally and absolutely perfect? Which of them all, when writing about himself, ever talks of feeling free from imperfection? On the contrary, men like David, and St. Paul, and St. John, declare in the strongest language that they feel in their own hearts weakness and sin. The holiest men of modern times have always been remarkable for deep humility. Have we ever seen holier men than the martyred John Bradford, or Hooker, or Usher, or Baxter, or Rutherford, or M'Cheyne? Yet no one can read the writings and letters of these men without seeing that they felt themselves "debtors to mercy and grace" every day, and the very last thing they ever laid claim to was perfection!

In face of such facts as these I must protest against the language used in many quarters, in these last days, about perfection. I must think that those who use it either know very little of the nature of sin, or of the attributes of God, or of their own hearts, or of the Bible, or of the meaning of words. When a professing Christian coolly tells me that he has got beyond such hymns as "Just as I am," and that they are below his present experience, though they suited him when he first took up religion, I must think his soul is in a very unhealthy state! When a man can talk coolly of the possibility of "living without sin" while in the body, and can actually say that he has "never had an evil thought for three months," I can only say that in my opinion he is a very ignorant Christian! I protest against such teaching as this. It not only does no good, but does immense harm. It disgusts and alienates from religion far-seeing men of the world, who know it is incorrect and untrue. It depresses some of the best of God's children, who feel they never can attain to "perfection" of this kind. It puffs up many weak brethren, who fancy they are something when they are nothing. In short, it is a dangerous delusion.

(4) In the fourth place, is it wise to assert so positively and violently, as many do, that the seventh chapter of the Epistle to the Romans does not describe the experience of the advanced saint, but the experience of the unregenerate man, or of the weak and un-established believer? I doubt it.

I admit fully that the point has been a disputed one for eighteen centuries, in fact ever since the days of St. Paul. I admit fully that eminent Christians like John and Charles Wesley, and Fletcher, a hundred years ago, to say nothing of some able writers of our own time, maintain firmly that St. Paul was not describing his own present experience when he wrote this seventh chapter. I admit fully that many cannot see what I and many others do see: viz., that Paul says nothing in this chapter which does not precisely tally with the recorded experience of the most eminent saints in every age, and that he does say several things which no unregenerate man or weak believer would ever think of saying, and cannot say. So, at any rate, it appears to me. But I will not enter into any detailed discussion of the chapter.[2]

What I do lay stress upon is the broad fact that the best commentators in every era of the Church have almost invariably applied the seventh chapter of Romans to advanced believers. The commentators who do not take this view have been, with a few bright exceptions, the Romanists, the Socinians, and the Arminians. Against them is arrayed the judgment of almost all the Reformers, almost all the Puritans, and the best modern Evangelical divines. I shall be told, of course, that no man is infallible, that the Reformers, Puritans, and modern divines I refer to may have been entirely mistaken, and the Romanists, Socinians, and Arminians may have been quite right! Our Lord has taught us, no doubt, to "call no man master." But while I ask no man to call the Reformers and Puritans "masters," I do ask people to read what they say on this subject, and answer their arguments, if they can. This has not been done yet! To say, as some do, that they do not want human "dogmas" and "doctrines," is no reply at all. The whole point at issue is, "What is the meaning of a passage of Scripture? How is the Seventh chapter of the Epistle to the Romans to be interpreted? What is the true sense of its words?" At any rate let us remember that there is a great fact which cannot be got over. On one side stand the opinions and interpretation of Reformers and Puritans, and on the other the opinions and interpretations of Romanists, Socinians, and Arminians. Let that be distinctly understood.

In the face of such a fact as this I must enter my protest against the sneering, taunting, contemptuous language which has been frequently used of late by some of the advocates of what I must call the Arminian view of the Seventh of Romans, in speaking of the opinions of their opponents. To say the least, such language is unseemly, and only defeats its own end. A cause which is defended by such language is deservedly suspicious. Truth needs no such weapons. If we cannot agree with men, we need not speak of their views with discourtesy and contempt. An opinion which is backed and supported by such men as the best Reformers and Puritans may not carry conviction to all minds in the nineteenth century, but at any rate it would be well to speak of it with respect.

(5) In the fifth place, is it wise to use the language which is often used in the present day about the doctrine of "Christ in us"? I doubt it. Is not this doctrine often exalted to a position which it does not occupy in Scripture? I am afraid that it is.

That the true believer is one with Christ and Christ in him, no careful reader of the New Testament will think of denying for a moment. There is, no doubt, a mystical union between Christ and the believer. With Him we died, with Him we were buried, with Him we rose again, with Him we sit in heavenly places. We have five plain texts where we are distinctly taught that Christ is "in us." (Rom. viii. 10; Gal. ii. 20; iv. 19; Eph. iii. 17; Col. iii. 11.) But we must be careful that we understand what we mean by the expression. That "Christ dwells in our hearts by faith," and carries on His inward work by His Spirit, is clear and plain. But if we mean to say that beside, and over, and above this there is some mysterious indwelling of Christ in a believer, we must be careful what we are about. Unless we take care, we shall find ourselves ignoring the work of the Holy Ghost. We shall be forgetting that in the Divine economy of man's salvation election is the special work of God the Father--atonement, mediation, and intercession, the special work of God the Son--and sanctification, the special work of God the Holy Ghost. We shall be forgetting that our Lord said, when He went away, that He would send us another Comforter, who should "abide with us" for ever, and, as it were, take His place. (John xiv. 16.) In short, under the idea that we are honouring Christ, we shall find that we are dishonouring His special and peculiar gift--the Holy Ghost. Christ, no doubt, as God, is everywhere--in our hearts, in heaven, in the place where two or three are met together in His name. But we really must remember that Christ, as our risen Head and High Priest, is specially at God's right hand interceding for us until He comes the second time; and that Christ carries on His work in the hearts of His people by the special work of His Spirit, whom He promised to send when He left the world. (John xv. 26.) A comparison of the ninth and tenth verses of the eighth chapter of Romans seems to me to show this plainly. It convinces me that "Christ in us" means Christ in us "by His Spirit." Above all, the words of St. John are most distinct and express: "Hereby we know that He abideth in us by the Spirit which He hath given us." (1 John iii. 24.)

In saying all this, I hope no one will misunderstand me. I do not say that the expression. "Christ in us" is unscriptural. But I do say that I see great danger of giving an extravagant and unscriptural importance to the idea contained in the expression; and I do fear that many use it now-a-days without exactly knowing what they mean, and unwittingly, perhaps, dishonour the mighty work of the Holy Ghost. If any readers think that I am needlessly scrupulous about the point, I recommend to their notice a curious book by Samuel Rutherford (author of the well-known letters), called "The Spiritual Antichrist." They will there see that two centuries ago the wildest heresies arose out of an extravagant teaching of this very doctrine of the "indwelling of Christ" in believers. They will find that Saltmarsh, and Dell, and Towne, and other false teachers, against whom good Samuel Rutherford contended, began with strange notions of "Christ in us," and then proceeded to build on the doctrine antinomianism, and fanaticism of the worst description and vilest tendency. They maintained that the separate, personal life of the believer was so completely gone, that it was Christ living in him who repented, and believed, and acted! The root of this huge error was a forced and unscriptural interpretation of such texts as "I live: yet not I, but Christ liveth in me." (Gal. ii. 20.) And the natural result of it was that many of the unhappy followers of this school came to the comfortable conclusion that believers were not responsible, whatever they might do! Believers, forsooth, were dead and buried; and only Christ lived in them, and undertook everything for them! The ultimate consequence was, that some thought they might sit still in a carnal security, their personal accountableness being entirely gone, and might commit any kind of sin without fear! Let us never forget that truth, distorted and exaggerated, can become the mother of the most dangerous heresies. When we speak of "Christ being in us," let us take care to explain what we mean. I fear some neglect this in the present day.

(6) In the sixth place, is it wise to draw such a deep, wide, and distinct line of separation between conversion and consecration, or the higher life, so called, as many do draw in the present day? Is this according to the proportion of God's Word? I doubt it.

There is, unquestionably, nothing new in this teaching. It is well known that Romish writers often maintain that the Church is divided into three classes--sinners, penitents, and saints. The modern teachers of this day who tell us that professing Christians are of three sorts--the unconverted, the converted, and the partakers of the "higher life" of complete consecration--appear to me to occupy very much the same ground! But whether the idea be old or new, Romish or English, I am utterly unable to see that it has any warrant of Scripture. The Word of God always speaks of two great divisions of mankind, and two only. It speaks of the living and the dead in sin--the believer and the unbeliever--the converted and the unconverted--the travellers in the narrow way and the travellers in the broad--the wise and the foolish--the children of God and the children of the devil. Within each of these two great classes there are, doubtless, various measures of sin and of grace; but it is only the difference between the higher and lower end of an inclined plane. Between these two great classes there is an enormous gulf; they are as distinct as life and death, light and darkness, heaven and hell. But of a division into three classes the Word of God says nothing at all! I question the wisdom of making new-fangled divisions which the Bible has not made, and I thoroughly dislike the notion of a second conversion.

That there is a vast difference between one degree of grace and another--that spiritual life admits of growth, and that believers should be continually urged on every account to grow in grace--all this I fully concede. But the theory of a sudden, mysterious transition of a believer into a state of blessedness and entire consecration, at one mighty bound, I cannot receive. It appears to me to be a man-made invention; and I do not see a single plain text to prove it in Scripture. Gradual growth in grace, growth in knowledge, growth in faith, growth in love, growth in holiness, growth in humility, growth in spiritual-mindedness--all this I see clearly taught and urged in Scripture, and clearly exemplified in the lives of many of God's saints. But sudden, instantaneous leaps from conversion to consecration I fail to see in the Bible. I doubt, indeed, whether we have any warrant for saying that a man can possibly be converted without being consecrated to God! More consecrated he doubtless can be, and will be as his grace increases; but if he was not consecrated to God in the very day that he was converted and born again, I do not know what conversion means. Are not men in danger of undervaluing and underrating the immense blessedness of conversion? Are they not, when they urge on believers the "higher life" as a second conversion, underrating the length, and breadth, and depth, and height, of that great first change which Scripture calls the new birth, the new creation, the spiritual resurrection? I may be mistaken. But I have sometimes thought, while reading the strong language used by many about "consecration," in the last few years, that those who use it must have had previously a singularly low and inadequate view of "conversion," if indeed they knew anything about conversion at all. In short, I have almost suspected that when they were consecrated, they were in reality converted for the first time!

I frankly confess I prefer the old paths. I think it wiser and safer to press on all converted people the possibility of continual growth in grace, and the absolute necessity of going forward, increasing more and more, and every year dedicating and consecrating themselves more, in spirit, soul, and body, to Christ. By all means let us teach that there is more holiness to be attained, and more of heaven to be enjoyed upon earth than most believers now experience. But I decline to tell any converted man that he needs a second conversion, and that he may some day or other pass by one enormous step into a state of entire consecration. I decline to teach it, because I cannot see any warrant for such teaching in Scripture. I decline to teach it, because I think the tendency of the doctrine is thoroughly mischievous, depressing the humble-minded and meek, and puffing up the shallow, the ignorant, and the self-conceited, to a most dangerous extent.

(7) In the seventh and last place, is it wise to teach believers that they ought not to think so much of fighting and struggling against sin, but ought rather to "yield themselves to God" and be passive in the hands of Christ? Is this according to the proportion of God's Word? I doubt it.

It is a simple fact that the expression "yield yourselves" is only to be found in one place in the New Testament, as a duty urged upon believers. That place is in the sixth chapter of Romans, and there within six verses the expression occurs five times. (See Rom. vi. 13-19.) But even there the word will not bear the sense of "placing ourselves passively in the hands of another." Any Greek student can tell us that the sense is rather that of actively "presenting" ourselves for use, employment, and service. (See Rom. xii. 1.) The expression therefore stands alone. But, on the other hand, it would not be difficult to point out at least twenty-five or thirty distinct passages in the Epistles where believers are plainly taught to use active personal exertion, and are addressed as responsible for doing energetically what Christ would have them do, and are not told to "yield themselves" up as passive agents and sit still, but to arise and work. A holy violence, a conflict, a warfare, a fight, a soldier's life, a wrestling, are spoken of as characteristic of the true Christian. The account of "the armour of God" in the sixth chapter of Ephesians, one might think, settles the question.[3] --Again, it would be easy to show that the doctrine of sanctification without personal exertion, by simply "yielding ourselves to God," is precisely the doctrine of the antinomian fanatics in the seventeenth century (to whom I have referred already, described in Rutherford's Spiritual Antichrist), and that the tendency of it is evil in the extreme.--Again, it would be easy to show that the doctrine is utterly subversive of the whole teaching of such tried and approved books as Pilgrim's Pro-Progress, and that if we receive it we cannot do better than put Bunyan's old book in the fire! If Christian in Pilgrim's Progress simply yielded himself to God, and never fought, or struggled, or wrestled, I have read the famous allegory in vain. But the plain truth is, that men will persist in confounding two things that differ--that is, justification and sanctification. In justification the word to be addressed to man is believe--only believe; in sanctification the word must be "watch, pray, and fight." What God has divided let us not mingle and confuse.

I leave the subject of my introduction here, and hasten to a conclusion. I confess that I lay down my pen with feelings of sorrow and anxiety. There is much in the attitude of professing Christians in this day which fills me with concern, and makes me full of fear for the future.

There is an amazing ignorance of Scripture among many, and a consequent want of established, solid religion. In no other way can I account for the ease with which people are, like children, "tossed to and fro, and carried about by every wind of doctrine." (Eph. iv. 14.) There is an Athenian love of novelty abroad, and a morbid distaste for anything old and regular, and in the beaten path of our forefathers. Thousands will crowd to hear a new voice and a new doctrine, without considering for a moment whether what they hear is true.--There is an incessant craving after any teaching which is sensational, and exciting, and rousing to the feelings.--There is an unhealthy appetite for a sort of spasmodic and hysterical Christianity. The religious life of many is little better than spiritual dram-drinking, and the "meek and quiet spirit" which St. Peter commends is clean forgotten, (1 Peter iii. 4.) Crowds, and crying, and hot rooms, and high-flown singing, and an incessant rousing of the emotions, are the only things which many care for.--Inability to distinguish differences in doctrine is spreading far and wide, and so long as the preacher is "clever" and "earnest," hundreds seem to think it must be all right, and call you dreadfully "narrow and uncharitable" if you hint that he is unsound I Moody and Haweis, Dean Stanley and Canon Liddon, Mackonochie and Pearsall Smith, all seem to be alike in the eyes of such people. All this is sad, very sad. But if, in addition to this, the true-hearted advocates of increased holiness are going to fall out by the way and misunderstand one another, it will be sadder still. We shall indeed be in evil plight.

For myself, I am aware that I am no longer a young minister. My mind perhaps stiffens, and I cannot easily receive any new doctrine. "The old is better." I suppose I belong to the old school of Evangelical theology, and I am therefore content with such teaching about sanctification as I find in the Life of Faith of Sibbes and of Manton, and in The Life, Walk, and Triumph of Faith of William Romaine. But I must express a hope that my younger brethren who have taken up new views of holiness will beware of multiplying causeless divisions. Do they think that a higher standard of Christian living is needed in the present day? So do I.--Do they think that clearer, stronger, fuller teaching about holiness is needed? So do I.--Do they think that Christ ought to be more exalted as the root and author of sanctification as well as justification? So do I.--Do they think that believers should be urged more and more to live by faith? So do I.--Do they think that a very close walk with God should be more pressed on believers as the secret of happiness and usefulness? So do I.--In all these things we agree. But if they want to go further, then I ask them to take care where they tread, and to explain very clearly and distinctly what they mean.

Finally, I must deprecate, and I do it in love, the use of uncouth and new-fangled terms and phrases in teaching sanctification. I plead that a movement in favour of holiness cannot be advanced by new-coined phraseology, or by disproportioned and one-sided statements--or by overstraining and isolating particular texts--or by exalting one truth at the expense of another--or by allegorizing and accommodating texts, and squeezing out of them meanings which the Holy Ghost never put in them--or by speaking contemptuously and bitterly of those who do not entirely see things with our eyes, and do not work exactly in our ways. These things do not make for peace: they rather repel many and keep them at a distance. The cause of true sanctification is not helped, but hindered, by such weapons as these. A movement in aid of holiness which produces strife and dispute among God's children is somewhat suspicious. For Christ's sake, and in the name of truth and charity, let us endeavour to follow after peace as well as holiness. "What God has joined together let not man put asunder."

It is my heart's desire, and prayer to God daily, that personal holiness may increase greatly among professing Christians in England, But I trust that all who endeavour to promote it will adhere closely to the proportion of Scripture, will carefully distinguish things that differ, and will separate "the precious from the vile." (Jer. xv. 19.)

ENDNOTE

[1] "There is a double justification by God: the one authoritative, the other declarative or demonstrative."--The first is St. Paul's scope, when he speaks of justification by faith without the deeds of the law. The second is St. James' scope, when he speaks of justification by works."--T. Goodwin on Gospel Holiness. Works, vol. vii, p. 181.

[2] Those who care to go into the subject will find it fully discussed in the Commentaries of Willet, Elton, Chalmers, and Haldane, and in Owen on Indwelling Sin, and in the work of Stafford on the Seventh of Romans.

[3] Old Sibbe's Sermon on "Victorious Violence" deserves the attention of all who have his works.--Vol. vii., p. 30.

HOLINESS

I. SIN

"Sin is the transgression of the law."--1 John iii. 4.

He that wishes to attain right views about Christian holiness, must begin by examining the vast and solemn subject of sin. He must dig down very low if he would build high. A mistake here is most mischievous. Wrong views about holiness are generally traceable to wrong views about human corruption. I make no apology for beginning this volume of papers about holiness by making some plain statements about sin.

The plain truth is that a right knowledge of sin lies at the root of all saving Christianity. Without it such doctrines as justification, conversion, sanctification, are "words and names" which convey no meaning to the mind. The first thing, therefore, that God does when He makes anyone a new creature in Christ, is to send light into his heart, and show him that he is a guilty sinner. The material creation in Genesis began with "light," and so also does the spiritual creation. God "shines into our hearts" by the work of the Holy Ghost, and then spiritual life begins. (2 Cor. iv. 6.)--Dim or indistinct views of sin are the origin of most of the errors, heresies, and false doctrines of the present day. If a man does not realize the dangerous nature of his soul's disease, you cannot wonder if he is content with false or imperfect remedies. I believe that one of the chief wants of the Church in the nineteenth century has been, and is, clearer, fuller teaching about sin.

(1) I shall begin the subject by supplying some definition of sin. We are all of course familiar with the terms "sin" and "sinners." We talk frequently of "sin" being in the world, and of men committing "sins." But what do we mean by these terms and phrases? Do we really know? I fear there is much mental confusion and haziness on this point. Let me try, as briefly as possible, to supply an answer.

I say, then, that "sin," speaking generally, is, as the Ninth Article of our Church declares, "the fault and corruption of the nature of every man that is naturally engendered of the offspring of Adam; whereby man is very far gone (quam longissime is the Latin) from original righteousness, and is of his own nature inclined to evil, so that the flesh lusteth alway against the spirit; and, therefore, in every person born into the world, it deserveth God's wrath and damnation." Sin, in short, is that vast moral disease which affects the whole human race, of every rank, and class, and name, and nation, and people, and tongue; a disease from which there never was but one born of woman that was free. Need I say that One was Christ Jesus the Lord?

I say, furthermore, that "a sin," to speak more particularly, consists in doing, saying, thinking, or imagining, anything that is not in perfect conformity with the mind and law of God. "Sin," in short, as the Scripture saith, is "the transgression of the law." (1 John iii. 4.)

The slightest outward or inward departure from absolute mathematical parallelism with God's revealed will and character constitutes a sin, and at once makes us guilty in God's sight.

Of course I need not tell any one who reads his Bible with attention, that a man may break God's law in heart and thought, when there is no overt and visible act of wickedness. Our Lord has settled that point beyond dispute in the Sermon on the Mount. (Matt. v. 21-28.) Even a poet of our own has truly said, "A man may smile and smile, and be a villain."

Again, I need not tell a careful student of the New Testament, that there are sins of omission as well as commission, and that we sin, as our Prayer-book justly reminds us, by "leaving undone the things we ought to do," as really as by "doing the things we ought not to do." The solemn words of our Master in the Gospel of St. Matthew place this point also beyond dispute. It is there written, "Depart, ye cursed, into everlasting fire:--for I was an hungered, and ye gave Me no meat; I was thirsty, and ye gave Me no drink." (Matt. xxv. 41, 42.) It was a deep and thoughtful saying of holy Archbishop Usher, just before he died--"Lord, forgive me all my sins, and specially my sins of omission."

But I do think it necessary in these times to remind my readers that a man may commit sin and yet be ignorant of it, and fancy himself innocent when he is guilty. I fail to see any Scriptural warrant for the modern assertion that "Sin is not sin to us until we discern it and are conscious of it." On the contrary, in the 4th and 5th chapters of that unduly neglected book, Leviticus, and in the 15th of Numbers, I find Israel distinctly taught that there were sins of ignorance which rendered people unclean, and needed atonement. (Levit. iv. 1-35; v. 14-19; Num. xv. 25-29.) And I find our Lord expressly teaching that "the servant who knew not his master's will and did it not," was not excused on account of his ignorance, but was "beaten" or punished. (Luke xii. 48.) We shall do well to remember, that when we make our own miserably imperfect knowledge and consciousness the measure of our sinfulness, we are on very dangerous ground. A deeper study of Leviticus might do us much good.

(2) Concerning the origin and source of this vast moral disease called "sin" I must say something. I fear the views of many professing Christians on this point are sadly defective and unsound. I dare not pass it by. Let us, then, have it fixed down in our minds that the sinfulness of man does not begin from without, but from within. It is not the result of bad training in early years. It is not picked up from bad companions and bad examples, as some weak Christians are too fond of saying. No! it is a family disease, which we all inherit from our first parents, Adam and Eve, and with which we are born. Created "in the image of God," innocent and righteous at first, our parents fell from original righteousness and became sinful and corrupt. And from that day to this all men and women are born in the image of fallen Adam and Eve, and inherit a heart and nature inclined to evil. "By one man sin entered into the world."--"That which is born of the flesh is flesh."--"We are by nature children of wrath."--"The carnal mind is enmity against God."--"Out of the heart (naturally as out of a fountain) proceed evil thoughts, adulteries," and the like. (John iii. 6; Ephes. ii. 3; Rom. viii. 7; Mark vii. 21.) The fairest babe that has entered life this year, and become the sunbeam of a family, is not, as its mother perhaps fondly calls it, a little "angel," or a little "innocent," but a little "sinner." Alas! as it lies smiling and crowing in its cradle, that little creature carries in its heart the seeds of every kind of wickedness! Only watch it carefully, as it grows in stature and its mind developes, and you will soon detect in it an incessant tendency to that which is bad, and a backwardness to that which is good. You will see in it the buds and germs of deceit, evil temper, selfishness, self-will, obstinacy, greediness, envy, jealousy, passion--which, if indulged and let alone, will shoot up with painful rapidity. Who taught the child these things?

Where did he learn them? The Bible alone can answer these questions!--Of all the foolish things that parents say about their children there is none worse than the common saying, "My son has a good heart at the bottom. He is not what he ought to be; but he has fallen into bad hands. Public schools are bad places. The tutors neglect the boys. Yet he has a good heart at the bottom."--The truth, unhappily, is diametrically the other way. The first cause of all sin lies in the natural corruption of the boy's own heart, and not in the school.

(3) Concerning the extent of this vast moral disease of man called sin, let us beware that we make no mistake. The only safe ground is that which is laid for us in Scripture. "Every imagination of the thoughts of his heart" is by nature "evil, and that continually."--"The heart is deceitful above all things, and desperately wicked," (Gen. vi. 5; Jer. xvii. 9.) Sin is a disease which pervades and runs through every part of our moral constitution and every faculty of our minds. The understanding, the affections, the reasoning powers, the will, are all more or less infected. Even the conscience is so blinded that it cannot be depended on as a sure guide, and is as likely to lead men wrong as right, unless it is enlightened by the Holy Ghost. In short, "from the sole of the foot even unto the head there is no soundness" about us. (Isa. i. 6.) The disease may be veiled under a thin covering of courtesy, politeness, good manners, and outward decorum; but it lies deep down in the constitution.

I admit fully that man has many grand and noble faculties left about him, and that in arts and sciences and literature he shows immense capacity. But the fact still remains that in spiritual things he is utterly "dead," and has no natural knowledge, or love, or fear of God. His best things are so interwoven and intermingled with corruption, that the contrast only brings out into sharper relief the truth and extent of the fall. That one and the same creature should be in some things so high and in others so low--so great and yet so little--so noble and yet so mean--so grand in his conception and execution of material things, and yet so grovelling and debased in his affections--that he should be able to plan and erect buildings like those to Carnac and Luxor in Egypt, and the Parthenon at Athens, and yet worship vile gods and goddesses, and birds, and beasts, and creeping things--that he should be able to produce tragedies like those of Æschylus and Sophocles, and histories like that of Thucydides, and yet be a slave to abominable vices like those described in the first chapter of the Epistle to the Romans--all this is a sore puzzle to those who sneer at "God's Word written," and scoff at us as Bibliolaters. But it is a knot that we can untie with the Bible in our hands. We can acknowledge that man has all the marks of a majestic temple about him--a temple in which God once dwelt, but a temple which is now in utter ruins--a temple in which a shattered window here, and a doorway there, and a column there, still give some faint idea of the magnificence of the original design, but a temple which from end to end has lost its glory and fallen from its high estate. And we say that nothing solves the complicated problem of man's condition but the doctrine of original or birth-sin and the crushing effects of the fall.

Let us remember, besides this, that every part of the world bears testimony to the fact that sin is the universal disease of all mankind. Search the globe from east to west and from pole to pole--search every nation of every clime in the four quarters of the earth--search every rank and class in our own country from the highest to the lowest--and under every circumstance and condition, the report will be always the same. The remotest islands in the Pacific Ocean, completely separate from Europe, Asia, Africa, and America, beyond the reach alike of Oriental luxury and Western arts and literature--islands inhabited by people ignorant of books, money, steam, and gunpowder--uncontaminated by the vices of modern civilization-- these very islands have always been found, when first discovered, the abode of the vilest forms of lust, cruelty, deceit, and superstition. If the inhabitants have known nothing else, they have always known how to sin! Everywhere the human heart is naturally "deceitful above all things, and desperately wicked." (Jer. xvii. 9.) For my part, I know no stronger proof of the inspiration of Genesis and' the Mosaic account of the origin of man, than the power, extent, and universality of sin. Grant that mankind have all sprung from one pair, and that this pair fell (as Gen. iii. tells us), and the state of human nature everywhere is easily accounted for. Deny it, as many do, and you are at once involved in inexplicable difficulties. In a word, the uniformity and universality of human corruption supply one of the most unanswerable instances of the enormous "difficulties of infidelity."

After all, I am convinced that the greatest proof of the extent and power of sin is the pertinacity with which it cleaves to man even after he is converted and has become the subject of the Holy Ghost's operations. To use the language of the Ninth Article, "this infection of nature doth remain--yea, even in them that are regenerate." So deeply planted are the roots of human corruption, that even after we are born again, renewed, "washed, sanctified, justified," and made living members of Christ, these roots remain alive in the bottom of our hearts, and, like the leprosy in the walls of the house, we never get rid of them until the earthly house of this tabernacle is dissolved. Sin, no doubt, in the believer's heart, has no longer dominion. It is checked, controlled, mortified, and crucified by the expulsive power of the new principle of grace. The life of a believer is a life of victory, and not of failure. But the very struggles which go on within his bosom, the fight that he finds it needful to fight daily, the watchful jealousy which he is obliged to exercise over his inner man, the contest between the flesh and the spirit, the inward "groanings" which no one knows but he who has experienced them--all, all testify to the same great truth, all show the enormous power and vitality of sin. Mighty indeed must that foe be who even when crucified is still alive! Happy is that believer who understands it, and while he rejoices in Christ Jesus has no confidence in the flesh; and while he says, "Thanks be unto God who giveth us the victory," never forgets to watch and pray lest he fall into temptation!

(4) Concerning the guilt, vileness, and offensivenesS of sin in the sight of God, my words shall be few. I say "few" advisedly. I do not think, in the nature of things, that mortal man can at all realize the exceeding sinfulness of sin in the sight of that holy and perfect One with whom we have to do. On the one hand, God is that eternal Being who "chargeth His angels with folly," and in whose sight the very "heavens are not clean." He is One who reads thoughts and motives as well as actions, and requires "truth in the inward parts." (Job xv. 18; xv. 15; Psa. li. 6.) We, on the other hand--poor blind creatures, here to-day and gone tomorrow, born in sin, surrounded by sinners, living in a constant atmosphere of weakness, infirmity, and imperfection--can form none but the most inadequate conceptions of the hideousness of evil. We have no line to fathom it, and no measure by which to gauge it. The blind man can see no difference between a masterpiece of Titian or Raphael, and the Queen's Head on a village signboard. The deaf man cannot distinguish between a penny whistle and a cathedral organ. The very animals whose smell is most offensive to us have no idea that they are offensive, and are not offensive to one another. And man, fallen man, I believe, can have no just idea what a vile thing sin is in the sight of that God whose handiwork is absolutely perfect--perfect whether we look through telescope or microscope--perfect in the formation of a mighty planet like Jupiter, with his satellites, keeping time to a second as he rolls round the sun--perfect in the formation of the smallest insect that crawls over a foot of ground. But let us nevertheless settle it firmly in our minds that sin is "the abominable thing that God hateth"--that God "is of purer eyes than to behold iniquity, and cannot look upon that which

is evil"--that the least transgression of God's law makes us "guilty of all"--that "the soul that sinneth shall die"--that "the wages of sin is death"--that God shall "judge the secrets of men"--that there is a worm that never dies, and a fire that is not quenched--that "the wicked shall be turned into hell"--and "shall go away into everlasting punishment"--and that "nothing that defiles shall in any wise enter heaven." (Jer. xliv. 4; Hab. i. 13; James ii. 10; Ezek. xviii. 4; Rom. vi. 23; Rom. ii. 16; Mark ix. 44; Ps. ix. 17; Matt. xxv. 46; Rev. xxi. 27.) These are indeed tremendous words, when we consider that they are written in the Book of a most merciful God!

No proof of the fulness of sin, after all, is so overwhelming and unanswerable as the cross and passion of our Lord Jesus Christ, and the whole doctrine of His substitution and atonement. Terribly black must that guilt be for which nothing but the blood of the Son of God could make satisfaction. Heavy must that weight of human sin be which made Jesus groan and sweat drops of blood in agony at Gethsemane, and cry at Golgotha, "My God, my God, why hast Thou forsaken Me?" (Matt. xxvii. 46.) Nothing, I am convinced, will astonish us so much, when we awake in the resurrection day, as the view we shall have of sin, and the retrospect we shall take of our own countless shortcomings and defects. Never till the hour when Christ comes the second time shall we fully realize the "sinfulness of sin." Well might George Whitfield say, "The anthem in heaven will be, What hath God wrought!"

(5) One point only remains to be considered on the subject of sin, which I dare not pass over. That point is its deceitfulness. It is a point of most serious importance, and I venture to think it does not receive the attention which it deserves. You may see this deceitfulness in the wonderful proneness of men to regard sin as less sinful and dangerous than it is in the sight of God; and in their readiness to extenuate it, make excuses for it, and minimize its guilt.--"It is but a little one! God is merciful! God is not extreme to mark what is done amiss! We mean well! One cannot be so particular! Where is the mighty harm? We only do as others!" Who is not familiar with this kind of language?--You may see it in the long string of smooth words and phrases which men have coined in order to designate things which God calls downright wicked and ruinous to the soul. What do such expressions as "fast," "gay," "wild," "unsteady," "thoughtless," "loose" mean? They show that men try to cheat themselves into the belief that sin is not quite so sinful as God says it is, and that they are not so bad as they really are.--You may see it in the tendency even of believers to indulge their children in questionable practices, and to bind their own eyes to the inevitable result of the love of money, of tampering with temptation, and sanctioning a low standard of family religion.--I fear we do not sufficiently realize the extreme subtlety of our soul's disease. We are too apt to forget that temptation to sin will rarely present itself to us in its true colours, saying, "I am your deadly enemy, and I want to ruin you for ever in hell." Oh, no! sin comes to us, like Judas, with a kiss; and like Joab, with an outstretched hand and flattering words. The forbidden fruit seemed good and desirable to Eve; yet it cast her out of Eden. The walking idly on his palace roof seemed harmless enough to David; yet it ended in adultery and murder. Sin rarely seems sin at first beginnings. Let us then watch and pray, lest we fall into temptation. We may give wickedness smooth names, but we cannot alter its nature and character in the sight of God. Let us remember St. Paul's words: "Exhort one another daily, lest any be hardened through the deceitfulness of sin." (Heb. iii. 13.) It is a wise prayer in our Litany, "From the deceits of the world, the flesh, and the devil, good Lord, deliver us."

And now, before I go further, let me briefly mention two thoughts which appear to me to rise with irresistible force out of the subject.

On the one hand, I ask my readers to observe what deep reasons we all have for humiliation and self-abasement. Let us sit down before the picture of sin displayed to us in the Bible, and consider what guilty, vile, corrupt creatures we all are in the sight of God. What need we all have of that entire change of heart called regeneration, new birth, or conversion! What a mass of infirmity and imperfection cleaves to the very best of us at our very best! What a solemn thought it is, that "without holiness no man shall see the Lord!" (Heb. xii. 14.) What cause we have to cry with the publican, every night in our lives, when we think of our sins of omission as well as commission, "God be merciful to me a sinner!" (Luke xviii. 13.) How admirably suited are the general and Communion Confessions of the Prayer-book to the actual condition of all professing Christians! How well that language suits God's children which the Prayer-book puts in the mouth of every Churchman before he goes up to the Communion Table--"The remembrance of our misdoings is grievous unto us; the burden is intolerable. Have mercy upon us, have mercy upon us, most merciful Father; for Thy Son our Lord Jesus Christ's sake, forgive us all that is past." How true it is that the holiest saint is in himself a miserable sinner," and a debtor to mercy and grace to the last moment of his existence!

With my whole heart I subscribe to that passage in Hooker's sermon on Justification, which begins, "Let the holiest and best things we do be considered. We are never better affected unto God than when we pray; yet when we pray, how are our affections many times distracted! How little reverence do we show unto the grand majesty of God unto whom we speak. How little remorse of our own miseries! How little taste of the sweet influence of His tender mercies do we feel! Are we not as unwilling many times to begin, and as glad to make an end, as if in saying, Call upon Me,' He had set us a very burdensome task? It may seem somewhat extreme, which I will speak; therefore, let every one judge of it, even as his own heart shall tell him, and not otherwise; I will but only make a demand! If God should yield unto us, not as unto Abraham--If fifty, forty, thirty, twenty--yea, or if ten good persons could be found in a city, for their sakes this city should not be destroyed; but, and if He should make us an offer thus large, search all the generations of men since the fall of our father Adam, find one man that hath done one action which hath passed from him pure, without any stain or blemish at all; and for that one man's only action neither man nor angel should feel the torments which are prepared for both. Do you think that this ransom to deliver men and angels could be found to be among the sons of men? The best things which we do have somewhat in them to be pardoned."[4]

That witness is true. For my part I am persuaded the more light we have, the more we see our own sinfulness: the nearer we get to heaven, the more we are clothed with humility. In every age of the Church you will find it true, if you will study biographies, that the most eminent saints--men like Bradford, Rutherford, and McCheyne--have always been the humblest men.

On the other hand, I ask my readers to observe how deeply thankful we ought to be for the glorious Gospel of the grace of God. There is a remedy revealed for man's need, as wide and broad and deep as man's disease. We need not be afraid to look at sin, and study its nature, origin, power, extent, and vileness, if we only look at the same time at the Almighty medicine provided for us in the salvation that is in Jesus Christ. Though sin has abounded, grace has much more abounded. Yes: in the everlasting covenant of redemption, to which Father, Son, and Holy Ghost are parties--in the Mediator of that covenant, Jesus Christ the righteous, perfect God and perfect Man in one Person--in the work that He did by dying for our sins and rising again for our justification--in the offices that He fills as our Priest, Substitute, Physician, Shepherd, and Advocate--in the precious blood He shed which can cleanse from all sin--in the everlasting righteousness that He brought in--in the perpetual intercession that He carries on as our Representative at God's right hand--in His power to save to the uttermost the chief of sinners, His willingness to receive and pardon the vilest, His readiness to bear with the weakest--in the grace of the Holy Spirit which He plants in the hearts of all His people, renewing, sanctifying and causing old things to pass away and all things to become new--in all this--and oh, what a brief sketch it is!--in all this, I say, there is a full, perfect, and complete medicine for the hideous disease of sin. Awful and tremendous as the right view of sin undoubtedly is, no one need faint and despair if he will take a right view of Jesus Christ at the same time. No wonder that old Flavel ends many a chapter of his admirable "Fountain of Life" with the touching words, "Blessed be God for Jesus Christ."

In bringing this mighty subject to a close, I feel that I have only touched the surface of it. It is one which cannot be thoroughly handled in a paper like this. He that would see it treated fully and exhaustively must turn to such masters of experimental theology as Owen, and Burgess, and Manton, and Charnock, and the other giants of the Puritan school. On subjects like this there are no writers to be compared to the Puritans. It only remains for me to point out some practical uses to which the whole doctrine of sin may be profitably turned in the present day.

(a) I say, then, in the first place, that a Scriptural view of sin is one of the best antidotes to that vague, dim, misty, hazy kind of theology which is so painfully current in the present age. It is vain to shut our eyes to the fact that there is a vast quantity of so-called Christianity now-a-days which you cannot declare positively unsound, but which, nevertheless, is not full measure, good weight, and sixteen ounces to the pound. It is a Christianity in which there is undeniably "something about Christ, and something about grace, and something about faith, and something about repentance, and something about holiness"; but it is not the real "thing as it is" in the Bible. Things are out of place, and out of proportion. As old Latimer would have said, it is a kind of "mingle-mangle," and does no good. It neither exercises influence on daily conduct, nor comforts in life, nor gives peace in death; and those who hold it often awake too late to find that they have got nothing solid under their feet. Now I believe the likeliest way to cure and mend this defective kind of religion is to bring forward more prominently the old Scriptural truth about the sinfulness of sin. People will never set their faces decidedly towards heaven, and live like pilgrims, until they really feel that they are in danger of hell. Let us all try to revive the old teaching about sin, in nurseries, in schools, in training colleges, in Universities. Let us not forget that "the law is good if we use it lawfully," and that "by the law is the knowledge of sin." (1 Tim. i. 8; Rom. iii. 20; vii. 7.) Let us bring the law to the front and press it on men's attention. Let us expound and beat out the Ten Commandments, and show the length, and breadth, and depth, and height of their requirements. This is the way of our Lord in the Sermon on the Mount. We cannot do better than follow His plan. We may depend upon it, men will never come to Jesus, and stay with Jesus, and live for Jesus, unless they really know why they are to come, and what is their need. Those whom the Spirit draws to Jesus are those whom the Spirit has convinced of sin. Without thorough conviction of sin, men may seem to come to Jesus and follow Him for a season, but they will soon fall away and return to the world.

(b) In the next place, a Scriptural view of sin is one of the best antidotes to the extravagantly broad and liberal theology which is so much in vogue at the present time. The tendency of modern thought is to reject dogmas, creeds, and every kind of bounds in religion. It is thought grand and wise to condemn no opinion whatsoever, and to pronounce all earnest and clever teachers to be trustworthy, however heterogeneous and mutually destructive their opinions may be.--Everything forsooth is true, and nothing is false! Everybody is right, and nobody is wrong! Everybody is likely to be saved, and nobody is to be lost!--The Atonement and Substitution of Christ, the personality of the devil, the miraculous element in Scripture, the reality and eternity of future punishment, all these mighty foundation-stones are coolly tossed overboard, like lumber, in order to lighten the ship of Christianity, and enable it to keep pace with modern science.--Stand up for these great verities, and you are called narrow, illiberal, old-fashioned, and a theological fossil! Quote a text, and you are told that all truth is not confined to the pages of an ancient Jewish Book, and that free inquiry has found out many things since the Book was completed!--Now, I know nothing so likely to counteract this modern plague as constant clear statements about the nature, reality, vileness, power, and guilt of sin. We must charge home into the consciences of these men of broad views, and demand a plain answer to some plain questions. We must ask them to lay their hands on their hearts, and tell us whether their favourite opinions comfort them in the day of sickness, in the hour of death, by the bedside of dying parents, by the grave of beloved wife or child. We must ask them whether a vague earnestness, without definite doctrine, gives them peace at seasons like these. We must challenge them to tell us whether they do not sometimes feel a gnawing "something" within, which all the free inquiry and philosophy and science in the world cannot satisfy. And then we must tell them that this gnawing "something" is the sense of sin, guilt, and corruption, which they are leaving out in their calculations. And, above all, we must tell them that nothing will ever make them feel rest, but submission to the old doctrines of man's ruin and Christ's redemption, and simple childlike faith in Jesus.

(c) In the next place, a right view of sin is the best antidote to that sensuous, ceremonial, formal kind of Christianity, which has swept over England like a flood in the last twenty-five years, and carried away so many before it. I can well believe that there is much that is attractive in this system of religion, to a certain order of minds, so long as the conscience is not fully enlightened. But when that wonderful part of our constitution called conscience is really awake and alive, I find it hard to believe that a sensuous ceremonial Christianity will thoroughly satisfy us. A little child is easily quieted and amused with gaudy toys, and dolls, and rattles, so long as it is not hungry; but once let it feel the cravings of nature within, and we know that nothing will satisfy it but food. Just so it is with man in the matter of his soul. Music, and flowers, and candles, and incense, and banners, and processions, and beautiful vestments, and confessionals, and man-made ceremonies of a semi-Romish character, may do well enough for him under certain conditions. But once let him "awake and arise from the dead," and he will not rest content with these things. They will seem to him mere solemn triflings, and a waste of time. Once let him see his sin, and he must see his Saviour. He feels stricken with a deadly disease, and nothing will satisfy him but the great Physician. He hungers and thirsts, and he must have nothing less than the bread of life. I may seem bold in what I am about to say; but I fearlessly venture the assertion, that four-fifths of the semi-Romanism of the last quarter of a century would never have existed if English people had been taught more fully and clearly the nature, vileness, and sinfulness of sin.

(d) In the next place, a right view of sin is one of the best antidotes to the overstrained theories of Perfection, of which we hear so much in these times. I shall say but little about this, and in saying it I trust I shall not give offence. If those who press on us perfection mean nothing more than an all-round consistency, and a careful attention to all the graces which make up the Christian character, reason would that we should not only bear with them, but agree with them entirely. By all means let us aim high.--But if men really mean to tell us that here in this world a believer can attain to entire freedom from sin, live for years in unbroken and uninterrupted communion with God, and feel for months together not so much as one evil thought, I must honestly say that such an opinion appears to me very unscriptural.--I go even further. I say that the opinion is very dangerous to him that holds it, and very likely to depress, discourage, and keep back inquirers after salvation. I cannot find the slightest warrant in God's Word for expecting such perfection as this while we are in the body. I believe the words of our Fifteenth Article are strictly true--that "Christ alone is without sin; and that all we, the rest, though baptized and born again in Christ, offend in many things; and if we say that we have no sin, we deceive ourselves, and the truth is not in us."--To use the language of our first Homily, "There be imperfections in our best works: we do not love God so much as we are bound to do, with all our hearts, mind, and power; we do not fear God so much as we ought to do; we do not pray to God but with many and great imperfections. We give, forgive, believe, live, and hope imperfectly; we speak, think, and do imperfectly; we fight against the devil, the world, and the flesh imperfectly. Let us, therefore, not be ashamed to confess plainly our state of imperfections."--Once more I repeat what I have said, the best preservative against this temporary delusion about perfection which clouds some minds--for such I hope I may call it--is a clear, full, distinct understanding of the nature, sinfulness, and deceitfulness of sin.

(e) In the last place, a Scriptural view of sin will prove an admirable antidote to them low views of personal holiness which are so painfully prevalent in these last days of the Church. This is a very painful and delicate subject, I know; but I dare not turn away from it. It has long been my sorrowful conviction that the standard of daily life among professing Christians in this country has been gradually falling. I am afraid that Christ-like charity, kindness, good-temper, unselfishness, meekness, gentleness, good-nature, self-denial, zeal to do good, and separation from the world, are far less appreciated than they ought to be, and than they used to be in the days of our fathers.

Into the causes of this state of things I cannot pretend to enter fully, and can only suggest conjectures for consideration. It may be that a certain profession of religion has become so fashionable and comparatively easy in the present age, that the streams which were once narrow and deep have become wide and shallow, and what we have gained in outward show we have lost in quality. It may be that the vast increase of wealth in the last twenty-five years has insensibly introduced a plague of worldliness, and self-indulgence, and love of ease into social life. What were once called luxuries are now comforts and necessaries, and self-denial and "enduring hardness" are consequently little known. It may be that the enormous amount of controversy which marks this age has insensibly dried up our spiritual life. We have too often been content with zeal for orthodoxy, and have neglected the sober realities of daily practical godliness. Be the causes what they may, I must declare my own belief that the result remains. There has been of late years a lower standard of personal holiness among believers than there used to be in the days of our fathers. The whole result is that the spirit is grieved! and the matter calls for much humiliation and searching of heart.

As to the best remedy for the state of things I have mentioned, I shall venture to give an opinion. Other schools of thought in the Churches must judge for themselves. The cure for Evangelical Churchmen, I am convinced, is to be found in a clearer apprehension of the nature and sinfulness of sin. We need not go back to Egypt, and borrow semi-Romish practices in order to revive our spiritual life. We need not restore the confessional, or return to monasticism or asceticism. Nothing of the kind! We must simply repent and do our first works. We must return to first principles. We must go back to "the old paths." We must sit down humbly in the presence of God, look the whole subject in the face, examine clearly what the Lord Jesus calls sin, and what the Lord Jesus calls "doing His will." We must then try to realize that it is terribly possible to live a careless, easy-going, half-worldly life, and yet at the same time to maintain Evangelical principles and call ourselves Evangelical people! Once let us see that sin is far viler, and far nearer to us, and sticks more closely to us than we supposed, and we shall be led, I trust and believe, to get nearer to Christ. Once drawn nearer to Christ, we shall drink more deeply out of His fullness, and learn more thoroughly to "live the life of faith" in Him, as St. Paul did. Once taught to live the life of faith in Jesus, and abiding in Him, we shall bear more fruit, shall find ourselves more strong for duty, more patient in trial, more watchful over our poor weak hearts, and more like our Master in all our little daily ways. Just in proportion as we realize how much Christ has done for us, shall we labour to do much for Christ. Much forgiven, we shall love much. In short, as the Apostle says, "with open face beholding as in a glass the glory of the Lord, we are changed into the same image even as by the Spirit of the Lord." (2 Cor. iii. 18.)

Whatever some may please to think or say, there can be no doubt that an increased feeling about holiness is one of the signs of the times. Conferences for the promotion of "spiritual life" are becoming common in the present day. The subject of "spiritual life" finds a place on Congress platforms almost every year. It has awakened an amount of interest and general attention throughout the land, for which we ought to be thankful. An^ movement, based on sound principles, which helps to deepen our spiritual life and increase our personal holiness, will be a real blessing to the Church of England. It will do much to draw us together and heal our unhappy divisions. It may bring down some fresh out-pouring of the grace of the Spirit, and be "life from the dead" in these later times. But sure I am, as I said in the beginning of this paper, we must begin low, if we would build high, I am convinced that the first step towards attaining a higher standard of holiness is to realize more fully the amazing sinfulness of sin.

ENDNOTE

[4] Hooker's "Learned Discourse of Justification."

II. SANCTIFICATION

"Sanctify them through Thy truth."--John xvii. 17.

"This is the will of God, even your sanctification."--1 Thess. iv. 3.

The subject of sanctification is one which many, I fear, dislike exceedingly. Some even turn from it with scorn and disdain. The very last thing they would like is to be a "saint," or a "sanctified" man. Yet the subject does not deserve to be treated in this way. It is not an enemy, but a friend.

It is a subject of the utmost importance to our souls. If the Bible be true, it is certain that unless we are "sanctified," we shall not be saved. There are three things which, according to the Bible, are absolutely necessary to the salvation of every man and woman in Christendom. These three are, justification, regeneration, and sanctification. All three meet in every child of God: he is both born again, and justified, and sanctified. He that lacks any one of these three things is not a true Christian in the sight of God, and dying in that condition will not be found in heaven and glorified in the last day.

It is a subject which is peculiarly seasonable in the present day. Strange doctrines have risen up of late upon the whole subject of sanctification. Some appear to confound it with justification. Others fritter it away to nothing, under the pretence of zeal for free grace, and practically neglect it altogether. Others are so much afraid of "works" being made a part of justification, that they can hardly find any place at all for "works" in their religion. Others set up a wrong standard of sanctification before their eyes, and failing to attain it, waste their lives in repeated secessions from church to church, chapel to chapel, and sect to sect, in the vain hope that they will find what they want. In a day like this, a calm examination of the subject, as a great leading doctrine of the Gospel, may be of great use to our souls.

I. Let us consider, firstly, the true nature of sanctification.

II. Let us consider, secondly, the visible marks of sanctification.

III. Let us consider, lastly, wherein justification and sanctification agree and are like one another, and wherein they differ and are unlike.

If, unhappily, the reader of these pages is one of those who care for nothing but this world, and make no profession of religion, I cannot expect him to take much interest in what I am writing. You will probably think it an affair of "words, and names," and nice questions, about which it matters nothing what you hold and believe. But if you are a thoughtful, reasonable, sensible Christian, I venture to say that you will find it worth while to have some clear ideas about sanctification.

I. In the first place, we have to consider the nature of sanctification. What does the Bible mean when it speaks of a "sanctified" man?

Sanctification is that inward spiritual work which the Lord Jesus Christ works in a man by the Holy Ghost, when He calls him to be a true believer. He not only washes him from his sins in His own blood, but He also separates him from his natural love of sin and the world, puts a new principle in his heart, and makes him practically godly in life. The instrument by which the Spirit effects this work is generally the Word of God, though He sometimes uses afflictions and providential visitations "without the Word." (1 Peter iii. 1.) The subject of this work of Christ by His Spirit is called in Scripture a "sanctified" man.[5]

He who supposes that Jesus Christ only lived and died and rose again in order to provide justification and forgiveness of sins for His people, has yet much to learn. Whether he knows it or not, he is dishonouring our blessed Lord, and making Him only a half Saviour. The Lord Jesus has undertaken everything that His people's souls require; not only to deliver them from the guilt of their sins by His atoning death, but from the dominion of their sins, by placing in their hearts the Holy Spirit; not only to justify them, but also to sanctify them. He is, thus, not only their "righteousness," but their "sanctification." (1 Cor. i. 30.) Let us hear what the Bible says: "For their sakes I sanctify myself, that they also might be sanctified."--"Christ loved the Church, and gave Himself for it; that He might sanctify and cleanse it."--"Christ gave Himself for us, that He might redeem us from all iniquity, and purify unto Himself a peculiar people, zealous of good works."--"Christ bore our sins in His own body on the tree, that we, being dead to sins, should live unto righteousness."--"Christ hath reconciled (you) in the body of His flesh through death, to present you holy and unblameable and unreproveable in His sight." (John xvii. 19; Ephes. v. 25; Titus ii. 14; 1 Peter ii. 24; Coloss. i. 22.) Let the meaning of these five texts be carefully considered. If words mean anything, they teach that Christ undertakes the sanctification, no less than the justification of His believing people. Both are alike provided for in that "everlasting covenant ordered in all things and sure," of which the Mediator is Christ. In fact, Christ in one place is called "He that sanctifieth," and His People, "they who are sanctified." (Heb. ii. 11.)

The subject before us is of such deep and vast importance, that it requires fencing, guarding, clearing up, and marking out on every side. A doctrine which is needful to salvation can never be too sharply developed, or brought too fully into light. To clear away the confusion between doctrines and doctrines, which is so unhappily common among Christians, and to map out the precise relation between truths and truths in religion, is one way to attain accuracy in our theology. I shall therefore not hesitate to lay before my readers a series of connected propositions or statements, drawn from Scripture, which I think will be found useful in defining the exact nature of sanctification.

(1) Sanctification, then, is the invariable result of that vital union with Christ which true faith gives to a Christian.--"He that abideth in Me, and I in him, the same bringeth forth much fruit." (John xv. 5.) The branch which bears no fruit is no living branch of the vine. The union with Christ which produces no effect on heart and life is a mere formal union, which is worthless before God. The faith which has not a sanctifying influence on the character is no better than the faith of devils. It is a "dead faith, because it is alone." It is not the gift of God. It is not the faith of God's elect. In short, where there is no sanctification of life, there is no real faith in Christ. True faith worketh by love. In constrains a man to live unto the Lord from a deep sense of gratitude for redemption. It makes him feel that he can never do too much for Him that died for him. Being much forgiven, he loves much. He whom the blood cleanses, walks in the light. He who has real lively hope in Christ, purifieth himself even as He is pure. (James ii. 17-20; Titus i. 1; Gal. v. 6; 1 John i. 7; iii. 3.)

(2) Sanctification, again, is the outcome and inseparable consequence of regeneration. He that is born again and made a new creature, receives a new nature and a new principle, and always lives a new life. A regeneration which a man can have, and yet live carelessly in sin or worldliness, is a regeneration invented by uninspired theologians, but never mentioned in Scripture. On the contrary, St. John expressly says, that "He that is born of God doth not commit sin--doeth righteousness--loveth the brethren--keepeth himself--and overcometh the world." (1 John ii. 29; iii. 9-14; v. 4-18.) In a word, where there is no sanctification there is no regeneration, and where there is no holy life there is no new birth. This is, no doubt, a hard saying to many minds; but, hard or not, it is simple Bible truth. It is written plainly, that he who is born of God is one whose "seed remaineth in him, and he cannot sin, because he is born of God." (1 John iii. 9.)

(3) Sanctification, again, is the only certain evidence of that indwelling of the Holy Spirit which is essential to salvation. "If any man have not the Spirit of Christ, he is none of His." (Rom. viii. 9.) The Spirit never lies dormant and idle within the soul: He always makes His presence known by the fruit He causes to be borne in heart, character, and life. "The fruit of the Spirit," says St. Paul, "is love, joy, peace, long-suffering, gentleness, goodness, faith, meekness, temperance," and such like. (Gal. v. 22.) Where these things are to be found, there is the Spirit: where these things are wanting, men are dead before God. The Spirit is compared to the wind, and, like the wind, He cannot be seen by our bodily eyes. But just as we know there is a wind by the effect it produces on waves, and trees, and smoke, so we may know the Spirit is in a man by the effects He produces in the man's conduct. It is nonsense to suppose that we have the Spirit, if we do not also "walk in the Spirit." (Gal. v. 25.) We may depend on it as a positive certainty, that where there is no holy living, there is no Holy Ghost. The seal that the Spirit stamps on Christ's people is sanctification. As many as are actually "led by the Spirit of God, they," and they only, "are the sons of God." (Rom. viii. 14.)

(4) Sanctification, again, is the only sure mark of God's election. The names and number of the elect are a secret thing, no doubt, which God has wisely kept in His own power, and not revealed to man. It is not given to us in this world to study the pages of the book of life, and see if our names are there. But if there is one thing clearly and plainly laid down about election, it is this--that elect men and women may be known and distinguished by holy lives. It is expressly written that they are "elect through sanctification--chosen unto salvation through sanctification--predestinated to be conformed to the image of God's Son--and chosen in Christ before the foundation of the world that they should be holy."--Hence, when St. Paul saw the working "faith" and labouring "love" and patient "hope" of the Thessalonian believers, he says, "I know your election of God." (1 Peter i. 2; 2 Thess. ii. 13; Rom. viii. 29; Eph. i. 4; 1 Thess. i. 3, 4.) He that boasts of being one of God's elect, while he is wilfully and habitually living in sin, is only deceiving himself, and talking wicked blasphemy. Of course it is hard to know what people really are, and many who make a fair show outwardly in religion, may turn out at last to be rotten-hearted hypocrites. But where there is not, at least, some appearance of sanctification, we may be quite certain there is no election. The Church Catechism correctly and wisely teaches that the Holy Ghost "sanctifieth all the elect people of God."

(5) Sanctification, again, is a thing that will always be seen. Like the Great Head of the Church, from whom it springs, it "cannot be hid." "Every tree is known by his own fruit." (Luke vi. 44.) A truly sanctified person may be so clothed with humility, that he can see in himself nothing but infirmity and defects. Like Moses, when he came down from the Mount,

he may not be conscious that his face shines. Like the righteous, in the mighty parable of the sheep and the goats, he may not see that he has done anything worthy of his Master's notice and commendation: "When saw we Thee an hungered, and fed Thee?" (Matt. xxv. 37.) But whether he sees it himself or not, others will always see in him a tone, and taste, and character, and habit of life unlike that of other men. The very idea of a man being "sanctified," while no holiness can be seen in his life, is flat nonsense and a misuse of words. Light may be very dim; but if there is only a spark in a dark room it will be seen. Life may be very feeble; but if the pulse only beats a little, it will be felt. It is just the same with a sanctified man: his sanctification will be something felt and seen, though he himself may not understand it. A "saint" in whom nothing can be seen but worldliness or sin, is a kind of monster not recognised in the Bible!

(6) Sanctification, again, is a thing for which every believer is responsible. In saying this I would not be mistaken. I hold as strongly as anyone that every man on earth is accountable to God, and that all the lost will be speechless and without excuse at the last day. Every man has power to "lose his own soul." (Matt. xvi. 26.) But while I hold this, I maintain that believers are eminently and peculiarly responsible, and under a special obligation to live holy lives. They are not as others, dead and blind and unrenewed: they are alive unto God, and have light and knowledge, and a new principle within them. Whose fault is it if they are not holy, but their own? On whom can they throw the blame if they are not sanctified, but themselves? God, who has given them grace and a new heart, and a new nature, has deprived them of all excuse if they do not live for His praise. This is a point which is far too much forgotten. A man who professes to be a true Christian, while he sits still, content with a very low degree of sanctification (if indeed he has any at all), and coolly tells you he "can do nothing," is a very pitiable sight, and a very ignorant man. Against this delusion let us watch and be on our guard. The Word of God always addresses its precepts to believers as accountable and responsible beings. If the Saviour of sinners gives us renewing grace, and calls us by His Spirit, we may be sure that He expects us to use our grace, and not to go to sleep. It is forgetfulness of this which causes many believers to "grieve the Holy Spirit," and makes them very useless and uncomfortable Christians.

(7) Sanctification, again, is a thing which admits of growth and degrees. A man may climb from one step to another in holiness, and be far more sanctified at one period of his life than another. More pardoned and more justified than he is when he first believes, he cannot be, though he may feel it more. More sanctified he certainly may be, because every grace in his new character may be strengthened, enlarged, and deepened. This is the evident meaning of our Lord's last prayer for His disciples, when He used the words, "Sanctify them"; and of St. Paul's prayer for the Thessalonians, "The very God of peace sanctify you." (John xvii. 17; 1 Thess. iv. 3.) In both cases the expression plainly implies the possibility of increased sanctification; while such an expression as "justify them" is never once in Scripture applied to a believer, because he cannot be more justified than he is. I can find no warrant in Scripture for the doctrine of "imputed sanctification." It is a doctrine which seems to me to confuse things that differ, and to lead to very evil consequences. Not least, it is a doctrine which is flatly contradicted by the experience of all the most eminent Christians. If there is any point on which God's holiest saints agree it is this: that they see more, and know more, and feel more, and do more, and repent more, and believe more, as they get on in spiritual life, and in proportion to the closeness of their walk with God. In short, they "grow in grace," as St. Peter exhorts believers to do; and "abound more and more," according to the words of St. Paul. (2 Pet. iii. 18; 1 Thess. iv. 1.)

(8) Sanctification, again, is a thing which depends greatly on a diligent use of Scriptural means. When I speak of "means," I have in view Bible-reading, private prayer, regular attendance on public worship, regular hearing of God's Word, and regular reception of the Lord's Supper. I lay it down as a simple matter of fact, that no one who is careless about such things must ever expect to make much progress in sanctification. I can find no record of any eminent saint who ever neglected them. They are appointed channels through which the Holy Spirit conveys fresh supplies of grace to the soul, and strengthens the work which He has begun in the inward man. Let men call this legal doctrine if they please, but I will never shrink from declaring my belief that there are no "spiritual gains without pains." I should as soon expect a farmer to prosper in business who contented himself with sowing his fields and never looking at them till harvest, as expect a believer to attain much holiness who was not diligent about his Bible-reading, his prayers, and the use of his Sundays. Our God is a God who works by means, and He will never bless the soul of that man who pretends to be so high and spiritual that he can get on without them.

(9) Sanctification, again, is a thing which does not prevent a man having a great deal of inward spiritual conflict. By conflict I mean a struggle within the heart between the old nature and the new, the flesh and the spirit, which are to be found together in every believer. (Gal. v. 17.) A deep sense of that struggle, and a vast amount of mental discomfort from it, are no proof that a man is not sanctified. Nay, rather, I believe they are healthy symptoms of our condition, and prove that we are not dead, but alive, A true Christian is one who has not only peace of conscience, but war within. He may be known by his warfare as well as by his peace. In saying this, I do not forget that I am contradicting the views of some well-meaning Christians, who hold the doctrine called "sinless perfection." I cannot help that. I believe that what I say is confirmed by the language of St. Paul in the seventh chapter of Romans. That chapter I commend to the careful study of all my readers. I am quite satisfied that it does not describe the experience of an unconverted man, or of a young and unestablished Christian; but of an old experienced saint in close communion with God. None but such a man could say, "I delight in the law of God after the inward man." (Rom. vii. 22.) I believe, furthermore, that what I say is proved by the experience of all the most eminent servants of Christ that have ever lived. The full proof is to be seen in their journals, their autobiographies, and their lives.--Believing all this, I shall never hesitate to tell people that inward conflict is no proof that a man is not holy, and that they must not think they are not sanctified because they do not feel entirely free from inward struggle. Such freedom we shall doubtless have in heaven; but we shall never enjoy it in this world. The heart of the best Christian, even at his best, is a field occupied by two rival camps, and the "company of two armies." (Cant. vi. 13.) Let the words of the Thirteenth and Fifteenth Articles be well considered by all Churchmen: "The infection of nature doth remain in them that are regenerated." "Although baptized and born again in Christ, we offend in many things; and if we say that we have no sin, we deceive ourselves, and the truth is not in us."[6]

(10) Sanctification, again, is a thing which cannot justify a man, and yet it pleases God. This may seem wonderful, and yet it is true. The holiest actions of the holiest saint that ever lived are all more or less full of defects and imperfections. They are either wrong in their motive or defective in their performance, and in themselves are nothing better than "splendid sins," deserving God's wrath and condemnation. To suppose that such actions can stand the severity of God's judgment, atone for sin, and merit heaven, is simply absurd. "By the deeds of the law shall no flesh be justified."--"We conclude that a man is justified by faith without the deeds of the law." (Rom. iii. 20-28.) The only righteousness in which we can appear be-

fore God is the righteousness of another--even the perfect righteousness of our Substitute and Representative, Jesus Christ the Lord. His work, and not our work, is our only title to heaven. This is a truth which we should be ready to die to maintain.--For all this, however, the Bible distinctly teaches that the holy actions of a sanctified man, although imperfect, are pleasing in the sight of God. "With such sacrifices God is well pleased." (Heb. xiii. 16.) "Obey your parents, for this is well pleasing to the Lord." (Col. iii. 20.) "We do those things that are pleasing in His sight." (1 John iii. 22.) Let this never be forgotten, for it is a very comfortable doctrine. Just as a parent is pleased with the efforts of his little child to please him, though it be only by picking a daisy or walking across a room, so is our Father in heaven pleased with the poor performances of His believing children. He looks at the motive, principle, and intention of their actions, and not merely at their quantity and quality. He regards them as members of His own dear Son, and for His sake, wherever there is a single eye, He is well-pleased. Those Churchmen who dispute this would do well to study the Twelfth Article of the Church of England.

(11) Sanctification, again, is a thing which will be found absolutely necessary as a witness to our character in the great day of judgment. It will be utterly useless to plead that we believed in Christ, unless our faith has had some sanctifying effect, and been seen in our lives. Evidence, evidence, evidence, will be the one thing wanted when the great white throne is set, when the books are opened, when the graves give up their tenants, when the dead are arraigned before the bar of God. Without some evidence that our faith in Christ was real and genuine, we shall only rise again to be condemned. I can find no evidence that will be admitted In that day, except sanctification. The question will not be how we talked and what we professed, but how we lived and what we did. Let no man deceive himself on this point. If anything is certain about the future, it is certain that there will be a judgment; and if anything is certain about judgment, it is certain that men's "works" and "doings" will be considered and examined in it. (John v. 29; 2 Cor. v. 10; Rev. xx. 13.) He that supposes works are of no importance, because they cannot justify us, is a very ignorant Christian. Unless he opens his eyes, he will find to his cost that if he comes to the bar of God without some evidence of grace, he had better never have been born.

(12) Sanctification, in the last place, is absolutely necessary in order to train and prepare us for heaven. Most men hope to go to heaven when they die; but few, it may be feared, take the trouble to consider whether they would enjoy heaven if they got there. Heaven is essentially a holy place; its inhabitants are all holy; its occupations are all holy. To be really happy in heaven, it is clear and plain that we must be somewhat trained and made ready for heaven while we are on earth. The notion of a purgatory after death, which shall turn sinners into saints, is a lying invention of man, and is nowhere taught in the Bible. We must be saints before we die, if we are to be saints afterwards in glory. The favourite idea of many, that dying men need nothing except absolution and forgiveness of sins to fit them for their great change, is a profound delusion. We need the work of the Holy Spirit as well as the work of Christ; we need renewal of the heart as well as the atoning blood; we need to be sanctified as well as to be justified. It is common to hear people saying on their death-beds, "I only want the Lord to forgive me my sins, and take me to rest." But those who say such things forget that the rest of heaven would be utterly useless if we had no heart to enjoy it! What could an unsanctified man do in heaven, if by any chance he got there? Let that question be fairly looked in the face, and fairly answered. No man can possibly be happy in a place where he is not in his element, and where all around him is not congenial to his tastes, habits, and character. When an eagle is happy in an iron cage, when a sheep is happy in the water, when an owl

is happy in the blaze of noonday sun, when a fish is happy on the dry land--then, and not till then, will I admit that the unsanctified man could be happy in heaven.[7]

I lay down these twelve propositions about sanctification with a firm persuasion that they are true, and I ask all who read these pages to ponder them well. Each of them would admit of being expanded and handled more fully, and all of them deserve private thought and consideration. Some of them may be disputed and contradicted; but I doubt whether any of them can be overthrown or proved untrue. I only ask for them a fair and impartial hearing. I believe in my conscience that they are likely to assist men in attaining clear views of sanctification.

II. I now proceed to take up the second point which I proposed to consider. That point is the visible evidence of sanctification. In a word, what are the visible marks of a sanctified man? What may we expect to see in him?

This is a very wide and difficult department of our subject. It is wide, because it necessitates the mention of many details which cannot be handled fully in the limits of a paper like this. It is difficult, because it cannot possibly be treated without giving offence. But at any risk truth ought to be spoken; and there is some kind of truth which especially requires to be spoken in the present day.

(1) True sanctification then does not consist in talk about religion. This is a point which ought never to be forgotten. The vast increase of education and preaching in these latter days makes it absolutely necessary to raise a warning voice. People hear so much of Gospel truth that they contract an unholy familiarity with its words and phrases, and sometimes talk so fluently about its doctrines that you might think them true Christians. In fact it is sickening and disgusting to hear the cool and flippant language which many pour out about "conversion--the Saviour--the Gospel--finding peace--free grace," and the like, while they are notoriously serving sin or living for the world. Can we doubt that such talk is abominable in God's sight, and is little better than cursing, swearing, and taking God's name in vain? The tongue is not the only member that Christ bids us give to His service. God does not want His people to be mere empty tubs, sounding brass and tinkling cymbals. We must be sanctified, not only "in word and in tongue, but in deed and truth." (1 John iii. 18.)

(2) True sanctification does not consist in temporary religious feelings. This again is a point about which a warning is greatly needed. Mission services and revival meetings are attracting great attention in every part of the land, and producing a great sensation. The Church of England seems to have taken a new lease of life, and exhibits a new activity; and we ought to thank God for it. But these things have their attendant dangers as well as their advantages. Wherever wheat is sown the devil is sure to sow tares. Many, it may be feared, appear moved and touched and roused under the preaching of the Gospel, while in reality their hearts are not changed at all. A kind of animal excitement from the contagion of seeing others weeping, rejoicing, or affected, is the true account of their case. Their wounds are only skin deep, and the peace they profess to feel is skin deep also. Like the stony-ground hearers, they "receive the Word with joy" (Matt. xiii. 20); but after a little they fall away, go back to the world, and are harder and worse than before. Like Jonah's gourd, they come up suddenly in a night and perish in a night. Let these things not be forgotten. Let us beware in this day of healing wounds slightly, and crying, Peace, peace, when there is no peace. Let us urge on every one who exhibits new interest in religion to be content with nothing short of the deep, solid, sanctifying work of the Holy Ghost. Reaction, after false religious excitement, is a most deadly disease of soul. When the devil is only temporarily cast out of a man in the heat of a

revival, and by and by returns to his house, the last state becomes worse than the first. Better a thousand times begin more slowly, and then "continue in the word" steadfastly, than begin in a hurry, without counting the cost, and by and by look back, with Lot's wife, and return to the world. I declare I know no state of soul more dangerous than to imagine we are born again and sanctified by the Holy Ghost, because we have picked up a few religious feelings.

(3) True sanctification does not consist in outward formalism and external devoutness. This is an enormous delusion, but unhappily a very common one. Thousands appear to imagine that true holiness is to be seen in an excessive quantity of bodily religion--in constant attendance on Church services, reception of the Lord's Supper, and observance of fasts and saints' days--in multiplied bowings and turnings and gestures and postures during public worship--in self-imposed austerities and petty self-denials--in wearing peculiar dresses, and the use of pictures and crosses. I freely admit that some people take up these things from conscientious motives, and actually believe that they help their souls. But I am afraid that in many cases this external religiousness is made a substitute for inward holiness; and I am quite certain that it falls utterly short of sanctification of heart. Above all, when I see that many followers of this outward, sensuous, and formal style of Christianity are absorbed in worldliness, and plunge headlong into its pomps and vanities, without shame, I feel that there is need of very plain speaking on the subject. There may be an immense amount of "bodily service," while there is not a jot of real sanctification.

(4) Sanctification does not consist in retirement from our place in life, and the renunciation of our social duties. In every age k has been a snare with many to take up this line in the pursuit of holiness. Hundreds of hermits have buried themselves in some wilderness, and thousands of men and women have shut themselves up within the walls of monasteries and convents, under the vain idea that by so doing they would escape sin and become eminently holy. They have forgotten that no bolts and bars can keep out the devil, and that, wherever we go, we carry that root of all evil, our own hearts. To become a monk, or a nun, or to join a House of of Mercy, is not the high road to sanctification. True holiness does not make a Christian evade difficulties, but face and overcome them. Christ would have His people show that His grace is not a mere hot-house plant, which can only thrive under shelter, but a strong, hardy thing which can flourish in every relation of life. It is doing our duty in that state to which God has called us--like salt in the midst of corruption, and light in the midst of darkness--which is a primary element in sanctification. It is not the man who hides himself in a cave, but the man who glorifies God as master or servant, parent or child, in the family and in the street, in business and in trade, who is the Scriptural type of a sanctified man. Our Master Himself said in His last prayer, "I pray not that Thou shouldest take them out of the world, but that Thou shouldest keep them from the evil." (John xvii. 15.)

(5) Sanctification does not consist in the occasional performance of right actions. It is the habitual working of a new heavenly principle within, which runs through all a man's daily conduct, both in great things and in small. Its seat is in the heart, and like the heart in the body, it has a regular influence on every part of the character. It is not like a pump, which only sends forth water when worked upon from without, but like a perpetual fountain, from which a stream is ever flowing spontaneously and naturally. Even Herod, when he heard John the Baptist, "did many things," while his heart was utterly wrong in the sight of God. (Mark vi. 20.) Just so there are scores of people in the present day who seem to have spasmodical fits of "goodness," as it is called, and do many right things under the influence of sickness, affliction, death in the family, public calamities, or a sudden qualm of conscience.

Yet all the time any intelligent observer can see plainly that they are not converted, and that they know nothing of "sanctification." A true saint, like Hezekiah, will be whole-hearted. He will "count God's commandments concerning all things to be right, and hate every false way." (2 Chron. xxxi. 21; Psalm cxix. 104.)

(6) Genuine sanctification will show itself in habitual respect to God's law, and habitual effort to live in obedience to it as the rule of life. There is no greater mistake than to suppose that a Christian has nothing to do with the law and the Ten Commandments, because he cannot be justified by keeping them. The same Holy Ghost who convinces the believer of sin by the law, and leads him to Christ for justification, will always lead him to a spiritual use of the law, as a friendly guide, in the pursuit of sanctification. Our Lord Jesus Christ never made light of the Ten Commandments; on the contrary, in His first public discourse, the Sermon on the Mount, He expounded them, and showed the searching nature of their requirements. St. Paul never made light of the law: on the contrary, he says, "The law is good, if a man use it lawfully."--"I delight in the law of God after the inward man", (1 Tim. i. 8; Rom. vii. 22.) He that pretends to be a saint, while he sneers at the Ten Commandments, and thinks nothing of lying, hypocrisy, swindling, ill-temper, slander, drunkenness, and breach of the seventh commandment, is under a fearful delusion. He will find it hard to prove that he is a "saint" in the last day!

(7) Genuine sanctification will show itself in an habitual endeavour to do Christ's will, and to live by His practical precepts. These precepts are to be found scattered everywhere throughout the four Gospels, and especially in the Sermon on the Mount. He that supposes they were spoken without the intention of promoting holiness, and that a Christian need not attend to them in his daily life, is really little better than a lunatic, and at any rate is a grossly ignorant person. To hear some men talk, and read some men's writings, one might imagine that our blessed Lord, when He was on earth, never taught anything but doctrine, and left practical duties to be taught by others! The slightest knowledge of the four Gospels ought to tell us that this is a complete mistake. What His disciples ought to be and to do is continually brought forward in our Lord's teaching. A truly sanctified man will never forget this. He serves a Master who said, "Ye are my friends if ye do whatsoever I command you." (John xv. 14.)

(8) Genuine sanctification will show itself in an habitual desire to live up to the standard which St. Paul sets before the Churches in his writings. That standard is to be found in the closing chapters of nearly all his Epistles. The common idea of many persons that St. Paul's writings are full of nothing but doctrinal statements and controversial subjects--justification, election, predestination, prophecy, and the like--is an entire delusion, and a melancholy proof of the ignorance of Scripture which prevails in these latter days. I defy anyone to read St. Paul's writings carefully without finding in them a large quantity of plain, practical directions about the Christian's duty in every relation of life, and about our daily habits, temper, and behaviour to one another. These directions were written down by inspiration of God for the perpetual guidance of professing Christians. He who does not attend to them may possibly pass muster as a member of a church or a chapel, but he certainly is not what the Bible calls a "sanctified" man.

(9) Genuine sanctification will show itself in habitual attention to the active graces which our Lord so beautifully exemplified, and especially to the grace of charity. "A new commandment I give unto you, that ye love one another; as I have loved you, that ye also love one another. By this shall all men know that ye are my disciples, if ye have love one to anoth-

er." (John xiii. 34, 35.) A sanctified man will try to do good in the world, and to lessen the sorrow and increase the happiness of all around him. He will aim to be like his Master, full of kindness and love to every one; and this not in word only, by calling people "dear," but by deeds and actions and self-denying work, according as he has opportunity. The selfish Christian professor, who wraps himself up in his own conceit of superior knowledge, and seems to care nothing whether others sink or swim, go to heaven or hell, so long as he walks to church or chapel in his Sunday best, and is called a "sound member"--such a man knows nothing of sanctification. He may think himself a saint on earth, but he will not be a saint in heaven. Christ will never be found the Saviour of those who know nothing of following His example. Saving faith and real converting grace will always produce some conformity to the image of Jesus.[8] (Coloss. iii. 10.)

(10) Genuine sanctification, in the last place, will show itself in habitual attention to the passive graces of Christianity. When I speak of passive graces, I mean those graces which are especially shown in submission to the will of God, and in bearing and for bearing towards one another. Few people, perhaps, unless they have examined the point, have an idea how much is said about these graces in the New Testament, and how important a place they seem to fill. This is the special point which St. Peter dwells upon in commending our Lord Jesus Christ's example to our notice: "Christ also suffered for us, leaving us an example, that we should follow His steps: Who did no sin, neither was guile found in His mouth: Who, when He was reviled, reviled not again; when He suffered, He threatened not; but committed Himself to Him that judgeth righteously." (1 Peter ii. 21-23.)--This is the one piece of profession which the Lord's prayer requires us to make: "Forgive us our trespasses, as we forgive them that trespass against us"; and the one point that is commented upon at the end of the prayer.--This is the point which occupies one-third of the list of the fruits of the Spirit, supplied by St. Paul. Nine are named, and three of these, "long-suffering, gentleness, and meekness," are unquestionably passive graces. (Gal. v. 22, 23.) I must plainly say that I do not think this subject is sufficiently considered by Christians. The passive graces are no doubt harder to attain than the active ones, but they are precisely the graces which have the greatest influence on the world. Of one thing I feel very sure--it is nonsense to pretend to sanctification unless we follow after the meekness, gentleness, long-suffering, and forgiveness of which the Bible makes so much. People who are habitually giving way to peevish and cross tempers in daily life, and are constantly sharp with their tongues, and disagreeable to all around them--spiteful people, vindictive people, revengeful people, malicious people--of whom, alas, the world is only too full!--all such know little, as they should know, about sanctification.

Such are the visible marks of a sanctified man. I do not say that they are all to be seen equally in all God's people. I freely admit that in the best they are not fully and perfectly exhibited. But I do say confidently, that the things of which i have been speaking are the Scriptural marks of sanctification, and that they who know nothing of them may well doubt whether they have any grace at all. Whatever others may please to say, I will never shrink from saying that genuine sanctification is a thing that can be seen, and that the marks I have endeavoured to sketch out are more or less the marks of a sanctified man.

III. I now propose to consider, in the last place, the distinction between justification and sanctification. Wherein do they agree, and wherein do they differ? This branch of our subject is one of great importance, though I fear it will not seem so to all my readers. I shall handle it briefly, but I dare not pass it over altogether. Too many are apt to look at nothing but the surface of things in religion, and regard nice distinctions in theology as questions of "words and names," which are of little real value. But I warn all who are in earnest about their souls, that the discomfort which arises from not "distinguishing things that differ" in Christian doctrine is very great indeed; and I especially advise them, if they love peace, to seek clear views about the matter before us. Justification and sanctification are two distinct things we must always remember. Yet there are points in which they agree and points in which they differ. Let us try to find out what they are.

In what, then, are justification and sanctification alike?

(a) Both proceed originally from the free grace of God. It is of His gift alone that believers are justified or sanctified at all.

(b) Both are part of that great work of salvation which Christ, in the eternal covenant, has undertaken on behalf of His people. Christ is the fountain of life, from which pardon and holiness both flow. The root of each is Christ.

(c) Both are to be found in the same persons. Those who are justified are always sanctified, and those who are sanctified are always justified. God has joined them together, and they cannot be put asunder.

(d) Both begin at the same time. The moment a person begins to be a justified person, he also begins to be a sanctified person. He may not feel it, but it is a fact.

(e) Both are alike necessary to salvation. No one ever reached heaven without a renewed heart as well as forgiveness, without the Spirit's grace as well as the blood of Christ, without a meetness for eternal glory as well as a title. The one is just as necessary as the other.

Such are the points on which justification and sanctification agree. Let us now reverse the picture, and see wherein they differ.

(a) Justification is the reckoning and counting a man to be righteous for the sake of another, even Jesus Christ the Lord. Sanctification is the actual making a man inwardly righteous, though it may be in a very feeble degree.

(b) The righteousness we have by our justification is not our own, but the everlasting perfect righteousness of our great Mediator Christ, imputed to us, and made our own by faith. The righteousness we have by sanctification is our own righteousness, imparted, inherent, and wrought in us by the Holy Spirit, but mingled with much infirmity and imperfection.

(c) In justification our own works have no place at all, and simple faith in Christ is the one thing needful. In sanctification our own works are of vast importance and God bids us fight, and watch, and pray, and strive, and take pains, and labour.

(d) Justification is a finished and complete work, and a man is perfectly justified the moment he believes. Sanctification is an imperfect work, comparatively, and will never be perfected until we reach heaven.

(e) Justification admits of no growth or increase: a man is as much justified the hour he first comes to Christ by faith as he will be to all eternity. Sanctification is eminently a progressive work, and admits of continual growth and enlargement so long as a man lives.

(f) Justification has special reference to our persons, our standing in God's sight, and our deliverance from guilt. Sanctification has special reference to our natures, and the moral renewal of our hearts.

(g) Justification gives us our title to heaven, and boldness to enter in. Sanctification gives us our meetness for heaven, and prepares us to enjoy it when we dwell there.

(h) Justification is the act of God about us, and is not easily discerned by others. Sanctification is the work of God within us, and cannot be hid in its outward manifestation from the eyes of men.

I commend these distinctions to the attention of all my readers, and I ask them to ponder them well. I am persuaded that one great cause of the darkness and uncomfortable feelings of many well-meaning people in the matter of religion, is their habit of confounding, and not distinguishing, justification and sanctification. It can never be too strongly impressed on our minds that they are two separate things. No doubt they cannot be divided, and everyone that is a partaker of either is a partaker of both. But never, never ought they to be confounded, and never ought the distinction between them to be forgotten.

It only remains for me now to bring this subject to a conclusion by a few plain words of application. The nature and visible marks of sanctification have been brought before us. What practical reflections ought the whole matter to raise in our minds?

(1) For one thing, let us all awake to a sense of the perilous state of many professing Christians. "Without holiness no man shall see the Lord"; without sanctification there is no salvation. (Heb. xii. 14.) Then what an enormous amount of so-called religion there is which is perfectly useless! What an immense proportion of church-goers and chapel-goers are in the broad road that leadeth to destruction! The thought is awful, crushing, and overwhelming. Oh, that preachers and teachers would open their eyes and realize the condition of souls around them! Oh, that men could be persuaded to "flee from the wrath to come "! If unsanctified souls can be saved and go to heaven, the Bible is not true. Yet the Bible is true and cannot lie! What must the end be!

(2) For another thing, let us make sure work of our own condition, and never rest till we feel and know that we are "sanctified" ourselves. What are our tastes, and choices, and likings, and inclinations? This is the great testing question. It matters little what we wish, and what we hope, and what we desire to be before we die. Where are we now? What are we doing? Are we sanctified or not? If not, the fault is all our own.

(3) For another thing, if we would be sanctified, our course is clear and plain--we must begin with Christ. We must go to Him as sinners, with no plea but that of utter need, and cast our souls on Him by faith, for peace and reconciliation with God. We must place ourselves in His hands, as in the hands of a good physician, and cry to Him for mercy and grace. We must wait for nothing to bring with us as a recommendation. The very first step towards sanctification, no less than justification, is to come with faith to Christ. We must first live and then work.

(4) For another thing, if we would grow in holiness and become more sanctified, we must continually go on as we began, and be ever making fresh applications to Christ. He is the Head from which every member must be supplied. (Ephes. iv. 16.) To live the life of daily faith in the Son of God, and to be daily drawing out of His fulness the promised grace and strength which He has laid up for His people--this is the grand secret of progressive sanctification. Believers who seem at a standstill are generally neglecting close communion with Jesus, and so grieving the Spirit. He that prayed, "Sanctify them," the last night before His crucifixion, is infinitely willing to help everyone who by faith applies to Him for help, and desires to be made more holy.

(5) For another thing, let us not expect too much from our own hearts here below. At our best we shall find in ourselves daily cause for humiliation, and discover that we are needy

debtors to mercy and grace every hour. The more light we have, the more we shall see our own imperfection. Sinners we were when we began, sinners we shall find ourselves as we go on; renewed, pardoned, justified--yet sinners to the very last. Our absolute perfection is yet to come, and the expectation of it is one reason why we should long for heaven.

(6) Finally, let us never be ashamed of making much of sanctification, and contending for a high standard of holiness. While some are satisfied with a miserably low degree of attainment, and others are not ashamed to live on without any holiness at all--content with a mere round of church-going and chapel-going, but never getting on, like a horse in a mill--let us stand fast in the old paths, follow after eminent holiness ourselves, and recommend it boldly to others. This is the only way to be really happy.

Let us feel convinced, whatever others may say, that holiness is happiness, and that the man who gets through life most comfortably is the sanctified man. No doubt there are some true Christians who from ill-health, or family trials, or other secret causes, enjoy little sensible comfort, and go mourning all their days on the way to heaven. But these are exceptional cases. As a general rule, in the long run of life, it will be found true that "sanctified" people are the happiest people on earth. They have solid comforts which the world can neither give nor take away. "The ways of wisdom are ways of pleasantness."--"Great peace have they that love Thy law."--It was said by One who cannot lie, "My yoke is easy, and my burden is light."--But it is also written, "There is no peace unto the wicked." (Prov iii. 17; Ps. cxix. 165; Matt. xi. 30; Is. xlviii. 22.)

P. S.

THE subject of sanctification is of such deep importance, and the mistakes made about it so many and great, that I make no apology for strongly recommending "Owen on the Holy Spirit" to all who want to study more thoroughly the whole doctrine of sanctification. No single paper like this can embrace it all.

I am quite aware that Owen's writings are not fashionable in the present day, and that many think fit to neglect and sneer at him as a Puritan! Yet the great divine who in Commonwealth times was Dean of Christ Church, Oxford, does not deserve to be treated in this way. He had more learning and sound knowledge of Scripture in his little finger than many who depreciate him have in their whole bodies. I assert unhesitatingly that the man who wants to study experimental theology will find no books equal to those of Owen and some of his contemporaries, for complete, Scriptural, and exhaustive treatment of the subjects they handle.

ENDNOTE

[5] There is mention in the Scripture of a twofold sanctification, and consequently in a twofold holiness. The first is common unto persons and things, consisting of the peculiar dedication, consecration, or separation of them unto the service of God, by His own appointment, whereby they become holy. Thus the priests and Levites of old, the ark, the altar, the tabernacle, and the temple, were sanctified and made holy; and, indeed, in all holiness whatever, there is a peculiar dedication and separation unto God. But in the sense mentioned, this was solitary and alone. No more belonged unto it but this sacred separation, nor was there any other effect of this sanctification. But, secondly, there is another kind of sanctification and holiness, wherein this separation to God is not the first thing done or intended, but

a consequent and effect thereof. This is real and internal, by the communicating of a principle of holiness unto our natures, attended with its exercise in acts and duties of holy obedience unto God. This is that which we inquire after."--John Owen on the Holy Spirit. Vol. iii, p. 370, Works, Goold's edition.

[6] "The devil's war is better than the devil's peace. Suspect dumb holiness. When the dog is kept out of doors he howls to be let in again."--"Contraries meeting, such as fire and water, conflict one with another.--When Satan findeth a sanctified heart, he tempteth with much importunity. Where there is much of God and of Christ, there are strong injections and fire-brands cast in at the windows, so that some of much faith have been tempted to doubt."--Rutherford's Trial of Faith, p. 403.

[7] "There is no imagination wherewith man is besotted, more foolish, none so pernicious, as this,--that persons not purified, not sanctified, not made holy in their life, should after-wards be taken into that state of blessedness which consists in the enjoyment of God. Neither can such persons enjoy God, nor would God be a reward to them.--Holiness indeed is perfected in heaven: but the beginning of it is invariably confined to this world."--Owen on Holy Spirit, p. 575. Goold's edition.

[8] "Christ in the Gospel is proposed to us as our pattern and example of holiness; and as it is a cursed imagination that this was the whole end of his life and death: namely, to exemplify and confirm the doctrine of holiness which He taught--so to neglect His being our example, in considering Him by faith to that end, and labouring after conformity to Him, is evil and pernicious. Wherefore let us be much in the contemplation of what He was, and what He did, and how in all duties and trials He carried Himself, until an image or idea of His perfect holiness is implanted in our minds, and we are made like unto Him thereby."--Owen on the Holy Ghost, p. 513. Goold's edition.

III. HOLINESS

"Holiness, without which no man shall see the Lord."--Heb. xii. 14.

The text which heads this page opens up a subject of deep importance. That subject is practical holiness. It suggests a question which demands the attention of all professing Christians--Are we holy? Shall we see the Lord?

That question can never be out of season. The wise man tells us, "There is a time to weep, and a time to laugh--a time to keep silence, and a time to speak" (Eccles. iii. 4, 7); but there is no time, no, not a day, in which a man ought not to be holy. Are we?

That question concerns all ranks and conditions of men. Some are rich and some are poor--some learned and some unlearned--some masters, and some servants; but there is no rank or condition in life in which a man ought not to be holy. Are we?

I ask to be heard to-day about this question. How stands the account between our souls and God? In this hurrying, bustling world, let us stand still for a few minutes and consider the matter of holiness. I believe I might have chosen a subject more popular and pleasant. I am sure I might have found one more easy to handle. But I feel deeply I could not have chosen one more seasonable and more profitable to our souls. It is a solemn thing to hear the Word of God saying, "Without holiness no man shall see the Lord." (Heb. xii. 14.)

I shall endeavour, by God's help, to examine what true holiness is, and the reason why it is so needful. In conclusion, I shall try to point out the only way in which holiness can be attained. I have already, in the second paper in this volume, approached this subject from a doctrinal side. Let me now try to present it to my readers in a more plain and practical point of view.

I. First, then, let me try to show what true practical holiness is--what sort of persons are those whom God calls holy.

A man may go great lengths, and yet never reach true holiness. It is not knowledge--Balaam had that: nor great profession--Judas Iscariot had that: nor doing many things--Herod had that: nor zeal for certain matters in religion--Jehu had that: nor morality and outward respectability of conduct--the young ruler had that: nor taking pleasure in hearing preachers--the Jews in Ezekiel's time had that: nor keeping company with godly people--Joab and Gehazi and Demas had that. Yet none of these was holy! These things alone are not holiness. A man may have any one of them, and yet never see the Lord.

What then is true practical holiness? It is a hard question to answer. I do not mean that there is any want of Scriptural matter on the subject. But I fear lest I should give a defective view of holiness, and not say all that ought to be said; or lest I should say things about it that ought not to be said, and so do harm. Let me, however, try to draw a picture of holiness, that we may see it clearly before the eyes of our minds. Only let it never be forgotten, when I have said all, that my account is but a poor imperfect outline at the best.

(a) Holiness is the habit of being of one mind with God, according as we find His mind described in Scripture. It is the habit of agreeing in God's judgment--hating what He hates--loving what He loves--and measuring everything in this world by the standard of His Word. He who most entirely agrees with God, he is the most holy man.

(b) A holy man will endeavour to shun every known sin, and to keep every known commandment. He will have a decided bent of mind toward God, a hearty desire to do His will--a greater fear of displeasing Him than of displeasing the world, and a love to all His ways. He will feel what Paul felt when he said,"I delight in the law of God after the inward man" (Rom. vii. 22), and what David felt when he said, "I esteem all Thy precepts concerning all things to be right, and I hate every false way." (Psalm cxix. 128.)

(c) A holy man will strive to be like our Lord Jesus Christ. He will not only live the life of faith in Him, and draw from Him all his daily peace and strength, but he will also labour to have the mind that was in Him, and to be "conformed to His image." (Rom. viii. 29.) It will be his aim to bear with and forgive others, even as Christ forgave us--to be unselfish, even as Christ pleased not Himself--to walk in love, even as Christ loved us--to be lowly-minded and humble, even as Christ made Himself of no reputation and humbled Himself. He will remember that Christ was a faithful witness for the truth--that He came not to do His own will--that it was His meat and drink to do His Father's will--that He would continually deny Himself in order to minister to others--that He was meek and patient under undeserved insults--that He thought more of godly poor men than of kings--that He was full of love and compassion to sinners--that He was bold and uncompromising in denouncing sin--that He sought not the praise of men, when He might have had it--that He went about doing good--that He was separate from worldly people--that He continued instant in prayer--that He would not let even His nearest relations stand in His way when God's work was to be done. These things a holy man will try to remember. By them he will endeavour to shape his course in life. He will lay to heart the saying of John, "He that saith he abideth in Christ ought himself also so to walk, even as He walked" (1 John ii. 6); and the saying of Peter, that "Christ suffered for us, leaving us an example that ye should follow His steps." (1 Peter ii. 21.) Happy is he who has learned to make Christ his "all," both for salvation and example! Much time would be saved, and much sin prevented, if men would oftener ask themselves the question, "What would Christ have said and done, if He were in my place?"

(d) A holy man will follow after meekness, longsuffering, gentleness, patience, kind tempers, government of his tongue. He will bear much, forbear much, overlook much, and be slow to talk of standing on his rights. We see a bright example of this in the behaviour of David when Shimei cursed him--and of Moses when Aaron and Miriam spake against him. (2 Sam. xvi. 10; Num. xii. 3.)

(e) A holy man will follow after temperance and self-denial. He will labour to mortify the desires of his body--to crucify his flesh with his affections and lusts--to curb his passions--to restrain his carnal inclinations, lest at any time they break loose. Oh, what a word is that of the Lord Jesus to the Apostles, "Take heed to yourselves, lest at any time your hearts be overcharged with surfeiting and drunkenness, and cares of this life" (Luke xxi. 34); and that of the Apostle Paul, "I keep under my body, and bring it into subjection, lest that by any means when I have preached to others, I myself should be a castaway." (1 Cor. ix. 27.)

(f) A holy man will follow after charity and brotherly kindness. He will endeavour to observe the golden rule of doing as he would have men do to him, and speaking as he would have men speak to him. He will be full of affection towards his brethren--towards their bodies, their property, their characters, their feelings, their souls. "He that loveth another," says Paul, "hath fulfilled the law." (Rom. xiii. 8.) He will abhor all lying, slandering, backbiting, cheating, dishonesty, and unfair dealing, even in the least things. The shekel and cubit of the sanctuary were larger than those in common use. He will strive to adorn his religion by all his outward demeanour, and to make it lovely and beautiful in the eyes of all around him. Alas, what condemning words are the 13th chapter of 1 Corinthians, and the Sermon on the Mount, when laid alongside the conduct of many professing Christians!

(g) A holy man will follow after a spirit of mercy and benevolence towards others. He will not stand all the day idle. He will not be content with doing no harm--he will try to do good. He will strive to be useful in his day and generation, and to lessen the spiritual wants and misery around him, as far as he can. Such was Dorcas, "full of good works and almsdeeds, which she did,"--not merely purposed and talked about, but did. Such an one was Paul: "I will very gladly spend and be spent for you," he says, "though the more abundantly I love you the less I be loved." (Acts ix. 36; 2 Cor. xii. 15.)

(h) A holy man will follow after purity of heart. He will dread all filthiness and uncleanness of spirit, and seek to avoid all things that might draw him into it. He knows his own heart is like tinder, and will diligently keep clear of the sparks of temptation. Who shall dare to talk of strength when David can fall? There is many a hint to be gleaned from the ceremonial law. Under it the man who only touched a bone, or a dead body, or a grave, or a diseased person, became at once unclean in the sight of God. And these things were emblems and figures. Few Christians are ever too watchful and too particular about this point.

(i) A holy man will follow after the fear of God. I do not mean the fear of a slave, who only works because he is afraid of punishment, and would be idle if he did not dread discovery. I mean rather the fear of a child, who wishes to live and move as if he was always before his father s face, because he loves him. What a noble example Nehemiah gives us of this! When he became Governor at Jerusalem he might have been chargeable to the Jews and required of them money for his support. The former Governors had done so. There was none to blame him if he did. But he says, "So did not I, because of the fear of God." (Nehem. v. 15.)

(j) A holy man will follow after humility. He will desire, in lowliness of mind, to esteem all others better than himself. He will see more evil in his own heart than in any other in the world. He will understand something of Abraham's feeling, when he says, "I am dust and ashes;"--and Jacob's, when he says, "I am less than the least of all Thy mercies;"--and Job's, when he says, "I am vile;"--and Paul's, when he says, "I am chief of sinners." Holy Bradford, that faithful martyr of Christ, would sometimes finish his letters with these words, "A most miserable sinner, John Bradford." Good old Mr. Grimshaw's last words, when he lay on his death-bed, were these, "Here goes an unprofitable servant."

(k) A holy man will follow after faithfulness in all the duties and relations in life. He will try, not merely to fill his place as well as others who take no thought for their souls, but even better, because he has higher motives, and more help than they. Those words of Paul should never be forgotten, "Whatever ye do, do it heartily, as unto the Lord,"--"Not slothful in business, fervent in spirit, serving the Lord." (Col. iii. 23; Rom. xii. 11.) Holy persons should aim at doing everything well, and should be ashamed of allowing themselves to do anything ill if they can help it. Like Daniel, they should seek to give no "occasion" against themselves, except "concerning the law of their God." (Dan. vi. 5.) They should strive to be good husbands and good wives, good parents and good children, good masters and good servants, good neighbours, good friends, good subjects, good in private and good in public, good in the place of business and good by their firesides. Holiness is worth little indeed, if it does not bear this kind of fruit. The Lord Jesus puts a searching question to His people, when He says, "What do ye more than others?" (Matt. v. 47.)

(l) Last, but not least, a holy man will follow after spiritual mindedness. He will endeavour to set his affections entirely on things above, and to hold things on earth with a very loose hand. He will not neglect the business of the life that now is; but the first place in his mind and thoughts will be given to the life to come. He will aim to live like one whose treasure is in heaven, and to pass through this world like a stranger and pilgrim travelling to his home. To commune with God in prayer, in the Bible, and in the assembly of His people--these things will be the holy man's chiefest enjoyments. He will value every thing and place and company, just in proportion as it draws him nearer to God. He will enter into something of David's feeling, when he says, "My soul followeth hard after Thee." "Thou art my portion." (Psalm lxiii. 8; cxix. 57.)

Such is the outline of holiness which I venture to sketch out. Such is the character which those who are called "holy" follow after. Such are the main features of a holy man.

But here let me say, I trust no man will misunderstand me. I am not without fear that my meaning will be mistaken, and the description I have given of holiness will discourage some tender conscience. I would not willingly make one righteous heart sad, or throw a stumbling-block in any believer's way.

I do not say for a moment that holiness shuts out the presence of indwelling sin. No: far from it. It is the greatest misery of a holy man that he carries about with him a "body of death;"--that often when he would do good "evil is present with him"; that the old man is clogging all his movements, and, as it were, trying to draw him back at every step he takes. (Rom. vii. 21.) But it is the excellence of a holy man that he is not at peace with indwelling sin, as others are. He hates it, mourns over it, and longs to be free from its company. The work of sanctification within him is like the wall of Jerusalem--the building goes forward "even in troublous times." (Dan. ix. 25.)

Neither do I say that holiness comes to ripeness and perfection all at once, or that these graces I have touched on must be found in full bloom and vigour before you can call a man holy. No: far from it. Sanctification is always a progressive work. Some men's graces are in the blade, some in the ear, and some are like full corn in the ear. All must have a beginning. We must never despise "the day of small things." And sanctification in the very best is an imperfect work. The history of the brightest saints that ever lived will contain many a "but," and "howbeit," and "notwithstanding," before you reach the end. The gold will never be without some dross--the light will never shine without some clouds, until we reach the heavenly Jerusalem. The sun himself has spots upon his face. The holiest men have many a blemish and defect when weighed in the balance of the sanctuary. Their life is a continual warfare with sin, the world, and the devil; and sometimes you will see them not overcoming, but overcome. The flesh is ever lusting against the spirit, and the spirit against the flesh, and "in many things they offend all." (Gal. v. 17; James iii. 2.)

But still, for all this, I am sure that to have such a character as I have faintly drawn, is the heart's desire and prayer of all true Christians. They press towards it, if they do not reach it.

They may not attain to it, but they always aim at it. It is what they strive and labour to be, if it is not what they are.

And this I do boldly and confidently say, that true holiness is a great reality. It is something in a man that can be seen, and known, and marked, and felt by all around him. It is light: if it exists, it will show itself. It is salt: if it exists, its savour will be perceived. It is a precious ointment: if it exists, its presence cannot be hid.

I am sure we should all be ready to make allowance for much backsliding, for much occasional deadness in professing Christians. I know a road may lead from one point to another, and yet have many a winding and turn; and a man may be truly holy, and yet be drawn aside by many an infirmity. Gold is not the less gold because mingled with alloy, nor light the less light because faint and dim, nor grace the less grace because young and weak. But after every allowance, I cannot see how any man deserves to be called "holy," who wilfully allows himself in sins, and is not humbled and ashamed because of them. I dare not call anyone "holy" who makes a habit of wilfully neglecting known duties, and wilfully doing what he knows God has commanded him not to do. Well says Owen, "I do not understand how a man can be a true believer unto whom sin is not the greatest burden, sorrow, and trouble."

Such are the leading characteristics of practical holiness. Let us examine ourselves and see whether we are acquainted with it. Let us prove our own selves.

II. Let me try, in the next place, to show some reasons why practical holiness is so important.

Can holiness save us? Can holiness put away sin--cover iniquities--make satisfaction for transgressions--pay our debt to God? No: not a whit. God forbid that I should ever say so. Holiness can do none of these things. The brightest saints are all "unprofitable servants." Our purest works are no better than filthy rags, when tried by the light of God's holy law. The white robe which Jesus offers, and faith puts on, must be our only righteousness--the name of Christ our only confidence--the Lamb's book of life our only title to heaven. With all our holiness we are no better than sinners. Our best things are stained and tainted with imperfection. They are all more or less incomplete, wrong in the motive or defective in the performance. By the deeds of the law shall no child of Adam ever be justified. "By grace are ye saved through faith, and that not of yourselves, it is the gift of God: not of works, lest any man should boast." (Ephes. ii. 8, 9.)

Why then is holiness so important? Why does the Apostle say, "Without it no man shall see the Lord"? Let me set out in order a few reasons.

(a) For one thing, we must be holy, because the voice of God in Scripture plainly commands it. The Lord Jesus says to His people, "Except your righteousness shall exceed the righteousness of the scribes and Pharisees, ye shall in no case enter into the kingdom of heaven." (Matt. v. 20.) "Be ye perfect, even as your Father which is in heaven is perfect." (Matt. v. 48.) Paul tells the Thessalonians, "This is the will of God, even your sanctification." (1 Thess. iv. 3.) And Peter says, "As He which hath called you is holy, so be ye holy in all manner of conversation;" because it is written, "Be ye holy, for I am holy." (1 Peter i. 15, 16.) "In this," says Leighton, "law and Gospel agree."

(b) We must be holy, because this is one grand end and purpose for which Christ came into the world. Paul writes to the Corinthians, "He died for all, that they which live should not henceforth live unto themselves, but unto Him which died for them and rose again." (2 Cor. v. 15.) And to the Ephesians, "Christ loved the Church, and gave Himself for it, that He might sanctify and cleanse it." (Ephes. v. 25, 26.) And to Titus, "He gave Himself for us, that He might redeem us from all iniquity, and purify unto Himself a peculiar people, zealous of good works." (Titus ii. 14.) In short, to talk of men being saved from the guilt of sin, without being at the same time saved from its dominion in their hearts, is to contradict the witness of all Scripture. Are believers said to be elect!--it is "through sanctification of the Spirit." Are they predestinated?--it is "to be conformed to the image of God's Son." Are they chosen?--it is "that they may be holy." Are they called?--is it "with a holy calling." Are they afflicted?--it is that they may be "partakers of holiness." Jesus is a complete Saviour. He does not merely take away the guilt of a believer's sin, He does more--He breaks its power, (1 Peter i. 2; Rom. viii. 29; Eph. i. 4; Heb. xii. 10.)

(c) We must be holy, because this is the only sound evidence that we have a saving faith in our Lord Jesus Christ. The Twelfth Article of our Church says truly, that "Although good works cannot put away our sins, and endure the severity of God's judgment, yet are they pleasing and acceptable to God in Christ, and do spring out necessarily of a true and lively faith; insomuch that by them a lively faith may be as evidently known as a tree discerned by its fruits." James warns us there is such a thing as a dead faith--a faith which goes no further than the profession of the lips, and has no influence on a man's character. (James ii. 17.) True saving faith is a very different kind of thing. True faith will always show itself by its fruits--it will sanctify, it will work by love, it will overcome the world, it will purify the heart. I know that people are fond of talking about death-bed evidences. They will rest on words spoken in the hours of fear, and pain, and weakness, as if they might take comfort in them about the friends they lose. But I am afraid in ninety-nine cases out of a hundred such evidences are not to be depended on. I suspect that, with rare exceptions, men die just as they have lived. The only safe evidence that we are one with Christ, and Christ in us, is holy life. They that live unto the Lord are generally the only people who die in the Lord. If we would die the death of the righteous, let us not rest in slothful desires only; let us seek to live His life. It is a true saying of Traill's, "That man's state is naught, and his faith unsound, that find not his hopes of glory purifying to his heart and life."

(d) We must be holy, because this is the only proof that we love the Lord Jesus Christ in sincerity. This is a point on which He has spoken most plainly, in the fourteenth and fifteenth chapters of John. "If ye love Me, keep my commandments."--"He that hath my command-ments and keepeth them, he it is that loveth Me."--"If a man love Me he will keep my words."--"Ye are my friends if ye do whatsoever I command you." (John xiv. 15, 21, 23; xv. 14.)--Plainer words than these it would be difficult to find, and woe to those who neglect them! Surely that man must be in an unhealthy state of soul who can think of all that Jesus suffered, and yet cling to those sins for which that suffering was undergone It was sin that wove the crown of thorns--it was sin that pierced our Lord's hands, and feet, and side--it was sin that brought Him to Gethsemane and Calvary, to the cross and to the grave. Cold must our hearts be if we do not hate sin and labour to get rid of it, though we may have to cut off the right hand and pluck out the right eye in doing it.

(e) We must be holy, because this is the only sound evidence that we are true children of God. Children in this world are generally like their parents. Some, doubtless, are more so, and some less--but it is seldom indeed that you cannot trace a kind of family likeness. And it is much the same with the children of God. The Lord Jesus says, "If ye were Abraham's chil-dren ye would do the works of Abraham."--"If God were your Father ye would love Me." (John viii. 39, 42.) If men have no likeness to the Father in heaven, it is vain to talk of their being His "sons." If we know nothing of holiness we may flatter ourselves as we please, but we have not got the Holy Spirit dwelling in us: we are dead, and must be brought to life again--we are lost, and must be found. "As many as are led by the Spirit of God, they," and they only, "are the sons of God." (Rom. viii. 14.) We must show by our lives the family we belong to.--We must let men see by our good conversation that we are indeed the children of the Holy One, or our son-ship is but an empty name. "Say not," says Gurnall, "that thou hast royal blood in thy veins, and art born of God, except thou canst prove thy pedigree by daring to be holy."

(f) We must be holy, because this is the most likely way to do good to others. We cannot live to ourselves only in this world. Our lives will always be doing either good or harm to those who see them. They are a silent sermon which all can read. It is sad indeed when they are a sermon for the devil's cause, and not for God's. I believe that far more is done for Christ's kingdom by the holy living of believers than we are at all aware of. There is a reality about such living which makes men feel, and obliges them to think. It carries a weight and influence with it which nothing else can give. It makes religion beautiful, and draws men to consider it, like a lighthouse seen afar off. The day of judgment will prove that many besides husbands have been won "without the word" by a holy life, (1 Pet. iii. 1.) You may talk to persons about the doctrines of the Gospels, and few will listen, and still fewer understand. But your life is an argument that none can escape. There is a meaning about holiness which not even the most unlearned can help taking in. They may not understand justification, but they can understand charity. I believe there is far more harm done by unholy and inconsistent Christians than we are aware of. Such men are among Satan's best allies. They pull down by their lives what ministers build with their lips. They cause the chariot wheels of the Gospel to drive heavily. They supply the children of this world with a never ending excuse for remaining as they are.--"I cannot see the use of so much religion," said an irreligious tradesman not long ago; "I observe that some of my customers are always talking about the Gospel, and faith, and election, and the blessed promises, and so forth; and yet these very people think nothing of cheating me of pence and half-pence, when they have an opportunity. Now, if religious persons can do such things, I do not see what good there is in religion."--I grieve to be obliged to write such things, but I fear that Christ's name is too often blasphemed because of the lives of Christians. Let us take heed lest the blood of souls should be required at our hands. From murder of souls by inconsistency and loose walking, good Lord, deliver us! Oh, for the sake of others, if for no other reason, let us strive to be holy!

(g) We must be holy, because our present comfort depends much upon it. We cannot be too often reminded of this. We are sadly apt to forget that there is a close connection between sin and sorrow, holiness and happiness, sanctification and consolation. God has so wisely ordered it, that our well-being and our well-doing are linked together. He has mercifully provided that even in this world it shall be man's interest to be holy. Our justification is not by works--our calling and election are not according to our works--but it is vain for anyone to suppose that he will have a lively sense of his justification, or an assurance of his calling, so long as he neglects good works, or does not strive to live a holy life. "Hereby we do know that we know Him, if we keep His commandments."--"Hereby we know that we are of the truth, and shall assure our hearts." (1 John ii. 3; iii. 19.) A believer may as soon expect to feel the sun's rays upon a dark and cloudy day, as to feel strong consolation in Christ while he does not follow Him fully. When the disciples forsook the Lord and fled, they escaped danger, but they were miserable and sad. When, shortly after, they confessed Him boldly before men, they were cast into prison and beaten; but we are told "they rejoiced that they were counted worthy to suffer shame for His name." (Acts v. 41.) Oh, for our own sakes, if there were no other reason, let us strive to be holy! He that follows Jesus most fully will always follow Him most comfortably.

(h) Lastly, we must be holy, because without holiness on earth we shall never be prepared to enjoy heaven. Heaven is a holy place. The Lord of heaven is a holy Being. The angels are holy creatures. Holiness is written on everything in heaven. The book of Revelation says expressly, "There shall in no wise enter into it anything that defileth, neither whatsoever worketh abomination, or maketh a lie." (Rev. xxi. 27.)

I appeal solemnly to everyone who reads these pages, How shall we ever be at home and happy in heaven, if we die unholy? Death works no change. The grave makes no alteration. Each will rise again with the same character in which he breathed his last. Where will our place be if we are strangers to holiness now?

Suppose for a moment that you were allowed to enter heaven without holiness. What would you do? What possible enjoyment could you feel there? To which of all the saints would you join yourself, and by whose side would you sit down? Their pleasures are not your pleasures, their tastes not your tastes, their character not your character. How could you possibly be happy, if you had not been holy on earth?

Now perhaps you love the company of the light and the careless, the worldly-minded and the covetous, the reveller and the pleasure-seeker, the ungodly and the profane. There will be none such in heaven.

Now perhaps you think the saints of God too strict and particular, and serious. You rather avoid them. You have no delight in their society. There will be no other company in heaven.

Now perhaps you think praying, and Scripture-reading, and hymn singing, dull and melancholy, and stupid work--a thing to be tolerated now and then, but not enjoyed. You reckon the Sabbath a burden and a weariness; you could not possibly spend more than a small part of it in worshipping God. But remember, heaven is a never-ending Sabbath. The inhabitants thereof rest not day or night, saying, "Holy, holy, holy, Lord God Almighty" and singing the praise of the Lamb. How could an unholy man find pleasure in occupation such as this?

Think you that such an one would delight to meet David, and Paul, and John, after a life spent in doing the very things they spoke against? Would he take sweet counsel with them, and find that he and they had much in common?--Think you, above all, that he would rejoice to meet Jesus, the Crucified One, face to face, after cleaving to the sins for which He died, after loving His enemies and despising His friends? Would he stand before Him with confidence, and join in the cry, "This is our God; we have waited for Him, we will be glad and rejoice in His salvation"? (Isa. xxv. 9.) Think you not rather that the tongue of an unholy man would cleave to the roof of his mouth with shame, and his only desire would be to be cast out! He would feel a stranger in a land he knew not, a black sheep amidst Christ's holy flock. The voice of Cherubim and Seraphim, the song of Angels and Archangels and all the company of heaven, would be a language he could not understand. The very air would seem an air he could not breathe. I know not what others may think, but to me it does seem clear that heaven would be a miserable place to an unholy man. It cannot be otherwise. People may say, in a vague way, "they hope to go to heaven;" but they do not consider what they say. There must be a certain "meetness for the inheritance of the saints in light." Our hearts must be somewhat in tune. To reach the holiday of glory, we must pass through the training school of grace. We must be heavenly-minded, and have heavenly tastes, in the life that now is, or else we shall never find ourselves in heaven, in the life to come.

And now, before I go any further, let me say a few words by way of application.

(1) For one thing, let me ask everyone who may read these pages, Are you holy? Listen, I pray you, to the question I put to you this day. Do you know anything of the holiness of which I have been speaking?

I do not ask whether you attend your church regularly--whether you have been baptized, and received the Lord's Supper--whether you have the name of Christian--I ask something more than all this: Are you holy, or are you not?

I do not ask whether you approve of holiness in others--whether you like to read the lives of holy people, and to talk of holy things, and to have on your table holy books--whether you mean to be holy, and hope you will be holy some day--I ask something further: Are you yourself holy this very day, or are you not?

And why do I ask so straitly, and press the question so strongly? I do it because the Scripture says, "Without holiness no man shall see the Lord." It is written, it is not my fancy--it is the Bible, not my private opinion--it is the word of God, not of man--"Without holiness no man shall see the Lord." (Heb. xii. 14.)

Alas, what searching, sifting words are these! What thoughts come across my mind, as I write them down! I look at the world, and see the greater part of it lying in wickedness. I look at professing Christians, and see the vast majority having nothing of Christianity but the name. I turn to the Bible, and I hear the Spirit saying, "Without holiness no man shall see the Lord."

Surely it is a text that ought to make us consider our ways, and search our hearts. Surely it should raise within us solemn thoughts, and send us to prayer.

You may try to put me off by saying "you feel much, and think much about these things: far more than many suppose." I answer, "This is not the point. The poor lost souls in hell do as much as this. The great question is not what you think, and what you feel, but what you do.

You may say, "It was never meant that all Christians should be holy, and that holiness, such as I have described, is only for great saints, and people of uncommon gifts." I answer, "I cannot see that in Scripture. I read that every man who hath hope in Christ purifieth himself." (1 John iii. 3.)--"Without holiness no man shall see the Lord."

You may say, "It is impossible to be so holy and to do our duty in this life at the same time: the thing cannot be done." I answer, "You are mistaken. It can be done. With Christ on your side nothing is impossible. It has been done by many. David, and Obadiah, and Daniel, and the servants of Nero's household, are all examples that go to prove it."

You may say, "If I were so holy I would be unlike other people." I answer, "I know it well. It is just what you ought to be. Christ's true servants always were unlike the world around them--a separate nation, a peculiar people;--and you must be so too, if you would be saved!"

You may say, "At this rate very few will be saved." I answer, "I know it. It is precisely what we are told in the Sermon on the Mount." The Lord Jesus said so 1,900 years ago. "Strait is the gate, and narrow is the way, that leadeth unto life, and few there be that find it." (Matt. vii. 14.) Few will be saved, because few will take the trouble to seek salvation. Men will not deny themselves the pleasures of sin and their own way for a little season. They turn their backs on an "inheritance incorruptible, undefiled, and that fadeth not away." "Ye will not come unto Me," says Jesus, "that ye might have life." (John v. 40.)

You may say, "These are hard sayings: the way is very narrow." I answer, "I know it. So says the Sermon on the Mount." The Lord Jesus said so 1,900 years ago. He always said that men must take up the cross daily, and that they must be ready to cut off hand or foot, if they would be His disciples. It is in religion as it is in other things, "there are no gains without pains." That which costs nothing is worth nothing.

Whatever we may think fit to say, we must be holy, if we would see the Lord. Where is our Christianity if we are not? We must not merely have a Christian name, and Christian knowledge, we must have a Christian character also. We must be saints on earth, if ever we mean to be saints in heaven. God has said it, and He will not go back: "Without holiness no man shall see the Lord." "The Pope's calendar," says Jenkyn, "only makes saints of the dead, but Scripture requires sanctity in the living." "Let not men deceive themselves," says Owen; "sanctification is a qualification indispensably necessary unto those who will be under the conduct of the Lord Christ unto salvation. He leads none to heaven but whom He sanctifies on the earth. This living Head will not admit of dead members."

Surely we need not wonder that Scripture says "Ye must be born again." (John iii. 7.) Surely it is clear as noon-day that many professing Christians need a complete change--new hearts, new natures--if ever they are to be saved. Old things must pass away--they must become new creatures. "Without holiness no man," be he who he may, "shall see the Lord."

(2) Let me, for another thing, speak a little to believers. I ask you this question, "Do you think you feel the importance of holiness as much as you should?"

I own I fear the temper of the times about this subject. I doubt exceedingly whether it holds that place which it deserves in the thoughts and attention of some of the Lord's people. I would humbly suggest that we are apt to overlook the doctrine of growth in grace, and that we do not sufficiently consider how very far a person may go in a profession of religion, and yet have no grace, and be dead in God's sight after all. I believe that Judas Iscariot seemed very like the other Apostles. When the Lord warned them that one would betray Him, no one said, "Is it Judas?" We had better think more about the Churches of Sardis and Laodicea than we do.

I have no desire to make an idol of holiness. I do not wish to dethrone Christ, and put holiness in His place. But I must candidly say, I wish sanctification was more thought of in this day than it seems to be, and I therefore take occasion to press the subject on all believers into whose hands these pages may fall. I fear it is sometimes forgotten that God has married together justification and sanctification. They are distinct and different things, beyond question, but one is never found without the other. All justified people are sanctified, and all sanctified are justified. What God has joined together let no man dare to put asunder. Tell me not of your justification, unless you have also some marks of sanctification. Boast not of Christ's work for you, unless you can show us the Spirit's work in you. Think not that Christ and the Spirit can ever be divided. I doubt not that many believers know these things, but I think it good for us to be put in remembrance of them. Let us prove that we know them by our lives. Let us try to keep in view this text more continually: "Follow holiness, without which no man shall see the Lord."

I must frankly say I wish there was not such an excessive sensitiveness on the subject of holiness as I sometimes perceive in the minds of believers. A man might really think it was a dangerous subject to handle, so cautiously is it touched! Yet surely when we have exalted Christ as "the way, the truth, and the life," we cannot err in speaking strongly about what should be the character of His people. Well says Rutherford, "The way that crieth down duties and sanctification, is not the way of grace. Believing and doing are blood-friends."

I would say it with all reverence, but say it I must--I sometimes fear if Christ were on earth now, there are not a few who would think His preaching legal; and if Paul were writing his Epistles, there are those who would think he had better not write the latter part of most of them as he did. But let us remember that the Lord Jesus did speak the Sermon on the Mount, and that the Epistle to the Ephesians contains six chapters and not four. I grieve to feel obliged to speak in this way, but I am sure there is a cause.

That great divine, John Owen, the Dean of Christ Church, used to say, more than two hundred years ago, that there were people whose whole religion seemed to consist in going about complaining of their own corruptions, and telling everyone that they could do nothing of themselves. I am afraid that after two centuries the same thing might be said with truth of some of Christ's professing people in this day. I know there are texts in Scripture which warrant such complaints. I do not object to them when they come from men who walk in the steps of the Apostle Paul, and fight a good fight, as he did, against sin, the devil, and the world. But I never like such complaints when I see ground for suspecting, as I often do, that they are only a cloak to cover spiritual laziness, and an excuse for spiritual sloth. If we say with Paul, "O wretched man that I am," let us also be able to say with him, "I press toward the mark." Let us not quote his example in one thing, while we do not follow him in another. (Rom. vii. 24; Philip. iii. 14.)

I do not set up myself to be better than other people, and if anyone asks, "What are you, that you write in this way?" I answer, "I am a very poor creature indeed." But I say that I cannot read the Bible without desiring to see many believers more spiritual, more holy, more single-eyed, more heavenly-minded, more whole-hearted than they are in the nineteenth century. I want to see among believers more of a pilgrim spirit, a more decided separation from the world, a conversation more evidently in heaven, a closer walk with God--and therefore I have written as I have.

Is it not true that we need a higher standard of personal holiness in this day? Where is our patience? Where is our zeal? Where is our love? Where are our works? Where is the power of religion to be seen, as it was in times gone by? Where is that unmistakable tone which used to distinguish the saints of old, and shake the world? Verily our silver has become dross, our wine mixed with water, and our salt has very little savour. We are all more than half asleep. The night is far spent, and the day is at hand. Let us awake, and sleep no more. Let us open our eyes more widely than we have done hitherto. "Let us lay aside every weight, and the sin that doth so easily beset us."--"Let us cleanse ourselves from all filthiness of flesh and spirit, and perfect holiness in the fear of God."--(Heb. xii. i; 2 Cor. vii. 1.) "Did Christ die," says Owen, "and shall sin live? Was He crucified in the world, and shall our affections to the world be quick and lively? Oh, where is the spirit of him, who by the cross of Christ was crucified to the world, and the world to him!"

III. Let me, in the last place, offer a word of advice to all who desire to be holy.

Would you be holy? Would you become a new creature? Then you must begin with Christ. You will do just nothing at all, and make no progress till you feel your sin and weakness, and flee to Him. He is the root and beginning of all holiness, and the way to be holy is to come to Him by faith and be joined to Him. Christ is not wisdom and righteousness only to His people, but sanctification also. Men sometimes try to make themselves holy first of all, and sad work they make of it. They toil and labour, and turn over new leaves, and make many changes; and yet, like the woman with the issue of blood, before she came to Christ, they feel "nothing bettered, but rather worse." (Mark v. 26.) They run in vain, and labour in vain; and little wonder, for they are beginning at the wrong end. They are building up a wall of sand; their work runs down as fast as they throw it up. They are baling water out of a leaky vessel: the leak gains on them, not they on the leak. Other foundation of "holiness" can no man lay than that which Paul laid, even Christ Jesus. "Without Christ we can do nothing." (John xv. 5.) It is a strong but true saying of Traill's, "Wisdom out of Christ is damning folly-- righteousness out of Christ is guilt and condemnation--sanctification out of Christ is filth and sin--redemption out of Christ is bondage and slavery."

Do you want to attain holiness? Do you feel this day a real hearty desire to be holy? Would you be a partaker of the Divine nature? Then go to Christ. Wait for nothing. Wait for nobody. Linger not. Think not to make yourself ready. Go and say to Him, in the words of that beautiful hymn--

Nothing in my hand I bring,

Simply to Thy cross I cling;

Naked, flee to Thee for dress;

Helpless, look to Thee for grace."

There is not a brick nor a stone laid in the work of our sanctification till we go to Christ. Holiness is His special gift to His believing people. Holiness is the work He carries on in their hearts, by the Spirit whom He puts within them. He is appointed a "Prince and a Saviour, to give repentance" as well as remission of sins.--"To as many as receive Him, He gives power to become sons of God." (Acts v. 31; John i. 12, 13.) Holiness comes not of blood--parents cannot give it to their children: nor yet of the will of the flesh--man cannot produce it in himself: nor yet of the will of man--ministers cannot give it you by baptism. Holiness comes from Christ. It is the result of vital union with Him, It is the fruit of being a living branch of the True Vine. Go then to Christ and say, "Lord, not only save me from the guilt of sin, but send the Spirit, whom Thou didst promise, and save me from its power. Make me holy. Teach me to do Thy will."

Would you continue holy? Then abide in Christ. He says Himself, "Abide in Me and I in you,--he that abideth in Me and I in him, the same beareth much fruit. (John xv. 4, 5.) It pleased the Father that in Him should all fulness dwell--a full supply for all a believer's wants. He is the Physician to whom you must daily go, if you would keep well. He is the Manna which you must daily eat, and the Rock of which you must daily drink. His arm is the arm on which you must daily lean, as you come up out of the wilderness of this world. You must not only be rooted, you must also be built up in Him. Paul was a man of God indeed--a holy man--a growing, thriving Christian--and what was the secret of it all? He was one to whom Christ was "all in all." He was ever "looking unto Jesus." "I can do all things," he says, "through Christ which strengthened me." "I live, yet not I, but Christ liveth in me. The life that I now live, I live by the faith of the Son of God." Let us go and do likewise. (Heb. xii. 2; Phil. iv. 13; Gal. ii. 20.)

May all who read these pages know these things by experience, and not by hearsay only. May we all feel the importance of holiness, far more than we have ever done yet! May our years be holy years with our souls, and then they will be happy ones! Whether we live, may we live unto the Lord; or whether we die, may we die unto the Lord; or if He comes for us, may we be found in peace, without spot, and blameless!

IV. THE FIGHT

"Fight the good fight of faith."--1 Timothy vi. 12.

IT is a curious fact that there is no subject about which most people feel such deep interest as "fighting." Young men and maidens, old men and little children, high and low, rich and poor, learned and unlearned, all feel a deep interest in wars, battles and fighting.

This is a simple fact, whatever way we may try to explain it. We should call that Englishman a dull fellow who cared nothing about the story of Waterloo, or Inkermann, or Balaclava or Lucknow. We should think that heart cold and stupid which was not moved and thrilled by the struggles at Sedan and Strasburg, and Metz, and Paris, during the war between France and Germany.

But there is another warfare of far greater importance than any war that was ever waged by man. It is a warfare which concerns not two or three nations only, but every Christian man and woman born into the world. The warfare I speak of is the spiritual warfare. It is the fight which everyone who would be saved must fight about his soul.

This warfare, I am aware, is a thing of which many know nothing. Talk to them about it, and they are ready to set you down as a madman, an enthusiast, or a fool. And yet it is as real and true as any war the world has ever seen. It has its hand-to-hand conflicts and its wounds. It has its watchings and fatigues. It has its sieges and assaults. It has its victories and its defeats. Above all, it has consequences which are awful, tremendous, and most peculiar. In earthly warfare the consequences to nations are often temporary and remediable. In the spiritual warfare it is very different. Of that warfare, the consequences, when the fight is over, are unchangeable and eternal.

It is of this warfare that St. Paul spoke to Timothy, when he wrote those burning words, "Fight the good fight of faith; lay hold on eternal life." It is of this warfare that I propose to speak in this paper. I hold the subject to be closely connected with that of sanctification and holiness. He that would understand the nature of true holiness must know that the Christian is "a man of war." If we would be holy we must fight.

I. The first thing I have to say is this: True Christianity is a fight.

True Christianity! Let us mind that word "true." There is a vast quantity of religion current in the world which is not true, genuine Christianity. It passes muster; it satisfies sleepy consciences; but it is not good money. It is not the real thing which was called Christianity eighteen hundred years ago. There are thousands of men and women who go to churches and chapels every Sunday, and call themselves Christians. Their names are in the baptismal register. They are reckoned Christians while they live. They are married with a Christian marriage service. They mean to be buried as Christians when they die. But you never see any "fight" about their religion! Of spiritual strife, and exertion, and conflict, and self-denial, and watching, and warring, they know literally nothing at all. Such Christianity may satisfy man, and those who say anything against it may be thought very hard and uncharitable; but it certainly is not the Christianity of the Bible. It is not the religion which the Lord Jesus founded, and His Apostles preached. It is not the religion which produces real holiness. True Christianity is "a fight."

The true Christian is called to be a soldier, and must behave as such from the day of his conversion to the day of his death. He is not meant to live a life of religious ease, indolence, and security. He must never imagine for a moment that he can sleep and doze along the way to heaven, like one travelling in an easy carriage. If he takes his standard of Christianity from the children of this world, he may be content with such notions; but he will find no countenance for them in the Word of God. If the Bible is the rule of his faith and practice, he will find his course laid down very plainly in this matter. He must "fight."

With whom is the Christian soldier meant to fight? Not with other Christians. Wretched indeed is that man's idea of religion who fancies that it consists in perpetual controversy! He who is never satisfied unless he is engaged in some strife between church and church, chapel and chapel, sect and sect, faction and faction, party and party, knows nothing yet as he ought to know. No doubt it may be absolutely needful sometimes to appeal to law courts, in order to ascertain the right interpretation of a Church's Articles, and rubrics, and formularies. But, as a general rule, the cause of sin is never so much helped as when Christians waste their strength in quarrelling with one another, and spend their time in petty squabbles.

No, indeed! The principal fight of the Christian is with the world, the flesh, and the devil. These are his never-dying foes. These are the three chief enemies against whom he must wage war. Unless he gets the victory over these three, all other victories are useless and vain. If he had a nature like an angel, and were not a fallen creature, the warfare would not be so essential. But with a corrupt heart, a busy devil, and an ensnaring world, he must either "fight" or be lost.

He must fight the flesh. Even after conversion he carries within him a nature prone to evil, and a heart weak and unstable as water. That heart will never be free from imperfection in this world, and it is a miserable delusion to expect it. To keep that heart from going astray, the Lord Jesus bids us "watch and pray." The spirit may be ready, but the flesh is weak. There is need of a daily struggle and a daily wrestling in prayer. "I keep under my body," cries St. Paul, "and bring it into subjection."'--"I see a law in my members warring against the law of my mind, and bringing me into captivity."--"O wretched man that I am, who shall deliver me from the body of this death?"--"They that are Christ's have crucified the flesh with the affections and lusts."--"Mortify your members which are upon the earth." (Mark xiv. 38; 1 Cor. ix. 27; Rom. vii. 23, 24; Gal. v. 24; Coloss. iii. 5.)

He must fight the world. The subtle influence of that mighty enemy must be daily resisted, and without a daily battle can never be overcome. The love of the world's good things--the fear of the world's laughter or blame--the secret desire to keep in with the world--the secret wish to do as others in the world do, and not to run into extremes--all these are spiritual foes which beset the Christian continually on his way to heaven, and must be conquered. "The friendship of the world is enmity with God: whosoever therefore will be a friend of the world is the enemy of God."--"If any man love the world, the love of the Father is not in him."--"The world is crucified to Me, and I unto the world."--"Whatsoever is born of God overcometh the world."--"Be not conformed to this world." (James iv. 4; 1 John ii. 15; Gal. vi. 14; 1 John v. 4; Rom. xii. 2.)

He must fight the devil. That old enemy of mankind is not dead. Ever since the fall of Adam and Eve he has been "going to and fro in the earth, and walking up and down in it," and striving to compass one great end--the ruin of man's soul. Never slumbering and never sleeping, he is always "going about as a lion seeking whom he may devour." An unseen enemy, he is always near us, about our path and about our bed, and spying out all our ways. A "murderer and a liar" from the beginning, he labours night and day to cast us down to hell. Sometimes by leading into superstition, sometimes by suggesting infidelity, sometimes by one kind of tactics and sometimes by another, he is always carrying on a campaign against our souls. "Satan hath desired to have you, that he may sift you as wheat." This mighty adversary must be daily resisted if we wish to be saved. But "this kind goeth not out" but by watching and praying, and fighting, and putting on the whole armour of God. The strong man armed will never be kept out of our hearts without a daily battle. (Job i. 7; 1 Peter v. 8; John viii. 44; Luke xxii. 31; Ephes. vi. 11.)

Some men may think these statements too strong. You fancy that I am going too far, and laying on the colours too thickly. You are secretly saying to yourself, that men and women in England may surely get to heaven without all this trouble and warfare and fighting. Listen to me for a few minutes and I will show you that I have something to say on God's behalf. Remember the maxim of the wisest General that ever lived in England--"In time of war it is the worst mistake to underrate your enemy, and try to make a little war." This Christian warfare is no light matter. Give me your attention and consider what I say. What saith the Scripture?-- "Fight the good fight of faith. Lay hold on eternal life.--"Endure hardness as a good soldier of Jesus Christ."--"Put on the whole armour of God, that ye may be able to stand against the wiles of the devil. For we wrestle not against flesh and blood, but against principalities, against powers, against the ruler of the darkness of this world, against spiritual wickedness in high places. Wherefore take unto you the whole armour of God, that you may be able to withstand in the evil day, and having done all to stand."--"Strive to enter in at the strait gate."--"Labour for the meat that endureth unto everlasting life."--"Think not that I came to send peace on the earth: I came not to send peace but a sword."--"He that hath no sword let him sell his garment and buy one."--"Watch ye, stand fast in the faith: quit you like men, be strong."--"War a good warfare, holding faith and a good conscience." (1 Tim. vi. 12; 2 Tim. ii. 3; Ephes. vi. 11-13; Luke xiii. 24; John vi. 27; Matt. x. 34; Luke xxii. 36; 1 Cor. xvi. 13; 1 Tim. i. 18, 19.) Words such as these appear to me clear, plain, and unmistakable. They all teach one and the same great lesson, if we are willing to receive it. That lesson is, that true Christianity is a struggle, a fight, and a warfare. He that pretends to condemn "fighting" and teaches that we ought to sit still and "yield ourselves to God," appears to me to misunderstand his Bible, and to make a great mistake.

What says the Baptismal Service of the Church of England? No doubt that Service is uninspired, and, like every uninspired composition, it has its defects; but to the millions of people all over the globe, who profess and call themselves English Churchmen, its voice ought to speak with some weight. And what does it say? It tells us that over every new member who is admitted into the Church of England the following words are used--"I baptize thee in the name of the Father, the Son, and the Holy Ghost."--"I sign this child with the sign of the cross, in token that hereafter he shall not be ashamed to confess the faith of Christ crucified, and manfully to fight under His banner against sin, the world, and the devil, and to continue Christ's faithful soldier and servant unto his life's end."--Of course we all know that in myriads of cases baptism is a mere form, and that parents bring their children to the font without faith or prayer or thought, and consequently receive no blessing. The man who supposes that baptism in such cases acts mechanically, like a medicine, and that godly and ungodly, praying and prayerless parents, all alike get the same benefit for their children, must be in a strange state of mind. But one thing, at any rate, is very certain. Every baptized Churchman is by his profession a "soldier of Jesus Christ," and is pledged "to fight under His banner against sin, the world, and the devil." He that doubts it had better take up his Prayer-book, and read, mark, and learn its contents. The worst thing about many very zealous Churchmen is their total ignorance of what their own Prayer-book contains.

Whether we are Churchmen or not, one thing is certain--this Christian warfare is a great reality, and a subject of vast importance. It is not a matter like Church government and ceremonial, about which men may differ, and yet reach heaven at last. Necessity is laid upon us. We must fight. There are no promises in the Lord Jesus Christ's Epistles to the Seven Churches, except to those who "overcome." Where there is grace there will be conflict. The believer is a soldier. There is no holiness without a warfare. Saved souls will always be found to have fought a fight.

It is a fight of absolute necessity. Let us not think that in this war we can remain neutral and sit still. Such a line of action may be possible in the strife of nations, but it is utterly impossible in that conflict which concerns the soul. The boasted policy of noninterference--the "masterly inactivity" which pleases so many statesmen--the plan of keeping quiet and letting things alone--all this will never do in the Christian warfare. Here at any rate no one can escape serving under the plea that he is "a man of peace." To be at peace with the world, the flesh and the devil, is to be at enmity with God, and in the broad way that leadeth to destruction. We have no choice or option. We must either fight or be lost.

It is a fight of universal necessity. No rank, or class, or age, can plead exemption, or escape the battle. Ministers and people, preachers and hearers, old and young, high and low, rich and poor, gentle and simple, kings and subjects, landlords and tenants, learned and unlearned--all alike must carry arms and go to war. All have by nature a heart full of pride, unbelief, sloth, worldliness, and sin. All are living in a world beset with snares, traps, and pitfalls for the soul. All have near them a busy, restless, malicious devil. All, from the queen in her palace down to the pauper in the workhouse, all must fight, if they would be saved.

It is a fight of perpetual necessity. It admits of no breathing time, no armistice, no truce. On week-days as well as on Sundays--in private as well as in public--at home by the family fireside as well as abroad--in little things like management of tongue and temper, as well as in great ones like the government of kingdoms--the Christian's warfare must unceasingly go on. The foe we have to do with keeps no holidays, never slumbers, and never sleeps. So long as we have breath in our bodies we must keep on our armour, and remember we are on an enemy's ground. "Even on the brink of Jordan," said a dying saint, "I find Satan nibbling at my heels." We must fight till we die.

Let us consider well these propositions. Let us take care that our own personal religion is real, genuine, and true. The saddest symptom about many so-called Christians is the utter absence of anything like conflict and fight in their Christianity. They eat, they drink, they dress, they work, they amuse themselves, they get money, they spend money, they go through a scanty round of formal religious services once or twice every week. But the great spiritual warfare--its watchings and strugglings, its agonies and anxieties, its battles and contests--of all this they appear to know nothing at all. Let us take care that this case is not our own. The worst state of soul is "when the strong man armed keepeth the house, and his goods are at peace"--when he leads men and women "captive at his will," and they make no resistance.

The worst chains are those which are neither felt nor seen by the prisoner. (Luke xi. 21; 2 Tim. ii. 26.)

We may take comfort about our souls if we know anything of an inward fight and conflict. It is the invariable companion of genuine Christian holiness. It is not everything, I am well aware, ut it is something. Do we find in our heart of hearts a spiritual struggle? Do we feel anything of the flesh lusting against the spirit and the spirit against the flesh, so that we cannot do the things we would? (Gal. v. 17.) Are we conscious of two principles within us, contending for the mastery? Do we feel anything of war in our inward man? Well, let us thank God for it! It is a good sign. It is strongly probable evidence of the great work of sanctification. All true saints are soldiers. Anything is better than apathy, stagnation, deadness, and indifference. We are in a better state than many. The most part of so-called Christians have no feeling at all. We are evidently no friends of Satan. Like the kings of this world, he wars not against his own subjects. The very fact that he assaults us should fill our minds with hope. I say again, let us take comfort. The child of God has two great marks about him, and of these two we have one. HE MAY BE KNOWN BY HIS INWARD WARFARE, AS WELL AS BY HIS INWARD PEACE.

II. I pass on to the second thing which I have to say in handling my subject: True Christianity is the fight of faith.

In this respect the Christian warfare is utterly unlike the conflicts of this world. It does not depend on the strong arm, the quick eye, or the swift foot. It is not waged with carnal weapons, but with spiritual. Faith is the hinge on which victory turns. Success depends entirely on believing.

A general faith in the truth of God's written Word is the primary foundation of the Christian soldier's character. He is what he is, does what he does, thinks as he thinks, acts as he acts, hopes as he hopes, behaves as he behaves, for one simple reason--he believes certain propositions revealed and laid down in Holy Scripture. "He that cometh to God must believe that He is, and that He is a Rewarder of them that diligently seek Him." (Heb. xi. 5.)

A religion without doctrine or dogma is a thing which many are fond of talking of in the present day. It sounds very fine at first. It looks very pretty at a distance. But the moment we sit down to examine and consider it, we shall find it a simple impossibility. We might as well talk of a body without bones and sinews. No man will ever be anything or do anything in religion, unless he believes something. Even those who profess to hold the miserable and uncomfortable views of the Deists are obliged to confess that they believe something. With all their bitter sneers against dogmatic theology and Christian credulity, as they call it, they themselves have a kind of faith.

As for true Christians, faith is the very backbone of their spiritual existence. No one ever fights earnestly against the world, the flesh and the devil, unless he has engraven on his heart certain great principles which he believes. What they are he may hardly know, and may certainly not be able to define or write down. But there they are, and, consciously or unconsciously, they form the roots of his religion. Wherever you see a man, whether rich or poor, learned or unlearned, wrestling manfully with sin, and trying to overcome it, you may be sure there are certain great principles which that man believes. The poet who wrote the famous lines:

> "For modes of faith let graceless zealots fight,
> He can't be wrong whose life is in the right,"

was a clever man, but a poor divine. There is no such thing as right living without faith and believing.

A special faith in our Lord Jesus Christ's person, work, and office, is the life, heart, and mainspring of the Christian soldier's character.

He sees by faith an unseen Saviour, who loved him, gave Himself for him, paid his debts for him, bore his sins, carried his transgressions, rose again for him, and appears in heaven for him as his Advocate at the right hand of God. He sees Jesus, and clings to Him. Seeing this Saviour and trusting in Him, he feels peace and hope, and willingly does battle against the foes of his soul.

He sees his own many sins--his weak heart, a tempting world, a busy devil; and if he looked only at them he might well despair. But he sees also a mighty Saviour, an interceding Saviour, a sympathizing Saviour--His blood, His righteousness, His everlasting priesthood-- and he believes that all this is his own. He sees Jesus, and casts his whole weight on Him. Seeing Him he cheerfully fights on, with a full confidence that he will prove "more than con- queror through Him that loved him." (Rom. viii. 37.)

Habitual lively faith in Christ's presence and readiness to help is the secret of the Chris- tian soldier fighting successfully.

It must never be forgotten that faith admits of degrees. All men do not believe alike, and even the same person has his ebbs and flows of faith, and believes more heartily at one time than another. According to the degree of his faith the Christian fights well or ill, wins victo- ries, or suffers occasional repulses, comes off triumphant, or loses a battle. He that has most faith will always be the happiest and most comfortable soldier. Nothing makes the anxieties of warfare sit so lightly on a man as the assurance of Christ's love and continual protection. Nothing enables him to bear the fatigue of watching, struggling, and wrestling against sin, like the indwelling confidence that Christ is on his side and success is sure. It is the "shield of faith" which quenches all the fiery darts of the wicked one.--It is the man who can say, "I know whom I have believed"--who can say in time of suffering, "I am not ashamed."--He who wrote those glowing words, "We faint not,"--"Our light affliction which endureth but for a moment worketh in us a far more exceeding and eternal weight of glory"--was the man who wrote with the same pen, "We look not at the things which are seen, but at the things which are not seen; for the things which are seen are temporal, but the things which are not seen are eternal."--It is the man who said, "I live by the faith of the Son of God," who said, in the same Epistle, "the world is crucified unto me, and I unto the world."--It is the man who said, "To me to live is Christ," who said, in the same Epistle, "I have learned in whatsoever state I am therewith to be content."--"I can do all things through Christ."--The more faith the more victory! The more faith the more inward peace! (Eph. vi. 16; 2 Tim. i. 12; 2 Cor. iv. 17, 18; Gal. ii. 20; vi. 14; Phil. i. 21; iv. 11, 13.)

I think it impossible to overrate the value and importance of faith. Well may the Apostle Peter call it "precious." (2 Pet. i. 1.) Time would fail me if I tried to recount a hundredth part of the victories which by faith Christian soldiers have obtained.

Let us take down our Bibles and read with attention the eleventh chapter of the Epistle to the Hebrews. Let us mark the long list of worthies whose names are thus recorded, from Abel down to Moses, even before Christ was born of the Virgin Mary, and brought life and immortality into full light by the Gospel. Let us note well what battles they won against the world, the flesh, and the devil. And then let us remember that believing did it all. These men looked forward to the promised Messiah. They saw Him that is invisible. "By faith the elders obtained a good report." (Heb. xi. 2-27.)

Let us turn to the pages of early Church history. Let us see how the primitive Christians held fast their religion even unto death, and were not shaken by the fiercest persecutions of heathen Emperors. For centuries there were never wanting men like Polycarp and Ignatius, who were ready to die rather than deny Christ. Fines, and prisons, and torture, and fire, and sword, were unable to crush the spirit of the noble army of martyrs. The whole power of imperial Rome, the mistress of the world, proved unable to stamp out the religion which began with a few fishermen and publicans in Palestine! And then let us remember that believing in an unseen Jesus was the Church's strength. They won their victory by faith.

Let us examine the story of the Protestant Reformation. Let us study the lives of its leading champions--Wycliffe, and Huss, and Luther, and Ridley, and Latimer, and Hooper. Let us mark how these gallant soldiers of Christ stood firm against a host of adversaries, and were ready to die for their principles. What battles they fought! What controversies they maintained! What contradiction they endured I What tenacity of purpose they exhibited against a world in arms! And then let us remember that believing in an unseen Jesus was the secret of their strength. They overcame by faith.

Let us consider the men who have made the greatest marks in Church history in the last hundred years. Let us observe how men like Wesley, and Whitfield, and Venn, and Romaine, stood alone in their day and generation, and revived English religion in the face of opposition from men high in office, and in the face of slander, ridicule, and persecution from nine-tenths of professing Christians in our land. Let us observe how men like William Wilberforce, and Havelock, and Hedley Vicars, have witnessed for Christ in the most difficult positions, and displayed a banner for Christ even at the regimental mess-table, or on the floor of the House of Commons. Let us mark how these noble witnesses never flinched to the end, and won the respect even of their worst adversaries. And then let us remember that believing in an unseen Christ is the key to all their characters. By faith they lived, and walked, and stood, and overcame.

Would anyone live the life of a Christian soldier? Let him pray for faith. It is the gift of God; and a gift which those who ask shall never ask for in vain. You must believe before you do. If men do nothing in religion, it is because they do not believe. Faith is the first step toward heaven.

Would anyone fight the fight of a Christian soldier successfully and prosperously? Let him pray for a continual increase of faith. Let him abide in Christ, get closer to Christ, tighten his hold on Christ every day that he lives. Let his daily prayer be that of the disciples--"Lord, increase my faith." (Luke xvii. 5.) Watch jealously over your faith, if you have any. It is the citadel of the Christian character, on which the safety of the whole fortress depends. It is the point which Satan loves to assail. All lies at his mercy if faith is overthrown. Here, if we love life, we must especially stand on our guard.

III. The last thing I have to say is this: True Christianity is a good fight.

"Good" is a curious word to apply to any warfare. All worldly war is more or less evil. No doubt it is an absolute necessity in many cases--to procure the liberty of nations, to prevent the weak from being trampled down by the strong--but still it is an evil. It entails an awful amount of bloodshed and suffering. It hurries into eternity myriads who are completely unprepared for their change. It calls forth the worst passions of man. It causes enormous waste and destruction of property. It fills peaceful homes with mourning widows and orphans. It spreads far and wide poverty, taxation, and national distress. It disarranges all the order of society. It interrupts the work of the Gospel and the growth of Christian missions. In short, war is an immense and incalculable evil, and every praying man should cry night and day, "Give peace in our time." And yet there is one warfare which is emphatically "good," and one fight in which there is no evil. That warfare is the Christian warfare. That fight is the fight of the soul.

Now what are the reasons why the Christian fight is a "good fight"? What are the points in which his warfare is superior to the warfare of this world? Let me examine this matter, and open it out in order. I dare not pass the subject and leave it unnoticed. I want no one to begin the life of a Christian soldier without counting the cost. I would not keep back from anyone that if he would be holy and see the Lord he must fight, and that the Christian fight though spiritual is real and severe. It needs courage, boldness, and perseverance. But I want my readers to know that there is abundant encouragement, if they will only begin the battle. The Scripture does not call the Christian fight "a good fight" without reason and cause. Let me try to show what I mean.

(a) The Christian's fight is good because fought under the best of generals. The Leader and Commander of all believers is our Divine Saviour, the Lord Jesus Christ--a Saviour of perfect wisdom, infinite love, and almighty power. The Captain of our salvation never fails to lead His soldiers to victory. He never makes any useless movements, never errs in judgment, never commits any mistake. His eye is on all His followers, from the greatest of them even to the least. The humblest servant in His army is not forgotten. The weakest and most sickly is cared for, remembered, and kept unto salvation. The souls whom He has purchased and redeemed with His own blood are far too precious to be wasted and thrown away. Surely this is good!

(b) The Christian's fight is good, because fought with the best of helps. Weak as each believer is in himself, the Holy Spirit dwells in him, and his body is a temple of the Holy Ghost. Chosen by God the Father, washed in the blood of the Son, renewed by the Spirit, he does not go a warfare at his own charges, and is never alone. God the Holy Ghost daily teaches, leads, guides, and directs him. God the Father guards him by His almighty power. God the Son intercedes for him every moment, like Moses on the mount, while he is fighting in the valley below. A threefold cord like this can never be broken! His daily provisions and supplies never fail. His commissariat is never defective. His bread and his water are sure. Weak as he seems in himself, like a worm, he is strong in the Lord to do great exploits. Surely this is good!

(c) The Christian fight is a good fight, because fought with the best of promises. To every believer belong exceeding great and precious promises--all Yea and Amen in Christ--promises sure to be fulfilled, because made by One who cannot lie, and has power as well as will to keep His word. "Sin shall not have dominion over you."--"The God of peace shall bruise Satan under your feet shortly."--"He that has begun a good work will perform it until the day of Jesus Christ."--"When thou passeth through the waters I will be with thee, and through the floods, they shall not overflow thee."--"My sheep shall never perish, neither shall anyone pluck them out of my hand."--"Him that cometh unto Me! will in no wise cast out."--"I will never leave thee, nor forsake thee."--"I am persuaded that neither death, nor life, nor things present, nor things to come, shall be able to separate us from the love of God, which is in Christ Jesus." (Rom. vi. 14; Rom. xvi. 20; Philip. i. 6; Isa. xliii. 2; John x. 28; John vi. 37; Heb.

xiii. 5; Rom. viii. 38.) Words like these are worth their weight in gold! Who does not know that promises of coming aid have cheered the defenders of besieged cities, like Lucknow, and raised them above their natural strength? Have we never heard that the promise of "help before night" had much to say to the mighty victory of Waterloo? Yet all such promises are as nothing compared to the rich treasure of believers, the eternal promises of God. Surely this is good!

(d) The Christian's fight is a good fight, because fought with the best of issues and results. No doubt it is a wa± in which there an; tremendous struggles, agonizing conflicts, wounds, bruises, watchings, fastings, and fatigue. But still every believer, without exception, is "more than conqueror through Him that loved him." (Rom. viii. 37.) No soldiers of Christ are ever lost, missing, or left dead on the battlefield. No mourning will ever need to be put on, and no tears to be shed for either private or officer in the army of Christ. The muster roll, when the last evening comes, will be found precisely the same that it was in the morning. The English Guards marched out of London to the Crimean campaign a magnificent body of men; but many of the gallant fellows laid their bones in a foreign grave, and never saw London again. Far different shall be the arrival of the Christian army in "the city which hath foundations, whose builder and maker is God." (Heb. xi. 10.) Not one shall be found lacking. The words of our great Captain shall be found true: "Of them which Thou hast given Me I have lost none." (John xviii. 9.) Surely this is good!

(e) The Christian's fight is good, because it does good to the soul of him that fights it. All other wars have a bad, lowering, and demoralising tendency. They call forth the worst passions of the human mind. They harden the conscience, and sap the foundations of religion and morality. The Christian warfare alone tends to call forth the best things that are left in man. It promotes humility and charity, it lessens selfishness and worldliness, it induces men to set their affections on things above. The old, the sick, the dying, are never known to repent of fighting Christ's battles against sin, the world, and the devil. Their only regret is that they did not begin to serve Christ long before. The experience of that eminent saint, Philip Henry, does not stand alone. In his last days he said to his family, "I take you all to record that a life spent in the service of Christ is the happiest life that a man can spend upon earth." Surely this is good!

(f) The Christian's fight is a good fight, because it does good to the world. All other wars have a devastating, ravaging, and injurious effect. The march of an army through a land is an awful scourge to the inhabitants. Wherever it goes it impoverishes, wastes, and does harm. Injury to persons, property, feelings, and morals invariably accompanies it. Far different are the effects produced by Christian soldiers. Wherever they live they are a blessing. They raise the standard of religion and morality. They invariably check the progress of drunkenness. Sabbath-breaking, profligacy, and dishonesty. Even their enemies are obliged to respect them. Go where you please, you will rarely find that barracks and garrisons do good to the neighbourhood. But go where you please, you will find that the presence of a few true Christians is a blessing. Surely this is good!

(g) Finally, the Christian's fight is good, because it ends in a glorious reward for all who fight it. Who can tell the wages that Christ will pay to all His faithful people? Who can estimate the good things that our Divine Captain has laid up for those who confess Him before men? A grateful country can give to her successful warriors medals, Victoria Crosses, pensions, peerages, honours, and titles. But it can give nothing that will last and endure for ever, nothing that can be carried beyond the grave. Palaces like Blenheim and Strathfieldsay can only be enjoyed for a few years. The bravest generals and soldiers must go down one day before the King of Terrors. Better, far better, is the position of him who fights under Christ's banner against sin, the world, and the devil. He may get little praise of man while he lives, and go down to the grave with little honour; but he shall have that which is far better, because far more enduring. He shall have "a crown of glory that fadeth not away." (1 Pet. v. 4.) Surely this is good!

Let us settle it in our minds that the Christian fight is a good fight--really good, truly good, emphatically good. We see only part of it as yet. We see the struggle, but not the end; we see the campaign, but not the reward; we see the cross, but not the crown. We see a few humble, broken-spirited, penitent, praying people, enduring hardships and despised by the world; but we see not the hand of God over them, the face of God smiling on them, the kingdom of glory prepared for them. These things are yet to be revealed. Let us not judge by appearances. There are more good things about the Christian warfare than we see.

And now let me conclude my whole subject with a few words of practical application. Our lot is cast in times when the world seems thinking of little else but battles and fighting. The iron is entering into the soul of more than one nation, and the mirth of many a fair district is clean gone. Surely in times like these a minister may fairly call on men to remember their spiritual warfare. Let me say a few parting words about the great fight of the soul.

(1) It may be you are struggling hard for the rewards of this world. Perhaps you are straining every nerve to obtain money, or place, or power, or pleasure. If that be your case, take care. Your sowing will lead to a crop of bitter disappointment. Unless you mind what you are about your latter end will be to lie down in sorrow.

Thousands have trodden the path you are pursuing, and have awoke too late to find it end in misery and eternal ruin. They have fought hard for wealth, and honour, and office, and promotion, and turned their backs on God, and Christ, and heaven, and the world to come. And what has their end been? Often, far too often, they have found out that their whole life has been a grand mistake. They have tasted by bitter experience the feelings of the dying statesman who cried aloud in his last hours, "The battle is fought: the battle is fought: but the victory is not won."

For your own happiness' sake resolve this day to join the Lord's side. Shake off your past carelessness and unbelief. Come out from the ways of a thoughtless, unreasoning world. Take up the cross, and become a good soldier of Christ. "Fight the good fight of faith," that you may be happy as well as safe.

Think what the children of this world will often do for liberty, without any religious principle. Remember how Greeks, and Romans, and Swiss, and Tyrolese, have endured the loss of all things, and even life itself, rather than bend their necks to a foreign yoke. Let their example provoke you to emulation. If men can do so much for a corruptible crown, how much more should you do for one which is incorruptible! Awake to a sense of the misery of being a slave. For life, and happiness, and liberty, arise and fight.

Fear not to begin and enlist under Christ's banner. The great Captain of your salvation rejects none that come to Him. Like David in the cave of Adullam, He is ready to receive all who apply to Him, however unworthy they may feel themselves. None who repent and believe are too bad to be enrolled in the ranks of Christ's army. All who come to Him by faith are admitted, clothed, armed, trained, and finally led on to complete victory. Fear not to begin this very day. There is yet room for you.

Fear not to go on fighting, if you once enlist. The more thorough and whole-hearted you are as a soldier, the more comfortable will you find your warfare. No doubt you will often meet with trouble, fatigue, and hard fighting, before your warfare is accomplished. But let none of these things move you. Greater is He that is for you than all they that be against you. Everlasting liberty or everlasting captivity are the alternatives before you. Choose liberty, and fight to the last.

(2) It may be you know something of the Christian warfare, and are a tried and proved soldier already. If that be your case, accept a parting word of advice and encouragement from a fellow-soldier. Let me speak to myself as well as to you. Let us stir up our minds by way of remembrance. There are some things which we cannot remember too well.

Let us remember that if we would fight successfully we must put on the whole armour of God, and never lay it aside till we die. Not a single piece of the armour can be dispensed with. The girdle of truth, the breastplate of righteousness, the shield of faith, the sword of the Spirit, the helmet of hope--each and all are needful. Not a single day can we dispense with any part of this armour. Well says an old veteran in Christ's army, who died 200 years ago, "In heaven we shall appear, not in armour, but in robes of glory. But here our arms are to be worn night and day. We must walk, work, sleep in them, or else we are not true soldiers of Christ." (Gurnall's Christian Armour.)

Let us remember the solemn words of an inspired warrior, who went to his rest 1,800 years ago: "No man that warreth entangleth himself with the affairs of this life; that he may please him who hath chosen him to be a soldier." (2 Tim. ii. 4.) May we never forget that saying!

Let us remember that some have seemed good soldiers for a little season, and talked loudly of what they would do, and yet turned back disgracefully in the day of battle.

Let us never forget Balaam, and Judas, and Demas, and Lot's wife. Whatever we are, and however weak, let us be real, genuine, true, and sincere.

Let us remember that the eye of our loving Saviour is upon us, morning, noon, and night. He will never suffer us to be tempted above that we are able to bear. He can be touched with the feeling of our infirmities, for He suffered Himself being tempted. He knows what battles and conflicts are, for He Himself was assaulted by the Prince of this world. Having such a High Priest, Jesus the Son of God, let us hold fast our profession. (Heb. iv. 14.)

Let us remember that thousands of soldiers before us have fought the same battle that we are fighting, and come off more than conquerors through Him that loved them. They overcame by the blood of the Lamb; and so also may we. Christ's arm is quite as strong as ever, and Christ's heart is just as loving as ever. He that saved men and women before us is one who never changes. He is "able to save to the uttermost all who come unto God by Him." Then let us cast doubts and fears away. Let us "follow them who through faith and patience inherit the promises," and are waiting for us to join them. (Heb. vii. 25; vi. 12.)

Finally, let us remember that the time is short, and the coming of the Lord draweth nigh. A few more battles and the last trumpet shall sound, and the Prince of Peace shall come to reign on a renewed earth. A few more struggles and conflicts, and then we shall bid an eternal good-bye to warfare, and to sin, to sorrow, and to death. Then let us fight on to the last, and never surrender. Thus saith the Captain of our salvation--"He that overcometh shall inherit all things; and I will be his God, and he shall be my son." (Rev. xxi. 7.)

Let me conclude all with the words of John Bunyan, in one of the most beautiful parts of Pilgrim's Progress. He is describing the end of one of his best and holiest pilgrims:--

"After this it was noised abroad that Mr. Valiant-for-truth was sent for by a summons, by the same party as the others. And he had this word for a token that the summons was true, The pitcher was broken at the fountain.' (Eccl. xii. 6.) When he understood it, he called for his friends, and told them of it. Then said he, I am going to my Father's house; and though with great difficulty I have got hither, yet now I do not repent me of all the troubles I have been at to arrive where I am. My sword I give to him that shall succeed me in my pilgrimage, and my courage and skill to him that can get it. My marks and scars I carry with me, to be a witness for me that I have fought His battles, who will now be my rewarder.' When the day that he must go home was come, many accompanied him to the river-side, into which, as he went down, he said, O death where is thy sting?' And as he went down deeper, he cried, O grave, where is thy victory?' So he passed over, and all the trumpets sounded for him on the other side."

May our end be like this! May we never forget that without fighting there can be no holiness while we live, and no crown of glory when we die!

V. THE COST

"Which of you, intending to build a house, sitteth not down first and counteth the cost?"--
-Luke xiv. 28.

THE text which heads this page is one of great importance. Few are the people who are not often obliged to ask themselves--"What does it cost?"

In buying property, in building houses, in furnishing rooms, in forming plans, in changing dwellings, in educating children, it is wise and prudent to look forward and consider. Many would save themselves much sorrow and trouble if they would only remember the question--"What does it cost?"

But there is one subject on which it is specially important to "count the cost." That subject is the salvation of our souls. What does it cost to be a true Christian? What does it cost to be a really holy man? This, after all, is the grand question. For want of thought about this, thousands, after seeming to begin well, turn away from the road to heaven, and are lost for ever in hell. Let me try to say a few words which may throw light on the subject.

I. I will show, firstly, what it costs to be a true Christian.

II. I will explain, secondly, why it is of such great importance to count the cost.

III. I will give, in the last place, some hints which may help men to count the cost rightly.

We are living in strange times. Events are hurrying on with singular rapidity. We never know "what a day may bring forth"; how much less do we know what may happen in a year!--We live in a day of great religious profession. Scores of professing Christians in every part of the land are expressing a desire for more holiness and a higher degree of spiritual life. Yet nothing is more common than to see people receiving the Word with joy, and then after two or three years falling away, and going back to their sins. They had not considered "what it costs" to be a really consistent believer and holy Christian. Surely these are times when we ought often to sit down and "count the cost," and to consider the state of our souls. We must mind what we are about. If we desire to be truly holy, it is a good sign. We may thank God for putting the desire into our hearts. But still the cost ought to be counted. No doubt Christ's way to eternal life is a way of pleasantness. But it is folly to shut our eyes to the fact that His way is narrow, and the cross comes before the crown.

I. I have, first, to show what it costs to be a true Christian.

Let there be no mistake about my meaning. I am not examining what it costs to save a Christian's soul. I know well that it costs nothing less than the blood of the Son of God to provide an atonement, and to redeem man from hell. The price paid for our redemption was nothing less than the death of Jesus Christ on Calvary. We "are bought with a price." "Christ gave Himself a ransom for all." (1 Cor. vi. 20; 1 Tim. ii. 6.) But all this is wide of the question.

The point I want to consider is another one altogether. It is what a man must be ready to give up if he wishes to be saved. It is the amount of sacrifice a man must submit to if he intends to serve Christ. It is in this sense that I raise the question, "What does it cost?" And I believe firmly that it is a most important one.

I grant freely that it costs little to be a mere outward Christian. A man has only got to attend a place of worship twice on Sunday, and to be tolerably moral during the week, and he has gone as far as thousands around him ever go in religion. All this is cheap and easy work: it entails no self-denial or self-sacrifice. If this is saving Christianity, and will take us to heaven when we die, we must alter the description of the way of life, and write, "Wide is the gate and broad is the way that leads to heaven!"

But it does cost something to be a real Christian, according to the standard of the Bible. There are enemies to be overcome, battles to be fought, sacrifices to be made, an Egypt to be forsaken, a wilderness to be passed through, a cross to be carried, a race to be run. Conversion is not putting a man in an arm-chair and taking him easily to heaven. It is the beginning of a mighty conflict, in which it costs much to win the victory. Hence arises the unspeakable importance of "counting the cost."

Let me try to show precisely and particularly what it costs to be a true Christian. Let us suppose that a man is disposed to take service with Christ, and feels drawn and inclined to follow Him. Let us suppose that some affliction, or some sudden death, or an awakening sermon, has stirred his conscience, and made him feel the value of his soul and desire to be a true Christian. No doubt there is everything to encourage him. His sins may be freely forgiven, however many and great. His heart may be completely changed, however cold and hard. Christ and the Holy Spirit, mercy and grace, are all ready for him. But still he should count the cost. Let us see particularly, one by one, the things that his religion will cost him.

(1) For one thing, it will cost him his self-righteousness. He must cast away all pride and high thoughts, and conceit of his own goodness. He must be content to go to heaven as a poor sinner saved only by free grace, and owing all to the merit and righteousness of another. He must really feel as well as say the Prayer-book words--that he has "erred and gone astray like a lost sheep," that he has "left undone the things he ought to have done, and done the things he ought not to have done, and that there is no health in him." He must be willing to give up all trust in his own morality, respectability, praying, Bible-reading, church-going, and sacrament-receiving, and to trust in nothing but Jesus Christ.

Now this sounds hard to some. I do not wonder. "Sir," said a godly ploughman to the well-known James Hervey, of Weston Favell, "it is harder to deny proud self than sinful self. But it is absolutely necessary." Let us set down this item first and foremost in our account. To be a true Christian it will cost a man his self-righteousness.

(2) For another thing, it will cost a man his sins. He must be willing to give up every habit and practice which is wrong in God's sight. He must set his face against it, quarrel with it, break off from it, fight with it, crucify it, and labour to keep it under, whatever the world around him may say or think. He must do this honestly and fairly. There must be no separate truce with any special sin which he loves. He must count all sins as his deadly enemies, and hate every false way. Whether little or great, whether open or secret, all his sins must be thoroughly renounced. They may struggle hard with him every day, and sometimes almost get the mastery over him. But he must never give way to them. He must keep up a perpetual war with his sins. It is written--"Cast away from you all your transgressions."--"Break off thy sins and iniquities."--"Cease to do evil."--(Ezek. xviii. 31; Daniel iv. 27; Isa. i. 16.)

This also sounds hard. I do not wonder. Our sins are often as dear to us as our children: we love them, hug them, cleave to them, and delight in them. To part with them is as hard as cutting off a right hand, or plucking out a right eye. But it must be done. The parting must come. "Though wickedness be sweet in the sinner's mouth, though he hide it under his tongue; though he spare it, and forsake it not," yet it must be given up, if he wishes to be saved. (Job xx. 12, 13.) He and sin must quarrel, if he and God are to be friends. Christ is willing to receive any sinners. But He will not receive them if they will stick to their sins. Let us set down that item second in our account. To be a Christian it will cost a man his sins.

(3) For another thing, it will cost a man his love of ease. He must take pains and trouble, if he means to run a successful race towards heaven. He must daily watch and stand on his guard, like a soldier on enemy's ground. He must take heed to his behaviour every hour of the day, in every company, and in every place, in public as well as in private, among strangers as well as at home. He must be careful over his time, his tongue, his temper, his thoughts, his imagination, his motives, his conduct in every relation of life. He must be diligent about his prayers, his Bible-reading, and his use of Sundays, with all their means of grace. In attending to these things he may come far short of perfection; but there is none of them that he can safely neglect. "The soul of the sluggard desireth, and hath nothing: but the soul of the diligent shall be made fat." (Prov. xiii. 4.)

This also sounds hard. There is nothing we naturally dislike so much as "trouble" about our religion. We hate trouble. We secretly wish we could have a "vicarious" Christianity, and could be good by proxy, and have everything done for us. Anything that requires exertion and labour is entirely against the grain of our hearts. But the soul can have "no gains without pains." Let us set down that item third in our account. To be a Christian it will cost a man his love of ease.

(4) In the last place, it will cost a man the favour of the world. He must be content to be thought ill of by man if he pleases God. He must count it no strange thing to be mocked, ridiculed, slandered, persecuted, and even hated. He must not be surprised to find his opinions and practices in religion despised and held up to scorn. He must submit to be thought by many a fool, an enthusiast, and a fanatic--to have his words perverted and his actions misrepresented. In fact, he must not marvel if some call him mad. The Master says--"Remember the word that I said unto you, The servant is not greater than his lord. If they have persecuted Me, they will also persecute you; if they have kept My saying, they will keep yours also." (John xv. 20.)

I dare say this also sounds hard. We naturally dislike unjust dealing and false charges, and think it very hard to be accused without cause. We should not be flesh and blood if we did not wish to have the good opinion of our neighbours. It is always unpleasant to be spoken against, and forsaken, and lied about, and to stand alone. But there is no help for it. The cup which our Master drank must be drunk by His disciples. They must be "despised and rejected of men." (Isa. liii. 3.) Let us set down that item last in our account. To be a Christian it will cost a man the favour of the world.

Such is the account of what it costs to be a true Christian. I grant the list is a heavy one. But where is the item that could be removed? Bold indeed must that man be who would dare to say that we may keep our self-righteousness, our sins, our laziness, and our love of the world, and yet be saved!

I grant it costs much to be a true Christian. But who in his sound senses can doubt that it is worth any cost to have the soul saved? When the ship is in danger of sinking, the crew think nothing of casting overboard the precious cargo. When a limb is mortified, a man will submit to any severe operation, and even to amputation, to save life. Surely a Christian should be willing to give up anything which stands between him and heaven. A religion that costs nothing is worth nothing! A cheap Christianity, without a cross, will prove in the end a useless Christianity, without a crown.

II. I have now, in the second place, to explain why "counting the cost" is of such great importance to man's soul.

I might easily settle this question by laying down the principle, that no duty enjoined by Christ can ever be neglected without damage. I might show how many shut their eyes throughout life to the nature of saving religion, and refuse to consider what it really costs to be a Christian. I might describe how at last, when life is ebbing away, they wake up, and make a few spasmodic efforts to turn to God. I might tell you how they find to their amazement that repentance and conversion are no such easy matters as they had supposed, and that it costs "a great sum" to be a true Christian. They discover that habits of pride and sinful indulgence, and love of ease, and worldliness, are not so easily laid aside as they had dreamed. And so, after a faint struggle, they give up in despair, and leave the world hopeless, graceless, and unfit to meet God! They had flattered themselves all their days that religion would be easy work when they once took it up seriously. But they open their eyes too late, and discover for the first time that they are ruined because they never "counted the cost."

But there is one class of persons to whom especially I wish to address myself in handling this part of my subject... It is a large class--an increasing class--and a class which in these days is in peculiar danger. Let me in a few plain words try to describe this class. It deserves our best attention.

The persons I speak of are not thoughtless about religion: they think a good deal about it. They are not ignorant of religion: they know the outlines of it pretty well. But their great defect is that they are not "rooted and grounded" in their faith. Too often they have picked up their knowledge second hand, from being in religious families, or from being trained in religious .ways, but have never worked it out by their own inward experience. Too often they have hastily taken up a profession of religion under the pressure of circumstances, from sentimental feelings, from animal excitement, or from a vague desire to do like others around them, but without any solid work of grace in their hearts. Persons like these are in a position of immense danger. They are precisely those, if Bible examples are worth anything, who need to be exhorted "to count the cost."

For want of "counting the cost" myriads of the children of Israel perished miserably in the wilderness between Egypt and Canaan. They left Egypt full of zeal and fervour, as if nothing could stop them. But when they found dangers and difficulties in the way, their courage soon cooled down. They had never reckoned on trouble. They had thought the promised land would be all before them in a few days. And so, when enemies, privations, hunger, and thirst began to try them, they murmured against Moses and God, and would fain have gone back to Egypt. In a word, they had "not counted the cost," and so lost everything, and died in their sins.

For want of "counting the cost," many of our Lord Jesus Christ's hearers went back after a time, and "walked no more with Him." (John vi. 66.) When they first saw His miracles, and heard His preaching, they thought "the kingdom of God would immediately appear." They cast in their lot with His Apostles, and followed Him without thinking of the consequences. But when they found that there were hard doctrines to be believed, and hard work to be done, and hard treatment to be borne, their fait gave way entirely, and proved to be nothing at all. In a word, they had not "counted the cost," and so made shipwreck of their profession.

For want of "counting the cost," King Herod returned to his old sins, and destroyed his soul. He liked to hear John the Baptist preach. He "observed" and honoured him as a just and holy man. He even "did many things" which were right and good. But when he found that he must give up his darling Herodias, his religion entirely broke down. He had not reckoned on this. He had not "counted the cost." (Mark vi. 20.)

For want of "counting the cost," Demas forsook the company of St. Paul, forsook the Gospel, forsook Christ, forsook heaven. For a long time he journeyed with the great Apostle of the Gentiles, and was actually a "fellow-labourer." But when he found he could not have the friendship of this world as well as the friendship of God, he gave up his Christianity and clave to the world. "Demas hath forsaken me," says St. Paul, "having loved this present world." (2 Tim. iv. 10.) He had not "counted the cost."

For want of "counting the cost," the hearers of powerful Evangelical preachers often come to miserable ends. They are stirred and excited into professing what they have not really experienced. They receive the Word with a "joy" so extravagant that it almost startles old Christians. They run for a time with such zeal and fervour that they seem likely to outstrip all others. They talk and work for spiritual objects with such enthusiasm that they make older believers feel ashamed. But when the novelty and freshness of their feelings is gone, a change comes over them. They prove to have been nothing more than stony-ground hearers. The description the great Master gives in the Parable of the Sower is exactly exemplified. "Temptation or persecution arises because of the Word, and they are offended." (Matt. xiii. 21.) Little by little their zeal melts away, and their love becomes cold. By and by their seats are empty in the assembly of God's people, and they are heard of no more among Christians. And why? They had "never counted the cost."

For want of "counting the cost," hundreds of professed converts, under religious revivals, go back to the world after a time, and bring disgrace on religion. They begin with a sadly mistaken notion of what is true Christianity. They fancy it consists in nothing more than a so-called "coming to Christ," and having strong inward feelings of joy and peace. And so, when they find, after a time, that there is a cross to be carried, that our hearts are deceitful, and that there is a busy devil always near us, they cool down in disgust, and return to their old sins. And why? Because they had really never known what Bible Christianity is, They had never learned that we must "count the cost."[9]

For want of "counting the cost," the children of religious parents often turn out ill, and bring disgrace on Christianity. Familiar from their earliest years with the form and theory of the Gospel--taught even from infancy to repeat great leading texts--accustomed every week to be instructed in the Gospel, or to instruct others in Sunday schools--they often grow up professing a religion without knowing why, or without ever having thought seriously about k. And then when the realities of grown-up life begin to press upon them, they often astound every one by dropping all their religion, and plunging right into the world. And why? They had never thoroughly understood the sacrifices which Christianity entails. They had never been taught to "count the cost."

These are solemn and painful truths. But they are truths. They all help to show the immense importance of the subject I am now considering. They all point out the absolute necessity of pressing the subject of this paper on all who profess a desire for holiness, and of crying aloud in all the churches--"Count the Cost."

I am bold to say that it would be well if the duty of "counting the cost" were more frequently taught than it is. Impatient hurry is the order of the day with many religionists. Instantaneous conversions, and immediate sensible peace, are the only results they seem to care for from the Gospel. Compared with these all other things are thrown into the shade. To produce them is the grand end and object, apparently, of all their labours. I say without hesitation that such a naked, one-sided mode of teaching Christianity is mischievous in the extreme.

Let no one mistake my meaning. I thoroughly approve of offering men a full, free, present, immediate salvation in Christ Jesus. I thoroughly approve of urging on man the possibility and the duty of immediate instantaneous conversion. In these matters I give place to no one. But I do say that these truths ought not to be set before men nakedly, singly, and alone. They ought to be told honestly what it is they are taking up, if they profess a desire to come out from the world and serve Christ. They ought not to be pressed into the ranks of Christ's army without being told what the warfare entails. In a word, they should be told honestly to "count the cost."

Does any one ask what our Lord Jesus Christ's practice was in this matter? Let him read what St. Luke records. He tells us that on a certain occasion "There went great multitudes with Him: and He turned and said unto them, If any come to Me, and hate not his father, and mother, and wife, and children, and brethren, and sisters, yea, and his own life also, he cannot be My disciple. And whosoever doth not bear his cross and come after Me, cannot be My disciple." (Luke xiv. 25-27.) I must plainly say, that I cannot reconcile this passage with the proceedings of many modern religious teachers. And yet, to my mind, the doctrine of it is as clear as the sun at noon-day. It shows us that we ought not to hurry men into professing discipleship, without warning them plainly to "count the cost."

Does any one ask what the practice of the eminent and best preachers of the Gospel has been in days gone by? I am bold to say that they have all with one mouth borne testimony to the wisdom of our Lord's dealing with the multitudes to which I have just referred. Luther, and Latimer, and Baxter, and Wesley, and Whitfield, and Berridge, and Rowland Hill, were all keenly alive to the deceitfulness of man's heart. They knew full well that all is not gold that glitters, that conviction is not conversion, that feeling is not faith, that sentiment is not grace, that all blossoms do not come to fruit. "Be not deceived," was their constant cry. "Consider well what you do. Do not run before you are called. Count the cost."

If we desire to do good, let us never be ashamed of walking in the steps of our Lord Jesus Christ. Work hard if you will, and have the opportunity, for the souls of others. Press them to consider their ways. Compel them with holy violence to come in, to lay down their arms, and to yield themselves to God. Offer them salvation, ready, free, full, immediate salvation. Press Christ and all His benefits on their acceptance. But in all your work tell the truth, and the whole truth. Be ashamed to use the vulgar arts of a recruiting serjeant. Do not speak only of the uniform, the pay, and the glory; speak also of the enemies, the battle, the armour, the watching, the marching, and the drill. Do not present only one side of Christianity. Do not keep back "the cross" of self-denial that must be carried, when you speak of the cross on which Christ died for our redemption. Explain fully what Christianity entails. Entreat men to repent and come to Christ; but bid them at the same time to "count the cost."

III. The third and last thing which I propose to do, is to give some hints which may help men to "count the cost" rightly.

Sorry indeed should I be if I did not say something on this branch of my subject. I have no wish to discourage any one, or to keep any one back from Christ's service. It is my heart's desire to encourage every one to go forward and take up the cross. Let us "count the cost" by all means, and count it carefully. But let us remember, that if we count rightly, and look on all sides, there is nothing that need make us afraid.

Let us mention some things which should always enter into our calculations in counting the cost of true Christianity. Set down honestly and fairly what you will have to give up and go through, if you become Christ's disciple. Leave nothing out. Put it all down. But then set down side by side the following sums which I am going to give you. Do this fairly and correctly, and I am not afraid for the result.

(a) Count up and compare, for one thing, the profit and the loss, if you are a true-hearted and holy Christian. You may possibly lose something in this world, but you will gain the salvation of your immortal soul. It is written--"What shall it profit a man, if he shall gain the whole world, and lose his own soul?" (Mark viii. 36.)

(b) Count up and compare, for another thing, the praise and the blame, if you are a true-hearted and holy Christian. You may possibly be blamed by man, but you will have the praise of God the Father, God the Son, and God the Holy Ghost. Your blame will come from the lips of a few erring, blind, fallible men and women. Your praise will come from the King of kings and Judge of all the earth. It is only those whom He blesses who are really blessed. It is written--"Blessed are ye when men shall revile you, and persecute you, and say all manner of evil against you falsely, for my sake. Rejoice and be exceeding glad, for great is your reward in heaven." (Matt. v. 11, 12.)

(c) Count up and compare, for another thing, the friends and the enemies, if you are a true-hearted and holy Christian. On the one side of you is the enmity of the devil and the wicked. On the other, you have the favour and friendship of the Lord Jesus Christ. Your enemies, at most, can only bruise your heel. They may rage loudly, and compass sea and land to work your ruin; but they cannot destroy you. Your Friend is able to save to the uttermost all them that come unto God by Him. None shall ever pluck His sheep out of His hand. It is written--"Be not afraid of them that kill the body, and after that have no more that they can do. But I will forewarn you whom ye shall fear: Fear Him, which after He hath killed hath power to cast into hell; yea, I say unto you, fear Him." (Luke xii. 5.)

(d) Count up and compare, for another thing, the life that now is and the life to come, if you are a true-hearted and holy Christian. The time present, no doubt, is not a time of ease. It is a time of watching and praying, fighting and struggling, believing and working. But it is only for a few years. The time future is the season of rest and refreshing. Sin shall be cast out. Satan shall be bound. And, best of all, it shall be a rest for ever. It is written--"Our light affliction, which is but for a moment, worketh for us a far more exceeding and eternal weight of glory; while we look not at the things which are seen, but at the things which are not seen: for the things which are seen are temporal; but the things which arc not seen are eternal." (2 Cor. iv. 17, 18.)

(e) Count up and compare, for another thing, the pleasures of sin and the happiness of God's service, if you are a true-hearted and holy Christian, The pleasures that the worldly man gets by his ways are hollow, unreal, and unsatisfying. They are like the fire of thorns, flashing and crackling for a few minutes, and then quenched for ever. The happiness that Christ gives to His people is something solid, lasting, and substantial. It is not dependent on health or circumstances. It never leaves a man, even in death. It ends in a crown of glory that fadeth not away. It is written--"The joy of the hypocrite is but for a moment."--"As the crackling of thorns under a pot, so is the laughter of the fool." (Job xx. 5; Eccl. vii. 6.) But it is also written--"Peace I leave with you, my peace give I unto you: not as the world giveth, give I unto you. Let not your heart be troubled, neither let it be afraid." (John xiv. 27.)

(f) Count up and compare, for another thing, the trouble that true Christianity entails, and the troubles that are in store for the wicked beyond the grave. Grant for a moment that Bible-reading, and praying, and repenting, and believing, and holy living, require pains and self-denial. It is all nothing compared to that "wrath to come" which is stored up for the impenitent and unbelieving. A single day in hell will be worse than a whole life spent in carrying the cross. The "worm that never dies, and the fire that is not quenched," are things which it passes man's power to conceive fully or describe. It is written--"Son, remember that thou in thy life-time receivedst thy good things, and likewise Lazarus evil things; but now he is comforted and thou art tormented." (Luke xvi. 25.)

(g) Count up and compare, in the last place, the number of those who turn from sin and the world and serve Christ, and the number of those who forsake Christ and return to the world. On the one side you will find thousands--on the other you will find none. Multitudes are every year turning out of the broad way and entering the narrow. None who really enter the narrow way grow tired ot it and return to the broad. The footsteps in the downward road are often to be seen turning out of it. The footsteps in the road to heaven are all one way. It is written--"The way of the wicked is darkness"--"The way of transgressors is hard." (Prov. iv. 19; xiii. 15.) But it is also written--"The path of the just is as the shining light, which shineth more and more unto the perfect day." (Prov. iv. 8.)

Such sums as these, no doubt, are often not done correctly. Not a few, I am well aware, are ever "halting between two opinions." They cannot make up their minds that it is worth while to serve Christ. The losses and gains, the advantages and disadvantages, the sorrows and the joys, the helps and the hindrances with that faith we shall set things down at their true value. Filled with that faith we shall neither add to the cross nor subtract from the crown. Our conclusions will be all correct. Our sum total will be without error.

(1) In conclusion, let every reader of this paper think seriously, whether his religion costs him anything at present. Very likely it costs you nothing. Very probably it neither costs you trouble, nor time, nor thought, nor care, nor pains, nor reading, nor praying, nor self-denial, nor conflict, nor working, nor labour of any kind. Now mark what I say. Such a religion as this will never save your soul. It will never give you peace while you live, nor hope while you die. It will not support you in the day of affliction, nor cheer you in the hour of death. A religion which costs nothing is worth nothing. Awake before it is too late. Awake and repent. Awake and be converted. Awake and believe. Awake and pray. Rest not till you can give a satisfactory answer to my question, "What does it cost?"

(2) Think, if you want stirring motives for serving God, what it cost to provide a salvation for your soul. Think how the Son of God left heaven and became Man, suffered on the cross, and lay in the grave, to pay your debt to God, and work out for you a complete redemption. Think of all this and learn that it is no light matter to possess an immortal soul. It is worth while to take some trouble about one's soul.

Ah, lazy man or woman, is it really come to this, that you will miss heaven for lack of trouble? Are you really determined to make shipwreck for ever, from mere dislike to exertion? Away with the cowardly, unworthy thought. Arise and play the man. Say to yourself, "Whatever it may cost, I will, at any rate, strive to enter in at the strait gate." Look at the cross of Christ, and take fresh courage. Look forward to death, judgment, and eternity, and be in earnest. It may cost much to be a Christian, but you may be sure it pays.

(3) If any reader of this paper really feels that he has counted the cost, and taken up the cross, I bid him persevere and press on. I dare say you often feel your heart faint, and are sorely tempted to give up in despair. Your enemies seem so many, your besetting sins so strong, your friends so few, the way so steep and narrow, you hardly know what to do. But still I say, persevere and press on.

The time is very short. A few more years of watching and praying, a few more tossings on the sea of this world, a few more deaths and changes, a few more winters and summers, and all will be over. We shall have fought our last battle, and shall need to fight no more.

The presence and company of Christ will make amends for all we suffer here below. When we see as we have been seen, and look back on the journey of life, we shall wonder at our own faintness of heart. We shall marvel that we made so much of our cross, and thought so little of our crown. We shall marvel that in "counting the cost" we could ever doubt on which side the balance of profit lay. Let us take courage. We are not far from home. IT MAY COST MUCH TO BE A TRUE CHRISTIAN AND A CONSISTENT BELIEVER; BUT IT PAYS.

ENDNOTE

[9] I should be very sorry indeed if the language I have used above about revivals was misunderstood. To prevent this I will offer a few remarks by way of explanation. For true revivals of religion no one can be more deeply thankful than I am. Wherever they may take place, and by whatever agents they may be effected, I desire to bless God for them, with all my heart. "If Christ is preached," I rejoice, whoever may be the preacher. If souls are saved, I rejoice, by whatever section of the Church the word of life has been ministered. But it is a melancholy fact that, in a world like this, you cannot have good without evil. I have no hesitation in saying, that one consequence of the revival movement has been the rise of a theological system which I feel obliged to call defective and mischievous in the extreme. The leading feature of the theological system I refer to, is this: an extravagant and disproportionate magnifying of three points in religion,--viz., instantaneous conversion--the invitation of unconverted sinners to come to Christ,--and the possession of inward joy and peace as a test of conversion. I repeat that these three grand truths (for truths they are) are so incessantly and exclusively brought forward, in some quarters, that great harm is done. Instantaneous conversion, no doubt, ought to be pressed on people. But surely they ought not to be led to suppose that there is no other sort of conversion, and that unless they are suddenly and powerfully converted to God, they are not converted at all. The duty of coming to Christ at once, "just as we are," should be pressed on all hearers. It is the very corner-stone of Gospel preaching. But surely men ought to be told to repent as well as to believe. They should be told why they are to come to Christ, and what they are to come for, and whence their need arises. The nearness of peace and comfort in Christ should be proclaimed to men. But surely they should be taught that the possession of strong inward joys and high frames of mind is not essential to justification, and that there may be true faith and true peace without such very triumphant feelings. Joy alone is no certain evidence of grace. The defects of the theological system I have in view appear to me to be these: (1) The work of the Holy Ghost in converting sinners is far too much narrowed and confined to one single way. Not all true converts are converted instantaneously, like Saul and the Philippian jailor. (2) Sinners are not

sufficiently instructed about the holiness of God's law, the depth of their sinfulness, and the real guilt of sin. To be incessantly telling a sinner to "come to Christ" is of little use, unless you tell him why he needs to come, and show him fully his sins. (3) Faith is not properly explained. In some cases people are taught that mere feeling is faith. In others they are taught that if they believe that Christ died for sinners they have faith! At this rate the very devils are believers! (4) The possession of inward joy and assurance is made essential to believing. Yet assurance is certainly not of the essence of saving faith. There may be faith when there is no assurance. To insist on all believers at once "rejoicing," as soon as they believe, is most unsafe. Some, I am quite sure, will rejoice without believing, while others will believe who cannot at once rejoice. (5) Last, but not least, the sovereignty of God in saving sinners, and the absolute necessity of preventing grace, are far too much overlooked. Many talk as if conversions could be manufactured at man's pleasure, and as if there were no such text as this, "It is not of him that willeth, nor of him that runneth, but of God that showeth mercy." (Rom. ix. 16.) The mischief done by the theological system I refer to is, I am persuaded, very great. On the one hand, many humble-minded Christians are totally discouraged and daunted. They fancy they have no grace because they cannot reach up to the high frames and feelings which are pressed on their attention. On the other side, many graceless people are deluded into thinking they are "converted," because under the pressure or animal excitement and temporary feelings they arc led to profess themselves Christians. And all this time the thoughtless and ungodly look on with contempt, and rind fresh reasons for neglecting religion altogether. The antidotes to the state of things I deplore are plain and few. (1) Let "all the counsel of God be taught" in Scriptural proportion; and let not two or three precious doctrines of the Gospel be allowed to overshadow all other truths. (2) Let repentance be taught fully as well as faith, and not thrust completely into the background. Our Lord Jesus Christ and St. Paul always taught both. (3) Let the variety of the Holy Ghost's works be honestly stated and admitted; and while instantaneous conversion is pressed on men, let it not be taught as a necessity. (4) Let those who profess to have found immediate sensible peace be plainly warned to try themselves well, and to remember that feeling is not faith, and that "patient continuance in well-doing" is the great proof that faith is true. (John viii. 31.) (5) Let the great duty of "counting the cost" be constantly urged on all who are disposed to make a religious profession, and let them be honestly and fairly told that there is warfare as well as peace, a cross as well as a crown, in Christ's service. I am sure that unhealthy excitement is above all things to be dreaded In religion, because it often ends in fatal, soul-ruining reaction and utter deadness. And when multitudes are suddenly brought under the power of religious impressions, unhealthy excitement is almost sure to follow. I have not much faith in the soundness of conversions when they are said to take places in masses and wholesale. It does not seem to me in harmony with God's general dealings in this dispensation. To my eyes it appears that God's ordinary plan is to call in individuals one by one. Therefore, when I hear of large numbers being suddenly converted all at one time, I hear of it with less hope than some. The healthiest and most enduring success in mission fields is certainly not where natives have come over to Christianity in a mass. The most satisfactory and firmest work at home does not always appear to me to be the work done in revivals. There are two passages of Scripture which I should like to have frequently and fully expounded in the present day by all who preach the Gospel, and specially by those who have anything to do with revivals. One passage is the parable of the sower, That parable is not recorded three times over without good reason and a deep meaning.--The other passage is our Lord's teaching about "counting the cost," and the words which He spoke to the "great multitudes" whom He saw following

Him. It is very noteworthy that He did not on that occasion say anything to flatter these volunteers or encourage them to follow Him. No: He saw what their case needed. He told them to stand still and "count the cost." (Luke xiv. 25, etc.) I am not sure that some modern preachers would have adopted this course of treatment.

VI. GROWTH

"Grow in grace, and in the knowledge of our Lord and Saviour Jesus Christ."--2 Peter iii. 18.

THE subject of the text which heads this page is one which I dare not omit in this volume about Holiness. It is one that ought to be deeply interesting to every true Christian. It naturally raises the questions, Do we grow in grace? Do we get on in our religion? Do we make progress?

To a mere formal Christian I cannot expect the inquiry to seem worth attention. The man who has nothing more than a kind of Sunday religion--whose Christianity is like his Sunday clothes, put on once a week, and then laid aside--such a man cannot, of course, be expected to care about "growth in grace." He knows nothing about such matters. "They are foolishness to him." (1 Cor. ii. 14.) But to every one who is in downright earnest about his soul, and hungers and thirsts after spiritual life, the question ought to come home with searching power. Do we make progress in our religion? Do we grow?

The question is one that is always useful, but especially so at certain seasons. A Saturday night, a Communion Sunday, the return of a birthday, the end of a year--all these are seasons that ought to set us thinking, and make us look within. Time is fast flying. Life is fast ebbing away. The hour is daily drawing nearer when the reality of our Christianity will be tested, and it will be seen whether we have built on "the rock" or on "the sand." Surely it becomes us from time to time to examine ourselves, and take account of our souls? Do we get on in spiritual things? Do we grow?

The question is one that is of special importance in the present day. Crude and strange opinions are floating in men's minds on some points of doctrine, and among others on the point of "growth in grace," as an essential part of true holiness. By some it is totally denied. By others it is explained away, and pared down to nothing. By thousands it is misunderstood, and consequently neglected. In a day like this it is useful to look fairly in the face the whole subject of Christian growth.

In considering this subject there are three things which I wish to bring forward and establish:--

I. The reality of religious growth. There is such a thing as "growth in grace."

II. The marks of religious growth. There are marks by which "growth in grace" may be known.

III. The means of religious growth. There are means that must be used by those who desire "growth in grace."

I know not who you are, into whose hands this paper may have fallen. But I am not ashamed to ask your best attention to its contents. Believe me, the subject is no mere matter of speculation and controversy. It is an eminently practical subject, if any is in religion. It is intimately and inseparably connected with the whole question of "sanctification." It is a leading mark of true saints that they grow. The spiritual health and prosperity, the spiritual happiness and comfort of every true-hearted and holy Christian, are intimately connected with the subject of spiritual growth.

I. The first point I propose to establish is this: There is such a thing as growth in grace.

That any Christian should deny this proposition is at first sight a strange and melancholy thing. But it is fair to remember that man's understanding is fallen no less than his will. Disagreements about doctrines are often nothing more than disagreements about the meaning of words. I try to hope that it is so in the present case. I try to believe that when I speak of "growth in grace" and maintain it, I mean one thing, while my brethren who deny it mean quite another. Let me therefore clear the way by explaining what I mean.

When I speak of "growth in grace," I do not for a moment mean that a believer's interest in Christ can grow. I do not mean that he can grow in safety, acceptance with God, or security. I do not mean that he can ever be more justified, more pardoned, more forgiven, more at peace with God, than he is the first moment that he believes. I hold firmly that the justification of a believer is a finished, perfect, and complete work; and that the weakest saint, though he may not know and feel it, is as completely justified as the strongest. I hold firmly that our election, calling, and standing in Christ admit of no degrees, increase, or diminution. If any one dreams that by "growth in grace" I mean growth in. justification he is utterly wide of the mark, and utterly mistaken about the whole point I am considering. I would go to the stake, God helping me, for the glorious truth, that in the matter of justification before God every believer is "complete in Christ." (Col. ii. 10.) Nothing can be added to his justification from the moment he believes, and nothing taken away.

When I speak of "growth in grace" I only mean increase in the degree, size, strength, vigour, and power of the graces which the Holy Spirit plants in a believer's heart. I hold that every one of those graces admits of growth, progress, and increase. I hold that repentance, faith, hope, love, humility, zeal, courage, and the like, may be little or great, strong or weak, vigorous or feeble, and may vary greatly in the same man at different periods of his life. When I speak of a man "growing in grace," I mean simply this--that1 his sense of sin is becoming deeper, his faith stronger, his hope brighter, his love more extensive, his spiritual-mindedness more marked. He feels more of the power of godliness in his own heart. He manifests more of it in his life. He is going on from strength to strength, from faith to faith, and from grace to grace. I leave it to others to describe such a man's condition by any words they please. For myself I think the truest and best account of him is this--he is "growing in grace."

One principal ground on which I build this doctrine of "growth in grace," is the plain language of Scripture. If words in the Bible mean anything, there is such a thing as "growth," and believers ought to be exhorted to "grow."--What says St. Paul? "Your faith groweth exceedingly." (2 Thess. i. 3) "We beseech you that ye increase more and more." (1 Thess. iv. 10.) "Increasing in the knowledge of God." (Col. i 10.) "Having hope, when your faith is increased." (2 Cor. x. 15.) "The Lord make you to increase in love." (1 Thess. iii. 12.) "That ye may grow up into Him in all things." (Eph. iv. 15.) "I pray that your love may abound more and more." (Phil. i. 9.) "We beseech you, as ye have received of us how ye ought to walk and to please God, so ye would abound more and more." (1 Thess. iv. 1.)--What says St. Peter? "Desire the sincere milk of the Word, that ye may grow thereby." (1 Pet. ii. 2.) "Grow in grace, and in the knowledge of our Lord and Saviour Jesus Christ." (2 Pet. iii. 18.) I know not what others think of such texts. To me they seem to establish the doctrine for which I contend, and to be incapable of any other explanation. Growth in grace is taught in the Bible. I might stop here and say no more.

The other ground, however, on which I build the doctrine of "growth in grace," is the ground of fact and experience. I ask any honest reader of the New Testament whether he cannot see degrees of grace in the New Testament saints whose histories are recorded, as plainly as the sun at noon-day?--I ask him whether he cannot see in the very same persons as great a difference between their faith and knowledge at one time and at another, as between the same man's strength when he is an infant and when he is a grownup man?--I ask him whether the Scripture does not distinctly recognise this in the language it uses, when it speaks of "weak" faith and "strong" faith, and of Christians as "new-born babes," "little children," "young men," and "fathers"? (1 Pet. ii. 2; John ii. 12-14.) I ask him, above all, whether his own observation of believers, now-a-days, does not bring him to the same conclusion?--What true Christian would not confess that there is as much difference between the degree of his own faith and knowledge when he was first converted, and his present attainments, as there is between a sapling and a full-grown tree? His graces are the same in principle; but they have grown. I know not how these facts strike others: to my eyes they seem to prove, most unanswerably, that "growth in grace" is a real thing.

I feel almost ashamed to dwell so long upon this part of my subject. In fact, if any man means to say that the faith, and hope, and knowledge, and holiness of a newly-converted person, are as strong as those of an old-established believer, and need no increase, it is waste of time to argue further. No doubt they are as real, but not so strong--as true, but not so vigorous--as much seeds of the Spirit's planting, but not yet so fruitful. And if any one asks how they are to become stronger, I say it must be by the same process by which all things having life increase--they must grow. And this is what I mean by "growth in grace."[10]

Let us turn away from the things I have been discussing to a more practical view of the great subject before us. I want men to look at "growth in grace" as a thing of infinite importance to the soul. I believe, whatever others may think, that our best interests are concerned in a right view of the question--Do we grow?

(a) Let us know then that "growth in grace" is the best evidence of spiritual health and prosperity. In a child, or a flower, or a tree, we are all aware that when there is no growth there is something wrong. Healthy life in an animal or vegetable will always show itself by progress and increase. It is just the same with our souls. If they are progressing and doing well they will grow.[11]

(b) Let us know, furthermore, that "growth in grace" is one way to be happy in our religion. God has wisely linked together our comfort and our increase in holiness. He has graciously made it our interest to press on and aim high in our Christianity. There is a vast difference between the amount of sensible enjoyment which one believer has in his religion compared to another. But you may be sure that ordinarily the man who feels the most "joy and peace in believing," and has the clearest witness of the Spirit in his heart, is the man who grows.

(c) Let us know, furthermore, that "growth in grace" is one secret of usefulness to others. Our influence on others for good depends greatly on what they see in us. The children of the world measure Christianity quite as much by their eyes as by their ears. The Christian who is always at a standstill, to all appearances the same man, with the same little faults, and weaknesses, and besetting sins, and petty infirmities, is seldom the Christian who does much good. The man who shakes and stirs minds, and sets the world thinking, is the believer who is continually improving and going forward. Men think there is life and reality when they see growth.[12]

(d) Let us know, furthermore, that "growth in grace" pleases God. It may seem a wonderful thing, no doubt, that anything done by such creatures as we are can give pleasure to the Most High God. But so it is. The Scripture speaks of walking so as to "please God." The Scripture says there are sacrifices with which "God is well-pleased." (1 Thess. iv. 1; Heb. xiii. 16.) The husbandman loves to see the plants on which he has bestowed labour flourishing and bearing fruit. It cannot but disappoint and grieve him to see them stunted and standing still. Now what does our Lord Himself say? "I am the true vine, and my Father is the husbandman."--"Herein is my Father glorified, that ye bear much fruit; so shall ye be my disciples." (John xv. 1, 8.) The Lord takes pleasure in all His people--but specially in those that grow.

(e) Let us know, above all, that "growth in grace" is not only a thing possible, but a thing for which believers are accountable. To tell an unconverted man, dead in sins, to "grow in grace" would doubtless be absurd. To tell a believer, who is quickened and alive to God, to grow, is only summoning him to a plain Scriptural duty. He has a new principle within him, and it is a solemn duty not to quench it. Neglect of growth robs him of privileges, grieves the Spirit, and makes the chariot wheels of his soul move heavily. Whose fault is it, I should like to know, if a believer does not grow in grace? The fault, I am sure, cannot be laid on God. He delights to "give more grace;" He "hath pleasure in the prosperity of His servants." (James iv. 6; Psa. xxxv. 27.) The fault, no doubt, is our own. We ourselves are to blame, and none else, if we do not grow.

II. The second point I propose to establish is this: There are marks by which growth in grace may be known.

Let me take it for granted that we do not question the reality of growth in grace and its vast importance.--So far so good. But you now want to know how any one may find out whether he is growing in grace or not? I answer that question, in the first place, y observing that we are very poor judges of our own condition, and that bystanders often know us better than we know ourselves. But I answer further, that there are undoubtedly certain great marks and signs of growth in grace, and that wherever you see these marks you see a "growing" soul. I will now proceed to place some of these marks before you in order.

(a) One mark of "growth in grace" is increased humility. The man whose soul is "growing," feels his own sinfulness and unworthiness more every year. He is ready to say with Job, "I am vile,"--and with Abraham, I am "dust and ashes,"--and with Jacob, "I am not worthy of the least of all Thy mercies,--and with David, "I am a worm,"--and with Isaiah, "I am a man of unclean lips,"--and with Peter, "I am a sinful man, O Lord." Job xl. 4; Gen. xviii. 27; xxxii. 10; Ps. xxii. 6; Isa. vi. 5; Luke v. 8.) The nearer he draws to God, and the more he sees of God's holiness and perfection, the more thoroughly is he sensible of his own countless imperfections. The further he journeys in the way to heaven, the more he understands what St. Paul means when he says, "I am not already perfect,"--"I am not meet to be called an Apostle,"--"I am less than the least of all saints,"--"I am chief of sinners." (Phil. iii. 12; 1 Cor. xv. 9; Ephes. iii. 8; 1 Tim. i. 15.) The riper he is for glory, the more, like the ripe corn, he hangs down his head. The brighter and clearer is his light, the more he sees of the shortcomings and infirmities of his own heart. When first converted, he would tell you he saw but little of them compared to what he sees now. Would anyone know whether he is growing in grace? Be sure that you look within for increased humility.[13]

(b) Another mark of "growth in grace" is increased faith and love towards our Lord Jesus Christ. The man whose soul is "growing," finds more in Christ to rest upon every year, and rejoices more that he has such a Saviour. No doubt he saw much in Him when first he believed. His faith laid hold on the atonement of Christ and gave him hope.--But as he grows in grace he sees a thousand things in Christ of which at first he never dreamed. His love and power--His heart and His intentions--His offices as Substitute, Intercessor, Priest, Advocate, Physician, Shepherd, and Friend, unfold themselves to a growing soul in an unspeakable manner. In short, he discovers a suitableness in Christ to the wants of his soul, of which the half was once not known to him. Would anyone know if he is growing in grace? Then let him look within for increased knowledge of Christ.

(c) Another mark of "growth in grace" is increased holiness of life and conversation. The man whose soul is "growing" gets more dominion over sin, the world, and the devil every year. He becomes more careful about his temper, his words, and his actions. He is more watchful over his conduct in every relation of life. He strives more to be conformed to the image of Christ in all things, and to follow Him as his example, as well as to trust in Him as his Saviour. He is not content with old attainments and former grace. He forgets the things that are behind and reaches forth unto those things which are before, making "Higher!" "Upward!" "Forward!" "Onward!" his continual motto. (Phil. iii. 13.) On earth he thirsts and longs to have a will more entirely in unison with God's will. In heaven the chief thing that he looks for, next to the presence of Christ, is complete separation from all sin. Would anyone know if he is growing in grace? Then let him look within for increased holiness.[14]

(d) Another mark of "growth in grace" is increased spirituality of taste and mind. The man whose soul is "growing" takes more interest in spiritual things every year. He does not neglect his duty in the world. He discharges faithfully, diligently, and conscientiously every relation of life, whether at home or abroad. But the things he loves best are spiritual things. The ways, and fashions, and amusements, and recreations of the world have a continually decreasing place in his heart. He does not condemn them as down right sinful, nor say that those who have anything to do with them are going to hell. He only feels that they have a constantly diminishing hold on his own affections, and gradually seem smaller and more trifling in his eyes. Spiritual companions, spiritual occupations, spiritual conversation, appear of ever-increasing value to him. Would anyone know if he is growing in grace? Then let him look within for increasing spirituality of taste.[15]

(e) Another mark of "growth in grace" is increase of charity. The man whose soul is "growing" is more full of love every year--of love to all men, but especially of love towards the brethren. His love will show itself actively in a growing disposition to do kindnesses, to take trouble for others, to be good-natured to everybody, to be generous, sympathizing, thoughtful, tender-hearted, and considerate. It will show itself passively in a growing disposition to be meek and patient toward all men, to put up with provocation and not stand upon rights, to bear and forbear much rather than quarrel. A growing soul will try to put the best construction on other people's conduct, and to believe all things and hope all things, even to the end. There is no surer mark of backsliding and falling off in grace than an increasing disposition to find fault, pick holes, and see weak points in others. Would any one know if he is growing in grace? Then let him look within for increasing charity.

(f) One more mark of "growth in grace" is increased zeal and diligence in trying to do good to souls. The man who is really "growing" will take greater interest in the salvation of sinners every year. Missions at home and abroad, efforts to increase religious light and diminish religious darkness--all these things will every year have a greater place in his attention. He will not become "weary in well-doing" because he does not see every effort succeed. He will not care less for the progress of Christ's cause on earth as he grows older, though he will learn to expect less. He will just work on, whatever the result may be--giving, praying, preaching, speaking, visiting, according to his position--and count his work its own reward. One of the surest marks of spiritual decline is a decreased interest about the souls of others and the growth of Christ's kingdom. Would any one know whether he is growing in grace? Then let him look within for increased concern about the salvation of souls.

Such are the most trustworthy marks of growth in grace. Let us examine them carefully, and consider what we know about them. I can well believe that they will not please some professing Christians in the present day. Those high-flying religionists, whose only notion of Christianity is that of a state of perpetual joy and ecstasy--who tell you that they have got far beyond the region of conflict and soul-humiliation--such persons no doubt will regard the marks I have laid down as "legal," "carnal," and "gendering to bondage." I cannot help that. I call no man master in these things. I only wish my statements to be tried in the balance of Scripture. And I firmly believe that what I have said is not only Scriptural, but agreeable to the experience of the most eminent saints in every age. Show me a man in whom the six marks I have mentioned can be found. He is the man who can give a satisfactory answer to the question, DO WE GROW?

III. The third and last thing I propose to consider is this:--The means that must be used by those who desire to grow in grace. The words of St. James must never be forgotten: "Every good gift and every perfect gift is from above, and cometh down from the Father of lights." (James i. 17.) This is no doubt as true of growth in grace as it is of everything else. It is the "gift of God." But still it must always be kept in mind that God is pleased to work by means. God has ordained means as well as ends. He that would grow in grace must use the means of growth.[16]

This is a point, I fear, which is too much overlooked by believers. Many admire growth in grace in others, and wish that they themselves were like them. But they seem to suppose that those who grow are what they are by some special gift or grant from God, and that as this gift is not bestowed on themselves they must be content to sit still. This is a grievous delusion, and one against which I desire to testify with all my might. I wish it to be distinctly understood that growth in grace is bound up with the use of means within the reach of all believers, and that, as a general rule, growing souls are what they are because they use these means.

Let me ask the special attention of my readers while I try to set forth in order the means of growth. Cast away for ever the vain thought that if a believer does not grow in grace it is not his fault. Settle it in your mind that a believer, a man quickened by the Spirit, is not a mere dead creature, but a being or mighty capacities and responsibilities. Let the words of Solomon sink down into your heart: "The soul of the diligent shall be made fat." (Prov. xiii. 4.)

(a) One thing essential to growth in grace is diligence in the use of private means of grace. By these I understand such means as a man must use by himself alone, and no one can use for him. I include under this head private prayer, private reading of the Scriptures, and private meditation and self-examination. The man who does not take pains about these three things must never expect to grow. Here are the roots of true Christianity. Wrong here, a man is wrong all the way through! Here is the whole reason why many professing Christians never seem to get on. They are careless and slovenly about their private prayers. They read their Bibles but little, and with very little heartiness of spirit. They give themselves no time for self-inquiry and quiet thought about the state of their souls.

It is useless to conceal from ourselves that the age we live in is full of peculiar dangers. It is an age of great activity, and of much hurry, bustle, and excitement in religion. Many are "running to and fro," no doubt, and "knowledge is increased." (Dan. xii. 4.) Thousands are ready enough for public meetings, sermon-hearing, or anything else in which there is "sensation." Few appear to remember the absolute necessity of making time to "commune with our hearts, and be still." (Psalm iv. 4.) But without this there is seldom any deep spiritual prosperity. I suspect that English Christians two hundred years ago read their Bibles more, and were more frequently alone with God, than they are in the present day. Let us remember this point! Private religion must receive our first attention, if we wish our souls to grow.

(b) Another thing which is essential to growth in grace is carefulness in the use of public means of grace. By these I understand such means as a man has within his reach as a member of Christ's visible Church. Under this head I include the ordinances of regular Sunday worship, the uniting with God's people in common prayer and praise, the preaching of the Word, and the Sacrament of the Lord's Supper. I firmly believe that the manner in which these public means of grace are used has much to say to the prosperity of a believer's soul. It is easy to use them in a cold and heartless way. The very familiarity of them is apt to make us careless. The regular return of the same voice, and the same kind of words, and the same ceremonies, is likely to make us sleepy, and callous, and unfeeling. Here is a snare into which too many professing Christians fall. If we would grow we must be on our guard here. Here is a matter in which the Spirit is often grieved and saints take great damage. Let us strive to use the old prayers, and sing the old hymns, and kneel at the old communion-rail, and hear the old truths preached, with as much freshness and appetite as in the year we first believed. It is a sign of bad health when a person loses relish for his food; and it is a sign of spiritual decline when we lose our appetite for means of grace. Whatever we do about public means, let us always do it "with our might." (Eccles. ix. 10.) This is the way to grow!

(c) Another thing essential to growth in grace is watchfulness over our conduct in the little matters of everyday life. Our tempers, our tongues, the discharge of our several relations of life, our employ ment of time--each and all must be vigilantly attended to if we wish our souls to prosper. Life is made up of days, and days of hours, and the little things of every hour are never so little as to be beneath the care of a Christian. When a tree begins to decay at root or heart, the mischief is first seen at the extreme end of the little branches. "He that despiseth little things," says an uninspired writer, "shall fall by little and little." That witness is true. Let others despise us, if they like, and call us precise and over-careful. Let us patiently hold on our way, remembering that "we serve a precise God," that our Lord's example is to be copied in the least things as well as the greatest, and that we must "take up our cross daily" and hourly, rather than sin. We must aim to have a Christianity which, like the sap of a tree, runs through every twig and leaf of our character, and sanctifies all. This is one way to grow!

(d) Another thing which is essential to growth in grace is caution about the company we keep and the friendships we form. Nothing perhaps affects a man's character more than the company he keeps. We catch the ways and tone of those we live and talk with, and unhappily get harm far more easily than good. Disease is infectious, but health is not. Now if a profess-ing Christian deliberately chooses to be intimate with those who are not friends of God and who cling to the world, his soul is sure to take harm. It is hard enough to serve Christ under any circumstances in such a world as this. But it is doubly hard to do it if we are friends of the thoughtless and ungodly. Mistakes in friendship or marriage-engagements are the whole reason why some have entirely ceased to grow. "Evil communications corrupt good man-ners." "The friendship of the world is enmity with God." (1 Cor. xv. 33; James iv. 4.) Let us seek friends that will stir us up about our prayers, our Bible-reading, and our employment of time--about our souls, our salvation, and a world to come. Who can tell the good that a friend's word in season may do, or the harm that it may stop? This is one way to grow.[17]

(e) There is one more thing which is absolutely essential to growth in grace--and that is regular and habitual communion with the Lord Jesus. In saying this, let no one suppose for a minute that I am referring to the Lord's Supper. I mean nothing of the kind. I mean that daily habit of intercourse between the believer and his Saviour, which can only be carried on by faith, prayer, and meditation. It is a habit, I fear, of which many believers know little. A man may be a believer and have his feet on the rock, and yet live far below his privileges. It is pos-sible to have "union" with Christ, and yet to have little if any "communion" with Him. But, for all that, there is such a thing.

The names and offices of Christ, as laid down in Scripture, appear to me to show unmis-takably that this "communion" between the saint and his Saviour is not a mere fancy, but a real true thing. Between the "Bridegroom" and his bride--between the "Head" and His mem-bers--between the "Physician" and His patients--between the "Advocate" and His clients--between the "Shepherd" and His sheep--between the "Master" and His scholars--there is evidently implied a habit of familiar intercourse, of daily application for things needed, of daily pouring out and unburdening our hearts and minds. Such a habit of dealing with Christ is clearly something more than a vague general trust in the work that Christ did for sinners. It is getting close to Him, and laying hold on Him with confidence, as a loving, personal Friend. Tins is what I mean by communion.

Now I believe that no man will ever grow in grace who does not know something exper-imentally of the habit of "communion." We must not be content with a general orthodox knowledge that justification is by faith and not by works, and that we put our trust in Christ. We must go further than this. We must seek to have personal intimacy with the Lord Jesus, and to deal with Him as a man deals with a loving friend. We must realize what it is to turn to Him first in every need, to talk to Him about every difficulty, to consult Him about every step, to spread before Him all our sorrows, to get Him to share in all our joys, to do all as in His sight, and to go through every day leaning on and looking to Him. This is the way that St. Paul lived: "The life which I now live in the flesh I live by the faith of the Son of God." "To me to live is Christ." (Gal. ii. 20; Phil. i. 21.) It is ignorance of this way of living that makes so many see no beauty in the book of Canticles. But it is the man who lives in this way, who keeps up constant communion with Christ--this is the man, I say emphatically, whose soul will grow.

I leave the subject of growth in grace here. Far more might be said about it, if time per-mitted. But I have said enough, I hope, to convince my readers that the subject is one of vast importance.--Let me wind up all with some practical applications.

(1) This book may fall into the hands of some who know nothing whatever about growth in grace. They have little or no concern about religion. A little proper Sunday church-going or

chapel-going makes up the sum and substance of their Christianity. They are without spiritual life, and of course they cannot at present grow. Are you one of these people? If you are, you are in a pitiable condition.

Years are slipping away and time is flying. Graveyards are filling up and families are thinning. Death and judgment are getting nearer to us all. And yet you live like one asleep about your soul! What madness! What folly! What suicide can be worse than this?

Awake before it be too late; awake, and arise from the dead, and live to God. Turn to Him who is sitting at the right hand of God, to be your Saviour and Friend. Turn to Christ, and cry mightily to Him about your soul. There is yet hope! He that called Lazarus from the grave is not changed. He that commanded the widow's son at Nain to arise from his bier can do miracles yet for your soul. Seek Him at once: seek Christ, if you would not be lost for ever. Do not stand still talking, and meaning, and intending, and wishing, and hoping. Seek Christ that you may live, and that living you may grow.

(2) This book may fall into the hands of some who ought to know something of growth in grace, but at present know nothing at all. They have made little or no progress since they were first converted. They seem to have "settled on their lees." (Zep. i. 12.) They go on from year to year content with old grace, old experience, old knowledge, old faith, old measure of attainment, old religious expressions, old set phrases. Like the Gibeonites, their bread is always mouldy, and their shoes are patched and clouted. They never appear to get on. Are you one of these people? If you are, you are living far below your privileges and responsibilities. It is high time to examine yourself.

If you have reason to hope that you are a true believer and yet do not grow in grace, there must be a fault, and a serious fault somewhere. It cannot be the will of God that your soul should stand still. "He giveth more grace." He "takes pleasure in the prosperity of His servants." (James iv. 6; Ps. xxxv. 27.) It cannot be for your own happiness or usefulness that your soul should stand still. Without growth you will never rejoice in the Lord. (Phil. iv. 4.) Without growth you will never do good to others. Surely this want of growth is a serious matter! It should raise in you great searchings of heart. There must be some "secret thing." (Job xv. 11.) There must be some cause.

Take the advice I give you. Resolve this very day that you will find out the reason of your standstill condition. Probe with a faithful and firm hand every corner of your soul. Search from one end of the camp to the other, till you find out the Achan who is weakening your hands. Begin with an application to the Lord Jesus Christ, the great Physician of souls, and ask Him to heal the secret ailment within you, whatever it may be. Begin as if you had never applied to Him before, and ask for grace to cut off the right hand and pluck out the right eye. But never, never be content, if your soul does not grow. For your peace sake, for your usefulness sake, for the honour of your Maker's cause, resolve to find out the reason why.

(3) This book may fall into the hands of some who are really growing in grace, but are not aware of it, and will not allow it. Their very growth is the reason why they do not see their growth! Their continual increase in humility prevents them feeling that they get on.[18] Like Moses, when he came down from the mount from communing with God, their faces shine. And yet, like Moses, they are not aware of it. (Ex. xxxiv. 29.) Such Christians, I grant freely, are not common. But here and there such are to be found. Like angels' visits, they are few and far between. Happy is the neighbourhood where such growing Christians live! To meet them and see them and be in their company, is like meeting and seeing a bit of "heaven upon earth."

Now what shall I say to such people? What can I say? What ought I to say? Shall I bid them awake to a consciousness of their growth and be pleased with it? I will do nothing of the kind.--Shall I tell them to plume themselves on their own attainments, and look at their own superiority to others? God forbid! I will do nothing of the kind.--To tell them such things would do them no good. To tell them such things, above all, would be useless waste of time. If there is any one feature about a growing soul which specially marks him, it is his deep sense of his own unworthiness. He never sees anything to be praised in himself. He only feels that he is an unprofitable servant and the chief of sinners. It is the righteous, in the picture of the judgment-day, who say, "Lord, when saw we Thee an hungred, and fed Thee?" (Matt. xxv. 37.) Extremes do indeed meet strangely sometimes. The conscience-hardened sinner and the eminent saint are in one respect singularly alike. Neither of them fully realizes his own condition. The one does not see his own sin, nor the other his own grace!

But shall I say nothing to growing Christians? Is there no word of counsel I can address to them? The sum and substance of all that I can say is to be found in two sentences: "Go forward!" "Go on!"

We can never have too much humility, too much faith in Christ, too much holiness, too much spirituality of mind, too much charity, too much zeal in doing good to others. Then let us be continually forgetting the things behind, and reaching forth unto the things before. (Phil. iii. 13.) The best of Christians in these matters is infinitely below the perfect pattern of his Lord. Whatever the world may please to say, we may be sure there is no danger of any of us becoming "too good."

Let us cast to the winds as idle talk the common notion that it is possible to be "extreme" and go "too far" in religion. This is a favourite He of the devil, and one which he circulates with vast industry. No doubt there are enthusiasts and fanatics to be found who bring evil report upon Christianity by their extravagances and follies. But if any one means to say that a mortal man can be too humble, too charitable, too holy, or too diligent in doing good, he must either be an infidel or a fool. In serving pleasure and money it is easy to go too far. But in following the things which make up true religion, and in serving Christ there can be no extreme.

Let us never measure our religion by that of others, and think we are doing enough if we have gone beyond our neighbours. This is another snare of the devil. Let us mind our own business. "What is that to thee?" said our Master on a certain occasion: "Follow thou Me." (John xxi. 22.) Let us follow on, aiming at nothing short of perfection. Let us follow on, making Christ's life and character our only pattern and example. Let us follow on, remembering daily that at our best we are miserable sinners. Let us follow on, and never forget that it signifies nothing whether we are better than others or not. At our very best we are far worse than we ought to be. There will always be room for improvement in us. We shall be debtors to Christ's mercy and grace to the very last. Then let us leave off looking at others and comparing ourselves with others. We shall find enough to do if we look at our own hearts.

Last, but not least, if we know anything of growth in grace, and desire to know more, let us not be surprised if we have to go through much trial and affliction in this world. I firmly believe it is the experience of nearly all the most eminent saints. Like their blessed Master they have been "men of sorrows, acquainted with grief," and "perfected through sufferings." (Isa. liii. 3; Heb. ii. 10.) It is a striking saying of our Lord, "Every branch in Me that beareth fruit, my Father purgeth it, that it may bring forth more fruit." (John xv. 2.) It is a melancholy fact, that constant temporal prosperity, as a general rule, is injurious to a believer's soul. We cannot stand it. Sickness, and losses, and crosses, and anxieties, and disappointments seem absolutely needful to keep us humble, watchful, and spiritual-minded. They are as needful as the pruning knife to the vine, and the refiner's furnace to the gold. They are not pleasant to flesh and blood. We do not like them, and often do not see their meaning. "No chastening for the present seemeth to be joyous, but grievous: nevertheless, afterward, it yieldeth the peaceable fruit of righteousness." (Heb. xii. 11.) We shall find that all worked for our good when we reach heaven. Let these thoughts abide in our minds, if we love growth in grace. When days of darkness come upon us, let us not count it a strange thing. Rather let us remember that lessons are learned on such days which would never have been learned in sunshine. Let us say to ourselves, "This also is for my profit, that I may be a partaker of God's holiness. It is sent in love. I am in God's best school. Correction is instruction. This is meant to make me grow."

I leave the subject of growth in grace here. I trust I have said enough to set some readers thinking about it. All things are growing older: the world is growing old; we ourselves are grow-older. A few more summers, a few more winters, a few more sicknesses, a few more sorrows, a few more weddings, a few more funerals, a few more meetings, and a few more partings, and then-- what? Why the grass will be growing over our graves!

Now would it not be well to look within, and put to our souls a simple question? In religion, in the things that concern our peace, in the great matter of personal holiness, are we getting on? DO WE GROW?

ENDNOTE

[10] "True grace is progressive, of a spreading, growing nature. It is with grace as it is with light: first, there is the day-break; then it shines brighter to the full noon-day. The saints are not only compared to stars for their light, but to trees for their growth, (Isa. lxi. 3; Hos. xiv. 5.) A good Christian is not like Hezekiah's sun that went backwards, nor Joshua's sun that stood still, but is always advancing in holiness, and increasing with the increase of God."-- Thomas Watson, Minister of St. Stephen's Walbrook, 1660. (Body of Divinity.)

[11] "The growth of grace is the best evidence of the truth of grace. Things that have not life will not grow. A picture will not grow. A stake in a hedge will not grow. But a plant that hath vegetative life will grow. The growing of grace shows it to be alive in the soul."--T. Watson, 1660.

[12] "Christian, as ever you would stir up others to exalt the God of grace, look to the exercise and improvement of your own graces. When poor servants live in a family, and see the faith, and love, and wisdom, and patience, and humility of a master, shining like the stars in heaven, it draws forth their hearts to bless the Lord that ever they came into such a family.-- When men's graces shine as Moses' face did, when their life, as one speaketh of Joseph's life, is a very heaven, sparkling with virtues as so many bright stars, how much others are stirred up to glorify God, and cry, These are Christians indeed! these are an honour to their God, a crown to their Christ, and a credit to their Gospel! Oh, if they were all such, we would be Christians too!"--T. Brooks, 1661. (Unsearchable Riches.)

[13] "The right manner of growth is to grow less in one's own eyes. I am a worm and no man.' (Psa. xxii. 6.) The sight of corruption and ignorance makes a Christian grow into a dislike of himself. He doth vanish in his own eyes. Job abhorred himself in the dust. (Job xlii. 6.) This is good, to grow out of conceit with oneself."--T. Watson. 1660.

¹⁴ "It is a sign of not growing in grace, when we are less troubled about sin. Time was when the least sin did grieve us (as the least hair makes the eye weep), but now we can digest sin without remorse. Time was when a Christian was troubled if he neglected closet prayer; now he can omit family prayer. Time was when vain thoughts did not trouble him; now he is not troubled for loose practices. There is a sad declension in religion; and grace is so far from growing that we can hardly perceive its puke to beat."--T. Watson. 1660.

¹⁵ "If now you would be rich in graces, look to your walking. It is not the knowing soul, nor the talking soul, but the close-walking soul, the obedient soul, that is rich. Others may be rich in notions, but none so rich in spiritual experience, and in all holy and heavenly graces, as close-walking Christians."--T. Brooks. 1661. "It is a sign of not growing in grace, when we grow more worldly. Perhaps once we were mounted into higher orbits, we did set our hearts on things above, and speak the language of Canaan. But now our minds are taken off heaven, we dig our comforts out of these lower mines, and with Satan compass the earth. It is a sign we are going down hill apace, and our grace is in a consumption. It is observable when nature decays, and people are near dying, they grow more stooping. And truly when men's hearts grow more stooping to the earth, and they can hardly lift up themselves to an heavenly thought, if grace be not dead, yet it is ready to die."--T. Watson. 1660.

¹⁶ "Experience will tell every Christian that the more strictly, and closely, and constantly he walketh with God, the stronger he groweth in duty. Infused habits are advantaged by exercise. As the fire that kindled the wood for sacrifices upon the altar first came down from heaven, but then was to be kept alive by the care and labour of the priests, so the habits of spiritual grace are indeed infused from God, and must be maintained by daily influences from God, yet with a concurrence also of our own labours, in waiting upon God, and exercising ourselves with godliness; and the more a Christian doth so exercise himself, the more strong he shall grow."--Collinges on Providence. 1678.

¹⁷ "Let them be thy choicest companions, that have made Christ their chiefest companion. Do not so much eye the outsides of men as their inside: look most to their internal worth. Many persons have their eyes upon the external garb of a professor. But give me a Christian that minds the internal worth of persons, that makes such as are most filled with the fulness of God his choicest and chiefest companions."--T. Brooks. 1661.

¹⁸ "Christians may be growing when they think they do not grow." There is that maketh himself poor, yet he is rich.' (Prov. xiii. 7.) The sight that Christians have of their defects in grace, and their thirst after greater measures of grace, makes them think they do not grow. He who covets a great estate, because he hath not so much as he desires thinks himself poor."-- T. Watson. 1660. "Souls may be rich in grace, and yet not know it, not perceive it. The child is heir to a crown or a great estate, but knows it not. Moses' face did shine, and others saw it, but he perceived it not. So many a precious soul is rich in grace, and others see it, and know it, and bless God for it, and yet the poor soul perceives it not.--Sometimes this arises from the soul's strong desires of spiritual riches. The strength of the soul's desires after spiritual riches doth often take away the very sense of growing spiritually rich. Many covetous men's desires are so strongly carried forth after earthly riches, that though they do grow rich, yet they cannot perceive it, they cannot believe it. It is just so with many a precious Christian: his desires after spiritual riches are so strong, that they take away the very sense of his growing rich in spirituals. Many Christians have much worth within them, but they see it not. It was a good man that said, The Lord was in this place and I knew it not.'--Again, this ariseth sometimes from men neglecting to cast up their accounts. Many men thrive and grow rich, and yet,

by neglecting to cast up their accounts, they cannot tell whether they go forward or backward. It is so with many precious souls. Again, this ariseth sometimes from the soul's too frequent casting up of its accounts. If a man should cast up his accounts once a week, or once a month, he may not be able to discern that he doth grow rich, and yet he may grow rich. But let him compare one year with another, and he shall clearly see that he doth grow rich.-- Again, this sometimes ariseth from the soul's mistakes in casting up its accounts. The soul many times mistakes: it is in a hurry, and then it puts down ten for a hundred, and a hundred for a thousand. Look, as hypocrites put down their counters for gold, their pence for pounds, and always prize themselves above the market, so sincere souls do often put down their pounds for pence, their thousands for hundreds, and still prize themselves below the market."--Thomas Brooks. 1661. (Unsearchable Riches)

VII. ASSURANCE

"I am now ready to be offered, and the time of my departure is at hand."

"I have fought a good fight, I have finished my course, I have kept the faith:

"Henceforth there is laid up for me a crown of righteousness, which the Lord, the righteous Judge, shall give me at that day: and not to me only, but unto all them also that love His appearing."--2 Tim. iv. 6, 7, 8.

IN the words of Scripture which head this page, we see the Apostle Paul looking three ways--downward, backward, forward; downward to the grave--backward to his own ministry--forward to that great day, the day of judgment!

It will do us good to stand by the Apostle's side a few minutes, and mark the words he uses. Happy is that soul who can look where Paul looked, and then speak as Paul spoke!

(a) He looks downward to the grave, and he does it without fear. Hear what he says:--

"I am ready to be offered."--I am like an animal brought to the place of sacrifice, and bound with cords to the very horns of the altar. The drink-offering, which generally accompanies the oblation, is already being poured out. The last ceremonies have been gone through. Every preparation has been made. It only remains to receive the death-blow, and then all is over.

"The time of my departure is at hand."--I am like a ship about to unmoor and put to sea. All on board is ready. I only wait to have the moorings cast off that fasten me to the shore, and I shall then set sail, and begin my voyage.

These are remarkable words to come from the lips of a child of Adam like ourselves! Death is a solemn thing, and never so much so as when we see it close at hand. The grave is a chilling, heart-sickening place, and it is vain to pretend it has no terrors. Yet here is a mortal man who can look calmly into the narrow "house appointed for all living," and say, while he stands upon the brink, "I see it all, and am not afraid."

(b) Let us listen to him again. He looks backward to his ministerial life, and he does it without shame. Hear what he says:--

"I have fought a good fight."--There he speaks as a soldier. I have fought that good fight with the world, the flesh, and the devil, from which so many shrink and draw back.

"I have finished my course."--There he speaks as one who has run for a prize. I have run the race marked out for me. I have gone over the ground appointed for me, however rough and steep. I have not turned aside because of difficulties, nor been discouraged by the length of the way. I am at last in sight of the goal.

"I have kept the faith."--There he speaks as a steward. I have held fast that glorious Gospel which was committed to my trust. I have not mingled it with man's traditions, nor spoiled its simplicity by adding my own inventions, nor allowed others to adulterate it without withstanding them to the face. "As a soldier --a runner--a steward," he seems to say, "I am not ashamed."

That Christian is happy who, as he quits the world, can leave such testimony behind him. A good conscience will save no man--wash away no sin--nor lift us one hair's breadth toward heaven. Yet a good conscience will be found a pleasant visitor at our bedside in a dying hour. There is a fine passage in Pilgrim's Progress which describes Old Honest's passage across the river of death. "The river," says Bunyan, "at that time overflowed its banks in some places; but Mr. Honest in his lifetime had spoken to one Good Conscience to meet him there; the which he also did, and lent him his hand, and so helped him over." We may be sure there is a mine of truth in that passage.

(c) Let us hear the Apostle once more. He looks forward to the great day of reckoning, and he does it without doubt. Mark his words:--

"Henceforth there is laid up for me a crown of righteousness, which the Lord, the righteous Judge, shall give me at that day: and not to me only, but unto all them also that love His appearing."--"A glorious reward," he seems to say, "is ready and laid up in store for me--even that crown which is only given to the righteous. In the great day of judgment the Lord shall give this crown to me, and to all beside me who have loved Him as an unseen Saviour, and longed to see Him face to face. My work on earth is over. This one thing now remains for me to look forward to, and nothing more."

Let us observe that the Apostle speaks without any hesitation or distrust. He regards the crown as a sure thing, as his own already. He declares with unfaltering confidence his firm persuasion that the righteous Judge will give it to him. Paul was no stranger to all the circumstances and accompaniments of that solemn day to which he referred. The great white throne--the assembled world--the open books--the revealing of all secrets--the listening angels--the awful sentence--the eternal separation of the lost and saved--all these were things with which he was well acquainted. But none of these things moved him. His strong faith overleaped them all, and he only saw Jesus, his all-prevailing Advocate, and the blood of sprinkling, and sin washed away. "A crown," he says, "is laid up for me." "The Lord Himself shall give it to me." He speaks as if he saw it all with his own eyes.

Such are the main things which these verses contain. Of most of them I shall not speak, because I want to confine myself to the special subject of this paper. I shall only try to consider one point in the passage. That point is the strong "assurance of hope," with which the Apostle looks forwards to his own prospects in the day of judgment.

I shall do this the more readily, because of the great importance which attaches to the subject of assurance, and the great neglect with which, I humbly conceive, it is often treated in this day.

But I shall do it at the same time with fear and trembling. I feel that I am treading on very difficult ground, and that it is easy to speak rashly and unscripturally in this matter. The road between truth and error is here especially a narrow pass; and if I shall be enabled to do good to some without doing harm to others, I shall be very thankful.

There are four things I wish to bring forward in speaking of the subject of assurance, and it may clear our way if I name them at once.

I. First, then, I will try to show that an assured hope, such as Paul here expresses, is a true and Scriptural thing.

II. Secondly, I will make this broad concession--that a man may never arrive at this assured hope, and yet be saved.

III. Thirdly, I will give some reasons why an assured hope is exceedingly to be desired.

IV. Lastly, I will try to point out some causes why an assured hope is so seldom attained.

I ask special attention of all who take an interest in the great subject of this volume. If I am not greatly mistaken, there is a very close connection between true holiness and assurance. Before I close this paper I hope to show my readers the nature of that connection. At present, I content myself with saying, that where there is the most holiness, there is generally the most assurance.

I. First, then, I will try to show that an assured hope is a true and Scriptural thing.

Assurance, such as Paul expresses in the verses which head this paper, is not a mere fancy or feeling. It is not the result of high animal spirits, or a sanguine temperament of body. It is a positive gift of the Holy Ghost, bestowed without reference to men's bodily frames or constitutions, and a gift which every believer in Christ ought to aim at and seek after.

In matters like these, the first question is this--What saith the Scripture? I answer that question without the least hesitation. The Word of God appears to me to teach distinctly that a believer may arrive at an assured confidence with regard to his own salvation.

I lay it down fully and broadly, as God's truth, that a true Christian, a converted man, may reach such a comfortable degree of faith in Christ, that in general he shall feel entirely confident as to the pardon and safety of his soul--shall seldom be troubled with doubts--seldom be distracted with fears--seldom be distressed by anxious questionings--and, in short, though vexed by many an inward conflict with sin, shall look forward to death without trembling, and to judgment without dismay.[19] This, I say, is the doctrine of the Bible.

Such is my account of assurance. I will ask my readers to mark it well. I say neither less nor more than I have here laid down.

Now such a statement as this is often disputed and denied. Many cannot see the truth of it at all.

The Church of Rome denounces assurance in the most unmeasured terms. The Council of Trent declares roundly that a "believer's assurance of the pardon of his sins is a vain and ungodly confidence;" and Cardinal Bellarmine, the well-known champion of Romanism, calls it "a prime error of heretics."

The vast majority of the worldly and thoughtless Christians among ourselves oppose the doctrine of assurance. It offends and annoys them to hear of it. They do not like others to feel comfortable and sure, because they never feel so themselves. Ask them whether their sins are forgiven, and they will probably tell you they do not know! That they cannot receive the doctrine of assurance is certainly no marvel.

But there are also some true believers who reject assurance, or shrink from it as a doctrine fraught with danger. They consider it borders on presumption. They seem to think it a proper humility never to feel sure, never to be confident, and to live in a certain degree of doubt and suspense about their souls. This is to be regretted, and does much harm.

I frankly allow there are some presumptuous persons who profess to feel a confidence for which they have no Scriptural warrant. There are always some people who think well of themselves when God thinks ill, just as there are some who think ill of themselves when God thinks well. There always will be such. There never yet was a Scriptural truth without abuses and counterfeits. God's election--man's impotence--salvation by grace--all are alike abused. There will be fanatics and enthusiasts as long as the world stands. But, for all this, assurance is a reality and a true thing; and God's children must not let themselves be driven from the use of a truth, merely because it is abused.[20]

My answer to all who deny the existence of real, well-grounded assurance, is simply this-- What saith the Scripture? If assurance be not there, I have not another word to say.

But does not Job say, "I know that my Redeemer liveth, and that He shall stand at the latter day upon the earth; and though after my skin worms destroy this body, yet in my flesh shall I see God"? (Job xix. 26, 26.)

Does not David say, "Though I walk through the valley of the shadow of death, I will fear no evil: for Thou art with me; Thy rod and Thy staff they comfort me "? (Psalm xxiii. 4.)

Does not Isaiah say, "Thou wilt keep him in perfect peace whose mind is stayed on Thee, because he trusteth in Thee"? (Isaiah xxvi. 3.)

And again, "The work of righteousness shall be peace; and the effect of righteousness quietness, and assurance for ever." (Isaiah xxxii. 17.)

Does not Paul say to the Romans, "I am persuaded that neither death, nor life, nor angels, nor principalities, nor powers, nor things present, nor things to come, nor height, nor depth, nor any other creature, shall be able to separate us from the love of God, which is in Christ Jesus our Lord"? (Rom. viii. 38, 39.)

Does he not say to the Corinthians, "We know that if our earthly house of this tabernacle were dissolved, we have a building of God, an house not made with hands, eternal in the heavens "? (2 Cor. v. 1.)

And again, "We are always confident, knowing that, whilst we are at home in the body, we are absent from the Lord." (2 Cor. v. 6.)

Does he not say to Timothy, "I know whom I have believed, and am persuaded that He is able to keep that which I have committed to Him"? (2 Tim. i. 12.)

And does he not speak to the Colossians of "the full assurance of understanding" (Coloss. ii. 2), and to the Hebrews of the "full assurance of faith," and the "full assurance of hope"? (Heb. vi. ii; x. 22.)

Does not Peter say expressly, "Give diligence to make your calling and election sure"? (2 Peter i. 10.)

Does not John say, "We know that we have passed from death unto life"? (1 John iii. 14.)

And again, "These things have I written unto you that believe on the name of the Son of God, that ye may know that ye have eternal life." (1 John v. 13.)

And again, "We know that we are of God." (1 John v. 19.)

What shall we say to these things? I desire to speak with all humility on any controverted point. I feel that I am only a poor fallible child of Adam myself. But I must say that in the passages I have just quoted I see something far higher than the mere "hopes" and "trusts," with which so many believers appear content in this day. I see the language of persuasion, confidence, knowledge--nay, I may almost say, of certainty. And I feel, for my own part, if I may take these Scriptures in their plain obvious meaning, the doctrine of assurance is true.

But my answer, furthermore, to all who dislike the doctrine of assurance, as bordering on presumption, is this:--It can hardly be presumption to tread in the steps of Peter, and Paul, of Job, and of John. They were all eminently humble and lowly-minded men, if ever any were; and yet they all speak of their own state with an assured hope. Surely this should teach us that deep humility and strong assurance are perfectly compatible, and that there is not any necessary connection between spiritual confidence and pride.[21]

My answer, furthermore, is that many have attained to such an assured hope as our text expresses, even in modern times. I will not concede for a moment that it was a peculiar privilege confined to the Apostolic day. There have been in our own land many believers, who have appeared to walk in almost uninterrupted fellowship with the Father and the Son--who have seemed to enjoy an almost unceasing sense of the light of God's reconciled countenance shining down upon them, and have left their experience on record. I could mention well-known names, if space permitted. The thing has been, and is--and that is enough.

My answer, lastly, is, It cannot be wrong to feel confidently in a matter where God speaks unconditionally--to believe decidedly when God promises decidedly--to have a sure persuasion of pardon and peace when we rest on the word and oath of Him that never changes. It is an utter mistake to suppose that the believer who feels assurance is resting on anything he sees in himself. He simply leans on the Mediator of the New Covenant, and the Scripture of truth. He believes the Lord Jesus means what He says, and takes Him at His word. Assurance after all is no more than a full-grown faith; a masculine faith that grasps Christ's promise with both hands--a faith that argues like the good centurion, If the Lord "speak the word only," I am healed. Wherefore then should I doubt? (Matt. viii. 8.)[22]

We may be sure that Paul was the last man in the world to build his assurance on anything of his own. He who could write himself down "chief of sinners" (1 Tim. i. 15), had a deep sense of his guilt and corruption. But then he had a still deeper sense of the length and breadth of Christ's righteousness imputed to him.--He who could cry, "O wretched man that I am" (Rom. vii. 24), had a clear view of the fountain of evil within his heart. But then he had a still clearer view of that other Fountain which can remove "all sin and uncleanness." He who thought himself "less than the least of all saints" (Ephes. iii. 8), had a lively and abiding feeling of his own weakness. But he had a still livelier feeling that Christ's promise, "My sheep shall never perish" (John x. 28), could not be broken.--Paul knew, if ever man did, that he was a poor, frail bark, floating on a stormy ocean. He saw, if any did, the rolling waves and roaring tempest by which he was surrounded. But then he looked away from self to Jesus, and was not afraid. He remembered that anchor within the veil, which is both "sure and steadfast." (Heb. vi. 19.) He remembered the word, and work, and constant intercession of Him that loved him and gave Himself for him. And this it was, and nothing else, that enabled him to say so boldly, "A crown is laid up for me, and the Lord shall give it to me;" and to conclude so surely, "The Lord will preserve me; I shall never be confounded."[23]

I may not dwell longer on this part of the subject. I think it will be allowed I have shown some good ground for the assertion I made, that assurance is a true thing.

II. I pass on to the second thing I spoke of. I said, a believer may never arrive at this assured hope, which Paul expresses, and yet be saved.

I grant this most freely. I do not dispute it for a moment. I would not desire to make one contrite heart sad that God has not made sad, or to discourage one fainting child of God, or to leave the impression that men have no part or lot in Christ, except they feel assurance.

A person may have saving faith in Christ, and yet never enjoy an assured hope, such as the Apostle Paul enjoyed. To believe and have a glimmering hope of acceptance is one thing; to have "joy and peace" in our believing, and abound in hope, is quite another. All God's children have faith; not all have assurance. I think this ought never to be forgotten.

I know some great and good men have held a different opinion. I believe that many excellent ministers of the Gospel, at whose feet I would gladly sit, do not allow the distinction I have stated. But I desire to call no man master. I dread as much as any one the idea of healing the the wounds of conscience slightly; but I should think any other view than that I have given, a most uncomfortable Gospel to preach, and one very likely to keep souls back a long time from the gate of life.[24]

I do not shrink from saying that by grace a man may have sufficient faith to flee to Christ; sufficient faith really to lay hold on Him--really to trust in Him--really to be a child of God-- really to be saved; and yet to his last day be never free from much anxiety, doubt, and fear.

"A letter," says an old writer, "may be written, which is not sealed; so grace may be written in the heart, yet the Spirit may not set the seal of assurance to it.

A child may be born heir to a great fortune, and yet never be aware of his riches; may live childish, die childish, and never know the greatness of his possessions. And so also a man may be a babe in Christ's family, think as a babe, speak as a babe, and, though saved, never enjoy a lively hope, or know the real privileges of his inheritance.

Let no man mistake my meaning when I dwell strongly on the reality, privilege, and importance of assurance. Do not do me the injustice to say, I teach that none are saved except such as can say with Paul, "I know and am persuaded--there is a crown laid up for me." I do not say so. I teach nothing of the kind.

Faith in the Lord Jesus Christ a man must have, beyond all question, if he is to be saved. I know no other way of access to the Father. I see no intimation of mercy, excepting through Christ. A man must feel his sins and lost estate--must come to Jesus for pardon and salvation--must rest his hope on Him, and on Him alone. But if he only has faith to do this, however weak and feeble that faith may be, I will engage, from Scripture warrants, he shall not miss heaven.

Never, never let us curtail the freeness of the glorious Gospel, or clip its fair proportions. Never let us make the gate more strait and the way more narrow than pride and the love of sin have made it already. The Lord Jesus is very pitiful, and of tender mercy. He does not regard the quantity of faith, but the quality: He does not measure its degree, but its truth. He will not break any bruised reed, nor quench any smoking flax. He will never let it be said that any perished at the foot of the cross. "Him that cometh unto Me," He says, "I will in no wise cast out." (John vi. 37.)[25]

Yes! Though a man's faith be no bigger than a grain of mustard seed, if it only brings him to Christ, and enables him to touch the hem of His garment, he shall be saved--saved as surely as the oldest saint in paradise--saved as completely and eternally as Peter, or John, or Paul. There are degrees in our sanctification. In our justification there are none. What is written, is written, and shall never fail: "Whosoever believeth on Him,"--not whosoever has a strong and mighty faith--"Whosoever believeth on Him shall not be ashamed." (Rom. x. 11.)

But all this time, be it remembered, the poor believing soul may have no full assurance of his pardon and acceptance with God. He may be troubled with fear upon fear, and doubt upon doubt. He may have many an inward question, and many an anxiety--many a struggle, and many a misgiving--clouds and darkness--storm and tempest to the very end.

I will engage, I repeat, that bare simple faith in Christ shall save a man, though he may never attain to assurance; but I will not engage it shall bring him to heaven with strong and abounding consolations. I will engage it shall land him safe in harbour; but I will not engage he shall enter that harbour in full sail, confident and rejoicing. I shall not be surprised if he reaches his desired haven weather-beaten and tempest-tossed, scarcely realizing his own safety, till he opens his eyes in glory.

I believe it is of great importance to keep in view this distinction between faith and assurance. It explains things which an inquirer in religion sometimes finds it hard to understand.

Faith, let us remember, is the root, and assurance is the flower. Doubtless you can never have the flower without the root; but it is no less certain you may have the root and not the flower.

Faith is that poor trembling woman who came behind Jesus in the press, and touched the hem of His garment. (Mark v. 25.) Assurance is Stephen standing calmly in the midst of his murderers, and saying, "I see the heavens opened, and the Son of man standing on the right hand of God." (Acts. vii. 56.)

Faith is the penitent thief, crying, "Lord, remember me." (Luke xxiii. 42.) Assurance is Job, sitting in the dust, covered with sores, saying, "I know that my Redeemer liveth" (Job xix. 25); "Though He slay me, yet will I trust Him." (Job xiii. 15.)

Faith is Peter's drowning cry, as he began to sink: "Lord save, me!" (Matt. xiv. 30.) Assurance is that same Peter declaring before the Council in after times, "This is the stone which was set at nought of you builders, which is become the head of the corner. Neither is there salvation in any other: for there is none other name under heaven given among men, whereby we must be saved." (Acts iv. 11, 12.)

Faith is the anxious, trembling voice, "Lord, I believe: help Thou my unbelief." (Mark ix. 24.) Assurance is the confident challenge, "Who shall lay anything to the charge of God's elect? Who is he that condemneth?" (Rom. viii. 33, 34.) Faith is Saul praying in the house of Judas at Damascus, sorrowful, blind, and alone. (Acts ix. 11.) Assurance is Paul, the aged prisoner, looking calmly into the grave, and saying, "I know whom I have believed. There is a crown laid up for me." (2 Tim. i. 12; iv. 8.)

Faith is life. How great the blessing! Who can describe or realize the gulf between life and death? "A living dog is better than a dead lion." (Eccles. ix. 4.) And yet life may be weak, sickly, unhealthy, painful, trying, anxious, weary, burdensome, joyless, smileless to the very end. Assurance is more than life. It is health, strength, power, vigour, activity, energy, manliness, beauty.

It is not a question of "saved or not saved," that lies before us, but of "privilege or no privilege."--It is not a question of peace or no peace, but of great peace or little peace.--It is not a question between the wanderers of this world and the school of Christ: it is one that belongs only to the school: it is between the first form and the last.

He that has faith does well. Happy should I be, if I thought all readers of this paper had it. Blessed, thrice blessed are they that believe! They are safe. They are washed. They are justified. They are beyond the power of hell. Satan, with all his malice, shall never pluck them out of Christ's hand. But he that has assurance does far better--sees more, feels more, knows more, enjoys more, has more days like those spoken of in Deuteronomy, even "the days of heaven upon the earth." (Deut. xi. 21.)[26]

III. I pass on to the third thing of which I spoke. I will give some reasons why an assured hope is exceedingly to be desired.

I ask special attention to this point. I heartily wish that assurance was more sought after than it is. Too many among those who believe begin doubting and go on doubting, live doubting and die doubting, and go to heaven in a kind of mist.

It would ill become me to speak in a slighting way of "hopes" and "trusts." But I fear many of us sit down content with them, and go no further. I should like to see fewer "perad-venturers" in the Lord's family, and more who could say, "I know and am persuaded." Oh, that all believers would covet the best gifts, and not be content with less! Many miss the full tide of blessedness the Gospel was meant to convey. Many keep themselves in a low and starved condition of soul, while their Lord is saying, "Eat and drink abundantly, O beloved." "Ask and receive, that your joy may be full." (Cant. v. 1; John xvi. 24.)

(1) Let us remember then, for one thing, that assurance is to be desired, because of the present comfort and peace it affords.

Doubts and fears have power to spoil much of the happiness of a true believer in Christ. Uncertainty and suspense are bad enough in any condition--in the matter of our health, our property, our families, our affections, our earthly callings--but never so bad as in the affairs of our souls. And so long as a believer cannot get beyond "I hope," and "I trust," he manifestly feels a degree of uncertainty about his spiritual state. The very words imply as much. He says "I hope," because he dares not say, "I know."

Now assurance goes far to set a child of God free from this painful kind of bondage, and thus ministers mightily to his comfort. It enables him to feel that the great business of life is a settled business, the great debt a paid debt, the great disease a healed disease, and the great work a finished work; and all other business, diseases, debts, and works, are then by compari-son small. In this way assurance makes him patient in tribulation, calm under bereavements, unmoved in sorrow, not afraid of evil tidings, in every condition content, for it gives him a fixedness of heart. It sweetens his bitter cups; it lessens the burden of his crosses; it smooths the rough places over which he travels; it lightens the valley of the shadow of death. It makes him always feel that he has something solid beneath his feet and something firm under his hands--a sure friend by the way, and a sure home at the end.[27]

Assurance will help a man to bear poverty and loss. It will teach him to say, "I know that I have in heaven a better and more enduring substance. Silver and gold have I none, but grace and glory are mine, and these can never make themselves wings and flee away. Though the fig tree shall not blossom, yet I will rejoice in the Lord." (Habak. iii. 17, 18.)

Assurance will support a child of God under the heaviest bereavements, and assist him to feel "It is well." An assured soul will say, "Though beloved ones are taken from me, yet Jesus is the same, and is alive for evermore. Christ, being raised from the dead, dieth no more. Though my house be not as flesh and blood could wish, yet I have an everlasting covenant, ordered in all things and sure." (2 Kings iv. 26; Heb. xiii. 8; Rom. vi. 9; 2 Sam. xxiii. 5.)

Assurance will enable a man to praise God, and be thankful, even in prison, like Paul and Silas at Philippi. It can give a believer songs even in the darkest night, and joy when all things seem going against him.[28] (Job xxxv. 10; Psalm xlii. 8.)

Assurance will enable a man to sleep with the full prospect of death on the morrow, like Peter in Herod's dungeon. It will teach him to say, "I will both lay me down in peace and sleep, for Thou, Lord, only makest me to dwell in safety." (Psalm iv. 8.)

Assurance can make a man rejoice to suffer shame for Christ's sake, as the Apostles did when put in prison at Jerusalem. (Acts v. 41.) It will remind him that he may "rejoice and be exceeding glad" (Matt. v. 12), and that there is in heaven an exceeding weight of glory that shall make amends for all. (2 Cor. iv. 17.)

Assurance will enable a believer to meet a violent and painful death without fear, as Stephen did in the beginning of Christ's Church, and as Cranmer, Ridley, Hooper, Latimer, Rogers, and Taylor did in our own land. It will bring to his heart the texts, "Be not afraid of them which kill the body, and after that have no more that they can do." (Luke xii. 4.) "Lord Jesus receive my spirit." (Acts vii. 59.)[29]

Assurance will support a man in pain and sickness, make all his bed, and smooth down his dying pillow. It will enable him to say, "If my earthly house fail, I have a building of God." (2 Cor. v. 1.) "I desire to depart and be with Christ." (Phil. i. 23.) "My flesh and my heart may fail, but God is the strength of my heart, and my portion for ever.[30] (Psalm lxxiii. 26.)

The strong consolation which assurance can give in the hour of death is a point of great importance. We may depend on it, we shall never think assurance so precious as when our turn comes to die. In that awful hour there are few believers who do not find out the value and privilege of an "assured hope," whatever they may have thought about it during their lives. General "hopes" and "trusts" are all very well to live upon while the sun shines and the body is strong; but when we come to die, we shall want to be able to say, "I know" and "I feel." The river of death is a cold stream, and we have to cross it alone. No earthly friend can help us. The last enemy, the king of terrors, is a strong foe. When our souls are departing, there is no cordial like the strong wine of assurance.

There is a beautiful expression in the Prayer-book service for the Visitation of the Sick: "The Almighty Lord, who is a most strong tower to all them that put their trust in Him, be now and evermore thy defence, and make thee know and feel that there is none other name under heaven, through whom thou mayest receive health and salvation, but only the name of our Lord Jesus Christ." The compilers of that service showed great wisdom there. They saw that when the eyes grow dim, and the heart grows faint, and the spirit is on the eve of departing, there must then be knowing and feeling what Christ has done for us, or else there cannot be perfect peace.[31]

(2) Let us remember, for another thing, that assurance is to be desired, because it tends to make a Christian an active working Christian.

None, generally speaking, do so much for Christ on earth as those who enjoy the fullest confidence of a free entrance into heaven, and trust not in their own works, but in the finished work of Christ. That sounds wonderful, I dare say, but it is true.

A believer who lacks an assured hope, will spend much of his time in inward searchings of heart about his own state. Like a nervous, hypochondriacal person, he will be full of his own ailments, his own doubtings and questionings, his own conflicts and corruptions. In short, you will often find he is so taken up with his internal warfare that he has little leisure for other things, and little time to work for God.

But a believer, who has, like Paul, an assured hope, is free from these harassing distractions. He does not vex his soul with doubts about his own pardon and acceptance. He looks at the everlasting covenant sealed with blood, at the finished work, and never-broken word of his Lord and Saviour, and therefore counts his salvation a settled thing. And thus he is able to give an undivided attention to the work of the Lord, and so in the long run to do more.[32]

Take, for an illustration of this, two English emigrants, and suppose them set down side by side in New Zealand or Australia. Give each of them a piece of land to clear and cultivate. Let the portions allotted to them be the same both in quantity and quality. Secure that land to them by every needful legal instrument; let it be conveyed as freehold to them and theirs for ever; let the conveyance be publicly registered, and the property made sure to them by every deed and security that man's ingenuity can devise.

Suppose then that one of them shall set to work to clear his land and bring it into cultivation, and labour at it day after day without intermission or cessation.

Suppose in the meanwhile that the other shall be continually leaving his work, and going repeatedly to the public registry to ask whether the land really is his own--whether there is not some mistake--whether after all there is not some flaw in the legal instruments which conveyed it to him.

The one shall never doubt his title, but just work diligently on. The other shall hardly ever feel sure of his title, and spend half his time in going to Sydney or Melbourne or Auckland, with needless inquiries about it.

Which now of these two men will have made most progress in a year's time? Who will have done the most for his land, got the greatest breadth of soil under tillage, have the best crops to show, be altogether the most prosperous?

Any one of common sense can answer that question. I need not supply an answer. There can only be one reply. Undivided attention will always attain the greatest success.

It is much the same in the matter of our title to "mansions in the skies." None will do so much for the Lord who bought him as the believer who sees his title clear, and is not distracted by unbelieving doubts, questionings, and hesitations. The joy of the Lord will be that man's strength. "Restore unto me," says David, "the joy of Thy salvation; then will I teach transgressors Thy ways." (Psalm li. 12.)

Never were there such working Christians as the Apostles. They seemed to live to labour. Christ's work was truly their meat and drink. They counted not their lives dear to themselves. They spent and were spent. They laid down ease, health, worldly comfort, at the foot of the cross. And one grand cause of this, I believe, was their assured hope. They were men who could say, "We know that we are of God, and the whole world lieth in wickedness." (1 John v. 19.)

(3) Let us remember, for another thing, that assurance is to be desired, because it tends to make a Christian a decided Christian.

Indecision and doubt about our own state in God's sight is a grievous evil, and the mother of many evils. It often produces a wavering and unstable walk in following the Lord. Assurance helps to cut many a knot, and to make the path of Christian duty clear and plain.

Many of whom we feel hopes that they are God's children, and have true grace, however weak, are continually perplexed with doubts in points of practice. "Should we do such and such a thing? shall we give up this family custom? Ought we to go into that company? How shall we draw the line about visiting? What is to be the measure of our dressing and our entertainments? Are we never, under any circumstances, to dance, never to touch a card, never to attend parties of pleasure?" These are a kind of question which seem to give them constant trouble. And often, very often, the simple root of their perplexity is, that they do not feel assured they are themselves children of God. They have not yet settled the point, which side of the gate they are on. They do not know whether they are inside the ark or not.

That a child of God ought to act in a certain decided way, they quite feel; but the grand question is, "Are they children of God themselves?" If they only felt they were so, they would go straightforward, and take a decided line. But not feeling sure about it, their conscience is for ever hesitating and coming to a deadlock. The devil whispers, "Perhaps after all you are only a hypocrite: what right have you to take a decided course? Wait till you are really a Christian." And this whisper too often turns the scale, and leads on to some miserable compromise or wretched conformity to the world!

I believe we have here one chief reason why so many in this day are inconsistent, trimming, unsatisfactory, and half-hearted in their conduct about the world. Their faith fails. They feel no assurance that they are Christ's, and so feel a hesitancy about breaking with the world. They shrink from laying aside all the ways of the old man, because they are not quite confident they have put on the new. In short, I have little doubt that one secret cause of "halting between two opinions" is want of assurance. When people can say decidedly, "The Lord, He is the God," their course becomes very clear. (1 Kings xviii. 39.)

(4) Let us remember, finally, that assurance is to be desired, because it tends to make the holiest Christians.

This, too, sounds wonderful and strange, and yet it is true. It is one of the paradoxes of the Gospel, contrary at first sight to reason and common sense, and yet it is a fact. Cardinal Bellarmine was seldom more wide of the truth than when he said, "Assurance tends to carelessness and sloth." He that is freely forgiven by Christ will always do much for Christ's glory, and he that enjoys the fullest assurance of this forgiveness will ordinarily keep up the closest walk with God. It is a faithful saying and worthy to be remembered by all believers, "He that hath this hope in Him purifieth himself, even as He is pure." (1 John iii. 3.) A hope that does not purify is a mockery, a delusion, and a snare.[33]

None are so likely to maintain a watchful guard over their own hearts and lives as those who know the comfort of living in close communion with God. They feel their privilege, and will fear losing it. They will dread falling from the high estate, and marring their own comforts, by bringing clouds between themselves and Christ. He that goes on a journey with little money about him takes little thought of danger, and cares little how late he travels. He, on the contrary, that carries gold and jewels will be a cautious traveller. He will look well to his roads, his lodgings, and his company, and run no risks. It is an old saying, however unscientific it may be, that the fixed stars are those which tremble most. The man that most fully enjoys the light of God's reconciled countenance, will be a man tremblingly afraid of losing its blessed consolations, and jealously fearful of doing anything to grieve the Holy Ghost.

I commend these four points to the serious consideration of all professing Christians. Would you like to feel the Everlasting Arms around you, and to hear the voice of Jesus daily drawing nigh to your soul, and saying, "I am thy salvation"?--Would you like to be a useful labourer in the vineyard in your day and generation?--Would you be known of all men as a bold, firm, decided, single-eyed, uncompromising follower of Christ?--Would you be eminently spiritually-minded and holy?--I doubt not some readers will say, "These are the very things our hearts desire. We long for them. We pant after them: but they seem far from us."

Now, has it never struck you that your neglect of assurance may possibly be the main secret of all your failures--that the low measure of faith which satisfies you may be the cause of your low degree of peace? Can you think it a strange thing that your graces are faint and languishing, when faith, the root and mother of them all, is allowed to remain feeble and weak?

Take my advice this day. Seek an increase of faith. Seek an assured hope of salvation like the Apostle Paul's. Seek to obtain a simple, childlike confidence in God's promises. Seek to be able to say with Paul, "I know whom I have believed: I am persuaded that He is mine, and I am His."

You have very likely tried other ways and methods and completely failed. Change your plan. Go upon another tack. Lay aside your doubts. Lean more entirely on the Lord's arm. Begin with implicit trusting. Cast aside your faithless backwardness to take the Lord at His word. Come and roll yourself, your soul, and your sins, upon your gracious Saviour. Begin with simple believing, and all other things shall soon be added to you.[34]

IV. I come now to the last thing of which I spoke. I promised to point out some probable causes why an assured hope is so seldom attained. I will do it very shortly.

This is a very serious question, and ought to raise in all of us great searchings of heart. Few, certainly, of Christ's people seem to reach up to this blessed spirit of assurance. Many comparatively believe, but few are persuaded. Many comparatively have saving faith, but few that glorious confidence which shines forth in the language of St. Paul. That such is the case, I think we must all allow.

Now, why is this so?--Why is a thing which two Apostles have strongly enjoined us to seek after, a thing of which few believers have any experimental knowledge in these fitter days? Why is an assured hope so rare?

I desire to offer a few suggestions on this point, with all humility. I know that many have never attained assurance, at whose feet I would gladly sit both in earth and heaven. Perhaps the Lord sees something in the natural temperament of some of His children, which makes assurance not good for them. Perhaps, in order to be kept in spiritual health, they need to be kept very low. God only knows. Still, after every allowance, I fear there are many believers without an assured hope, whose case may too often be explained by causes such as these.

(1) One most common cause, I suspect, is a defective view of the doctrine of justification.

I am inclined to think that justification and sanctification are insensibly confused together in the minds of many believers. They receive the Gospel truth--that there must be something done in us, as well as something done for us, if we are true members of Christ: and so far they are right. But then, without being aware of it, perhaps, they seem to imbibe the idea that their justification is, in some degree, affected by something within themselves. They do not clearly see that Christ's work, not their own work--either in whole or in part, either directly or indirectly--is alone the ground of our acceptance with God; that justification is a thing entirely without us, for which nothing whatever is needful on our part but simple faith--and that the weakest believer is as fully and completely justified as the strongest.[35]

Many appear to forget that we are saved and justified as sinners, and only sinners; and that we never can attain to anything higher, if we live to the age of Methuselah. Redeemed sinners, justified sinners, and renewed sinners doubtless we must be--but sinners, sinners, sinners, we shall be always to the very last. They do not seem to comprehend that there is a wide difference between our justification and our sanctification. Our justification is a perfect finished work, and admits of no degrees. Our sanctification is imperfect and incomplete, and will be so to the last hour of our life. They appear to expect that a believer may at some period of his life be in a measure free from corruption, and attain to a kind of inward perfection. And not finding this angelic state of things in their own hearts, they at once conclude there must be something very wrong in their state. And so they go mourning all their days--oppressed with fears that they have no part or lot in Christ, and refusing to be comforted.

Let us weigh this point well. If any believing soul desires assurance, and has not got it, let him ask himself, first of all, if he is quite sure he is sound in the faith, if he knows how to distinguish things that differ, and if his eyes are thoroughly clear in the matter of justification. He must know what it is simply to believe and to be justified by faith before he can expect to feel assured.

In this matter, as well as in many others, the old Galatian heresy is the most fertile source of error, both in doctrine and in practice. People ought to seek clearer views of Christ, and what Christ has done for them. Happy is the man who really understands "justification by faith without the deeds of the law."

(2) Another common cause of the absence of assurance is, slothfulness about growth in grace.

I suspect many true believers hold dangerous and unscriptural views on this point; I do not of course mean intentionally, but they do hold them. Many appear to think that, once converted, they have little more to attend to, and that a state of salvation is a kind of easy chair, in which they may just sit still, lie back, and be happy. They seem to fancy that grace is given them that they may enjoy it, and they forget that it is given, like a talent, to be used, employed, and improved. Such persons lose sight of the many direct injunctions "to increase--to grow--to abound more and more--to add to our faith," and the like; and in this little-doing condition, this sitting-still state of mind, I never marvel that they miss assurance.

I believe it ought to be our continual aim and desire to go forward, and our watchword on every returning birthday, and at the beginning of every year, should be, "More and more" (1 Thess. iv. 1): more knowledge--more faith--more obedience--more love. If we have brought forth thirtyfold, we should seek to bring forth sixty; and if we have brought forth sixty, we should strive to bring forth a hundred. The will of the Lord is our sanctification, and it ought to be our will too. (Matt. xiii. 23; 1 Thess. iv. 3.)

One thing, at all events, we may depend upon--there is an inseparable connection between diligence and assurance. "Give diligence" says Peter, "to make your calling and election sure." (2 Peter i. 10.) "We desire," says Paul, "that every one of you do show the same diligence to the full assurance of hope unto the end." (Heb. vi. 11.) "The soul of the diligent," says Solomon, "shall be made fat." (Prov. xiii. 4.) There is much truth in the old maxim of the Puritans: "Faith of adherence comes by hearing, but faith of assurance comes not without doing."

Is any reader of this paper one of those who desires assurance, but has not got it? Mark my words. You will never get it without diligence, however much you may desire it. There are no gains without pains in spiritual things, any more than in temporal. "The soul of the sluggard desireth and hath nothing." (Prov. xiii. 4.)[36]

(3) Another common cause of a want of assurance is an inconsistent walk in life.

With grief and sorrow I feel constrained to say that I fear nothing more frequently prevents men attaining an assured hope than this. The stream of professing Christianity in this day is far wider than it formerly was, and I am afraid we must admit at the same time it is much less deep.

Inconsistency of life is utterly destructive of peace of conscience. The two things are incompatible. They cannot and they will not go together. If you will have your besetting sins, and cannot make up your minds to give them up--if you will shrink from cutting off the right hand and plucking out the right eye when occasion requires it--I will engage you will have no assurance.

A vacillating walk--a backwardness to take a bold and decided line--a readiness to conform to the world--a hesitating witness for Christ--a lingering tone of religion--a flinching from a high standard of holiness and spiritual life--all these make up a sure receipt for bringing a blight upon the garden of your soul.

It is vain to suppose you will feel assured and persuaded of your own pardon and acceptance with God, unless you count all God's commandments concerning all things to be right, and hate every sin, whether great or small. (Psalm cxix. 128.) One Achan allowed in the camp of your heart will weaken your hands and lay your consolations low in the dust. You must be daily sowing to the Spirit, if you are to reap the witness of the Spirit. You will not find and feel that all the Lord's ways are ways of pleasantness, unless you labour in all your ways to please the Lord.[37]

I bless God that our salvation in no wise depends on our own works. By grace we are saved--not by works of righteousness--through faith--without the deeds of the law. But I never would have any believer for a moment forget that our sense of salvation depends much on the manner of our living. Inconsistency will dim our eyes, and bring clouds between us and the sun. The sun is the same behind the clouds, but you will not be able to see its brightness or enjoy its warmth, and your soul will be gloomy and cold. It is in the path of well doing that the day-spring of assurance will visit you, and shine down upon your heart.

"The secret of the Lord," says David, "is with them that fear Him, and He will show them His covenant." (Psalm xxv. 14.)

"To him that ordereth his conversation aright, will I show the salvation of God." (Psalm l. 23.)

"Great peace have they which love Thy law, and nothing shall offend them." (Psalm cxix. 165.)

"If we walk in the light, as He is in the light, we have fellowship one with another." (1 John i. 7.)

"Let us not love in word, neither in tongue; but in deed and in truth; and hereby we know that we are of the truth, and shall assure our hearts before Him." (1 John iii. 18, 19.)

"Hereby we do know that we know Him, if we keep His commandments." (1 John ii. 3.)

Paul was a man who exercised himself to have always a conscience void of offence toward God and toward man. (Acts xxiv. 16.) He could say with boldness, "I have fought the good fight, I have kept the faith." I do not therefore wonder that the Lord enabled him to add with confidence, "Henceforth there is a crown laid up for me, and the Lord shall give it me at that day."

If any believer in the Lord Jesus desires assurance, and has not got it, let him think over this point also. Let him look at his own heart, look at his own conscience, look at his own life, look at his own ways, look at his own home. And perhaps when he has done that, he will be able to say, "There is a cause why I have no assured hope."

I leave the three matters I have just mentioned to the private consideration of every reader of this paper. I am sure they are worth examining. May we examine them honestly. And may the Lord give us understanding in all things.

(1) And now in closing this important inquiry, let me speak first to those readers who have not yet given themselves to the Lord, who have not yet come out from the world, chosen the good part, and followed Christ.

I ask you then to learn from this subject, the privileges and comforts of a true Christian.

I would not have you judge of the Lord Jesus Christ by His people. The best of servants can give you but a faint idea of that glorious Master. Neither would I have you judge of the privileges of His kingdom, by the measure of comfort to which many of His people attain. Alas, we are most of us poor creatures! We come short, very short, of the blessedness we might enjoy. But, depend upon it, there are glorious things in the city of our God, which they who have an assured hope taste, even in their lifetime. There are lengths and breadths of peace and consolation there, which it has not entered into your heart to conceive. There is bread enough and to spare in our Father's house, though many of us certainly eat but little of it, and continue weak. But the fault must not be laid to our Master's charge: it is all our own.

And, after all, the weakest child of God has a mine of comforts within him, of which you know nothing. You see the conflicts and tossings of the surface of his heart, but you see not the pearls of great price which are hidden in the depths below. The feeblest member of Christ would not change conditions with you. The believer who possesses the least assurance is far better off than you are. He has a hope, however faint, but you have none at all. He has a portion that will never be taken from him, a Saviour that will never be taken from him, a Saviour that will never forsake him, a treasure that fadeth not away, however little he may realize it all at present. But, as for you, if you die as you are, your expectations will all perish. Oh, that you were wise! Oh, that you understood these things! Oh, that you would consider your latter end!

I feel deeply for you in these latter days of the world, if I ever did. I feel deeply for those whose treasure is all on earth, and whose hopes are all on this side of the grave. Yes! when I see old kingdoms and dynasties shaking to the very foundation--when I see, as we all saw a few years ago, kings and princes and rich men and great men fleeing for their fives, and scarce knowing where to hide their heads--when I see property dependent on public confidence melting like snow in the spring, and public stocks and funds losing their value--when I see these things, I feel deeply for those who have no better portion than this world can give them, and no place in that kingdom which cannot be removed.[38]

Take advice of a minister of Christ this very day. Seek durable riches--a treasure that cannot be taken from you--a city which hath lasting foundations. Do as the Apostle Paul did. Give yourself to the Lord Jesus Christ, and seek that incorruptible crown He is ready to bestow. Take His yoke upon you, and learn of Him. Come away from a world which will never really satisfy you, and from sin which will bite like a serpent, if you cleave to it, at last. Come to the Lord Jesus as lowly sinners, and He will receive you, pardon you, give you His renewing Spirit, fill you with peace. This shall give you more real comfort than the world has ever done. There is a gulf in your heart which nothing but the peace of Christ can fill. Enter in and share our privileges. Come with us, and sit down by our side.

(2) Lastly, let me turn to all believers who read these pages, and speak to them a few words of brotherly counsel.

The main thing that I urge upon you is this--if you have not got an assured hope of your own acceptance in Christ, resolve this day to seek it. Labour for it. Strive after it. Pray for it. Give the Lord no rest till you "know whom you have believed."

I feel, indeed, that the small amount of assurance in this day, among those who are reckoned God's children, is a shame and a reproach. "It is a thing to be heavily bewailed," says old Traill, "that many Christians have lived twenty or forty years since Christ called them by His grace, yet doubting in their life." Let us call to mind the earnest "desire" Paul expresses, that "every one" of the Hebrews should seek after full assurance; and let us endeavour, by God's blessing, to roll this reproach away. (Heb. vi. 11.)

Believing reader, do you really mean to say that you have no desire to exchange hope for confidence, trust for persuasion, uncertainty for knowledge? Because weak faith will save you, will you therefore rest content with it? Because assurance is not essential to your entrance into heaven, will you therefore be satisfied without it upon earth? Alas, this is not a healthy state of soul to be in; this is not the mind of the Apostolic day! Arise at once and go forward. Stick not at the foundations of religion: go on to perfection. Be not content with a day of small things. Never despise it in others, but never be content with it yourself.

Believe me, believe me, assurance is worth the seeking. You forsake your own mercies when you rest content without it. The things I speak are for your peace. If it is good to be sure in earthly things, how much better is it to be sure in heavenly things! Your salvation is a fixed and certain thing. God knows it. Why should not you seek to know it too? There is nothing unscriptural in this. Paul never saw the Book of Life, and yet Paul says, "I know and am persuaded."

Make it then your daily prayer that you may have an increase of faith. According to your faith will be your peace. Cultivate that blessed root more, and sooner or later, by God's blessing, you may hope to have the flower. You may not perhaps attain to full assurance all at once. It is good sometimes to be kept waiting: we do not value things which we get without trouble. But though it tarry, wait for it. Seek on, and expect to find.

There is one thing, however, of which I would not have you ignorant:--You must not be surprised if you have occasional doubts, after you have got assurance. You must not forget you are on earth, and not in heaven. You are still in the body, and have indwelling sin: the flesh will lust against the spirit to the very end. The leprosy will never be out of the walls of the old house till death takes it down. And there is a devil, too, and a strong devil: a devil who tempted the Lord Jesus, and gave Peter a fall; and he will take care you know it. Some doubts there always will be. He that never doubts has nothing to lose. He that never fears possesses nothing truly valuable. He that is never jealous knows little of deep love. Be not discouraged: you shall be more than conqueror through Him that loved you.

Finally, do not forget that assurance is a thing which may be lost for a season, even by the brightest Christians, unless they take care.

Assurance is a most delicate plant. It needs daily, hourly watching, watering, tending, cherishing. So watch and pray the more when you have got it. As Rutherford says, "Make much of assurance." Be always upon your guard. When Christian slept in the arbour, in Pilgrim's Progress, he lost his certificate. Keep that in mind.

David lost assurance for many months by falling into transgression. Peter lost it when he denied his Lord. Each found it again undoubtedly, but not till after bitter tears. Spiritual darkness comes on horseback, and goes away on foot. It is upon us before we know that it is coming. It leaves us slowly, gradually, and not till after many days. It is easy to run down hill. It is hard work to climb up. So remember my caution--when you have the joy of the Lord, watch and pray.

Above all, grieve not the Spirit. Quench not the Spirit. Vex not the Spirit. Drive Him not to a distance, by tampering with small bad habits and little sins. Little jarrings between husbands and wives make unhappy homes, and petty inconsistencies, known and allowed, will bring in a strangeness between you and the Spirit.

Hear the conclusion of the whole matter.

The man who walks with God in Christ most closely will generally be kept in the greatest peace.

The believer who follows the Lord most fully and aims at the highest degree of holiness will ordinarily enjoy the most assured hope, and have the clearest persuasion of his own salvation.

NOTE

Extracts from English Divines, showing that there is a difference between faith and assurance--that a believer may be justified and accepted with God, and yet not enjoy a comfortable knowledge and persuasion of his own safety--and that the weakest faith in Christ, if it be true, will save a man as surely as the strongest.

(1) "The mercy of God is greater than all the sins in the world. But we sometimes are in such a case, that we think we have no faith at all; or if we have any, it is very feeble and weak. And therefore these are two things: to have faith, and to have the feeling of faith. For some men would fain have the feeling of faith, but they cannot attain unto it; and yet they must not despair, but go forward in calling upon God, and it will come at the length: God will open their hearts, and let them feel His goodness."--Bishop Larimer's Sermons. 1552.

(2) "Weak faith may fail in the applying, or in the apprehension and appropriating of Christ's benefits to a man's own self. This is to be seen in ordinary experience. For many a man there is of humble and contrite heart, that serveth God in spirit and truth, yet is not able to say, without great doublings and waverings, I know and am fully assured that my sins are pardoned. Now shall we say that all such are without faith? God forbid.

"This weak faith will as truly apprehend God's merciful promises for the pardon of sin as strong faith, though not so soundly. Even as a man with a palsied hand can stretch it out as well to receive a gift at the hand of a king as he that is more sound, though it may be not so firmly and steadfastly."--Exposition of the Creed, by William Perkins, Minister of Christ in the University of Cambridge. 1612.

(3) "This certainty of our salvation, spoken of by Paul, rehearsed by Peter, and mentioned by David (Psalm iv. 7), is that special fruit of faith, which breedeth spiritual joy and inward peace, which passeth all understanding. True it is, all God's children have it not. One thing is the tree, and another thing is the fruit of the tree: one thing is faith, and another thing is the fruit of faith. And that remnant of God's elect which feel the want of this faith, have notwith-

standing faith."--Sermons by Richard Greenham, Minister and Preacher of the Word of God. 1612.

(4) "Some think they have no faith at all, because they have no full assurance. Yet the fairest fire that can be will have some smoke."--The Bruised Reed, by Richard Sibbes, Master of Catherine Hall, Cambridge, and Preacher of Gray's Inn, London. 1630.

(5) "The act of faith is to apply Christ to the soul; and this the weakest faith can do as well as the strongest, if it be true. A child can hold a staff as well, though not so strongly, as a man. The prisoner through a hole sees the sun, though not so perfectly as they in the open air. They that saw the brazen serpent, though a great way off, yet were healed.

"The least faith is as precious to the believer's soul as Peter's or Paul's faith was to themselves; for it lays hold upon Christ and brings eternal salvation."--An Exposition of the Second Epistle General of Peter, by the Rev. Thomas Adams, Rector of St. Gregory's, London. 1633.

(6) "Weak faith is true faith--as precious, though not so great as strong faith: the same Holy Ghost the author, the same Gospel the instrument.

"If it never proves great, yet weak faith shall save; for it interests us in Christ, and makes Him and all His benefits ours. For it is not the strength of our faith that saves, but the truth of our faith--not the weakness of our faith that condemns, but the want of faith; for the least faith layeth hold on Christ, and so will save us. Neither are we saved by the worth or quantity of our faith, but by Christ, who is laid hold on by a weak faith as well as a strong. Just as a weak hand that can put meat into the mouth shall feed and nourish the body as well as if it were a strong hand; seeing the body is not nourished by the strength of the hand, but by the goodness of the meat."--The Doctrine of Faith, by John Rogers, Preacher of God's Word, at Dedham, in Essex. 1634.

(7) "It is one thing to have a thing surely, another thing to know I have it surely. We seek many things that we have in our hands, and we have many things that we think we have lost. So a believer, who hath a sure belief, yet doth not always know that he so believeth. Faith is necessary to salvation: but full assurance that I do believe is not of like necessity."--Ball on Faith. 1637.

(8) "There is a weak faith, which yet is true; and although it be weak, yet, because it is true, it shall not be rejected of Christ.

"Faith is not created perfect at the first, as Adam was; but is like a man in the ordinary course of nature, who is first an instrument, then a child, then a youth, then a man.

"Some utterly reject all weak ones, and tax all weakness in faith with hypocrisy. Certainly these are either proud or cruel men.

"Some comfort and establish those who are weak, saying, Be quiet. Thou hast faith and grace enough, and art good enough: thou needest no more, neither must thou be too righteous.' (Eccles. vii. 16.) These are soft, but not safe, cushions: these are fawning flatterers, and not faithful friends.

"Some comfort and exhort, saying, Be of good cheer: He who hath begun a good work will also finish it in you; therefore pray that His grace may abound in you; yea, do not sit still, but go forward, and march on in the way of the Lord.' (Heb. vi. 1.) Now this is the safest and best course."--Questions, Observations, etc., upon the Gospel according to St. Matthew, by

Richard Ward, sometime Student at Cambridge, and Preacher of the Gospel in London. 1640.

(9) "A man may be in the favour of God, in the state of grace, a justified man before God, and yet want the sensible assurance of His salvation, and of the favour of God in Christ.

"A man may have saving grace in him, and not perceive it himself; a man may have true justifying faith in him, and not have the use and operation of it, so far as to work in him a comfortable assurance of his reconciliation with God. Nay, I will say more: a man may be in the state of grace, and have true justifying faith in him, and yet be so far from sensible assurance of it in himself, as in his own sense and feeling he may seem to be assured of the contrary. Job was certainly in this case when he cried unto God, Wherefore hidest Thou Thy face and boldest me for Thine enemy?' (Job xiii. 24.)

"The weakest faith will justify. If thou canst receive Christ and rest upon Him, even with the weakest faith, it will serve thy turn. Take heed thou think not it is the strength of thy faith that justifieth thee. No, no: it is Christ and His perfect righteousness which thy faith receiveth and resteth upon, that doth it. He that hath the feeblest and weakest hand may receive an alms and apply a sovereign plaster to his wound, as well as he that hath the strongest, and receive as much good by it too."--Lectures upon the 51st Psalmy preached at Ashby-de-la-Zouch, by Arthur Hildersam, Minister of Jesus Christ. 1642.

(10) "Though your grace be never so weak, if ye have truth of grace, you have as great a share in the righteousness of Christ for your justification as the strong Christian hath. You have as much of Christ imputed to you as any other."--Sermons by William Bridge, formerly Fellow of Emmanuel College, Cambridge, and Pastor of the Church of Christ, in Great Yarmouth. 1648.

(1) "There are some who are true believers, and yet weak in faith. They do indeed receive Christ and free grace, but it is with a shaking hand; they have, as divines say, the faith of adherence; they will stick to Christ, as theirs. But they want the faith of evidence; they cannot see themselves as His. They are believers, but of little faith; they hope that Christ will not cast them off, but are not sure that He will take them up."--Sips of Sweetness, or Consolation for Weak Relievers, by John Durant, Preacher in Canterbury Cathedral. 1649.

(12) "I know, thou sayest, that Jesus Christ came into the world to save sinners: and that Whosoever believeth in Him shall not perish, but have eternal life.' (John iii. 15.) Neither can I know but that, in a sense of my own sinful condition, I do cast myself in some measure upon my Saviour, and lay some hold upon His all-sufficient redemption: but, alas, my apprehensions of Him are so feeble, as that they can afford no sound comfort to my soul!

"Courage, my son. Were it that thou lookedst to be justified, and saved by the power of the very act of thy faith, thou hadst reason to be disheartened with the conscience of the weakness thereof; but now that the virtue and efficacy of this happy work is in the object apprehended by thee, which is the infinite merits and mercy of thy God and Saviour, which cannot be abated by thine infirmities, thou hast cause to take heart to thyself, and cheerfully to expect His salvation.

"Understand thy case aright. Here is a double hand, that helps us up toward Heaven. Our hand of faith lays hold upon our Saviour; our Saviour's hand of mercy and plenteous redemption lays hold on us. Our hold of Him is feeble and easily loosed; His hold of us is strong and irresistible.

"If work were stood upon, a strength of hand were necessary; but now that only taking and receiving of a precious gift is required, why may not a weak hand do that as well as a strong? As well, though not as forcibly."--Bishop Hall's "Balm of Gilead." 1650.

(13) "I find not salvation put upon the strength of faith, but the truth of faith--not upon the brightest degree, but upon any degree of faith. It is not said, If you have such a degree of faith you shall be justified and saved; but simply believing is required. The lowest degree of true faith will do it; as Romans x. 9, If thou shalt confess with thy mouth the Lord Jesus, and shalt believe in thine heart that God hath raised Him from the dead, thou shalt be saved.' The thief upon the cross had not attained to such high degrees of faith: he by one act, and that of a weak faith, was justified and saved. (Luke xxiii. 42.)"--Exposition of the Prophet E^ekiel, by William Greenhill, Rector of Stepney, London, and Chaplain to the Dukes of York and Gloucester. 1650.

(14) "A man may have true grace that hath not the assurance of the love and favour of God, or the remission of his sins, and salvation of his soul. A man may be God's, and yet he not know it; his estate may be good, and yet he not see it; he may be in a safe condition, when he is not in a comfortable position. All may be well with him in the court of glory, when he would give a thousand worlds that all were but well in the court of conscience.

"Assurance is requisite to the well-being of a Christian, but not to the being; it is requisite to the consolation of a Christian, but not to the salvation of a Christian; it is requisite to the well-being of grace, but not to the mere being of grace. Though a man cannot be saved without faith, yet he may be saved without assurance. God hath in many places of the Scripture declared that without faith there is no salvation; but God hath not in any one place of Scripture declared that without assurance there is no salvation."--Heaven on Earth, by Thomas Brooks, Preacher of the Gospel, at St. Margaret's, Fish Street Hill, London. 1654.

(15) "You that can clear this to your own hearts that you have faith, though it be weak, be not discouraged, be not troubled. Consider that the smallest degree of faith is true, is saving faith as well as the greatest. A spark of fire is as true fire as any is in the element of fire. A drop of water is as true water as any is in the ocean. So the least grain of faith is as true faith, and as saving as the greatest faith in the world.

"The least bud draws sap from the root as well as the greatest bough. So the weakest measure of faith doth as truly ingraft thee into Christ, and by that draw life from Christ, as well as the strongest. The weakest faith hath communion with the merits and blood of Christ as well as the strongest.

"The least faith marries the soul to Christ. The weakest faith hath as equal a share in God's love as the strongest. We are beloved in Christ, and the least measure of faith makes us members of Christ. The least faith hath equal right to the promises as the strongest. And therefore let not our souls be discouraged for weakness."--Nature and Royalties of Faith, by Samuel Bolton, D.D., of Christ's College, Cambridge. 1657.

(16) "Some are afraid they have no faith at all, because they have not the highest degree of faith, which is full assurance, or because they want the comfort which others attain to, even joy unspeakable and full of glory. But for the rolling of this stone out of the way, we must remember there are several degrees of faith. It is possible thou mayest have faith, though not the highest degree of faith, and so joy in the Spirit. That is rather a point of faith than faith itself. It is indeed rather a living by sense than a living by faith, when we are cheered up with continual cordials. A stronger faith is required to live upon God without comfort, than when

God shines in on our spirit with abundance of joy."--Matthew Lawrence, Preacher at Ipswich, on Faith. 1657.

(17) "If any person abroad have thought that a special and full persuasion of the pardon of their sin was of the essence of faith, let them answer for it. Our divines at home generally are of another judgment. Bishop Davenant and Bishop Prideaux, and others, have shown the great difference between recumbrance and assurance, and they all do account and call assurance, a daughter, fruit, and consequent of faith. And the late learned Arrowsmith tells us, that God seldom bestows assurance upon believers till they are grown in grace: for, says he, there is the same difference between faith of recumbence and faith of assurance, as is between reason and learning. Reason is the foundation of learning; so, as there can be no learning if reason be wanting (as in beasts), in like manner there can be no assurance where there is no faith of adherence. Again: as reason well exercised m the study of arts and sciences arises to learning; so faith being well exercised on its proper object, and by its proper fruits, arises to assurance. Further, as by negligence, non- attendance, or some violent disease, learning may be lost, while reason doth abide; so by temptation, or by spiritual sloth, assurance may be lost, while saving faith may abide. Lastly, as all men have reason, but all men are not learned; so all regenerate persons have faith to comply savingly with the gospel method of salvation, but all true believers have not assurance."--Sermon by R. Fair dough, Fellow of Immanuel College, Cambridge, in the Morning Exercises, preached at Southwark. 1660.

(18) We must distinguish between weakness of faith and nullity. A weak faith is true. The bruised reed is but weak, yet it is such as Christ will not break. Though thy faith be but weak, yet be not discouraged. A weak faith may receive a strong Christ; a weak hand can tie the knot in marriage as well as a strong; a weak eye might have seen the brazen serpent. The promise is not made to strong faith, but to true. The promise doth not say, Whosoever hath a giant faith that can remove mountains, that can stop the mouth of lions, shall be saved; but whosoever believes, be his faith never so small.

"You may have the water of the Spirit poured on you in sanctification, though not the oil of gladness in assurance; there may be faith of adherence, and not of evidence; there may be life in the root where there is no fruit in the branches, and faith in the heart where no fruit of assurance."--A Body of Divinity, by Thomas Watson, formerly Minister of St. Stephen's, Walbrook, London. 1660.

(19) "Many of God's dear children for a long time may remain very doubtful as to their present and eternal condition, and know not what to conclude, whether they shall be damned or whether they shall be saved. There are believers of several growths in the Church of God,--fathers, young men, children, and babes; and as in most families there are more babes and children than grown men, so in the Church of God there are more weak, doubting Christians than strong ones, grown up to a full assurance. A babe may be born, and yet not know it; so a man may be born again, and yet not be sure of it.

"We make a difference betwixt saving faith, as such, and a full persuasion of the heart. Some of those that shall be saved may not be certain that they shall be saved; for the promise is made to the grace ot faith, and not to the evidence of it--to faith as true, and not to faith as strong. They may be sure of heaven, and yet in their own sense not assured of heaven."--Sermon by Rev. Thomas Doolittle, of Pembroke Hall, Cambridge, and sometime Rector of St. Alphege, London, in the Morning Exercises, at Cripplegate. 1661.

(20) "Is it not necessary to justification to be assured that my sins are pardoned, and that I am justified? No: that is no act of faith as it justifieth, but an effect and fruit that followeth after justification.

"It is one thing for a man to have his salvation certain, another thing to be certain that it is certain.

"Even as a man fallen into a river, and like to be drowned, as he is carried down with the flood, espies the bough of a tree hanging over the river, which he catcheth at, and clings unto with all his might to save him, and seeing no other way of succour but that, ventures his life upon it. This man, so soon as he has fastened on this bough, is in a safe condition, though all troubles, fears, and terrors are not presently out of his mind, until he comes to himself, and sees himself quite out of danger. Then he is sure he is safe; but he was safe before he was sure. Even so it is with a believer. Faith is but the espying of Christ as the only means to save, and the reaching out of the heart to lay hold upon Him. God hath spoke the word, and made the promise to His Son: I believe Him to be the only Saviour, and remit my soul to Him to be saved by His mediation. So soon as the soul can do this, God imputeth the righteousness of His Son unto it, and it is actually justified in the court of heaven, though it is not presently quieted and pacified in the court of conscience. That is done afterwards: in some sooner, in some later, by the fruits and effects of justification."--Archbishop Usher's "Body of Divinity." 1670.

(21) "There are those who doubt, because they doubt, and multiply distrust upon itself, concluding that they have no faith, because they find so much and so frequent doubting within them. But this is a great mistake. Some doublings there may be, where there is even much faith; and a little faith there may be, where there is much doubting.

"Our Saviour requires, and delights in a strong, firm believing on Him, though the least and weakest He rejects not."--Archbishop Leighton's Lectures on the first nine chapters of St. Matthew's Gospel. 1670.

(22) "Many formerly, and those of the highest remark and eminency, have placed true faith in no lower degree than assurance, or the secure persuasion of the pardon of their sins, the acceptation of their persons, and their future salvation.

"But this, as it is very sad and uncomfortable for thousands of doubting and deserted souls, concluding all those to fall short of grace who fall short of certainty, so hath it given the Papists too great advantage.

"Faith is not assurance. But this doth sometimes crown and reward a strong, vigorous and heroic faith; the Spirit of God breaking in upon the soul with an evidencing light, and scattering all that darkness, and those fears and doubts which before beclouded it."--Bishop Hopkins on the Covenants. 1680.

(23) "A want of assurance is not unbelief. Drooping spirits may be believers. There is a manifest distinction made between faith in Christ, and the comfort of that faith--between believing to eternal life, and knowing we have eternal life. There is a difference between a child's having a right to an estate, and his full knowledge of the title.

"The character of faith may be written in the heart, as letters engraven upon a seal, yet filled with so much dust as not to be distinguished. The dust hinders the reading of the letters, yet doth not raze them out."--Discourses by Stephen Charnock, of Emmanuel College, Cambridge. 1680.

(24) "Some rob themselves of their own comfort by placing saving faith in full assurance. Faith, and sense of faith, are two distinct and separable mercies; you may have truly received Christ, and not receive the knowledge or assurance of it. Some there be that say, Thou art our God,' of whom God never said, You are my people', these have no authority to be called the sons of God: others there are, of whom God saith, These are my people,' yet they dare not call God their God'; these have authority to be called the sons of God, yet know it not. They have received Christ, that is their safety; but they have not yet received the knowledge and assurance of it, that is their trouble. . . . The father owns his child in the cradle, who yet knows him not to be his father."--Method of Grace, by John Flavel, Minister of the Gospel at Dartmouth, Devon. 1680.

(25) "It is confessed weak faith hath as much peace with God, through Christ, as another hath by strong faith, but not so much bosom peace.

"Weak faith will as surely land the Christian in heaven as strong faith, for it is impossible the least dram of true grace should perish, being all incorruptible seed; but the weak, doubting Christian is not like to have so pleasant a voyage thither as another with strong faith. Though all in the ship come safe to shore, yet he that is all the way sea-sick hath not so comfortable a voyage as he that is strong and healthful."--The Christian in Complete Armour, by William Gurnall, sometime Ejector of Lavenham, Suffolk. 1680.

(26) "Be not discouraged if it doth not yet appear to you that you were given by the Father to the Son. It may be, though you do not see it. Many of the given do not for a long time know it; yea, I see no great danger in saying that not a few of the given to the Son may be in darkness, and doubts, and fears about it, till the last and brightest day declare it, and till the last sentence proclaims it.

"If, therefore, any of you be in the dark about your own election, be not discouraged: it may be, though you do not know it."--Sermons on the Lord's Prayer, by Robert Traill, Minister of the Gospel, in London, and sometime at Cranbrook, Kent. 1690.

(27) "Assurance is not essential to the being of faith. It is a strong faith; but we read likewise of a weak faith, little faith, faith like a grain of mustard seed. True saving faith in Jesus Christ is only distinguishable by its different degrees; but in every degree and in every subject, it is universally of the same kind."--Sermons, by the Key. John Newton, sometime Vicar of Olney, and Rector of St. Mary, Woolnoth, London. 1767.

(28) "There is no reason why weak believers should conclude against themselves. Weak faith unites as really with Christ as strong faith--as the least bud in the vine is drawing sap and life from the root, no less than the strongest branch. Weak believers, therefore, have abundant cause to be thankful; and while they reach after growth in grace, ought not to overlook what they have already received."--Letter of Rev. Henry Venn. 1784.

(29) "The faith necessary and sufficient for our salvation is not assurance. Its tendency doubtless is to produce that lively expectation of the Divine favour which will issue in a full confidence. But the confidence is not itself the faith of which we speak, nor is it necessarily included in it: nay, it is a totally distinct thing.

"Assurance will generally accompany a high degree of faith. But there are sincere persons who are endued with only small measures of grace, or in whom the exercise of that grace may be greatly obstructed. When such defects or hindrances prevail, many fears and distresses may be expected to arise."--The Christian System, by the Rev. Thomas Robinson, Vicar of St. Mary's, Leicester. 1795.

(30) "Salvation, and the joy of salvation, are not always contemporaneous; the latter does not always accompany the former in present experience.

"A sick man may be under a process of recovery, and yet be in doubt concerning the restoration of his health. Pain and weakness may cause him to hesitate. A child may be heir to Ms estate or kingdom, and yet derive no joy from the prospect of his future inheritance. He may be unable to trace his genealogy, or to read his title-deeds, and the testament of his father; or with a capacity of reading them he may be unable to understand their import, and his guardian may for a time deem it right to suffer him to remain in ignorance. But his ignorance does not affect the validity of his title.

"Personal assurance of salvation is not necessarily connected with faith. They are not essentially the same. Every believer might indeed infer, from the effect produced in his own heart, his own safety and privileges; but many who truly believe are unskilful in the word of righteousness, and fail of drawing the conclusion from Scriptural premises which they would be justified in drawing."--Lectures on the 51st Psalm, by the Rev. Thomas Biddulph, Minister of St. James's, Bristol. 1830. 134

ENDNOTE

[19] "Full assurance that Christ hath delivered Paul from condemnation, yea, so full and real as produceth thanksgiving and triumphing in Christ, may and doth consist with complaints and outcries of a wretched condition for the indwelling of the body of sin."--Rutherford's Triumph of Faith. 1645.

[20] We do not vindicate every vain pretender to the witness of the spirit'; we are aware that there are those in whose professions of religion we can see nothing but their forwardness and confidence to recommend them. But let us not reject any doctrine of revelation through an over-anxious fear of consequences."--Robinson's Christian System. "True assurance is built upon a Scripture basis: presumption hath no Scripture to show for its warrant; it is like a will without seal and witnesses, which is null and void in law. Presumption wants both the witness of the Word and the seal of the Spirit. Assurance always keeps the heart in a lowly posture; but presumption is bred of pride. Feathers fly up, but gold descends; he who hath this golden assurance, his heart descends in humility."--Watson's Body of Divinity. 1650. "Presumption is joined with looseness of life; persuasion with a tender conscience; that dares sin because it is sure, this dares not for fear of losing assurance. Persuasion will not sin, because it cost her Saviour so dear; presumption will sin, because grace doth abound. Humility is the way to heaven. They that are proudly secure of their going to heaven do not so often come thither as they that are afraid of going to hell."--Adams on Second Epistle of Peter. 1633.

[21] "They are quite mistaken that think faith and humility are inconsistent; they not only agree well together, but they cannot be parted."--Traill.

[22] "To be assured of our salvation," Augustine saith, "is no arrogant stoutness; it is our faith. It is no pride; it is devotion. It is no presumption; it is God's promise."--Bishop Jewell's Defence of the Apology. 1570 "If the ground of our assurance rested in and on ourselves, it might justly be called presumption; but the Lord and the power of His might being grounded thereof, they either know not what is the might of His power, or else too lightly esteem it, who account assured confidence thereon presumption."--Gouge's Whole Armour of God. 1647. "Upon what ground is this certainty built? Surely not upon anything that is in us. Our

assurance of perseverance is grounded wholly upon God. If we look upon ourselves, we see cause of fear and doubting; but if we look up to God, we shall find cause enough for assurance."--Hildersam on John iv. 1632. "Our hope is not hung upon such an untwisted thread as, I imagine so,' or It is likely'; but the cable, the strong rope of our fastened anchor, is the oath and promise of Him who is eternal verity. Our salvation is fastened with God's own hand, and Christ's own strength, to the strong stake of God's unchangeable nature."--Rutherford's Letters. 1637.

[23] "Never did a believer in Jesus Christ die or drown in his voyage to heaven. They will all be found safe and sound with the Lamb on Mount Zion. Christ loseth none of them; yea, nothing of them. (John vi. 39.) Not a bone of a believer is to be seen in the field of battle. They are all more than conquerors through Him that loved them." (Rom. viii. 37.)--Traill.

[24] The reader who would like to hear more about this point is referred to a Note at the end of this paper, in which he will find extracts from several well-known English Divines, supporting the view here maintained. The extracts are too long for insertion in this page.

[25] "He that believeth on Jesus shall never be confounded. Never was any; neither shall you, if you believe. It was a great word of faith spoken by a dying man, who had been converted in a singular way, betwixt his condemnation and execution: his last words were these, spoken with a mighty shout: Never man perished with his face towards Christ Jesus.'"--Traill.

[26] "The greatest thing that we can desire, next to the glory of God, is our own salvation; and the sweetest thing we can desire is the assurance of our salvation. In this life we cannot get higher than to be assured of that which in the next life is to be enjoyed. All saints shall enjoy a heaven when they leave this earth; some saints enjoy a heaven while they are here on earth."--Joseph Caryl. 1653.

[27] "It was a saying of Bishop Latimer to Ridley, When I live in a settled and steadfast assurance about the state of my soul, methinks than I am as bold as a lion. I can laugh at all trouble: no affliction daunts me. But when I am eclipsed in my comforts, I am of so fearful a spirit that I could run into a very mouse-hole."--Quoted by Christopher Love. 1653. "Assurance will assist us in all duties: it will arm us against all temptations; It will answer all objections; it will sustain us in all conditions into which the saddest of times can bring us. If God be for us, who can be against us?'"--Bishop Reynolds on Hosea xiv. 1642. "We cannot come amiss to him that hath assurance. God is his. Hath he lost a friend?--his father lives. Hath he lost an only child?--God hath given him His only Son. Hath he scarcity of bread?--God hath given him the finest of the wheat, the bread of life. Are his comforts gone?--he hath a Comforter. Doth he meet with storms?--he knows where to put in for harbour. God is his Portion, and heaven is his haven."--Thomas Watson. 1662.

[28] These were John Bradford's words in prison, shortly before his execution: "I have no request to make. If Queen Mary gives me my life, I will thank her; if she will banish me, I will thank her; if she will burn me, I will thank her; if she will condemn me to perpetual imprisonment, I will thank her." This was Rutherford's experience when banished to Aberdeen: "How blind are my adversaries, who sent me to a banqueting house, and not to a prison or a place of exile." "My prison is a palace to me, and Christ's banqueting house."--Letters.

[29] These were the last words of Hugh Mackail on the scaffold, at Edinburgh, 1666: "Now I begin my intercourse with God, which shall never be broken off. Farewell, father and mother, friends and relations; farewell, the world and all its delights; farewell, meat and drinks; farewell, sun, moon and stars. Welcome, God and Father; welcome, sweet Lord Jesus,

the Mediator of the new covenant; welcome, blessed Spirit of grace, and God of all consolation; welcome, glory; welcome, eternal life; welcome, death. O Lord, into Thy hands I com-commit my spirit; for Thou hast redeemed my soul, O Lord God of truth!"

[30] These were Rutherford's words on his death-bed: "O that all my brethren did know what a Master I have served, and what peace I have this day! I shall sleep in Christ, and when I awake I shall be satisfied with His likeness." 1661. These were Baxter's words on his death-bed: "I bless God I have a well-grounded assurance of my eternal happiness, and great peace and comfort within." Towards the close he was asked how he did. The answer was, "Almost well." 1691.

[31] "The least degree of faith takes away the sting of death, because it takes away guilt; but the full assurance of faith breaks the very teeth and jaws of death, by taking away the fear and dread of it."--Fairclough's Sermon in the Morning Exercises.

[32] "Assurance would make us active and lively in God's service: it would excite prayer, quicken obedience. Faith would make us walk, but assurance would make us run--we should think we could never do enough for God. Assurance would be as wings to the bird, as weights to the clock, to set all the wheels of obedience a-running."--Thomas Watson. "Assurance will make a man fervent, constant, and abundant in the work of the Lord. When the assured Christian hath done one work, he is calling out for another.-- What is next, Lord, says the assured soul, what is nest? An assured Christian will put his hand to any work, he will put his neck in any yoke for Christ--he never thinks he hath done enough, he always thinks he had done too little; and when he hath done all he can, he sits down, saying, I am an unprofitable servant".--Thomas Brooks.

[33] "The true assurance of salvation which the Spirit of God hath wrought in any heart hath that force to restrain a man from looseness of life, and to knit his heart in love and obedience to God, as nothing else hath in all the world. It is certainly either the want of faith and assurance of God's love, or a false and carnal assurance of it, that is the true cause of all the licentiousness that reigns in the world."--Hildersam 51st Psalm. "None walk so evenly with God, as they who are assured of the love of God. Faith is the mother of obedience, and sureness of trust makes way for strictness of life. When men are loose from Christ, they are loose in point of duty, and their floating belief is soon discovered in their inconstancy and unevenness of walking. We do not, with alacrity, engage in that of the success of which we are doubtful; and, therefore, when we know not whether God will accept us or not, when we are off and on in point of trust, we are just so in the course of our lives, and serve God by fits and starts. It is the slander of the world to think assurance an idle doctrine."--Manton's Exposition of James. 1660. "Who is more obliged, or who feels the obligation to observance more cogently--the son who knows his near relation, and knows his father loves him, or the servant that hath great reason to doubt it? Fear is a weak and impotent principle, in comparison of love. Terrors may awaken: love enlivens. Terrors may almost persuade': love over-persuades. Sure am I that a believer's knowledge that his Beloved is his, and he is his Beloved's (Cant. vi. 3), is found by experience to lay the most strong and cogent obligations upon him to loyalty and faithfulness to the Lord Jesus. For as to him that believes Christ is precious (1 Peter ii. 7), so to him that knows he believes Christ is so much the more precious, even the chiefset of ten thousand.'" (Cant. v. 10)--Fairclough's Sermon in Morning Exercises. 1660. "Is it necessary that men should be kept in continual dread of damnation, in order to render them circumspect and ensure their attention to duty? Will not the well-grounded expectation of heaven prove far more efficacious? Love is the noblest and strangest principle of

obedience; nor can it be but that a sense of God's love to us will increase our desire to please Him."--Robinson's Christian System.

34 "That which breeds so much perplexity is, that we would invert God's order. If I knew,' say some, that the promise belonged to me, and Christ was a Saviour to me, I could believe': that is to say, I would first see and then believe. But the true method is just the contrary: I had fainted,' says David, unless I had believed to see the goodness of the Lord.' He believed it first, and saw it afterwards."--Archbishop Leighton. "It is a weak and ignorant, but common thought of Christians, that they ought not to look for heaven, nor trust Christ for eternal glory, till they be well advanced in holiness and meetness for it. But as the first sanctification of our natures flows from out faith and trust in Christ for acceptance, so our further sanctification and meetness for glory flows from the renewed and repeated exercise of faith in Him."--Traill.

35 The Westminster Confession of Faith gives an admirable account of justification: "Those whom God effectually calleth, He also freely justified!--not by infusing righteousness into them, but by pardoning their sins, and by accounting and accepting their persons as righteous; not for anything wrought in them or done by them, but for Christ's sake alone; not by imputing faith itself, the act of believing, or any other evangelical obedience, to them, as their righteousness; but by imputing the obedience and righteousness of Christ unto them, they receiving and resting on Him and His righteousness by faith."

36 "Whose fault is it that thy interest in Christ is not put out of question? Were Christians more in self-examination, more close in walking with God, and if they had more near communion with God and were more in acting of faith, this shameful darkness and doubting would quickly vanish."--Traill. "A lazy Christian shall always want four things: viz., comfort, content, confidence, and assurance. God hath made a separation between joy and idleness, between assurance and laziness; and, therefore, it is impossible for thee to bring these together that God hath put so far asunder."--Thomas Brooks. "Are you in depths and doubts, staggering and uncertain, not knowing what is your condition, nor whether you have any interest in the forgiveness that is of God? Are you tossed up and down between hopes and fears, and want peace, consolation, and establishment? Why lie you upon your faces? Get up: watch, pray, fast, meditate, offer violence to your lusts and corruptions; fear not, startle not at their crying to be spared; press unto the throne of grace by prayer, supplications, importunities, restless requests--this is the way to take the kingdom of God. These things are not peace, are not assurance; but they are part of the means God hath appointed for the attainment of them."--Owen on the 130th Psalm.

37 "Would'st thou have thy hope strong? Then keep thy conscience pure: thou canst not defile one without weakening the other. The godly person that is loose and careless in his holy walking will soon find his hope languishing. All sin disposeth the soul that tampers with it to trembling fears and shakings of heart."--Gurnall. "One great and too common cause of distress is the secret maintaining some known sin: it puts out the eye of the soul, or dimmeth it and stupefies it, that it can neither see nor feel its own condition; but especially it provoketh God to withdraw Himself, His comforts, and the assistance of His Spirit."--Baxter's Saints' Rest. "The stars which have least circuit are nearest the pole; and men whose earths are least entangled with the world are always nearest to God and to the assurance of His favour. Worldly Christians, remember this. You and the world must part, or else assurance and your souls will never meet."--Thomas Brooks.

[38] "They are doubly miserable that have neither heaven nor earth, temporals nor eternals, made sure to them in changing times."--Thomas Brooks.

[39] "None have assurance at all times. As in a walk that is shaded with trees and chequered with light and shadow, some tracks and paths in it are dark and others are sunshine. Such is usually the life of the most assured Christian."--Bishop Hopkins. "It is very suspicious, that that person is a hypocrite that is always in the same frame, let him pretend it to be never so good."--Traill.

VIII. MOSES-- AN EXAMPLE

"By faith Moses, when he was come to years, refused to be called the son of Pharaoh's daughter:
"Choosing rather to suffer affliction with the people of God, than to enjoy the pleasures of sin for a season;
"Esteeming the reproach of Christ greater riches than the treasures in Egypt: for he had respect unto the rec-
ompense of the reward."--Hebrews xi. 24-26.

THE characters of God's most eminent saints, as drawn and described in the Bible, form a most useful part of Holy Scripture. Abstract doctrines, and principles, and precepts, are all most valuable in their way; but after all, nothing is more helpful than a pattern or example. Do we want to know what practical holiness is? Let us sit down and study the picture of an eminently holy man. I propose in this paper to set before my readers the history of a man who lived by faith, and left us a pattern of what faith can do in promoting holiness of character. To all who want to know what "living by faith" means, I offer Moses as an example.

The eleventh chapter of the Epistle to the Hebrews, from which my text is taken, is a great chapter: it deserves to be printed in golden letters. I can well believe it must have been most cheering and encouraging to a converted Jew. I suppose no members of the early Church found so much difficulty in a profession of Christianity as the Hebrews did. The way was narrow to all, but preeminently so to them. The cross was heavy to all but surely they had to carry double weight. And this chapter would refresh them like a cordial--it would be as "wine to those that be of heavy hearts." Its words would "be pleasant as the honey-comb, sweet to the soul, and health to the bones." (Prov. xxxi. 6; xvi. 24.)

The three verses I am going to explain are far from being the least interesting in the chapter. Indeed I think few, if any, have so strong a claim on our attention. And I will explain why I say so.

It seems to me that the work of faith described in the story of Moses comes home more especially to our own case. The men of God who are named in the former part of the chapter are all examples to us beyond question. But we cannot literally do what most of them did, however much we may drink into their spirit. We are not called upon to offer a literal sacrifice like Abel--or to build a literal ark like Noah--or to leave our country literally, and dwell in tents, and offer up our Isaac like Abraham. But the faith of Moses comes nearer to us. It seems to operate in a way more familiar to our own experience. It made him take up a line of conduct such as we must sometimes take up ourselves in the present day, each in our own walk of life, if we would be consistent Christians, And for this reason I think these three verses deserve more than ordinary consideration.

Now I have nothing but the simplest things to say about them. I shall only try to show the greatness of the things Moses did, and the principle on which he did them. And then perhaps we shall be better prepared for the practical instruction which the verses appear to hold out to every one who will receive it.

I. First, then, I will speak of what Moses gave up and refused.

Moses gave up three things for the sake of his soul. He felt that his soul would not be saved if he kept them--so he gave them up. And in so doing, I say that he made three of the greatest sacrifices that man's heart can possibly make. Let us see.

(1) He gave up rank and greatness.

"He refused to be called the son of Pharaoh's daughter." We all know his history. The daughter of Pharaoh had preserved his life, when he was an infant. She had gone further than that: she had adopted him and educated him as her own son.

If some writers of history may be trusted, she was Pharaoh's only child. Some go so far as to say that in the common order of things, Moses would one day have been King of Egypt![40] That may be, or may not; we cannot tell. It is enough for us to know that, from his connection with Pharaoh's daughter, Moses might have been, if he had pleased, a very great man. If he had been content with the position in which he found himself at the Egyptian court, he might easily have been among the first (if not the very first) in all the land of Egypt.

Let us think, for a moment, how great this temptation was.

Here was a man of like passions with ourselves. He might have had as much greatness as earth can well give. Rank, power, place, honour, titles, dignities--all were before him, and within his grasp. These are the things for which many men are continually struggling. These are the prizes which there is an incessant race in the world around us to obtain. To be somebody, to be looked up to, to raise themselves in the scale of society, to get a handle to their names--these are the very things for which many sacrifice time, and thought, and health, and life itself. But Moses would not have them as a gift. He turned his back upon them. He refused them. He gave them up!

(2) And more than this--he refused pleasure.

Pleasure of every kind, no doubt, was at his feet, if he had liked to take it up--sensual pleasure, intellectual pleasure, social pleasure--whatever could strike his fancy. Egypt was a land of artists, a residence of learned men, a resort of everyone who had skill, or science of any description. There was nothing which could feed the "lust of the flesh, the lust of the eye, or the pride of life," which one in the place of Moses might not easily have commanded and possessed as his own. (1 John ii. 16.)

Let us think again, how great was this temptation also.

Pleasure, be it remembered, is the one thing for which millions live. They differ, perhaps, in their views of what makes up real pleasure, but all agree in seeking first and foremost to obtain it. Pleasure and enjoyment in the holidays is the grand object to which a schoolboy looks forward. Pleasure and satisfaction in making himself independent is the mark on which the young man in business fixes his eye. Pleasure and ease in retiring from business with a fortune is the aim which the merchant sets before him. Pleasure and bodily comfort at his own home is the sum of the poor man's wishes. Pleasure and fresh excitement in politics, in travelling, in amusements, in company, in books--this is the goal towards which the rich man is straining. Pleasure is the shadow which all alike are hunting--high and low, rich and poor, old and young, one with another--each, perhaps, pretending to despise his neighbour for seeking it--each in his own way seeking it for himself--each secretly wondering that he does not find it--each firmly persuaded that somewhere or other it is to be found. This was the cup that Moses had before his lips. He might have drunk as deeply as he liked of earthly pleasure; but he would not have it. He turned his back upon it. He refused it. He gave it up!

(3) And more than this--he refused riches.

"The treasures in Egypt" is an expression that seems to tell of boundless wealth which Moses might have enjoyed, had he been content to remain with Pharaoh's daughter. We may well suppose these "treasures" would have been a mighty fortune. Enough is still remaining in Egypt to give us some faint idea of the money at its King's disposal. The pyramids, and obelisks, and temples, and statues are still standing there as witnesses. The ruins at Carnac, and Luxor, and Denderah, and many other places, are still the mightiest buildings in the world. They testify to this day that the man who gave up Egyptian wealth, gave up something which even our English minds would find it hard to reckon up and estimate.

Let us think once more, how great was this temptation.

Let us consider, for a moment, the power of money--the immense influence that "the love of money" obtains over men's minds. Let us look around us and observe how men covet it, and what amazing pains and trouble they will go through to obtain it. Tell them of an is-land many thousand miles away, where something may be found which may be profitable, if imported, and at once a fleet of ships will be sent to get it. Show them a way to make 1 per cent, more of their money, and they will reckon you among the wisest of men--they will al-most fall down and worship you. To possess money seems to hide defects--to cover over faults--to clothe a man with virtues. People can get over much, if you are rich! But here is a man who might have been rich, and would not. He would not have Egyptian treasures. He turned his back upon them. He refused them. He gave them up!

Such were the things that Moses refused--rank, pleasure, riches, all three at once.

Add to all this that he did it deliberately. He did not refuse these things in a hasty fit of youthful excitement.--He was forty years old. He was in the prime of life. He knew what he was about. He was a highly educated man, "learned in all the wisdom of the Egyptians." (Acts vii. 22.) He could weigh both sides of the question.

Add to it that he did not refuse them because he was obliged. He was not like the dying man, who tells us "he craves nothing more in this world;" and why?--Because he is leaving the world, and cannot keep it. He was not like the pauper, who makes a merit of necessity, and says "he does not want riches"; and why?--Because he cannot get them. He was not like the old man who boasts that "he has laid aside worldly pleasures;" and why?--Because he is worn out, and cannot enjoy them. No! Moses refused what he might have enjoyed. Rank, pleasure, and riches did not leave him, but he left them.

And then judge whether I am not right in saying that his was one of the greatest sacrifices mortal man ever made. Others have refused much, but none, I think, so much as Moses. Others have done well in the way of self-sacrifice and self-denial, but he excels them all.

II. And now let me go on to the second thing I wish to consider. I will speak of what Moses chose.

I think his choices as wonderful as his refusals. He chose three things for his soul's sake. The road to salvation led through them, and he followed it; and in so doing he chose three of the last things that man is ever disposed to take up.

(1) For one thing he chose suffering and affliction.

He left the ease and comfort of Pharaoh's court, and openly took part with the children of Israel. They were an enslaved and persecuted people--an object of distrust, suspicion, and hatred; and anyone who befriended them was sure to taste something of the bitter cup they were daily drinking.

To the eye of sense there seemed no chance of their deliverance from Egyptian bondage, without a long and doubtful struggle. A settled home and country for them must have appeared a thing never likely to be obtained, however much desired. In fact, if ever man seemed to be choosing pain, trials, poverty, want, distress, anxiety, perhaps even death, with his eyes open, Moses was that man.

Let us think how wonderful was this choice.

Flesh and blood naturally shrink from pain. It is in us all to do so. We draw back by a kind of instinct from suffering, and avoid it if we can. If two courses of action are set before us, which both seem right, we generally take that which is the least disagreeable to flesh and blood. We spend our days in fear and anxiety when we think affliction is coming near us, and use every means to escape it. And when it does come, we often fret and murmur under the burden of it; and if we can only bear it patiently, we count it a great matter.

But look here! Here is a man of like passions with ourselves, and he actually chooses affliction! Moses saw the cup of suffering that was before him if he left Pharaoh's court, and he chose it, preferred it, and took it up.

(2) But he did more than this, he chose the company of a despised people.

He left the society of the great and wise, among whom he had been brought up, and joined himself to the Children of Israel. He who had lived from infancy in the midst of rank, and riches, and luxury, came down from his high estate, and cast in his lot with poor men-- slaves, serfs, helots, pariahs, bondservants, oppressed, destitute, afflicted, tormented-- labourers in the brick-kiln.

How wonderful, once more, was this choice!

Generally speaking, we think it enough to carry our own troubles. We may be sorry for others whose lot is to be mean and despised.--We may even try to help them--we may give money to raise them--we may speak for them to those on whom they depend; but here we generally stop.

But here is a man who does far more. He not merely feels for despised Israel, but actually goes down to them, adds himself to their society, and lives with them altogether. You would wonder if some great man in Grosvenor or Belgrave Square were to give up house, and fortune, and position in society, and go to live on a small allowance in some narrow lane in Bethnal Green, for the sake of doing good. Yet this would convey a very faint and feeble notion of the kind of thing that Moses did. He saw a despised people, and he chose their company in preference to that of the noblest in the land. He became one with them--their fellow, their companion in tribulation, their ally, their associate, and their friend.

(3) But he did even more. He chose reproach and scorn.

Who can conceive the torrent of mockery and ridicule that Moses would have to stem, in turning away from Pharaoh's court to join Israel! Men would tell him he was mad, foolish, weak, silly, out of his mind. He would lose his influence; he would forfeit the favour and good opinion of all among whom he had lived. But none of these things moved him. He left the court and joined the slaves!

Let us think again, what a choice this was!

There are few things more powerful than ridicule and scorn. It can do far more than open enmity and persecution. Many a man who would march up to a cannon's mouth, or lead a forlorn hope, or storm a breach, has found it impossible to face the mockery of a few companions, and has flinched from the path of duty to avoid it. To be laughed at! To be made a joke of! To be jested and sneered at! To be reckoned weak and silly! To be thought a fool!--There is nothing grand in all this, and many, alas, cannot make up their minds to undergo it!

Yet here is a man who made up his mind to it, and did not shrink from the trial. Moses saw reproach and scorn before him, and he chose them, and accepted them for his portion.

Such then were the things that Moses chose: affliction--the company of a despised people--and scorn.

Set down beside all this, that Moses was no weak, ignorant, illiterate person, who did not know what he was about. You are specially told he was "mighty in words and in deeds;" and yet he chose as he did! (Acts vii. 22.)

Set down, too, the circumstances of his choice. He was not obliged to choose as he did. None compelled him to take such a course. The things he took up did not force themselves upon him against his will. He went after them; they did not come after him. All that he did, he did of his own free choice--voluntarily, and of his own accord.

And then judge whether it is not true that his choices were as wonderful as his refusals. Since the world began, I suppose, none ever made such a choice as Moses did in our text.

III. And now let me go on to a third thing:--let me speak of the principle which moved Moses, and made him do as he did.

How can this conduct of his be accounted for? What possible reason can be given for it? To refuse that which is generally called good, to choose that which is commonly thought evil, this is not the way of flesh and blood. This is not the manner of man; this requires some explanation. What will that explanation be?

We have the answer in the text. I know not whether its greatness or its simplicity is more to be admired. It all lies in one little word, and that word is "faith."

Moses had faith. Faith was the mainspring of his wonderful conduct. Faith made him do as he did, choose what he chose, and refuse what he refused. He did it all because he believed.

God set before the eyes of his mind His own will and purpose. God revealed to him that a Saviour was to be born of the stock of Israel, that mighty promises were bound up in these children of Abraham, and yet to be fulfilled, that the time for fulfilling a portion of these promises was at hand; and Moses put credit in this, and believed. And every step in his wonderful career, every action in his journey through life after leaving Pharaoh's court--his choice of seeming evil, his refusal of seeming good--all, all must be traced up to this fountain; all will be found to rest on this foundation. God had spoken to him, and he had faith in God's word.

He believed that God would keep His promises--that what He had said He would surely do, and what He had covenanted He would surely perform.

He believed that with God nothing was impossible. Reason and sense might say that the deliverance of Israel was out of the question: the obstacles were too many, the difficulties too great. But faith told Moses that God was all-sufficient. God had undertaken the work, and it would be done.

He believed that God was all wise. Reason and sense might tell him that his line of action was absurd; that he was throwing away useful influence, and destroying all chance of benefiting his people, by breaking with Pharaoh's daughter. But faith told Moses that if God said "Go this way," it must be the best.

He believed that God was all merciful. Reason and sense might hint that a more pleasant manner of deliverance might be found, that some compromise might be effected, and many hardships be avoided. But faith told Moses that God was love, and would not give His people one drop of bitterness beyond what was absolutely needed.

Faith was a telescope to Moses. It made him see the goodly land afar off--rest, peace, and victory, when dim-sighted reason could only see trial and barrenness, storm and tempest, weariness and pain,

Faith was an interpreter to Moses. It made him pick out a comfortable meaning in the dark commands of God's handwriting, while ignorant sense could see nothing in it but mystery and foolishness.

Faith told Moses that all this rank and greatness was of the earth, earthy, a poor, vain, empty thing, frail, fleeting, and passing away; and that there was no true greatness like that of serving God. He was the king, he the true nobleman who belonged to the family of God. It was better to be last in heaven than first in hell.

Faith told Moses that worldly pleasures were "pleasures of sin." They were mingled with sin, they led on to sin, they were ruinous to the soul, and displeasing to God. It would be small comfort to have pleasure while God was against him. Better suffer and obey God, than be at ease and sin.

Faith told Moses that these pleasures after all were only for a "season." They could not last; they were all short-lived; they would weary him soon; he must leave them all in a few years.

Faith told him that there was a reward in heaven for the believer far richer than the treasures in Egypt, durable riches, where rust could not corrupt, nor thieves break through and steal. The crown there would be incorruptible; the weight of glory would be exceeding and eternal;--and faith bade him look away to an unseen heaven if his eyes were dazzled with Egyptian gold.

Faith told Moses that affliction and suffering were not real evils.--They were the school of God, in which He trains the children of grace for glory--the medicines which are needful to purify our corrupt wills--the furnace which must burn away our dross--the knife which must cut the ties that bind us to the world.

Faith told Moses that the despised Israelites were the chosen people of God. He believed that to them belonged the adoption, and the covenant, and the promises, and the glory; that of them the seed of the woman was one day to be born, who should bruise the serpent's head; that the special blessing of God was upon them; that they were lovely and beautiful in His eyes--and that it was better to be a doorkeeper among the people of God than to reign in the palaces of wickedness.

Faith told Moses that all the reproach and scorn poured out on him was "the reproach of Christ";--that it was honourable to be mocked and despised for Christ's sake--that whoso persecuted Christ's people was persecuting Christ Himself--and that the day must come when His enemies would bow before Him and lick the dust. All this, and much more, of which I cannot speak particularly, Moses saw by faith. These were the things he believed, and believing, did what he did. He was persuaded of them, and embraced them--he reckoned them as certainties--he regarded them as substantial verities--he counted them as sure as if he had seen them with his own eyes--he acted on them as realities--and this made him the man that he was. He had faith. He believed.

Marvel not that he refused greatness, riches, and pleasure.--He looked far forward. He saw with the eye of faith kingdoms crumbling into dust--riches taking to themselves wings and fleeing away--pleasures leading on to death and judgment--and Christ only and His little flock enduring for ever.

Wonder not that he chose affliction, a despised people, and reproach.--He beheld things below the surface. He saw with the eye of faith affliction lasting but for a moment--reproach rolled away, and ending in everlasting honour--and the despised people of God reigning as kings with Christ in glory.

And was he not right? Does he not speak to us, though dead, this very day? The name of Pharaoh's daughter has perished, or at any rate is extremely doubtful.--The city where Pharaoh reigned is not known.--The treasures in Egypt are gone.--But the name of Moses is known wherever the Bible is read, and is still a standing witness that "whoso liveth by faith, happy is he."

IV. And now let me wind up all by trying to set forth in order some practical lessons, which appear to me to follow, as legitimate consequences, from this history of Moses.

What has all this to do with us? some men will say. We do not live in Egypt--we have seen no miracles--we are not Israelites--we are weary of the subject.

Stay a little, if this be the thought of your heart, and by God's help I will show you that all may learn here, and all may be instructed. He that would live a Christian life, and be a really holy man, let him mark the history of Moses and get wisdom.

(1) For one thing, if you would ever be saved, you must make the choice that Moses made--you must choose God before the world.

Mark well what I say. Do not overlook this, though all the rest be forgotten. I do not say that the statesman must throw up his office, and the rich man forsake his property. Let no one fancy that I mean this. But I say, if a man would be saved, whatever be his rank in life, he must be prepared for tribulation. He must make up his mind to choose much which seems evil, and to give up and refuse much which seems good.

I dare say this sounds strange language to some who read these pages. I know well you may have a certain form of religion, and find no trouble in your way. There is a common, worldly kind of Christianity in this day, which many have, and think they have enough--a cheap Christianity which offends nobody, and is worth nothing. I am not speaking of religion of this kind.

But if you really are in earnest about your soul--if your religion is something more than a mere fashionable Sunday cloak--if you are determined to live by the Bible--if you are resolved to be a New Testament Christian, then, I repeat, you will soon find you must carry a cross.--You must endure hard things, you must suffer on behalf of your soul, as Moses did, or you cannot be saved.

The world in the nineteenth century is what it always was. The hearts of men are still the same. The offence of the cross is not ceased. God's true people are still a despised little flock.

True Evangelical religion still brings with it reproach and scorn. A real servant of God will still be thought by many a weak enthusiast and a fool.

But the matter comes to this. Do you wish your soul to be saved? Then remember, you must choose whom you will serve. You cannot serve God and mammon. You cannot be on two sides at once. You cannot be a friend of Christ and a friend of the world at the same time. You must come out from the children of this world, and be separate; you must put up with much ridicule, trouble, and opposition, or you will be lost for ever. You must be willing to think and do things which the world considers foolish, and to hold opinions which are only held by a few. It will cost you something. The stream is strong, and you have to stem it. The way is narrow and steep, and it is no use saying it is not. But depend on it, there can be no saving religion without sacrifices and self-denial.

Now are you making any sacrifices? Does your religion cost you anything? I put it to your conscience in all affection and tenderness.--Are you, like Moses, preferring God to the world, or not? I beseech you not to take shelter under that dangerous word "we": "we ought," and "we hope," and "we mean," and the like. I ask you plainly, What are you doing yourself? Are you willing to give up anything which keeps you back from God? or are you clinging to the Egypt of the world, and saying to yourself, "I must have it, I must have it: I cannot tear myself away"? Is there any cross in your Christianity? Are there any sharp corners in your religion, anything that ever jars and comes in collision with the earthly-mindedness around you? or is all smooth and rounded-off, and comfortably fitted into custom and fashion? Do you know anything of the afflictions of the Gospel? Is your faith and practice ever a subject of scorn and reproach? Are you thought a fool by anyone because of your soul? Have you left Pharaoh's daughter, and heartily joined the people of God? Are you venturing all on Christ? Search and see.

These are hard inquiries and rough questions. I cannot help it. I believe they are founded on Scripture truths. I remember it is written, "There went great multitudes with Jesus, and He turned, and said unto them, If any man come to Me and hate not his father, and mother, and wife, and children, and brethren, and sisters, yea and his own life, also, he cannot be my disciple. And whosoever doth not bear his cross, and come after Me, cannot be my disciple." (Luke xiv. 25-27.) Many, I fear, would like glory, who have no wish for grace. They would fain have the wages, but not the work; the harvest, but not the labour; the reaping, but not the sowing; the reward, but not the battle. But it may not be. As Bunyan says, "the bitter must go before the sweet." If there is no cross, there will be no crown.

(2) The second thing I say is this--nothing mil ever enable you to choose God before the world, except faith.

Nothing else will do it. Knowledge will not, feeling will not, a regular use of outward forms will not, good companions will not. All these may do something, but the fruit they produce has no power of continuance: it will not last. A religion springing from such sources will only endure so long as there is no "tribulation of persecution because of the Word"; but as soon as there is any, it will dry up. It is a clock without mainspring or weights; its face may be beautiful, you may turn its fingers round, but it will not go. A religion that is to stand must have a living foundation, and there is none other but faith.

There must be a real heartfelt belief that God's promises are sure and to be depended on; a real belief that what God says in the Bible is all true, and that every doctrine contrary to this is false, whatever anyone may say. There must be a real belief that all God's words are to be received, however hard and disagreeable to flesh and blood, and that His way is right and all others wrong. This there must be, or you will never come out from the world, take up the cross, follow Christ, and be saved.

You must learn to believe promises better than possessions; things unseen better than things seen; things in heaven out of sight better than things on earth before your eyes; the praise of the invisible God better than the praise of visible man. Then, and then only, you will make a choice like Moses, and prefer God to the world.

Now I ask every reader of this paper, have you got this faith? If you have, you will find it possible to refuse seeming good, and choose seeming evil.--You will think nothing of to-day's losses, in the hope of to-morrow's gains.--You will follow Christ in the dark, and stand by Him to the very last. If you have not, I warn you, you will never war a good warfare, and "so run as to obtain."--You will soon be offended and turn back to the world.

Above all this there must be a real abiding faith in the Lord Jesus Christ. The life that you live in the flesh you must live by faith of the Son of God. There must be a settled habit of continually leaning on Jesus, looking unto Jesus, drawing out of Jesus, and using Him as the manna of your soul. You must strive to be able to say, "To me to live is Christ." "I can do all things through Christ which strengthened me." (Philip. i. 21; iv. 13.)

This was the faith by which the old saints obtained a good report. This was the weapon by which they overcame the world. This made them what they were.

This was the faith that made Noah go on building Ms ark, while the world looked on and mocked--and Abraham give the choice of the land to Lot, and dwell on quietly in tents--and Ruth cleave to Naomi, and turn away from her country and her gods--and Daniel continue in prayer, though he knew the lions' den was prepared--and the three children refuse to worship idols, though the fiery furnace was before their eyes--and Moses forsake Egypt, not fearing the wrath of Pharaoh. All these acted as they did because they believed. They saw the difficulties and troubles of this course. But they saw Jesus by faith above them all, and they pressed on. Well may the Apostle Peter speak of faith as "precious faith." (2 Peter i. 1.)

(3) The third thing I say is this--the true reason why so many are worldly and ungodly persons is that they have no faith.

We must be aware that multitudes of professing Christians would never think for a moment of doing as Moses did. It is useless to speak smooth things, and shut your eyes to the fact. That man must be blind who does not see thousands around him who are daily preferring the world to God--placing the things of time before the things of eternity, and the things of the body before the things of the soul. We may not like to admit this, and we try hard to blink the fact. But so it is.

And why do they do so? No doubt they will all give us reasons and excuses. Some will talk of the snares of the world--some of the want of time--some of the peculiar difficulties of their position--some of the cares and anxieties of life, some of the strength of temptation--some of the power of passions--some of the effects of bad companions. But what does it come to after all? There is a far shorter way to account for the state of their souls--they do not believe. One simple sentence, like Aaron's rod, will swallow up all their excuses--they have no faith.

They do not really think what God says is true. They secretly flatter themselves with the notion, "It will surely not be fulfilled--there must surely be some other way to heaven beside that which ministers speak of--there cannot surely be so much danger of being lost." In short, they do not put implicit confidence in the words that God has written and spoken, and so do not act upon them. They do not thoroughly believe hell, and so do not flee from it--nor heaven, and so do not seek it--nor the guilt of sin, and so do not turn from it--nor the holiness of God, and so do not fear Him--nor their need of Christ, and so do not trust in Him, nor love Him. They do not feel confidence in God, and so venture nothing for Him. Like the boy Passion, in Pilgrim's Progress, they must have their good things now. They do not trust God, and so they cannot wait.

Now how is it with ourselves? Do we believe all the Bible? Let us ask ourselves that question. Depend on it, it is a much greater thing to believe all the Bible than many suppose. Happy is the man who can lay his hand on his heart and say, "I am a believer."

We talk of infidels sometimes as if they were the rarest people in the world. And I grant that open avowed infidelity is happily not very common now. But there is a vast amount of practical infidelity around us, for all that, which is as dangerous in the end as the principles of Voltaire and Paine. There are many who Sunday after Sunday repeat the creed, and make a point of declaring their belief in all that the Apostolic and Nicene forms contain. And yet these very persons will live all the week as if Christ had never died, and as if there were no judgment, and no resurrection of the dead, and no life everlasting at all. There are many who will say, "Oh, we know it all," when spoken to about eternal things and the value of their souls. And yet their lives show plainly they know not anything as they ought to know; and the saddest part of their state is that they think they do!

It is an awful truth, and worthy of all consideration, that knowledge not acted upon, in God's sight, is not merely useless and unprofitable. It is much worse than that. It will add to our condemnation and increase our guilt in the judgment day. A faith that does not influence a man's practice is not worthy of the name. There are only two classes in the Church of Christ--those who believe and those who do not. The difference between the true Christian and the mere outward professor just lies in one word--the true Christian is like Moses, "He has faith"; the mere outward professor has none. The true Christian believes, and therefore lives as he does; the mere professor does not believe, and therefore is what he is. Oh, where is our faith? Let us not be faithless, but believing.

(4) The last thing I say is this--the true secret of doing great things for God is to have great faith.

I believe that we are all apt to err on this point. We think too much, and talk too much, about graces, and gifts, and attainments, and do not sufficiently remember that faith is the root and mother of them all. In walking with God, a man will go just as far as he believes, and no further. His life will always be proportioned to his faith. His peace, his patience, his courage, his zeal, his works--all will be according to his faith.

You read the lives of eminent Christians, of such men as Wesley, or Whitefield, or Venn, or Martyn, of Bickersteth, or Simeon, or M'Cheyne. And you are disposed to say, "What wonderful gifts and graces these men had!" I answer, you should rather give honour to the mother-grace which God puts forward in the eleventh chapter of the Epistle to the Hebrews--you should give honour to their faith. Depend on it, faith was the mainspring in the character of each and all.

I can fancy someone saying, "They were so prayerful--that made them what they were." I answer, why did they pray much?--Simply because they had much faith. What is prayer, but faith speaking to God?

Another perhaps will say, "They were so diligent and laborious--that accounts for their success." I answer, why were they so diligent?--Simply because they had faith. What is Christian diligence, but faith at work?

Another will tell me, "They were so bold--that rendered them so useful." I answer, why were they so bold?--Simply because they had much faith. What is Christian boldness, but faith honestly doing its duty?

And another will cry, "It was their holiness and spirituality--that gave them their weight." For the last time I answer, what made them holy?--Nothing but a living, realizing spirit of faith. What is holiness, but faith visible and faith incarnate?

Now does any reader of this paper desire to grow in grace, and in the knowledge of our Lord Jesus Christ? Would you bring forth much fruit? Would you be eminently holy and useful? Would you be bright, and shine as a light in your day? Would you, like Moses, make it clear as noonday that you have chosen God before the world? I dare be sure that every believer will reply, "Yes! yes! yes! these are the things we long for and desire."

Then take the advice I give you this day--go and cry to the Lord Jesus Christ, as the disciples did, "Lord, increase our faith." Faith is the root of a real Christian's character. Let your root be right, and your fruit will soon abound. Your spiritual prosperity will always be according to your faith. He that believeth shall not only be saved, but shall never thirst--shall overcome--shall be established--shall walk firmly on the waters of this world--and shall do great works.

Reader, if you believe the things contained in this paper, and desire to be a thoroughly holy man, begin to act on your belief. Take Moses for your example. Walk in his steps. Go and do likewise.

ENDNOTE

[40] In Eastern countries the liberty to adopt children who are not blood-relatives, and to give them the privileges of sons, is notoriously carried out most extensively.

IX. LOT-- A BEACON

"He lingered."--Gen. xix. 16."

THE Holy Scriptures, which were written for our learning, contain beacons as well as patterns. They show us examples of what we should avoid, as well as examples of what we should follow. The man whose name heads this page is set for a beacon to the whole Church of Christ. His character is put before us in one little word--"He lingered." Let us sit down and look at this beacon for a few minutes. Let us consider Lot.

Who is this man that lingered?--It is the nephew of faithful Abraham. And when did he linger?--The very morning Sodom was to be destroyed. And where did he linger?--Within the walls of Sodom itself. And before whom did he linger?--Under the eyes of the two angels, who were sent to bring him out of the city. Even then "he lingered!"

The words are solemn, and full of food for thought. They ought to sound like a trumpet in the ears of all who make any profession of religion. I trust they will make every reader of this paper think. Who knows but they are the very words your soul requires? The voice of the Lord Jesus commands you to "remember Lot's wife." (Luke xvii. 32.) The voice of one of His ministers invites you this day to remember Lot.

Let me try to show--

I. What Lot was himself;

II. What the text already quoted tells you of him;

III. What reasons may account for his lingering;

IV. What kind of fruit his lingering brought forth.

I ask the special attention of all who have reason to hope they are real Christians, and desire to live holy lives. Let it be a settled principle in our minds, if we follow holiness, that we must not "linger."

Once more, I say, "Lot is a beacon."

I. What was Lot?

This is a most important point. If I leave it unnoticed, I shall perhaps miss that class of professing Christians I want especially to benefit. If I did not make it quite clear, many would perhaps say, after reading this paper, "Ah! Lot was a bad man--a poor, wicked, dark creature-- an unconverted man--a child of this world!--no wonder he lingered."

But mark now what I say. Lot was nothing of the kind. Lot was a true believer--a converted person--a real child of God--a justified soul--a righteous man.

Has any one of my readers grace in his heart?--So also had Lot. Has any one of my readers a hope of salvation?--So also had Lot. Is any one of my readers a traveller in the narrow way which leads unto life?--So also was Lot.

Let no one think this is only my private opinion--a mere arbitrary fancy of my own--a notion unsupported by Scripture. Let no one suppose I want him to believe it merely because I say it. The Holy Ghost has placed the matter beyond controversy, by calling him "just" and "righteous" (2 Peter ii. 7, 8), and has given us good evidence of the grace that was in him.

One evidence is, that he lived in a wicked place, "seeing and hearing" evil all around him (2 Peter ii. 8), and yet was not wicked himself. Now to be a Daniel in Babylon--an Obadiah in Ahab's house--an Abijah in Jeroboam's family--a saint in Nero's court, and a "righteous man" in Sodom, a man must have the grace of God. Without grace it would be impossible.

Another evidence is that he "vexed his soul with the unlawful deeds" he beheld around him. (2 Peter ii. 8.) He was wounded, grieved, pained, and hurt at the sight of sin. This was feeling like holy David, who says, "I beheld the transgressors, and was grieved, because they kept not Thy word." "Rivers of waters run down mine eyes, because they keep not Thy law." (Psalm cxix. 136, 158.) This was feeling like St. Paul, who says, "I have great sorrow and continual heaviness in my heart--for my brethren, my kinsmen according to the flesh." (Rom. ix. 2, 3.) Nothing will account for this but the grace of God.

Another evidence is that he "vexed his soul from day to day" with the unlawful deeds he saw. (2 Peter ii. 8.) He did not at length become cool and lukewarm about sin, as many do. Familiarity and habit did not take off the fine edge of his feelings, as too often is the case. Many a man is shocked and startled at the first sight of wickedness, and yet becomes at last so accustomed to see it, that he views it with comparative unconcern. This is especially the case with those who live in towns and cities, or with English people who travel on the Continent. Such persons often become utterly indifferent about Sabbath-breaking, and many forms of open sin. But it was not so with Lot. And this, again, is a great mark of the reality of his grace.

Such an one was Lot--a just and righteous man, a man sealed and stamped as an heir of heaven by the Holy Ghost Himself.

Before we pass on, let us remember that a true Christian may have many a blemish, many a defect, many an infirmity, and yet be a true Christian nevertheless. We do not despise gold because it is mixed with much dross. We must not undervalue grace because it is accompanied by much corruption. Read on, and you will find that Lot paid dearly for his "lingering." But do not forget, as you read, that Lot was a child of God.

II. Let us pass on to the second thing I spoke of. What does the text, already quoted, tell us about Lot's behaviour?

The words are wonderful and astounding: "He lingered."--The more we consider the time and circumstances, the more wonderful we shall think them.

Lot knew the awful condition of the city in which he stood. "The cry" of its abominations "had waxen great before the Lord." (Gen. xix. 13.) And yet "he lingered."

Lot knew the fearful judgment coming down on all within its walls. The angels had said plainly, "The Lord hath sent us to destroy it." (Gen. xix. 13.) And yet "he lingered."

Lot knew that God was a God who always kept His word, and if He said a thing would surely do it. He could hardly be Abraham's nephew, and live long with him, and not be aware of this. Yet "he lingered."

Lot believed there was danger--for he went to his sons-in-law, and warned them to flee. "Up!" he said, "Get you out of this place; for the Lord will destroy this city." (Gen. xix. 14.) And yet "he lingered."

Lot saw the angels of God standing by, waiting for him and his family to go forth. He heard the voice of those ministers of wrath ringing in his ears to hasten him--"Arise! take thy wife and thy two daughters which are here; lest thou be consumed in the iniquity of the city." (Gen. xix. 15.) And yet "he lingered."

He was slow when he should have been quick--backward when he should have been forward--trifling when he should have been hastening--loitering when he should have been hurrying--cold when he should have been hot. It is passing strange! It seems almost incredible! It appears too wonderful to be true! But the Spirit writes it down for our learning. And so it was.

And yet, wonderful as it may appear at first sight, I fear there are many of the Lord Jesus Christ's people very like Lot.

I ask every reader of this paper to mark well what I say. I repeat it that there may be no mistake about my meaning. I have shown you that Lot "lingered."--I say that there are many Christian men and Christian women in this day very like Lot.

There are many real children of God who appear to know far more than they live up to, and see far more than they practise, and yet continue in this state for many years. Wonderful that they go as far as they do, and yet go no further!

They acknowledge the Head, even Christ, and love the truth. They like sound preaching, and assent to every article of Gospel doctrine, when they hear it. But still there is an indescribable something which is not satisfactory about them. They are constantly doing things which disappoint the expectations of their ministers, and of more advanced Christian friends. Marvellous that they should think as they do, and yet stand still!

They believe in heaven, and yet seem faintly to long for it; and in hell, and yet seem little to fear it, They love the Lord Jesus; but the work they do for Him is small. They hate the devil; but they often appear to tempt him to come to them. They know the time is short; but they live as if it were long. They know they have a battle to fight; yet a man might think they were at peace. They know they have a race to run; yet they often look like people sitting still. They know the Judge is at the door, and there is wrath to come; and yet they appear half asleep. Astonishing they should be what they are, and yet be nothing more!

And what shall we say of these people? They often puzzle godly friends and relations. They often cause great anxiety. They often give rise to great doubts and searchings of heart. But they may be classed under one sweeping description: they are all brethren and sisters of Lot. They linger.

These are they who get the notion into their minds that it is impossible for all believers to be so very holy and very spiritual! They allow that eminent holiness is a beautiful thing. They like to read about it in books, and even to see it occasionally in others. But they do not think that all are meant to aim at so high a standard. At any rate, they seem to make up their minds it is beyond their reach.

These are they who get into their heads false ideas of charity, as they call it. They are morbidly afraid of being illiberal and narrow-minded, and are always flying into the opposite extreme. They would fain please everybody, and suit everybody, and be agreeable to everybody. But they forget they ought first to be sure that they please God.

These are they who dread sacrifices, and shrink from self-denial. They never appear able to apply our Lord's command, to "take up the cross," and "cut off the right hand and pluck out the right eye." (Matt. v. 29, 30.) They cannot deny that our Lord used these expressions, but they never find a place for them in their religion. They spend their lives in trying to make the gate more wide, and the cross more light. But they never succeed.

These are they who are always trying to keep in with the world. They are ingenious in discovering reasons for not separating decidedly, and in framing plausible excuses for attending questionable amusements, and keeping up questionable friendships. One day you are told of their attending a Bible-reading: the next day perhaps you hear of their going to a ball. One day they fast, or go to the Lord's table and receive the sacrament: another day they go to the race-course in the morning and the opera at night. One day they are almost in hysterics under the sermon of some sensational preacher: another day they are weeping over some novel. They are constantly labouring to persuade themselves that to mix a little with worldly people on their own ground does good. Yet in their case it is very clear they do no good, and only get harm.

These are they who cannot find it in their hearts to quarrel with their besetting sin, whether it be sloth, indolence, ill-temper, pride, selfishness, impatience, or what it may. They allow it to remain a tolerably quiet and undisturbed tenant of their hearts. They say, "it is their health, or their constitutions, or their temperaments, or their trials, or their way. Their father, or mother, or grandmother, was so before themselves, and they are sure they cannot help it." And when you meet after the absence of a year or so, you hear the same thing!

But all, all, all may be summed up in one single sentence. They are the brethren and sisters of Lot. They linger.

Ah, if you are a lingering soul, you are not happy! You know you are not. It would be strange indeed if you were so. Lingering is the sure destruction of a happy Christianity. A lingerer's conscience forbids him to enjoy inward peace.

Perhaps at one time you did run well. But you have left your first love--you have never felt the same comfort since, and you never will till you return to your "first works." (Rev. ii. 5.) Like Peter, when the Lord Jesus was taken prisoner, you are following the Lord afar off; and, like him, you will find the way not pleasant, but hard.

Come and look at Lot. Come and mark Lot's history. Come and consider Lot's "lingering," and be wise.

III. Let us next consider the reasons that may account for Lot's lingering.

This is a question of great importance, and I ask most serious attention to it. To know the root of a disease is one step towards a remedy. He that is forewarned is forearmed.

Who is there among the readers of this paper that feels secure, and has no fear of lingering? Come and listen while I tell you a few passages of Lot's history. Do as he did, and it will be a miracle indeed if you do not get into the same state of soul at last.

One thing then I observe in Lot is this--he made a wrong choice in early life.

There was a time when Abraham and Lot lived together. They both became rich, and could live together no longer. Abraham, the elder of the two, in the true spirit of humility and courtesy, gave Lot the choice of the country, when they resolved to part company: "If thou," he said, "wilt take the left hand, then I will go to the right; or if thou depart to the right hand, then I will go to the left." (Gen. xiii. 9.)

And what did Lot do?--We are told he saw that the plains of Jordan, near Sodom, were rich, fertile, and well watered. It was a good land for cattle, and full of pastures. He had large flocks and herds, and it just suited his requirements. And this was the land he chose for a residence, simply because it was a rich, "well watered land." (Gen. xiii. 10.)

It was near the town of Sodom! He cared not for that.--The men of Sodom, who would be his neighbours, were wicked! It mattered not.--They were sinners before God exceedingly! It made no difference to him.--The pasture was rich. The land was good. He wanted such a country for his flocks and herds. And before that argument all scruples and doubts, if indeed he had any, at once went down.

He chose by sight, and not by faith. He asked no counsel of God, to preserve him from mistakes. He looked to the things of time, and not of eternity. He thought of his worldly profit, and not of his soul. He considered only what would help him in this life. He forgot the solemn business of the life to come. This was a bad beginning.

But I observe also that Lot mixed with sinners when there was no occasion for his doing so.

We are first told that he "pitched his tent toward Sodom." (Gen. xiii. 12.) This, as I have already shown, was a great mistake.

But the next time he is mentioned, we find him actually living in Sodom itself. The Spirit says expressly, "He dwelt in Sodom." (Gen. xiv. 12.) His tents were left. The country was forsaken. He occupied a house in the very streets of that wicked town.

We are not told the reason of this change. We are not aware that any occasion could have arisen for it. We are sure there could have been no command of God. Perhaps his wife liked the town better than the country, for the sake of society. It is plain she had no grace herself. Perhaps she persuaded Lot it was needful for the advantage of his daughters, that they might marry, and get settled in life. Perhaps the daughters urged living in the town for the sake of gay company: they were evidently light-minded young women. Perhaps Lot liked it himself, in order to make more of his flocks and herds. Men never want reasons to confirm their wills. But one thing is very clear--Lot dwelt in the midst of Sodom without good cause.

When a child of God does these two things which I have named, we never need be surprised if we hear, by and by, unfavourable accounts about his soul. We never need wonder if he becomes deaf to the warning voice of affliction, as Lot was (Gen. xiv. 12), and turns out a lingerer in the day of trial and danger, as Lot did.

Make a wrong choice in life--an unscriptural choice--and settle yourself down unnecessarily in the midst of worldly people, and I know no surer way to damage your own spirituality, and to go backward about your eternal concerns. This is the way to make the pulse of your soul beat feebly and languidly. This is the way to make the edge of your feeling about sin become blunt and dull. This is the way to dim the eyes of your spiritual discernment, till you can scarcely distinguish good from evil, and stumble as you walk. This is the way to bring a moral palsy on your feet and limbs, and make you go tottering and trembling along the road to Zion, as if the grasshopper was a burden. This is the way to sell the pass to your worst enemy--to give the devil vantage-ground in the battle--to tie your arms in fighting--to fetter your legs in running--to dry up the sources of your strength--to cripple your energies--to cut off your own hair, like Samson, and give yourself into the hands of the Philistines, to put out your own eyes, grind at the mill, and become a slave.

I call on every reader of this paper to mark well what I am saying. Settle these things down in your mind. Do not forget them. Recollect them in the morning. Recall them to memory at night. Let them sink down deeply into your heart. If ever you would be safe from "lingering," beware of needless mingling with worldly people. Beware of Lot's choice! If you would not settle down into a dry, dull, sleepy, lazy, barren, heavy, carnal, stupid, torpid state of soul, beware of Lot's choice!

(a) Remember this in choosing a dwelling-place, or residence. It is not enough that the house is comfortable--the situation good--the air fine--the neighbourhood pleasant--the rent or price small--the living cheap. There are other things yet to be considered. You must think of your immortal soul. Will the house you think of help you towards heaven or hell?--Is the Gospel preached within an easy distance?--Is Christ crucified within reach of your door?--Is there a real man of God near, who will watch over your soul? I charge you, if you love life, not to overlook this. Beware of Lot's choice.

(b) Remember this in choosing a calling, a place, or profession in life. It is not enough that the salary is high--the wages good--the work light--the advantages numerous--the prospects of getting on most favourable. Think of your soul, your immortal soul. Will it be prospered or drawn back? Will you have your Sundays free, and be able to have one day in the week for your spiritual business? I beseech you, by the mercies of God, to take heed what you do. Make no rash decision. Look at the place in every light--the light of God as well as the light of the world. Gold may be bought too dear. Beware of Lot's choice.

(c) Remember this in choosing a husband or wife, if you are unmarried. It is not enough that your eye is pleased--that your tastes are met--that your mind find congeniality--that there is amiability and affection--that there is a comfortable home for life. There needs something more than this. There is a life yet to come. Think of your soul, your immortal soul. Will it be helped upwards or dragged downwards by the union you are planning?--Will it be made more heavenly, or more earthly--drawn nearer to Christ, or to the world?--Will its religion grow in vigour, or will it decay?--I pray you, by all your hopes of glory, allow this to enter into your calculations. "Think," as old Baxter said, and "think, and think again," before you commit yourself. "Be not unequally yoked." (2 Cor. vi. 14.) Matrimony is nowhere named among the means of conversion. Remember Lot's choice.

(d) Remember this, if you are ever offered a situation on a railway.--It is not enough to have good pay and regular employment--the confidence of the directors, and the best chance of rising to a higher post. These things are very well in their way, but they are not everything. How will your soul fare if you serve a railway company that runs Sunday trains? What day in the week will you have for God and eternity? What opportunities will you have for hearing the Gospel preached? I solemnly warn you to consider this. It will profit you nothing to fill your purse, if you bring leanness and poverty on your soul. Beware of selling your Sabbath for the sake of a good place! Remember Esau's mess of pottage. Beware of Lot's choice!

Some reader may perhaps think, "A believer need not fear; he is a sheep of Christ, he will never perish, he cannot come to much harm. It cannot be that such small matters can be of great importance."

Well, you may think so. But I warn you, if you neglect these matters, your soul will never prosper. A true believer will certainly not be cast away, although he may linger. But if he does linger, it is vain to suppose that his religion will thrive. Grace is a tender plant. Unless you cherish it and nurse it well, it will soon become sickly in this evil world. It may droop, though it cannot die. The brightest gold will soon become dim when exposed to a damp atmosphere. The hottest iron will soon become cold. It requires pains and toil to bring it to a red heat: it requires nothing but letting alone, or a little cold water to become black and hard.

You may be an earnest, zealous Christian now. You may feel like David in his prosperity: "I shall never be moved." (Psalm xxx. 6.) But be not deceived. You have only got to walk in Lot's steps and make Lot's choice, and you will soon come to Lot's state of soul. Allow yourself to do as he did, presume to act as he acted, and be very sure you will soon discover you have become a wretched "lingerer" like him. You will find, like Samson, the presence of the Lord is no longer with you. You will prove, to your own shame, an undecided, hesitating man, in the day of trial. There will come a canker on your religion, and eat out its vitality without your knowing it. There will come a slow consumption on your spiritual strength, and waste it away insensibly. And at length you will wake up to find your hands hardly able to do the Lord's work, and your feet hardly able to carry you along the Lord's way, and your faith no bigger than a grain of mustard seed; and this, perhaps, at some turning point in your life, at a time when the enemy is coming in like a flood, and your need is the sorest.

Ah, if you would not become a lingerer in religion, consider these things! Beware of doing what Lot did!

IV. Let us inquire now what kind of fruit Lot's lingering spirit bore at last.

I would not pass over this point for many reasons, and especially in the present day. There are not a few who will feel disposed to say, "After all, Lot was saved: he was justified--he got to heaven. I want no more. If I do but get to heaven, I shall be content." If this be the thought of your heart, just stay a moment, and listen to me a little longer. I will show you one or two things in Lot's history which deserve attention, and may perhaps induce you to alter your mind.

I think it of first importance to dwell upon this subject. I always will contend that eminent holiness and eminent usefulness are most closely connected--that happiness and "following the Lord fully" go side by side--and that if believers will linger, they must not expect to be useful in their day and generation, or to be very saintly and Christlike, or to enjoy great comfort and peace in believing,

(a) Let us mark, then, for one thing, that Lot did no good among the inhabitants of Sodom.

Lot probably lived in Sodom many years. No doubt he had many precious opportunities for speaking of the things of God, and trying to turn away souls from sin. But Lot seems to have effected just nothing at all. He appears to have had no weight or influence with the people who lived around him. He possessed none of that respect and reverence which even the men of the world will frequently concede to a bright servant of God.

Not one righteous person could be found in all Sodom, outside the walls of Lot's home. Not one of his neighbours believed his testimony. Not one of his acquaintances honoured the Lord whom he worshipped. Not one of his servants served his master's God. Not one of "all the people from every quarter" cared a jot for his opinion when he tried to restrain their wickedness. "This one fellow came in to sojourn," said they, "and he will needs be a judge."

(Gen. xix. 9.) His life carried no weight; his words were not listened to; his religion drew none to follow him.

And, truly, I do not wonder! As a general rule, lingering souls do no good to the world and bring no credit to God's cause. Their salt has too little savour to season the corruption around them. They are not "Epistles of Christ" who can be "known and read of all." (2 Cor. iii. 2.) There is nothing magnetic, and attractive, and Christ-reflecting about their ways. Let us remember this.

(b) Let us mark, for another thing, that Lot helped none of his family, relatives^ or connections towards heaven.

We are not told how large his family was. But this we know--he had a wife and two daughters at least, in the day he was called out of Sodom, if he had not more children besides.

But whether Lot's family was large or small, one thing, I think, is perfectly clear--there was not one among them all that feared God!

When he "went out and spake to his sons-in-law, which married his daughters," and warned them to flee from the judgments coming on Sodom, we are told, "he seemed to them as one that mocked." (Gen. xix. 14.) What fearful words those are! It was as good as saying, "Who cares for anything you say?" So long as the world stands, those things will be a painful proof of the contempt with which a "lingerer" in religion is regarded.

And what was Lot's wife? She left the city in his company, but she did not go far. She had not faith to see the need of such a speedy flight. She left her heart in Sodom when she began to flee. She looked back from behind her husband, in spite of the plainest" command not to do so (Gen. xix. 17), and was at once turned into a pillar of salt.

And what were Lot's two daughters? They escaped, indeed, but only to do the devil's work. They became their father's tempters to wickedness, and led him to commit the foulest of sins.

In short, Lot seems to have stood alone in his family! He was not made the means of keeping one soul back from the gates of hell!

And I do not wonder. Lingering souls are seen through by their own families; and, when seen through, they are despised. Their nearest relatives understand inconsistency, if they understand nothing else in religion. They draw the sad, but not unnatural, conclusion, "Surely, if he believed all he professes to believe, he would not go on as he does." Lingering parents seldom have godly children. The eye of the child drinks in far more than the ear. A child will always observe what you do much more than what you say. Let us remember this.

(c) Let us mark, for a third thing, that Lot left no evidences Mind him when he died.

We know but little about Lot after his flight from Sodom, and all that we do know is unsatisfactory.

His pleading for Zoar, because it was "a little one,"--his departure from Zoar afterwards--and his conduct in the cave--all, all tell the same story. All show the weakness of the grace that was in him, and how low the state of soul into which he had fallen.

We know not how long he lived after his escape. We know not where he died, or when he died--whether he saw Abraham again--what was the manner of his death--what he said or what he thought. All these are hidden things. We are told of the last days of Abraham, Isaac, Jacob, Joseph, David--but not one word about Lot. Oh, what a gloomy deathbed the deathbed of Lot must have been!

The Scripture appears to draw a veil around him on purpose. There is a painful silence about his latter end. He seems to go out like an expiring lamp, and to leave an ill-savour behind him. And had we not been specially told in the New Testament that Lot was "just" and "righteous," I verily believe we should have doubted whether Lot was a saved soul at all.

But I do not wonder at his sad end. Lingering believers will generally reap according as they have sown. Their lingering often meets them when their spirit is departing. They have little peace at the last. They reach heaven, to be sure; but they reach it in poor plight, weary and footsore, in weakness and tears, in darkness and storm. They are saved, but "saved so as by fire." (1 Cor. iii. 15.)

I ask every reader of this paper to consider the three things which I have just mentioned. Do not misunderstand my meaning. It is amazing to observe how readily people catch at the least excuse for misunderstanding the things that concern their souls!

I do not tell you that believers who do not "linger" will, as a matter of course, be great instruments of usefulness to the world. Noah preached one hundred and twenty years, and none believed him. The Lord Jesus was not esteemed by His own people, the Jews.

Nor yet do I tell you that believers who do not linger, will, as a matter of course, be the means of converting their families and relatives. David's children were, many of them, ungodly. The Lord Jesus was not believed on even by His own brethren.

But I do say it is almost impossible not to see some connection between Lot's evil choice and Lot's lingering--and between Lot's lingering and his unprofitableness to his family and the world. I believe the Spirit meant us to see it. I believe the Spirit meant to make him a beacon to all professing Christians. And I am sure the lessons I have tried to draw from the whole history deserve serious reflection.

And now let me speak a few parting words to all who read this paper, and especially to all who call themselves believers in Christ.

I have no wish to make your hearts sad. I do not want to give you a gloomy view of the Christian course. My only object is to give you friendly warnings. I desire your peace and comfort. I would fain see you happy as well as safe--and joyful, as well as justified. I speak as I have done for your good.

You live in days when a lingering, Lot-like religion abounds. The stream of profession is far broader than it once was, but far less deep in many places. A certain kind of Christianity is almost fashionable now. To belong to some party in the Church of England, and show a zeal for its interests--to talk about the leading controversies of the day--to buy popular religious books as fast as they come out, and lay them on your table--to attend meetings--to subscribe to Societies--to discuss the merits of preachers--to be enthusiastic and excited about every new form of sensational religion which crops up--all these are now comparatively easy and common attainments. They no longer make a person singular. They require little or no sacrifice. They entail no cross.

But to walk closely with God--to be really spiritually-minded--to behave like strangers and pilgrims--to be distinct from the world in employment of time, in conversation, in amusements, in dress--to bear a faithful witness for Christ in all places--to leave a savour of our Master in every society--to be prayerful, humble, unselfish, good-tempered, quiet, easily pleased, charitable, patient, meek--to be jealously afraid of all manner of sin, and tremblingly alive to our danger from the world--these, these are still rare things! They are not common among those who are called true Christians, and, worst of all, the absence of them is not felt and bewailed as it should be.

In a day like this I venture to offer counsel to every believing reader of this paper. Do not turn away from it. Do not be angry with me for plain speaking. I bid you "give diligence to make your calling and election sure," (2 Peter i. 10.) I bid you not to be slothful--not to be careless, not to be content with a small measure of grace--not be satisfied with being a little better than the world. I solemnly warn you not to attempt doing what never can be done--I mean, to serve Christ and yet keep in with the world. I call upon you, and beseech you to be a whole-hearted Christian, to follow after eminent holiness, to aim at a high degree of sanctification, to live a consecrated life, to present your body a "living sacrifice" unto God, to "walk in the spirit." (Rom. xii. 1; Gal. v. 25.) I charge you, and exhort you--by all your hopes of heaven and desires of glory, if you would be happy, if you would be useful--do not be a lingering soul.

Would you know what the times demand?--The shaking of nations--the uprooting of ancient things--the overturning of kingdoms--the stir and restlessness of men's minds--what do they say? They all cry aloud--Christian! do not linger!

Would you be found ready for Christ at His second appearing--your loins girded--your lamp burning--yourself bold, and prepared to meet Him? Then do not linger!

Would you enjoy much sensible comfort in your religion--feel the witness of the Spirit within you--know whom you have believed--and not be a gloomy, complaining, sour, downcast, and melancholy Christian? Then do not linger!

Would you enjoy strong assurance of your own salvation, in the day of sickness, and on the bed of death?--Would you see with the eye of faith heaven opening and Jesus rising to receive you? Then do not linger!

Would you leave great broad evidences behind you when you are gone?--Would you like us to lay you in the grave with comfortable hope, and talk of your state after death without a doubt? Then do not linger!

Would you be useful to the world in your day and generation?--Would you draw men from sin to Christ, adorn your doctrine, and make your Master's cause beautiful and attractive in their eyes? Then do not linger!

Would you help your children and relatives towards heaven, and make them say, "We will go with you"?--and not make them infidels and despisers of all religion? Then do not linger!

Would you have a great crown in the day of Christ's appearing, and not be the least and smallest star in glory, and not find yourself the last and lowest in the kingdom of God? Then do not linger!

Oh, let not one of us linger! Time does not--death does not--judgment does not--the devil does not--the world does not. Neither let the children of God linger.

Does any reader of this paper feel that he is a lingerer? Has your heart felt heavy, and your conscience sore, while you have been reading these pages? Does something within you whisper, "I am the man"? Then listen to what I am saying.--It is not well with your soul. Awake, and try to do better.

If you are a lingerer, you must go to Christ at once and be cured.--You must use the old remedy; you must bathe in the old fountain. You must turn again to Christ and be healed. The way to do a thing is to do it. Do this at once!

Think not for a moment your case is past recovery. Think not, because you have been long living in a dry, sleepy, and heavy state of soul, that there is no hope of revival. Is not the Lord Jesus Christ an appointed Physician for all spiritual ailments? Did He not cure every form of disease when He was upon earth? Did He not cast out every kind of devil? Did He not raise poor backsliding Peter, and put a new song in his mouth? Oh, doubt not, but earnestly believe that He will yet revive His work within you! Only return from lingering, and confess your folly, and come--come at once to Christ. Blessed are the words of the prophet: "Only acknowledge thine iniquity."--"Return, ye backsliding children, and I will heal your backsliding." (Jerem. iii. 13, 22.)

And let us all remember the souls of others, as well as our own. If at any time we see any brother or sister lingering, let us try to awaken them--try to arouse them--try to stir them up. Let us all "exhort one another" as we have opportunity. "Let us provoke unto love and good works." (Heb. iii. 13; x. 24.) Let us not be afraid to say to each other, "Brother, or sister, have you forgotten Lot? Awake! and remember Lot!--Awake, and linger no more."

X. A WOMAN TO BE REMEMBERED

"Remember Lot's Wife."--Luke xvii. 32.

THERE are few warnings in Scripture more solemn than that which heads this page. The Lord Jesus Christ says to us, "Remember Lot's wife."

Lot's wife was a professor of religion: her husband was a "righteous man." (2 Peter ii. 8.) She left Sodom with him on the day when Sodom was destroyed; she looked back towards the city from behind her husband, against God's express command; she was struck dead at once, and turned into a pillar of salt. And the Lord Jesus Christ holds her up as a beacon to His Church: He says, "Remember Lot's wife."

It is a solemn warning, when we think of the person Jesus names. He does not bid us remember Abraham, or Isaac, or Jacob, or Sarah, or Hannah, or Ruth. No: He singles out one whose soul was lost for ever. He cries to us, "Remember Lot's wife."

It is a solemn warning, when we consider the subject Jesus is upon. He is speaking of His own second coming to judge the world: He is describing the awful state of unreadiness in which many will be found. The last days are on His mind, when He says, "Remember Lot's wife."

It is a solemn warning, when we think of the person who gives it. The Lord Jesus is full of love, mercy, and compassion: He is one who will not break the bruised reed nor quench the smoking flax. He could weep over unbelieving Jerusalem, and pray for the men that crucified Him; yet even He thinks it good to remind us of lost souls. Even He says, "Remember Lot's wife."

It is a solemn warning, when we think of the persons to whom it was first given. The Lord Jesus was speaking to His disciples: He was not addressing the scribes and Pharisees, who hated Him, but Peter, James, and John, and many others who loved Him; yet even to them He thinks it good to address a caution. Even to them He says, "Remember Lot's wife."

It is a solemn warning, when we consider the manner in which it was given. He does not merely say, "Beware of following--take heed of imitating--do not be like Lot's wife." He uses a different word: He says, "Remember." He speaks as if we were all in danger of forgetting the subject; He stirs up our lazy memories; He bids us keep the case before our minds. He cries, "Remember Lot's wife."

I propose to examine the lessons which Lot's wife is meant to teach us. I am sure that her history is full of useful instruction to the Church. The last days are upon us; the second coming of the Lord Jesus draws nigh; the danger of worldliness is yearly increasing in the Church. Let us be provided with safeguards and antidotes against the disease that is around us; and, not least, let us become familiar with the story of Lot's wife.

There are three things which I shall do, in order to bring the subject before our minds in order.

I. I will speak of the religious privileges which Lot's wife enjoyed.

II. I will speak of the sin which Lot's wife committed.

III. I will speak of the judgment which God inflicted upon her.

I. I will first speak of the religious privileges which Lot's wife enjoyed.

In the days of Abraham and Lot, true saving religion was scarce upon earth: there were no Bibles, no ministers, no churches, no tracts, no missionaries. The knowledge of God was confined to a few favoured families; the greater part of the inhabitants of the world were living in darkness, ignorance, superstition, and sin. Not one in a hundred perhaps had such good example, such spiritual society, such clear knowledge, such plain warnings as Lot's wife. Compared with millions of her fellow-creatures in her time, Lot's wife was a favoured woman.

She had a godly man for her husband: she had Abraham, the father of the faithful, for her uncle by marriage. The faith, the knowledge, and the prayers of these two righteous men could have been no secret to her. It is impossible that she could have dwelt in tents with them for any length of time, without knowing whose they were and whom they served. Religion with them was no mere formal business; it was the ruling principle of their lives and the mainspring of all their actions. All this Lot's wife must have seen and known. This was no small privilege.

When Abraham first received the promises, it is probable Lot's wife was there. When he built his altar by his tent between Hai and Bethel, it is probable she was there. When her husband was taken captive by Chedorlaomer, and delivered by God's interference, she was there. When Melchizedek, king of Salem, came forth to meet Abraham with bread and wine, she was there. When the angels came to Sodom and warned her husband to flee, she saw them; when they took them by the hand and led them out of the city, she was one of those whom they helped to escape. Once more, I say, these were no small privileges.

Yet what good effect had all these privileges on the heart of Lot's wife? None at all. Notwithstanding all her opportunities and means of grace--notwithstanding all her special warnings and messages from heaven, she lived and died graceless, godless, impenitent, and unbelieving. The eyes of her understanding were never opened; her conscience was never really aroused and quickened; her will was never really brought into a state of obedience to God; her affections were never really set upon things above. The form of religion which she had was kept up for fashion's sake and not from feeling: it was a cloak worn for the sake of pleasing her company, but not from any sense of its value. She did as others did around her in Lot's house: she conformed to her husband's ways: she made no opposition to his religion: she allowed herself to be passively towed along in his wake: but all this time her heart was wrong in the sight of God. The world was in her heart, and her heart was in the world. In this state she lived, and in this state she died.

In all this there is much to be learned: I see a lesson here which is of the deepest importance in the present day. You live in times when there are many persons just like Lot's wife: come and hear the lesson which her case is meant to teach.

Learn, then, that the mere possession of religious privileges mil save no one's soul. You may have spiritual advantages of every description; you may live in the full sunshine of the richest opportunities and means of grace; you may enjoy the best of preaching and the choicest instruction; you may dwell in the midst of light, knowledge, holiness, and good company. All this may be, and yet you yourself may remain unconverted, and at last be lost for ever.

I dare say this doctrine sounds hard to some readers. I know that many fancy they want nothing but religious privileges in order to become decided Christians. They are not what they ought to be at present, they allow; but their position is so hard, they plead, and their difficulties are so many. Give them a godly husband, or a godly wife--give them godly companions, or a godly master--give them the preaching of the Gospel--give them privileges, and then they would walk with God.

It is all a mistake. It is an entire delusion. It requires something more than privileges to save souls. Joab was David's captain; Gehazi was Elisha's servant; Demas was Paul's companion; Judas Iscariot was Christ's disciple; and Lot had a worldly, unbelieving wife. These all died in their sins. They went down to the pit in spite of knowledge, warnings, and opportunities; and they all teach us that it is not privileges alone that men need. They need the grace of the Holy Ghost.

Let us value religious privileges, but let us not rest entirely upon them. Let us desire to have the benefit of them in all our movements in life, but let us not put them in the place of Christ. Let us use them thankfully, if God grants them to us, but let us take care that they produce some fruit in our heart and life. If they do not do good, they often do positive harm: they sear the conscience, they increase responsibility, they aggravate condemnation. The same fire which melts the wax hardens the clay; the same sun which makes the living tree grow, dries up the dead tree, and prepares it for burning. Nothing so hardens the heart of man as a barren familiarity with sacred things. Once more I say, it is not privileges alone which make people Christians, but the grace of the Holy Ghost. Without that no man will ever be saved.

I ask the members of Evangelical congregations, in the present day, to mark well what I am saying. You go to Mr. A's, or Mr. B's church: you think him an excellent preacher; you delight in his sermons; you cannot hear anyone else with the same comfort; you have learned many things since you attended his ministry; you consider it a great privilege to be one of his hearers! All this is very good. It is a privilege. I should be thankful if ministers like yours were multiplied a thousandfold. But after all, what have you got in your heart? Have you yet received the Holy Ghost? If not, you are no better than Lot's wife.

I ask the servants of religious families to mark well what I am saying. It is a great privilege to live in a house where the fear of God reigns. It is a privilege to hear family prayers morning and evening, to hear the Word of God regularly expounded, to have a quiet Sunday, and to be able always to go to church. These are the things that you ought to seek after when you try to get a situation; these are the things which make a really good place. High wages and light work will never make up for a constant round of worldliness, Sabbath-breaking, and sin. But take heed that you do not rest content with these things: do not suppose because you have all these spiritual advantages, that you will of course go to heaven. You must have grace in your own heart, as well as attend family prayers. If not, you are at present no better than Lot's wife.

I ask the children of religious parents to mark well what I am saying. It is the highest privilege to be the child of a godly father and mother, and to be brought up in the midst of many prayers. It is a blessed thing indeed to be taught the Gospel from our earliest infancy, and to hear of sin, and Jesus, and the Holy Spirit, and holiness, and heaven, from the first moment we can remember anything. But, oh, take heed that you do not remain barren and unfruitful in the sunshine of all these privileges: beware lest your heart remains hard, impenitent and worldly, notwithstanding the many advantages you enjoy. You cannot enter the kingdom of God on the credit of your parents' religion. You must eat the bread of life for yourself, and have the witness of the Spirit in your own heart. You must have repentance of your own, faith of your own, and sanctification of your own. If not, you are no better than Lot's wife.

I pray God that all professing Christians, in these days, may lay these things to heart. May we never forget that privileges alone cannot save us. Light and knowledge, and faithful preaching, and abundant means of grace, and the company of holy people are all great blessings and advantages. Happy are they that have them! But, after all, there is one thing without which privileges are useless: that one thing is the grace of the Holy Ghost. Lot's wife had many privileges: but Lot's wife had no grace.

II. I will next speak of the sin which Lot's wife committed.

The history of her sin is given by the Holy Ghost in few and simple words--"She looked back from behind her husband, and she became a pillar of salt." We are told no more than this. There is a naked solemnity about the history. The sum and substance of her transgression lies in these three words, "She looked back."

Does that sin seem small in the eyes of any reader of this paper? Does the fault of Lot's wife appear a trifling one to be visited with such a punishment? This is the feeling, I dare say, that rises in some hearts. Give your attention while I reason with you on the subject. There was far more in that look than strikes you at first sight: it implied far more than it expressed. Listen, and you shall hear.

(a) That look was a little thing, but revealed the true character of Lot's wife. Little things will often show the state of a man's mind even better than great ones, and little symptoms are often the signs of deadly and incurable diseases. The apple that Eve ate was a little thing, but it proved that she had fallen from innocence and become a sinner. A crack in an arch seems a little thing, but it proves that the foundation is giving way, and the whole fabric is unsafe. A little cough in a morning seems an unimportant ailment, but it is often an evidence of failing in the constitution, and leads on to decline, consumption, and death. A straw may show which way the wind blows, and one look may show the rotten condition of a sinner's heart. (Matt. v. 28.)

(b) That look was a little thing, but it told of disobedience in Lot's wife. The command of the angel was strait and unmistakable: "Look not behind thee." (Gen. xix. 17.) This command Lot's wife refused to obey. But the Holy Ghost says, that "to obey is better than sacrifice," and that "rebellion is as the sin of witchcraft." (1 Sam. xv. 22, 23.) When God speaks plainly by His Word, or by His messengers, man's duty is clear.

(c) That look was a little thing, but it told of proud unbelief in Lot's wife. She seemed to doubt whether God was really going to destroy Sodom: she appeared not to believe there was any danger, or any need for such hasty flight. But without faith it is impossible to please God. (Heb. xi. 6.) The moment a man begins to think he knows better than God, and that God does not mean anything when He threatens, his soul is in great danger. When we cannot see the reason of God's dealings, our duty is to hold our peace and believe.

(d) That look was a little thing, but it told of secret love of the world in Lot's wife. Her heart was in Sodom, though her body was outside. She had left her affections behind when she fled from her home. Her eye turned to the place where her treasure was, as the compass-needle turns to the pole. And this was the crowning point of her sin. "The friendship of the world is enmity with God." (James iv. 4.) "If any man love the world, the love of the Father is not in him." (1 John ii. 15.)

I ask the special attention of my readers to this part of our subject. I believe it to be the part to which the Lord Jesus particularly intends to direct our minds. I believe He would have us observe that Lot's wife was lost by looking back to the world. Her profession was at one time fair and specious, but she never really gave up the world. She seemed at one time in the road to safety, but even then the lowest and deepest thoughts of her heart were for the world. The immense danger of worldliness is the grand lesson which the Lord Jesus means us to learn. Oh, that we may all have an eye to see and a heart to understand!

I believe there never was a time when warnings against worldliness were so much needed by the Church of Christ as they are at the present day. Every age is said to have its own peculiar epidemic disease: the epidemic disease to which the souls of Christians are liable just now is the love of the world. It is a pestilence that walketh in darkness, and a sickness that destroyeth at noonday. It "hath cast down many wounded; yea, many strong men have been wounded by it." I would fain raise a warning voice, and try to arouse the slumbering consciences of all who make a profession of religion. I would fain cry aloud, "Remember the sin of Lot's wife." She was no murderess, no adulteress, no thief--but she was a professor of religion, and she looked back.

There are thousands of baptized persons in our churches who are proof against immorality and infidelity, and yet fall victims to the love of the world. There are thousands who run well for a season, and seem to bid fair to reach heaven, but by and by give up the race, and turn their backs on Christ altogether. And what has stopped them? Have they found the Bible not true? Have they found the Lord Jesus fail to keep His word? No: not at all. But they have caught the epidemic disease: they are infected with the love of this world. I appeal to every true-hearted Evangelical minister who reads this paper: I ask him to look round his congregation. I appeal to every old-established Christian: I ask him to look round the circle of his acquaintance. I am sure that I am speaking the truth. I am sure that it is high time to remember the sin of Lot's wife.

(a) How many children of religious families begin well and end ill! In the days of their childhood they seem full of religion. They can repeat texts and hymns in abundance; they have spiritual feel ings and convictions of sin; they profess to love the Lord Jesus and desire after heaven; they take pleasure in going to church and hearing sermons; they say things which are treasured up by their fond parents as indications of grace; they do things which make relations say, "What manner of child will this be?" But, alas, how often their goodness vanishes like the morning cloud, and like the dew that passes away! The boy becomes a young man, and cares for nothing but amusements, field-sports, revelling, and excess. The girl becomes a young woman, and cares for nothing but dress, gay company, novel-reading, and excitement. Where is the spirituality which once appeared to promise so fair? It is all gone: it is buried; it is overflowed by the love of the world. They walk in the steps of Lot's wife. They look back.

(b) How many married people do well in religion to all appear ance, until their children begin to grow up--and then they fall away! In the early years of their married life they seem to follow Christ diligently, and to witness a good confession. They regularly attend the preaching of the Gospel: they are fruitful in good works; they are never seen in vain and dissipated society. Their faith and practice are both sound, and walk hand in hand. But, alas, how often a spiritual blight comes over the household when a young family begins to grow up, and sons and daughters have to be brought forward in life. A leaven of worldliness begins to appear in their habits, dress, entertainments, and employment of time. They are no longer strict about the company they keep and the places they visit. Where is the decided fine of separation which they once observed? Where is the unswerving abstinence from worldly amusements which once marked their course? It is all forgotten. It is all laid aside, like an old almanack. A change has come over them: the spirit of the world has taken possession of their hearts. They walk in the steps of Lot's wife. They look back.

(c) How many young women seem to love decided religion until they are twenty or twenty-one, and then lose all! Up to this time of their life their conduct in religious matters is all that could be desired. They keep up habits of private prayer; they read their Bibles diligently; they visit the poor, when they have opportunity; they teach in Sunday schools, when there is an opening; they minister to the temporal and spiritual wants of the poor; they like religious friends; they love to talk on religious subjects: they write letters lull or religious expressions and religious experience. But, alas, how often they prove unstable as water, and are ruined by the love of the world! Little by little they fall away and lose their first love. Little by little the "things seen" push out of their minds the "things unseen," and, like the plague of locusts, eat up every green thing in their souls. Step by step they go back from the decided position they once took up. They cease to be jealous about sound doctrine; they pretend to find out that it is "uncharitable" to think one person has more religion than another; they discover it is "exclusive" to attempt any separation from the customs of society. By and by they give their affections to some man who makes no pretence to decided religion. At last they end by giving up the last remnant of their own Christianity, and becoming thorough children of the world. They walk in the steps of Lot's wife. They look back.

(d) How many communicants in our churches were at one time zealous and earnest professors, and have now become torpid, formal, and cold! Time was when none seemed so much alive in religion as they were: none were so diligent in their attendance on the means of grace; none were so anxious to promote the cause of the Gospel, and so ready for every good work; none were so thank ful for spiritual instruction; none were apparently so desirous to grow in grace. But now, alas, everything seems altered! The "love of other things" has taken possession of their hearts, and choked the good seed of the Word. The money of the world, the rewards of the world, the literature of the world, the honours of the world, have now the first place in their affections. Talk to them, and you will find no response about spiritual things. Mark their daily conduct, and you will see no zeal about the kingdom of God. A religion they have indeed, but it is living religion no more. The spring of their former Christianity is dried up and gone; the fire of the spiritual machine is quenched and cold: earth has put out the flame which once burned so brightly. They have walked in the steps of Lot's wife. They have looked back.

(e) How many clergymen work hard in their profession for a few years, and then become lazy and indolent from the love of this present world I At the outset of their ministry they seem willing to spend and be spent for Christ: they are instant in season and out of season; their preaching is lively and their churches are filled. Their congregations are well looked after: cottage lectures, prayer-meetings, house-to-house visitation, are their weekly delight. But, alas, how often after "beginning in the Spirit" they end "in the flesh," and, like Samson, are shorn of their strength in the lap of that Delilah, the world! They are preferred to some rich living; they marry a worldly wife; they are puffed up with pride, and neglect study and prayer. A nipping frost cuts off the spiritual blossoms which once bade so fair. Their preaching loses its unction and power; their week-day work becomes less and less; the society they mix in becomes less select; the tone of their conversation becomes more earthly. They cease to disregard the opinion of man: they imbibe a morbid fear of "extreme views," and are filled with a cautious dread of giving offence. And at last the man who at one time seemed likely to be a real successor of the apostles and a good soldier of Christ, settles down on his lees as a clerical gardener, farmer, or diner-out, by whom nobody is offended and nobody is saved. His church becomes half empty; his influence dwindles away; the world has bound him hand and foot. He has walked in the steps of Lot's wife. He has looked back.[41]

It is sad to write of these things, but it is far more sad to see them. It is sad to observe how professing Christians can blind their consciences by specious arguments on this subject, and can defend positive worldliness by talking of the "duties of their station," the "courtesies of life," and the necessity of having a "cheerful religion."

It is sad to see how many a gallant ship launches forth on the voyage of life with every prospect of success and, springing this leak of worldliness, goes down with all her freight in full view of the harbour of safety. It is saddest of all to observe how many flatter themselves it is all right with their souls when it is all wrong, by reason of this love of the world. Grey hairs are here and there upon them, and they know it not. They began with Jacob, and David, and Peter, and they are likely to end with Esau, and Saul, and Judas Iscariot. They began with Ruth, and Hannah, and Mary, and Persis, and they are likely to end with Lot's wife.

Beware of a half-hearted religion. Beware of following Christ from any secondary motive--to please relations and friends--to keep in with the custom of the place or family in which you reside--to appear respectable and have the reputation of being religious. Follow Christ for His own sake, if you follow Him at all. Be thorough, be real, be honest, be sound, be whole-hearted. If you have any religion at all, let your religion be real. See that you do not sin the sin of Lot's wife.

Beware of ever supposing that you may go too far in religion, and of secretly trying to keep in with the world. I want no reader of this paper to become a hermit, a monk, or a nun: I wish every one to do his real duty in that state of life to which he is called. But I do urge on every professing Christian who wishes to be happy, the immense importance of making no compromise between God and the world. Do not try to drive a hard bargain, as if you wanted to give Christ as little of your heart as possible, and to keep as much as possible of the things of this life. Beware lest you overreach yourself, and end by losing all. Love Christ with all your heart, and mind, and soul, and strength. Seek first the kingdom of God, and believe that then all other things shall be added to you. Take heed that you do not prove a copy of the character John Bunyan draws--Mr. Facing-both-ways. For your happiness' sake, for your usefulness' sake, for your safety's sake, for your soul's sake, beware of the sin of Lot's wife. Oh, it is a solemn saying of our Lord Jesus, "No man having put his hand to the plough and looking back is fit for the kingdom of God." (Luke ix. 62.)

III. I will now speak, in the last place, of the punishment which God inflicted on Lot's wife.

The Scripture describes her end in few and simple words. It is written that "she looked back and became a pillar of salt." A miracle was wrought to execute God's judgment on this guilty woman. The same Almighty hand which first gave her life, took that life away in the twinkling of an eye. From living flesh and blood she was turned into a pillar of salt.

That was a fearful end for a soul to come to! To die at any time is a solemn thing. To die amidst kind friends and relations, to die calmly and quietly in one's bed, to die with the prayers of godly men still sounding in your ears, to die with a good hope through grace in the full assurance of salvation, leaning on the Lord Jesus, buoyed up by Gospel promises--to die even so, I say, is a serious business. But to die suddenly and in a moment, in the very act of sin, to die in full health and strength, to die by the direct interposition of an angry God--this is fearful indeed. Yet this was the end of Lot's wife. I cannot blame the prayer-book Litany, as some do, for retaining this petition, "From sudden death, good Lord, deliver us."

That was a hopeless end for a soul to come to! There are cases where one hopes, as it were, against hope, about the souls of those we see go down to the grave. We try to persuade ourselves that our poor departed brother or sister may have repented unto salvation at the last moment, and laid hold on the hem of Christ's garment at the eleventh hour. We call to mind God's mercies; we remember the Spirit's power; we think on the case of the penitent thief; we whisper to ourselves, that saving work may have gone on even on that dying bed which the dying person had not strength to tell. But there is an end of all such hopes when a person is suddenly cut down in the very act of sin. Charity itself can say nothing when the soul has been summoned away in the very midst of wickedness, without even a moment's time for thought or prayer. Such was the end of Lot's wife. It was a hopeless end. She went to hell.

But it is good for us all to mark these things. It is good to be reminded that God can punish sharply those who sin wilfully, and that great privileges misused bring down great wrath on the soul. Pharaoh saw all the miracles which Moses worked--Korah, Dathan, and Abiram had heard God speaking from Mount Sinai--Hophni and Phinehas were sons of God's High Priest--Saul lived in the full light of Samuel's ministry--Ahab was often warned by Elijah the prophet--Absalom enjoyed the privilege of being one of David's children--Belshazzar had Daniel the prophet hard by his door--Ananias and Sapphira joined the Church in the days when the apostles were working miracles--Judas Iscariot was a chosen companion of our Lord Jesus Christ Himself. But they all sinned with a high hand against light and knowledge; and they were all suddenly destroyed without remedy. They had no time or space for repentance. As they lived, so they died: as they were, they hurried away to meet God. They went with all their sins upon them, unpardoned, unrenewed, and utterly unfit for heaven. And being dead they yet speak. They tell us, like Lot's wife, that it is a perilous thing to sin against light, that God hates sin, and that there is a hell.

I feel constrained to speak freely to my readers on the subject of hell. Suffer me to use the opportunity which the end of Lot's wife affords. I believe the time is come when it is a positive duty to speak plainly about the reality and eternity of hell. A flood of false doctrine has lately broken in upon us. Men are beginning to tell us "that God is too merciful to punish souls for ever--that there is a love of God lower even than hell--and that all mankind, however wicked and ungodly some of them may be, will sooner or later be saved." We are invited to leave the old paths of apostolic Christianity. We are told that the views of our fathers about hell, and the devil, and punishment, are obsolete and old-fashioned. We are to embrace what is called a "kinder theology," and treat hell as a Pagan fable, or a bugbear to frighten children and fools. Against such false teaching I desire, for one, to protest. Painful, sorrowful, distressing as the controversy may be, we must not blink it, or refuse to look the subject in the face. I, for one, am resolved to maintain the old position, and to assert the reality and eternity of hell.

Believe me, this is no mere speculative question. It is not to be classed with disputes about liturgies and Church government. It is not to be ranked with mysterious problems, like the meaning of Ezekiel's temple or the symbols of Revelation. It is a question which lies at the very foundation of the whole Gospel. The moral attributes of God, His justice, His holiness, His purity, are all involved in it. The necessity of personal faith in Christ, and the sanctification of the Spirit, are all at stake. Once let the old doctrine about hell be overthrown, and the whole system of Christianity is unsettled, unscrewed, unpinned, and thrown into disorder.

Believe me, the question is not one in which we are obliged to fall back on the theories and inventions of man. The Scripture has spoken plainly and fully on the subject of hell. I hold it to be impossible to deal honestly with the Bible, and to avoid the conclusions to which it will lead us on this point. If words mean anything, there is such a place as hell. If texts are to be interpreted fairly, there are those who will be cast into it. If language has any sense belonging to it, hell is for ever. I believe that the man who finds arguments for evading the evidence of the Bible on this question has arrived at a state of mind in which reasoning is useless. For my own part, it seems just as easy to argue that we do not exist, as to argue that the Bible does not teach the reality and eternity of hell.

(a) Settle it firmly in your mind, that the same Bible which teaches that God in mercy and compassion sent Christ to die for sinners, does also teach that God hates sin, and must from His very nature punish all who cleave to sin, or refuse the salvation He has provided. The very same chapter which declares, "God so loved the world," declares also, that "the wrath of God abideth" on the unbeliever. (John iii. 16, 36.) The very same Gospel which is launched into the earth with the blessed tidings, "He that believeth and is baptized shall be saved," proclaims in the same breath, "He that believeth not shall be damned." (Mark xvi. 16.)

(b) Settle it firmly in your mind that God has given us proof upon proof in the Bible that He will punish the hardened and unbelieving, and that He can take vengeance on His enemies, as well as show mercy on the penitent. The drowning of the old world by the flood--the burning of Sodom and Gomorrah--the overthrow of Pharaoh and all his host in the Red Sea--the judgment on Korah, Dathan, and Abiram--the utter destruction of the seven nations of Canaan--all teach the same awful truth. They are all given to us as beacons, and signs, and warnings, that we may not provoke God. They are all meant to lift up the corner of the curtain which hangs over things to come, and to remind us that there is such a thing as the wrath of God. They all tell us plainly that "the wicked shall be turned into hell." (Psalm ix. 17.)

(c) Settle it firmly in your mind, that the Lord Jesus Christ Himself has spoken most plainly about the reality and eternity of hell. The parable of the rich man and Lazarus contains things which should make men tremble. But it does not stand alone. No lips have used so many words to express the awfulness of hell, as the lips of Him who spake as never man spake, and who said "The word which ye hear is not Mine, but the Father's which sent Me." (John xiv. 24.) Hell, hell fire, the damnation of hell, eternal damnation, the resurrection of damnation, everlasting fire, the place of torment, destruction, outer darkness, the worm that never dies, the fire that is not quenched, the place of weeping, wailing, and gnashing of teeth, everlasting punishment--these, these are the words which the Lord Jesus Christ Himself employs. Away with the miserable nonsense which people talk in this day, who tell us that the ministers of the Gospel should never speak of hell! They only show their own ignorance, or their own dishonesty, when they talk in such a manner. No man can honestly read the four Gospels and fail to see that he who would follow the example of Christ must speak of hell.

(d) Settle it, lastly, in your mind, that the comforting ideas which the Scripture gives us of heaven are at an end, if we once deny the reality or eternity of hell. Is there no future separate abode for those who die wicked and ungodly? Are all men, after death, to be mingled together in one confused multitude? Why then, heaven will be no heaven at all! It is utterly impossible for two to dwell happily together except they be agreed.--Is there to be a time when the term of hell and punishment will be over? Are the wicked after ages of misery to be admitted into heaven? Why then, the need of the sanctification of the Spirit is cast aside and despised! I read that men can be sanctified and made meet for heaven on earth: I read nothing of any sanctification in hell. Away with such baseless and unscriptural theories! The eternity of hell is as clearly affirmed in the Bible as the eternity of heaven. Once allow that hell is not eternal, and you may as well say that God and heaven are not eternal. The same Greek word which is used in the expression, "everlasting punishment," is the word that Is used by the Lord Jesus in the expression, "life eternal," and by St. Paul in the expression, "everlasting God." (Matt. xxv. 46; Rom. xvi. 26.)

I know that all this sounds dreadful in many ears. I do not wonder. But the only question we have to settle is this--Is it Scriptural? Is it true? I maintain firmly that it is so: and I maintain that professing Christians ought to be often reminded that they may be lost and go to hell.

I know that it is easy to deny all plain teaching about hell, and to make it odious by invidious names. I have often heard of "narrow-minded views, and old-fashioned notions, and brimstone theology," and the like. I have often been told that "broad" views are wanted in the present day. I wish to be as broad as the Bible, neither less nor more. I say that he is the narrow-minded theologian, who pares down such parts of the Bible as the natural heart dislikes, and rejects any portion of the counsel of God.

God knows that I never speak of hell without pain and sorrow. I would gladly offer the salvation of the Gospel to the very chief of sinners. I would willingly say to the vilest and most profligate of mankind on his deathbed, "Repent, and believe on Jesus, and thou shalt be saved." But God forbid that I should ever keep back from mortal man that Scripture reveals a hell as well as heaven, and that the Gospel teaches that men may be lost as well as saved. The watchman who keeps silent when he sees a fire, is guilty of gross neglect--the doctor who tells us we are getting well when we are dying, is a false friend; and the minister who keeps back hell from his people in his sermons is neither a faithful nor a charitable man.

Where is the charity of keeping back any portion of God's truth? He is the kindest friend who tells me the whole extent of my danger. Where is the use of hiding the future from the impenitent and the ungodly? Surely it is like helping the devil, if we do not tell them plainly that "the soul that sinneth shall surely die." Who knows but the wretched carelessness of many baptized persons arises from this, that they have never been told plainly of hell? Who can tell but thousands might be converted, if ministers would urge them more faithfully to flee from the wrath to come? Verily, I fear we are many of us guilty in this matter: there is a morbid tenderness amongst us which is not the tenderness of Christ. We have spoken of mercy, but not of judgment; we have preached many sermons about heaven, but few about hell: we have been carried away by the wretched fear of being thought "low, vulgar and fanatical." We have forgotten that He who judgeth us is the Lord, and that the man who teaches the same doctrine that Christ taught cannot be wrong.

If you would ever be a healthy Scriptural Christian, I entreat you to give hell a place in your theology. Establish it in your mind as a fixed principle, that God is a God of judgment, as well as of mercy; and that the same everlasting counsels which laid the foundation of the bliss of heaven, have also laid the foundation of the misery of hell. Keep in full view of your mind that all who die unpardoned and unrenewed, are utterly unfit for the presence of God and must be lost for ever. They are not capable of enjoying heaven: they could not be happy there. They must go to their own place: and that place is hell.--Oh, it is a great thing in these days of unbelief to believe the whole Bible!

If you would ever be a healthy and Scriptural Christian, I entreat you to beware of any ministry which does not plainly teach the reality and eternity of hell. Such a ministry may be soothing and pleasant, but it is far more likely to lull you to sleep than to lead you to Christ, or build you up in the faith. It is impossible to leave out any portion of God's truth without spoiling the whole. That preaching is sadly defective which dwells exclusively on the mercies of God and the joys of heaven, and never sets forth the terrors of the Lord and the miseries of hell. It may be popular, but it is not Scriptural: it may amuse and gratify, but it will not save. Give me the preaching which keeps back nothing that God has revealed. You may call it stern and harsh; you may tell us that to frighten people is not the way to do them good. But you are forgetting that the grand object of the Gospel is to persuade men to "flee from the wrath to come," and that it is vain to expect men to flee unless they are afraid. Well would it be for many professing Christians if they were more afraid about their souls than they now are!

If you desire to be a healthy Christian, consider often what your own end will be. Will it be happiness, or will it be misery? Will it be the death of the righteous, or will it be a death without hope, like that of Lot's wife? You cannot live always: there must be an end one day. The last sermon will one day be heard; the last prayer will one day be prayed; the last chapter in the Bible will one day be read--meaning, wishing, hoping, intending, resolving, doubting, hesitating--all will at length be over. You will have to leave this world and to stand before a holy God. Oh, that you would be wise! Oh, that you would consider your latter end!

You cannot trifle for ever: a time will come when you must be serious. You cannot put off your soul's concerns for ever: a day will come when you must have a reckoning with God. You cannot be always singing, and dancing, and eating, and drinking, and dressing, and read-ing, and laughing, and jesting, and scheming, and planning, and money-making. The summer insects cannot always sport in the sunshine; the cold chilly evening will come at last, and stop their sport for ever. So will it be with you. You may put off religion now, and refuse the counsel of God's ministers: but the cool of the day is drawing on, when God will come down to speak with you. And what will your end be? Will it be a hopeless one, like that of Lot's wife?

I beseech you, by the mercies of God, to look this question fairly in the face. I entreat you not to stifle conscience by vague hopes of God's mercy, while your heart cleaves to the world. I implore you not to drown convictions by childish fancies about God's love, while your daily ways and habits show plainly that "the love of the Father is not in you." There is mercy in God, like a river--but it is for the penitent believer in Christ Jesus. There is a love in God towards sinners which is unspeakable and unsearchable--but it is for those who "hear Christ's voice and follow Him." Seek to have an interest in that love. Break off every known sin; come out boldly from the world; cry mightily to God in prayer; cast yourself wholly and unreservedly on the Lord Jesus for time and eternity; lay aside every weight. Cling to nothing, however dear, which interferes with your soul's salvation; give up everything, however pre-cious, which comes between you and heaven. This old shipwrecked world is fast sinking beneath your feet: the one thing needful is to have a place in the lifeboat and get safe to shore. Give diligence to make your calling and election sure. Whatever happens to your house and property, see that you make sure of heaven. Oh, better a million times be laughed at and thought extreme in this world than go down to hell from the midst of the congregation and end like Lot's wife!

And now, let me conclude this paper by offering to all who read it, a few questions to impress the subject on their consciences. You have seen the history of Lot's wife--her privileges, her sin, and her end. You have been told of the uselessness of privileges without the gift of the Holy Ghost, of the danger of worldliness, and of the reality of hell. Suffer me to wind up all by a few direct appeals to your own heart. In a day of much light, and knowledge, and profession, I desire to set up a beacon to preserve souls from shipwreck. I would fain moor a buoy in the channel of all spiritual voyagers, and paint upon it, "Remember Lot's wife."

(a) Are you careless about the second Advent of Christ? Alas, many are! They live like the men of Sodom, and the men of Noah's day: they eat, and drink, and plant, and build, and marry, and are given in marriage, and behave as if Christ was never going to return. If you are such an one, I say to you this day, Take care: "Remember Lot's wife."

(b) Are you lukewarm, and cold in your Christianity? Alas, many are! They try to serve two masters: they labour to keep friends both with God and mammon. They strive to be a kind of spiritual bat, neither one thing nor the other: not quite a thorough-going Christian, but not quite men of the world. If you are such an one, I say to you this day, Take care: "Remember Lot's wife."

(c) Are you halting between two opinions, and disposed to go back to the world? Alas, many are! They are afraid of the cross: they secretly dislike the trouble and reproach of decided religion. They are weary of the wilderness and the manna, and would fain return to Egypt, if they could. If you are such an one, I say to you this day, Take care: "Remember Lot's wife."

(d) Are you secretly cherishing some besetting sin? Alas, many are! They go far in a profession of religion; they do many things that are right, and are very like the people of God. But there is always some darling evil habit, which they cannot tear from their heart. Hidden worldliness, or covetousness, or lust, sticks to them like their skin. They are willing to see all their idols broken, but this one. If you are such an one, I say to you this day, Take care: "Remember Lot's wife."

(e) Are you trifling with little sins? Alas, many are! They hold the great essential doctrines of the Gospel. They keep clear of all gross profligacy, or open breach of God's law; but they are painfully careless about little inconsistencies, and painfully ready to make excuses for them. "It is only a little temper, or a little levity, or a little thoughtlessness, or a little forgetfulness"--they tell us: "God does not take account of such little matters. We are none of us perfect: God will never require it."--If you are such an one, I say to you this day, Take care: "Remember Lot's wife."

(f) Are you resting on religious privileges? Alas, many do! They enjoy the opportunity of hearing the Gospel regularly preached, and of attending many ordinances, and means of grace: and they settle down on their lees. They seem to be "rich, and increased with goods, and have need of nothing" (Rev. iii. 17); while they have neither faith, nor grace, nor spiritual-mindedness nor meetness for heaven. If you are such an one, I say to you this day, Take care: "Remember Lot's wife."

(g) Are you trusting to your religious knowledge? Alas, many do! They are not ignorant, as other men: they know the difference between true doctrine and false. They can dispute, they can reason, they can argue, they can quote texts; but all this time they are not converted, and they are yet dead in trespasses and sins. If you are such an one, I say to you this day, Take care: "Remember Lot's wife."

(h) Are you making some profession of religion, and yet clinging to the world? Alas, many do! They aim at being thought Christians. They like the credit of being serious, steady, proper, regular, church-going people; yet all the while their dress, their tastes, their companions, their entertainments tell plainly they are of the world. If you are such an one, I say to you this day, Take care: "Remember Lot's wife."

(i) Are you trusting that you will have a death-bed repentance? Alas, many do so! They know they are not what they ought to be: they are not yet born again, and fit to die. But they flatter themselves that when their last illness comes they shall have time to repent and lay hold on Christ, and go out of the world pardoned, sanctified, and meet for heaven. They forget that people often die very suddenly, and that as they live they generally die. If you are such an one, I say to you this day, Take care: Remember Lot's wife."

(j) Do you belong to an Evangelical congregation? Many do, and, alas, go no further! They hear the truth Sunday after Sunday and remain as hard as the nether-millstone. Sermon after sermon sounds in their ears. Month after month they are invited to repent, to believe, to come to Christ, and to be saved. Year after year passes away, and they are not changed. They keep their seat under the teaching of a favourite minister, and they also keep their favourite sins. If you are such an one, I say to you this day, Take care: "Remember Lot's wife."

Oh, may these solemn words of our Lord Jesus Christ be deeply graven on all our hearts! May they awaken us when we feel sleepy--revive us when we feel dead--sharpen us when we feel dull--warm us when we feel cold! May they prove a spur to quicken us when we are falling back, and a bridle to check us when we are turning side I May they be a shield to defend us when Satan casts a subtle temptation at our heart; and a sword to fight with, when he says boldly, "Give up Christ, come back to the world, and follow me!" Oh, may we say, in such hours of trial, "Soul, remember thy Saviour's warning! Soul, soul, hast thou forgotten His words? Soul, soul, REMEMBER LOT'S WIFE!'"

ENDNOTE

[41] "Remember Dr. Dodd! I myself heard him tell his own flock, whom he was lecturing in his house, that he was obliged to give up that method of helping their souls, because it exposed him to so much reproach. He gave it up, and fell from one compliance to another with his corrupt nature; and under what reproach did he die!" (He was hanged for forgery.) Venn's Life and Letters, p. 238. Edit. 1853.

XI. CHRIST'S GREATEST TROPHY

"And one of the malefactors which were hanged railed on Him, saying, If Thou be Christ, save Thyself and us.

"But the other answering rebuked him, saying, Dost not thou fear God, seeing thou art in the same condemnation?

"And we indeed justly; for we receive the due reward of our deeds: but this Man hath done nothing amiss.

"And he said unto Jesus, Lord, remember me when Thou comest into Thy kingdom.

"And Jesus said unto him, Verily I say unto thee, To-day shalt thou be with Me in paradise."--Luke xxiii. 39-43.

There are few passages in the New Testament which are more familiar to men's ears than the verses which head this chapter. They contain the well-known story of "the penitent thief."

And it is right and good that these verses should be well known. They have comforted many troubled minds; they have brought peace to many uneasy consciences; they have been a healing balm to many wounded hearts; they have been a medicine to many sin-sick souls; they have smoothed down not a few dying pillows. Wherever the Gospel of Christ is preached, they will always be honoured, loved, and had in remembrance.

I wish to say something about these verses. I will try to unfold the leading lessons which they are meant to teach. I cannot see the peculiar mental state of anyone into whose hands this paper may fall. But I can see truths in this passage which no man can ever know too well. Here is the greatest trophy which Christ ever won.

I. First of all, we are meant to learn from these verses, Christ's power and willingness to save sinners.

This is the main doctrine to be gathered from the history of the penitent thief. It teaches us that which ought to be music in the ears of all who hear it--it teaches us that Jesus Christ is "mighty to save." (Isa. lxiii. 1.)

I ask anyone to say whether a case could look more hopeless and desperate than that of this penitent thief once did?

He was a wicked man--a malefactor--a thief, if not a murderer. We know this, for such only were crucified. He was suffering a just punishment for breaking the laws. And as he had lived wicked, so he seemed determined to die wicked--for at first, when he was crucified, he railed on our Lord.

And he was a dying man. He hung there, nailed to a cross, from which he was never to come down alive. He had no longer power to stir hand or foot. His hours were numbered: the grave was ready for him. There was but a step between him and death.

If ever there was a soul hovering on the brink of hell, it was the soul of this thief. If ever there was a case that seemed lost, gone, and past recovery, it was his. If ever there was a child of Adam whom the devil made sure of as his own, it was this man.

But see now what happened. He ceased to rail and blaspheme, as he had done at the first: he began to speak in another manner altogether. He turned to our blessed Lord in prayer. He prayed Jesus to "remember him when he came into His kingdom." He asked that his soul might be cared for, his sins pardoned, and himself thought of in another world. Truly this was a wonderful change!

And then mark what kind of answer he received. Some would have said he was too wicked a man to be saved; but it was not so. Some would have fancied it was too late: the door was shut, and there was no room for mercy; but it proved not too late at all. The Lord Jesus returned him an immediate answer--spoke kindly to him--assured him he should be with Him that day in paradise--pardoned him completely--cleansed him thoroughly from his sins--received him graciously--justified him freely--raised him from the gates of hell, gave him a title to glory. Of all the multitude of saved souls, none ever received so glorious an assurance of his own salvation as did this penitent thief. Go over the whole list, from Genesis to Revelation, and you will find none who had such words spoken to him as these--"To-day shalt thou be with Me in paradise."

I believe the Lord Jesus never gave so complete a proof of His power and will to save, as He did upon this occasion. In the day when He seemed most weak, He showed that He was a strong deliverer. In the hour when His body was racked with pain, He showed that He could feel tenderly for others. At the time when He Himself was dying, He conferred on a sinner eternal life.

Now, have I not a right to say, Christ is "able to save to the uttermost them that come unto God by Him"? (Heb. vii. 25.) Behold the proof of it. If ever sinner was too far gone to be saved, it was this thief. Yet he was plucked as a brand from the fire.

Have I not a right to say, Christ will receive any poor sinner who comes to Him with the prayer of faith, and cast out none? Behold the proof of it. If ever there was one that seemed too bad to be received, this was the man. Yet the door of mercy was wide open even for him.

Have I not a right to say, By grace ye may be saved through faith, not of works: fear not, only believe? Behold the proof of it. This thief was never baptized; he belonged to no visible Church; he never received the Lord's Supper; he never did any work for Christ; he never gave money to Christ's cause! But he had faith, and so he was saved.

Have I not a right to say, The youngest faith will save a man's soul, if it only be true? Behold the proof of it. This man's faith was only one day old; but it led him to Christ, and preserved him from hell.

Why then should any man or woman despair with such a passage as this in the Bible? Jesus is a Physician who can cure hopeless cases. He can quicken dead souls, and call the things which be not as though they were.

Never should any man or woman despair! Jesus is still the same now that He was eighteen hundred years ago. The keys of death and hell are in His hand. When He opens none can shut.[42]

What though your sins be more in number than the hairs of your head? What though your evil habits have grown with your growth, and strengthened with your strength? What though you have hitherto hated good, and loved evil, all the days of your life? These things are sad indeed; but there is hope, even for you. Christ can heal you: Christ can raise you from your low estate. Heaven is not shut against you. Christ is able to admit you, if you will humbly commit your soul into His hands.

Are your sins forgiven? If not, I set before you this day a full and free salvation. I invite you to follow the steps of the penitent thief: come to Christ and live. I tell you that Jesus is very pitiful, and of tender mercy. I tell you He can do everything that your soul requires. Though your sins be as scarlet, He can make them white as snow; though they be red like crimson, they shall be as wool. Why should you not be saved as well as another? Come unto Christ and live.

Are you a true believer? If you are, you ought to glory in Christ. Glory not in your own faith, your own feelings, your own knowledge, your own prayers, your own amendment, your own diligence. Glory in nothing but Christ. Alas! The best of us know but little of that merciful and mighty Saviour. We do not exalt Him and glory in Him enough. Let us pray that we may see more of the fulness there is in Him.

Do you ever try to do good to others? If you do, remember to tell them about Christ. Tell the young, tell the poor, tell the aged, tell the ignorant, tell the sick, tell the dying--tell them all about Christ. Tell them of His power, and tell them of His love; tell them of His doings, and tell them of His feelings; tell them what He has done for the chief of sinners; tell them what He is willing to do to the last day of time: tell it them over and over again. Never be tired of speaking of Christ. Say to them broadly and fully, freely and unconditionally, unreservedly and undoubtingly, "Come unto Christ, as the penitent thief did: come unto Christ, and you shall be saved."

II. The second lesson we are meant to learn from this passage is this.--If some are saved in the very hour of death, others are not.

This is a truth that never ought to be passed over, and I dare not leave it unnoticed. It is a truth that stands out plainly in the sad end of the other malefactor, and is only too often forgotten. Men forget that there were "two thieves."

What became of the other thief who was crucified? Why did he not turn from his sin, and call upon the Lord? Why did he remain hardened and impenitent? Why was he not saved? It is useless to try to answer such questions. Let us be content to take the fact as we find it, and see what it is meant to teach us..

We have no right whatever to say this thief was a worse man than his companion: there is nothing to prove it. Both plainly were wicked men; both were receiving the due reward of their deeds; both hung by the side of our Lord Jesus Christ; both heard Him pray for His murderers, both saw Him suffer patiently. But while one repented, the other remained hardened; while one began to pray, the other went on railing; while one was converted in his last hours, the other died a bad man, as he had lived; while one was taken to paradise, the other went to his own place--the place of the devil and his angels.

Now these things are written for our warning. There is warning, as well as comfort in these verses, and that is a very solemn warning too.

They tell me loudly, that though some may repent and be converted on their deathbeds, it does not at all follow that all will. A deathbed is not always a saving time.

They tell me loudly, that two men may have the same opportunities of getting good for their souls, may be placed in the same position, see the same things, and hear the same things--and yet only one of the two shall take advantage of them, repent, believe and be saved.

They tell me, above all, that repentance and faith are the gifts of God and are not in a man's own power; and that if anyone flatters himself he can repent at his own time, choose his own season, seek the Lord when he pleases, and, like the penitent thief, be saved at the very last--he may find at length he is greatly deceived.

And it is good and profitable to bear this in mind. There is an immense amount of delusion in the world on this very subject. I see many allowing life to slip away, quite unprepared to die. I see many allowing that they ought to repent, but always putting off their own repentance. And I believe one grand reason is, that most men suppose they can turn to God just when they like! They wrest the parable of the labourer in the vineyard, which speaks of the eleventh hour, and use it as it never was meant to be used. They dwell on the pleasant part of the verses I am now considering, and forget the rest. They talk of the thief that went to paradise, and was saved, and they forget the one who died as he had lived--and was lost.[43]

I entreat every man of common sense who reads this paper, to take heed that he does not fall into this mistake.

Look at the history of men in the Bible, and see how often these notions I have been speaking of are contradicted. Mark well how many proofs there are that two men may have the same light offered them, and only one use it; and that no one has a right to take liberties with God's mercy, and presume he will be able to repent just when he likes.

Look at Saul and David. They lived about the same time; they rose from the same rank in life; they were called to the same position in the world; they enjoyed the ministry of the same prophet, Samuel; they reigned the same number of years!--Yet one was saved, and the other lost.

Look at Sergius Paulus and Gallio. They were both Roman governors; they were both wise and prudent men in their generation; they both heard the Apostle Paul preach! But one believed and was baptised--the other "cared for none of those things." (Acts xviii. 17.)

Look at the world around you. See what is going on continually under your eyes. Two sisters will often attend the same ministry, listen to the same truths, hear the same sermons; and yet only one shall be converted unto God, while the other remains totally unmoved. Two friends often read the same religious book: one is so moved by it, that he gives up all for Christ; the other sees nothing at all in it, and continues the same as before. Hundreds have read Doddridge's Rise and Progress without profit: with Wilberforce it was one of the beginnings of spiritual life. Thousands have read Wilberforce's Practical View of Christianity and laid it down again unaltered: from the time Legh Richmond read it he became another man. No man has any warrant for saying, "Salvation is in my own power."

I do not pretend to explain these things. I only put them before you as great facts; and I ask you to consider them well.

You must not misunderstand me. I do not want to discourage you. I say these things in all affection, to give you warning of danger. I do not say them to drive you back from heaven.--I say them rather to draw you on, and bring you to Christ, while He can be found.

I want you to beware of presumption. Do not abuse God's mercy and compassion. Do not continue in sin, I beseech you, and think you can repent, and believe, and be saved, just when you like, when you please, when you will, and when you choose. I would always set before you an open door. I would always say, "While there is life there is hope." But if you would be wise, put nothing off that concerns your soul.

I want you to beware of letting slip good thoughts and godly convictions, if you have them. Cherish them and nourish them, lest you lose them for ever. Make the most of them, lest they take to themselves wings and flee away. Have you an inclination to begin praying? Put it in practice at once. Have you an idea of beginning really to serve Christ? Set about it at once. Are you enjoying any spiritual light? See that you live up to your light. Trifle not with opportunities, lest the day come when you will want to use them, and not be able. Linger not, lest you become wise too late.

You may say, perhaps, "It is never too late to repent." I answer--"That is right enough: but late repentance is seldom true. And I say further, you cannot be certain if you put off repenting, you will repent at all."

You may say, "Why should I be afraid?--the penitent thief was saved." I answer--"That is true: but look again at the passage which tells you that the other thief was lost."

III. The third lesson we are meant to learn from these verses Is this: The Spirit always leads saved souls in one way.

This is a point that deserves particular attention, and is often overlooked. Men look at the broad fact that the penitent thief was saved when he was dying, and they look no further.

They do not consider the evidences this thief left behind him. They do not observe the abundant proof he gave of the work of the Spirit in his heart. And these proofs I wish to trace out. I wish to show you that the Spirit always works in one way, and that--whether He converts a man in an hour, as He did the penitent thief, or whether by slow degrees, as He does others--the steps by which He leads souls to heaven are always the same.

Let me try to make this clear to everyone who reads this paper, I want to put you on your guard. I want you to shake off the common notion that there is some easy, royal road to heaven from a dying bed. I want you thoroughly to understand, that every saved soul goes through the same experience, and that the leading principles of the penitent thief's religion were just the same as those of the oldest saint that ever lived.

(a) See then, for one thing, how strong was the faith of this man.

He called Jesus "Lord." He declared his belief that He would have a "kingdom." He believed that He was able to give him eternal life and glory, and in this belief prayed to Him. He maintained His innocence of all the charges brought against Him. "This Man." said he, he hath done nothing amiss." Others perhaps may have thought the Lord innocent--none said so openly but this poor dying man.

And when did all this happen? It happened when the whole nation had denied Christ-- shouting, "Crucify Him, crucify Him: we have no king but Caesar,"--when the chief priests and Pharisees had condemned and found Him "guilty of death,"--when even His own disciples had forsaken Him and fled--when He was hanging, faint, bleeding, and dying on the cross, numbered with transgressors, and accounted accursed. This was the hour when the thief believed in Christ, and prayed to Him I Surely such faith was never seen since the world began.[44]

The disciples had seen mighty signs and miracles. They had seen the dead raised with a word--and lepers healed with a touch --the blind receiving sight--the dumb made to speak-- the lame made to walk. They had seen thousands fed with a few loaves and fishes. They had seen their Master walking on the water as on dry land. They had all of them heard Him speak as no man ever spake, and hold out promises of good things yet to come. They had some of them had a foretaste of His glory in the mount of transfiguration. Doubtless their faith was "the gift of God," but still they had much to help it.

The dying thief saw none of the things I have mentioned. He only saw our Lord in agony, and in weakness, in suffering, and in pain. He saw Him undergoing a dishonourable punishment; deserted, mocked, despised, blasphemed. He saw Him rejected by all the great, and wise, and noble of His own people--His strength dried up like a potsherd, His life drawing nigh to the grave. (Ps. xxii. 15; lxxxviii. 3.) He saw no sceptre, no royal crown, no outward dominion, no glory, no majesty, no power, no signs of might. And yet the dying thief believed, and looked forward to Christ's kingdom.

Would you know if you have the Spirit? Then mark the question I put to you this day.--Where is your faith in Christ?

(b) See, for another thing, what a right sense of sin the thief had. He says to his companion, "We receive the due reward of our deeds." He acknowledges his own ungodliness, and the justice of his punishment. He makes no attempt to justify himself, or excuse his wickedness. He speaks like a man humbled and self-abased by the remembrance of past iniquities. This is what all God's children feel. They are ready to allow they are poor, hell-deserving sinners. They can say with their hearts as well as with their lips, "We have left undone the things that we ought to have done, and we have done those things that we ought not to have done, and there is no health in us."

Would you know if you have the Spirit? Then mark my question.--Do you feel your sins?

(c) See, for another thing, what brotherly love the thief showed to his companion. He tried to stop his railing and blaspheming, and bring him to a better mind. "Dost not thou fear God," he says, "seeing thou art in the same condemnation?" There is no surer mark of grace than this I Grace shakes a man out of his selfishness, and makes him feel for the souls of others. When the Samaritan woman was converted, she left her water-pot, and ran to the city, saying, "Come, see a man that told me all things that ever I did: is not this the Christ?" (John iv. 28, 29.) When Saul was converted, immediately he went to the synagogue at Damascus and testified to his brethren of Israel that "Christ was the Son of God." (Acts ix. 20.) Would you know if you have the Spirit? Then where is your charity and love to souls?

In one word, you see in the penitent thief a finished work of the Holy Ghost. Every part of the believer's character may be traced in him. Short as his life was after conversion, he found time to leave abundant evidence that he was a child of God. His faith, his prayer, his humility, his brotherly love, are unmistakable witnesses of the reality of his repentance. He was not a penitent in name only, but in deed and m truth.

Let no man therefore think, because the penitent thief was saved, that men can be saved without leaving any evidence of the Spirit's work. Let such an one consider well what evidences this man left behind, and take care.

It is mournful to hear what people sometimes say about what they call deathbed evidences. It is perfectly fearful to observe how little satisfies some persons, and how easily they can persuade themselves that their friends have gone to heaven. They will tell you when their relative is dead and gone, that "he made such a beautiful prayer one day--or that he talked so well--or that he was so sorry for his old ways and intended to live so differently if he got better--or that he craved nothing in this world--or that he liked people to read to him, and pray with him." And because they have this to go upon, they seem to have a comfortable hope that he is saved! Christ may never have been named--the way of salvation may never have been in the least mentioned. But it matters not; there was a little talk of religion, and so they are content!

Now I have no desire to hurt the feelings of anyone who reads this paper, but I must and will speak plainly upon this subject.

Once for all, let me say, that as a general rule, nothing is so unsatisfactory as deathbed evidences. The things that men say, and the feelings they express when sick and frightened, are little to be depended on. Often, too often, they are the result of fear, and do not spring from the ground of the heart. Often, too often, they are things said by rote; caught from the lips of ministers and anxious friends, but evidently not felt. And nothing can prove all this more clearly than the well-known fact, that the great majority of persons who make promises of amendment on a sick bed, and then for the first time talk about religion, if they recover, go back to sin and the world.

When a man has lived a life of thoughtlessness and folly, I want something more than a few fair words and good wishes to satisfy me about his soul, when he comes to his deathbed. It is not enough for me that he will let me read the Bible to him, and pray by his bedside--that he says, "he has not thought so much as he ought of religion, and he thinks he should be a different man if he got better." All this does not content me: it does not make me feel happy about his state. It is very well as far as it goes, but it is not conversion. It is very well in its way, but it is not faith in Christ. Until I see conversion, and faith in Christ, I cannot and dare not feel satisfied. Others may feel satisfied if they please, and after their friend's death say, they hope he is gone to heaven. For my part, I would rather hold my tongue and say nothing. I would be content with the least measure of repentance and faith in a dying man, even though it be no bigger than a grain of mustard seed. But to be content with anything less than repentance and faith, seems to me next door to infidelity.

What kind of evidence do you mean to leave behind as to the state of your soul? Take example by the penitent thief, and you will do well.

When we have carried you to your narrow bed, let us not have to hunt up stray words, and scraps of religion, in order to make out that you were a true believer. Let us not have to say in a hesitating way one to another, "I trust he is happy; he talked so nicely one day; and he seemed so pleased with a chapter in the Bible on another occasion; and he liked such a person, who is a good man." Let us be able to speak decidedly as to your condition. Let us have some solid proof of your repentance, your faith, and your holiness, so that none shall be able for a moment to question your state. Depend on it, without this, those you leave behind can feel no solid comfort about your soul. We may use the form of religion at your burial, and express charitable hopes. We may meet you at the churchyard gate and say, "Blessed are the dead that die in the Lord." But this will not alter your condition! If you die without conversion to God--without repentance, and without faith--your funeral will only be the funeral of a lost soul; you had better never have been born.

IV. We are meant, in the next place, to learn from these verses, that believers in Christ when they die are with the Lord.

This you may gather from our Lord's words to the penitent thief: "This day shalt thou be with Me in paradise." And you have an expression very like it in the Epistle to the Philippians, where Paul says he has a desire to "depart and be with Christ." (Phil. i. 23.)

I shall say but little on this subject. I would simply lay it before you, for your own private meditations. To my own mind it is very full of comfort and peace.

Believers after death are "with Christ." That answers many a difficult question, which otherwise might puzzle man's busy, restless mind. The abode of dead saints, their joys, their feelings, their happiness, all seem met by this simple expression--they are "with Christ."

I cannot enter into full explanations about the separate state of departed believers. It is a high and deep subject, such as man's mind can neither grasp nor fathom. I know their happiness falls short of what it will be when their bodies are raised again, in the resurrection at the last day, and Jesus returns to earth. Yet I know also they enjoy a blessed rest, a rest from labour--a rest from sorrow--a rest from pain--and a rest from sin. But it does not follow because I cannot explain these things, that I am not persuaded they are far happier than they ever were on earth. I see their happiness in this very passage, "They are with Christ," and when I see that, I see enough.

If the sheep are with the Shepherd--if the members are with the Head--if the children of Christ's family are with Him who loved them and carried them all the days of their pilgrimage on earth, all must be well, all must be right.

I cannot describe what kind of place paradise is, because I cannot understand the condition of a soul separate from the body. But I ask no brighter view of paradise than this--that Christ is there.[45] All other things in the picture which imagination draws of the state between death and resurrection, are nothing in comparison of this. How He is there, and in what way He is there, I know not. Let me only see Christ in paradise when my eyes close in death, and that sufficeth me. Well does the Psalmist say, "In Thy presence is fulness of joy." (Psa. xvi. 11.) It was a true saying of a dying girl, when her mother tried to comfort her by describing what paradise would be. "There," she said to the child, "there you will have no pains, and no sickness; there you will see your brothers and sisters who have gone before you, and will be always happy." "Ah, mother!" was the reply, "but there is one thing better than all, and that is, Christ will be there."

It may be you do not think much about your soul. It may be you know little of Christ as your Saviour, and have never tasted by experience that He is precious. And yet perhaps you hope to go to paradise when you die. Surely this passage is one that should make you think. Paradise is a place where Christ is. Then can it be a place that you would enjoy??

It may be you are a believer, and yet tremble at the thought of the grave. It seems cold and dreary. You feel as if all before you was dark and gloomy, and comfortless. Fear not, but be encouraged by this text. You are going to paradise, and Christ will be there.

V. The last thing we are meant to learn from these verses is this: The eternal portion of every man's soul is close to him.

"To-day," says our Lord to the penitent thief, "to-day shalt thou be with Me in paradise." He names no distant period--He does not talk of His entering into a state of happiness as a thing "far away," He speaks of to-day--"this very day in which thou art hanging on the cross."

How near that seems! How awfully near that word brings our everlasting dwelling-place! Happiness or misery--sorrow or joy--the presence of Christ or the company of devils--all are close to us. "There is but a step," says David, "between me and death." (1 Sam. xx. 3.) There is but a step, we may say, between ourselves and either paradise or hell.

We none of us realize this as we ought to do. It is high time to shake off the dreamy state of mind in which we live on this matter. We are apt to talk and think, even about believers, as if death was a long journey--as if the dying saint had embarked on a long voyage. It is all wrong, very wrong! Their harbour and their home is close by, and they have entered it.

Some of us know by bitter experience what a long and weary time it is between the death of those we love, and the hour when we bury them out of our sight. Such weeks are the slowest, saddest, heaviest weeks in all our lives. But, blessed be God, the souls of departed saints are free from the very moment their last breath is drawn. While we are weeping, and the coffin is preparing, and the mourning being provided, and the last painful arrangements being made, the spirits of our beloved ones are enjoying the presence of Christ. They are freed for ever from the burden of the flesh. They are "where the wicked cease from troubling, and the weary be at rest." (Job iii. 17.)

The very moment that believers die they are in paradise. Their battle is fought: their strife is over. They have passed through that gloomy valley we must one day tread; they have gone over that dark river we must one day cross. They have drunk that last bitter cup which sin has mingled for man: they have reached that place where sorrow and sighing are no more. Surely we should not wish them back again! We should not weep for them, but for ourselves.

We are warring still, but they are at peace. We are labouring, but they are at rest. We are watching, but they are sleeping. We are wearing our spiritual armour, but they have for ever put it off. We are still at sea, but they are safe in harbour. We have tears, but they have joy. We are strangers and pilgrims, but as for them they are at home. Surely, better are the dead in Christ than the living! Surely the very hour the poor saint dies, he is at once higher and happier than the highest upon earth.[46]

I fear there is a vast amount of delusion on this point. I fear that many, who are not Roman Catholics, and profess not to believe in purgatory, have, notwithstanding, some strange ideas in their minds about the immediate consequences of death.

I fear that many have a sort of vague notion that there is some interval or space of time between death and their eternal state. They fancy they shall go through a kind of purifying change, and that though they die unfit for heaven, they shall yet be found meet for it after all!

But this is an entire mistake. There is no change after death: there is no conversion in the grave: there is no new heart given after the last breath is drawn. The very day we go, we launch for ever: the day we go from this world, we begin an eternal condition. From that day there is no spiritual alteration--no spiritual change. As we die, so we shall receive our portion after death: as the tree falls, so it must lie.

If you are an unconverted man, this ought to make you think, Do you know you are close to hell? This very day you might die; and if you died out of Christ you would open your eyes at once in in hell, and in torment.

If you are a true Christian, you are far nearer heaven than you think. This very day if the Lord should take you, you would find yourself in paradise. The good land of promise is near to you. The eyes that you closed in weakness and pain would open at once on a glorious rest, such as my tongue cannot describe.

And now let me say a few words in conclusion, and I have done.

(1) This paper may fall into the hands of some humble-hearted and contrite sinner.--Are you that man? Then here is encouragement for you. See what the penitent thief did, and do likewise. See how he prayed; see how he called on the Lord Jesus Christ; see what an answer of peace he obtained. Brother or sister, why should not you do the same? Why should not you also be saved?

(2) This paper may fall into the hands of some proud and presumptuous man of the world.--Are you that man? Then take warning. See how the impenitent thief died as he had lived and beware lest you come to a like end. Oh, erring brother or sister, be not too confident, lest you die in your sins! Seek the Lord while He may be found. Turn you, turn: why will you die?

(3) This paper may fall into the hands of some professing believer in Christ. Are you such an one? Then take the penitent thief's religion as a measure by which to prove your own. See that you know something of true repentance and saving faith, of real humility and fervent charity. Brother or sister, do not be satisfied with the world's standard of Christianity. Be of one mind with the penitent thief, and you will be wise.

(4) This paper may fall into the hands of someone who is mourning over departed believers.--Are you such an one? Then take comfort from this Scripture. See how your beloved ones are in the best of hands. They cannot be better off. They never were so well in their lives as they are now. They are with Jesus, whom their souls loved on earth. Oh, cease from your selfish mourning I Rejoice rather that they are freed from trouble, and have entered into rest.

(5) And this paper may fall into the hands of some aged servant of Christ. Are you such an one? Then see from these verses how near you are to home. Your salvation is nearer than when you first believed. A few more days of labour and sorrow, and the King of kings shall send for you; and in a moment your warfare shall be at end, and all shall be peace.

ENDNOTE

[42] "O Saviour, what a precedent is this of Thy free and powerful grace! Where Thou wilt give, what unworthiness can bar us from Thy mercy? When Thou wilt give, what time can prejudice our vocation? Who can despair of Thy goodness, when he, that in the morning was posting to hell, is in the evening with Thee in Paradise?"--Bishop Hall.

[43] "He that puts off his repentance and seeking for pardon to the very last, in reliance upon this example, does but tempt God, and turn that to his own poison, which God intended for better ends. "The mercies of God are never recorded in Scripture for man's presumption, and the failings of men never for imitation."--Lightfoot. Sermon. 1684. "Most ungrateful and foolish is the conduct of those who take encouragement from the penitent thief to put off repentance to a dying moment; most ungrateful in perverting the grace of their Redeemer into an occasion of renewing their provocations against Him; and most foolish to imagine that what our Lord did in so singular circumstances, is to be drawn into an ordinary precedent."--Doddridge.

[44] "I know not that since the creation of the world there ever was a more remarkable and striking example of faith."--Calvin/s Commentary on the Gospels. "A great faith that can see the sun under so thick a cloud; that can discover a Christ, a Saviour, under such a poor, scorned, despised, crucified Jesus, and call Him Lord. "A great faith that could see Christ's kingdom through His cross, and grave, and death, and when there was so little sign of a kingdom, and pray to be remembered In that kingdom."--Lightfoot. Sermon. 1684. "The penitent thief was the first confessor of Christ's heavenly kingdom--the first martyr who bore testimony to the holiness of His sufferings--and the first apologist for His oppressed innocence."--Quesnel on the Gospel. "Probably there are few saints in glory who ever honoured Christ more illustriously than this dying sinner."--Doddridge. "Is this the voice of a thief or a disci-

ple? Give me leave, O Saviour, to borrow Thine own words, Verily I have not found so great faith, no not in Israel.' He saw Thee hanging miserably by him, and yet styles Thee Lord. He saw Thee dying, and yet talks of Thy kingdom. He felt himself dying, yet talks of a future remembrance, O faith, stronger than death, which can look beyond the cross at a crown; beyond dissolution at a remembrance of life and glory! Which of Thine eleven were heard to speak so gracious a word to Thee in these Thy last pangs?"--Bishop Hall.

[45] "We ought not to enter into curious and subtle arguments about the place of paradise. Let us rest satisfied with knowing that those who are engrafted by faith into the body of Christ are partakers of life, and there enjoy after death a blessed and joyful rest, until the perfect glory of the heavenly life is fully manifested by the coming of Christ."--Calvin's Commentary on the Gospels.

[46] "We give Thee hearty thanks, for that it hath pleased Thee to deliver this our brother out of the miseries of this sinful world."--Church of England Burial Service. "I have some of the best news to impart. One beloved by you has accomplished her warfare; has received an answer to her prayers, and everlasting joy rests upon her head. My dear wife, the source of my best earthly comfort for twenty years, departed on Tuesday."--Venn's Letter to Stillingfleet, announcing the death of his wife.

XII. THE RULER OF THE WAVES

"And there arose a great storm of wind, and the waves beat into the ship, so that it was now full.

"And He was in the hinder part of the ship, asleep on a pillow: and they awake Him, and say unto Him, Master, carest Thou not that we perish?

"And He arose, and rebuked the wind, and said unto the sea, Peace, be still. And the wind ceased, and there was a great calm.

"And He said unto them, Why are ye so fearful. How is it that ye have no faith?"--Mark iv. 37-40.

IT would be well if professing Christians in modern days studied the four Gospels more than they do. No doubt all Scripture is profitable. It is not wise to exalt one part of the Bible at the expense of another. But I think it should be good for some who are very familiar with the Epistles, if they knew a little more about Matthew, Mark, Luke, and John.

Now why do I say this? I say it because I want professing Christians to know more about Christ. It is well to be acquainted with all the doctrines and principles of Christianity. It is better to be acquainted with Christ Himself. It is well to be familiar with faith, and grace, and justification, and sanctification. They are all matters "pertaining to the King." But it is far better to be familiar with Jesus Himself, to see the King's own face, and to behold His beauty. This is one secret of eminent holiness. He that would be conformed to Christ's image, and become a Christ-like man, must be constantly studying Christ Himself.

Now the Gospels were written to make us acquainted with Christ. The Holy Ghost has told us the story of His life and death--His sayings and His doings, four times over. Four different, inspired hands have drawn the picture of the Saviour. His ways, His manners, His feelings, His wisdom, His grace, His patience, His love, His power, are graciously unfolded to us by four different witnesses. Ought not the sheep to be familiar with the Shepherd? Ought not the patient to be familiar with the Physician? Ought not the bride to be familiar with the Bridegroom? Ought not the sinner to be familiar with the Saviour? Beyond doubt it ought to be so. The Gospels were written to make men familiar with Christ, and therefore I wish men to study the Gospels.

On whom must we build our souls if we would be accepted with God? We must build on the rock, Christ. From whom must we draw that grace of the Spirit which we daily need in order to be fruitful? We must draw from the vine, Christ. To whom must we look for sympathy when earthly friends fail us or die? We must look to our elder brother, Christ. By whom must our prayers be presented, if they are to be heard on high? They must be presented by our advocate, Christ. With whom do we hope to spend the thousand years of glory, and the after eternity? With the King of kings, Christ. Surely we cannot know this Christ too well! Surely there is not a word, nor a deed, nor a day, nor a step, nor a thought in the record of

His life, which ought not to be precious to us. We should labour to be familiar with every line that is written about Jesus.

Come now, and let us study a page in our Master's history. Let us consider what we may learn from the verses of Scripture which stand at the head of this paper. You there see Jesus crossing the lake of Galilee, in a boat with His disciples. You see a sudden storm arise while He is asleep. The waves beat into the boat and fill it. Death seems to be close at hand. The frightened disciples awake their Master and cry for help. He arises and rebukes the wind and the waves, and at once there is a calm. He mildly reproves the faithless fears of His companions, and all is over. Such is the picture. It is one full of deep instruction. Come now, and let us examine what we are meant to learn.

1. Let us learn, first of all, that following Christ will not prevent our having earthly sorrows and troubles.

Here are the chosen disciples of the Lord Jesus in great anxiety. The faithful little flock which believed when priests, and scribes, and Pharisees were all alike unbelieving, is allowed by the Shepherd to be much disquieted. The fear of death breaks in upon them like an armed man. The deep water seems likely to go over their souls. Peter, James, and John, the pillars of the Church about to be planted in the world, are much distressed.

Perhaps they had not reckoned on all this. Perhaps they had expected that Christ's service would at any rate lift them above the reach of earthly trials. Perhaps they thought that He who could raise the dead, and heal the sick, and feed multitudes with a few loaves, and cast out devils with a word--He would never allow His servants to be sufferers upon earth. Perhaps they had supposed He would always grant them smooth journeys, fine weather, an easy course, and freedom from trouble and care.

If the disciples thought so, they were much mistaken. The Lord Jesus taught them that a man may be one of His chosen servants, and yet have to go through many an anxiety, and endure many a pain.

It is good to understand this clearly. It is good to understand that Christ's service never did secure a man from all the ills that flesh is heir to, and never will. If you are a believer, you must reackon on having your share of sickness and pain, of sorrow and tears, of losses and crosses, of deaths and bereavements, of partings and separations, of vexations and disappointments, so long as you are in the body. Christ never undertakes that you shall get to heaven without these. He has undertaken that all who come to Him shall have all things pertaining to life and godliness; but He has never undertaken that He will make them prosperous, or rich, or healthy, and that death and sorrow shall never come to their family.

I have the privilege of being one of Christ's ambassadors. In His name I can offer eternal fife to any man, woman, or child who is willing to have it. In His name I do offer pardon, peace, grace, glory, to any son or daughter of Adam who reads this paper. But I dare not offer that person worldly prosperity as a part and parcel of the Gospel. I dare not offer him long life, an increased income, and freedom from pain. I dare not promise the man who takes up the cross and follows Christ, that in the following he shall never meet with a storm.

I know well that many do not like these terms. They would prefer having Christ and good health--Christ and plenty of money--Christ and no deaths in their family--Christ and no wearing cares--Christ and a perpetual morning without clouds. But they do not like Christ and the cross--Christ and tribulation--Christ and the conflict--Christ and the howling wind--Christ and the storm.

Is this the secret thought of anyone who is reading this paper? Believe me, if it is, you are very wrong. Listen to me, and I will try to show you you have yet much to learn.

How should you know who are true Christians, if following Christ was the way to be free from trouble? How should we discern the wheat from the chaff, if it were not for the winnowing of trial? How should we know whether men served Christ for His own sake or from selfish motives, if His service brought health and wealth with it as a matter of course? The winds of winter soon show us which of the trees are evergreen and which are not. The storms of affliction and care are useful in the same way. They discover whose faith is real, and whose is nothing but profession and form.

How would the great work of sanctification go on in a man if he had no trial? Trouble is often the only fire which will burn away the dross that clings to our hearts. Trouble is the pruning-knife which the great Husbandman employs in order to make us fruitful in good works. The harvest of the Lord's field is seldom ripened by sunshine only. It must go through its days of wind, and rain, and storm.

If you desire to serve Christ and be saved, I entreat you to take the Lord on His own terms. Make up your mind to meet with your share of crosses and sorrows, and then you will not be surprised. For want of understanding this, many seem to run well for a season, and then turn back in disgust, and are cast away.

If you profess to be a child of God, leave to the Lord Jesus to sanctify you in His own way. Rest satisfied that He never makes any mistakes. Be sure that He does all things well. The winds may howl around you, and the waters swell. But fear not, "He is leading you by the right way, that He may bring you to a city of habitation." (Psalm cvii. 7.)

II. Let us learn, in the second place, that the Lord Jesus Christ is truly and really Man.

There are words used in this little history which, like many other passages in the Gospel, bring out this truth in a very striking way. We are told that when the waves began to break on the ship, Jesus was in the hinder part, "asleep on a pillow." He was weary; and who can wonder at it, after reading the account given in the fourth chapter of Mark? After labouring all day to do good to souls--after preaching in the open air to vast multitudes, Jesus was fatigued. Surely if the sleep of the labouring man is sweet, much more sweet must have been the sleep of our blessed Lord!

Let us settle in our minds this great truth, that Jesus Christ was verily and indeed Man. He was equal to the Father in all things, and the eternal God. But He was also Man, and took part of flesh and blood, and was made like unto us in all things, sin only excepted. He had a body like our own. Like us, He was born of a woman. Like us, He grew and increased in stature. Like us, He was often hungry and thirsty, and faint and weary. Like us, He ate and drank, rested and slept. Like us, He sorrowed, and wept, and felt. It is all very wonderful, but so it is. He that made the heavens went to and fro as a poor, weary Man on earth! He that ruled over principalities and powers in heavenly places, took on Him a frail body like our own. He that might have dwelt for ever in the glory which He had with the Father, amidst the praises of legions of angels, came down to earth and dwelt as a Man among sinful men. Surely this fact alone is an amazing miracle of condescension, grace, pity, and love.

I find a deep mine of comfort in this thought, that Jesus is perfect Man no less than perfect God. He in whom I am told by Scripture to trust is not only a great High Priest, but a feeling High Priest. He is not only a powerful Saviour, but a sympathising Saviour, He is not only the Son of God, mighty to save, but the Son of man, able to feel.

170

Who does not know that sympathy is one of the sweetest things left to us in this sinful world? It is one of the bright seasons in our dark journey here below, when we can find a person who enters into our troubles, and goes along with us in our anxieties--who can weep when we weep, and rejoice when we rejoice.

Sympathy is far better than money, and far rarer too. Thousands can give who know not what it is to feel. Sympathy has the greatest power to draw us and to open our hearts. Proper and correct counsel often falls dead and useless on a heavy heart. Cold advice often makes us shut up, shrink, and withdraw into ourselves, when tendered in the day of trouble. But genuine sympathy in such a day will call out all our better feelings, if we have any, and obtain an influence over us when nothing else can. Give me the friend who, though poor in gold and silver, has always ready a sympathizing heart.

Our God knows all this well. He knows the very secrets of man's heart. He knows the ways by which that heart is most easily approached, and the springs by which that heart is most readily moved. He has wisely provided that the Saviour of the Gospel should be feeling as well as mighty. He has given us one who has not only a strong hand to pluck us as brands from the burning, but a sympathizing heart on which the labouring and heavy-laden may find rest.

I see a marvellous proof of love and wisdom in the union of two natures in Christ's person. It was marvellous love in our Saviour to condescend to go through weakness and humiliation for our sakes, ungodly rebels as we are. It was marvellous wisdom to fit Himself in this way to be the very Friend of friends, who could not only save man, but meet him on his own ground. I want one able to perform all things needful to redeem my soul. This Jesus can do, for He is the eternal Son of God. I want one able to understand my weakness and infirmities, and to deal gently with my soul, while tied to a body of death. This again Jesus can do, for He was the Son of man, and had flesh and blood like my own. Had my Saviour been God only, I might perhaps have trusted Him, but I never could have come near to Him without fear. Had my Saviour been Man only, I might have loved Him, but I never could have felt sure that He was able to take away my sins. But, blessed be God, my Saviour is God as well as Man, and Man as well as God--God, and so able to deliver me--Man, and so able to feel with me. Almighty power and deepest sympathy are met together in one glorious person, Jesus Christ, my Lord. Surely a believer in Christ has a strong consolation. He may well trust, and not be afraid.

If any reader of this paper knows what it is to go to the throne of grace for mercy and pardon, let him never forget that the Mediator by whom he draws near to God is the Man Christ Jesus.

Your soul's business is in the hand of a High Priest who can be touched with the feeling of your infirmities. You have not to do with a being of so high and glorious a nature that your mind can in no wise comprehend Him. You have to do with Jesus, who had a body like your own and was a Man upon earth like yourself. He well knows that world through which you are struggling, for He dwelt in the midst of it thirty-three years. He well knows "the contradictions of sinners," which so often discourages you, for He endured it Himself. (Heb. xii. 3.) He well knows the art and cunning of your spiritual enemy, the devil, for He wrestled with him in the wilderness. Surely, with such an advocate you may well feel bold.

If you know what it is to apply to the Lord Jesus for spiritual comfort in earthly troubles, you should well remember the days of His flesh, and His human nature.

You are applying to One who knows your feelings by experience, and has drunk deep of the bitter cup, for He was "a Man of sorrows, and acquainted with grief." (Isa. liii. 3.) Jesus knows the heart of a man--the bodily pains of a man--the difficulties of a man, for he was a Man Himself, and had flesh and blood upon earth. He sat wearied by the well at Sychar. He wept over the grave of Lazarus at Bethany. He sweat great drops of blood at Gethsemane. He groaned with anguish at Calvary.

He is no stranger to your sensations. He is acquainted with everything that belongs to human nature, sin only excepted.

(a) Are you poor and needy? So also was Jesus. The foxes had holes, and the birds of the air had nests, but the Son of man had not where to lay His head. He dwelt in a despised city. Men used to say, "Can any good thing come out of Nazareth?" (John i. 46.) He was esteemed a carpenter's son. He preached in a borrowed boat, rode into Jerusalem on a borrowed ass, and was buried in a borrowed tomb.

(b) Are you alone in the world, and neglected by those who ought to love you? So also was Jesus. He came unto His own, and they received Him not. He came to be a Messiah to the lost sheep of the house of Israel, and they rejected Him. The princes of this world would not acknowledge Him. The few that followed Him were publicans and fishermen. And even these at the last forsook Him, and were scattered every man to his own place.

(c) Are you misunderstood, misrepresented, slandered, and persecuted? So also was Jesus. He was called a glutton and a wine-bibber, a friend of publicans, a Samaritan, a madman, and a devil. His character was belied. False charges were laid against Him. An unjust sentence was passed upon Him, and, though innocent, He was condemned as a malefactor, and as such died on the cross.

(d) Does Satan tempt you, and offer horrid suggestions to your mind? So also did he tempt Jesus. He bade Him to distrust God's fatherly providence. "Command these stones to be made bread." He proposed to Him to tempt God by exposing Himself to unnecessary danger. "Cast Thyself down" from the pinnacle of the temple. He suggested to Him to obtain the kingdoms of the world for His own, by one little act of submission to himself. "All these things will I give Thee, if Thou wilt fall down and worship me." (Matt. iv. 1-10.)

(e) Do you ever feel great agony and conflict of mind? Do you feel in darkness as if God had left you? So did Jesus. Who can tell the extent of the sufferings of mind He went through in the garden? Who can measure the depth of His soul's pain when He cried, "My God! my God! why hast Thou forsaken me?" (Matt. xxvii. 46.)

It is impossible to conceive a Saviour more suited to the wants of man's heart than our Lord Jesus Christ--suited not only by His power, but by His sympathy--suited not only by His divinity, but by His humanity. Labour, I beseech you, to get firmly impressed on your mind that Christ, the refuge of souls, is Man as well as God. Honour Him as King of kings, and Lord of lords. But while you do this, never forget that He had a body and was a Man. Grasp this truth and never let it go. The unhappy Socinian errs fearfully when he says that Christ was only Man, and not God. But let not the rebound from that error make you forget that while Christ was very God He was also very Man.

Listen not for a moment to the wretched argument of the Roman Catholic when he tells you that the Virgin Mary and the saints are more sympathizing than Christ. Answer him that such an argument springs from ignorance of the Scriptures and of Christ's true nature. Answer him, that you have not so learned Christ as to regard Him only as an austere Judge and a being to be feared. Answer him, that the four Gospels have taught you to regard Him as the most loving and sympathizing of friends, as well as the mightiest and most powerful of Saviours. Answer him, that you want no comfort from saints and angels, from the Virgin Mary or from Gabriel, so long as you can repose your weary soul on THE MAN CHRIST JESUS.

III. Let us learn, in the third place, that there may be much weakness and infirmity, even in a true Christian.

You have a striking proof of this in the conduct of the disciples here recorded, when the waves broke over the ship. They awoke Jesus in haste. They said to Him, in fear and anxiety, "Master, carest Thou not that we perish? "

There was impatience. They might have waited till their Lord thought fit to arise from His sleep.

There was unbelief. They forgot that they were in the keeping of One who had all power in His hand. "We perish."

There was distrust. They spoke as if they doubted their Lord's care and thoughtfulness for their safety and well-being. "Carest Thou not that we perish?"

Poor faithless men! What business had they to be afraid? They had seen proof upon proof that all must be well so long as the Bridegroom was with them. They had witnessed repeated examples of His love and kindness towards them, sufficient to convince them that He would never let them come to real harm. But all was forgotten in the present danger. Sense of immediate peril often makes men have a bad memory. Fear is often unable to reason from past experience. They heard the winds. They saw the waves. They felt the cold waters beating over them. They fancied death was close at hand. They could wait no longer in suspense. "Carest Thou not," said they, "that we perish?"

But, after all, let us understand this is only a picture of what is constantly going on among believers in every age. There are too many disciples, I suspect, at this very day, like those who are here described.

Many of God's children get on very well so long as they have no trials. They follow Christ very tolerably in the time of fair weather. They fancy they are trusting Him entirely. They flatter themselves they have cast every care on Him. They obtain the reputation of being very good Christians.

But suddenly some unlooked-for trial assails them. Their property makes itself wings and flies away. Their own health fails. Death comes up into their house. Tribulation or persecution ariseth, because of the word. And where now is their faith? Where is the strong confidence they thought they had? Where is their peace, their hope, their resignation? Alas, they are sought for and not found. They are weighed in the balances and found wanting. Fear, and doubt, and distress, and anxiety, break in upon them like a flood, and they seem at their wits' end. I know that this is a sad description. I only put it to the conscience of every real Christian, whether it is not correct and true.

The plain truth is that there is no literal and absolute perfection among true Christians, so long as they are in the body. The best and brightest of God's saints is but a poor mixed being. Converted, renewed, and sanctified though he be, he is still compassed with infirmity. There is not a just man upon earth that always doeth good and sinneth not. In many things we offend all. A man may have true saving faith, and yet not have it always close at hand, and ready to be used. (Eccles. vii. 20; James iii. 2.)

Abraham was the father of the faithful. By faith he forsook his country and his kindred, and went out according to the command of God, to a land he had never seen. By faith he was content to dwell in the land as a stranger, believing that God would give it to him for an inheritance. And yet this very Abraham was so far overcome by unbelief, that he allowed Sarah to be called his sister, and not his wife, through the fear of man. Here was great infirmity. Yet there have been few greater saints than Abraham.

David was a man after God's own heart. He had faith to go out to battle with the giant Goliath when he was but a youth. He publicly declared his belief that the Lord who delivered him from the paw of the lion and bear, would deliver him from this Philistine. He had faith to believe God's promise that he should one day be King of Israel, though he was owned by few followers--though Saul pursued him like a partridge on the mountains and there often seemed but a step between him and death. And yet this very David at one time was so far overtaken by fear and unbelief that he said, "I shall one day perish by the hand of Saul." (1 Sam. xxvii. 1.) He forgot the many wonderful deliverances he had experienced at God's hand. He only thought of his present danger, and took refuge among the ungodly Philistines. Surely here was great infirmity. Yet there have been few stronger believers than David.

I know it is easy for a man to reply, "All this is very true, but k does not excuse the fears of the disciples. They had Jesus actually with them. They ought not to have been afraid. I should never have been so cowardly and faithless as they were!" I tell the man who argues in that way, that he knows little of his own heart. I tell him no one knows the length and breadth of his own infirmities if he has not been tempted. No one can say how much weakness might appear in himself if he was placed in circumstances to call it forth.

Does any reader of this paper think that he believes in Christ? Do you feel such love and confidence in Him that you cannot understand being greatly moved by any event that could happen? It is all well. I am glad to hear it. But has this faith been tried? Has this confidence been put to the test? If not, take heed of condemning these disciples hastily. Be not highminded, but fear. Think not because your heart is in a lively frame now, that such a frame will always last. Say not, because your feelings are warm and fervent to-day, "to-morrow shall be as to-day, and much more abundant." Say not, because your heart is lifted up just now with a strong sense of Christ's mercy, "I shall never forget Him as long as I live." Oh, learn to abate something of this flattering estimate of yourself. You do not know yourself thoroughly. There are more things in your inward man than you are at present aware of. The Lord may leave you as He did Hezekiah, to show you all that is in your heart. (2 Chron. xxxii. 31.) Blessed is he that is "clothed with humility."--"Happy is he that feareth always." "Let him that thinketh he standeth take heed lest he fall." (1 Pet. v. 5; Prov. xxviii. 14; 1 Cor. x. 12.)

Why do I dwell on this? Do I want to apologize for the corruptions of professing Christians, and excuse their sins? God forbid!--Do I want to lower the standard of sanctification, and countenance anyone in being a lazy, idle soldier of Christ? God forbid!--Do I want to wipe out the broad line of distinction between the converted and the unconverted, and to wink at inconsistencies? Once more I say, God forbid!--I hold strongly that there is a mighty difference between the true Christian and the false, between the believer and the unbeliever, between the children of God and the children of the world. I hold strongly that this difference is not merely one of faith, but of life--not only one of profession, but of practice. I hold strongly that the ways of the believer should be as distinct from those of the unbeliever, as bitter from sweet, light from darkness, heat from cold.

But I do want young Christians to understand what they must expect to find in themselves. I want to prevent their being stumbled and puzzled by the discovery of their own weakness and infirmity. I want them to see that they may have true faith and grace, in spite of all the devil's whispers to the contrary, though they feel within doubts and fears. I want them to observe that Peter, and James, and John, and their brethren were true disciples, and yet not so spiritual but that they could be afraid. I do not tell them to make the unbelief of the disciples an excuse for themselves. But I do tell them that it shows plainly, that so long as they are in the body they must not expect faith to be above the reach of fear.

Above all, I want all Christians to understand what they must expect in other believers. You must not hastily conclude that a man has no grace merely because you see in him some corruption-There are spots on the face of the sun; and yet the sun shines brightly and enlightens the whole world. There is quartz and dross mixed up with many a lump of gold that comes from Australia; and yet who thinks the gold on that account worth nothing at all? There are flaws in some of the finest diamonds in the world; and yet they do not prevent their being rated at a priceless value. Away with this morbid squeamishness which makes many ready to excommunicate a man if he only has a few faults! Let us be more quick to see grace and more slow to see imperfections! Let us know that, if we cannot allow there is grace where there is corruption, we shall find no grace in the world. We are yet in the body. The devil is not dead. We are not yet like the angels. Heaven has not yet begun. The leprosy is not out of the walls of the house, however much we may scrape them, and never will be till the house is taken down. Our bodies are indeed the temple of the Holy Ghost, but not a perfect temple until they are raised or changed. Grace is indeed a treasure, but a treasure in earthen vessels. It is possible for a man to forsake all for Christ's sake, and yet to be overtaken occasionally with doubts and fears.

I beseech every reader of this paper to remember this. It is a lesson worth attention. The Apostles believed in Christ, loved Christ, and gave up all to follow Christ. And yet you see in this storm the Apostles were afraid. Learn to be charitable in your judgment of them. Learn to be moderate in your expectations from your own heart. Contend to the death for the truth that no man is a true Christian who is not converted, and is not a holy man. But allow that a man may be converted, have a new heart, and be a holy man, and yet be liable to infirmity, doubts and fears.

IV. Let us learn, in the fourth place, the power of the Lord Jesus Christ.

You have a striking example of His power in the history upon which I am now dwelling. The waves were breaking into the ship where Jesus was. The terrified disciples awoke Him, and cried for help. "He arose and rebuked the wind, and said unto the sea, Peace, be still. And the wind ceased, and there was a great calm." This was a wonderful miracle. No one could do this but one who was almighty.

Make the winds cease with a word! Who does not know that it is a common saying, in order to describe an impossibility, "You might as well speak to the wind!" Yet Jesus rebukes the wind and at once it ceases. This was power.

Calm the waves with a voice! What reader of history does not know that a mighty King of England tried in vain to stop the tide rising on the shore? Yet here is one who says to raging waves in a storm, "Peace, be still," and at once there was a calm. Here was power.

It is good for all men to have clear views of the Lord Jesus Christ's power. Let the sinner know that the merciful Saviour to whom he is urged to flee, and in whom he is invited to trust, is nothing less than the Almighty, and has power over all flesh to eternal life. (Rev. i. 8; John xvii. 2.) Let the anxious inquirer understand that if he will only venture on Jesus, and take up the cross, he ventures on One who has all power in heaven and earth. (Matt. xxviii. 18.) Let the believer remember as he journeys through the wilderness, that his Mediator, and Advocate, and Physician, and Shepherd, and Redeemer, is Lord of lords, and King of kings, and that through Him all things may be done. (Rev. xvii. 14; Phil. iv. 13.) Let all study the subject, for it deserves to be studied.

(a) Study it in His works of creation. "All things were made by Him, and without Him was not any thing made that was made." (John i. 3.) The heavens and all their glorious host of inhabitants--the earth and all that it contains--the sea and all that is in it--all creation, from the sun on high to the least worm below, was the work of Christ. He spake and they came into being. He commanded and they began to exist. That very Jesus, who was born of a poor woman at Bethlehem and lived in a carpenter's house at Nazareth, had been the Former of all things. Was not this power?

(b) Study it in His works of providence, and the orderly continuance of all things in the world. "By Him all things consist." (Col. i. 17.) Sun, moon, and stars roll round in a perfect system. Spring, summer, autumn, and winter follow one another in regular order. They continue to this day and fail not, according to the ordinance of Him who died on Calvary. (Psalm cxix. 91.) The kingdoms of this world rise and increase, and decline and pass away. The rulers of the earth plan, and scheme, and make laws, and change laws, and war, and pull down one and raise up another. But they little think that they rule only by the will of Jesus and that nothing happens without the permission of the Lamb of God. They do not know that they and their subjects are all as a drop or water in the hand of the crucified One, and that He increaseth the nations and diminishes the nations, just according to His mind. Is not this power?

(c) Study the subject not least in the miracles worked by our Lord Jesus Christ during the three years of His ministry upon earth. Learn from the mighty works which He did, that the things which are impossible with man are possible with Christ. Regard every one of His miracles as an emblem and figure of spiritual things. See in it a lovely picture of what He is able to do for your soul. He that could raise the dead with a word can just as easily raise man from the death of sin. He that could give sight to the blind, hearing to the deaf, and speech to the dumb, can also make sinners to see the kingdom of God, hear the joyful sound of the Gospel, and speak forth the praise of redeeming love. He that could heal leprosy with a touch, can heal any disease of heart. He that could cast out devils can bid every besetting sin yield to His grace. Oh, begin to read Christ's miracles in this light! Wicked, and bad, and corrupt as you may feel, take comfort in the thought that you are not beyond Christ's power to heal. Remember that in Christ there is not only a fulness of mercy, but a fulness of power.

(d) Study the subject in particular as placed before you this day. I dare be sure your heart has sometimes been tossed to and fro like the waves in a storm. You have found it agitated like the waters of the troubled sea when it cannot rest. Come and hear this day that there is One who can give you rest. Jesus can say to your heart, whatever may be its ailment, "Peace, be still I "

What though your conscience within be lashed by the recollection of countless transgressions, and torn by every gust of temptation? What though the remembrance of past hideous profligacy be grievous unto you, and the burden intolerable? What though your heart seems full of evil, and sin appears to drag you whither it will like a slave? What though the devil rides to and fro over your soul like a conqueror, and tells you it is vain to struggle against him, there is no hope for you? I tell you there is One who can give even you pardon and peace. My Lord and Master Jesus Christ can rebuke the devil's raging, can calm even your soul's misery, and say even to you, "Peace, be still!" He can scatter that cloud of guilt which now weighs you down. He can bid despair depart. He can drive fear away. He can remove the spirit of bondage and fill you with the spirit of adoption. Satan may hold your soul like a strong man armed, but Jesus is stronger than he, and when He commands, the prisoners must go free. Oh, if any troubled reader wants a calm within, let him go this day to Jesus Christ and all shall yet be well!

But what if your heart be right with God, and yet you are pressed down with a load of earthly trouble? What if the fear of poverty is tossing you to and fro and seems likely to overwhelm you? What if pain of body be racking you to distraction day after day? What if you are suddenly laid aside from active usefulness, and compelled by infirmity to sit still and do nothing? What if death has come into your home and taken away your Rachael, or Joseph, or Benjamin and left you alone, crushed to the ground with sorrow? What if all this has happened? Still there is comfort in Christ. He can speak peace to wounded hearts as easily as calm troubled seas. He can rebuke rebellious wills as powerfully as raging winds. He can make storms of sorrow abate and silence tumultuous passions as surely as He stopped the Galilean storm. He can say to the heaviest anxiety, "Peace, be still!" The floods of care and tribulation may be mighty, but Jesus sits upon the waterfloods and is mightier than the waves of the sea. (Psalm xciii. 4.) The winds of trouble may howl fiercely round you, but Jesus holds them in His hand and can stay them when He lists. Oh, if any reader of this paper is broken-hearted, and care-worn, and sorrowful, let him go to Jesus Christ and cry to Him, and he shall be refreshed. "Come unto Me," He says, "all ye that labour and are heavy laden, and I will give you rest." (Matt. xi. 28.)

I invite all who profess and call themselves Chris dans, to take large views of Christ's power. Doubt anything else if you will, but never doubt Christ's power. Whether you do not secretly love sin, may be doubtful. Whether you are not privately clinging to the world, may be doubtful. Whether the pride of your nature is not rising against the idea of being saved as a poor sinner by grace, may be doubtful. But one thing is not doubtful, and that is that Christ is "able to save to the uttermost," and will save you, if you will let Him. (Heb. vii. 25.)

V. Let us learn, in the last place, how tenderly and patiently the Lord Jesus deals with weak believers.

We see this truth brought out in His words to His disciples, when the wind ceased and there was a calm. He might well have rebuked them sharply. He might well have reminded them of all the great things He had done for them and reproved them for their cowardice and mistrust. But there is nothing of anger in the Lord's words. He simply asks two questions. "Why are ye so fearful? How is it that ye have no faith?"

The whole of our Lord's conduct towards His disciples on earth deserves close considera-tion, it throws a beautiful light on the compassion and longsuffering that there is in Him. No master surely ever had scholars so slow to learn their lessons as Jesus had in the Apostles. No scholars surely ever had so patient and forbearing a teacher as the Apostles had in Christ. Gather up all the evidence on this subject that lies scattered through the Gospels, and see the truth of what I say.

At no time of our Lord's ministry did the disciples seem to comprehend fully the object of His coming into the world. The humiliation, the atonement, the crucifixion, were hidden

177

things to them. The plainest words and clearest warnings from their Master of what was going to befall Him seemed to have had no effect on their minds. They understood not. They perceived not. It was hid from their eyes. Once Peter even tried to dissuade our Lord from suffering. "Be it far from Thee, Lord," he said, "this shall not be unto Thee." (Matt. xvi. 22; Luke xviii. 34; ix. 45.)

Frequently you will see things in their spirit and demeanour which are not at all to be commended. One day we are told they disputed among themselves who should be greatest. (Mark ix. 34.) Another day they considered not His miracles and their hearts were hardened. (Mark vi. 52.) Once two of them wished to call down fire from heaven upon a village, because it did not receive them. (Luke ix. 54.) In the garden of Gethsemane the three best of them slept when they should have watched and prayed. In the hour of His betrayal they all forsook Him and fled, and worst of all, Peter, the most forward of the twelve, denied his Master three times with an oath.

Even after the resurrection, you see the same unbelief and hardness of heart cling to them; though they saw their Lord with their eyes, and touched Him with their hands, even then some doubted. So weak were they in faith! So slow of heart were they to "believe all that the prophets had spoken." (Luke xxiv. 25.) So backward were they in understanding the meaning of our Lord's words, and actions, and life, and death.

But what do you see in our Lord's behaviour towards these disciples all through His ministry? You see nothing but unchanging pity, compassion, kindness, gentleness, patience, long-suffering, and love. He does not cast them off for their stupidity. He does not reject them for their unbelief. He does not dismiss them for ever for cowardice. He teaches them as they are able to bear. He leads them on step by step, as a nurse does an infant when it first begins to walk. He sends them kind messages as soon as He is risen from the dead. "Go," He said to the women, "Go tell my brethren that they go into Galilee, and there they shall see Me." (Matt. xxviii. 10.) He gathers them round Himself once more. He restores Peter to his place, and bids him "feed His sheep." (John xxi. 17.) He condescends to sojourn with them forty days before He finally ascends. He commissions them to go forth as His messengers, and preach the Gospel to the Gentiles. He blesses them in parting, and encourages them with that gracious promise, "I am with you always, even unto the end of the world." (Matt. xxviii. 20.) Truly this was a love that passeth knowledge. This is not the manner of man.

Let all the world know that the Lord Christ is very pitiful, and of tender mercy. He will not break the bruised reed, nor quench the smoking flax. As a father pitieth his children, so He pitieth them that fear Him. As one whom his mother comforteth, so will He comfort His people. (James v. 11; Matt. xii. 20; Ps. ciii. 13; Isa. lxvi. 13.) He cares for the lambs of His flock as well as for the old sheep. He cares for the sick and feeble ones of His fold as well as for the strong. It is written that He will carry them in His bosom, rather than let one of them be lost. (Isaiah xl. 11.) He cares for the least members of His body, as well as for the greatest. He cares for the babes of His family as well^as the grownup men. He cares for the tenderest little plants in His garden as well as for the cedar of Lebanon. All are in His book of life, and all are under His charge. All are given to Him in an everlasting covenant, and He has undertaken, in spite of all weaknesses, to bring every one safe home. Only let a sinner lay hold on Christ by faith and then, however feeble, Christ's word is pledged to him, "I will never leave thee nor forsake thee." He may correct him occasionally in love. He may gently reprove him at times. But He will never, never give him up. The devil shall never pluck him from Christ's hand.

Let all the world know that the Lord Jesus will not cast away His believing people because of shortcomings and infirmities. The husband does not put away his wife because he finds failings in her. The mother does not forsake her infant because it is weak, feeble and ignorant. And the Lord Christ does not cast off poor sinners who have committed their souls into His hands because He sees in them blemishes and imperfections. Oh, no! It is His glory to pass over the faults of His people, and heal their backslidings--to make much of their weak graces and to pardon their many faults. The eleventh of Hebrews is a wonderful chapter. It is marvellous to observe how the Holy Ghost speaks of the worthies whose names are recorded in that chapter. The faith of the Lord's people is there brought forward and had in remembrance. But the faults of many a one, which might easily have been brought up also, are left alone, and not mentioned at all.

Who is there now among the readers of this paper that feels desires after salvation, but is afraid to become decided, lest by-and-by he should fall away? Consider, I beseech you, the tenderness and patience of the Lord Jesus and be afraid no more. Fear not to take up the cross and come out boldly from the world. That same Lord and Saviour who bore with the disciples is ready and willing to bear with you. If you stumble, He will raise you. If you err, He will gently bring you back. If you faint, He will revive you. He will not lead you out of Egypt, and then suffer you to perish in the wilderness. He will conduct you safe into the promised land. Only commit yourself to His guidance, and then, my soul for yours, He shall carry you safe home. Only hear Christ's voice, and follow Him, and you shall never perish.

Who is there among the readers of this paper that has been converted and desires to do his Lord's will? Take example, this day, by your Master's gentleness and long-suffering, and learn to be tender-hearted and kind to others. Deal gently with young beginners. Do not expect them to know everything and understand everything all at once. Take them by the hand. Lead them on and encourage them. Believe all things, and hope all things, rather than make that heart sad which God would not have made sad. Deal gently with backsliders. Do not turn your back on them as if their case was hopeless. Use every lawful means to restore them to their former place. Consider yourself, and your often infirmities, and do as you would be done by. Alas, there is a painful absence of the Master's mind among many of His disciples. There are few churches, I fear, in the present day, which would have received Peter into communion again for many a long year, after denying His Lord. There are few believers ready to do the work of Barnabas--willing to take young converts by the hand, and encourage them at their first beginnings. Verily we want an outpouring of the Spirit upon believers almost as much as upon the world.

And now, I have only to ask my readers to make a practical use of the lessons I have brought before them. You have heard this day five things.

First. That Christ's service will not secure you against troubles. The holiest saints are liable to them.

Second. That Christ is very Man as well as God.

Third. That believers may have much weakness and infirmity, and yet be true believers.

Fourth. That Christ has all power: and

Fifth. That Christ is full of patience and kindness towards His people. Remember these five lessons, and you will do well.

Bear with me a few moments while I say a few words to impress the things you have been reading more deeply on your heart.

(1) This paper will very likely be read by some who know nothing of Christ's service by experience, or of Christ Himself.

There are only too many who take no interest whatever in the things about which I have been writing. Their treasure is all below. They are wholly taken up with the things of the world. They care nothing about the believer's conflict, and struggles, and infirmities, and doubts, and fears.

They care little whether Christ did miracles or not. It is all a matter of words, and names, and forms, about which they do not trouble themselves. They are without God in the world.

If perchance you are such a man as this, I can only warn you solemnly that your present course cannot last. You will not live for ever. There must be an end. Grey hairs, age, sickness, infirmities, death--all, all are before you, and must be met one day. What will you do when that day comes?

Remember my words this day. You will find no comfort when sick and dying, unless Jesus Christ is your friend. You will, discover, to your sorrow and confusion, that however much men may talk and boast, they cannot do without Christ when they come to their deathbed. You may send for ministers, and get them to read prayers, and give you the sacrament. You may go through every form and ceremony of Christianity. But if you persist in living a careless and worldly life, and despising Christ in the morning of your days, you must not be surprised if Christ leaves you to yourself in your latter end. Alas! these are solemn words, and are often sadly fulfilled: "I will laugh at your calamity; I will mock when your fear cometh." (Prov. i. 26.)

Come then, this day, and be advised by one who loves your soul. Cease to do evil. Learn to do well. Forsake the foolish, and go in the path of understanding. Cast away that pride which hangs about your heart, and seek the Lord Jesus while He may be found. Cast away that spiritual sloth which is palsying your soul, and resolve to take trouble about your Bible, your prayers, and your Sundays. Break off from a world which can never really satisfy you, and seek that treasure which alone is truly incorruptible. Oh, that the Lord's own words might find a place in your conscience! "How long, ye simple ones, will ye love simplicity? and the scorners delight in their scorning, and fools hate knowledge? Turn you at my reproof: behold I will pour out my Spirit unto you, I will make known my words unto you." (Prov. i. 22, 23.) I believe the crowning sin of Judas Iscariot was that he would not seek pardon and turn again to his Lord. Beware, lest that be your sin also.

(2) This paper will probably fall into the hands of some who love the Lord Jesus, and believe in Him, and yet desire to love Him better.

If you are such a man, suffer the word of exhortation and apply it to your heart.

For one thing, keep before your mind, as an ever-present truth, that the Lord Jesus is an actual, living Person, and deal with Him as such.

I fear the personality of our Lord is sadly lost sight of by many professors in the present day. Their talk is more about salvation than about the Saviour--more about redemption than about the Redeemer--more about justification than about Jesus--more about Christ's work than about Christ's person. This a great fault, and one that fully accounts for the dry and sapless character of the religion of many professors.

As ever, you would grow in grace and have joy and peace in believing, beware of falling into this error. Cease to regard the Gospel as a mere collection of dry doctrines. Look at it rather as the revelation of a mighty, living Being in whose sight you are daily to live. Cease to regard it as a mere set of abstract propositions and abstruse principles and rules. Look at it as the introduction to a glorious, personal Friend. This is the kind of Gospel that the Apostles preached. They did not go about the world telling men of love, and mercy, and pardon, in the abstract. The leading subject of all their sermons was the loving heart of an actual living Christ. This is the kind of Gospel which is most calculated to promote sanctification and meetness for glory. Nothing, surely, is so likely to prepare us for that heaven where Christ's personal presence will be all, and that glory where we shall meet Christ face to face, as to realize communion with Christ, as an actual living Person here on earth. There is all the difference in the world between an idea and a person.

For another thing, try to keep before your mind, as an ever-present truth, that the Lord Jesus is utterly unchanged.

That Saviour, in whom you trust, is the same yesterday, to-day, and for ever. He knows no variableness, nor shadow of turning. Though high in heaven at God's right hand, He is just the same in heart that He was 1900 years ago on earth. Remember this and you will do well.

Follow Him all through Pits journeys to and fro in Palestine. Mark how He received all that came to Him and cast out none. Mark how He had an ear to listen to every tale of sorrow, a hand to help every case of distress, a heart to feel for all who needed sympathy. And then say to yourself, "This same Jesus is He who is my Lord and Saviour. Place and time have made no difference in Him. What He was, He is, and will be for evermore."

Surely this thought will give life and reality to your daily religion. Surely this thought will give substance and shape to your expectation of good things to come. Surely it is matter for joyful reflection, that He who was thirty-three years upon earth, and whose life we read in the Gospels, is the very Saviour in whose presence we shall spend eternity.

The last word of this paper shall be the same as the first. I want men to read the four Gospels more than they do. I want men to become better acquainted with Christ. I want unconverted men to know Jesus, that they may have eternal life through Him. I want believers to know Jesus better, that they may become more happy, more holy, and more meet for the inheritance of the saints in light. He will be the holiest man who learns to say with St. Paul, "To me to live is Christ." (Phil. i. 21.)

XIII. THE CHURCH WHICH CHRIST BUILDS

"Upon this rock I will build my church, and the gates of hell shall not prevail against it."--Matt. xvi. 18.

DO we belong to the Church which is built upon a rock? Are we members of the only Church in which our souls can be saved?--These are serious questions. They deserve serious consideration. I ask the attention of all who read this paper, while I try to show the one true, holy, Catholic Church, and to guide men's feet into the only safe fold. "What is this Church? What is it like? What are its marks? Where is it to be found?" On all these points I have something to say. I am going to unfold the words of our Lord Jesus Christ, which stand at the head of this page. He declares, "Upon this rock I will build my Church, and the gates of hell shall not prevail against it."

There are five things in these famous words which demand our attention:--

I. A Building: "My Church."

II. A Builder: Christ says, "I will build my Church."

III. A Foundation: "Upon this rock I will build my Church."

IV. Perils Implied: "The gates of hell."

V. Security Asserted: "The gates of hell shall not prevail against it."

The whole subject demands special attention in the present day. Holiness, we must never forget, is the prominent characteristic of all who belong to the one true Church.

I. We have, firstly, a Building mentioned in the text. The Lord Jesus Christ speaks of "my Church."

Now what is this Church? Few inquiries can be made of more importance than this. For want of due attention to this subject, the errors that have crept into the world are neither few nor small.

The Church of our text is no material building. It is no temple made with hands of wood, or brick, or stone, or marble. It is a company of men and women.--It is no particular visible Church on earth. It is not the Eastern Church or the Western Church. It is not the Church of England or the Church of Scotland.--Above all, it certainly is not the Church of Rome. The Church of our text is one that makes far less show than any visible Church in the eyes of man, but is of far more importance in the eyes of God.

The Church of our text is made up of all true believers in the Lord Jesus Christ, of all who are really holy and converted people. It comprehends all who have repented of sin, and fled to Christ by faith, and been made new creatures in Him. It comprises all God's elect, all who have received God's grace, all who have been washed in Christ's blood, all who have been clothed in Christ's righteousness, all who have been born again and sanctified by Christ's Spirit. All such, of every name, and rank, and nation, and people, and tongue, compose the Church of our text. This is the body of Christ. This is the flock of Christ. This is the bride. This is the Lamb's wife. This is "the holy Catholic and Apostolic Church" of the Apostles' Creed and the Nicene Creed. This is "the blessed company of all faithful people," spoken of in the Communion Service of the Church of England. This is "THE CHURCH ON THE ROCK."

The members of this Church do not all worship God in the same way, or use the same form of government. Some of them are governed by bishops and some of them by elders. Some of them use a prayer-book when they meet for public worship and some of them use none. The thirty-fourth Article of the Church of England most wisely declares, "It is not necessary that ceremonies should be in all places one and alike." But the members of this Church all come to one throne of grace. They all worship with one heart. They are all led by one Spirit. They are all really and truly holy. They can all say "Alleluia," and they can all reply, "Amen."

This is that Church to which all visible churches on earth are servants and handmaidens. Whether they are Episcopalian, Independent, or Presbyterian, they all serve the interests of the one true Church. They are the scaffolding behind which the great building is carried on. They are the husk under which the living kernel grows. They have their various degrees of usefulness. The best and worthiest of them is that which trains up most members for Christ's true Church. But no visible church has any right to say, "We are the only True Church. We are the men, and wisdom shall die with us." No visible Church should ever dare to say, "We shall stand for ever. The gates of hell shall not prevail against me."

This is that Church to which belong the Lord's gracious promises of preservation, continuance, protection, and final glory.--"Whatsoever," says Hooker, "we read in Scripture concerning the endless love and saving mercy which God showeth towards His Churches, the only proper subject thereof is this Church, which we properly term the mystical body of Christ."--Small and despised as the true Church may be in this world, it is precious and honourable in the sight of God. The temple of Solomon in all its glory was mean and contemptible in comparison with that Church which is built upon a rock.

I trust the things I have just been saying will sink down into the minds of all who read this paper. See that you hold sound doctrine upon the subject of "the Church." A mistake here may lead on to dangerous and soul-ruining errors. The Church which is made up of true believers is the Church for which we, who are ministers, are specially ordained to preach. The Church which comprises all who repent and believe the Gospel is the Church to which we desire you to belong. Our work is not done, and our hearts are not satisfied until you are made a new creature, and are a member of the one true Church. Outside of the Church which is "built on the rock" there can be NO SALVATION.

II. I pass on to the second point to which I propose to invite your attention. Our text contains not merely a building, but a Builder. The Lord Jesus Christ declares, "I will build my Church."

The true Church of Christ is tenderly cared for by all the three Persons in the blessed Trinity. In the plan of salvation revealed in the Bible, beyond doubt God the Father chooses, God the Son redeems, and God the Holy Ghost sanctifies every member of Christ's mystical body. God the Father, God the Son, and God the Holy Ghost, three Persons and one God, co-operate for the salvation of every saved soul. This is truth, which ought never to be forgotten. Nevertheless, there is a peculiar sense in which the help of the Church is laid on the Lord Jesus Christ. He is peculiarly and pre-eminently the Redeemer and Saviour of the Church. Therefore it is that we find Him saying in our text, "I will build--the work of building is my special work."

It is Christ who calls the members of the Church in due time. They are "the called of Jesus Christ." (Rom. i. 6.) It is Christ who quickens them. "The Son quickeneth whom He will." (John v. 21.) It is Christ who washes away their sins. He "has loved us, and washed us from our sins in His own blood." (Rev. i. 5.) It is Christ who gives them peace. "Peace I leave with you, my peace I give unto you." (John xiv. 27.) It is Christ who gives them eternal life. "I give unto them eternal life, and they shall never perish." (John x. 28.) It is Christ who grants them repentance. "Him hath God exalted to be a Prince and a Saviour, to give repentance." (Acts v. 31.) It is Christ who enables them to become God's children. "To as many as received Him, to them gave He power to become the sons of God." (John i. 12.) It is Christ who carries on the work within them when it is begun "Because I live, ye shall live also." (John xiv. 19.) In short, it has "pleased the Father that in Christ should all fullness dwell." (Coloss. i. 19.) He is the author and finisher of faith. He is the life. He is the head. From Him every joint and member of the mystical body of Christians is supplied. Through Him they are kept from falling. He shall preserve them to the end, and present them faultless before the Father's throne with exceeding great joy. He is all things in all believers.

The mighty agent by whom the Lord Jesus Christ carries out this work in the members of His Church is without doubt the Holy Ghost. He it is who is ever renewing, awakening, convincing, leading to the cross, transforming, taking out of the world stone after stone, and adding to the mystical building. But the great chief Builder, who has undertaken to execute the work of redemption and bring it to completion, is the Son of God, the "Word who was made flesh." It is Jesus Christ who "builds."

In building the true Church, the Lord Jesus condescends to use many subordinate instruments. The ministry of the Gospel, the circulation of the Scriptures, the friendly rebuke, the word spoken in season, the drawing influence of afflictions--all, all are means and appliances by which His work is carried on, and the Spirit conveys life to souls. But Christ is the great superintending Architect, ordering, guiding, directing all that is done. Paul may plant, and Apollos water, but God giveth the increase, (1 Cor. iii. 6.) Ministers may preach and writers may write, but the Lord Jesus Christ alone can build. And except He builds, the work stands still.

Great is the wisdom wherewith the Lord Jesus Christ builds His Church! All is done at the right time, and in the right way. Each stone in its turn is put in its right place. Sometimes He chooses great stones, and sometimes He chooses small stones. Sometimes the work goes on fast, and sometimes it goes on slowly. Man is frequently impatient and thinks that nothing is doing. But man's time is not God's time. A thousand years in His sight are but as a single day. The great Builder makes no mistakes. He knows what He is doing. He sees the end from the beginning. He works by a perfect, unalterable, and certain plan. The mightiest conceptions of architects, like Michelangelo and Wren, are mere trifling and child's play in comparison with Christ's wise counsels respecting His Church.

Great is the condescension and mercy which Christ exhibits in building His Church! He often chooses the most unlikely and roughest stones, and fits them into a most excellent work. He despises none, and rejects none, on account of former sins and past transgressions.

He often makes Pharisees and Publicans become pillars of His house. He delights to show mercy. He often takes the most thoughtless and ungodly, and transforms them into polished corners of His spiritual temple.

Great is the power which Christ displays in building His Church! He carries on His work in spite of opposition from the world, the flesh, and the devil. In storm, in tempest, through troublous times, silently, quietly, without noise, without stir, without excitement, the building progresses, like Solomon's temple. "I will work," He declares, "and who shall let it?" (Isaiah xliii. 13.)

The children of this world take little or no interest in the building of this Church. They care nothing for the conversion of souls. What are broken spirits and penitent hearts to them? What is conviction of sin, or faith in the Lord Jesus to them? It is all "foolishness" in their eyes. But while the children of this world care nothing, there is joy in the presence of the angels of God. For the preserving of the true Church, the laws of nature have oftentimes been suspended. For the good of that Church, all the providential dealings of God in this world are ordered and arranged. For the elect's sake, wars are brought to an end, and peace is given to a nation. Statesmen, rulers, emperors, kings, presidents, heads of governments, have their schemes and plans, and think them of vast importance. But there is another work going on of infinitely greater moment, for which they are only the "axes and saws" in God's hands. (Isai. x. 15.) That work is the erection of Christ's spiritual temple, the gathering in of living stones into the one true Church.

We ought to feel deeply thankful that the building of the true Church is laid on the shoulders of One that is mighty. If the work depended on man, it would soon stand still. But, blessed be God, the work is in the hands of a Builder who never fails to accomplish His designs! Christ is the almighty Builder. He will carry on His work, though nations and visible Churches may not know their duty. Christ will never fail. That which He has undertaken He will certainly accomplish.

III.--I pass on to the third point which I propose to consider--The Foundation upon which this Church is built. The Lord Jesus Christ tells us, "Upon this rock will I build my Church."

What did the Lord Jesus Christ mean when He spoke of this foundation? Did He mean the Apostle Peter, to whom He was speaking? I think assuredly not. I can see no reason, if He meant Peter, why He did not say, "Upon thee" will I build my Church. If He had meant Peter, He would surely have said, I will build my Church on thee, as plainly as He said, "to thee will I give the keys."--No, it was not the person of the Apostle Peter, but the good confession which the Apostle had just made! It was not Peter, the erring, unstable man, but the mighty truth which the Father had revealed to Peter. It was the truth concerning Jesus Christ Himself which was the rock. It was Christ's Mediatorship, and Christ's Messiahship. It was the blessed truth that Jesus was the promised Saviour, the true Surety, the real Intercessor between God and man. This was the rock, and this the foundation, upon which the Church of Christ was to be built.

The foundation of the true Church was laid at a mighty cost. It needed that the Son of God should take our nature upon Him, and in that nature live, suffer, and die, not for His own sins, but for ours. It needed that in that nature Christ should go to the grave, and rise again. It needed that in that nature Christ should go up to heaven, to sit at the right hand of God, having obtained eternal redemption for all His people. No other foundation could have met the necessities of lost, guilty, corrupt, weak, helpless sinners.

That foundation, once obtained, is very strong. It can bear the weight of the sins of all the world. It has borne the weight of all the sins of all the believers who have built on it. Sins of thought, sins of the imagination, sins of the heart, sins of the head, sins which everyone has seen, and sins which no man knows, sins against God, and sins against man, sins of all kinds and descriptions--that mighty rock can bear the weight of all these sins, and not give way. The mediatorial office of Christ is a remedy sufficient for all the sins of all the world.

To this one foundation every member of Christ's true Church is joined. In many things believers are disunited and disagreed. In the matter of their soul's foundation they are all of one mind. Whether Episcopalians or Presbyterians, Baptists or Methodists, believers all meet at one point. They are all built on the rock. Ask where they get their peace, and hope, and joyful expectation of good things to come. You will find that all flows from that one mighty source, Christ the Mediator between God and man, and the office that Christ holds, as the High Priest and Surety of sinners.

Look to your foundation, if you would know whether or not you are a member of the one true Church. It is a point that may be known to yourself. Your public worship we can see; but we cannot see whether you are personally built upon the rock. Your attendance at the Lord's table we can see; but we cannot see whether you are joined to Christ, and one with Christ, and Christ in you. Take heed that you make no mistake about your own personal salvation. See that your own soul is upon the rock. Without this, all else is nothing. Without this, you will never stand in the day of judgment. Better a thousand times in that day to be found in a cottage "upon the rock," than in a palace upon the sand!

IV. I proceed in the fourth place to speak of the Implied Trials of the Church, to which our text refers. There is mention made of "the gates of hell." By that expression we are meant to understand the power of the prince of hell, even the devil. (Compare Psalm ix. 13; cvii. 18; Isa. xxxviii. 10.)

The history of Christ's true Church has always been one of conflict and war. It has been constantly assailed by a deadly enemy, Satan, the prince of this world. The devil hates the true Church of Christ with an undying hatred. He is ever stirring up opposition against all its members. He is ever urging the children of this world to do his will, and to injure and harass the people of God. If he cannot bruise the head, he will bruise the heel. If he cannot rob the believers of heaven, he will vex them by the way.

Warfare with the powers of hell has been the experience of the whole body of Christ for six thousand years. It has always been a bush burning, though not consumed--a woman fleeing into the wilderness, but not swallowed up. (Exod. iii. 2; Rev. xii. 6, 16.) The visible Churches have their times of prosperity and seasons of peace, but never has there been a time of peace for the true Church. Its conflict is perpetual. Its battle never ends.

Warfare with the powers of hell is the experience of every individual member of the true Church. Each has to fight. What are the lives of all the saints, but records of battles? What were such men as Paul, and James, and Peter, and John, and Polycarp, and Chrysostom, and Augustine, and Luther, and Calvin, and Latimer, and Baxter, but soldiers engaged in a constant warfare? Sometimes the persons of the saints have been assailed, and sometimes their property. Sometimes they have been harassed by calumnies and slanders, and sometimes by open persecution. But in one way or another the devil has been continually warring against the Church. The "gates of hell" have been continually assaulting the people of Christ.

We who preach the Gospel can hold out to all who come to Christ, "exceeding great and precious promises." (2 Pet. i. 4.) We can offer boldly to you, in our Master's name, the peace of God which passeth all understanding. Mercy, free grace, and full salvation, are offered to every one who will come to Christ, and believe on Him. But we promise you no peace with the world, or with the devil. We warn you, on the contrary, that there must be warfare so long as you are in the body. We would not keep you back, or deter you from Christ's service. But we would have you "count the cost," and fully understand what Christ's service entails. (Luke xiv. 28.)

(a) Marvel not at the enmity of the gates of hell. "If ye were of the world, the world would love his own." (John xv. 19.) So long as the world is the world, and the devil the devil, so long there must be warfare, and believers in Christ must be soldiers. The world hated Christ, and the world will hate true Christians, as long as the earth stands. As the great reformer, Luther, said, "Cain will go on murdering Abel so long as the Church is on earth."

(b) Be prepared for the enmity of the gates of hell. Put on the whole armour of God. The tower of David contains a thousand bucklers, all ready for the use of God's people. The weapons of our warfare have been tried by millions of poor sinners like ourselves, and have never been found to fail.

(c) Be patient under the enmity of the gates of hell. It is all working together for your good. It tends to sanctify. It will keep you awake. It will make you humble. It will drive you nearer to the Lord Jesus Christ. It will wean you from the world. It will help to make you pray more. Above all, it will make you long for heaven. It will teach you to say with heart as well as lips, "Come, Lord Jesus. Thy kingdom come."

(d) Be not cast down by the enmity of hell. The warfare of the true child of God is as much a mark of grace as the inward peace which he enjoys. No cross, no crown! No conflict, no saving Christianity! "Blessed are ye," said our Lord Jesus Christ, "when men shall revile you, and persecute you, and say all manner of evil against you falsely, for my sake." If you are never persecuted for religion's sake, and all men speak well of you, you may well doubt whether you belong to "the Church on the rock." (Matt. v. 11; Luke vi. 26.)

V. There remains one thing more to be considered--the Security of the true Church of Christ. There is a glorious promise given by the Builder, "The gates of hell shall not prevail."

He who cannot lie has pledged His word that all the powers of hell shall never overthrow His Church. It shall continue, and stand, in spite of every assault. It shall never be overcome. All other created things perish and pass away, but not the Church which is built on the rock.

Empires have risen and fallen in rapid succession. Egypt, Assyria, Babylon, Persia, Tyre, Carthage, Rome, Greece, Venice.--Where are all these now? They were all the creations of man's hand, and have passed away. But the true Church of Christ lives on.

The mightiest cities have become heaps of ruins. The broad walls of Babylon have sunk to the ground. The palaces of Nineveh are covered with mounds of dust. The hundred gates of Thebes are only matters of history. Tyre is a place where fishermen hang their nets. Carthage is a desolation. Yet all this time the true Church stands. The gates of hell do not prevail against it.

The earliest visible Churches have in many cases decayed and perished. Where is the Church of Ephesus and the Church of Antioch? Where is the Church of Alexandria and the Church of Constantinople? Where are the Corinthian, and Philippian, and Thessalonian Churches? Where, indeed, are they all? They departed from the Word of God. They were proud of their bishops, and synods, and ceremonies, and learning, and antiquity. They did not glory in the true cross of Christ. They did not hold fast the Gospel. They did not give the Lord Jesus His rightful office, or faith its rightful place. They are now among the things that have been. Their candlestick has been taken away. But all this time the true Church has lived on.

Has the true Church been oppressed in one country? It has fled to another.--Has it been trampled on and oppressed in one soil? It has taken root and flourished in some other climate.--Fire, sword, prisons, fines, penalties, have never been able to destroy its vitality. Its persecutors have died and gone to their own place, but the Word of God has lived, and grown, and multiplied. Weak as this true Church may appear to the eye of man, it is an anvil which has broken many a hammer in times past, and perhaps will break many more before the end. "He that lays hands on it, is touching the apple of his eye." (Zech. ii. 8.)

The promise of our text is true of the whole body of the true Church. Christ will never be without witness in the world. He has had a people in the worst of times. He had seven thousand in Israel even in the days of Ahab. There are some now, I believe, in dark places of the Roman and Greek Churches, who, in spite of much weakness, are serving Christ. The devil may rage horribly. The Church in some countries may be brought exceedingly low. But the gates of hell shall never entirely "prevail."

The promise of our text is true of every individual member of the Church. Some of God's people have been so much cast down and disquieted, that they have despaired of their safety. Some have fallen sadly, as David and Peter did. Some have departed from the faith for a time, like Cranmer and Jewell. Many have been tried by cruel doubts and fears. But all have got safe home at last, the youngest as well as the oldest, the weakest as well as the strongest.--And so it will be to the end. Can you prevent tomorrow's sun from rising? Can you prevent the tide in the Bristol Channel from ebbing and flowing? Can you prevent the planets moving in their respective orbits? Then, and then alone, can you prevent the salvation of any believer, however feeble--the final safety of any living stone in that Church which is built upon the rock, however small or insignificant that stone may appear.

The true Church is Christ's body. Not one bone in that mystical body shall ever be broken.--The true Church is Christ's bride. Those whom God has joined in everlasting covenant, shall never be put asunder.--The true Church is Christ's flock. When the lion came and took a lamb out of David's flock, David arose and delivered the lamb from his mouth. Christ will do the same. He is David's greater son. Not a single sick lamb in Christ's flock shall perish. He will say to His Father in the last day, "Of them which Thou gavest Me I have lost none." (John xviii. 9.)--The true Church is the wheat of the earth. It may be sifted, winnowed, buffeted, tossed to and fro. But not one grain shall! be lost. The tares and chaff shall be burned. The wheat shall be gathered into the barn.--The true Church is Christ's army. The Captain of our salvation loses none of His soldiers. His plans are never defeated. His supplies never fail. His muster-roll is the same at the end as it was at the beginning. Of the men that marched gallantly out of England many years ago in the Crimean war, how many ever came back! Regiments that went forth, strong and cheerful, with bands playing and banners flying, laid their bones in a foreign land and never returned to their native country. But it is not so with Christ's army. Not one of His soldiers shall be missing at last. He Himself declares, "They shall never perish." (John x. 28.)

The devil may cast some of the members of the true Church into prison. He may kill, and burn, and torture, and hang. But after he has killed the body, there is nothing more that he can do. He cannot hurt the soul. When the French troops took Rome years ago, they found on the walls of a prison cell, under the Inquisition, the words of a prisoner. Who he was, we know not. But his words are worthy of remembrance. "Though dead, he yet speaketh." He had written on the walls, very likely after an unjust trial and a still more unjust excommunication, the following striking words:--"Blessed Jesus, they cannot cast me out of Thy true Church." That record is true! Not all the power of Satan can cast out of Christ's true Church one single believer.

I trust that no reader of this paper will ever allow fear to prevent his beginning to serve Christ. He to whom you commit your soul has all power in heaven and earth, and He will keep you. He will never let you be cast away. Relatives may oppose. Neighbours may mock. The world may slander, and ridicule, and jest, and sneer. Fear not! Fear not! The powers of hell shall never prevail against your soul. Greater is He that is for you, than all they that are against you.

Fear not for the Church of Christ when ministers die, and saints are taken away. Christ can ever maintain His own cause. He will raise up better servants and brighter stars. The stars are all in His right hand. Leave off all anxious thought about the future. Cease to be cast down by the measures of statesmen, or the plots of wolves in sheep's clothing. Christ will ever provide for His own Church. Christ will take care that "The gates of hell shall not prevail against it." All is going on well, though our eyes may not see it. The kingdoms of this world shall yet become the kingdoms of our God, and of His Christ.

I will now conclude this paper with a few words of practical application.

(1) My first word of application shall be a question. What shall that question be? What shall I ask? I will return to the point with which I began. I will go back to the first sentence with which I opened my paper. I ask you, whether you are a member of the one true Church of Christ? Are you in the highest, the best sense, a "churchman" in the sight of God? You know now what I mean. I look far beyond the Church of England. I am not speaking of church or chapel. I speak of "the Church built upon the rock." I ask you, with all solemnity-- Are you a member of that Church? Are you joined to the great Foundation? Are you on the rock? Have you received the Holy Ghost? Does the Spirit witness with your spirit, that you are one with Christ, and Christ with you?--I beseech you, in the name of God, to lay to heart these questions, and to ponder them well. If you are not converted, you do not yet belong to the "Church of the Rock."

Let every reader of this paper take heed to himself, if he cannot give a satisfactory answer to my inquiry. Take heed, take heed, that you do not make shipwreck of your soul to all eternity. Take heed, lest at last the gates of hell prevail against you, the devil claim you as his own, and you be cast away for ever. Take heed, lest you go down to the pit from the land of Bibles, and in the full light of Christ's Gospel. Take heed, lest you are found at the left hand of Christ at last--a lost Episcopalian or a lost Presbyterian, a lost Baptist or a lost Methodist--lost because, with all your zeal for your own party and your own communion table, you never joined the one true Church.

(2) My second word of application shall be an invitation. I address it to every one who is not yet a true believer. I say to you, come and join the one true Church without delay. Come and join yourself to the Lord Jesus Christ in an everlasting covenant not to be forgotten.

Consider well what I say. I charge you solemnly not to mistake the meaning of my invitation. I do not bid you leave the visible Church to which you belong. I abhor all idolatry of forms and parties. I detest a proselytising spirit. But I do bid you come to Christ and be saved. The day of decision must come some time. Why not this very hour? Why not to-day, while it is called to-day?--Why not this very night, ere the sun rises to-morrow morning?-- Come to Him who died for sinners on the cross, and invites all sinners to come to Him by faith and be saved. Come to my Master, Jesus Christ. Come, I say, for all things are now ready. Mercy is ready for you. Heaven is ready for you. Angels are ready to rejoice over you. Christ is ready to receive you. Christ will receive you gladly, and welcome you among His children. Come into the ark.--The flood of God's wrath will soon break upon the earth; come into the ark and be safe.

Come into the lifeboat of the one true Church. This old world will soon break into pieces! Hear you not the tremblings of it? The world is but a wreck hard upon a sandbank. The night is far spent--the waves are beginning to rise--the wind is getting up--the storm will soon shatter the old wreck. But the lifeboat is launched, and we, the ministers of the Gospel, beseech you to come into the lifeboat and be saved.--We beseech you to arise at once and come to Christ.

Dost thou ask, "How can I come? My sins are too many. I am too wicked yet. I dare not come."--Away with the thought! It is a temptation of Satan. Come to Christ as a sinner. Come just as you are. Hear the words of that beautiful hymn:--

"Just as I am, without one plea,

But that Thy blood was shed for me,

And that Thou bid'st me come to Thee,

O Lamb of God I come."

This is the way to come to Christ. You should come waiting for nothing and tarrying for nothing. You should come as a hungry sinner to be filled--as a poor sinner to be enriched--as a bad, undeserving sinner to be clothed with righteousness. So coming, Christ would receive you. "Him that cometh" to Christ, He "will in no wise cast out." Oh I come, come to Jesus Christ. Come into "the true Church" by faith and be saved.

(3) Last of all, let me give a word of exhortation to all believers into whose hands this paper may fall.

Strive to live a holy life. Walk worthy of the Church to which you belong. Live like citizens of heaven. Let your light shine before men, so that the world may profit by your conduct. Let them know whose you are, and whom you serve. Be epistles of Christ, known and read of all men--written in such clear letters that none can say of you, "I know not whether this man be a member of Christ or not." He that knows nothing of real, practical holiness is no member of "the Church on the Rock,"

Strive to live a courageous life. Confess Christ before men. Whatever station you occupy, in that station confess Christ. Why should you be ashamed of Him? He was not ashamed of you on the cross. He is ready to confess you now before His Father in heaven. Why should you be ashamed of Him? Be bold. Be very bold. The good soldier is not ashamed of his uniform. The true believer ought never to be ashamed of Christ.

Strive to live a joyful life. Live like men who look for that blessed hope--the second coming of Jesus Christ. This is the prospect to which we should all look forward. It is not so much the thought of going to heaven as of heaven coming to us, that should fill our minds.

"There is a good time coming" for all the people of God--a good time for all the Church of Christ--a good time for all believers--a bad time for the impenitent and unbelieving, but a good time for true Christians. For that good time, let us wait, and watch, and pray.

The scaffolding will soon be taken down.--The last stone will soon be brought out.--The top-stone will be placed upon the edifice. Yet a little time, and the full beauty of the Church which Christ is building shall be clearly seen.

The great Master Builder will soon come Himself. A building shall be shown to assembled worlds in which there shall be no imperfection. The Saviour and the saved shall rejoice together. The whole universe shall acknowledge that in the building of Christ's Church all was well done. "Blessed"--it shall be said in that day, if it was never said before--"BLESSED ARE ALL THEY WHO BELONG TO THE CHURCH ON THE ROCK!"

XIV. VISIBLE CHURCHES WARNED

"He that hath an ear, let him hear what the Spirit saith unto the Churches."--Rev. iii. 22.

I SUPPOSE I may take it for granted that every reader of this paper belongs to some visible Church of Christ. I do not ask now whether you are an Episcopalian, or a Presbyterian, or an Independent. I only suppose that you would not like to be called an Atheist or an Infidel. You attend the public worship of some visible, particular, or national body of professing Christians.

Now, whatever the name of your Church may be, I invite your special attention to the verse of Scripture before your eyes. I charge you to remember that the words of that verse concern yourself. They are written for your learning, and for all who call themselves Christians. "He that hath an ear, let him hear what the Spirit saith unto the Churches."

This verse is repeated seven times over in the second and third chapters of the book of Revelation. Seven different letters does the Lord Jesus there send by the hand of His servant John to the seven Churches of Asia. Seven times over He winds up His letter by the same solemn words, "He that hath an ear, let him hear what the Spirit saith unto the Churches."

Now the Lord God is perfect in all His works. He does nothing by chance. He caused no part of the Scriptures to be written by chance. In all His dealings you may trace design, purpose and plan. There was design in the size and orbit of each planet. There was design in the shape and structure of the least fly's wing. There was design in every verse of the Bible. There was design in every repetition of a verse, wherever it took place. There was design in the sevenfold repetition of the verse before our eyes. It had a meaning, and we were intended to observe it.

This verse appears to me to call the special attention of all true Christians to the seven "Epistles to the Churches." I believe it was meant to make believers take particular notice of the things which these seven Epistles contain.

Let me try to point out certain leading truths which these seven Epistles seem to me to teach. They are truths for the times we live in--truths for the latter days--truths which we cannot know too well--truths which it would be good for us all to know and feel far better than we do.

I. I ask my readers to observe in the first place, that the Lord Jesus, in all the seven Epistles, speaks of nothing but matters of doctrine, practice, warning, and promise.

I ask you to look over these seven Epistles to the Churches, quietly and at your leisure, and you will soon see what I mean,

You will observe that the Lord Jesus sometimes finds fault with false doctrines, and ungodly, inconsistent practices, and rebukes them sharply.

You will observe that He sometimes praises faith, patience, work, labour, perseverance, and bestows on these graces high commendation.

You will sometimes find Him enjoining repentance, amendment, return to the first love, renewed application to Himself--and the like.

But I want you to observe that you will not find the Lord in any of the epistles dwelling upon Church government or ceremonies. He says nothing about sacraments or ordinances. He makes no mention of liturgies or forms. He does not instruct John to write one word about baptism, or the Lord's Supper, or the apostolical succession of ministers. In short, the leading principles of what may be called "the sacramental system" are not brought forward in any one of the seven epistles from first to last.

Now why do I dwell on this?--I do it because many professing Christians in the present day would have us believe these things are of first, of cardinal, of paramount importance.

There are not a few who seem to hold that there can be no Church without a bishop--and no godliness without a liturgy.--They appear to believe that to teach the value of the sacraments is the first work of a minister, and to keep to their parish church the first business of a people.

Now let no man misunderstand me when I say this. Do not run away with the notion that I see no importance in sacraments. On the contrary, I regard them as great blessings to all who receive them "rightly, worthily, and with faith." Do not fancy that I attach no value to Episcopacy, a liturgy, and the parochial system. On the contrary, I consider that a Church well-administered, which has these three things, and an Evangelical ministry, is a far more complete and useful Church than one in which they are not to be found.

But this I say, that sacraments, Church government, the use of a liturgy, the observance of ceremonies and forms, are all as nothing compared to faith, repentance, and holiness. And my authority for so saying is the whole tenor of our Lord's words to the seven Churches.

I never can believe, if a certain form of Church government was so important as some say, that the great Head of the Church would have said nothing about it here. I should have expected to have found something said about it to Sardis and Laodicea. But I find nothing at all. And I think that silence is a great fact.

I cannot help remarking just the same fact in Paul's parting words to the Ephesian elders. (Acts xx. 27-35.) He was then leaving them for ever. He was giving his last charge on earth, and spoke as one who would see the faces of his hearers no more. And yet there is not a word in the charge about the sacraments and Church government. If ever there was a time for speaking of them, it was then. But he says nothing at all; and I believe it was an intentional silence.

Now here lies one reason why we, who, rightly or wrongly, are called Evangelical clergy, do not preach about bishops, and the Prayer-book, and ordinances more than we do. It is not because we do not value them in their place, proportion, and way. We do value them as really and truly as any, and are thankful for them. But we believe that repentance toward God, faith toward our Lord Jesus Christ, and a holy conversation, are subjects of far more importance to men's souls. Without these no man can be saved. These are the first and most weighty matters, and therefore on these we dwell.

Here again lies one reason why we so often urge on men not to be content with the mere outward part of religion. You must have observed that we often warn you not to rest on Church membership and Church privileges. We tell you not to be satisfied all is right because you come to church on Sunday and come up to the Lord's table. We often urge you to remember that he is not a Christian who is one outwardly--that you must be "born again"--that you must have a "faith that worketh by love "--that there must be a "new creation" by the Spirit in your heart. We do it because this seems to us the mind of Christ. These are the kind of things He dwells upon, when writing seven times over to seven different Churches. We feel that if we follow Him we cannot greatly err.

I am aware that men charge us with taking "low views" of the subjects to which I have adverted. It is a small thing that our views are thought "low," so long as our consciences tell us they are Scriptural. High ground, as it is called, is not always safe ground. What Balaam said must be our answer, "What the Lord saith that will I speak." (Numbers xxiv. 13.)

The plain truth is, there are two distinct and separate systems of Christianity in England at the present day. It is useless to deny it. Their existence is a great fact and one that cannot be too clearly known.

According to one system, religion is a mere corporate business. You are to belong to a certain body of people. By virtue of your membership of this body, vast privileges, both for time and eternity, are conferred upon you. It matters little what you are and what you feel. You are not to try yourself by your feelings. You are a member of a great ecclesiastical corporation. Then all its privileges and immunities are your own. Do you belong to the one true, visible corporation? That is the grand question.

According to the other system, religion is eminently a personal business between yourself and Christ. It will not save your soul to be an outward member of any ecclesiastical body whatever, however sound that body may be. Such membership will not wash away one sin, or give you confidence in the day of judgment. There must be personal faith in Christ--personal dealings between yourself and God--personal felt communion between your own heart and the Holy Ghost. Have you this personal faith? Have you this felt work of the Spirit in your soul? This is the grand question. If not, you will be lost.

This last system is the system which those who are called Evangelical ministers cleave to and teach. They do so because they are satisfied that it is the system of Holy Scripture. They do so because they are convinced that any other system is productive of most dangerous consequences, and calculated to delude men fatally as to their actual state. They do so because they believe it to be the only system of teaching which God will bless, and that no Church will flourish so much as that in which repentance, faith, conversion, and the work of the Spirit are the grand subjects of the minister's sermon.

Once more I say, let us often look carefully over the seven "Epistles to the Churches."

II. I ask my readers, in the second place, to observe that in every epistle the Lord Jesus says, I know thy works.

That repeated expression is very striking. It is not for nothing that we read these words seven times over.

To one Church the Lord Jesus says, I know thy labour and patience--to another, thy tribulation and poverty--to a third, thy charity, and service, and faith. But to all, He uses the words I now dwell on: "I know thy works." It is not, "I know thy profession--thy desires--thy resolutions--thy wishes,"--but thy works. "I know thy works."

The works of a professing Christian are of great importance. They cannot save your soul. They cannot justify you. They cannot wipe out your sins. They cannot deliver you from the wrath of God. But it does not follow because they cannot save you, that they are of no importance. Take heed and beware of such a notion. The man who thinks so is fearfully deceived.

I often think I could willingly die for the doctrine of justification by faith without the deeds of the law. But I must earnestly contend, as a general principle, that a man's works are the evidence of a man's religion. If you call yourself a Christian, you must show it in your daily ways and daily behaviour. Call to mind that the faith of Abraham and of Rahab was proved by their works. (James ii. 21-25.) Remember it avails you and me nothing to profess we know God, if in works we deny Him. (Titus i. 16.) Remember the words of the Lord Jesus, "Every tree is known by its own fruit." (Luke vi. 44.)

But whatever the works of a professing Christian may be, Jesus says, "I know them!" "His eyes are in every place, beholding the evil and the good." (Prov. xv. 3.) You never did an action, however private, but Jesus saw it. You never spoke a word, no, not even in a whisper, but Jesus heard it. You never wrote a letter, even to your dearest friend, but Jesus read it. You never thought a thought, however secret, but Jesus was familiar with it. His eyes are as a flaming fire. The darkness is no darkness with Him. All things are open and manifest before Him. He says to every one, "I know thy works."

(a) The Lord Jesus knows the works of all impenitent and unbelieving souls, and will one day punish them. They are not forgotten in heaven, though they may be upon earth. When the great white throne is set, and the books are opened, the wicked dead will be judged "according to their works."

(b) The Lord Jesus knows the works of His own people, and weighs them. "By Him actions are weighed." (1 Sam. ii. 3.) He knows the why and the wherefore of the deeds of all believers. He sees their motives in every step they take. He discerns how much is done for His sake, and how much is done for the sake of praise. Alas! not a few things are done by believers which seem very good to you and me, but are rated very low by Christ.

(c) The Lord Jesus knows the works of all His own people, and will one day reward them. He never overlooks a kind word or a kind deed done in His name. He will own the least fruit of faith, and declare it before the world in the day of His appearing. If you love the Lord Jesus and follow Him, you may be sure your work and labour shall not be in vain in the Lord. The works of those that die in the Lord "shall follow them." (Rev. xiv. 13.) They shall not go before them, nor yet by their side, but they shall follow them, and be owned in the day of Christ's appearing. The parable of the pounds shall be made good. "Every man shall receive his own reward, according to his own labour." (1Cor. iii. 8.) The world knows you not, for it knows not your Master. But Jesus sees and knows all. "I know thy works."

Think what a solemn warning there is here to all worldly and hypocritical professors of religion. Let all such read, mark, and digest these words. Jesus says to you, "I know thy works." You may deceive me or any other minister; it is easy to do so. You may receive the bread and wine from my hands, and yet be cleaving to iniquity in your hearts. You may sit under the pulpit of an Evangelical preacher, week after week, and hear his words with a serious face, but believe them not. But remember this, you cannot deceive Christ. He who discovered the deadness of Sardis and the lukewarmness of Laodicea, sees you through and through, and will expose you at the last day, except you repent.

Oh! believe me, hypocrisy is a losing game. It will never answer to seem one thing and be another; to have the name of Christian, and not the reality. Be sure, if your conscience smites you and condemns you in this matter--be sure your sin will find you out. The eye that saw

Achan steal the golden wedge and hide it, is upon you. The book that recorded the deeds of Gehazi, and Ananias, and Sapphira, is recording your ways. Jesus mercifully sends you a word of warning to-day. He says, "I know thy works." But think also what encouragement there is here for every honest and true-hearted believer. To you also Jesus says, "I know thy works." You see no beauty in any action that you do. All seems imperfect, blemished, and defiled. You are often sick at heart of your own short-comings. You often feel that your whole life is one great arrear, and that every day is either a blank or a blot. But know now that Jesus can see some beauty in everything that you do from a conscientious desire to please Him. His eye can discern excellence in the least thing which is a fruit of His own Spirit. He can pick out the grains of gold from amidst the dross of your performances, and sift the wheat from amidst the chaff, in all your doings. Your tears are all put into His bottle. Your endeavours to do good to others, however feeble, are written in His book of remembrance. The least cup of cold water given in His name shall not lose its reward. He does not forget your work and labour of love, however little the world may regard it.

It is very wonderful; but so it is. Jesus loves to honour the work of His Spirit in His people, and to pass over their frailties. He dwells on the faith of Rahab, but not on her lie. He commends His Apostles for continuing with Him in His temptations, and passes over their ignorance and want of faith. (Luke xxii. 28.) "Like as a father pitieth his children, so the Lord pitieth them that fear Him." (Ps. ciii. 13.) And as a father finds a pleasure in the least acts of his children, of which a stranger knows nothing, so I suppose the Lord finds a pleasure in our poor feeble efforts to serve Him.

But it is all very wonderful. I can well understand the righteous in the day of judgment saying, "Lord, when saw we Thee an hungered and fed Thee, or thirsty and gave Thee drink? When saw we Thee a stranger, and took Thee in? or naked, and clothed Thee? Or when saw we Thee sick or in prison, and came unto Thee?" (Matt. xxv. 37-39.) It may well seem incredible and impossible that they can have done anything worth naming in the great day! Yet so it is. Let all believers take the comfort of it. The Lord says, "I know thy works." It ought to humble you. But it ought not to make you afraid.

III. I ask my readers to observe, in the third and last place, that in every epistle the Lord Jesus makes a promise to the man that overcomes.

Seven times over Jesus gives to the Churches exceeding great and precious promises. Each is different, and each full of strong consolation: but each is addressed to the overcoming Christian. It is always "he that overcometh," or "to him that overcometh." I ask you to take notice of this.

Every professing Christian is the soldier of Christ. He is bound by his baptism to fight Christ's battle against sin, the world, and the devil. The man that does not do this breaks his vow. He is a spiritual defaulter. He does not fulfil the engagements made for him. The man that does not do this is practically renouncing his Christianity. The very fact that he belongs to a Church, attends a Christian place of worship, and calls himself a Christian is a public declaration that he desires to be reckoned a soldier of Jesus Christ.

Armour is provided for the professing Christian, if he will only use it. "Take unto you," says Paul to the Ephesians, "the whole armour of God." "Stand, having your loins girt about with truth, and having on the breastplate of righteousness." "Take the helmet of salvation, and the sword of the Spirit, which is the Word of God." "Above all, take the shield of faith." (Ephes. vi. 13-17.) And not least, the professing Christian has the best of leaders: Jesus the

Captain of Salvation, through whom he may be more than conqueror--the best of provisions, the bread and water of life--and the best of pay promised to him: an eternal weight of glory.

All these are ancient things. I will not be drawn off from my subject in order to dwell on them now.

The one point I want to impress upon your soul just now is this, that the true believer is not only a soldier, but a victorious soldier.--He not only professes to fight on Christ's side against sin, the world, and the devil, but he does actually fight and overcome.

Now this is one. grand distinguishing mark of true Christians. Other men, perhaps, like to be numbered in the ranks of Christ's army. Other men may have lazy wishes, and languid desires after the crown of glory. But it is the true Christian alone who does the work of a soldier. He alone fairly meets the enemies of his soul--really fights with them, and in that fight overcomes them.

One great lesson I want men to learn from these seven epistles is this, that if you would prove you are born again and going to heaven, you must be a victorious soldier of Christ. If you would make it clear that you have any title to Christ's precious promises, you must fight the good fight in Christ's cause, and in that fight you must conquer.

Victory is the only satisfactory evidence that you have a saving religion. You like good sermons perhaps. You respect the Bible, and read it occasionally. You say your prayers night and morning. You have family prayers, and give to Religious Societies. I thank God for this. It is an very good. But how goes the battle? How does the great conflict go on all this time? Are you overcoming the love of the world and the fear of man? Are you overcoming the passions, tempers, and lusts of your own heart? Are you resisting the devil and making him flee from you? How is it in this matter? You must either rule or serve sin, and the devil, and the world. There is no middle course. You must either conquer or be lost.

I know well it is a hard battle that you have to fight, and I want you to know it too. You must fight the good fight of faith, and endure hardships, if you would lay hold of eternal life. You must make up your mind to a daily struggle, if you would reach heaven. There may be short roads to heaven invented by man; but ancient Christianity, the good old way, is the way of the cross--the way of conflict. Sin, the world, and the devil must be actually mortified, resisted, and overcome.

This is the road that saints of old have trodden in, and left their record on high.

(a) When Moses refused the pleasures of sin in Egypt, and chose affliction with the people of God--this was overcoming: he overcame the love of pleasure.

(b) When Micaiah refused to prophesy smooth things to king Ahab, though he knew he would be persecuted if he spoke the truth--this was overcoming: he overcame the love of ease.

(c) When Daniel refused to give up praying, though he knew the den of lions was prepared for him--this was overcoming: he overcame the fear of death.

(d) When Matthew rose from the receipt of custom at our Lord's bidding, left all and followed Him--this was overcoming: he overcame the love of money.

(e) When Peter and John stood up boldly before the council and said, "We cannot but speak the things we have seen and heard"--this was overcoming: they overcame the fear of man.

(f) When Saul the Pharisee gave up all his prospects of preferment among the Jews, and preached that very Jesus whom he had once persecuted--this was overcoming: he overcame the love of man's praise.

The same kind of thing which these men did you must also do if you would be saved. They were men of like passions with yourself, and yet they overcame. They had as many trials as you can possibly have, and yet they overcame. They fought. They wrestled. They struggled. You must do the same.

What was the secret of their victory?--their faith. They believed on Jesus, and believing were made strong. They believed on Jesus, and believing were held up. In all their battles, they kept their eyes on Jesus, and He never left them nor forsook them. "They overcame by the blood of the Lamb, and the word of their testimony," and so may you. (Rev. xii. 11.)

I set these words before you. I ask you to lay them to heart. Resolve, by the grace of God, to be an overcoming Christian.

I fear much for many professing Christians. I see no sign of fighting in them, much less of victory. They never strike one stroke on the side of Christ. They are at peace with His enemies. They have no quarrel with sin.--I warn you, this is not Christianity. This is not the way to heaven.

I often fear much for those who hear the Gospel regularly, i fear lest you become so familiar with the sound of its doctrines, that insensibly you become dead to its power. I fear lest your religion should sink down into a little vague talk about your own weakness and corruption, and a few sentimental expressions about Christ, while real, practical fighting on Christ's side is altogether neglected. Oh! beware of this state of mind. "Be doers of the word, and not hearers only." No victory--no crown! Fight and overcome! (James i. 22.)

Young men and women, and specially those who have been brought up in religious families, I fear much for you. I fear lest you get a habit of giving way to every temptation. I fear lest you become afraid of saying, "No!" to the world and the devil--and, when sinners entice you, think it least trouble to consent. Beware, I do beseech you, of giving way. Every concession will make you weaker. Go into the world resolved to fight Christ's battle--and fight your way on.

Believers in the Lord Jesus, of every Church and rank in life, I feel much for you. I know your course is hard. I know it is a sore battle you have to fight. I know you are often tempted to say, "It is of no use," and to lay down your arms altogether.

Cheer up, dear brethren and sisters. Take comfort, I entreat you. Look at the bright side of your position. Be encouraged to fight on. The time is short. The Lord is at hand. The night is far spent. Millions as weak as you have fought the same fight. Not one of all those millions has been finally led captive by Satan. Mighty are your enemies--but the Captain of your salvation is mightier still.--His arm, His grace, and His Spirit shall hold you up. Cheer up. Be not cast down.

What though you lose a battle or two? You shall not lose all. What though you faint sometimes? You shall not be quite cast down. What though you fall seven times? You shall not be destroyed. Watch against sin, and sin shall not have dominion over you. Resist the devil, and he shall flee from you. Come out boldly from the world, and the world shall be obliged to let you go. You shall find yourselves in the end more than conquerors--you shall "overcome."

Let me draw from the whole subject a few words of application, and then I have done.

(1) For one thing, let me warn all who are living only for the world, to take heed what they are doing. You are enemies to Christ, though you may not know it. He marks your ways, though you turn your backs on Him, and refuse to give Him your hearts. He is observing your daily life, and reading your daily ways. There will yet be a resurrection of all your thoughts, words and actions. You may forget them, but God does not. You may be careless about them, but they are carefully marked down in the book of remembrance. Oh! worldly man, think of this! Tremble, tremble and repent.

(2) For another thing, let me warn all formalists and self-righteous people to take heed that they are not deceived. You fancy you will go to heaven because you go regularly to church. You indulge an expectation of eternal life, because you are always at the Lord's table, and are never missing in your pew. But where is your repentance? Where is your faith? Where are your evidences of a new heart? Where is the work of the Spirit? Where are your evidences of regeneration? Oh, formal Christian, consider these questions! Tremble, tremble and repent.

(3) For another thing, let me warn all careless members of Churches to beware lest they trifle their souls into hell. You live on year after year as if there was no battle to be fought with sin, the world, and the devil. You pass through life a smiling, laughing, gentlemanlike or lady-like person, and behave as if there was no devil, no heaven, and no hell. Oh, careless Churchman, or careless Dissenter, careless Episcopalian, careless Presbyterian, careless Independent, careless Baptist, awake to see eternal realities in their true light! Awake and put on the armour of God! Awake and fight hard for life! Tremble, tremble and repent.

(4) For another thing, let me warn every one who wants to be saved, not to be content with the world's standard of religion. Surely, no man with his eyes open can fail to see that the Christianity of the New Testament is something far higher and deeper than the Christianity of most professing Christians. The formal, easy-going, do-little thing which most people call religion, is evidently not the religion of the Lord Jesus. The things that He praises in these seven Epistles are not praised by the world. The things that He blames are not things in which the world sees any harm. Oh, if you would follow Christ, be not content with the world's Christianity! Tremble, tremble and repent.

(5) In the last place, let me warn every one who professes to be a believer in the Lord Jesus, not to be content with a little religion.

Of all sights in the Church of Christ, I know none more painful to my own eyes than a Christian contented and satisfied with a little grace, a little repentance, a little faith, a little knowledge, a little charity, and a little holiness. I do beseech and entreat every believing soul that reads this tract not to be that kind of man. If you have any desires after usefulness--if you have any wishes to promote your Lord's glory--if you have any longings after much inward peace--be not content with a little religion.

Let us rather seek, every year we live, to make more spiritual progress than we have done--to grow in grace, and in the knowledge of the Lord Jesus--to grow in humility and self-acquaintance--to grow in spirituality and heavenly-mindedness--to grow in conformity to the image of our Lord.

Let us beware of leaving our first love like Ephesus--of becoming lukewarm like Laodicea--of tolerating false practices like Pergamos--of tampering with false doctrine like Thyatira--of becoming half dead, ready to die, like Sardis.

Let us rather covet the best gifts. Let us aim at eminent holiness. Let us endeavour to be like Smyrna and Philadelphia. Let us hold fast what we have already, and continually seek to have more. Let us labour to be unmistakable Christians. Let it not be our distinctive character that we are men of science--or men of literary attainments--or men of the world--or men of pleasure, or men of business--but "men of God." Let us so live that all may see that to us the things of God are the first things, and the glory of God the first aim in our lives--to follow Christ our grand object in time present--to be with Christ our grand desire in time to come.

Let us live in this way, and we shall be happy. Let us live in this way, and we shall do good to the world. Let us live in this way, and we shall leave good evidence behind us when we are buried. Let us live in this way, and the Spirit's word to the Churches will not have been spoken to us in vain.

XV. "LOVEST THOU ME?"

"Lovest thou Me?"--John xxi. 16.

THE question which heads this paper was addressed by Christ to the Apostle Peter. A more important question could not be asked. Nineteen hundred years have passed away since the words were spoken. But to this very day the inquiry is most searching and useful.

A disposition to love somebody is one of the commonest feelings which God has implanted in human nature. Too often, unhappily, people set their affection on unworthy objects. I want this day to claim a place for Him who alone is worthy of all our hearts' best feelings. I want men to give some of their love to that Divine Person who loved us, and gave Himself for us. In all their loving, I would have them not forget TO LOVE CHRIST.

Suffer me to press this mighty subject upon the attention of every reader of this paper. This is no matter for mere enthusiasts and fanatics. It deserves the consideration of every reasonable Christian who believes the Bible. Our very salvation is bound up with it. Life or death, heaven or hell, depend on our ability to answer the simple question "Do you love Christ? "

There are two points which I wish to bring forward in opening up this subject.

I. In the first place, let me show the peculiar feeling of a true Christian towards Christ--he loves Him.

A true Christian is not a mere baptized man or woman. He is something more. He is not a person who only goes, as a matter of form, to a church or chapel on Sundays and lives all the rest of the week as if there was no God. Formality is not Christianity. Ignorant lip-worship is not true religion. The Scripture speaketh expressly: "They are not all Israel which are of Israel." (Rom. ix. 6.) The practical lesson of those words is clear and plain. All are not true Christians who are members of the visible Church of Christ.

The true Christian is one whose religion is in his heart and life. It is felt by himself in his heart. It is seen by others in his conduct and life. He feels his sinfulness, guilt and badness, and repents. He sees Jesus Christ to be that Divine Saviour whom his soul needs, and commits himself to Him. He puts off the old man with his corrupt and carnal habits and puts on the new man. He lives a new and holy life, fighting habitually against the world, the flesh and the devil. Christ Himself is the corner-stone of his Christianity. Ask him in what he trusts for the forgiveness of his many sins, and he will tell you in the death of Christ.--Ask him in what righteousness he hopes to stand innocent at the judgment day, and he will tell you it is the righteousness of Christ.--Ask him by what pattern he tries to frame his life, and he will tell you that it is the example of Christ.

But, beside all this, there is one thing in a true Christian which is eminently peculiar to him. That thing is love to Christ. Knowledge, faith, hope, reverence, obedience, are all marked features in a true Christian's character. But his picture would be very imperfect if you omitted his "love" to his Divine Master. He not only knows, trusts, and obeys. He goes further than this--he loves.

This peculiar mark of a true Christian is one which we find mentioned several times in the Bible. "Faith toward our Lord Jesus Christ" is an expression which many Christians are familiar with. Let it never be forgotten that love is mentioned by the Holy Ghost in almost as strong terms as faith. Great as the danger is of him "that believeth not," the danger of him that "loveth not" is equally great. Not believing and not loving are both steps to everlasting ruin.

Hear what St. Paul says to the Corinthians: "If any man love not the Lord Jesus Christ, let him be Anathema Maran-atha." (1 Cor. 22.) St. Paul allows no way of escape to the man who does not love Christ. He leaves him no loophole or excuse. A man may lack clear head-knowledge and yet be saved. He may fail in courage and be overcome by the fear of man, like Peter. He may fall tremendously, like David, and yet rise again. But if a man does not love Christ he is not in the way of life. The curse is yet upon him. He is on the broad road that leadeth to destruction.

Hear what St. Paul says to the Ephesians, "Grace be with all them that love our Lord Jesus Christ in sincerity." (Eph. vi. 24.) The Apostle is here sending his good wishes, and declaring his good will to all true Christians. Many of them, no doubt, he had never seen. Many of them in the early Churches, we may be very sure, were weak in faith, and knowledge, and self-denial. How, then, shall he describe them in sending his message? What words can he use which will not discourage the weaker brethren? He chooses a sweeping expression which exactly describes all true Christians under one common name. All had not attained to the same degree, whether in doctrine or practice. But all loved Christ in sincerity.

Hear what our Lord Jesus Christ Himself says to the Jews, "If God were your Father, ye would love Me." (John viii. 42.) He saw His misguided enemies satisfied with their spiritual condition, on the one single ground that they were children of Abraham. He saw them, like many ignorant Christians of our own day, claiming to be God's children for no better reasons than this: that they were circumcised and belonged to the Jewish Church. He lays down the broad principle that no man is a child of God who does not love God's only begotten Son. No man has a right to call God "Father" who does not love Christ. Well would it be for many Christians if they were to remember that this mighty principle applies to them as well as to the Jews. No love to Christ--then no sonship to God I

Hear once more what our Lord Jesus Christ said to the Apostle Peter after He rose from the dead. Three times He asked him the question, "Simon, son of Jonas, lovest thou Me." (John xxi. 15-17.) The occasion was remarkable. He meant gently to remind His erring disciple of His thrice-repeated fall. He desired to call forth from him a new confession of faith before publicly restoring to him his commission to feed the Church. And what was the question that He asked him? He might have said:--"Believest thou? Art thou converted? Are thou ready to confess Me? Wilt thou obey Me?" He uses none of these expressions. He simply says, "lovest thou Me?" This is the point, He would have us know, on which a man's Christianity hinges. Simple as the question sounded, it was most searching. Plain and easy to be understood by the most unlearned poor man, it contains matter which tests the reality of the most advanced apostle. If a man truly loves Christ, all is right--if not, all is wrong.

Would you know the secret of this peculiar feeling towards Christ which distinguishes the true Christian? You have it in the words of St. John, "We love Him because He first loved us." (1 John iv. 19.) That text, no doubt, applies specially to God the Father. But it is no less true of God the Son.

A true Christian loves Christ for all He has done for him. He has suffered in his stead, and died for him on the cross. He has redeemed him from the guilt, the power, and the consequences of sin, by His blood. He has called him by His Spirit to self-knowledge, repentance, faith, hope, and holiness. He has forgiven all his many sins and blotted them out. He has freed him from the captivity of the world, the flesh, and the devil. He has taken him from the brink of hell, placed him in the narrow way, and set his face toward heaven. He has given him light instead of darkness, peace of conscience instead of uneasiness, hope instead of uncertainty, life instead of death. Can you wonder that the true Christian loves Christ?

And he loves Him besides, for all that He is still doing. He feels that He is daily washing away his many shortcomings and infirmities, and pleading his soul's cause before God. He is daily supplying all the needs of his soul, and providing him with an hourly provision of mercy and grace. He is daily leading him by His Spirit to a city of habitation, bearing with him when he is weak and ignorant, raising him up when he stumbles and falls, protecting him against his many enemies, preparing an eternal home for him in heaven. Can you wonder that the true Christian loves Christ?

Does the debtor in jail love the friend who unexpectedly and undeservedly pays all his debts, supplies him with fresh capital, and takes him into partnership with himself? Does the prisoner in war love the man who at the risk of his own life breaks through the enemy's lines, rescues him, and sets him free? Does the drowning sailor love the man who plunges into the sea, dives after him, catches him by the hair of his head, and by a mighty effort saves him from a watery grave? A very child can answer such questions as these. Just in the same way, and upon the same principles, a true Christian loves Jesus Christ.

(a) This love to Christ is the inseparable companion of saving faith. A faith of devils, a mere intellectual faith, a man may have without love, but not that faith which saves. Love cannot usurp the office of faith. It cannot justify. It does not join the soul to Christ. It cannot bring peace to the conscience. But where there is real justifying faith in Christ, there will always be heart-love to Christ. He that is really forgiven is the man who will really love. (Luke vii. 47.) If a man has no love to Christ, you may be sure he has no faith.

(b) Love to Christ is the mainspring of work for Christ. There is little done for His cause on earth from sense of duty, or from knowledge of what is right and proper. The heart must be interested before the hands will move and continue moving. Excitement may galvanize the Christian's hands into a fitful and spasmodic activity. But there will be no patient continuance in well-doing, no unwearied labour in missionary work at home or abroad, without love. The nurse in a hospital may do her duty properly and well, may give the sick man his medicine at the right time, may feed him, minister to him, and attend to all his wants. But there is a vast difference between that nurse and a wife tending the sick-bed of a beloved husband, or a mother watching over a dying child. The one acts from a sense of duty--the other from affection and love. The one does her duty because she is paid for it--the other is what she is because of her heart. It is just the same in the matter of the service of Christ. The great workers of the Church--the men who have led forlorn hopes in the mission-field and turned the world upside down, have all been eminently lovers of Christ.

Examine the characters of Owen and Baxter, of Rutherford and George Herbert, of Leighton and Hervey, of Whitfield and Wesley, of Henry Martyn and Judson, of Bickersteth and Simeon, of Hewitson and M'Cheyne, of Stowell and M'Neile. These men have left a mark on the world. And what was the common feature of their characters? They all loved Christ. They not only held a creed. They loved a Person, even the Lord Jesus Christ.

(c) Love to Christ is the point which we ought specially to dwell upon in teaching religion to children. Election, imputed righteousness, original sin, justification, sanctification, and even faith itself, are matters which sometimes puzzle a child of tender years. But love to Jesus seems far more within reach of their understanding. That He loved them even to His death, and that they ought to love Him in return, is a creed which meets the span of their minds. How true it is that "out of the mouths of babes and sucklings Thou hast perfected praise!" (Matt. xxi. 16.) There are myriads of Christians who know every article of the Athanasian, Nicene, and Apostolic Creeds, and yet know less of real Christianity than a little child who only knows that he loves Christ.

(d) Love to Christ is the common meeting-point of believers of every branch of Christ's Church on earth. Whether Episcopalian or Presbyterian, Baptist or Independent, Calvinist or Arminian, Methodist or Moravian, Lutheran or Reformed, Established or Free--here, at least, they are agreed. About forms and ceremonies, about Church government and modes of worship, they often differ widely. But on one point, at any rate, they are united. They have all one common feeling towards Him on whom they build their hope of salvation. They "love the Lord Jesus Christ in sincerity." (Ephes. vi. 24.) Many of them, perhaps, are ignorant of systematic divinity and could argue but feebly in defence of their creed. But they all know what they feel toward Him who died for their sins.--"I cannot speak much for Christ, sir," said an old, uneducated Christian woman to Dr. Chalmers; "but if I cannot speak for Him, I could die for Him!"

(e) Love to Christ will be the distinguishing mark of all saved souls in heaven. The multitude which no man can number will all be of one mind. Old differences will be merged in one common feeling. Old doctrinal peculiarities, fiercely wrangled for upon earth, will be covered over by one common sense of debt to Christ. Luther and Zwingle will no longer dispute. Wesley and Toplady will no longer waste time in controversy. Churchmen and Dissenters will no longer bite and devour one another. All will find themselves joining with one heart and voice in that hymn of praise, "Unto Him that loved us, and washed us from our sin in His own blood, and hath made us kings and priests unto God and his Father; to Him be glory and dominion for ever and ever. Amen." (Rev. i. 5-6.)

The words which John Bunyan puts in the mouth of Mr. Standfast as he stood in the river of death are very beautiful. He said, "This river has been a terror to many; yea, the thoughts of it also have often frightened me. But now methinks I stand easy: my foot is fixed upon that on which the priests that bear the ark stood while Israel went over Jordan. The waters indeed are to the palate bitter, and to the stomach cold; yet the thoughts of what I am going to, and of the convoy that waits for me on the other side, lie as a glowing coal at my heart. I see myself now at the end of my journey; my toilsome days are ended. I am going to see that Head which was crowned with thorns, and that Face which was spit upon for me. I have formerly lived by hearing and faith, but now I go where I shall live by sight, and be with Him in whose company I delight myself. I have loved to hear my Lord spoken of; and wherever I have seen the print of His shoe in the earth, there I have coveted to set my foot too. His name has been to me a civet-box; yea, sweeter than all perfumes! His voice to me has been most sweet; and His countenance I have more desired than they that have desired the light of the sun!" Happy are they that know something of this experience! He that would be in tune for heaven must know something of love to Christ. He that dies ignorant of that love had better never have been born.

II. Let me show, in the second place, the peculiar marks by which love to Christ makes itself known.

The point is one of vast importance. If there is no salvation without love to Christ--if he that does not love Christ is in peril of eternal condemnation, it becomes us all to find out very distinctly what we know about this matter. Christ is in heaven, and we are upon earth. In what way shall the man be discerned that loves Him?

Happily the point is one which it is not very hard to settle. How do we know whether we love any person here upon earth? In what way and manner does love show itself between people in this world--between husband and wife--between parent and child--between brother and sister--between friend and friend? Let these questions be answered by common sense and observations, and I ask no more. Let these questions be honestly answered, and the knot before us is untied. How does affection show itself among ourselves?

(a) If we love a person, we like to think about him. We do not need to be reminded of him. We do not forget his name, or his appearance, or his character, or his opinions, or his tastes, or his position, or his occupation. He comes up before our mind's eye many a time in the day. Though perhaps far distant, he is often present in our thoughts. Well, it is just so between the true Christian and Christ! Christ "dwells in his heart," and is thought of more or less every day. (Ephes. iii. 17.) The true Christian does not need to be reminded that he has a crucified Master. He often thinks of Him. He never forgets that He has a day, a cause, and a people, and that of His people he is one. Affection is the real secret of a good memory in religion. No worldly man can think much about Christ, unless Christ is pressed upon his notice, because he has no affection for Him. The true Christian has thoughts about Christ every day that he lives, for this one simple reason, that he loves Him.

(b) If we love a person, we like to hear about him. We find a pleasure in listening to those who speak of him. We feel an interest in any report which others make of him. We are all attention when others talk about him and describe his ways, his sayings, his doings, and his plans. Some may hear him mentioned with utter indifference, but our own hearts bound within us at the very sound of his name. Well, it is just so between the true Christian and Christ! The true Christian delights to hear something about his Master. He likes those sermons best which are full of Christ. He enjoys that society most in which people talk of the things which are Christ's. I have read of an old Welsh believer who used to walk several miles every Sunday to hear an English clergyman preach, though she did not understand a word of English. She was asked why she did so. She replied that this clergyman named the name of Christ so often in his sermons that it did her good. She loved even the name of her Saviour.

(c) If we love a person, we like to read about him. What intense pleasure a letter from an absent husband gives to a wife, or a letter from an absent son to his mother. Others may see little worth notice in the letter. They can scarcely take the trouble to read it through. But those who love the writer see something in the letter which no one else can. They carry it about with them as a treasure. They read it over and over again. Well, it is just so between the true Christian and Christ! The true Christian delights to read the Scriptures, because they tell him about his beloved Saviour. It is no wearisome task with him to read them. He rarely needs remind ing to take his Bible with him when he goes a journey. He cannot be happy without it. And why is all this? It is because the Scriptures testify of Him whom his soul loves, even Christ.

(d) If we love a person, we like to please him. We are glad to consult his tastes and opinions, to act upon his advice, and do the things which he approves. We even deny ourselves to meet his wishes, abstain from things which we know he dislikes, and learn things to do which we are not naturally inclined, because we think it will give him pleasure. Well, it is just so between the true Christian and Christ! The true Christian studies to please Him, by being holy both in body and spirit. Show him anything in his daily practice that Christ hates, and he will give it up. Show him anything that Christ delights in, and he will follow after it. He does not murmur at Christ's requirements as being too strict and severe, as the children of the world do. To him Christ's commandments are not grievous and Christ's burden is light. And why is all this? Simply because he loves Him.

(e) If we love a person, we like his friends. We are favourably inclined to them, even before we know them. We are drawn to them by the common tie of common love to one and the same person. When we meet them we do not feel that we are altogether strangers. There is a bond of union between us. They love the person that we love, and that alone is an introduction. Well, it is just so between the true Christian and Christ! The true Christian regards all Christ's friends as his friends, members of the same body, children of the same family, soldiers in the same army, travellers to the same home. When he meets them, he feels as if he had long known them. He is more at home with them in a few minutes than he is with many worldly people after an acquaintance of several years. And what is the secret of all this? It is simply affection to the same Saviour, and love to the same Lord.

(f) If we love a person, we are jealous about his name and honour. We do not like to hear him spoken against without speaking up for him and defending him. We feel bound to maintain his interests and his reputation. We regard the person who treats him ill with almost as much disfavour as if he had ill-treated us. Well, it is just so between the true Christian and Christ. The true Christian regards with a godly jealousy all efforts to disparage his Master's word, or name, or Church, or day. He will confess Him before princes, if need be, and be sensitive of the least dishonour put upon Him. He will not hold his peace and suffer his Master's cause to be put to shame without testifying against it. And why Is all this? Simply because he loves Him.

(g) If we love a person, we like to talk to him. We tell him all our thoughts, and pour out all our heart to him. We find no difficulty in discovering subjects of conversation. However silent and reserved we may be to others, we find it easy to talk to a much-loved friend. However often we may meet, we are never at a loss for matter to talk about. We have always much to say, much to ask about, much to describe, much to communicate. Well, it is just so between the true Christian and Christ! The true Christian finds no difficulty in speaking to his Saviour. Every day he has something to tell Him, and he is not happy unless he tells it. He speaks to Him in prayer every morning and night. He tells Him his wants and desires, his feelings and his fears. He asks counsel of Him in difficulty. He asks comfort of Him in trouble. He cannot help it. He must converse with his Saviour continually, or he would faint by the way. And why is this? Simply because he loves Him.

(h) Finally, if we love a person, we like to be always with him. Thinking, and hearing, and reading, and occasionally talking are all well in their way. But when we really love people we want something more. We long to be always in their company. We wish to be continually in their society, and to hold communion with them without interruption or farewell. Well, it is just so between the true Christian and Christ. The heart of a true Christian longs for that blessed day when he will see his Master face to face, and go out no more. He longs to have done with sinning and repenting, and believing, and to begin that endless life when he shall see as he has been seen, and sin no more. He has found it sweet to live by faith, and he feels it will be sweeter still to live by sight. He has found it pleasant to hear of Christ, and talk of Christ, and read of Christ. How much more pleasant will it be to see Christ with his own eyes, and never to leave Him any more! "Better," he feels, "is the sight of the eyes than the wandering of the desires" (Eccles. vi. 9.) And why is all this? Simply because he loves Him.

Such are the marks by which true love may be discovered. They are all plain, simple, and easy to be understood. There is nothing dark, abstruse, and mysterious about them. Use them honestly, and handle them fairly, and you cannot fail to get some light on the subject of this paper.

Perhaps you had a beloved son in the army at the time of a great war. Perhaps he was actively engaged in that war, and in the very midst of the struggle. Cannot you remember how strong, and deep, and anxious your feelings were about that son?--That was love!

Perhaps you have known what it is to have a beloved husband in the navy, often called from home by duty, often separated from you for many months and even years. Cannot you recollect your sorrowful feelings at that time of separation?--That was love!

Perhaps you have at this moment a beloved brother in London, launched for the first time amidst the temptations of a great city, in order to make his way in business. How will he turn out? How will he get on? Will you ever see him again? Do you not know that you often think about that brother?--That is affection!

Perhaps you are engaged to be married to a person every way suited to you. But prudence makes it necessary to defer the marriage to a distant period, and duty makes it necessary to be at a distance from the one you have promised to make your wife. Must you not confess that she is often in your thoughts?--Must you not confess that you like to hear of her, and hear from her, and that you long to see her?--That is affection!

I speak of things that are familiar to everyone. I need not dwell upon them any further. They are as old as the hills. They are understood all over the world. There is hardly a branch of Adam's family that does not know something of affection and love. Then let it never be said that we cannot find out whether a Christian really loves Christ. It can be known; it may be discovered; the proofs are all ready to your hand. You have heard them this very day. Love to the Lord Jesus Christ is no hidden, secret, impalpable thing. It is like the light--it will be seen. It is like sound--it will be heard. It is like heat--it will be felt. Where it exists it cannot be hid. Where it cannot be seen you may be sure there is none.

It is time for me to draw this paper to a conclusion. But I cannot end without an effort to press its subject home to the individual conscience of each into whose hands it has fallen. I do it in all love and affection. My heart's desire and prayer to God, in writing this paper, is to do good to souls.

1. Let me ask you, for one thing, to look the question in the face which Christ asked of Peter, and try to answer it for yourself. Look at it seriously. Examine it carefully. Weigh it well. After reading all that I have said about it, can you honestly say that you love Christ?

It is no answer to tell me that you believe the truth of Christianity, and hold the articles of the Christian faith. Such religion as this will never save your soul. The devils believe in a certain way, and tremble. (James ii. 19.) True, saving Christianity is not the mere believing a certain set of opinions, and holding a certain set of notions. Its essence is knowing, trusting, and loving a certain living Person who died for us--even Christ the Lord. The early Christians, like Phoebe, and Persis, and Tryphena, and Tryphosa, and Gaius, and Philemon, knew little, probably, of dogmatic theology. But they all had this grand leading feature in their religion, they loved Christ.

It is no answer to tell me that you disapprove of a religion of feelings. If you mean by that that you dislike a religion consisting of nothing but feelings, I agree with you entirely. But if you mean to shut out feelings altogether, you can know little of Christianity. The Bible teaches us plainly that a man may have good feelings without any true religion. But it teaches us no less plainly that there can be no true religion without some feeling towards Christ.

It is vain to conceal that if you do not love Christ, your soul is in great danger. You can have no saving faith now while you live. You are unfit for heaven if you die. He that lives without love to Christ can be sensible of no obligation to Him. He that dies without love to Christ could never be happy in that heaven where Christ is all, and in all. Awake to know the peril of your position. Open your eyes. Consider your ways, and be wise. I can only warn you as a friend. But I do it with all my heart and soul. May God grant that this warning may not be in vain!

2. In the next place, if you do not love Christ, let me tell you plainly what is the reason. You have no sense of debt to Him. You have no feeling of obligation to Him. You have no abiding recollection of having got anything from Him. This being the case it is not likely, it is not probable, it is not reasonable that you should love Him.

There is but one remedy for this state of things. That remedy is self-knowledge, and the teaching of the Holy Ghost. The eyes of your understanding must be opened. You must find out what you are by nature. You must discover that grand secret, your guilt and emptiness in God's sight.

Perhaps you never read your Bible at all, or only read an occasional chapter as a mere matter of form, without interest, understanding, or self-application. Take my advice this day, and change your plan. Begin to read the Bible like a man in earnest, and never rest till you become familiar with it. Read what the law of God requires, as expounded by the Lord Jesus in the fifth of St. Matthew. Read how St. Paul describes human nature in the first two chapters of his Epistle to the Romans. Study such passages as these with prayer for the Spirit's teaching, and then say whether you are not a debtor to God and a debtor in mighty need of a Friend like Christ.

Perhaps you are one who has never known anything of real, hearty, business-like prayer. You have been used to regard religion as an affair of churches, chapels, forms, services, and Sundays, but not as a thing requiring the serious, heartfelt attention of the inward man. Take my advice this day and change your plan. Begin the habit of real, earnest pleading with God about your soul. Ask Him for light, teaching, and self-knowledge. Beseech Him to show you anything you need to know for the saving of your soul. Do this with all your heart and mind, and I have no doubt that before long you will feel your need of Christ.

The advice I offer may seem simple and old-fashioned. Do not despise it on that account. It is the good old way in which millions have walked already and found peace to their souls. Not to love Christ is to be in imminent danger of eternal ruin. To see your need of Christ and your amazing debt to Christ is the first step towards loving Him. To know yourself and find out your real condition before God is the only way to see your need. To search God's Book and ask God for light in prayer is the right course by which to attain saving knowledge. Do not be above taking the advice I offer. Take it and be saved.

(3) In the last place, if you really know anything of love towards Christ, accept two parting words of comfort and counsel. The Lord grant they may do you good.

For one thing, if you love Christ in deed and truth, rejoice in the thought that you have good evidence about the state of your soul. Love, I tell you this day, is an evidence of grace.

What though you are sometimes perplexed with doubts and fears? What though you find it hard to say whether your faith is genuine and your grace real? What though your eyes are often so dimmed with tears that you cannot clearly see your calling and election of God? Still there is ground for hope and strong consolation if your heart can testify that you love Christ. Where there is true love, there is faith and grace. You would not love Him if He had not done something for you. Your very love is a token for good.

For another thing, if you love Christ, never be ashamed to let others see it and know it. Speak for Him. Witness for Him. Live for Him. Work for Him. If He has loved you and washed you from your sins in His own blood, you never need shrink from letting others know that you feel it, and love Him in return.

"Man," said a thoughtless, ungodly English traveller to a North American Indian convert, "Man, what is the reason that you make so much of Christ, and talk so much about Him? What has this Christ done for you, that you should make so much ado about Him?"

The converted Indian did not answer him in words. He gathered together some dry leaves and moss and made a ring with them on the ground. He picked up a live worm and put it in the middle of the ring. He struck a light and set the moss and leaves on fire. The flame soon rose and the heat scorched the worm. It writhed in agony, and after trying in vain to escape on every side, curled itself up in the middle, as if about to die in despair. At that moment the Indian reached forth his hand, took up the worm gently and placed it on his bosom. "Stranger," he said to the Englishman, "Do you see that worm? I was that perishing creature. I was dying in my sins, hopeless, helpless, and on the brink of eternal fire. It was Jesus Christ who put forth the arm of His power. It was Jesus Christ who delivered me with the hand of His grace, and plucked me from everlasting burnings. It was Jesus Christ who placed me, a poor sinful worm, near the heart of His love. Stranger, that is the reason why I talk of Jesus Christ and make much of Him. I am not ashamed of it, because I love Him."

If we know anything of love to Christ, may we have the mind of this North American Indian! May we never think that we can love Christ too well, live to Him too thoroughly, confess Him too boldly, lay ourselves out for Him too heartily! Of all the things that will surprise us in the resurrection morning, this, I believe, will surprise us most: that we did not love Christ more before we died.

XVI. WITHOUT CHRIST

"Ye were without Christ."--Ephes. ii. 12.

THE text which heads this paper describes the state of the Ephesians before they became Christians. But that is not all. It describes the state of every man and woman in England who is not converted to God. A more miserable state cannot be conceived! It is bad enough to be without money, or without health, or without home, or without friends. But it is far worse to be "without Christ."

Let us examine the text this day, and see what it contains. Who can tell but it may prove a message from God to some reader of this paper?

1. Let us consider, in the first place, when it can be said of a man that he is "without Christ."

The expression "without Christ," be it remembered, is not one of my own invention. The words were not first coined by me, but were written under the inspiration of the Holy Ghost. They were used by St. Paul when he was reminding the Ephesian Christians what their former condition was, before they heard the Gospel and believed. Ignorant and dark no doubt they had been, buried in idolatry and heathenism, worshippers of the false goddess Diana. But all this he passes over completely. He seems to think that this would only partially describe their state. So he draws a picture, of which the very first feature is the expression before us: "At that time ye were without Christ." (Ephes. ii. 12.) Now what does the expression mean?

(a) A man is "without Christ" when he has no head-knowledge of Him. Millions, no doubt, are in this condition. They know not who Christ is--nor what He has done--nor what He taught--nor why He was crucified--nor where He is now--nor what He is to mankind. In short, they are entirely ignorant of Him. The heathen, of course, who never yet heard the Gospel come first under this description. But unhappily they do not stand alone. There are thousands of people living in England at this very day who have hardly any clearer ideas about Christ than the very heathen. Ask them what they know about Jesus Christ, and you will be astounded at the gross darkness which covers their minds. Visit them on their death-beds and you will find that they can tell you no more about Christ than about Mahomet. Thousands are in this state in country parishes, and thousands in towns. And about all such persons but one account can be given. They are "without Christ."

I am aware that some modern divines do not take the view which I have just stated. They tell us that all mankind have a part and interest in Christ, whether they know Him or not. They say that all men and women, however ignorant while they live, shall be taken by Christ's mercy to heaven when they die! Such views, I firmly believe, cannot be reconciled with God's Word. It is written, "This is life eternal, that they might know Thee the only true God, and

Jesus Christ, whom Thou hast sent." (John xvii. 3.) It is one of the marks of the wicked, on whom God shall take vengeance at the last day, that they "know not God." (2 Thess. i. 8.) An unknown Christ is no Saviour. What shall be the state of the heathen after death?--how shall the savage, who never heard the Gospel, be judged?--in what manner will God deal with the helplessly ignorant and uneducated?--all these are questions which we may safely let alone. We may rest assured that "the Judge of all the earth will do right." (Gen. xviii. 25.) But we must not fly in the face of Scripture. If Bible words mean anything, to be ignorant of Christ is to be "without Christ."

(b) But this is not all. A man is "without Christ" when he has no heart-faith in Him as his Saviour. It is quite possible to know all about Christ, and yet not to put our trust in Him. There are multitudes who know every article of the Belief, and can tell you glibly that Christ was "born of the Virgin Mary, suffered under Pontius Pilate, was crucified, dead, and buried." They learned it at school. They have it sticking fast in their memories. But they make no practical use of their knowledge. They put their trust in something which is not "Christ." They hope to go to heaven because they are moral and well-conducted--because they say their prayers and go to Church--because they have been baptized and go to the Lord's Table. But as to a lively faith in God's mercy through Christ--a real, intelligent confidence in Christ's blood and righteousness and intercession--these are things of which they know nothing at all. And of all such persons I can see but one true account. They are "without Christ."

I am aware that many do not admit the truth of what I have just said. Some tell us that all baptized people are members of Christ by virtue of their baptism. Others tell us that where there is a head-knowledge, we have no right to question a person's interest in Christ. To these views I have only one plain answer. The Bible forbids us to say that any man is joined to Christ until he believes. Baptism is no proof that we are joined to Christ. Simon Magus was baptized, and yet was distinctly told that he had "no part or lot in this matter." (Acts viii. 21.) Head-knowledge is no proof that we are joined to Christ. The devils know Christ well enough, but have no portion in Him. God knows, no doubt, who are His from all eternity. But man knows nothing of anyone's justification until he believes. The grand question is, "Do we believe?" It is written, "He that believeth not the Son shall not see life; but the wrath of God abideth on him." "He that believeth not shall be damned." (John iii. 36; Mark xvi. 16.) If Bible words mean anything, to be without faith is to be "without Christ."

(c) But I have yet one thing more to say. A man is "without Christ" when the Holy Spirit's work cannot be seen in his life. Who can avoid seeing, if he uses his eyes, that myriads of professing Christians know nothing of inward conversion of heart? They will tell you that they believe the Christian religion; they go to their places of worship with tolerable regularity; they think it a proper thing to be married and buried with all the ceremonies of the Church; they would be much offended if their Christianity were doubted. But where is the Holy Ghost to be seen in their lives? What are their hearts and affections set upon? Whose is the image and superscription that stands out in their tastes, and habits, and ways? Alas, there can only be one reply! They know nothing experimentally of the renewing, sanctifying work of the Holy Ghost. They are yet dead to God. And of all such, only one account can be given. They are "without Christ."

I am well aware, again, that few will admit this. The vast majority will tell you that it is extreme, and wild, and extravagant to require so much in Christians, and to press on every one conversion. They will say that it is impossible to keep up the high standard which I have just referred to, without going out of the world; and that we may surely go to heaven without being such very great saints. To all this I can only reply, What saith the Scripture? What saith the Lord? It is written, "Except a man be born again, he cannot see the kingdom of God."--"Except ye be converted, and become as little children, ye shall not enter into the kingdom of heaven."--"He that saith he abideth in Christ, ought himself also so to walk, even as He walked."--"If any man have not the Spirit of Christ, he is none of His." (John iii. 3; Matt. xviii. 3; 1 John ii. 6; Rom. viii. 9.) The Scripture cannot be broken. If Bible words mean anything, to be without the Spirit is to be "without Christ."

I commend the three propositions I have just laid down to your serious and prayerful consideration. Mark well what they come to. Examine them carefully on every side. In order to have a saving interest in Christ, knowledge, faith, and the grace of the Holy Ghost are absolutely needful. He that is without them is "without Christ."

How painfully ignorant are many! They know literally nothing about religion. Christ, and the Holy Ghost, and faith, and grace, and conversion, and sanctification are mere "words and names" to them. They could not explain what they mean, if it were to save their lives. And can such ignorance as this take anyone to heaven? Impossible! Without knowledge, "without Christ!"

How painfully self-righteous are many! They can talk complacently about having "done their duty," and being "kind to everybody," and having always "kept to their Church," and having "never been so very bad" as some--and therefore they seem to think they must go to heaven! And as to deep sense of sin and simple faith in Christ's blood and sacrifice, these seem to have no place in their religion. Their talk is all of doing and never of believing. And will such self-righteousness as this land anyone in heaven? Never! Without faith, "without Christ!"

How painfully ungodly are many! They live in the habitual neglect of God's Sabbath, God's Bible, God's ordinances, and God's sacraments. They think nothing of doing things which God has flatly forbidden. They are constantly living in ways which are directly contrary to God's commandments. And can such ungodliness end in salvation? Impossible! Without the Holy Ghost, "without Christ!"

I know well that at first sight these statements seem hard, and sharp, and rough, and severe. But after all, are they not God's truth as revealed to us in Scripture? If truth, ought they not to be made known? If necessary to be known, ought they not to be plainly laid down? If I know anything of my own heart, I desire above all things to magnify the riches of God's love to sinners. I long to tell all mankind what a wealth of mercy and loving-kindness there is laid up in God's heart for all who will seek it. But I cannot find anywhere that ignorant, and unbelieving, and unconverted people have any part in Christ! If I am wrong, I shall be thankful to anyone who will show me a more excellent way. But till I am shown it, I must stand fast on the positions I have already laid down. I dare not forsake them, lest I be found guilty of handling God's Word deceitfully. I dare not be silent about them, lest the blood of souls be required at my hands. The man without knowledge, without faith, and without the Holy Ghost, is a man "without Christ!"

II. Let me now turn to another point which I wish to consider. What is the actual condition of a man "without Christ"?

This is a branch of our present subject that demands very special attention. Thankful indeed should I be if I could exhibit it in its true colours. I can easily imagine some reader saying to himself, "Well, suppose I am without Christ, where is the mighty harm? I hope God will be merciful. I am no worse than many others. I trust all will be right at last." Listen to me, and, by God's help, I will try to show that you are sadly deceived. "Without Christ" all will not be right, but all desperately wrong.

(a) For one thing, to be without Christ is to be without God. The Apostle St. Paul told the Ephesians as much as this in plain words. He ends the famous sentence which begins, "Ye were without Christ," by saying, "Ye were without God in the world." And who that thinks can wonder? That man can have very low ideas of God who does not conceive Him a most pure, and holy, and glorious, and spiritual Being. That man must be very blind who does not see that human nature is corrupt, and sinful, and defiled. How then can such a worm as man draw near to God with comfort? How can he look up to Him with confidence and not feel afraid? How can he speak to Him, have dealings with Him, look forward to dwelling with Him, without dread and alarm? There must be a Mediator between God and man, and there is but One that can fill the office. That One is Christ.

Who art thou that talkest of God's mercy and God's love separate from and independent of Christ? There is no such love and mercy recorded in Scripture. Know this day that God out of Christ is "a consuming fire." (Heb. xii. 29.) Merciful He is, beyond all question: rich in mercy, plenteous in mercy. But His mercy is inseparably connected with the mediation of His beloved Son Jesus Christ. It must flow through Him as the appointed channel, or it cannot flow at all. It is written, "He that honoureth not the Son, honoureth not the Father which hath sent Him."--"I am the way, the truth, and the life: No man cometh unto the Father but by Me." (John v. 23; xiv. 6.) "Without Christ" we are without God.

(b) For another thing, to be without Christ is to be without peace. Every man has a conscience within him, which must be satisfied before he can be truly happy. So long as this conscience is asleep or half dead, so long, no doubt, he gets along pretty well. But as soon as a man's conscience wakes up, and he begins to think of past sins, and present failings, and future judgment, at once he finds out that he needs something to give him inward rest. But what can do it? Repenting, and praying, and Bible-reading, and church-going, and sacrament-receiving, and self-mortification may be tried, and tried in vain. They never yet took off the burden from anyone's conscience. And yet peace must be had!

There is only one thing can give peace to the conscience, and that is the blood of Jesus Christ sprinkled on it. A clear understanding that Christ's death was an actual payment of our debt to God, and that the merit of that death is made over to man when he believes, is the grand secret of inward peace. It meets every craving of conscience. It answers every accusation. It calms every fear. It is written, "These things I have spoken unto you, that in Me ye might have peace." "He is our peace." "Being justified by faith, we have peace with God through our Lord Jesus Christ." (John xvi. 33; Ephes. ii. 14; Rom. v. 1.) We have peace through the blood of His cross: peace like a deep mine--peace like an everflowing stream. But "without Christ" we are without peace.

(e) For another thing, to be without Christ is to be without hope. Hope of some sort or other almost everyone thinks he possesses. Rarely indeed will you find a man who will boldly tell you that he has no hope at all about his soul. But how few there are that can give "a reason of the hope that is in them!" (1 Pet. iii. 15.) How few can explain it, describe it, and show its foundations! How many a hope is nothing better than a vague, empty feeling, which the day of sickness and the hour of death will prove to be utterly useless--impotent alike to comfort or to save.

There is but one hope that has roots, life, strength and solidity, and that is the hope which is built on the great rock of Christ's work and office as man's Redeemer. "Other foundation can no man lay than that is laid, which is Jesus Christ." (1 Cor. iii. 11.) He that buildeth on this cornerstone "shall not be confounded." About this hope there is reality. It will bear looking at and handling. It will meet every enquiry. Search it through and through, and you will find no flaw whatever in it. All other hopes besides this are worthless. Like summer-dried fountains, they fail man just when his need is the sorest. They are like unsound ships, which look well so long as they lie quiet in harbour, but when the winds and the waves of the ocean begin to try them, their rotten condition is discovered, and they sink beneath the waters. There is no such thing as a good hope without Christ, and "without Christ" is to have "no hope." (Eph. ii. 12.)

(d) For another thing, to be without Christ is to be without heaven. In saying this I do not merely mean that there is no entrance into heaven, but that "without Christ" there could be no happiness in being there. A man without a Saviour and Redeemer could never feel at home in heaven. He would feel that he had no lawful right or title to be there: boldness and confidence and ease of heart would be impossible. Amidst pure and holy angels, under the eyes of a pure and holy God, he could not hold up his head: he would feel confounded and ashamed. It is the very essence of all true views of heaven that Christ is there.

Who art thou that dreamest of a heaven in which Christ has no place? Awake to know thy folly. Know that in every description of heaven which the Bible contains, the presence of Christ is one essential feature. "In the midst of the throne," says St, John, "stood a Lamb as it had been slain." The very throne of heaven is called the "throne of God and of the Lamb."--"The Lamb is the light of heaven, and the temple of it."--The saints who dwell in heaven are to be "fed by the Lamb," and "led to living fountains of waters." The meeting of the saints in heaven is called, "the marriage supper of the Lamb." (Rev. v. 6; xxii. 3; xxi. 22, 23; vii. 17; xix. 9.) A heaven without Christ would not be the heaven of the Bible. To be "without Christ" is to be without heaven.

I might easily add to these things. I might tell you that to be without Christ is to be without fife, without strength, without safety, without foundation, without a friend in heaven, without righteousness. None so badly off as those that are without Christ!

What the ark was to Noah, what the passover lamb was to Israel in Egypt, what the manna, the smitten rock, the brazen serpent, the pillar of cloud and fire, the scapegoat, were to the tribes in the wilderness, all this the Lord Jesus is meant to be to man's soul. None so destitute as those that are without Christ!

What the root is to the branches, what the air is to our lungs, what food and water are to our bodies, what the sun is to creation, all this and much more Christ is intended to be to us. None so helpless, none so pitiable as those that are without Christ!

I grant that, if there were no such things as sickness and death--if men and women never grew old, and lived on this earth for ever--the subject of this paper would be of no importance. But you must know that sickness, death, and the grave are sad realities.

If this life were all--if there were no judgment, no heaven, no hell, no eternity--it would be mere waste of time to trouble yourself with such inquiries as this tract suggests. But you have got a conscience. You know well that there is a reckoning-day beyond the grave. There is a judgment yet to come.

Surely the subject of this paper is no light matter. It is not a small thing, and one that does not signify. It demands the attention of every sensible person. It lies at the very root of that all-important question, the salvation of our souls. To be "without Christ" is to be most miserable.

(1) And now I ask every one who has read this paper through to examine himself and find out his own precise condition. Are you without Christ?

Do not allow life to pass away without some serious thoughts and self-inquiry. You cannot always go on as you do now. A day must come when eating, and drinking, and sleeping, and dressing, and making merry, and spending money, will have an end. There will be a day when your place will be empty and you will be only spoken of as one dead and gone. And where will you be then^ if you have lived and died without thought about your soul, without God, and without Christ? Oh, remember, it is better a thousand times to be without money, and health, and friends, and company, and good cheer, than to be without Christ!

(2) If you have lived without Christ hitherto, I invite you in all affection to change your course without delay. Seek the Lord Jesus while He may be found. Call upon Him while He is near. He is sitting at God's right hand, able to save to the uttermost everyone who comes to Him, however sinful and careless he may have been. He is sitting at God's right hand, willing to hear the prayer of every one who feels that his past life has been all wrong, and wants to be set right. Seek Christ, seek Christ without delay. Acquaint yourself with Him. Do not be ashamed to apply to Him. Only become one of Christ's friends this year, and you will say one day it was the happiest year that you ever had.

(3) If you have become one of Christ's friends already, I exhort you to be a thankful man. Awake to a deeper sense of the infinite mercy of having an Almighty Saviour, a title to heaven, a home that is eternal, a Friend that never dies! A few more years and all our family gatherings will be over. What a comfort to think that we have in Christ something that we can never lose!

Awake to a deeper sense of the sorrowful state of those who are "without Christ." We are often reminded of the many who are without food, or clothing, or school, or church. Let us pity them, and help them, as far as we can. But let us never forget that there are people whose state is far more pitiable. Who are they? The people "without Christ!"

Have we relatives "without Christ"? Let us feel for them, pray for them, speak to the King about them, strive to recommend the Gospel to them. Let us leave no stone unturned in our efforts to bring them to Christ.

Have we neighbours "without Christ"? Let us labour in every way for their souls' salvation. The night cometh when none can work. Happy is he who lives under the abiding conviction that to be "in Christ" is peace, safety, and happiness; and that to be "without Christ" is to be on the brink of destruction.

XVII. THIRST RELIEVED

"In the last day, that great day of the feast, Jesus stood and cried, saying, If any man thirst, let him come unto Me, and drink. He that believeth on Me, as the Scripture hath said, out of his belly shall flow rivers of living water."--John vii. 37. 38.

THE text which heads this chapter contains one of those mighty sayings of Christ which deserve to be printed in letters of gold. All the stars in heaven are bright and beautiful; yet even a child can see that one star excelleth another in glory. All Scripture is given by inspiration of God; but that heart must indeed be cold and dull which does not feel that some verses are peculiarly rich and full. Of such verses this text is one.

In order to see the whole force and beauty of the text, we must remember the place, the time, and the occasion when it comes in.

The place, then, was Jerusalem, the metropolis of Judaism, and the stronghold of priests and scribes, of Pharisees and Sadducees.--The occasion was the Feast of Tabernacles, one of those great annual feasts when every Jew, if he could, went up to the temple, according to the law.--The time was "the last day of the feast," when all the ceremonies were drawing to a close, when the water drawn from the fountain of Siloam, according to traditional custom, had been solemnly poured on the altar, and nothing remained for worshippers but to return home.

At this critical moment, our Lord Jesus Christ "stood" forward on a prominent place, and spoke to the assembled crowds. I doubt not He read their hearts. He saw them going away with aching consciences and unsatisfied minds, having got nothing from their blind teachers the Pharisees and Sadducees, and carrying away nothing but a barren recollection of pompous forms. He saw and pitied them, and cried aloud, like a herald, "If any man thirst, let him come unto Me and drink."--That this was all our Lord said on this memorable occasion, I take leave to doubt. I suspect it is only the key-note of His address. But this, I imagine, was the first sentence that fell from His lips: "If any man thirst, let him come unto Me." If anyone wants living, satisfying water, let him come unto ME.

Let me remind my readers, in passing, that no prophet or apostle ever took on himself to use such language as this. "Come with us," said Moses to Hobab (Num. x. 29); "Come to the waters," says Isaiah (Isa. lv. 1); "Behold the Lamb," says John the Baptist (John i. 29); "Believe on the Lord Jesus Christ," says St. Paul (Acts xvi. 31) But no one except Jesus of Nazareth ever said, "Come to ME." That fact is very significant. He that said,"Come to Me," knew and felt, when He said it, that He was the eternal Son of God, the promised Messiah, the Saviour of the world.

There are three points in this great saying of our Lord to which I now propose to direct attention.

I. You have a case supposed: "If any man thirst."

II. You have a remedy proposed: "Let him come unto Me, and drink."

III. You have a promise held out: "He that believeth on Me, as the Scripture hath said, out of his belly shall flow rivers of living waters."

Each of these points concerns all into whose hands this paper may fall. On each of them I have somewhat to say.

I. In the first place, then, you have a case supposed. Our Lord says, "If any man thirst."

Bodily thirst is notoriously the most painful sensation to which the frame of mortal man is liable. Read the story of the miserable sufferers in the black hole at Calcutta.--Ask anyone who has travelled over desert plains under a tropical sun.--Hear what any old soldier will tell you is the chief want of the wounded on a battlefield.--Remember what the crews of ships lost in mid-ocean, tossed for days in boats without water, go through.--Mark the awful words of the rich man in the parable: "Send Lazarus that he may dip the tip of his finger in water to cool my tongue: for I am tormented in this flame." (Luke xvi. 24.) The testimony is unvarying. There is nothing so terrible and hard to bear as thirst.

But if bodily thirst is so painful, how much more painful is thirst of soul? Physical suffering is not the worst part of eternal punishment. It is a light thing, even in this world, compared to the suffering of the mind and inward man. To see the value of our souls, and find out they are in danger of eternal ruin--to feel the burden of unforgiven sin, and not to know where to turn for relief--to have a conscience sick and ill at ease, and to be ignorant of the remedy--to discover that we are dying, dying daily, and yet unprepared to meet God--to have some clear view of our own guilt and wickedness, and yet to be in utter darkness about absolution--this is the highest degree of pain--the pain which drinks up soul and spirit, and pierces joints and marrow! And this no doubt is the thirst of which our Lord is speaking. It is thirst after pardon, forgiveness, absolution, and peace with God. It is the craving of a really awakened conscience, wanting satisfaction and not knowing where to find it, walking through dry places and unable to get rest.

This is the thirst which the Jews felt when Peter preached to them on the day of Penetcost. It is written that they were "pricked In their heart, and said, Men and brethren, what shall we do?" (Acts ii. 37.)

This is the thirst which the Philippian jailor felt, when he awoke to consciousness of his spiritual danger and felt the earthquake making the prison reel under his feet. It is written that he "came trembling, and fell down before Paul and Silas, and brought them out, saying, Sirs, what must I do to be saved?" (Acts xvi. 30.)

This is the thirst which many of the greatest servants of God seem to have felt when light first broke in on their minds. Augustine seeking rest among the Manichean heretics and finding none--Luther groping after truth among monks in Erfurt Monastery--John Bunyan agonizing amidst doubts and conflicts in his Elstow cottage--George Whitefield groaning under self-imposed austerities, for want of clear teaching, when an undergraduate at Oxford-- all have left on record their experience. I believe they all knew what our Lord meant when He spoke of "thirst."

And surely it is not too much to say that all of us ought to know something of this thirst, if not as much as Augustine, Luther, Bunyan, or Whitefield. Living as we do in a dying world- -knowing as we do, if we will confess it, that there is a world beyond the grave, and that after death comes the judgment--feeling, as we must do in our better moments, what poor, weak, unstable, defective creatures we all are, and how unfit to meet God--conscious as we must be in our inmost heart of hearts, that on our use of time depends our place in eternity--we ought to feel and to realise something like "thirst" for a sense of peace with the living God. But alas, nothing proves so conclusively the fallen nature of man as the general, common want of spiritual appetite! For money, for power, for pleasure, for rank, for honour, for distinction--for all these the vast majority are now intensely thirsting. To lead forlorn hopes, to dig for gold, to storm a breach, to try to hew a way through thick-ribbed ice to the North Pole, for all these objects there is no lack of adventurers and volunteers. Fierce and unceasing is the competition for these corruptible crowns! But few indeed, by comparison, are those who thirst after eternal life. No wonder that the natural man is called in Scripture "dead," and "sleeping," and blind, and deaf. No wonder that he is said to need a second birth and a new creation. There is no surer symptom or mortification in the body than the loss of all feeling. There is no more painful sign of an unhealthy state of soul than an utter absence or spiritual thirst. Woe to that man of whom the Saviour can say, "Thou knowest not that thou art wretched, and miserable, and poor, and blind, and naked." (Rev. iii. 17.)

But who is there among the readers of this paper that feels the burden of sin, and longs for peace with God? Who is there that really feels the words of our Prayer-book Confession: "I have erred and strayed like a lost sheep--there is no health in me--I am a miserable offender"? Who is there that enters into the fullness of our Communion Service, and can say with truth, "The remembrance of my sins is grievous, and the burden of them is intolerable"? You are the man that ought to thank God. A sense of sin, guilt, and poverty of soul, is the first stone laid by the Holy Ghost when He builds a spiritual temple. He convinces of sin. Light was the first thing called into being in the material creation. (Gen. i. 3.) Light about our own state is the first work in the new creation. Thirsting soul, I say again, you are the person who ought to thank God. The kingdom of God is near you. It is not when we begin to feel good, but when we feel bad, that we take the first step towards heaven. Who taught thee that thou wast naked? Whence came this inward light? Who opened thine eyes and made thee see and feel? Know this day that flesh and blood hath not revealed these things unto thee, but our Father which is in heaven. Universities may confer degrees, and schools may impart knowledge of all mysteries, but they cannot make men feel sin. To realise our spiritual need, and feel true spiritual thirst, is the A B C in saving Christianity.

It is a great saying of Elihu, in the book of Job--"God looketh upon men, and if any say, I have sinned, and perverted that which was right, and it profited me not; He will deliver his soul from death, and his life shall see the light." (Job xxxiii. 27, 28.) Let him that knows anything of spiritual "thirst" not be ashamed. Rather let him lift up his head and begin to hope. Let him pray that God would carry on the work He has begun, and make him feel more.

II. I pass from the case supposed to the remedy proposed. "If any man thirst," says our blessed Lord Jesus Christ, "let him come unto Me, and drink."

There is a grand simplicity about this little sentence which cannot be too much admired. There is not a word in it of which the literal meaning is not plain to a child. Yet, simple as it appears, it is rich in spiritual meaning. Like the Koh-i-noor diamond, which you may carry between finger and thumb, it is of unspeakable value. It solves that mighty problem which all the philosophers of Greece and Rome could never solve--"How can man have peace with God? "Place it in your memory side by side with six other golden sayings of your Lord. "I am the Bread of life: he that cometh unto me shall never hunger; and he that believeth on me shall never thirst."--"I am the Light of the world: he that followeth me shall not walk in darkness, but shall have the light of life."--"I am the Door: by me if any man enter in, he shall be saved."--"I am the Way, the Truth, and the Life: no man cometh unto the Father but by me."--"Come unto me, all ye that labour and are heavy laden, and I will give you rest."--" Him that cometh to me I will in no wise cast out."--Add to these six texts the one before you to-day. Get the whole seven by heart. Rivet them down in your mind, and never let them go. When your feet touch the cold river, on the bed of sickness and in the hour of death, you will find these seven texts above all price. (John vi. 35; viii. 12; x. 9; xiv. 6; Matt. xi. 28; John vi. 37.)

For what is the sum and substance of these simple words? It is this. Christ is that Fountain of living water which God has graciously provided for thirsting souls. From Him, as out of the rock smitten by Moses, there flows an abundant stream for all who travel through the wilderness of this world. In Him, as our Redeemer and Substitute, crucified for our sins and raised again for our justification, there is an endless supply of all that men can need--pardon, absolution, mercy, grace, peace, rest, relief, comfort, and hope.

This rich provision Christ has bought for us at the price of His own precious blood. To open this wondrous fountain He suffered for sin, the just for the unjust, and bore our sins in His own body on the tree. He was made sin for us, who knew no sin, that we might be made the righteousness of God in Him. (1 Peter ii. 24; iii. 18; 2 Cor. v. 21.) And now He is sealed and appointed to be the Reliever of all who are labouring and heavy laden, and the Giver of living water to all who thirst. It is His office to receive sinners. It is His pleasure to give them pardon, life, and peace. And the words of the text are a proclamation He makes to all mankind--"If any man thirst, let him come unto Me, and drink."

The efficacy of a medicine depends in great measure on the manner in which it is used. The best prescription of the best physician is useless if we refuse to follow the directions which accompany it. Suffer the word of exhortation, while I offer some caution and advice about the Fountain of living water.

(a) He that thirsts and wants relief must come to Christ Himself. He must not be content with coming to His Church and His ordinances, or to the assemblies of His people for prayer and praise. He must not stop short even at His holy table, or rest satisfied with privately opening his heart to His ordained ministers. Oh, no! he that is content with only drinking these waters "shall thirst again." (John iv. 13.) He must go higher, further, much further than this. He must have personal dealings with Christ Himself: all else in religion is worthless without Him. The King's palace, the attendant servants, the richly furnished banqueting house, the very banquet itself--all are nothing unless we speak with the King. His hand alone can take the burden off our backs and make us feel free. The hand of man may take the stone from the grave and show the dead; but none but Jesus can say to the dead, "Come forth and live." (John xi. 41-43.) We must deal directly with Christ.

(b) Again: he that thirsts and wants relief from Christ must actually come to Him. It is not enough to wish, and talk, and mean, and intend, and resolve, and hope. Hell, that awful reality, is truly said to be paved with good intentions. Thousands are yearly lost in this fashion, and perish miserably just outside the harbour. Meaning and intending they live; meaning and intending they die. Oh, no! we must "arise and come!" If the prodigal son had been content with saying, "How many hired servants of my father have bread enough and to spare, and I perish with hunger! I hope some day to return home," he might have remained for ever among the swine. It was when he arose and came to his father that his father ran to meet him, and said, "Bring forth the best robe and put it on him.--Let us eat and be merry." (Luke

xv. 20-23.) Like him, we must not only "come to ourselves" and think, but we must actually come to the High Priest, to Christ. We must come to the Physician.

(c) Once again: he that thirsts and wants to come to Christ must remember that simple faith is the one thing required. By all means let him come with a penitent, broken and contrite heart; but let him not dream of resting on that for acceptance. Faith is the only hand that can carry the living water to our lips. Faith is the hinge on which all turns in the matter of our justification. It is written again and again that "whosoever believeth shall not perish, but have eternal life." (John iii. 15, 16.) "To him that worketh not, but believeth on Him that justifieth the ungodly, his faith is counted for righteousness." (Rom. iv. 5.) Happy is he that can lay hold on the principle laid down in that matchless hymn--

> Just as I am! without one plea
> But that Thy blood was shed for me,
> And that Thou bidst me come to Thee--
> O Lamb of God, I come!

How simple this remedy for thirst appears! But oh, how hard it is to persuade some persons to receive it! Tell them to do some great thing, to mortify their bodies, to go on pilgrimage, to give all their goods to feed the poor, and so to merit salvation, and they will try to do as they are bid. Tell them to throw overboard all idea of merit, working, or doing, and to come to Christ as empty sinners, with nothing in their hands, and, like Naaman, they are ready to turn away in disdain. (2 Kings v. 12.) Human nature is always the same in every age. There are still some people just like the Jews, and some like the Greeks. To the Jews Christ crucified is still a stumbling-block, and to the Greeks foolishness. Their succession, at any rate, has never ceased! Never did our Lord say a truer word than that which He spoke to the proud scribes in the Sanhedrim--"ye will not come unto Me that ye might have life." (John v. 40.)

But, simple as this remedy for thirst appears, it is the only cure for man's spiritual disease, and the only bridge from earth to heaven. Kings and their subjects, preachers and hearers, masters and servants, high and low, rich and poor, learned and unlearned, all must alike drink of this water of life, and drink in the same way. For eighteen centuries men have laboured to find some other medicine for weary consciences; but they have laboured in vain. Thousands, after blistering their hands, and growing grey in hewing out "broken cisterns which can hold no water" (Jer. ii. 13), have been obliged to come back at last to the old Fountain, and have confessed in their latest moments that here, in Christ alone, is true peace.

And simple as the old remedy for thirst may appear, it is the root of the inward life of all God's greatest servants in all ages. What have the saints and martyrs been in every era of Church history, but men who came to Christ daily by faith, and found "His flesh meat indeed and His blood drink indeed?" (John vi. 55.) What have they all been but men who lived the life of faith in the Son of God, and drank daily out of the fulness there is in Him? (Gal. ii. 20.) Here, at all events, the truest and best Christians, who have made a mark on the world, have been of one mind. Holy Fathers and Reformers, holy Anglican divines and Puritans, holy Episcopalians and Nonconformists, have all in their best moments borne uniform testimony to the value of the Fountain of life. Separated and contentious as they may sometimes have been in their lives, in their deaths they have not been divided. In their last struggle with the king of terrors they have simply clung to the cross of Christ, and gloried in nothing but the "precious blood," and the Fountain open for all sin and uncleanness.

How thankful we ought to be that we live in a land where the great remedy for spiritual thirst is known--in a land of open Bibles, preached Gospel, and abundant means of grace--in a land where the efficacy of Christ's sacrifice is still proclaimed, with more or less fulness, in 20,000 pulpits every Sunday! We do not realise the value of our privileges. The very familiarity of the manna makes us think of it just as Israel loathed "the light bread" in the wilderness. (Num. xxi. 5.) But turn to the pages of a heathen philosopher like the incomparable Plato, and see how he groped after light like one blindfolded, and wearied himself to find the door. The humblest peasant who grasps the four "comfortable words" of our beautiful Communion Service in the Prayer-book knows more of the way of peace with God than the Athenian sage.--Turn to the accounts which trustworthy travellers and missionaries give of the state of the heathen who have never heard the Gospel. Read of the human sacrifices in Africa, and the ghastly, self-imposed tortures of the devotees of Hindostan, and remember they are all the result of an unquenched "thirst" and a blind and unsatisfied desire to get near to God. And then learn to be thankful that your lot is cast in a land like your own. Alas, I fear God has a controversy with us for our unthankfulness! Cold indeed, and dead, must that heart be which can study the condition of Africa, China, and Hindostan, and not thank God that he lives in Christian England.

III. I turn, in the last place, to the promise held out to all who come to Christ. "He that believeth on Me, as the Scripture hath said, out of his belly shall flow rivers of living water."

The subject of Scripture promises is a vast and most interesting one. I doubt whether it receives the attention which it deserves in the present day. "Clarke's Scripture Promises" is an old book which is far less studied now, I suspect, than it was in the days of our fathers. Few Christians realize the number, and length, and breadth, and depth, and height, and variety of the precious "shalls" and "wills" laid up in the Bible for the special benefit and encouragement of all who will use them.

Yet promise lies at the bottom of nearly all the transactions of man with man in the affairs of this life. The vast majority of Adam's children in every civilized country are acting every day on the faith of promises. The labourer on the land works hard from Monday morning to Saturday night, because he believes that at the end of the week he shall receive his promised wages. The soldier enlists in the army, and the sailor enters his name on the ship's books in the navy, in the full confidence that those under whom they serve will at some future time give them their promised pay. The humblest maid-servant in a family works on from day to day at her appointed duties, in the belief that her mistress will give her the promised wages. In the business of great cities, among merchants, and bankers, and tradesmen, nothing could be done without incessant faith in promises. Every man of sense knows that cheques and bills, and promissory notes, are the only means by which the immense majority of mercantile affairs can possibly be carried on. Men of business are compelled to act by faith and not by sight. They believe promises, and expect to be believed themselves. In fact, promises, and faith in promises, and actions springing from faith in promises, are the back-bone of nine-tenths of all the dealings of man with his fellow-men throughout Christendom.

Now promises, in like manner, in the religion of the Bible, are one grand means by which God is pleased to approach the soul of man. The careful student of Scripture cannot fail to observe that God is continually holding out inducements to man to listen to Him, obey Him, and serve Him, and undertaking to do great things, if man will only attend and believe. In short, as St. Peter says, "There are given to us exceeding great and precious promises." (2 Pet. i. 4.) He who has mercifully caused all Holy Scripture to be written for our learning has shown His perfect knowledge of human nature, by spreading over the Book a perfect wealth of promises, suitable to every kind of experience and every condition of life. He seems to say, "Would you know what I undertake to do for you? Do you want to hear my terms? "--"Take up the Bible and read."

But there is one grand difference between the promises of Adam's children and the promises of God, which ought never to be forgotten. The promises of man are not sure to be fulfilled. With the best wishes and intentions, he cannot always keep his word. Disease and death may step in like an armed man, and take away from this world him that promises. War, or pestilence, or famine, or failure of crops, or hurricanes, may strip him of his property, and make it impossible for him to fulfil his engagements. The promises of God, on the contrary, are certain to be kept. He is Almighty: nothing can prevent His doing what He has said. He never changes: He is always "of one mind": and with Him there is "no variableness or shadow of turning." (Job xxiii. 13; James 1. 17.) He will always keep His word. There is one thing which, as a little girl once told her teacher, to her surprise, God cannot do: "It is impossible for God to lie." (Heb. vi. 18.) The most unlikely and improbable things, when God has once said He will do them, have always come to pass. The destruction of the old world by a flood, and the preservation of Noah in the ark, the birth of Isaac, the deliverance of Israel from Egypt, the raising of David to the throne of Saul, the miraculous birth of Christ, the resurrection of Christ, the scattering of the Jews all over the earth, and their continued preservation as a distinct people--who could imagine events more unlikely and improbable than these? Yet God said they should be, and in due time they all came to pass. In truth, with God it is just as easy to do a thing as to say it. Whatever He promises, He is certain to perform.

Concerning the variety and riches of Scripture promises, far more might be said than it is possible to say in a short paper like this. Their name is legion. The subject is almost inexhaustible. There is hardly a step in man's life, from childhood to old age, hardly any position in which man can be placed, for which the Bible has not held out encouragement to everyone who desires to do right in the sight of God. There are "shalls" and "wills" in God's treasury for every condition. About God's infinite mercy and compassion--about His readiness to receive all who repent and believe--about His willingness to forgive, pardon, and absolve the chief of sinners--about His power to change hearts and alter our corrupt nature--about the encouragements to pray, and hear the Gospel, and draw near to the throne of grace--about strength for duty, comfort in trouble, guidance in perplexity, help in sickness, consolation in death, support under bereavement, happiness beyond the grave, reward in glory--about all these things there is an abundant supply of promises in the Word. No one can form an idea of its abundance unless he carefully searches the Scriptures, keeping the subject steadily in view. If anyone doubts it, I can only say, "Come and see." Like the Queen of Sheba at Solomon's Court, you will soon say, "The half was not told me." (1 Kings x. 7.)

The promise of our Lord Jesus Christ which heads this paper is somewhat peculiar. It is singularly rich in encouragement to all who feel spiritual thirst, and come to Him for relief, and therefore it deserves peculiar attention. Most of our Lord's promises refer specially to the benefit of the person to whom they are addressed. The promise before us takes a far wider range: it seems to refer to many others beside those to whom He spoke. For what says He?-- "He that believeth on Me, as the Scripture hath said" (and everywhere teaches), "out of his belly shall flow rivers of living water. But this spake He of the Spirit, which they that believe on Him should receive." Figurative undoubtedly are these words--figurative, like the earlier words of the sentence--figurative, like "thirst" and "drinking." But all the figures of Scripture contain great truth; and what the figure before us was meant to convey I will now try to show.

(1) For one thing, then, I believe our Lord meant that he who comes to Him by faith shall receive an abundant supply of everything that he can desire for the relief of his own soul's wants. The Spirit shall convey to him such an abiding sense of pardon, peace and hope, that it shall be in his inward man like a well-spring, never dry. He shall feel so satisfied with "the things of Christ," which the Spirit shall show him (John xvi. 15), that he shall rest from spiritual anxiety about death, judgment, and eternity. He may have his seasons of darkness and doubt, through his own infirmities or the temptations of the devil. But, speaking generally, when he has once come to Christ by faith, he shall find in his heart of hearts an unfailing fountain of consolation. This, let us understand, is the first thing which the promise before us contains. "Only come to Me, poor anxious soul," our Lord seems to say--"Only come to Me, and thy spiritual anxiety shall be relieved. I will place in thy heart, by the power of the Holy Spirit, such a sense of pardon and peace, through My atonement and intercession, that thou shalt never completely thirst again. Thou mayest have thy doubts, and fears, and conflicts, while thou art in the body. But once having come to Me, and taken Me for thy Saviour, thou shalt never feel thyself entirely hopeless. The condition of thine inward man shall be so thoroughly changed that thou shalt feel as if there were within thee an ever-flowing spring of water."

What shall we say to these things? I declare my own belief that whenever a man or woman really comes to Christ by faith, he finds this promise fulfilled. He may possibly be weak in grace, and have many misgivings about his own condition. He may possibly not dare to say that he is converted, justified, sanctified, and meet for the inheritance of the saints in light. But, for all that, I am bold to say, the humblest and feeblest believer in Christ has got something within him which he would not part with, though he may not yet fully understand it. And what is that "something"? It is just that "river of living water" which begins to run in the heart of every child of Adam as soon as he comes to Christ and drinks. In this sense I believe this wonderful promise of Christ is always fulfilled.

(2) But is this all that is contained in the promise which heads this paper? By no means. There yet remains much behind. There is more to follow. I believe our Lord meant us to understand that he who comes to Him by faith shall not only have an abundant supply of everything which he needs for his own soul, but shall also become a source of blessing to the souls of others. The Spirit who dwells in him shall make him a fountain of good to his fellow-men, so that at the last day there shall be found to have flowed from him "rivers of living water."

This is a most important part of our Lord's promise, and opens up a subject which is seldom realized and grasped by many Christians. But it is one of deep interest, and deserves far more attention than it receives. I believe it to be a truth of God. I believe that just as "no man liveth unto himself" (Rom. xiv. 7), so also no man is converted only for himself; and that the conversion of one man or woman always leads on, in God's wonderful providence, to the conversion of others. I do not say for a moment that all believers know it. I think it far more likely that many live and die in the faith, who are not aware that they have done good to any soul. But I believe the resurrection morning and the judgment day, when the secret history of all Christians is revealed, will prove that the full meaning of the promise before us has never failed. I doubt if there will be a believer who will not have been to some one or other a "river of living water"--a channel through whom the Spirit has conveyed saving grace. Even the penitent thief, short as his time was after he repented, has been a source of blessing to thousands of souls!

(a) Some believers are "rivers of living water" while they live. Their words, their conversation, their preaching, their teaching, are all means by which the water of life has flowed into the hearts of their fellow-men. Such, for example, were the Apostles, who wrote no Epistles, and only preached the Word. Such were Luther, and Whitefield, and Wesley, and Berridge, and Rowlands, and thousands of others, of whom I cannot now speak particularly.

(b) Some believers are "rivers of living water" when they die. Their courage in facing the king of terrors, their boldness in the most painful sufferings, their unswerving faithfulness to Christ's truth even at the stake, their manifest peace on the edge of the grave--all this has set thousands thinking, and led hundreds to repent and believe. Such, for example, were the primitive martyrs whom the Roman Emperors persecuted. Such were John Huss, and Jerome of Prague. Such were Cranmer, Ridley, Latimer, Hooper, and the noble army of Marian martyrs. The work that they did at their deaths, like Samson, was far greater than the work done in their lives.

(c) Some believers are "rivers of living water" long after they die. They do good by their books and writings in every part of the world, long after the hands which held the pen are mouldering in the dust. Such men were Bunyan, and Baxter, and Owen, and George Herbert, and Robert M'Cheyne. These blessed servants of God do more good probably by their books at this moment, than they did by their tongues when they were alive. "Being dead they yet speak." (Heb. xi. 4.)

(d) Finally, there are some believers who are "rivers of living water" by the beauty of their daily conduct and behaviour. There are many quiet, gentle, consistent Christians who make no show and no noise in the world, and yet insensibly exercise a deep influence for good on all around them. They "win without the Word." (1 Peter iii. 1.) Their love, their kindness, their sweet temper, their patience, their unselfishness, tell silently on a wide circle, and sow seeds of thought and self-inquiry in many minds. It was a fine testimony of an old lady who died in great peace, saying that under God she owed her salvation to Mr. Whiteneld:--"It was not any sermon that he preached; it was not anything that he ever said to me. It was the beautiful consistency and kindness of his daily life, in the house where he was staying, when I was a little girl. I said to myself, if I ever have any religion, Mr. Whitefield's God shall be my God."

Let us all lay hold on this view of our Lord's promise, and never forget it. Think not for a moment that your own soul is the only soul that will be saved if you come to Christ by faith and follow Him. Think of the blessedness of being a "river of living water" to others. Who can tell that you may not be the means of bringing many others to Christ? Live, and act, and speak, and pray, and work, keeping this continually in view. I knew a family, consisting of a father, mother, and ten children, in which true religion began with one of the daughters; and when it began she stood alone, and all the rest of the family were in the world. And yet, before she died, she saw both her parents and all her brothers and sisters converted to God, and all this, humanly speaking, began from her influence! Surely, in the face of this, we need not doubt that a believer may be to others a "river of living water." Conversions may not be in your time, and you may die without seeing them. But never doubt that conversion generally leads to conversions, and that few go to heaven alone. When Grimshaw, of Haworth, the apostle of the north, died, he left his son graceless and godless. Afterwards the son was converted, never having forgotten his father's advice and example. And his last words were,

"What will my old father say when he sees me in heaven?" Let us take courage and hope on, believing Christ's promise.

(1) And now, before I close this paper, let me ask you a plain question. Do you know anything of spiritual thirst? Have you ever felt anything of genuine deep concern about your soul?--I fear that many know nothing about it. I have learned, by the painful experience of the third of a century, that people may go on for years attending God's house and yet never feel their sins, or desire to be saved. The cares of this world, the love of pleasure, the "lust of other things" choke the good seed every Sunday, and make it unfruitful. They come to church with hearts as cold as the stone pavement on which they walk. They go away as thoughtless and unmoved as the old marble busts which look down on them from the monuments on the walls. Well, it may be so; but I do not despair of anyone, so long as he is alive. That grand old bell in St. Paul's Cathedral, London, which has struck the Hours for so many years, is seldom heard by many during the business hours of the day. The roar and din of traffic in the streets have a strange power to deaden its sound, and prevent men hearing it. But when the daily work is over, and desks are locked, and doors are closed, and books are put away, and quiet reigns in the great city, the case is altered. As the old bell at night strikes eleven, and twelve, and one, and two, and three, thousands hear it who never heard it during the day. And so I hope it will be with many an one in the matter of his soul. Now, in the plenitude of health and strength, in the hurry and whirl of business, I fear the voice of your conscience is often stifled, and you cannot hear it. But the day may come when the great bell of conscience will make itself heard, whether you like it or not. The time may come when, laid aside in quietness, and obliged by illness to sit still, you may be forced to look within, and consider your soul's concerns. And then, when the great bell of awakened conscience is sounding in your ears, I trust that many a man who reads this paper may hear the voice of God and repent, may learn to thirst, and learn to come to Christ for relief. Yes, I pray God you may be taught to feel before it be too late!

(2) But do you feel anything at this very moment? Is your conscience awake and working? Are you sensible of spiritual thirst, and longing for relief? Then hear the invitation which I bring you in my Master's name this day:--"If any man," no matter who he may be--if any man, high or low, rich or poor, learned or unlearned--"if any man thirst, let him come to Christ and drink." Hear and accept that invitation without delay. Wait for nothing. Wait for nobody. Who can tell that you may not wait for "a convenient season" till it be too late? The hand of a living Redeemer is now held out from heaven; but it may be withdrawn. The Fountain is open now; but it may soon be closed for ever. "If any man thirst, let him come and drink" without delay. Though you have been a great sinner, and have resisted warnings, counsel, and sermons, yet come.--Though you have sinned against light and knowledge, against a father's advice, and a mother's tears, though you have lived for years without a Sabbath, and without prayer, yet come.--Say not that you know not how to come, that you do not understand what it is to believe, that you must wait for more light. Will a tired man say that he is too tired to lie down? or a drowning man, that he knows not how to lay hold on the hand stretched out to help him? or the shipwrecked sailor, with a life-boat alongside the stranded hulk, that he knows not how to jump in? Oh, cast away these vain excuses! Arise, and come! The door is not shut. The fountain is not yet closed. The Lord Jesus invites you. It is enough that you feel thirsting, and desire to be saved. Come: come to Christ without delay. Who ever came to the fountain for sin and found it dry? Who ever went unsatisfied away?

(3) But have you come to Christ already, and found relief? Then come nearer, nearer still. The closer your communion with Christ, the more comfort you will feel. The more you daily live by the side of the Fountain, the more you shall feel in yourself "a well of water springing up into everlasting life." (John iv. 14.) You shall not only be blessed yourself, but be a source of blessing to others.

In this evil world you may not perhaps feel all the sensible comfort you could desire. But remember you cannot have two heavens. Perfect happiness is yet to come. The devil is not yet bound. There is "a good time coming" for all who feel their sins and come to Christ, and commit their thirsting souls to His keeping. When He comes again they will be completely satisfied. They will remember all the way by which they were led, and see the need-be of everything that befell them. Above all, they will wonder that they could ever live so long without Christ, and hesitate about coming to Him.

There is a pass in Scotland called Glencroe, which supplies a beautiful illustration of what heaven will be to the souls who come to Christ. The road through Glencroe carries the traveller up a long and steep ascent, with many a little turn and winding in its course. But when the top of the pass is reached, a stone is seen by the wayside with these simple words inscribed upon it:--"Rest, and be thankful." Those words describe the feelings with which every thirsting one who comes to Christ will enter heaven. The summit of the narrow way will at length be ours. We shall cease from our weary journeyings, and sit down in the kingdom of God. We shall look back on all the way of our lives with thankfulness, and see the perfect wisdom of every step in the steep ascent by which we were led. We shall forget the toil of the upward journey in the glorious rest. Here, in this world, our sense of rest in Christ at best is feeble and partial: we hardly seem at times to taste fully "the living water." But when that which is perfect is come, then that which is imperfect shall be done away. "When we awake up after His likeness we shall be satisfied." (Psalm xvii. 15.) We shall drink out of the river of His pleasures and thirst no more.

NOTE

THERE is a passage in an old writer which throws so much light on some points mentioned in this paper, that I make no excuse for giving it to the reader in its entirety. It comes from a work which is little known and less read. It has done me good, and I think it may do good to others.

"When a man is awakened, and brought to that that all must be brought to, or to worse, What shall I do to be saved?' (Acts xvi. 30, 31), we have the apostolic answer to it: Believe on the Lord Jesus Christ, and thou shalt be saved, and thy house.' This answer is so old that with many it seems out of date. But it is still and will ever be fresh, and new, and savoury, and the only resolution of this grand case of conscience, as long as conscience and the world lasts. No wit or art of man will ever find a crack or flaw in it, or devise another or a better answer; nor can any but this alone heal rightly the wound of an awakened conscience.

"Let us set this man to seek resolution and relief in this case of some masters in our Israel. According to their principles they must say to him, Repent, and mourn for your known sins, and leave them and loath them; and God will have mercy on you.' Alas!' (saith the poor man), my heart is hard, and I cannot repent aright: yea, I find my heart more hard and vile than when I was secure in sin.' If you speak to this man of qualifications for Christ, he knows nothing of them; if of sincere obedience, his answer is native and ready: Obedience is the work of a living man, and sincerity is only in a renewed soul.' Sincere obedience is, therefore, as impossible to a dead unrenewed sinner as perfect obedience is. Why should not the right answer be given to the awakened sinner: Believe on the Lord Jesus Christ, and you shall be saved'? Tell him what Christ is, what He hath done and suffered to obtain eternal redemption for sinners, and that according to the will of God and His Father. Give him a plain downright narrative of the Gospel salvation wrought out by the Son of God; tell him the history and mystery of the Gospel plainly. It may be the Holy Ghost will work faith thereby, as He did m those first fruits of the Gentiles. (Acts x. 44.)

"If he ask, What warrant he hath to believe on Jesus Christ? tell him that he hath utter indispensable necessity for it; for without believing on Him, he must perish eternally. Tell him that he hath God's gracious offer of Christ and all His redemption; with a promise, that upon accepting the offer by faith, Christ and salvation with Him is his. Tell him that he hath God's express commandment (1 John iii. 23) to believe on Christ's name; and that he should make conscience of obeying it, as well as any command in the moral law. Tell him of Christ's ability and good-will to save; that no man was ever rejected by Him that cast himself upon Him; that desperate cases are the glorious triumphs of His art of saving. Tell him that there is no midst (or medium) between faith and unbelief; that there is no excuse for neglecting the one and continuing in the other; that believing on the Lord Jesus for salvation is more pleasing to God than all obedience to His law; and that unbelief is the most provoking to God, and the most damning to man, of all sins. Against the greatness of his sins, the curse of the law, and the severity of God as Judge, there is no relief to be held forth to him, but the free and boundless grace of God in the merit of Christ's satisfaction by the sacrifice of Himself.

"If he should say, What is it to believe on Jesus Christ? As to this, I find no such question in the Word; but that all did some way understand the notion of it: the Jews that did not believe on Him (John vi. 28-30); the chief priests and Pharisees (John vii. 48); the blind man. (John ix. 35.) When Christ asked him, Believest thou on the Son of God? he answered, Who is He, Lord, that I may believe on Him? Immediately, when Christ had told him (verse 37), he saith not, What is it to believe on Him? but, Lord, I believe; and worshipped Him: and so both professed and acted faith in Him. So the father of the lunatic (Mark ix. 23, 24) and the eunuch (Acts viii. 37), they all, both Christ's enemies and His disciples, knew that faith in Him was a believing that the Man Jesus of Nazareth was the Son of God, the Messiah, and Saviour of the world, so as to receive and look for salvation in His name. (Acts iv. 12.) This was the common report, published by Christ and His apostles and disciples, and known by all that heard it.

"If he yet ask, What he is to believe? you tell him, that he is not called to believe that he is in Christ, and that his sins are pardoned, and he a justified man; but that he is to believe God's record concerning Christ, (1 John v. 10-12.) And this record is, that God giveth (that is, offereth) to us eternal Life in His Son Jesus Christ; and that all that with the heart believe this report, and rest their souls on these glad tidings, shall be saved. (Rom. x. 9-11.) And thus he is to believe, that he may be justified. (Gal. ii. 16.)

"If he still say that this believing is hard, this is a good doubt, but easily resolved. It bespeaks a man deeply humbled. Anybody may see his own impotence to obey the law of God fully; but few find the difficulty of believing. For his relief and resolution ask him, What it is he finds makes believing difficult to him? Is it unwillingness to be justified and saved? Is it unwillingness to be so saved by Jesus Christ, to the praise of God's grace in Him, and to the voiding of all boasting in himself? This he will surely deny. Is it a distrust of the truth of the Gospel record? This he dare not own. Is it a doubt of Christ's ability or good-will to save?

This is to contradict the testimony of God in the Gospel. Is it because he doubts of an interest in Christ and His redemption? You tell him that believing on Christ makes up the interest in Him.

"If he say that he cannot believe on Jesus Christ because of the difficulty of the acting this faith, and that a Divine power is needful to draw it forth, which he finds not, you must tell him that believing in Jesus Christ is no work, but a resting on Jesus Christ. You must tell him that this pretence is as unreasonable as if a man, wearied with a journey and not able to go one step further, should argue, I am so tired, that I am not able to lie down,' when indeed he can neither stand nor go. The poor wearied sinner can never believe on Jesus Christ till he finds he can do nothing for himself; and in his first believing doth always apply himself to Christ for salvation, as a man hopeless and helpless in himself. And by such reasonings with him from the Gospel, the Lord will (as He hath often done) convey faith, and joy and peace by believing."--Robert Traill's works, 1696. Vol. I, 266-269.

XVIII. "UNSEARCHABLE RICHES"

"Unto me, who am less than the least of all saints, is this grace given, that I should preach among the Gentiles the unsearchable riches of Christ." Ephesians iii. 8.

IF we heard that sentence read for the first time, I think we should all feel it was a very remarkable one, even though we did not know by whom it was written. It is remarkable on account of the bold and striking figures of speech which it contains. "Less than the least of all saints;"--"Unsearchable riches of Christ;"--these are indeed "thoughts that breathe and words that burn."

But the sentence is doubly remarkable when we consider the man who wrote it. The writer was none other than the great Apostle of the Gentiles, St. Paul--the leader of that noble little Jewish army which went forth from Palestine nineteen centuries ago, and turned the world upside down--that good soldier of Christ who left a deeper mark on mankind than any born of woman, except his sinless Master--a mark which abides to this very day. Surely such a sentence from the pen of such a man demands peculiar attention.

Let us fix our eyes steadily on this text, and notice in it three things:--

I. First, what St. Paul says of himself. He says, "I am less than the least of all saints."

II. Secondly, what St. Paul says of his ministerial office. He says, "Grace is given unto me to preach."

III. Thirdly, what St. Paul says of the great subject of his preaching. He calls it "the unsearchable riches of Christ."

I trust that a few words on each of these three points may help to fasten down the whole text in memories, consciences, hearts, and minds.

I. In the first place, let us notice what St. Paul says of himself.

The language he uses is singularly strong. The founder of famous Churches, the writer of fourteen inspired epistles, the man who was "not behind the very chiefest apostles," "in labours more abundant, in stripes above measure, in prisons more frequent, in deaths oft,"--the man who "spent and was spent" for souls, and "counted all things but loss for Christ,"--the man who could truly say, "To me to live is Christ, and to die is gain,"--what do we find him saying of himself? He employs an emphatic comparative and superlative. He says, "I am less than the least of all saints." What a poor creature is the least saint! Yet St. Paul says, "I am less than that man."

Such language as this, I suspect, is almost unintelligible to many who profess and call themselves Christians. Ignorant alike of the Bible and their own hearts, they cannot understand what a saint means when he speaks so humbly of himself and his attainments. "It is a mere fashion of speaking," they will tell you; "it can only mean what St. Paul used to be, when he was a novice, and first began to serve Christ." So true it is that "the natural man receiveth not the things of the Spirit of God." (1 Cor. ii. 14.) The prayers, the praises, the conflicts, the fears, the hopes, the joys, the sorrows of the true Christian, the whole experience of the seventh of Romans--all, all are "foolishness" to the man of the world. Just as the blind man is no judge of a Reynolds, or a Gainsborough, and the deaf cannot appreciate Handel's Messiah, so the unconverted man cannot fully understand an apostle's lowly estimate of himself.

But we may rest assured that what St. Paul wrote with his pen, he testily felt in his heart. The language of our text does not stand alone. It is even exceeded in other places. To the Philippians he says, "I have not attained, nor am I already perfect: I follow after." To the Corinthians he says, "I am the least of the apostles, which am not meet to be called an apostle." To Timothy he says, "I am chief of sinners." To the Romans he cries, "Wretched man that I am I who shall deliver me from the body of this death?" (Phil. iii. 12; 1 Cor. xv. 9; 1 Tim. i. 15; Rom. vii. 24.) The plain truth is that St. Paul saw in his own heart of hearts far more defects and infirmities than he saw in anyone else. The eyes of his understanding were so fully opened by the Holy Spirit of God that he detected a hundred things wrong in himself which the dull eyes of other men never observed at all. In short, possessing great spiritual light, he had great insight into his own natural corruption, and was clothed from head to foot with humility, (1 Peter v. 5.)

Now let us clearly understand that humility like St. Paul's was not a peculiar characteristic of the great apostle of the Gentiles. On the contrary, it is one leading mark of all the most eminent saints of God in every age. The more real grace men have in their hearts, the deeper is their sense of sin. The more light the Holy Ghost pours into their souls, the more do they discern their own infirmities, defilements, and darkness. The dead soul feels and sees nothing; with life comes clear vision, a tender conscience and spiritual sensibility. Observe what lowly expressions Abraham, and Jacob, and Job, and David, and John the Baptist, used about themselves. Study the biographies of modern saints like Bradford, and Hooker, and George Herbert, and Beveridge, and Baxter, and McCheyne. Mark how one common feature of character belongs to them all--a very deep sense of sin.

Superficial and shallow professors in the warmth of their first love may talk, if they will, of perfection. The great saints, in every era of Church history, from St. Paul down to this day, have always been "clothed with humility."

He that desires to be saved, among the readers of this paper, let him know this day that the first steps towards heaven are a deep sense of sin and a lowly estimate of ourselves. Let him cast away that weak and silly tradition that the beginning of religion is to feel ourselves "good" Let him rather grasp that grand Scriptural principle, that we must begin by feeling "bad"; and that until we really feel "bad" we know nothing of true goodness or saving Christianity. Happy is he who has learned to draw near to God with the prayer of the publican, "God be merciful to me a sinner." (Luke xviii. 13.)

Let us all seek humility. No grace suits man so well What are we that we should be proud? Of all creatures born into the world, none is so dependent as the child of Adam. Physically looked at, what body requires such care and attention, and is such a daily debtor to half creation for food and clothing, as the body of man? Mentally looked at, how little do the wisest men know (and they are but few), and how ignorant the vast majority of mankind are, and what misery do they create by their own folly! "We are but of yesterday," says the book of Job, "and know nothing." (Job viii. 9.) Surely there is no created being on earth or in heaven that ought to be so humble as man.

Let us seek humility. There is no grace which so befits an English churchman. Our matchless Prayer-book, from first to last, puts the humblest language into the mouths of all who use it. The sentences at the beginning of morning and evening prayer, the General Confession, the Litany, the Communion Service--all, all are replete with lowly-minded and self-abasing expressions. All, with one harmonious voice, supply Church of England worshippers with clear teaching about our right position in the sight of God.

Let us all seek more humility, if we know anything of it now. The more we have of it, the more Christlike we shall be. It is written of our blessed Master (though in Him there was no sin) that "being in the form of God He thought it not robbery to be equal with God: but made Himself of no reputation, and took upon Him the form of a servant, and was made in the likeness of men: and being found in fashion as a man, He humbled Himself, and became obedient unto death, even the death of the cross." (Phil. ii. 6-8.) And let us remember the words which precede that passage "Let this mind be in you which was also in Christ Jesus." Depend on it, the nearer men draw to heaven, the more humble do they become. In the hour of death, with one foot in the grave, with something of the light of heaven shining down upon them, hundreds of great saints and Church dignitaries--such men as Selden, Bishop Butler, Archbishop Longley--have left on record their confession, that never till that hour did they see their sins so clearly and feel so deeply their debt to mercy and grace. Heaven alone, I suppose, will fully teach us how humble we ought to be. Then only, when we stand within the veil, and look back on all the way of life by which we were led, then only shall we completely understand the need and beauty of humility. Strong language like St. Paul's will not appear to us too strong in that day. No: indeed! We shall cast our crowns before the throne, and realize what a great divine meant when he said, "The anthem in heaven will be, What hath God wrought."

II. In the second place, let us notice what St. Paul says of his ministerial office.

There is a grand simplicity in the Apostle's words about this subject. He says, "Grace is given unto me that I should preach." The meaning of the sentence is plain: "To me is granted the privilege of being a messenger of good news. I have been commissioned to be a herald of glad tidings."--Of course we cannot doubt that St. Paul's conception of the minister's office included the administration of the sacraments, and the doing all other things needful for the edifying of the body of Christ. But here, as in other places, it is evident that the leading idea continually before his mind was that the chief business of a minister of the New Testament is to be a preacher, an evangelist, God's ambassador, God's messenger, and the proclaimer of God's good news to a fallen world. He says in another place, "Christ sent me not to baptize, but to preach the Gospel." (1 Cor. i. 17.)

I fail to see that St. Paul ever supports the favourite theory that there was intended to be a sacerdotal ministry, a sacrificing priesthood in the Church of Christ. There is not a word in the Acts or in his Epistles to the Churches to warrant such a notion. It is nowhere written, "God hath set some in the Church, first apostles, then priests." (1 Cor. xii. 28.) There is a conspicuous absence of the theory in the Pastoral Epistles to Timothy and Titus, where, if anywhere, we might have expected to find it. On the contrary, in these very Epistles, we read such expressions as these, "God hath manifested His Word through preaching," "I am appointed a preacher." "I am ordained a preacher." "That by me the preaching might be fully known." (1 Tim. ii. 7; 2 Tim. i. 11; 2 Tim. iv. 17; Tit. i. 3.) And, to crown all, one of his last injunctions to his friend Timothy, when he leaves him in charge of an organized Church, is this pithy sentence, "Preach the Word." (2 Tim. iv. 2.) In short, I believe St. Paul would have us understand that, however various the works for which the Christian minister is set apart, his first, foremost, and principal work is to be the preacher and proclaimer of God's Word.

But, while we refuse to allow that a sacrificing priesthood has any warrant of Scripture, let us beware in these days that we do not rush into the extreme of undervaluing the office which the minister of Christ holds. There is some danger in this direction. Let us grasp firmly certain fixed principles about the Christian ministry, and, however strong our dislike of priesthood and aversion to Romanism, let nothing tempt us to let these principles slip out of our hands. Surely there is solid middle ground between a grovelling idolatry of sacerdotalism on one hand, and a disorderly anarchy on the other. Surely it does not follow, because we will not be Papists in this matter of the ministry, that we must needs be Quakers or Plymouth Brethren.[47] This, at any rate, was not in the mind of St. Paul.

(a) For one thing, let us settle it firmly in our minds that the ministerial office is a Scriptural Institution. I need not weary you with quotations to prove this point. I will simply advise you to read the Epistles to Timothy and Titus and judge for yourselves. If these Epistles do not authorize a ministry, there is, to my mind, no meaning in words. Take a jury of the first twelve intelligent, honest, disinterested, unprejudiced men you can find, and set them down with a New Testament to examine this question by them selves: "Is the Christian ministry a Scriptural thing or not?" I have no doubt what their verdict would be.

(b) For another thing, let us settle it in our minds that the ministerial office is a most wise and useful provision of God. It secures the regular maintenance of all Christ's ordinances and means of grace. It provides an undying machinery for promoting the awakening of sinners and the edification of saints. All experience proves that everybody's business soon becomes nobody's business; and if this is true in other matters, it is no less true in the matter of religion. Our God is a God of order, and a God who works by means, and we have no right to expect His cause to be kept up by constant miraculous interpositions, while His servants stand idle. For the uninterrupted preaching of the Word and administration of the sacraments, no better plan can be devised than the appointment of a regular order of men who shall give themselves wholly to Christ's business.

(c) For another thing, let us settle it firmly in our minds that the ministerial office is an honourable privilege. It is an honour to be the Ambassador of a King: the very person of such an officer of state is respected, and called legally sacred. It is an honour to bear the tidings of a victory such as Trafalgar and Waterloo: before the invention of telegraphs it was a highly coveted distinction. But how much greater honour is it to be the ambassador of the King of kings, and to proclaim the good news of the conquest achieved on Calvary! To serve directly such a Master, to carry such a message, to know that the results of our work, if God shall bless it, are eternal, this is indeed a privilege. Other labourers may work for a corruptible crown, but the minister of Christ for an incorruptible. Never is a land in worse condition than when the ministers of religion have caused their office to be ridiculed and despised. It is a tremendous word in Malachi: "I have made you contemptible and base before all the people, according as ye have not kept my ways." (Malachi ii. 9.) But, whether men will hear or forbear, the office of a faithful ambassador is honourable. It was a fine saying of an old missionary on his death-bed, who died at the age of ninety-six, "The very best thing that a man can do is to preach the Gospel."

Let me leave this branch of my subject with an earnest request that all who pray will never forget to make supplications and prayers and intercession for the ministers of Christ--that there never may be wanting a due supply of them at home and in the mission field--that they may be kept sound in the faith and holy in their lives, and that they make take heed to themselves as well as to the doctrine. (1 Tim. iv. 16.)

Oh, remember that while our office is honourable, useful, and Scriptural, it is also one of deep and painful responsibility! We watch for souls "as those who must give account" at the judgment day. (Heb. xiii. 17.) If souls are lost through unfaithfulness, their blood will be required at our hands. If we had only to read services and administer sacraments, to wear a peculiar dress and go through a round of ceremonies, and bodily exercises, and gestures, and postures, our position would be comparatively light. But this is not all. We have got to deliver our Master's message--to keep back nothing that is profitable---to declare all the counsel of God. If we tell our congregations less than the truth or more than the truth, we may ruin for ever immortal souls. Life and death are in the power of the preacher's tongue. "Woe is unto us if we preach not the Gospel!" (1 Cor. ix. 16.)

Once more I say, Pray for us. Who is sufficient for these things? Remember the old saying of the Fathers: "None are in more spiritual danger than ministers." It is easy to criticise and find fault with us. We have a treasure in earthen vessels. We are men of like passions with yourselves, and not infallible. Pray for us in these trying, tempting, controversial days, that our Church may never lack bishops, priests, and deacons who are sound in the faith, bold as lions, "wise as serpents, and yet harmless as doves." (Matt. x. 16.) The very man who said "Grace is given me to preach," is the same man who said, in another place, "Pray for us, that the word of the Lord may have free course, and be glorified, and that we may be delivered from unreasonable and wicked men: for all men have not faith." (2 Thess. iii. 1, 2.)

III. Let us now notice, in the last place, what St. Paul says of the great subject of his preaching. He calls it "the unsearchable riches of Christ."

That the converted man of Tarsus should preach "Christ" is no more than we might expect from his antecedents. Having found peace through the blood of the cross himself, we may be sure he would always tell the story of the cross to others. He never wasted precious time in exalting a mere rootless morality, in descanting on vague abstractions and empty platitudes--such as "the true," and "the noble," and "the earnest," and "the beautiful," and "the germs of goodness in human nature," and the like. He always went to the root of the matter, and showed men their great family disease, their desperate state as sinners, and the Great Physician needed by a sin-sick world.

That he should preach Christ among "the Gentiles" again, is in keeping with all we know of his line of action in all places and among all people. Wherever he travelled and stood up to preach --at Antioch, at Lystra, at Philippi, at Athens, at Corinth, at Ephesus, among Greeks or Romans, among learned or unlearned, among Stoics and Epicureans, before rich or poor, barbarians, Scythians, bond, or free--Jesus and His vicarious death, Jesus and His resurrection, was the keynote of his sermons. Varying his mode of address according to his audience, as he wisely did, the pith and heart of his preaching was Christ crucified.

But in the text before us, you will observe, he uses a very peculiar expression, an expression which unquestionably stands alone in his writings--"the unsearchable riches of Christ" It is the strong, burning language of one who always remembered his debt to Christ's mercy and grace, and loved to show how intensely he felt it by his words. St. Paul was not a man to act or speak by halves. (Quicquid fecit valdé fecit.) He never forgot the road to Damascus, the house of Judas in the street called Strait, the visit of good Ananias, the scales falling from his eyes, and his own marvellous passage from death to life. These things are always fresh and green before his mind; and so he is not content to say, "Grace is given me to preach Christ." No: he amplifies his subject. He calls it "the unsearchable riches of Christ."

But what did the Apostle mean when he spoke of "unsearchable riches"? This is a hard question to answer. No doubt he saw in Christ such a boundless provision for all the wants of man's soul that he knew no other phrase to convey his meaning. From whatever standpoint he beheld Jesus, he saw in Him far more than mind could conceive, or tongue could tell. What he precisely intended must necessarily be matter of conjecture. But it may be useful to set down in detail some of the things which most probably were in his mind. It may, it must, it ought to be useful. For after all, let us remember, these "riches of Christ" are riches which you and I need in England just as much as St. Paul; and, best of all, these "riches" are treasured up in Christ for you and me as much as they were 1900 years ago. They are still there. They are still offered freely to all who are willing to have them. They are still the property of everyone who repents and believes. Let us glance briefly at some of them.

(a) Set down, first and foremost, in your minds that there are unsearchable riches in Christ's person. That miraculous union of perfect Man and perfect God in our Lord Jesus Christ is a great mystery, no doubt, which we have no line to fathom. It is a high thing; and we cannot attain to it. But, mysterious as that union may be, it is a mine of comfort and consolation to all who can rightly regard it. Infinite power and infinite sympathy are met together and combined in our Saviour. If He had been only Man He could not have saved us. If He had been only God (I speak with reverence) He could not have been "touched with the feeling of our infirmities," nor "suffered Himself being tempted." (Heb. ii. 18; iv. 15.) As God, He is mighty to save; and as Man, He is exactly suited to be our Head, Representative, and Friend. Let those who never think deeply, taunt us, if they will, with squabbling about creeds and dogmatic theology. But let thoughtful Christians never be ashamed to believe and hold fast the neglected doctrine of the Incarnation, and the union of two natures in our Saviour. It is a rich and precious truth that our Lord Jesus Christ is both "God and Man."

(b) Set down, next, in your minds that there are unsearchable riches in the work which Christ accomplished for us, when He lived on earth, died, and rose again. Truly and indeed, "He finished the work which His Father gave Him to do." (John xvii. 4)--the work of atonement for sin, the work of reconciliation, the work of redemption, the work of satisfaction, the work of substitution as "the just for the unjust." It pleases some men, I know, to call these short phrases "man-made theological terms, human dogmas," and the like. But they will find it hard to prove that each of these much-abused phrases does not honestly contain the substance of plain texts of Scripture; which, for convenience sake, like the word Trinity, divines have packed into a single word. And each phrase is very rich.

(c) Set down, next, in your minds that there are unsearchable riches in the offices which Christ at this moment fills, as He lives for us at the right hand of God. He is at once our Mediator, our Advocate, our Priest, our Intercessor, our Shepherd, our Bishop, our Physician, our Captain, our King, our Master, our Head, our Forerunner, our Elder Brother, the Bridegroom of our souls. No doubt these offices are worthless to those who know nothing of vital religion. But to those who live the life of faith, and seek first the kingdom of God, each office is precious as gold.

(d) Set down, next, in your minds that there are unsearchable riches in the names and titles which are applied to Christ in the Scriptures. Their number is very great, every careful

Bible-reader knows, and I cannot of course pretend to do more than select a few of them. Think for a moment of such titles as the Lamb of God--the bread of life--the fountain of living waters--the light of the world--the door--the way--the vine--the rock--the corner stone--the Christian's robe--the Christian's altar. Think of all these names, I say, and consider how much they contain. To the careless, worldly man they are mere "words," and nothing more; but to the true Christian each title, if beaten out and developed, will be found to have within its bosom a wealth of blessed truth.

(e) Set down, lastly, in your minds that there are unsearchable riches in the characteristic qualities, attributes, dispositions, and intentions of Christ's mind towards man, as we find them revealed in the New Testament. In Him there are riches of mercy, love, and com passion for sinners--riches of power to cleanse, pardon, forgive, and to save to the uttermost--riches of willingness to receive all who come to Him repenting and believing--riches of ability to change by His Spirit the hardest hearts and worst characters--riches of tender patience to bear with the weakest believer--riches of strength to help His people to the end, notwithstanding every foe without and within--riches of sympathy for all who are cast down and bring their troubles to Him--and last, but not least, riches of glory to reward, when He comes again to raise the dead and gather His people to be with Him in His kingdom. Who can estimate these riches? The children of this world may regard them with indifference, or turn away from them with disdain; but those who feel the value of their souls know better. They will say with one voice, "There are no riches like those which are laid up in Christ for His people."

For, best of all, these riches are unsearchable. They are a mine which, however long it may be worked, is never exhausted. They are a fountain which, however many draw its waters, never runs dry. The sun in heaven has been shining for thousands of years, and giving light, and life, and warmth, and fertility to the whole surface of the globe. There is not a tree or a flower in Europe, Asia, Africa, or America which is not a debtor to the sun. And still the sun shines on for generation after generation, and season after season, rising and setting with unbroken regularity, giving to all, taking from none, and to all ordinary eyes the same in light and heat that it was in the day of creation, the great common benefactor of mankind. Just so it is, if any illustration can approach the reality, just so it is with Christ. He is still "the Sun of righteousness" to all mankind. (Malachi iv. 2.) Millions have drawn from Him in days gone by, and looking to Him have lived with comfort, and with comfort died. Myriads at this moment are drawing from Him daily supplies of mercy, grace, peace, strength, and help, and find "all fulness" dwelling in Him. And yet the half of the riches laid up in Him for mankind, I doubt not, is utterly unknown! Surely the Apostle might well use that phrase, "the unsearchable riches of Christ."

Let me now conclude this paper with three words of practical application. For convenience sake I shall put them in the form of questions, and I invite each reader of this volume to examine them quietly and try to give them an answer.

(1) First, then, let me ask you what you think of yourself? What St. Paul thought of himself you have seen and heard. Now, what are your thoughts about yourself? Have you found out that grand foundation-truth that you are a sinner, a guilty sinner in the sight of God?

The cry for more education in this day is loud and incessant. Ignorance is universally deplored. But, you may depend, there is no ignorance so common and so mischievous as ignorance of ourselves. Yes: men may know all arts, and sciences, and languages, and political economy, and state-craft, and yet be miserably ignorant of their own hearts and their own state before God.

Be very sure that self-knowledge is the first step towards heaven. To know God's unspeakable perfection, and our own immense imperfection--to see our own unspeakable defectiveness and corruption, is the A B C in saving religion. The more real inward light we have, the more humble and lowly-minded we shall be, and the more we shall understand the value of that despised thing, the Gospel of Christ. He that thinks worst of himself and his own doings is perhaps the best Christian before God. Well would it be for many if they would pray, night and day, this simple prayer--"Lord, show me myself."

(2) Secondly, what do you think of the ministers of Christ? Strange as that question may seem, I verily believe that the kind of answer a man would give to it, if he speaks honestly, is very often a fair test of the state of his heart.

Observe, I am not asking what you think of an idle, worldly, inconsistent clergyman--a sleeping watchman and faithless shepherd. No! I ask what you think of the faithful minister of Christ, who honestly exposes sin, and pricks your conscience. Mind how you answer that question. Too many, nowadays, like only those ministers who prophesy smooth things and let their sins alone, who flatter their pride and amuse their intellectual taste, but who never sound an alarm, and never tell them of a wrath to come. When Ahab saw Elijah, he said, "Hast thou found me, O mine enemy?" (1 Kings xxi. 20.) When Micaiah was named to Ahab, he cried, "I hate him because he doth not prophesy good of me, but evil." (1 Kings xxii. 8.) Alas, there are many like Ahab in the nineteenth century! They like a ministry which does not make them uncomfortable, and send them home ill at ease. How is it with you? Oh, believe me, he is the best friend who tells you the most truth! It is an evil sign in the Church when Christ's witnesses are silenced, or persecuted, and men hate him who reproveth. (Isaiah xxix. 21.) It was a solemn saying of the prophet to Amaziah: "Now I know that God hath determined to destroy thee, because thou has done this, and not hearkened to my counsel." (2 Chron. xxv. 16.)

(3) Last of all, what do you think of Christ Himself? Is He great or little in your eyes? Does He come first or second in your estimation? Is He before or behind His Church, His ministers, His sacraments, His ordinances? Where is He in your heart and your mind's eye?

After all, this is the question of questions! Pardon, peace, rest of conscience, hope in death, heaven itself--all hinge upon our answer. To know Christ is life eternal. To be without Christ is to be without God. "He that hath the Son hath life; and he that hath not the Son of God hath not life." (1 John v. 12.) The friends of purely secular education, the enthusiastic advocates of reform and progress, the worshippers of reason, and intellect, and mind, and science, may say what they please, and do all they can to mend the world. But they will find their labour in vain if they do not make allowance for the fall of man, if there is no place for Christ in their schemes. There is a sore disease at the heart of mankind, which will baffle all their efforts, and defeat all their plans, and that disease is sin. Oh, that people would only see and recognize the corruption of human nature, and the uselessness of all efforts to improve man which are not based on the remedial system of the Gospel! Yes: the plague of sin is in the world, and no waters will ever heal that plague except those which flow from the fountain for all sin--a crucified Christ.

But, to wind up all, where is boasting? As a great divine said on his death-bed, "We are all of us only half awake." The best Christian among us knows but little of his glorious Saviour, even after he had learned to believe. We see through a glass darkly. We do not realize the "unsearchable riches" there are in Him. When we wake up after His likeness in another world, we shall be amazed that we knew Him so imperfectly, and loved Him so little Let us seek to know Him better now, and live in closer communion with Him. So living, we shall feel no need of human priests and earthly confessionals. We shall feel "I have all and abound: I want nothing more. Christ dying for me on the cross--Christ ever interceding for me at God's right hand--Christ dwelling in my heart by faith--Christ soon coming again to gather me and all His people together to part no more, Christ is enough for me. Having Christ, I have unsearchable riches.'"

"The good I have is from His stores supplied,
The ill is only what He deems the best;
He for my Friend, I'm rich with nought beside,
And poor without Him, though of all possess'd:
Changes may come, I take or I resign,
Content while I am His, and He is mine.

"While here, alas! I know but half His love,
But half discern Him, and but half adore;
But when I meet Him in the realms above,
I hope to love Him better, praise Him more,
And feel, and tell, amid the choir divine,
How fully I am His, and He is mine."

ENDNOTE

[47] Every well-informed person knows that, to the apprehension of most people, the Quakers and Plymouth Brethren appear to ignore the ministerial office altogether.

XIX. WANTS OF THE TIMES

"Men that had understanding of the times."--1 Chronicles xii. 32.

THESE words were written about the tribe of Issachar, in the days when David first began to reign over Israel. It seems that after Saul's unhappy death, some of the tribes of Israel were undecided what to do. "Under which king?" was the question of the day in Palestine. Men doubted whether they should cling to the family of Saul, or accept David as their king. Some hung back, and would not commit themselves; others came forward boldly, and declared for David. Among these last were many of the children of Issachar; and the Holy Ghost gives them a special word of praise. He says, "They were men that had understanding of the times."

I cannot doubt that this sentence, like every sentence in Scripture, was written for our learning. These men of Issachar are set before us as a pattern to be imitated and an example to be followed; for it is a most important thing to understand the times in which we live, and to know what those times require. The wise men in the court of Ahasuerus "knew the times." (Esther i. 13.) Our Lord Jesus Christ blames the Jews because they "knew not the time of their visitation," and did not "discern the signs of the times." (Matt. xvi. 3; Luke xix. 44.) Let us take heed lest we fall into the same sin. The man who is content to sit ignorantly by his own fireside, wrapped up in his own private affairs, and has no public eye for what is going on in the Church and the world, is a miserable patriot, and a poor style of Christian. Next to our Bibles and our own hearts, our Lord would have us study our own times.

Now I propose in this paper to consider what our own times require at our hands. All ages have their own peculiar dangers for professing Christians, and all consequently demand special attention to peculiar duties. I ask my readers to give me their minds for a few minutes while I try to show them what the times require of English Christians, and particularly of English Churchmen. There are five points which I propose to bring before you, and I shall speak of them plainly and without reserve. "If the trumpet give an uncertain sound, who shall prepare himself to the battle?" (1 Cor. xiv. 8.)

I. First and foremost, the times require of us a bold and unflinching maintenance of the entire truth of Christianity, and the Divine authority of the Bible.

Our lot is cast in an age of abounding unbelief, scepticism, and, I fear I must add, infidelity. Never, perhaps, since the days of Celsus, Porphyry, and Julian, was the truth of revealed religion so openly and unblushingly assailed, and never was the assault so speciously and plausibly conducted. The words which Bishop Butler wrote in 1736 are curiously applicable to our own days:--"It is come to be taken for granted by many persons, that Christianity is not even a subject of inquiry; but that it is now at length discovered to be fictitious. And accordingly they treat it as if, in the present age, this was an agreed point among all people of discernment, and nothing remained but to set it up as a principal subject of mirth and ridicule, as it were by way of reprisals for its having so long interrupted the pleasures of the world." (Butter's Analogy, Introduction.) I often wonder what the good Bishop would have now said, if he had lived in the present day.

In reviews, magazines, newspapers, lectures, essays, and sometimes even in sermons, scores of clever writers are incessantly waging war against the very foundations of Christianity. Reason, science, geology, anthropology, modern discoveries, free thought, are all boldly asserted to be on their side. No educated person, we are constantly told nowadays, can really believe supernatural religion, or the plenary inspiration of the Bible, or the possibility of miracles. Such ancient doctrines as the Trinity, the deity of Christ, the personality of the Holy Spirit, the atonement, the obligation of the Sabbath, the necessity and efficacy of prayer, the existence of the devil, and the reality of future punishment, are quietly put on the shelf as useless old Almanacs, or contemptuously thrown overboard as lumber! And all this is done so cleverly, and with such an appearance of candour and liberality, and with such compliments to the capacity and nobility of human nature, that multitudes of unstable Christians are carried away as by a flood, and become partially unsettled, if they do not make complete shipwreck of faith.

The existence of this plague of unbelief must not surprise us for a moment. It is only an old enemy in a new dress, an old disease in a new form. Since the day when Adam and Eve fell, the devil has never ceased to tempt men not to believe God, and has said, directly or indirectly, "Ye shall not die even if you do not believe." In the latter days especially we have warrant of Scripture for expecting an abundant crop of unbelief:--"When the Son of man cometh, shall He find faith on the earth?"--"Evil men and seducers shall wax worse and worse."--"There shall come in the last days scoffers." (Luke xviii. 8; 2 Tim. iii. 13; 2 Peter iii. 3.) Here in England scepticism is that natural rebound from semi-popery and superstition, which many wise men have long predicted and expected. It is precisely that swing of the pendulum which far-sighted students of human nature looked for; and it has come.

But as I tell you not to be surprised at the widespread scepticism of the times, so also I must urge you not to be shaken in mind by it, or moved from your steadfastness. There is no real cause for alarm. The ark of God is not in danger, though the oxen seem to shake it. Christianity has survived the attacks of Hume and Hobbes and Tindal--of Collins and Woolston and Bolingbroke and Chubb--of Voltaire and Payne and Holyoak. These men made a great noise in their day, and frightened weak people; but they produced no more effect than idle travellers produce by scratching their names on the great pyramid of Egypt. Depend on it, Christianity in like manner will survive the attacks of the clever writers of these times. The startling novelty of many modern objections to Revelation, no doubt, makes them seem more weighty than they really are. It does not follow, however, that hard knots cannot be untied because our fingers cannot untie them, or formidable difficulties cannot be explained because our eyes cannot see through or explain them. When you cannot answer a sceptic, be content to wait for more light; but never forsake a great principle. In religion, as in many scientific questions, said Faraday, "the highest philosophy is often a judicious suspense of judgment." He that believeth shall not make haste: he can afford to wait.

When sceptics and infidels have said all they can, we must not forget that there are three great broad facts which they have never explained away; and I am convinced they never can, and never will. Let me tell you briefly what they are. They are very simple facts, and any plain man can understand them.

(a) The first fact is Jesus Christ Himself. If Christianity is a mere invention of man, and the Bible is not from God, how can infidels explain Jesus Christ? His existence in history, they cannot deny. How is it that without force or bribery, without arms or money, He has made such an immensely deep mark on the world, as He certainly has? Who was He? What was He? Where did He come from? How is it that there never has been one like Him, neither before nor after, since the beginning of historical times? They cannot explain it. Nothing can explain it but the great foundation principle of revealed religion, that Jesus Christ is God, and His Gospel is all true.

(b) The second fact is the Bible itself. If Christianity is a mere invention of man, and the Bible is of no more authority than any other uninspired volume, how is it that the Book is what it is? How is it that a Book written by a few Jews in a remote corner of the earth--written at distant periods without consort or collusion among the writers--written by members of a nation which, compared to Greeks and Romans, did nothing for literature--how is it that this Book stands entirely alone, and there is nothing that even approaches it, for high views of God, for true views of man, for solemnity of thought, for grandeur of doctrine, and for purity of morality? What account can the infidel give of this Book, so deep, so simple, so wise, so free from defects? He cannot explain its existence and nature on his principles. We only can do that who hold that the Book is Supernatural and of God.

(c) The third fact is the effect which Christianity has produced on the world. If Christianity is a mere invention of man, and not a supernatural, Divine revelation, how is it that it has wrought such a complete alteration in the state of mankind? Any well-read man knows that the moral difference between the condition of the world, before Christianity was planted and since Christianity took root, is the difference between night and day, the kingdom of heaven and the kingdom of the devil. At this very moment, I defy anyone to look at the map of the world, and compare the countries where men are Christians with those where men are not Christians, and to deny that these countries are as different as light and darkness, black and white. How can any infidel explain this on his principles? He cannot do it. We only can who believe that Christianity came down from God, and is the only Divine religion in the world.

Whenever you are tempted to be alarmed at the progress of infidelity, look at the three facts I have just mentioned, and cast your fears away. Take up your position boldly behind the ramparts of these three facts, and you may safely defy the utmost efforts of modern sceptics. They may often ask you a hundred questions you cannot answer, and start ingenious problems about various readings, or inspiration, or geology, or the origin of man, or the age of the world, which you cannot solve. They may vex and irritate you with wild speculations and theories, of which at the time you cannot prove the fallacy, though you feel it. But be calm and fear not. Remember the three great facts I have named, and boldly challenge sceptics to explain them. away. The difficulties of Christianity no doubt are great; but, depend on it, they are nothing compared to the difficulties of infidelity.

II. In the second place, the times require at our hands distinct and decided views of Christian doctrine.

I cannot withhold my conviction that the professing Church of the nineteenth century is as much damaged by laxity and indistinctness about matters of doctrine within, as it is by sceptics and unbelievers without. Myriads of professing Christians nowadays seem utterly unable to distinguish things that differ. Like people afflicted with colour-blindness, they are incapable of discerning what is true and what is false, what is sound and what is unsound. If a preacher of religion is only clever and eloquent and earnest, they appear to think he is all right, however strange and heterogeneous his sermons may be. They are destitute of spiritual sense, apparently, and cannot detect error. Popery or Protestantism, an atonement or no atonement, a personal Holy Ghost or no Holy Ghost, future punishment or no future punishment, High Church or Low Church or Broad Church, Trinitarianism, Arianism, or Unitarianism, nothing comes amiss to them: they can swallow it all, if they cannot digest it! Carried away by a fancied liberality and charity, they seem to think everybody is right and nobody is wrong, every clergyman is sound and none are unsound, everybody is going to be saved and nobody going to be lost. Their religion is made up of negatives; and the only positive thing about them is that they dislike distinctness and think all extreme and decided and positive views are very naughty and very wrong!

These people live in a kind of mist or fog. They see nothing clearly, and do not know what they believe. They have not made up their minds about any great point in the Gospel, and seem content to be honorary members of all schools of thought. For their lives they could not tell you what they think is truth about justification, or regeneration, or sanctification, or the Lord's Supper, or baptism, or faith, or conversion, or inspiration, or the future state. They are eaten up with a morbid dread of controversy and an ignorant dislike of party spirit; and yet they really cannot define what they mean by these phrases. The only point you can make out is that they admire earnestness and cleverness and charity, and cannot believe that any clever, earnest, charitable man can ever be in the wrong! And so they live on undecided; and too often undecided they drift down to the grave, without comfort in their religion, and, I am afraid, often without hope.

The explanation of this boneless, nerveless, jelly-fish condition of soul is not difficult to find. To begin with, the heart of man is naturally in the dark about religion--has no intuitive sense of truth--and really needs instruction and illumination. Besides this, the natural heart in most men hates exertion in religion, and cordially dislikes patient, painstaking inquiry. Above all, the natural heart generally likes the praise of others, shrinks from collision, and loves to be thought charitable and liberal. The whole result is that a kind of broad religious "agnosticism" just suits an immense number of people, and specially suits young persons. They are content to shovel aside all disputed points as rubbish, and if you charge them with indecision, they will tell you: "I do not pretend to understand controversy; I decline to examine controverted points. I daresay it is all the same in the long run."--Who does not know that such people swarm and abound everywhere?

Now I do beseech all who read this paper to beware of this undecided state of mind in religion. It is a pestilence which walketh in darkness, and a destruction that killeth in noonday. It is a lazy, idle frame of soul which, doubtless, saves men the trouble of thought and investigation; but it is a frame of soul for which there is no warrant in the Bible, nor yet in the Articles or Prayer-book of the Church of England. For your own soul's sake, dare to make up your mind what you believe, and dare to have positive, distinct views of truth and error. Never, never be afraid to hold decided doctrinal opinions; and let no fear of man and no morbid dread of being thought party-spirited, narrow, or controversial, make you rest contented with a bloodless, boneless, tasteless, colourless, lukewarm, undogmatic Christianity.

Mark what I say. If you want to do good in these times, you must throw aside indecision, and take up a distinct, sharply-cut, doctrinal religion. If you believe little, those to whom you try to do good will believe nothing. The victories of Christianity, wherever they have been won, have been won by distinct doctrinal theology; by telling men roundly of Christ's vicarious death and sacrifice; by showing them Christ's substitution on the cross, and His precious blood; by teaching them justification by faith, and bidding them believe on a crucified Saviour; by preaching ruin by sin, redemption by Christ, regeneration by the Spirit; by lifting up the brazen serpent; by telling men to look and five--to believe, repent, and be converted. This--this is the only teaching which for eighteen centuries God has honoured with success, and is honouring at the present day both at home and abroad. Let the clever advocates of a broad and undogmatic theology--the preachers of the Gospel of earnestness, and sincerity and cold morality--let them, I say, show us at this day any English village or parish, or city, or town, or district, which has been evangelized without "dogma," by their principles. They cannot do it, and they never will. Christianity without distinct doctrine is a powerless thing. It may be beautiful to some minds, but it is childless and barren. There is no getting over facts. The good that is done in the earth may be comparatively small. Evil may abound, and ignorant impatience may murmur and cry out that Christianity has failed. But, depend on it, if we want to "do good" and shake the world, we must fight with the old apostolic weapons, and stick to "dogma." No dogma, no fruits! No positive Evangelical doctrine, no evangelization!

Mark once more what I say. The men who have done most for the Church of England, and made the deepest mark on their day and generation, have always been men of most decided and distinct doctrinal views. It is the bold, decided, outspoken man, like Capel Molyneux, or our grand old Protestant champion Hugh McNeile, who makes a deep impression, and sets people thinking, and "turns the world upside down." It was "dogma" in the apostolic ages which emptied the heathen temples and shook Greece and Rome. It was "dogma" which awoke Christendom from its slumbers at the time of the Reformation and spoiled the Pope of one third of his subjects. It was "dogma" which 100 years ago revived the Church of England in the days of Whitfield, Wesley, Venn, and Romaine, and blew up our dying Christianity into a burning flame. It is "dogma" at this moment which gives power to every successful mission, whether at home or abroad. It is doctrine--doctrine, clear, ringing doctrine--which, like the ram's horns at Jericho, casts down the opposition of the devil and sin. Let us cling to decided doctrinal views, whatever some may please to say in these times, and we shall do well for ourselves, well for others, well for the Church of England, and well for Christ's cause in the world.

III. In the third place, the times require of us an awakened and livelier sense of the unscriptural and soul-ruining character of Romanism.

This is a painful subject; but it imperatively demands some plain speaking.

The facts of the case are very simple. No intelligent observer can fail to see that the tone of public feeling in England about Romanism has undergone a great change in the last forty years. Father Oakley, the well-known pervert, an ally of Cardinal Newman, asserts this triumphantly in a recent number of the Contemporary Review. And I am sorry to say that, in my judgment, he speaks the truth. There is no longer that general dislike, dread, and aversion to Popery, which was once almost universal in this realm. The edge of the old British feeling about Protestantism seems blunted and dull. Some profess to be tired of all religious controversy, and are ready to sacrifice God's truth for the sake of peace.--Some look on Romanism as simply one among many English forms of religion, and neither worse nor better than others.--Some try to persuade us that Romanism is changed, and not nearly so bad as it used to be.--Some boldly point to the faults of Protestants, and loudly cry that Romanists are quite as good as ourselves.--Some think it fine and liberal to maintain that we have no right to think anyone wrong who is in earnest about his creed.--And yet the two great historical facts, (a) that ignorance, immorality, and superstition reigned supreme in England 400 years ago under

Popery, (b) that the Reformation was the greatest blessing God ever gave to this land--both these are facts which no one but a Papist ever thought of disputing fifty years ago! In the present day, alas, it is convenient and fashionable to forget them! In short, at the rate we are going, I shall not be surprised if it is soon proposed to repeal the Act of Settlement and to allow the Crown of England to be worn by a Papist.

The causes of this melancholy change of feeling are not hard to discover.

(a) It arises partly from the untiring zeal of the Romish Church herself. Her agents never slumber or sleep. They compass sea and land to make one proselyte. They creep in everywhere, like the Egyptian frogs, and leave no stone unturned, in the palace or the workhouse, to promote their cause, (b) It has been furthered immensely by the proceedings of the Ritualistic party in the Church of England. That energetic and active body has been vilifying the Reformation and sneering at Protestantism for many years, with only too much success. It has corrupted, leavened, blinded, and poisoned the minds of many Churchmen by incessant misrepresentation. It has gradually familiarized people with every distinctive doctrine and practice of Romanism--the real presence--the mass--auricular confession and priestly absolution--the sacerdotal character of the ministry--the monastic system--and a histrionic, sensuous, showy style of public worship--and the natural result is, that many simple people see no mighty harm in downright genuine Popery! Last, but not least, the spurious liberality of the ay we live in helps on the Romeward tendency. It is fashionable now to say that all sects should be equal--that the State should have nothing to do with religion--that all creeds should be regarded with equal favour and respect--and that there is a substratum of common truth at the bottom of all kinds of religion, whether Buddhism, Mohammedanism, or Christianity! The consequence is that myriads of ignorant folk begin to think there is nothing peculiarly dangerous in the tenets of Papists any more than in the tenets of Methodists, Independents, Presbyterians, or Baptists--and that we ought to let Romanism alone and never expose its unscriptural and Christ-dishonouring character.

The consequences of this changed tone of feeling, I am bold to say, will be most disastrous and mischievous, unless it can be checked. Once let Popery get her foot again on the neck of England and there will be an end of all our national greatness. God will forsake us and we shall sink to the level of Portugal and Spain. With Bible-reading discouraged--with private judgment forbidden--with the way to Christ's cross narrowed or blocked up--with priest-craft re-established--with auricular confession set up in every parish--with monasteries and nunneries dotted over the land--with women everywhere kneeling like serfs and slaves at the feet of clergymen--with men casting off all faith, and becoming sceptics--with schools and colleges made seminaries of Jesuitism--with free thought denounced and anathematized--with all these things the distinctive manliness and independence of the British character will gradually dwindle, wither, pine away, and be destroyed; and England will be ruined. And all these things, I firmly believe, will come unless the old feeling about the value of Protestantism can be revived.

I warn all who read this paper, and I warn my fellow-churchmen in particular, that the times require you to awake and be on your guard. Beware of Romanism and beware of any religious teaching which, wittingly or unwittingly, paves the way to it. I beseech you to realize the painful fact that the protestantism of this country is gradually ebbing away, and I entreat you, as Christians and patriots to resist the growing tendency to forget the blessings of the English Reformation.

For Christ's sake, for the sake of the Church of England, for the sake of our country, for the sake of our children, let us not drift back to Romish ignorance, superstition, priestcraft, and immorality. Our fathers tried Popery long ago, for centuries, and threw it off at last with disgust and indignation. Let us not put the clock back and return to Egypt. Let us have no peace with Rome till Rome adjures her errors and is at peace with Christ. Till Rome does that, the vaunted re-union of Western Churches, which some talk of, and press upon our notice, is an insult to Christianity.

Read your Bibles and store your minds with Scriptural arguments. A Bible-reading laity is a nation's surest defence against error. I have no fear for English Protestantism if the English laity will only do their duty. Read your Thirty-nine Articles and "Jewell's Apology," and see how those neglected documents speak of Romish doctrines. We clergymen, I fear, are often sadly to blame. We break the first Canon, which bids us preach four times every year against the Pope's supremacy! Too often we behave as if "giant Pope" was dead and buried, and never name him. Too often, for fear of giving offence, we neglect to show our people the real nature and evil of Popery.

I entreat my readers, beside the Bible and Articles, to read history and see what Rome did in days gone by. Read how she trampled on your country's liberties, plundered your forefathers' pockets, and kept the whole nation ignorant, superstitious, and immoral. Read how Archbishop Laud ruined Church and State, and brought himself and King Charles to the scaffold by his foolish, obstinate, and God-displeasing effort to unprotestantize the Church of England. Read how the last Popish King of England, James the second, lost his crown by his daring attempt to put down protestantism and reintroduce Popery. And do not forget that Rome never changes. It is her boast and glory that she is infallible, and always the same.

Read facts, standing out at this minute on the face of the globe, if you will not read history. What has made Italy and Sicily what they were till very lately? Popery.--What has made the South American States what they are? Popery.--What has made Spain and Portugal what they are? Popery.--What has made Ireland what she is in Munster, Leinster, and Connaught? Popery.--What makes Scotland, the United States, and our own beloved England the powerful, prosperous countries they are, and I pray God they may long continue? I answer, unhesitatingly, Protestantism--a free Bible and the principles of the Reformation. Oh, think twice before you cast aside the principles of the Reformation! Think twice before you give way to the prevailing tendency to favour Popery and go back to Rome.

The Reformation found Englishmen steeped in ignorance and left them in possession of knowledge--found them without Bibles and placed a Bible in every parish--found them in darkness and left them in comparative light--found them priest-ridden and left them enjoying the liberty which Christ bestows--found them strangers to the blood of atonement, to faith and grace and real holiness, and left them with the key to these things in their hands--found them blind and left them seeing--found them slaves and left them free. For ever let us thank God for the Reformation! It lighted a candle which we ought never to allow to be extinguished or to burn dim. Surely I have a right to say that the times require of us a renewed sense of the evils of Romanism, and of the enormous value of the Protestant Reformation!

IV. In the fourth place, the times require of us a higher standard of personal holiness, and an increased attention to practical religion in daily life.

I must honestly declare my conviction that, since the days of the Reformation, there never has been so much profession of religion without practice, so much talking about God without walking with Him, so much hearing God's words without doing them, as there is in

England at this present date. Never were there so many empty tubs and tinkling cymbals! Never was there so much formality and so little reality. The whole tone of men's minds on what constitutes practical Christianity seems lowered. The old golden standard of the behaviour which becomes a Christian man or woman appears debased and degenerated. You may see scores of religious people (so-called) continually doing things which in days gone by would have been thought utterly inconsistent with vital religion. They see no harm in such things as card-playing, theatre-going, dancing, incessant novel-reading, and Sunday-travelling, and they cannot in the least understand what you mean by objecting to them! The ancient tenderness of conscience about such things seems dying away and becoming extinct, like the dodo; and when you venture to remonstrate with young communicants who indulge in them, they only stare at you as an old-fashioned, narrow-minded, fossilized person and say, "Where is the harm?" In short, laxity of ideas among young men, and "fastness" and levity among young women, are only too common characteristics of the rising generation of Christian professors.

Now in saying all this I would not be mistaken. I disclaim the slightest wish to recommend an ascetic religion. Monasteries, nunneries, complete retirement from the world, and refusal to do our duty in it, all these I hold to be unscriptural and mischievous nostrums. Nor can I ever see my way clear to urging on men an ideal standard of perfection for which I find no warrant in God's Word, a standard which is unattainable in this life, and hands over the management of the affairs of society to the devil and the wicked. No: I always wish to promote a genial, cheerful, manly religion, such as men may carry everywhere and yet glorify Christ.

The pathway to a higher standard of holiness which I commend to the attention of my readers is a very simple one, so simple that I can fancy many smiling at it with disdain. But, simple as it is, it is a path sadly neglected and overgrown with weeds, and it is high time to direct men into it. We need then to examine more closely our good old friends the ten commandments. Beaten out, and properly developed as they were by Bishop Andrews and the Puritans, the two tables of God's law are a perfect mine of practical religion. I think it an evil sign of our day that many clergymen neglect to have the commandments put up in their new, or restored, churches, and coolly tell you "they are not wanted now!" I believe they never were wanted so much!--We need to examine more closely such portions of our Lord Jesus Christ's teaching as the Sermon on the Mount. How rich is that wonderful discourse in food for thought! What a striking sentence that is, "Except your righteousness exceed the righteousness of the scribes and Pharisees, ye shall in no case enter the kingdon of heaven." (Matt. v. 20.) Alas, that text is rarely used!--Last, but not least, we need to study more closely the latter part of nearly all St. Paul's Epistles to the Churches. They are far too much slurred over and neglected. Scores of Bible readers, I am afraid, are well acquainted with the first eleven chapters of the Epistle to the Romans, but know comparatively little of the five last. When Thomas Scott expounded the Epistle to the Ephesians at the old Lock Chapel, he remarked that the congregations became much smaller when he reached the practical part of that blessed book! Once more I say you may think my recommendations very simple. I do not hesitate to affirm that attention to them would by God's blessing be most useful to Christ's cause. I believe it would raise the standard of English Christianity about such matters as home religion, separation from the world, diligence in the discharge of relative duties, unselfishness, good temper, and general spiritual-mindedness, to a pitch which it seldom attains now.

There is a common complaint in these latter days that there is a want of power in modern Christianity, and that the true Church of Christ, the body of which He is the Head, does not shake the world in the twentieth century as it used to do in former years. Shall I tell you in plain words what is the reason? It is the low tone of life which is so sadly prevalent among professing believers. We want more men and women who walk with God and before God, like Enoch and Abraham. Though our numbers at this date far exceed those of our Evangelical forefathers, I believe we fall far short of them in our standard of Christian practice. Where is the self-denial, the redemption of time, the absence of luxury and self-indulgence, the unmistakable separation from earthly things, the manifest air of being always about our Master's business, the singleness of eye, the simplicity of home life, the high tone of conversation in society, the patience, the humility, the universal courtesy which marked so many of our forerunners seventy or eighty years ago? Yes: where is it indeed? We have inherited their principles and we wear their armour, but I fear we have not inherited their practice. The Holy Ghost sees it, and is grieved; and the world sees it, and despises us. The world sees it, and cares little for our testimony. It is life, life--a heavenly, godly, Christ-like life--depend on it, which influences the world. Let us resolve, by God's blessing, to shake off this reproach. Let us awake to a clear view of what the times require of us in this matter. Let us aim at a much higher standard of practice. Let the time past suffice us to have been content with a half-and-half holiness. For the time to come, let us endeavour to walk with God, to be "thorough" and unmistakable in our daily life, and to silence, if we cannot convert, a sneering world.

V. In the fifth and last place, the times require of us more regular and steady perseverance in the old ways of getting good for our souls.

I think no intelligent Englishman can fail to see that there has been of late years an immense increase of what I must call, for want of a better phrase, public religion in the land. Services of all sorts are strangely multiplied. Places of worship are thrown open for prayer and preaching and administration of the Lord's Supper, at least ten times as much as they were fifty years ago. Services in cathedral naves, meetings in large public rooms like the Agricultural Hall and Mildmay Conference Building, Mission Services carried on day after day and evening after evening--all these have become common and familiar things. They are, in fact, established institutions of the day, and the crowds who attend them supply plain proof that they are popular. In short, we find ourselves face to face with the undeniable fact that the last quarter of the nineteenth century is an age of an immense amount of public religion.

Now I am not going to find fault with this. Let no one suppose that for a moment. On the contrary, I thank God for the revival of the old apostolic plan of "aggressiveness" in religion, and the evident spread of a desire "by all means to save some." (1 Cor. ix. 22.) I thank God for shortened services, home missions, and evangelistic movements like that of Moody and Sankey. Anything is better than torpor, apathy, and inaction. "If Christ is preached I rejoice, yea, and will rejoice." (Phil. i. 18.) Prophets and righteous men in England once desired to see those things, and never saw them. If Whitfield and Wesley had been told in their day that a time would come when English Archbishops and Bishops would not only sanction mission services but take an active part in them, I can hardly think they would have believed it. Rather, I suspect, they would have been tempted to say, like the Samaritan nobleman in Elisha's time, "If the Lord would make windows in heaven, might this thing be." (2 Kings vii. 2.)

But while we are thankful for the increase of public religion, we must never forget that, unless it is accompanied by private religion, it is of no real solid value, and may even produce most mischievous effects. Incessant running after sensational preachers, incessant attendance at hot, crowded meetings, protracted to late hours, incessant craving after fresh excitement and highly-spiced pulpit novelties--all this kind of thing is calculated to produce a very unhealthy style of Christianity; and, in many cases, I am afraid, the end is utter ruin of soul. For, unhappily, those who make public religion everything, are often led away by mere temporary emotions, after some grand display of ecclesiastical oratory, into professing far more than they really feel. After this, they can only be kept up to the mark, which they imagine they have reached, by a constant succession of religious excitements. By and by, as with opium-eaters and dram-drinkers, there comes a time when their dose loses its power, and a feeling of exhaustion and discontent begins to creep over their minds. Too often, I fear, the conclusion of the whole matter is a relapse into utter deadness and unbelief, and a complete return to the world. And all results from having nothing but a public religion! Oh, that people would remember that it was not the wind, or the fire, or the earthquake, which showed Elijah the presence of God, but "the still, small voice." (1 Kings xix. 12.)

Now I desire to lift up a warning voice on this subject. I want to see no decrease of public religion, remember: but I do want to promote an increase of that religion which is private--private between each man and his God. The root of a plant or tree makes no show above ground. If you dig down to it and examine it, it is a poor, dirty, coarse-looking thing, and not nearly so beautiful to the eye as the fruit, or leaf, or flower. But that despised root, nevertheless, is the true source of all the life, health, vigour and fertility which your eyes see, and without it the plant or tree would soon die. Now private religion is the root of all vital Christianity. Without it, we may make a brave show in the meeting or on the platform, and sing loud, and shed many tears, and have a name to live and the praise of man. But without it we have no wedding garment, and are "dead before God." I tell my readers plainly that the times require of us all more attention to our private religion.

(a) Let us pray more heartily in private, and throw our whole souls more into our prayers. There are live prayers and there are dead prayers--prayers that cost us nothing and prayers which often cost us strong crying and tears. What are yours? When great professors backslide in public, and the Church is surprised and shocked, the truth is that they had long ago backslidden on their knees. They had neglected the throne of grace.

(b) Let us read our Bibles in private more, and with more pains and diligence. Ignorance of Scripture is the root of all error and makes a man helpless in the hand of the devil. There is less private Bible-reading, I suspect, than there was fifty years ago. I never can believe that so many English men and women would have been "tossed to and fro with every wind of doctrine," some falling into scepticism, some rushing into the wildest and narrowest fanaticism, and some going over to Rome, if there had not grown up a habit of lazy, superficial, careless, perfunctory reading of God's Word. "Ye do err not knowing the Scriptures." (Matt. xxii. 29.) The Bible in the pulpit must never supersede the Bible at home.

(c) Let us cultivate the habit of keeping up more private meditation and communion with Christ. Let us resolutely make time for getting alone occasionally, for talking with our own souls like David, for pouring out our hearts to our Great High Priest, Advocate, and Confessor at the right hand of God. We want more auricular confession: but not to man. The confessional we want is not a box in the vestry, but the throne of grace. I see some professing Christians always running about after spiritual food, always in public, and always out of breath and in a hurry, and never allowing themselves leisure to sit down quietly to digest, and take stock of their spiritual condition. I am never surprised if such Christians have a dwarfish, stunted religion and do not grow, and if, like Pharaoh's lean kine, they look no better for their public religious feasting, but rather worse. Spiritual prosperity depends immensely on our private religion, and private religion cannot nourish unless we determine that by God's help we will make time, whatever trouble it may cost us, for thought, for prayer, for the Bible, and for private communion with Christ. Alas! That saying of our Master is sadly overlooked: "Enter into thy closet and shut the door." (Matt. vi. 6.)

Our Evangelical forefathers had far fewer means and opportunities than we have. Full religious meetings and crowds, except occasionally at a Church or in a field when such men as Whitfield, or Wesley, or Rowlands preached, these were things of which they knew nothing. Their proceedings were neither fashionable nor popular, and often brought on them more persecution and abuse than praise. But the few weapons they used, they used well. With less noise and applause from man they made, I believe, a far deeper mark for God on their generation than we do, with all our Conferences, and Meetings, and Mission rooms, and Halls, and multiplied religious appliances. Their converts, I suspect, like the old-fashioned cloths and linens, wore better, and lasted longer, and faded less, and kept colour, and were more stable, and rooted, and grounded than many of the new-born babes of this day. And what was the reason of all this? Simply, I believe, because they gave more attention to private religion than we generally do. They walked closely with God and honoured Him in private, and so He honoured them in public. Oh, let us follow them as they followed Christ! Let us go and do likewise.

Let me now conclude this paper with a few words of practical application.

(1) First of all, would you understand what the times require of you in reference to your own soul? Listen, and I will tell you. You live in times of peculiar spiritual danger. Never perhaps were there more traps and pitfalls in the way to heaven: never certainly were those traps so skilfully baited and those pitfalls so ingeniously made. Mind what you are about. Look well to your goings. Ponder the paths of your feet. Take heed lest you come to eternal grief and ruin your own soul. Beware of practical infidelity under the specious name of free thought. Beware of a helpless state of indecision about doctrinal truth under the plausible idea of not being party spirited, and under the baneful influence of so-called liberality and charity. Beware of frittering away life in wishing, and meaning, and hoping for the day of decision, until the door is shut and you are given over to a dead conscience and die without hope. Awake to a sense of your danger. Arise and give diligence to make your calling and election sure, whatever else you leave uncertain. The kingdom of God is very nigh. Christ the Almighty Saviour, Christ the sinner's Friend, Christ and eternal life, are ready for you if you will only come to Christ. Arise and cast away excuses: this very day Christ calleth you. Wait not for company if you cannot have It; wait for nobody. The times, I repeat, are desperately dangerous. If only few are in the narrow way of life, resolve that by God's help you at any rate will be among the few.

(2) In the next place, would you understand what the times require of all Christians in reference to the souls of others? Listen, and I will tell you. You live in times of great liberty and abounding opportunities of doing good. Never were there so many open doors of usefulness, so many fields white to the harvest. Mind that you use those open doors, and try to reap those fields. Try to do a little good before you die. Strive to be useful. Determine that, by God's help, you will leave the world a better world in the day of your burial than it was in the day you were born. Remember the souls of relatives, friends and companions; remember that God often works by weak instruments, and try with holy ingenuity to lead them to Christ.

The time is short: the sand is running out of the glass of this old world; then redeem the time, and endeavour not to go to heaven alone. No doubt you cannot command success. It is not certain that your efforts to do good will always do good to others: but it is quite certain that they will always do good to yourself. Exercise, exercise, is one grand secret of health, both for body and soul. "He that watereth shall be watered himself." (Prov. ii. 25.) It is a deep and golden saying of our Master's, but seldom understood in its full meaning--"It is more blessed to give than to receive." (Acts xx. 35.)

(3) In the last place, would you understand what the times require of you in reference to the Church of England? Listen to me, and I will tell you. No doubt you live in days when our time- honoured Church is in a very perilous, distressing, and critical position. Her rowers have brought her into troubled waters. Her very existence is endangered by Papists, Infidels, and Liberationists without. Her life-blood is drained away by the behaviour of traitors, false friends, and timid officers within. Nevertheless, so long as the Church of England sticks firmly to the Bible, the Articles, and the principles of the Protestant Reformation, so long I advise you strongly to stick to the Church. When the Articles are thrown overboard and the old flag is hauled down, then, and not till then, it will be time for you and me to launch the boats and quit the wreck. At present, let us stick to the old ship.

Why should we leave her now, like cowards, because she is in difficulties and the truth cannot be maintained within her pale without trouble? How can we better ourselves? To whom can we go? Where shall we find better prayers? In what communion shall we find so much good being done, in spite of the existence of much evil? No doubt there is much to sadden us; but there is not a single visible Church on earth at this day doing better. There is not a single communion where there are no clouds, and all is serene. "The evils everywhere are mingled with the good:" the wheat never grows without tares. But for all that, there is much to gladden us, more Evangelical preaching than there ever was before in the land, more work done both at home and abroad. If old William Romaine, of St. Anne's, Blackfriars, who stood alone with some half-a-dozen others in London last century, had lived to see what our eyes see, he would have sharply rebuked our faintheartedness and unthankfulness. No! the battle of the Reformed Church of England is not yet lost, in spite of semi-popery and scepticism, whatever jealous onlookers without and melancholy grumblers within may please to say. As Napoleon said at four o'clock on the battlefield of Marengo, "there is yet time to win a victory." If the really loyal members of the Church will only stand by her boldly, and not look coolly at one another, and refuse to work the same fire-engine, or man the same lifeboat--if they will not squabble and quarrel and "fall out by the way," the Church of England will live and not die, and be a blessing to our children's children. Then let us set our feet down firmly and stand fast in our position. Let us not be in a hurry to quit the ship because of a few leaks: let us rather man the pumps, and try to keep the good ship afloat. Let us work on, and fight on, and pray on, and stick to the Church of England. The Churchman who walks in these lines, I believe, is the Churchman who "understands the times."

XX. "CHRIST IS ALL"

"Christ is all."--Colossians iii. 11.

THE words of the text which heads this page are few, short, and soon spoken; but they contain great things. Like those golden sayings, "To me to live is Christ"--"I live, yet not I, but Christ liveth in me "--they are singularly rich and suggestive. (Phil. i. 21; Gal. ii. 20.)

These three words are the essence and substance of Christianity. If our hearts can really go along with them, it is well with our souls. If not, we may be sure we have yet much to learn.

Let me try to set before my readers in what sense "Christ is all"; and let me ask them, as they read, to judge themselves honestly, that they may not make shipwreck in the judgment of the last day.

I purposely close this volume with a paper on this remarkable text. Christ is the main-spring both of doctrinal and practical Christianity. A right knowledge of Christ is essential to a right knowledge of sanctification as well as justification. He that follows after holiness will make no progress unless he gives to Christ His rightful place. I began the volume with a plain statement about sin. Let me end it with an equally plain statement about Christ.

I. First of all, let us understand that Christ is all, in all the counsels of God concerning man.

(a) There was a time when this earth had no being. Solid as the mountains look, bound-less as the sea appears, high as the stars in heaven look--they once did not exist. And man, with all the high thoughts he now has of himself, was a creature unknown.

And where was Christ then?

Even then Christ was "with God "--and "was God"--and was "equal with God." (John i. 1; Phil. ii. 6.) Even then He was the beloved Son of the Father: "Thou lovedst Me," He says, "before the foundation of the world."--"I had glory with Thee before the world began."--"I was set up from everlasting, from the beginning, or ever the earth was." (John xvii. 5, 24; Prov. viii. 23.) Even then He was the Saviour "foreordained before the foundation of the world" (1 Peter i. 20), and believers were "chosen in Him." (Ephes. i. 4.)

(b) There came a time when this earth was created in its present order. Sun, moon and stars--sea, land and all their inhabitants, were called into being and made out of chaos and confusion. And, last of all, man was formed out of the dust of the ground.

And where was Christ then?

Hear what the Scripture says: "All things were made by Him, and without Him was not any thing made that was made." (John i. 3.) "By Him were all things created, that are in heav-en and that are in earth." (Colos. i. 16.) "And Thou, Lord, in the beginning hast laid the foundation of the earth; and the heavens are the works of Thine hands." (Heb. i. 10.) "When He prepared the heavens, I was there: when He set a compass upon the face of the depth: when He established the clouds above: when He strengthened the foundations of the deep: when He gave to the sea His decree, that the water should not pass His commandment: when He appointed the foundations of the earth: then I was by Him, as one brought up with Him." (Prov. viii. 27-30.) Can we wonder that the Lord Jesus, in His preaching, should continually draw lessons from the book of nature? When He spoke of the sheep, the fish, the ravens, the corn, the lilies, the fig-tree, the vine--He spoke of things which He Himself had made.

(c) There came a day when sin entered the world.--Adam and Eve ate the forbidden fruit, and fell. They lost that holy nature in which they were first formed. They forfeited the friendship and favour of God and became guilty, corrupt, helpless, hopeless sinners. Sin came as a barrier between themselves and their holy Father in heaven. Had He dealt with them according to their deserts, there had been nothing before them but death, hell, and everlasting ruin.

And where was Christ then?

In that very day He was revealed to our trembling parents, as the only hope of salvation. The very day they fell, they were told that "the seed of the woman should yet bruise the serpent's head,"--that a Saviour born of a woman should overcome the devil and win for sinful man an entrance to eternal life. (Gen. iii. 15.) Christ was held up as the true light of the world, in the very day of the fall; and never has any name been made known from that day by which souls could be saved, excepting His. By Him all saved souls have entered heaven, from Adam downwards; and without Him none have ever escaped hell.

(d) There came a time when the world seemed sunk and buried in ignorance of God. After 4,000 years the nations of the earth appeared to have clean forgotten the God that made them. Egyptian, Assyrian, Persian, Grecian, and Roman empires had done nothing but spread superstition and idolatry. Poets, historians, philosophers had proved that, with all their intellectual powers, they had no right knowledge of God; and that man, left to himself, was utterly corrupt. "The world, by wisdom, knew not God." (1 Cor. i. 21.) Excepting a few despised Jews in a corner of the earth, the whole world was dead in ignorance and sin.

And what did Christ do then?

He left the glory He had had from all eternity with the Father, and came down into the world to provide a salvation. He took our nature upon Him, and was born as a man. As a man He did the will of God perfectly, which we all had left undone: as a man He suffered on the cross the wrath of God which we ought to have suffered. He brought in everlasting righteousness for us. He redeemed us from the curse of a broken law. He opened a fountain for all sin and uncleanness. He died for our sins. He rose again for our justification. He ascended to God's right hand, and there sat down, waiting till His enemies should be made His footstool. And there He sits now, offering salvation to all who will come to Him, interceding for all who believe in Him, and managing by God's appointment all that concerns the salvation of souls.

(e) There is a time coming when sin shall be cast out from this world.--Wickedness shall not always flourish unpunished--Satan shall not always reign--creation shall not always groan, being burdened. There shall be a time of restitution of all things. There shall be a new heaven and a new earth, wherein dwelleth righteousness, and the earth shall be full of the knowledge of the Lord as the waters cover the sea. (Rom. viii. 22; Acts iii. 21; 2 Pet. iii. 13; Isa. xi. 9.)

And where shall Christ be then? And what shall He do?

Christ Himself shall be King. He shall return to this earth and make all things new. He shall come in the clouds of heaven with power and great glory, and the kingdoms of the world shall become His. The heathen shall be given to Him for His inheritance, and the uttermost parts of the earth for His possession. To Him every knee shall bow, and every tongue shall confess that He is Lord. His dominion shall be an everlasting dominion which shall not pass away, and His kingdom that which shall not be destroyed. (Matt. xxiv. 30; Rev. xi. 15; Psalm ii. 8; Phil. ii. 10, 11; Dan. vii. 14.)

(f) There is a day coming when all men shall be judged. The sea shall give up the dead which are in it, and death and hell shall deliver up the dead which are in them. All that sleep in the grave shall awake and come forth, and all shall be judged according to their works. (Rev. xx. 13; Dan. xii. 2.)

And where will Christ be then?

Christ Himself will be the Judge. "The Father hath committed all judgment unto the Son."--"When the Son of man shall come in His glory, then shall He sit upon the throne of His glory:--and before Him shall be gathered all nations: and He shall separate them one from another, as a shepherd divideth the sheep from the goats."--"We must all appear before the judgment seat of Christ: that every one may receive the things done in his body, according to that he hath done, whether it be good or bad." (John v. 22; Matt. xxv. 32; 2 Cor. v. 10.)

Now if any reader of this paper thinks little of Christ, let him know this day that he is very unlike God! You are of one mind, and God is of another. You think it enough to give Christ a little honour--a little reverence--a little respect. But in all the eternal counsels of God the Father, in creation, redemption, restitution, and judgment--in all these, Christ is "all."

Surely we shall do well to consider these things. Surely it is not written in vain, "He that honoureth not the Son, honoureth not the Father which hath sent Him." (John v. 23.)

II. In the second place, let us understand that "Christ is all" in the inspired books which make up the Bible.

In every part of both Testaments, Christ is to be found--dimly and indistinctly at the beginning--more clearly and plainly in the middle--fully and completely at the end--but really and substantially everywhere.

Christ's sacrifice and death for sinners, and Christ's kingdom and future glory, are the light we must bring to bear on any book of Scripture we read. Christ's cross and Christ's crown are the clue we must hold fast if we would find our way through Scripture difficulties. Christ is the only key that will unlock many of the dark places of the Word. Some people complain that they do not understand the Bible. And the reason is very simple. They do not use the key. To them the Bible is like the hieroglyphics in Egypt. It is a mystery, just because they do not know and employ the key.

(a) It was Christ crucified who was set forth in every Old Testament sacrifice. Every animal slain and offered on an altar was a practical confession that a Saviour was looked for who would die for sinners--a Saviour who should take away man's sin, by suffering, as his Substitute and Sin-bearer, in his stead, (1 Peter iii. 18.) It is absurd to suppose that an unmeaning slaughter of innocent beasts, without a distinct object in view, could please the eternal God!

(b) It was Christ to whom Abel looked when he offered a better sacrifice than Cain. Not only was the heart of Abel better than that of his brother, but he showed his knowledge of vicarious sacrifice and his faith in an atonement. He offered the firstlings of his flock, with the blood thereof, and in so doing declared his belief that without shedding of blood there is no remission. (Heb. xi. 4.)

(c) It was Christ of whom Enoch prophesied in the days of abounding wickedness before the flood.--"Behold," he said, "the Lord cometh with ten thousands of His saints, to execute judgment upon all." (Jude 15.)

(d) It was Christ to whom Abraham looked when he dwelt in tents in the land of promise. He believed that in his seed--in one born of his family--all the nations of the earth should be blessed. By faith he saw Christ's day, and was glad. (John viii. 56.)

(e) It was Christ of whom Jacob spoke to his sons, as he lay dying. He marked out the tribe out of which He would be born, and foretold that "gathering together" unto Him which is yet to be accomplished. "The sceptre shall not depart from Judah, nor the law-giver from between his feet, until Shiloh come, and unto Him shall the gathering of the people be." (Gen. xlix. 10.)

(f) It was Christ who was the substance of the ceremonial law which God gave to Israel by the hand of Moses. The morning and evening sacrifice--the continual shedding of blood--the altar--the mercy-seat--the high priest--the passover--the day of atonement--the scape-goat:--all these were so many pictures, types, and emblems of Christ and His work. God had compassion upon the weakness of His people. He taught them "Christ" line upon line, and, as we teach little children, by similitudes. It was in this sense especially that "the law was a schoolmaster to lead" the Jews "unto Christ." (Gal. iii. 24.)

(g) It was Christ to whom God directed the attention of Israel by all the daily miracles which were done before their eyes in the wilderness. The pillar of cloud and fire which guid-ed them--the manna from heaven which every morning fed them--the water from the smitten rock which followed them--all and each were figures of Christ. The brazen serpent, on that memorable occasion when the plague of fiery serpents was sent upon them, was an emblem of Christ. (1 Cor. x. 4; John iii. 14.)

(h) It was Christ of whom all the Judges were types. Joshua, and David, and Gideon, and Jephthah, and Samson, and all the rest whom God raised up to deliver Israel from captivity--all were emblems of Christ. Weak and unstable and faulty as some of them were, they were set for example of better things in the distant future. All were meant to remind the tribes of that far higher Deliverer who was yet to come.

(i) It was Christ of whom David the king was a type. Anointed and chosen when few gave him honour--despised and rejected by Saul and all the tribes of Israel--persecuted and obliged to flee for his life--a man of sorrow all his life, and yet at length a conqueror--in all these things David represented Christ.

(j) It was Christ of whom all the prophets from Isaiah to Malachi spoke. They saw through a glass darkly. They sometimes dwelt on His sufferings, and sometimes on His glory that should follow. (1 Peter i. 11.) They did not always mark out for us the distinction be-tween Christ's first coming and Christ's second coming. Like two candles in a straight line, one behind the other, they sometimes saw both the advents at the same time, and spoke of them in one breath. They were sometimes moved by the Holy Ghost to write of the times of Christ crucified, and sometimes of Christ's kingdom in the latter days. But Jesus dying, or Jesus reigning, was the thought you will ever find uppermost in their minds.

(k) It is Christ, I need hardly say, of whom the whole New Testament is full. The Gospels are "Christ" living, speaking, and moving among men. The Acts are "Christ" preached, published, and proclaimed. The Epistles are "Christ" written of, explained, and exalted. But all through, from first to last, there is one name above every other, and that is the name of Christ.

I charge every reader of this paper to ask himself frequently what the Bible is to him. Is it a Bible in which you have found nothing more than good moral precepts and sound advice? Or is it a Bible in which you have found Christ? Is it a Bible in which "Christ is all "? If not, I tell you plainly, you have hitherto used your Bible to very little purpose. You are like a man who studies the solar system and leaves out in his studies the sun, which is the centre of all. It is no wonder if you find your Bible a dull book!

III. In the third place, let us understand that "Christ is all" in the religion of all true Christians on earth.

In saying this, I wish to guard myself against being misunderstood. I hold the absolute necessity of the election of God the Father, and the sanctification of God the Spirit, in order to effect the salvation of everyone that is saved. I hold that there is a perfect harmony and unison in the action of the three Persons of the Trinity, in bringing any man to glory, and that all three co-operate and work a joint work in his deliverance from sin and hell. Such as the Father is, such is the Son, and such is the Holy Ghost. The Father is merciful, the Son is merciful, the Holy Ghost is merciful. The same three who said at the beginning, "Let us create," said also, "Let us redeem and save." I hold that everyone who reaches heaven will ascribe all the glory of his salvation to Father, Son and Holy Ghost, three Persons in one God.

But, at the same time, I see clear proof in Scripture that it is the mind of the blessed Trinity that Christ should be prominently and distinctly exalted in the matter of saving souls. Christ is set forth as the "Word," through whom God's love to sinners is made known. Christ's incarnation and atoning death on the cross are the great corner-stone on which the whole plan of salvation rests. Christ is the way and door, by which alone approaches to God are to be made. Christ is the root into which all elect sinners must be grafted. Christ is the only meeting-place between God and man, between heaven and earth, between the Holy Trinity and the poor sinful child of Adam. It is Christ whom God the Father has "sealed" and appointed to convey life to a dead world. (John vi. 27.) It is Christ to whom the Father has given a people to be brought to glory. It is Christ of whom the Spirit testifies, and to whom He always leads a soul for pardon and peace. In short, it has "pleased the Father that in Christ all fulness should dwell." (Coloss. i. 19.) What the sun is in the firmament of heaven, that Christ is in true Christianity.

I say these things by way of explanation. I want my readers clearly to understand that in saying "Christ is all," I do not mean to shut out the work of the Father and of the Spirit. Now let me show what I do mean.

(a) Christ is all in a sinner's justification before God.

Through Him alone we can have peace with a Holy God, By Him alone we can have admission into the presence of the Most High, and stand there without fear. "We have boldness and access with confidence by the faith of Him." In Him alone can God be just, and justify the ungodly. (Ephes. iii. 12; Rom. iii. 26.)

Wherewith can any mortal man come before God? What can we bring as a plea for acquittal before that Glorious Being, in whose eyes the very heavens are not clean?

Shall we say that we have done our duty to God? Shall we say that we have done our duty to our neighbour? Shall we bring forward our prayers?--our regularity?--our morality?--our amendments?--our church-going? Shall we ask to be accepted because of any of these?

Which of these things will stand the searching inspection of God's eye. Which of them will actually justify us? Which of them will carry us clear through judgment, and land us safe in glory?

None, none, none! Take any commandment of the ten, and let us examine ourselves by it. We have broken it repeatedly. We cannot answer God one of a thousand.--Take any of us, and look narrowly into our ways--and we are nothing but sinners. There is but one verdict: we are all guilty--all deserve hell--all ought to die. Wherewith can we come before God?

We must come in the name of Jesus--standing on no other ground--pleading no other plea than this, "Christ died on the cross for the ungodly, and I trust in Him. Christ died for me, and I believe on Him."

The garment of our Elder Brother--the righteousness of Christ--this is the only robe which can cover us and enable us to stand in the light of heaven without shame.

The name of Jesus is the only name by which we shall obtain an entrance through the gate of eternal glory. If we come to that gate in our own names, we are lost, we shall not be admitted, we shall knock in vain. If we come in the name of Jesus, it is a passport and Shibboleth, and we shall enter and live.

The mark of the blood of Christ is the only mark that can save us from destruction. When the angels are separating the children of Adam in the last day, if we are not found marked with that atoning blood, we had better never have been born.

Oh, let us never forget that Christ must be "all" to that soul who would be justified!--We must be content to go to heaven as beggars--saved by free grace, simply as believers in Jesus-- or we shall never be saved at all.

Is there a thoughtless, worldly soul among the readers of this book? Is there one who thinks to reach heaven by saying hastily at the last, "Lord have mercy on me" without Christ? Friend, you are sowing misery for yourself, and unless you alter you will awake to endless woe.

Is there a proud, formal soul among the readers of this book? Is there anyone thinking to make himself fit for heaven and good enough to pass muster by his own doings?--Brother, you are building a Babel, and you will never reach heaven in your present state.

But is there a labouring, heavy-laden one among the readers of this book? Is there one who wants to be saved, and feels a vile sinner? I say to such an one, "Come to Christ, and He shall save you. Come to Christ, and cast the burden of your soul on Him. Fear not: only believe."

Do you fear wrath? Christ can deliver you from the wrath to come.--Do you feel the curse of a broken law? Christ can redeem you from the curse of the law.--Do you feel far away? Christ has suffered, to bring you nigh to God.--Do you feel unclean? Christ's blood can cleanse all sin away.--Do you feel imperfect? You shall be complete in Christ.--Do you feel as if you were nothing? Christ shall be "all in all" to your soul.--Never did saint reach heaven with any tale but this, "I was washed and made white in the blood of the Lamb." (Rev. vii. 14.)

(b) But again, Christ is not only all in the justification of a true Christian, but He is also all in his sanctification.

I would not have anyone misunderstand me. I do not mean for a moment to undervalue the work of the Spirit. But this I say, that no man is ever holy till he comes to Christ and is united to Him. Till then his works are dead works, and he has no holiness at all.--First you must be joined to Christ, and then you shall be holy. "Without Him--separate from Him--you can do nothing." (John xv. 5.)

And no man can grow in holiness except he abides in Christ. Christ is the great root from which every believer must draw his strength to go forward. The Spirit is His special gift, His purchased gift for His people. A believer must not only "receive Christ Jesus the Lord," but "walk in Him, and be rooted and built up in Him." (Col. ii. 6, 7.)

Would you be holy? Then Christ is the manna you must daily eat, like Israel in the wilderness of old. Would you be holy? Then Christ must be the rock from which you must daily drink the living water. Would you be holy? Then you must be ever looking unto Jesus--looking at His cross, and learning fresh motives for a closer walk with God--looking at His example, and taking Him for your pattern. Looking at Him, you would become like Him. Looking at Him, your face would shine without your knowing it. Look less at yourself and more at Christ, and you will find besetting sins dropping off and leaving you, and your eyes enlightened more and more every day. (Heb. xii. 2; 2 Cor. iii. 18.)

The true secret of coming up out of the wilderness is to come up "leaning on the Beloved." (Cant. viii. 5.) The true way to be strong is to realize our weakness and to feel that Christ must be all. The true way to grow in grace is to make use of Christ as a fountain for every minute's necessities. We ought to employ Him as the prophet's wife employed the oil--not only to pay our debts, but to live on also. We should strive to be able to say, "The life that I now live in the flesh I live by the faith of the Son of God, who loved me, and gave Himself for me." (2 Kings iv. 7; Gal. ii. 20.)

I pity those who try to be holy without Christ! Your labour is all in vain. You are putting money in a bag with holes. You are pouring water into a sieve. You are rolling a huge round stone uphill. You are building up a wall with untempered mortar. Believe me, you are beginning at the wrong end. You must come to Christ first, and He shall give you His sanctifying Spirit. You must learn to say with Paul, "I can do all things through Christ which strengtheneth me." (Phil. iv. 13.)

(c) But again, Christ is not only all in the sanctification of a true Christian, but all in his comfort in time present.

A saved soul has many sorrows. He has a body like other men--weak and frail. He has a heart like other men--and often a more sensitive one, too. He has trials and losses to bear like others--and often more. He has his share of bereavements, deaths, disappointments, crosses. He has the world to oppose--a place in life to fill blamelessly--unconverted relatives to bear with patiently--persecutions to endure--and a death to die.

And who is sufficient for these things? What shall enable a believer to bear all this? Nothing but "the consolation there is in Christ." (Phil. ii. 1.)

Jesus is indeed the brother born for adversity. He is the friend that sticketh closer than a brother, and He alone can comfort His people. He can be touched with the feeling of their infirmities, for He suffered Himself. (Heb. iv. 15.) He knows what sorrow is, for He was a Man of sorrows. He knows what an aching body is, for His body was racked with pain. He cried, "All my bones are out of joint." (Ps. xxii. 14.) He knows what poverty and weariness are, for He was often wearied and had not where to lay His head. He knows what family unkindness is, for even His brethren did not believe Him. He had no honour in His own house.

And Jesus knows exactly how to comfort His afflicted people. He knows how to pour in oil and wine into the wounds of the spirit--how to fill up gaps in empty hearts--how to speak a word in season to the weary--how to heal the broken heart--how to make all our bed in sickness--how to draw nigh when we are faint, and say, "Fear not: I am thy salvation." (Lam. iii. 57.)

We talk of sympathy being pleasant. There is no sympathy like that of Christ. In all our afflictions He is afflicted. He knows our sorrows. In all our pain He is pained, and like the good Physician, He will not measure out to us one drop of sorrow too much. David once said, "In the multitude of my thoughts within me, Thy comforts delight my soul." (Ps. xciv. 19.) Many a believer, I am sure, could say as much. "If the Lord Himself had not stood by me, the deep waters would have gone over my soul," (Ps. cxxiv. 5.)

How a believer gets through all his troubles appears wonderful. How he is carried through the fire and water he passes through seems past comprehension. But the true account of it is just this--that Christ is not only justification and sanctification, but consolation also.

Oh, you who want unfailing comfort, I commend you to Christ! In Him alone there is no failure. Rich men are disappointed in their treasures. Learned men are disappointed in their books. Husbands are disappointed in their wives. Wives are disappointed in their husbands. Parents are disappointed in their children. Statesmen are disappointed when, after many a struggle, they attain place and power. They find out, to their cost, that it is more pain than pleasure--that it is disappointment, annoyance, incessant trouble, worry, vanity, and vexation of spirit. But no man was ever disappointed in Christ.

(d) But as Christ is all in the comforts of a true Christian in time present, so Christ is all in his hopes for time to come.

Few men and women, I suppose, are to be found who do not indulge in hopes of some kind about their souls. But the hopes of the vast majority are nothing but vain fancies. They are built on no solid foundation. No living man but the real child of God--the sincere, thoroughgoing Christian--can give a reasonable account of the hope that is in him. No hope is reasonable which is not Scriptural.

A true Christian has a good hope when he looks forward: the worldly man has none. A true Christian sees light in the distance: the worldly man sees nothing but darkness. And what is the hope of a true Christian? It is just this--that Jesus Christ is coming again, coming without sin--coming with all His people, coming to wipe away every tear--coming to raise His sleeping saints from the grave--coming to gather together all His family, that they may be for ever with Him.

Why is a believer patient? because he looks for the coming of the Lord. He can bear hard things without murmuring. He knows the time is short. He waits quietly for the King.

Why is he moderate in all things? Because he expects his Lord soon to return. His treasure is in heaven, his good things are yet to come. The world is not his rest, but an inn; and an inn is not home. He knows that "He that shall come will soon come, and will not tarry." Christ is coming, and that is enough. (Heb. x. 37.)

This is indeed a "blessed hope!" (Titus ii. 13.) Now is the school-time--then the eternal holiday. Now is the tossing on the waves of a troublesome world--then the quiet harbour. Now is the scattering--then the gathering. Now is the time of sowing--then the harvest. Now is the working season--then the wages. Now is the cross--then the crown.

People talk of their "expectations" and hopes from this world. None have such solid expectations as a saved soul. He can say, "My soul, wait thou only upon God; my expectation is from Him." (Ps. lxii. 5.)

In all true saving religion Christ is all: all in justification--all in comfort--all in hope. Blessed is that mother's child that knows it, and far more blessed is he that feels it too. Oh that men would prove themselves, and see what they know of it for their own souls!

IV. One thing more I will add, and then I have done. Let us understand that Christ will be all in heaven.

I cannot dwell long on this point. I have not power, if I had space and room. I can ill describe things unseen and a world unknown. But this I know, that all men and women who reach heaven will find that even there also "Christ is all."

Like the altar in Solomon's temple, Christ crucified will be the grand object in heaven. That altar struck the eye of every one who entered the temple gates. It was a great brazen altar, twenty cubits broad--as broad as the front of the temple itself. (2 Chron. iii. 4; iv. 1.) So in like manner will Jesus fill the eyes of all who enter glory. In the midst of the throne and surrounded by adoring angels and saints, there will be "the Lamb that was slain." And "the Lamb shall be the light" of the place. (Rev. v. 6; xxi. 23.)

The praise of the Lord Jesus will be the eternal song of all the inhabitants of heaven. They will say with a loud voice, "Worthy is the Lamb that was slain. Blessing, and honour, and glory, and power, be to Him that sitteth on the throne, and to the Lamb for ever and ever." (Rev. v. 12. 13.)

The service of the Lord Jesus will be one eternal occupation of all the inhabitants of heaven. We shall "serve Him day and night in His temple." (Rev. vii. 13.) Blessed is the thought that we shall at length attend on Him without distraction, and work for Him without weariness.

The presence of Christ Himself shall be one everlasting enjoyment of the inhabitants of heaven. We shall "see His face," and hear His voice, and speak with Him as friend with friend. (Rev. xxii. 4.) Sweet is the thought that whosoever may be wanting at the marriage supper, the Master Himself will be there. His presence will satisfy all our wants. (Ps. xvii. 15.)

What a sweet and glorious home heaven will be to those who have loved the Lord Jesus Christ in sincerity! Here we live by faith in Him, and find peace, though we see Him not. There we shall see Him face to face, and find He is altogether lovely. "Better" indeed will be the "sight of the eyes than the wandering of the desire!" (Eccles. vi. 9.)

But alas, how little fit for heaven are many who talk of "going to heaven" when they die, while they manifestly have no saving faith, and no real acquaintance with Christ. You give Christ no honour here. You have no communion with Him. You do not love Him. Alas! what could you do in heaven? It would be no place for you. Its joys would be no joys for you. Its happiness would be a happiness into which you could not enter. Its employments would be a weariness and a burden to your heart. Oh, repent and change before it be too late!

I trust I have shown how deep are the foundations of that little expression, "Christ is all."

I might easily add to the things I have said, if space permitted. The subject is not exhausted. I have barely walked over the surface of it. There are mines of precious truth connected with it which I have left unopened.

I might show how Christ ought to be all in a visible Church. Splendid religious buildings, numerous religious services, gorgeous ceremonies, troops of ordained men, all, all are nothing in the sight of God, if the Lord Jesus Himself in all His offices is not honoured, magnified, and exalted. That Church is but a dead carcase in which Christ is not "all."

I might show how Christ ought to be all in a ministry. The great work which ordained men are intended to do, is to lift up Christ. We are to be like the pole on which the brazen serpent was hung. We are useful so long as we exalt the great object of faith, but useful no further. We are to be ambassadors to carry tidings to a rebellious world about the King's Son, and if we teach men to think more about us and our office than about Him, we are not fit for our place. The Spirit will never honour that minister who does not testify of Christ--who does not make Christ "all."

I might show how language seems exhausted in the Bible, in describing Christ's various offices. I might describe how figures seem endless which are employed in unfolding Christ's fulness. The High Priest, the Mediator, the Redeemer, the Saviour, the Advocate, the Shepherd, the Physician, the Bridegroom, the Head, the Bread of Life, the Light of the World, the Way, the Door, the Vine, the Rock, the Fountain, the Sun of Righteousness, the Forerunner, the Surety, the Captain, the Prince of Life, the Amen, the Almighty, the Author and Finisher of Faith, the Lamb of God, the King of Saints, the Wonderful, the Mighty God, the Counsellor, the Bishop of Souls--all these, and many more, are names given to Christ in Scripture. Each is a fountain of instruction and comfort for everyone who is willing to drink of it. Each supplies matter for useful meditation.

But I trust I have said enough to throw light on the point I want to impress on the minds of all who read this paper. I trust I have said enough to show the immense importance of the practical conclusions with which I now desire to finish the subject.

(1) Is Christ all? Then let us learn the utter uselessness of a christless religion.

There are only too many baptized men and women who practically know nothing at all about Christ. Their religion consists in a few vague notions and empty expressions. "They trust they are no worse than others. They keep to their church. They try to do their duty. They do nobody any harm. They hope God will be merciful to them. They trust the Almighty will pardon their sins, and take them to heaven when they die." This is about the whole of their religion!

But what do these people know practically about Christ? Nothing: nothing at all! What experimental acquaintance have they with His offices and work, His blood, His righteousness, His mediation, His priesthood, His intercession? None: none at all! Ask them about a saving faith--ask them about being born again of the Spirit--ask them about being sanctified in Christ Jesus. What answer will you get? You are a barbarian to them. You have asked them simple Bible questions. But they know no more about them experimentally than a Buddhist or a Turk. And yet this is the religion of hundreds and thousands of people who are called Christians, all over the world!

If any reader of this paper is a man of this kind, I warn him plainly that such Christianity will never take him to heaven. It may do very well in the eye of man. It may pass muster very decently at the vestry-meeting, in the place of business, in the House of Commons, or in the streets. But it will never comfort you. It will never satisfy your conscience. It will never save your soul.

I warn you plainly that all notions and theories about God being merciful without Christ, and excepting through Christ, are baseless delusions and empty fancies. Such theories are as purely an idol of man's invention as the idol of Juggernaut. They are all of the earth, earthy. They never came down from heaven. The God of heaven has sealed and appointed Christ as the one only Saviour and way of life, and all who would be saved must be content to be saved by Him, or they will never be saved at all.

Let every reader take notice. I give you fair warning this day. A religion without Christ will never save your soul.

(2) Let me say another thing. Is Christ all? Then LEARN THE ENORMOUS FOLLY OF JOINING ANYTHING WITH CHRIST IN THE MATTER OF SALVATION.

There are multitudes of baptized men and women who profess to honour Christ, but in reality do Him great dishonour. They give Christ a certain place in their system of religion, but not the place which God intended Him to fill. Christ alone is not "all in all" to their souls.--No! It is either Christ and the Church--or Christ and the sacraments--or Christ and His ordained ministers--or Christ and their own repentance--or Christ and their own good-ness--or Christ and their own prayers--or Christ and their own sincerity and charity, on which they practically rest their souls.

If any reader of this paper is a Christian of this kind, I warn him also plainly, that his reli-gion is an offence to God. You are changing God's plan of salvation into a plan of your own devising. You are in effect deposing Christ from His throne, by giving the glory due to Him to another.

I care not who it is that teaches such religion and on whose word you build. Whether he be Pope or Cardinal, Archbishop or Bishop, Dean or Archdeacon, Presbyter or Deacon, Episcopalian or Presbyterian, Baptist or Independent, Wesleyan or Plymouth brother, who-soever adds anything to Christ teaches you wrong.

I care not what it is that you add to Christ. Whether it be the necessity of joining the Church of Rome, or of being an Episcopalian, or of becoming a Free Churchman, or of giv-ing up the Liturgy, or of being dipped--whatever you may practically add to Christ in the matter of salvation, you do Christ an injury.

Take heed what you are doing. Beware of giving to Christ's servants the honour due to none but Christ. Beware of giving the Lord's ordinances the honour due unto the Lord. Be-ware of resting the burden of your soul on anything but Christ, and Christ alone.

(3) Let me say another thing. Is Christ all? Then LET ALL WHO WANT TO BE SAVED, APPLY DIRECT TO CHRIST.

There are many who hear of Christ with the ear and believe all they are told about Him. They allow that there is no salvation excepting in Christ. They acknowledge that Jesus alone can deliver them from hell and present them faultless before God.

But they seem never to get beyond this general acknowledgment. They never fairly lay hold on Christ for their own souls. They stick fast in a state of wishing, and wanting, and feeling, and intending, and never get any further. They see what we mean: they know it is all true. They hope one day to get full benefit of it: but at present they get no benefit whatever.

The world is their "all." Politics are their "all." Pleasure is their "all." Business is their "all." But Christ is not their all.

If any reader of this paper is a man of this kind, I warn him also plainly, he is in a bad state of soul. You are as truly in the way to hell in your present condition, as Judas Iscariot, or Ahab, or Cain. Believe me, there must be actual faith in Christ, or else Christ died in vain so far as you are concerned. It is not looking at the bread that feeds the hungry man but the actual eating of it. It is not gazing on the lifeboat that saves the shipwrecked sailor, but actually getting into it. It is not knowing and believing that Christ is a Saviour that can save your soul, unless there are actual transactions between you and Christ. You must be able to say, "Christ is my Saviour, because I have come to Him by faith, and taken Him for my own."-- "Much of religion," said Luther, "turns on being able to use possessive pronouns. Take from me the word my.' and you take from me God!"

Hear the advice I give you this day, and act upon it at once. Stand still no longer, waiting for some imaginary frames and feelings which will never come. Hesitate no longer under the idea that you must first of all obtain the Spirit and then come to Christ. Arise and come to Christ just as you are. He waits for you, and is as willing to save as He is mighty. He is the appointed Physician for sin-sick souls. Deal with Him as you would with your doctor about the cure of a disease of your body. Make a direct application to Him and tell Him all your wants. Take with you words this day, and cry mightily to the Lord Jesus for pardon and peace, as the thief did on the cross. Do as that man did: cry, "Lord, remember me." (Luke xxiii. 42.) Tell Him you have heard that He receives sinners, and that you are such. Tell Him you want to be saved and ask Him to save you. Rest not till you have actually tasted for yourself that the Lord is gracious. Do this and you shall find, sooner or later, if you are really in earnest, that "Christ is all."

(4) One more thing let me add. Is Christ all? Then LET ALL HIS CONVERTED PEOPLE DEAL WITH HIM AS IF THEY REALLY BELIEVED IT. LET THEM LEAN ON HIM AND TRUST HIM FAR MORE THAN THEY HAVE EVER DONE YET.

Alas, there are many of the Lord's people who live far below their privileges! There are many truly Christian souls who rob themselves of their own peace, and forsake their own mercies. There are many who insensibly join their own faith, or the work of the Spirit in their own hearts, to Christ, and so miss the fullness of Gospel peace. There are many who make little progress in their pursuit of holiness, and shine with a very dim light. And why is all this? Simply because in nineteen cases out of twenty men do not make Christ all in all.

Now I call on every reader of this paper who is a believer, I beseech him for his own sake, to make sure that Christ is really and thoroughly his all in all. Beware of allowing yourself to mingle anything of your own with Christ.

Have you faith? It is a priceless blessing. Happy indeed are they who are willing and ready to trust Jesus. But take heed you do not make a Christ of your faith. Rest not on your own faith, but on Christ.

Is the work of the Spirit in your soul? Thank God for it. It is a work that shall never be overthrown. But oh, beware, lest, unaware to yourself, you make a Christ of the work of the Spirit! Rest not on the work of the Spirit, but on Christ.

Have you any inward feelings of religion and experience of grace. Thank God for it. Thousands have no more religious feeling than a cat or dog. But oh, beware lest you make a

Christ of your feelings and sensations! They are poor, uncertain things and sadly dependent on our bodies and outward circumstances. Rest only on Christ.

Learn, I entreat you, to look more and more at the great object of faith, Jesus Christ, and to keep your mind dwelling on Him. So doing you would find faith, and all the other graces, grow, though the growth at the time might be imperceptible to yourself. He that would prove a skilful archer must not look at the arrow, but at the mark.

Alas, I fear there is a great piece of pride and unbelief still sticking in the hearts of many believers! Few seem to realize how much they need a Saviour. Few seem to understand how thoroughly they are indebted to Him. Few seem to comprehend how much they need Him every day. Few seem to feel how simply and like a child they ought to hang their souls on Him. Few seem to be aware how full of love He is to His poor, weak people, and how ready to help them! And few therefore seem to know the peace, and joy, and strength, and power to live a godly life, which is to be had in Christ.

Change you plan, reader, if your conscience tells you you are guilty: change your plan, and learn to trust Christ more. Physicians love to see patients coming to consult them: it is their office to receive the sickly and, if possible, to effect cures. The advocate loves to be employed: it is his calling. The husband loves his wife to trust him and lean upon him: it is his delight to cherish her and promote her comfort. And Christ loves His people to lean on Him, to rest in Him, to call on Him, to abide in Him.

Let us all learn and strive to do so more and more. Let us live on Christ. Let us live in Christ. Let us live with Christ. Let us live to Christ. So doing, we shall prove that we fully realize that "Christ is all." So doing, we shall feel great peace, and attain more of that "holiness without which no man shall see the Lord." (Heb. xii. 14.)

XXI. EXTRACTS FROM OLD WRITERS

THE passages I append from Traill and Brooks on the subject of Holiness appear to me so valuable that I make no apology for introducing them.

They are the product of an age when, I am obliged to say, experimental religion was more deeply studied and far better understood than it is now.

(I.) Reverend Robert Trail, sometime Minister of Cranbrook, Kent. 1696.

"Concerning sanctification, there are three things that I would speak to.

"I. What sanctification is.

"II. Wherein it agrees with justification.

"III. Wherein it differs from justification.

"I. What is sanctification? It is a great deal better to feel it than to express it,

"Sanctification is the same with regeneration; the same with the renovation of the whole man. Sanctification is the forming and the framing of the new creature; it is the implanting and engraving the image of Christ upon the poor soul. It is what the Apostle breathed after-- That Christ might be formed in them' (Gal. iv. 19); That they might bear the image of the heavenly." (1 Cor. xv. 49)

"There are but two men only that all the world is like; and so will it fare with them, as they are like the one, or like the other: the first Adam, and the second Adam. Every man by nature is like the first Adam and like the devil: for the devil and the first fallen Adam were like one another. Ye are of your father the devil.' saith our Lord (John viii. 44), and he was a murderer from the beginning.' All the children of the first Adam are the devil's children, there is no difference here. And all the children of the other sort are like to Jesus Christ, the second Adam; and when His image shall be perfected in them, then they shall be perfectly happy. As we have also borne the image of the earthly, so shall we also bear the image of the heavenly.' (1 Cor. xv. 49.) Pray observe; we bear the image of the earthly by being born in sin and misery; we bear the image of the earthly by living in sin and misery; and we bear the image of the earthly by dying in sin and misery; and we bear the image of the earthly in the rottenness of the grave; and we bear the image of the heavenly Adam when we are sanctified by His Spirit. This image increases in us according to our growth in sanctification: and we perfectly bear the image of the heavenly Adam when we are just like the Man Christ, both in soul and body, perfectly happy, and perfectly holy; when we have overcome death by His grace, as He overcame it by His own strength. It will never be known how like believers are to Jesus Christ, till they are risen again: when they shall arise from their graves, like so many little suns shining in glory and brightness. Oh, how like will they be to Jesus Christ! though His personal transcendent glory will be His property and prerogative to all eternity.

"II. Wherein are justification and sanctification alike? I answer, in many things.

" 1st. They are like one another as they are the same in their author; it is God that justifieth, and it is God that sanctifies. Who shall lay anything to the charge of God's elect? it is God that justifieth.' (Rom. viii. 33.) I am the Lord that doth sanctify you, is a common word in the Old Testament. (Ex. xxxi. 13; Lev. xx. 8.)

"2ndly. They are alike and the same in their rise, being both of free grace; justification is an act of free grace, and sanctification is the same. Not by works of righteousness which we have done, but according to His mercy, He saved us by the washing of regeneration, and the renewing of the Holy Ghost.' (Tit. iii. 5.) They are both of grace.

"3rdly. They are alike in that they are both towards the same persons. Never a man is justified but he is also sanctified; and never a man is sanctified but he is also justified; all the elect of God, all the redeemed, have both these blessings passing upon them.

"4thly. They are alike as to the time, they are the same in time. It is a hard matter for us to talk or think of time when we are speaking of the works of God: these saving works of His are always done at the same time; a man is not justified before he is sanctified, though it may be conceived so in order of nature, yet at the same time the same grace works both. Such were some of you,' saith the Apostle, but ye are washed, but ye are sanctified, but ye are justified in the name of the Lord Jesus, and by the Spirit of our God.' (1 Cor. vi. 11.)

"5thly. They are the same as to the operation of them by the same means, that is, by the Word of God: we are justified by the Word, sentencing us to eternal life by the promise; and we are also sanctified by the power of the same Word. Now ye are clean,' saith our Lord, through the Word that I have spoken unto you.' (John xv. 3.) That He might sanctify and cleanse His Church,' saith the Apostle, with the washing of water by the Word.' (Eph. v. 26.)

"6th and lastly. They are the same as to their equal necessity to eternal life. I do not say as to their equal order, but as to their equal necessity: that is, as it is determined that no man who is not justified shall be saved, so it is determined that no man who is not sanctified shall be saved: no unjustified man can be saved, and no unsanctified man can be saved. They are of equal necessity in order to the possessing of eternal life.

"III. Wherein do justification and sanctification differ? This is a matter of great concernment for people's practice and daily exercise; wherein they differ. They agree in many things, as has just now been declared, but they likewise differ vastly.

"1st. Justification is an act of God about the state of a man's person; but sanctification is the work of God about the nature of a man: and these two are very different, as I shall illustrate by a similitude. Justification is an act of God as a judge about a delinquent, absolving him from a sentence of death; but sanctification is an act of God about us, as a physician, in curing us of a mortal disease. There is a criminal that conies to the bar, and is arraigned for high treason; the same criminal has a mortal disease, that he may die of, though there was no judge on the bench to pass the sentence of death upon him for his crime. It is an act of grace which absolves the man from the sentence of the law, that he shall not suffer death for his treason--that saves the man's life. But notwithstanding this, unless his disease be cured, he may die quickly after, for all the judge's pardon. Therefore, I say, justification is an act of God as a gracious Judge, sanctification is a work of God as a merciful Physician; David joins them both together. (Ps. ciii. 3.) Who forgiveth all thine inqiuities, who healeth all thy diseases.' It is promised, That iniquity shall not be your ruin (Ezek. xviii. 30), in the guilt of it; that is justification: and it shall not be your ruin, in the power of it; there lies sanctification.

"2ndly. Justification is an act of God's grace upon the account of the righteousness of another, but sanctification is a work of God, infusing a righteousness into us. Now there is a great difference between these two: for the one is by imputation, the other by infusion.

"In justification, the sentence of God proceeds this way: the righteousness that Christ wrought out by His life and death, and the obedience that He paid to the law of God, is reckoned to the guilty sinner for his absolution; so that when a sinner comes to stand at God's bar, when the question is asked, Hath not this man broken the law of God? Yes, saith God; yes, saith the conscience of the poor sinner, I have broken it in innumerable ways. And doth not the law condemn thee to die for thy transgression? Yes, saith the man; yes, saith the law of God, the law knows nothing more but this; the soul that sinneth must die.' Well, then, but Is there no hope in this case? Yes, and Gospel grace reveals this hope. There is One that took sin on Him, and died for our sins, and His righteousness is reckoned for the poor sinner's justification; and thus we are absolved. We are absolved in justification by God's reckoning on our account, on our behalf, and for our advantage, what Christ hath done and suffered for us.

"In sanctification the Spirit of God infuses a holiness into the soul. I do not say He infuses a righteousness; for I would fain have these words, righteousness and holiness, better distinguished than generally they are. Righteousness and holiness are, in this case, to be kept vastly asunder. Our righteousness is without us; our holiness is within us, it is our own; the Apostle plainly makes that distinction. Not having mine own righteousness.' (Phil. iii. 9.) It is our own, not originally, but our own inherently; not our own so us to be of our own working, but our own because it is indwelling in us. But our righteousness is neither our own originally nor inherently; it is neither wrought out by us, nor doth it dwell in us; but it is wrought out by Jesus Christ, and it eternally dwells in Him, and is only to be pleaded by faith, by a poor creature. But our holiness, though it be not our own originally, yet it is our own inherently, it dwells in us: this is the distinction that the Apostle makes. That I may be found in Him, not having my own righteousness, which is of the law, but that which is through the faith of Christ, the righteousness which is of God by faith.' (Phil. iii. 9.)

"3rdly. Justification is perfect, but sanctification is imperfect; and here lies a great difference between them. Justification, I say, is perfect, and admits of no degrees; admits of no decays, admits of no intermission, nor of any interruption: but sanctification admits of all these. When I say justification is perfect, I mean, that every justified man is equally and perfectly justified. The poorest believer that is this day in the world, is justified as much as ever the Apostle Paul was; and every true believer is as much justified now as he will be a thousand years hence. Justification is perfect in all them that are partakers of it, and to all eternity; it admits of no degrees. And the plain reason of it is this--the ground of it is the perfect righteousness of Jesus Christ, and the entitling us to it is by an act of God the gracious Judge, and that act stands for ever; and if God justifies, who is he that shall condemn? (Rom. viii. 33.) But sanctification is an imperfect, incomplete, changeable thing. One believer is more sanctified than another. I am apt to believe that the Apostle Paul was more sanctified the first hour of his conversion, than any man this day in the world.

"Sanctification differs greatly as to the persons that are partakers of it; and it differs greatly too as to the same man; for a true believer, a truly sanctified man, may be more holy and sanctified at one time than at another. There is a work required of us--to be perfecting holiness in the fear of God (2 Cor. vii. 1). But we are nowhere required to be perfecting righteousness in the sight of God; for God hath brought in a perfect righteousness, in which we stand; but we are to take care, and to give diligence to perfect holiness in the fear of God. A saint in glory is more sanctified than ever he was, for he is perfectly so; but he is not more justified than he was. Nay, a saint in heaven is not more justified than a believer on earth is: only they know it better, and the glory of that light in which they see it, discovers it more brightly and more clearly to them."

From Traill's Sermons, upon 1 Pet. i. 1-3, vol. 4, p. 71. Edinburgh edition of Traill's Works. 1810.

(2.) Rev. Thomas Brooks, Rector of St. Margaret, Fish Street Hill, London. 1662.

"Consider the necessity of holiness. It is impossible that ever you should be happy, except you are holy. No holiness here, no happiness hereafter. The Scripture speaks of three bodily inhabitants of heaven--Enoch, before the law; Elijah, under the law; and Jesus Christ, under the Gospel: all three eminent in holiness, to teach us, that even in an ordinary course there is no going to heaven without holiness. There are many thousand thousands now in heaven, but not one unholy one among them all; there is not one sinner among all those saints; not one goat among all those sheep; not one weed among all those flowers; not one thorn or prickle among all those roses; not one pebble among all those glistering diamonds. There is not one Cain among all those Abels; nor one Ishmael among all those Isaacs; nor one Esau among all those Jacobs in heaven. There is not one Ham among all the patriarchs; not one Saul among all the prophets; nor one Judas among all the apostles; nor one Demas among all the preachers; nor one Simon Magus among all the professors.

"Heaven is only for the holy man, and the holy man is only for heaven: heaven is a garment of glory, that is only suited to him that is holy. God, who is truth itself, and cannot lie, hath said it, that without holiness no man shall see the Lord. Mark that word no man.' Without holiness the rich man shall not see the Lord; without holiness the poor man shall not see the Lord; without holiness the nobleman shall not see the Lord; without holiness the mean man shall not see the Lord; without holiness the prince shall not see the Lord; without holiness the peasant shall not see the Lord; without holiness the ruler shall not see the Lord; without holiness the ruled shall not see the Lord; without holiness the learned man shall not see the Lord; without holiness the ignorant man shall not see the Lord; without holiness the husband shall not see the Lord; without holiness the wife shall not see the Lord; without holiness the father shall not see the Lord; without holiness the child shall not see the Lord; without holiness the master shall not see the Lord; without holiness the servant shall not see the Lord. For faithful and strong is the Lord of hosts that hath spoken it.' (Josh. xxiii. 14.)

"In this day some cry up one form, some another; some cry up one Church state, some another; some cry up one way, some another; but certainly the way of holiness is the good old way (Jer. vi. 16); it is the King of kings' highway to heaven and happiness: And a highway shall be there, and a way, and it shall be called The way of holiness; the unclean shall not pass over it; but it shall be for those: the wayfaring men, though fools, shall not err therein.' (Isa. xxxv. 8.) Some men say, Lo, here is the way; other men say, Lo, there is the way; but certainly the way of holiness is the surest, the safest, the easiest, the noblest, and the shortest way to happiness.

"Among the heathen, no man could enter into the temple of honour, but must first enter the temple of virtue. There is no entering the temple of happiness, except you enter into the temple of holiness. Holiness must first enter into you, before you can enter into God's holy hill. As Samson cried out, Give me water, or I die'; or as Rachel cried out, Give me children, or I die'; so all unsanctified souls may well cry out, Lord, give me holiness, or I die: give me holiness or I eternally die. If the angels, those princes of glory, fall once from their holiness, they shall be for ever excluded from everlasting happiness and blessedness. If Adam in paradise fall from his purity, he shall quickly be driven out from the presence of Divine glory. Augustine would not be a wicked man, an unholy man, one hour for all the world, because he did not know but that he might die that hour; and should he die in an unholy estate, he knew he should be for ever separated from the presence of the Lord and the glory of His power.

"O, sirs, do not deceive your own souls; holiness is of absolute necessity; without it you shall never see the Lord. (2 Thess. i. 8-10.) It is not absolutely necessary that you should be great or rich in the world; but it is absolutely necessary that you should be holy: it is not absolutely necessary that you should enjoy health, strength, friends, liberty, life; but it is absolutely necessary that you should be holy. A man may see the Lord without worldly prosperity, but he can never see the Lord except he be holy. A man may to heaven, to happiness, without honour or worldly glory, but he can never to heaven, to happiness, without holiness. Without holiness here, no heaven hereafter. And there shall in no wise enter into it anything that defileth.' (Rev. xxi. 27.) God will at last shut the gates of glory against every person that is without heart-purity.

"Ah, sirs, holiness is a flower that grows not in Nature's garden. Men are not born with holiness in their hearts, as they are born with tongues in their mouths: holiness is of a Divine offspring: it is a pearl of price, that is to be found in no nature but a renewed nature, m no bosom but a sanctified bosom. There is not the least beam or spark of holiness in any natural man in the world. Every imagination of the thoughts of man's heart is only evil continually.' (Gen. vi. 5.) How can man be clean that is born of a woman?' (Job xxv. 4.) The interrogation carries in it a strong negation, How can man be clean?' that is, man cannot be clean that is born of a woman: a man that is born of a woman is born in sin, and born both under wrath and under the curse. And who can bring a clean thing out of an unclean?' But we are all as an unclean thing, and all our righteousnesses are as filthy rags.' (Job xiv. 4; Isa. lxiv. 6.) There is none righteous, no not one; there is none that understandeth, there is none that seeketh after God.' (Rom. iii. 10, 11.) Every man by nature is a stranger, yea, an enemy to holiness. (Rom. viii. 7.) Every man that comes into this world comes with his face towards sin and hell, and with his back upon God and holiness.

"Such is the corruption of our nature, that, propound any Divine good to it, it is entertained as fire by water, or wet wood, with hissing. Propound any evil, then it is like fire to straw; it is like the foolish satyr that made haste to kiss the fire; it is like that unctuous matter which, the naturalists say, sucks and snatches the fire to it, with which it is consumed. All men are born sinners, and there is nothing but an infinite power that can make them saints. All men would be happy, and yet they naturally loathe to be holy. By all which you may clearly see that food is not more necessary for the preservation of natural life, than holiness is necessary for the preservation and salvation of the soul. If a man had the wisdom of Solomon, the strength of Samson, the courage of Joshua, the policy of Ahithophel, the dignities of Haman, the power of Ahasuerus, and the eloquence of Apollos, yet all those without holiness would never save him. The days and times wherein we live call aloud for holiness. If you look upon them as days and times of grace, what greater and higher engagements to holiness were ever put upon a people, than those that God hath put upon us, who enjoy so many ways, means, and helps to make us holy? Oh, the pains, the care, the cost, the charge, that

God hath been at, and that God is daily at, to make us holy! Hath He not sent, and doth He not still send His messengers, rising up early, and going to bed late, and all to provoke you to be holy? Have not many of them spent their time, and spent their strength, and spent their spirits, and spent their lives to make you holy? O, sirs, what do holy ordinances call for, but holy hearts and holy lives? What do days of light call for, but walking in the light, and casting off the deeds of darkness? What is the voice of all the means of grace, but this, Oh, labour to be gracious? And what is the voice of the Holy Spirit, but this, Oh, labour to be holy? And what is the voice of all the miracles of mercy that God hath wrought in the midst of you, but this, Be ye holy, be ye holy'? O, sirs, what could the Lord have done that He hath not done to make you holy? Hath He not lifted you up to heaven in respect of holy helps? Hath He not to this very day followed you close with holy offers, and holy entreaties, and holy counsels, and holy encouragements, and all to make you holy? And will you be loose still, and proud still, and worldly still, and malicious still, and envious still, and contentious still, and unholy still? Oh, what is this, but to provoke the Lord to put out all the lights of heaven, to drive your teachers into corners, to remove your candlesticks, and to send His everlasting Gospel, that hath stood long a tip-toe, among a people that may more highly prize it, and dearly love it, and stoutly defend it, and conscientiously practise it, than you have done to this very day? (Rev. ii. 4, 5; Isa. xlii. 25.) I suppose there is nothing more evident than that the times and seasons wherein we live call aloud upon every one to look after holiness, and to labour for holiness. Never complain of the times, but cease to do evil, and labour to do well, and all will be well; get but better hearts and better lives, and you will quickly see better times. (Isa. i. 16-19.)

From Brooks' "Crown and Glory of Christianity; or, Holiness the only way to Happiness"--Brooks' Works, vol. 4, pp. 151-153, 187-188.--Grosart's edition. 1866.

SELECTED TEXTS AND SERMONS

THE BEST FRIEND

"This is my Friend!" —Song of Solomon 4:16

A friend is one of the greatest blessings on earth. Tell me not of money — love is better than gold; sympathy is better than lands. He is the poor man — who has no friends! This world is full of sorrow — because it is full of sin. It is a dark place. It is a lonely place. It is a disappointing place. The brightest sunbeam in it, is a friend. Friendship halves our troubles — and doubles our joys!

A real friend is scarce and rare. There are many who will eat, and drink, and laugh with us in the sunshine of prosperity. There are few who will stand by us in the days of darkness — few who will love us when we are sick, helpless, and poor — few, above all, who will care for our souls! Does any reader of this paper want a real friend? I write to recommend one to your notice this day. I know of One "who sticks closer than a brother!" (Proverbs 18:24.) I know of One who is ready to be your friend for time and for eternity, if you will receive Him. Hear me, while I try to tell you something about Him.

The friend I want you to know is Jesus Christ. Happy is that family in which Christ has the foremost place! Happy is that person whose chief friend is Christ!

I. Do we want a friend in NEED? Such a friend is the Lord Jesus Christ!

Man is the neediest creature on God's earth, because he is a sinner. There is no need as great as that of sinners: poverty, hunger, thirst, cold, sickness — all are nothing in comparison. Sinners need pardon — and they are utterly unable to provide it for themselves; they need deliverance from a guilty conscience and the fear of death — and they have no power of their own to obtain it. This need, the Lord Jesus Christ came into the world to relieve. "He came into the world to save sinners!" (1 Tim. 1:15.)

We are all by nature, poor dying creatures. From the king on his throne, to the pauper in the workhouse — we are all sick of a mortal disease of soul. Whether we know it or not, whether we feel it or not — we are all dying daily. The plague of sin is in our blood. We cannot cure ourselves — we are hourly getting worse and worse! All this, the Lord Jesus undertook to remedy. He came into the world to bring in health and cure; He came to deliver us "from the second death;" He came "to abolish death, and bring life and immortality to light through the Gospel." (Jeremiah 33:6; Rev. 2:11; 2 Tim. 1:10.)

We are all by nature imprisoned debtors. We owed our God millions — and had nothing to pay. We were wretched bankrupts, without hope of freeing ourselves. We could never have freed ourselves from our load of liabilities, and were daily getting more deeply indebted. All this the Lord Jesus saw, and undertook to remedy. He engaged to "ransom and redeem us." He came to "proclaim liberty to the captives, and the opening of the prison to those who are bound." "He came to redeem us from the curse of the law." (Hos. 13:14; Isaiah 41:1; Galatians 3:13.)

We were all by nature shipwrecked and cast away. We could never have reached the harbor of everlasting life. We were sinking in the midst of the waves — hopeless, helpless, and powerless; tied and bound by the chain of our sins, foundering under the burden of our own guilt, and likely to become a prey to the devil. All this the Lord Jesus saw and undertook to remedy. He came down from Heaven to be our "mighty helper." He came to "seek and to save those who are lost;" and to "deliver us from going down into the pit." (Psalm 89:19; Luke 19:10; Job 33:24.)

Could we have been saved without the Lord Jesus Christ coming down from Heaven? It would have been utterly impossible. The wisest men of Egypt, and Greece, and Rome never found out the way to peace with God. Without the friendship of Christ — we would all have been lost for evermore in Hell. Was the Lord Jesus Christ obliged to come down to save us? Oh, no! no! It was His own free love, mercy, and pity — which brought Him down. He came unsought and unasked — because He was gracious.

Let us think on these things. Search all history from the beginning of the world — look around the whole circle of those you know and love — you never heard of such friendship among men. There never was such a real friend in need as Jesus Christ!

II. Do you want a friend in DEED? Such a friend is the Lord Jesus Christ.

The true extent of a man's friendship must be measured by his deeds. Tell me not what he says, and feels, and wishes; tell me not of his words and letters — tell me rather what he does. "A friend is measured by what he does." The doings of the Lord Jesus Christ for man are the grand proof of His friendly feeling towards him. Never were there such acts of kindness and self-denial — as those which He has performed on our behalf. He has not loved us in word only — but in deed.

For our sakes, He took our nature upon Him, and was born of a woman. He who was very God, and equal with the Father, laid aside His glory for a season, and took upon Him flesh and blood like our own. The almighty Creator of all things — became a little babe like any of us, and experienced all our bodily weaknesses and infirmities, sin only excepted. "Though He was rich — He became poor; that we through His poverty — might be rich." (2 Corinthians 8:9.)

For our sakes, He lived thirty-three years in this evil world, despised and rejected by men, a man of sorrows, and acquainted with grief. Though He was King of kings — He had nowhere to lay His head; though He was Lord of lords — He was often weary, and hungry, and thirsty, and poor. "He took on Him the form of a servant, and humbled Himself." (Philippians 3:7, 8.)

For our sakes, He suffered the most painful of all deaths, even the death of the cross! Though innocent, and without fault, He allowed Himself to be condemned, and found guilty. He who was the Prince of Life — was led as a lamb to the slaughter, and poured out His soul unto death. He "died for us." (1 Thessalonians 5:10.)

Was He obliged to do this? Oh, no! He might have summoned to His help, more than twelve legions of angels, and scattered His enemies with a word. He suffered voluntarily and of His own free will, to make atonement for our sins. He knew that nothing but the sacrifice of His body and blood — could ever make peace between sinful man and a holy God. He laid down His life — to pay the price of our redemption. He died — that we might live. He suffered — that we might reign. He bore shame — that we might receive glory. "He suffered for sins, the just for the unjust, that He might bring us to God." "God made him who had no sin to be sin for us — so that in him we might become the righteousness of God." (1 Peter 3:18; 2 Corinthians 5:21.)

Such friendship as this surpasses man's understanding. Friends who would die for those who love them — we may have heard of sometimes. But who can find a man who would lay down his life for those that hate him? Yet this is what Jesus has done for us. "Christ died for the ungodly. God commends His love towards us, in that while we were yet sinners — Christ died for us. When we were God's enemies — we were reconciled to him through the death of his Son!" (Romans 5:6, 8, 10.)

Ask all the tribes of mankind, from one end of the world to the other — and you will nowhere hear of a deed like this! None was ever so high and stooped down so low — as Jesus the Son of God! None ever gave so costly a proof of his friendship! None ever paid so much and endured so much to do good to others. Never was there such a friend in deed as Jesus   Christ!

III. Do we want a MIGHTY and POWERFUL friend? Such a friend is Jesus Christ.

Power to help, is that which few possess in this world. Many have desire enough to do good to others — but no power. They feel for the sorrows of others, and would gladly relieve them if they could; they can weep with their friends in affliction — but are unable to take their grief away. But though man is weak — Christ is strong; though the best of our earthly friends is feeble — Christ is almighty! "All power is given unto Him in Heaven and earth." (Matthew 28:18.) No one can do so much for those whom He befriends, as Jesus Christ. Others can befriend their bodies a little — He can befriend both body and soul. Others can do a little for them in time — He can be a friend both for time and eternity!

(a) He is able to pardon and save the very chief of sinners. He can deliver the most guilty conscience from all its burdens, and give it perfect peace with God. He can wash away the vilest stains of wickedness, and make a man whiter than snow in the sight of God. He can clothe a poor weak child of Adam in everlasting righteousness, and give him a title to Heaven that can never be overthrown. In a word, He can give any one of us peace, hope, forgiveness, and reconciliation with God — if we will only trust in Him. "The blood of Jesus Christ cleanses from all sin!" (1 John 1:7.)

(b) He is able to convert the hardest of hearts, and create in man a new spirit. He can take the most thoughtless and ungodly people, and give them another mind by the Holy Spirit whom He puts in them. He can cause old things to pass away, and all things to become new. He can make them love the things which they once hated — and hate the things which they once loved. "He can give them power to become the sons of God." "If any man is in Christ — he is a new creature." (John 1:12; 2 Corinthians 5:17.)

(c) He is able to preserve to the end all who believe in Him, and become His disciples. He can give them grace to overcome the world, the flesh and the devil, and fight a good fight until the last. He can . . .lead them on safely in spite of every temptation, carry them home through a thousand dangers, and keep them faithful, though they stand alone and have none to help them. "He is able to save them to the uttermost, all who come unto God by Him." (Hebrews 7:25.)

(d) He is able to give those who love Him the best of gifts. He can give them in this life — inward comforts, which money can never buy — peace in poverty, joy in sorrow, patience in suffering. He can give them in death — bright hopes, which enable them to walk through the dark valley without fear. He can give them after death — an unfading crown of glory, and a reward compared to which, the Queen of England has nothing to bestow.

This is power indeed! This is true greatness! This is real strength! Go and look at the poor Hindu idolater, seeking peace in vain by afflicting his body; and, after fifty years of self-imposed suffering, unable to find it. Go and look at the benighted Romanist, giving money to his priest to pray for his soul — and yet dying without comfort. Go and look at rich men, spending thousands in search of happiness — and yet always discontented and unhappy. Then turn to Jesus, and think what He can do, and is daily doing for all who trust Him. Think how He . . .

> heals all the broken-hearted,
> comforts all the sick,
> cheers all the poor that trust in Him,
> and supplies all their daily need.
> The fear of man is strong,
> the opposition of this evil world is mighty,
> the lusts of the flesh rage horribly,
> the fear of death is terrible,
> the devil is a roaring lion seeking whom he may devour
> — but Jesus is stronger than them all, Jesus can make us conquerors over all these foes!

And then say whether there was ever was so mighty a friend as Jesus Christ.

IV. Do we want a LOVING and affectionate friend? Such a friend is Jesus Christ.

Kindness is the very essence of true friendship. Money and advice and help lose half their grace, if not given in a loving manner. What kind of love is that of the Lord Jesus toward man? It is called, "A love that surpasses knowledge." (Ephesians 3:19.)

Love shines forth in His reception of sinners. He refuses none who come to Him for salvation, however unworthy they may be. Though their lives may have been most wicked, though their sins may be more in number than the stars of Heaven — the Lord Jesus is ready to receive them, and give them pardon and peace! There is no end to His compassion! There are no bounds to His pity! He is not ashamed to befriend those whom the world casts off as hopeless. There are none too bad, too filthy, and too much diseased with sin — to be admitted into His home! He is willing to be the friend of any sinner. He has kindness and mercy and healing medicine for all. He has long proclaimed this to be His rule: "Whoever comes unto Me — I will never cast out." (John 6:37.)

Love shines forth in His dealings with sinners, after they have believed in Him and become His friends. He is very patient with them, though their conduct is often very trying and provoking. He is never tired of hearing their complaints — however often they may come to Him. He sympathizes deeply in all their sorrows. He knows what pain is — He is "acquainted with grief" (Is. 53:3.) In all their afflictions, He is afflicted. He never allows them to be tempted above what they are able to bear. He supplies them with daily grace for their daily conflict. Their poor services are acceptable to Him. He is as well pleased with them as a parent is with his child's endeavors to speak and walk. He has caused it to be written in His book, that "He takes pleasure in His people," and that "He takes pleasure in those who fear Him." (Psalm 147:11; 119:4.)

There is no love on earth that can even be named together with this! We love those in whom we see something that deserves our affection, or those who are our relatives — but the Lord Jesus loves sinners in whom there is no good thing. We love those from whom we get some return for our affection — but the Lord Jesus loves those who can do little or nothing for Him, compared to what He does for them. We love where we can give some reason for loving — but the great Friend of sinners draws His reasons out of His own everlasting compassion. His love is purely unselfish — purely free. Never, never was there so truly loving a friend as Jesus Christ.

V. Do we want a WISE prudent friend? Such a friend is the Lord Jesus Christ.

Man's friendship is sadly blind. He often injures those he loves by injudicious kindness. He often errs in the counsel he gives — he often leads his friends into trouble by bad advice, even when he means to help them. He sometimes keeps them back from the way of life, and entangles them in the vanities of the world, when they have well near escaped. The friendship of the Lord Jesus is not so — it always does us good, and never evil.

The Lord Jesus never spoils His friends by extravagant indulgence. He gives them everything that is really for their benefit. He withholds nothing from them that is really good. He requires them to take up their cross daily and follow Him. He bids them endure hardships as good soldiers. He calls on them to fight the good fight against the world, the flesh, and the devil. His people often dislike it at the time, and think it hard — but when they reach Heaven, they will see it was all well done.

The Lord Jesus makes no mistakes in managing His friends' affairs. He orders all their concerns with perfect wisdom — all things happen to them at the right time, and in the right way. He gives them . . . as much of sickness — and as much of health, as much of poverty — and as much of riches, as much of sorrow — and as much of joy — as He sees their souls require.

He leads them by the right way to bring them to the city of habitation. He mixes their bitterest cups like a wise physician, and takes care that they have not a drop too little — or too much. His people often misunderstand His dealings — they are silly enough to imagine their course of life might have been better ordered. But in the resurrection-day, they will thank God that not their will — but Christ's will was done.

Look round the world and see the harm which people are continually getting from their friends. Mark how much more ready men are to encourage one another in worldliness and levity — than to provoke to love and good works. Think how often they meet together, not for the better — but for the worse; not to quicken one another's souls in the way to Heaven — but to confirm one another in the love of this present world. Alas, there are thousands who are wounded unexpectedly in the house of their friends!

And then turn to the great Friend of sinners, and see how different a thing is His friendship from that of man. Listen to Him as He walks by the way with His disciples — mark how He comforts, reproves, and exhorts with perfect wisdom. Observe how He times His visits to those He loves — as to Mary and Martha at Bethany. Hear how He converses, as He dines on the shore of the sea of Galilee: "Simon, son of Jonah, do you love Me?" (John 21:16.)

His company is always sanctifying.

His gifts are always for our soul's good.

His kindness is always wise.

His fellowship is always to edification.

One day with the Son of Man — is better than a thousand in the society of earthly friends! One hour spent in private communion with Him — is better than a year in kings' palaces. Never, never was there such a wise friend as Jesus Christ.

VI. Do we want a TRIED and PROVED friend? Such a friend is Jesus Christ.

Six thousand years have passed away since the Lord Jesus began His work of befriending mankind. During that long period of time, He has had many friends in this world. Millions on millions, unhappily, have refused His offers, and been miserably lost forever; but thousands on thousands have enjoyed the mighty privilege of His friendship and been saved. He has had great experience.

(a) He has had friends of every rank and station in life. Some of them were kings and rich men, like David, and Solomon, and Hezekiah, and Job. Some of them were very poor in this world, like the shepherds of Bethlehem, and James, and John, and Andrew. But they were all alike Christ's friends.

(b) He has had friends of every age that man can pass through. Some of them never knew Him until they were advanced in years, like Manasseh, and Zacchaeus, and probably the Ethiopian Eunuch. Some of them were His friends even from their earliest childhood, like Joseph, and Samuel, and Josiah, and Timothy. But they were all alike Christ's friends.

(c) He has had friends of every possible temperament and disposition. Some of them were simple plain men, like Isaac. Some of them were mighty in word and deed, like Moses. Some of them were fervent and warm-hearted, like Peter. Some of them were gentle and retiring spirits, like John. Some of them were active and stirring, like Martha. Some of them loved to sit quietly at His feet, like Mary. Some dwelt unknown among their own people, like the Shunamite. Some have gone everywhere and turned the world upside down, like Paul. But they were all alike Christ's friends.

(d) He has had friends of every condition in life. Some of them were married, and had sons and daughters, like Enoch. Some of them lived and died unmarried, like Daniel and John the Baptist. Some of them were often sick, like Lazarus and Epaphroditus. Some of them were strong to labor, like Persis, and Tryphena, and Tryphosa. Some of them were masters, like Abraham and Cornelius. Some of them were servants, like the saints in Nero's household. Some of them had bad servants, like Elisha. Some of them had bad masters like Obadiah. Some of them had bad wives and children, like David. But they were all alike Christ's friends.

(e) He has had friends of almost every nation, and people, and tongue. He has had friends in hot countries and in cold; friends among nations highly civilized, and friends among the simplest and rudest tribes. His book of life contains the names of Greeks and Romans, of Jews and Egyptians, of bond and of free. There are to be found on its lists . . .reserved Englishmen and cautious Scotsmen, impulsive Irishmen and fiery Welshmen, volatile Frenchmen and dignified Spaniards, refined Italians and solid Germans, crude Africans and refined Hindus, cultivated Chinese and half-savage New Zealanders.But they were all alike Christ's friends!

All these have made trial of Christ's friendship, and proved it to be good. They all found nothing lacking when they began — they all found nothing lacking as they went on. No lack, no defect, no deficiency was ever found by any one of them, in Jesus Christ. Each found his own soul's needs fully supplied; each found every day, that in Christ there was enough and to spare. Never, never was there a friend so fully tried and proved as Jesus Christ.

VII. Last — but not least, do we want an UNFAILING friend? Such a friend is the Lord Jesus Christ.

The saddest part of all the good things of earth is their instability.

Riches make themselves wings and flee away;

youth and beauty are but for a few years;

strength of body soon decays;

mind and intellect are soon exhausted.

> All is perishing.
>
> All is fading.
>
> All is passing away.

But there is one splendid exception to this general rule, and that is the friendship of Jesus Christ.

The Lord Jesus is a friend who never changes. There is no fickleness about Him. Those whom He loves — He loves unto the end. Husbands have been known to forsake their wives; parents have been known to cast off their children; human vows and promises of faithfulness have often been forgotten. Thousands have been neglected in their poverty and old age — who were honored by all when they were rich and young. But Christ never changed His feelings towards one of His friends. He is "the same yesterday, today, and forever." (Hebrews 13:8.)

The Lord Jesus never goes away from His friends. There is never a parting and good-bye between Him and His people. From the time that He makes His abode in the sinner's heart — He abides in it forever. The world is full of leave-takings and departures; death and the lapse of time break up the most united family; sons go forth to make their way in life; daughters are married, and leave their father's house forever. Scattering, scattering, scattering — is the yearly history of the happiest home. How many we have tearfully watched as they drove away from our doors, whose pleasant faces we have never seen again! How many we have sorrowfully followed to the grave — and then come back to a cold, silent, lonely, and blank fireside! But, thanks be to God, there is One who never leaves His friends! The Lord Jesus is He who has said, "I will never leave you, nor forsake you." (Hebrews 13:5.)

The Lord Jesus goes with His friends wherever they go. There is no possible separation between Him and those whom He loves. There is no place or position on earth that can divide them from the great Friend of their souls. When the path of duty calls them far away from home — He is their companion. When they pass through the fire and water of fierce tribulation — He is with them. When they lie down on the bed of sickness — He stands by them and makes all their trouble work for good. When they go down the valley of the shadow of death, and friends and relatives stand still and can go no further — He goes down by their side. When they wake up in the unknown world of Paradise — they are still with Him. When they rise with a new body at the judgment day — they will not be alone. He will own them for His friends, and say, "They are mine! Deliver them and let them go free." He will make good His own words: "I am with you always, even unto the end of the world." (Matthew 28:20.)

Look around the world, and see how failure is written on all men's schemes. Count up the partings, and separations, and disappointments, and bereavements which have happened under your own knowledge. Think what a privilege it is that there is One at least who never fails, and in whom no one was ever disappointed! Never, never was there so unfailing a friend as Jesus Christ!

And now, allow me to conclude this paper with a few plain words of APPLICATION. I know not who you are or in what state your soul may be; but I am sure that the words I am about to say deserve your serious attention. Oh, that this paper may not find you heedless of spiritual things! Oh, that you may be able to give a few thoughts to Christ!

(1) Know then, for one thing, that I call upon you to seriously consider whether Christ is your Friend, and you are His.

There are thousands on thousands, I grieve to say, who are not Christ's friends. Baptized in His name, members of a Christian Church, attendants on His means of grace — all this they are, no doubt. But they are not Christ's friends.

Do they hate the sins which Jesus died to put away? No.

Do they love the Savior who came into the world to save them? No.

Do they care for the souls which were so precious in His sight? No.

Do they delight in the His Word? No.

Do they try to speak with the Friend of sinners in prayer? No.

Do they seek close fellowship with Him? No.

Oh, reader, is this your case? How is it with you? Are you or are you not, one of Christ's friends?

(2) Know, in the next place, that if you are not one of Christ's friends — then you are a poor miserable being.

I write this down deliberately. I do not say it without thought. I say that if Christ is not your friend — then you are a poor, miserable being.

You are in the midst of a failing, sorrowful world — and you have no real source of comfort, or refuge for a time of need. You are a dying creature — and you are not ready to die. You have sins — and they are not forgiven. You are going to be judged — and you are not prepared to meet God: you might be — but you refuse to use the one only Mediator and Advocate. You love the world better than Christ. You refuse the great Friend of sinners, and you have no friend in Heaven to plead your cause. Yes, it is sadly true! You are a poor, miserable being! It matters nothing what your income is — without Christ's friendship, you are very poor.

(3) Know, in the third place, that if you really want a friend — then Christ is willing to become your friend.

He has long wanted you to join His people, and He now invites you by my hand. He is ready to receive you, all unworthy as you may feel, and to write your name down in the list of His friends. He is ready to pardon all the past, to clothe you with righteousness, to give you His Spirit, to make you His own dear child. All He asks you to do, is to come to Him.

He bids you to come with all your sins; only acknowledging your vileness, and confessing that you are ashamed. Just as you are — waiting for nothing — unworthy of anything in yourself — Jesus bids you come and be His friend.

Oh, come and be wise! Come and be safe. Come and be happy. Come and be Christ's friend.

(4) Know, in the last place, that if Christ is your friend — then you have great privileges, and ought to walk worthy of them.

Seek every day to have closer communion with Him who is your Friend, and to know more of His grace and power. True Christianity is not merely the believing a certain set of dry theological propositions — it is to live in daily personal communication with an actual living person — Jesus the Son of God. "To me," said Paul, "to live is Christ." (Philippians 1:21.)

Seek every day to glorify your Lord and Savior in all your ways. "He who has a friend, should show himself friendly" (Proverbs 18:24), and no man surely is under such mighty obligations as the friend of Christ. Avoid everything which would grieve your Lord. Fight hard against besetting sins, against inconsistency, against backwardness to confess Him before men. Say to your soul, whenever you are tempted to that which is wrong, "Soul, soul — is this your kindness to your Friend?"

Think, above all, of the mercy which has been shown you, and learn to rejoice daily in your Friend! What though your body is bowed down with disease? What though your poverty and trials are very great? What though your earthly friends forsake you, and you are alone in the world? All this may be true; but if you are in Christ, then you have a Friend, a mighty Friend, a loving Friend, a wise Friend, a Friend that never fails. Oh, think, think much upon your friend! Yet in a little while, your Friend shall come to take you home, and you shall dwell with Him forever. Yet in a little while, you shall see as you have been seen, and know as you have been known. And then you shall hear assembled worlds confess, that he is the rich and happy man, who has had Christ for his friend!

CHRIST'S GREATEST TROPHY

"And one of the malefactors which were hanged railed on him, saying, If thou be Christ, save thyself and us. But the other answering rebuked him, saying, Dost not thou fear God, seeing thou art in the same condemnation? And we indeed justly; for we receive the due reward of our deeds: but this man hath done nothing amiss. And he said unto Jesus, Lord, remember me when thou comest into thy kingdom. And Jesus said unto him, Verily I say unto thee, Today shalt thou be with me in paradise." —Luke 23:39-43

There are few passages in the New Testament which are more familiar to men's ears than the verses which head this message. They contain the well known story of 'the penitent thief.'

And it is right and good that these verses should be well known. They have comforted many troubled minds; they have brought peace to many uneasy consciences; they have been a healing balm to many wounded hearts; they have been a medicine to many sin–sick souls; they have smoothed down not a few dying pillows. Wherever the gospel of Christ is preached, they will always be honored, loved and had in remembrance.

I wish to say something about these verses. I will try to unfold the Leading lessons which they are meant to teach. I cannot see the peculiar mental state of anyone into whose hands this message may fall. But I can see truths in this passage which no man can ever know too well. Here is the greatest trophy which Christ ever won.

1. Christ's power and willingness to save sinners

This is the main doctrine to be gathered from the history of the penitent thief. It teaches us that which ought to be music in the ears of all who hear it: it teaches us that Jesus Christ is 'mighty to save' (Isa. 63:1).

I ask anyone to say whether a case could look more hopeless and desperate than that of this penitent thief once did.

He was a wicked man, a malefactor, a thief, if not a murderer. We know this, for such only were crucified. He was suffering a just punishment for breaking the laws. And as he had lived wicked, so he seemed determined to die wicked, for at first, when he was crucified, he railed on our Lord.

And he was a dying man. He hung there, nailed to a cross, from which he was never to come down alive. He had no longer power to stir hand or foot. His hours were numbered; the grave was ready for him. There was but a step between him and death.

If ever there was a soul hovering on the brink of hell, it was the soul of this thief. If ever there was a case that seemed lost, gone and past recovery, it was his. If ever there was a child of Adam whom the devil made sure of as his own, it was this man.

But see now what happened. He ceased to rail and blaspheme, as he had done at the first; he began to speak in another manner altogether. He turned to our blessed Lord in prayer. He prayed Jesus to 'remember him when He came into His kingdom'. He asked that his soul might be cared for, his sins pardoned and himself thought of in another world. Truly this was a wonderful change!

And then mark what kind of answer he received. Some would have said he was too wicked a man to be saved; but it was not so. Some would have fancied it was too late, the door was shut, and there was no room for mercy; but it proved not too late at all. The Lord Jesus returned him an immediate answer, spoke kindly to him, assured him he should be with Him that day in paradise, pardoned him completely, cleansed him thoroughly from his sins, received him graciously, justified him freely, raised him from the gates of hell, gave him a title to glory. Of all the multitude of saved souls, none ever received so glorious an assurance of his own salvation as did this penitent thief. Go over the whole list, from Genesis to Revelation, and you will find none who had such words spoken to him as these 'Today shall you be with Me in paradise.'

I believe the Lord Jesus never gave so complete a proof of His power and will to save, as He did upon this occasion. In the day when He seemed most weak, He showed that He was a strong deliverer. In the hour when His body was racked with pain, He showed that He could feel tenderly for others. At the time when He Himself was dying, He conferred on a sinner eternal life.

Now, have I not a right to say, 'Christ is able to save to the uttermost them that come unto God by Him?' (Heb. 7:25) Behold the proof of it. If ever sinner was too far gone to be saved, it was this thief. Yet he was plucked as a brand from the fire.

Have I not a right to say, 'Christ will receive any poor sinner who comes to Him with the prayer of faith, and cast out none?' Behold the proof of it. If ever there was one that seemed too bad to be received, this was the man. Yet the door of mercy was wide open even for him.

Have I not a right to say, 'By grace you may be saved through faith, not of works fear not, only believe?' Behold the proof of it. This thief was never baptized; he belonged to no visible church; he never received the Lord's Supper; he never did any work for Christ; he never gave money to Christ's cause! But he had faith, and so he was saved.

Have I not a right to say, 'The youngest faith will save a man's soul, if it only be true,?' Behold the proof of it. This man's faith was only one day old; but it led him to Christ, and preserved him from hell.

Why then should any man or woman despair with such a passage as this in the Bible? Jesus is a Physician who can cure hopeless cases. He can quicken dead souls, and call the things which be not as though they were.

Never should any man or woman despair! Jesus is still the same now that He was eighteen hundred years ago. The keys of death and hell are in His hand. When He opens none can shut.

What though your sins be more in number than the hairs of your head? What though your evil habits have grown with your growth, and strengthened with your strength? What though you have hitherto hated good and loved evil all the days of your life? These things are sad indeed, but there is hope, even for you. Christ can heal you, Christ can raise you from your low estate. Heaven is not shut against you. Christ is able to admit you, if you will humbly commit your soul into His hands.

Are your sins forgiven? If not, I set before you this day a full and free salvation. I invite you to follow the steps of the penitent thief come to Christ and live. I tell you that Jesus is very pitiful, and of tender mercy. I tell you He can do everything that your soul requires. Though your sins be as scarlet, He can make them white as snow; though they be red like crimson, they shall be as wool. Why should you not be saved as well as another? Come unto Christ and live.

Are you a true believer? If you are, you ought to glory in Christ. Glory not in your own faith, your own feelings, your own knowledge, your own prayers, your own amendment, your own diligence. Glory in nothing but Christ. Alas! the best of us know but little of that merciful and mighty Savior. We do not exalt Him and glory in Him enough. Let us pray that we may see more of the fullness there is in Him.

Do you ever try to do good to others? If you do, remember to tell them about Christ. Tell the young, tell the poor, tell the aged, tell the ignorant' tell the sick, tell the dying—tell them all about Christ. Tell them of His power, and tell them of His love; tell them of His doings, and tell them of His feelings; tell them what He has done for the chief of sinners; tell them what He is willing to do to the last day of time; tell it them over and over again. Never be tired of speaking of Christ. Say to them broadly and fully, freely and unconditionally, unreservedly and undoubtingly, 'Come unto Christ, as the penitent thief did; come unto Christ, and you shall be saved.'

2. If some are saved in the very hour of death, others are not

This is a truth that never ought to be passed over, and I dare not leave it unnoticed. It is a truth that stands out plainly in the sad end of the other malefactor, and is only too often forgotten. Men forget that there were 'two thieves.'

What became of the other thief who was crucified? Why did he not turn from his sin, and call upon the Lord? Why did he remain hardened and impenitent? Why was he not saved? It is useless to try to answer such questions. Let us be content to take the fact as we find it, and see what it is meant to teach us.

We have no right whatever to say this thief was a worse man than his companion there is nothing to prove it. Both plainly were wicked men; both were receiving the due reward of their deeds; both hung by the side of our Lord Jesus Christ; both heard Him pray for His murderers, both saw Him suffer patiently. But while one repented, the other remained hardened; while one began to pray, the other went on railing; while one was converted in his last hours, the other died a bad man, as he had lived; while one was taken to paradise, the other went to his own place—the place of the devil and his angels.

Now these things are written for our warning. There is warning, as well as comfort in these verses, and that is a very solemn warning, too.

They tell me loudly, that though some may repent and be converted on their deathbeds, it does not at all follow that all will. A deathbed is not always a saving time.

They tell me loudly, that two men may have the same opportunities of getting good for their souls, may be placed in the same position, see the same things and hear the same things, and yet only one of the two shall take advantage of them, repent, believe and be saved.

They tell me, above all, that repentance and faith are the gifts of God and are not in a man's own power; and that if any one flatters himself he can repent at his own time, choose his own season, seek the Lord when he pleases and, like the penitent thief, be saved at the very last, he may find at length he is greatly deceived.

And it is good and profitable to bear this in mind. There is an immense amount of delusion in the world on this very subject. I see many allowing life to slip away, quite unprepared to die. I see many allowing that they ought to repent, but always putting off their own repentance. And I believe one grand reason is, that most men suppose they can turn to God just when they like! They wrest the parable of the laborer in the vineyard, which speaks of the eleventh hour, and use it as it never was meant to be used. They dwell on the pleasant part of the verses I am now considering, and forget the rest. They talk of the thief that went to paradise and was saved, and they forget the one who died as he had lived and was lost.

I entreat every man of common sense who reads this message to take heed that he does not fall into this mistake.

Look at the history of men in the Bible, and see how often these notions I have been speaking of are contradicted. Mark well how many proofs there are that two men may have the same light offered them, and only one use it, and that no one has a right to take liberties with God's mercy, and presume he will be able to repent just when he likes.

Look at Saul and David. They lived about the same time; they rose from the same rank in life; they were called to the same position in the world; they enjoyed the ministry of the same prophet, Samuel; they reigned the same number of years! Yet one was saved, and the other lost

Look at Sergius Paulus and Gallio. They were both Roman governors; they were both wise and prudent men in their generation; they both heard the apostle Paul preach! But one believed and was baptized, the other 'cared for none of those things' (Acts 18:17).

Look at the world around you. See what is going on continually under your eyes. Two sisters will often attend the same ministry, listen to the same truths, hear the same sermons, and yet only one shall be converted unto God, while the other remains totally unmoved. Two friends often read the same religious book one is so moved by it, that he gives up all for Christ, the other sees nothing at all in it, and continues the same as before. Hundreds have read Doddridge's Rise and Progress without profit: with Wilberforce it was one of the beginnings of spiritual life. Thousands have read Wilberforce's Practical View of Christianity and laid it down again unaltered from the time Leigh Richmond read it he became another man. No man has any warrant for saying, 'Salvation is in my own power.'

I do not pretend to explain these things. I only put them before you as great facts; and I ask you to consider them well.

You must not misunderstand me. I do not want to discourage you. I say these things in all affection, to give you warning of danger. I do not say them to drive you back from heaven. I say them rather to draw you on, and bring you to Christ, while He can be found.

I want you to beware of presumption. Do not abuse God's mercy and compassion. Do not continue in sin, I beseech you, and do you think can repent and believe and be saved, just when you like, when you please, when you will and when you choose. I would always set before you an open door. I would always say, 'While there is life there is hope,' But if you would be wise, put nothing off that concerns your soul.

I want you to beware of letting slip good thoughts and godly convictions, if you have them. Cherish them and nourish them, lest you lose them for ever. Make the most of them, lest they take to themselves wings and flee away. Have you an inclination to begin praying? Put it in practice at once. Have you an idea of beginning really to serve Christ? Set about it at once. Are you enjoying any spiritual light? See that you live up to your light. Trifle not with opportunities, lest the day come when you will want to use them, and not be able. Linger not, lest you become wise too late.

You may say, perhaps, 'It is never too late to repent.' I answer, 'That is right enough; but late repentance is seldom true.' And I say further, you cannot be certain if you put off repenting, you will repent at all.

You may say, 'Why should I be afraid? The penitent thief was saved.' I answer, 'That is true; but look again at the passage which tells you that the other thief was lost.'

3. The Spirit always leads saved souls in one way

This is a point that deserves particular attention, and is often overlooked. Men look at the broad fact that the penitent thief was saved when he was dying, and they look no further.

They do not consider the evidences this thief left behind him. They do not observe the abundant proof he gave of the work of the Spirit in his heart. And these proofs I wish to trace out. I wish to show you that the Spirit always works in one way, and that, whether He converts a man in an hour, as He did the penitent thief, or whether by slow degrees, as He does others, the steps by which He leads souls to heaven are always the same.

Let me try to make this clear to everyone who reads this message. I want to put you on your guard. I want you to shake off the common notion that there is some easy royal road to heaven from a dying bed. I want you thoroughly to understand, that every saved soul goes through the same experience, and that the leading principles of the penitent thief's religion were just the same as those of the oldest saint that ever lived.

a. See how strong this man's faith was. He called Jesus 'Lord.' He declared his belief that He would have a 'kingdom.' He believed that He was able to give him eternal life and glory, and in this belief prayed to Him. He maintained His innocence of all the charges brought against Him. 'This Man,' said he, 'has done nothing amiss.' Others perhaps may have thought the Lord innocent—none said so openly but this poor dying man.

And when did all this happen? It happened when the whole nation had denied Christ, shouting, 'Crucify Him, crucify Him we have no king but Caesar'; when the chief priests and Pharisees had condemned and found Him 'guilty of death'; when even His own disciples had forsaken Him and fled; when He was hanging, faint, bleeding and dying on the cross, numbered with transgressors, and accounted accursed. This was the hour when the thief believed in Christ, and prayed to Him! Surely such faith was never seen since the world began.

The disciples had seen mighty signs and miracles. They had seen the dead raised with a word and lepers healed with a touch, the blind receiving sight, the dumb made to speak, the lame made to walk. They had seen thousands fed with a few loaves and fishes. They had seen their Master walking on the water as on dry land. They had all of them heard Him speak as no man ever spoke, and hold out promises of good things yet to come. They had some of them had a foretaste of His glory in the mount of transfiguration. Doubtless their faith was 'the gift of God,' but still they had much to help it.

The dying thief saw none of the things I have mentioned. He only saw our Lord in agony, and in weakness, in suffering and in pain. He saw Him undergoing a dishonorable punishment, deserted, mocked, despised, blasphemed. He saw Him rejected by all the great and wise and noble of His own people, His strength dried up like a potsherd, His life drawing near to the grave (Ps. 22:15; 88:3). He saw no scepter, no royal crown, no outward dominion, no glory, no majesty, no power, no signs of might. And yet the dying thief believed, and looked forward to Christ's kingdom.

Would you know if you have the Spirit? Then mark the question I put to you this day: where is your faith in Christ?

b. See what a right sense of sin the thief had. He says to his companion, 'We receive the due reward of our deeds.' He acknowledges his own ungodliness, and the justice of his punishment. He makes no attempt to justify himself, or excuse his wickedness. He speaks like a man humbled and self–abased by the remembrance of past iniquities. This is what all God's children feel. They are ready to allow they are poor hell–deserving sinners. They can say with their hearts as well as with their lips 'We have left undone the things that we ought to have done, and we have done those things that we ought not to have done, and there is no health in us.'

Would you know if you have the Spirit? Then mark my question do you feel your sins?

c. See what brotherly love the thief showed to his companion. He tried to stop his railing and blaspheming, and bring him to a better mind. 'Does not you fear God', he says, 'seeing you are in the same condemnation?' There is no surer mark of grace than this! Grace shakes a man out of his selfishness, and makes him feel for the souls of others. When the Samaritan woman was converted, she left her water pot, and ran to the city, saying, 'Come, see a man which told me all things that ever I did is not this the Christ?' (John 4:28, 29). When Saul was converted, immediately he went to the synagogue at Damascus, and testified to his brethren of Israel that 'Christ was the Son of God' (Acts 9:20).

Would you know if you have the Spirit? Then where is your charity and love to souls?

In one word, you see in the penitent thief a finished work of the Holy Spirit. Every part of the believer's character may be traced in him. Short as his life was after conversion, he found time to leave abundant evidence that he was a child of God. His faith, his prayer, his humility, his brotherly love, are unmistakable witnesses of the reality of his repentance. He was not a penitent in name only, but in deed and in truth.

Let no man therefore think, because the penitent thief was saved, that men can be saved without leaving any evidence of the Spirit's work. Let such an one consider well what evidences this man left behind, and take care.

It is mournful to hear what people sometimes say about what they call deathbed evidences. It is perfectly fearful to observe how little satisfies some people, and how easily they can persuade themselves that their friends have gone to heaven. They will tell you when their relative is dead and gone, that 'he made such a beautiful prayer one day', or that 'he talked so well', or that 'he was so sorry for his old ways, and intended to live so differently if he got better', or that 'he craved nothing in this world', or that 'he liked people to read to him, and pray with him'. And because they have this to go upon, they seem to have a comfortable hope that he is saved! Christ may never have been named, the way of salvation may never have been in the least mentioned. But it matters not; there was a little talk of religion, and so they are content!

Now I have no desire to hurt the feelings of anyone who reads this message, but I must and will speak plainly upon this subject.

Once for all, let me say, that as a general rule, nothing is so unsatisfactory as deathbed evidences. The things that men say, and the feelings they express when sick and frightened, are little to be depended on. Often, too often, they are the result of fear, and do not spring from the ground of the heart. Often, too often, they are things said by rote, caught from the lips of ministers and anxious friends, but evidently not felt. And nothing can prove all this more clearly than the well–known fact, that the great majority of people who make promises of amendment on a sick bed, and then for the first time talk about religion, if they recover, go back to sin and the world.

When a man has lived a life of thoughtlessness and folly, I want something more than a few fair words and good wishes to satisfy me about his soul, when he comes to his deathbed. It is not enough for me that he will let me read the Bible to him, and pray by his bedside, that he says, he has 'not thought so much as he ought of religion, and he thinks he should be a different man if he got better.' All this does not content me; it does not make me feel happy about his state. It is very well as far as it goes, but it is not conversion. It is very well in its way, but it is not faith in Christ. Until I see conversion, and faith in Christ, I cannot and dare not feel satisfied. Others may feel satisfied if they please, and after their friend's death say, they hope he is gone to heaven. For my part I would rather hold my tongue and say nothing. I would be content with the least measure of repentance and faith in a dying man, even though it be no bigger than a grain of mustard seed. But to be content with anything less than repentance and faith seems to me next door to infidelity.

What kind of evidence do you mean to leave behind as to the state of your soul? Take example by the penitent thief, and you will do well.

When we have carried you to your narrow bed, let us not have to hunt up stray words and scraps of religion, in order to make out that you were a true believer. Let us not have to say in a hesitating way one to another, 'I trust he is happy; he talked so nicely one day, and he seemed so pleased with a chapter in the Bible on another occasion, and he liked such a person, who is a good man.' Let us be able to speak decidedly as to your condition. Let us have some solid proof of your repentance, your faith and your holiness, so that none shall be able for a moment to question your state. Depend on it, without this, those you leave behind can feel no solid comfort about your soul. We may use the form of religion at your burial, and express charitable hopes. We may meet you at the churchyard gate, and say, 'Blessed are the dead that die in the Lord.' But this will not alter your condition! If you die without conversion to God, without repentance, and without faith, your funeral will only be the funeral of a lost soul; you had better never have been born.

4. Believers in Christ when they die are with the Lord

We are meant, in the next place, to learn from these verses, that believers in Christ when they die are with the Lord.

This you may gather from our Lord's words to the penitent thief: 'This day shall you be with Me in paradise.' And you have an expression very like it in the Epistle to the Philippines, where Paul says he has a desire to 'depart and be with Christ' (Phil. 1:23).

I shall say but little on this subject. I would simply lay it before you, for your own private meditations. To my own mind it is very full of comfort and peace.

Believers after death are 'with Christ.' That answers many a difficult question, which otherwise might puzzle man's busy, restless mind. The abode of dead saints, their joys, their feelings, their happiness, all seem met by this simple expression—they are 'with Christ.'

I cannot enter into full explanations about the separate state of departed believers. It is a high and deep subject, such as man's mind can neither grasp nor fathom. I know their happiness falls short of what it will be when their bodies are raised again, in the resurrection at the last day, and Jesus returns to earth. Yet I know also they enjoy a blessed rest, a rest from labor a rest from sorrow, a rest from pain—and a rest from sin. But it does not follow because I cannot explain these things, that I am not persuaded they are far happier than they ever were on earth. I see their happiness in this very passage they are 'with Christ,' and when I see that I see enough.

If the sheep are with the Shepherd, if the members are with the Head, if the children of Christ's family are with Him who loved them and carried them all the days of their pilgrimage on earth, all must be well, all must be right.

I cannot describe what kind of place paradise is, because I cannot understand the condition of a soul separate from the body. But I ask no brighter view of paradise than this—that Christ is there. All other things, in the picture which imagination draws of the state between death and resurrection, are nothing in comparison of this. How He is there, and in what way He is there, I know not. Let me only see Christ in paradise when my eyes close in death, and that suffices me. Well does the psalmist say, 'In Your presence is fullness of joy' (Ps. 16:11). It was a true saying of a dying girl, when her mother tried to comfort her by describing what paradise would be. 'There,' she said to the child, 'there you will have no pains, and no sickness; there you will see your brothers and sisters, who have gone before you, and will be always happy.' 'Ah, mother,' was the reply, 'but there is one thing better than all, and that is, Christ will be there!'

It may be you do not think much about your soul. It may be you know little of Christ as your Savior. and have never tasted by experience that He is precious. And yet perhaps you hope to go to paradise when you die. Surely this passage is one that should make you think. Paradise is a place where Christ is. Then can it be a place that you would enjoy?

It may be you are a believer, and yet tremble at the thought of the grave. It seems cold and dreary. You feel as if all before you was dark and gloomy and comfortless. Fear not, but be encouraged by this text. You are going to paradise, and Christ will be there.

5. The eternal portion of every man's soul is close to him

'Today,' says our Lord to the penitent thief, 'today shall you be with Me in paradise.' He names no distant period; He does not talk of His entering into a state of happiness as a thing 'far away.' He speaks of today—'this very day in which you are hanging on the cross.'

How near that seems! How awfully near that word brings our everlasting dwelling–place! Happiness or misery, sorrow or joy, the presence of Christ or the company of devils—all are close to us. 'There is but a step,' says David, 'between me and death' (1 Sam. 20:3). There is but a step, we may say, between ourselves and either paradise or hell.

We none of us realize this as we ought to do. It is high time to shake off the dreamy state of mind in which we live on this matter. We are apt to talk and think, even about believers, as if death was a long journey, as if the dying saint had embarked on a long voyage. It is all wrong, very wrong! Their harbor and their home is close by, and they have entered it.

Some of us know by bitter experience what a long and weary time it is between the death of those we love and the hour when we bury them out of our sight. Such weeks are the slowest, saddest, heaviest weeks in all our lives.. But, blessed be God, the souls of departed saints are free from the very moment their last breath is drawn. While we are weeping, and the coffin is preparing, and the mourning being provided, and the last painful arrangements being made, the spirits of our beloved ones are enjoying the presence of Christ. They are freed forever from the burden of the flesh. They are 'where the wicked cease troubling, and the weary be at rest' (Job 3:17).

The very moment that believers die they are in paradise. Their battle is fought; their strife is over. They have passed through that gloomy valley we must one day tread; they have gone over that dark river we must one day cross. They have drunk that last bitter cup which sin has mingled for man; they have reached that place where sorrow and sighing are no more. Surely we should not wish them back again! We should not weep for them, but for ourselves.

We are warring still, but they are at peace. We are laboring, but they are at rest. We are watching, but they are sleeping. We are wearing our spiritual amour, but they have forever put it off. We are still at sea, but they are safe in harbor We have tears, but they have joy. We are strangers and pilgrims, but as for them they are at home. Surely, better are the dead in Christ than the living! Surely the very hour the poor saint dies, he is at once higher and happier than the highest upon earth.

I fear there is a vast amount of delusion on this point. I fear that many, who are not Roman Catholics, and profess not to believe in purgatory, have, notwithstanding, some strange ideas in their minds about the immediate consequences of death.

I fear that many have a sort of vague notion that there is some interval or space of time between death and their eternal state. They fancy they shall go through a kind of purifying change, and that though they die unfit for heaven, they shall yet be found meet for it after all!

But this is an entire mistake. There is no change after death; there is no conversion in the grave; there is no new heart given after the last breath is drawn. The very day we go, we launch forever; the day we go from this world, we begin an eternal condition. From that day there is no spiritual alteration, no spiritual change. As we die, so we shall receive our portion after death; as the tree falls, so it must lie.

If you are an unconverted man, this ought to make you think. Do you know you are close to hell? This very day you might die; and if you died out of Christ, you would open your eyes at once in hell, and in torment.

If you are a true Christian, you are far nearer heaven than you think This very day if the Lord should take you, you would find yourself in paradise. The good land of promise is near to you. The eyes that you closed in weakness and pain would open at once on a glorious rest, such as my tongue cannot describe.

And now let me say a few words in conclusion:

1. This message may fall into the hands of some humble–hearted and contrite sinner. Are you that man? Then here is encouragement for you. See what the penitent thief did, and do likewise. See how he prayed; see how he called on the Lord Jesus Christ; see what an answer of peace he obtained. Brother or sister, why should not you do the same? Why should not you also be saved?

2. This message may fall into the hands of some proud and presumptuous man of the world. Are you that man? Then take warning. See how the impenitent thief died as he had lived and beware lest you come to a like end. Oh, erring brother or sister, be not too confident, lest you die in your sins! Seek the Lord while He may be found. Turn you, turn; why will you die?

3. This message may fall into the hands of some professing believer in Christ. Are you such an one? Then take the penitent thief's religion as a measure by which to prove your own. See that you know something of true repentance and saving faith, of real humility and fervent charity. Brother or sister, do not be satisfied with the world's standard of Christianity. Be of one mind with the penitent thief, and you will be wise.

4. This message may fall into the hands of someone who is mourning over departed believers. Are you such an one? Then take comfort from this Scripture. See how your beloved ones are in the best of hands They cannot be better off. They never were so well in their lives as they are now. They are with Jesus, whom their souls loved on earth. Oh, cease from your selfish mourning! Rejoice rather that they are freed from trouble, and have entered into rest.

5. And this message may fall into the hands of some aged servant of Christ. Are you such an one? Then see from these verses how near you are to home. Your salvation is nearer than when you first believed. A few more days of labor and sorrow. and the King of kings shall send for you, and in a moment your warfare shall be at end, and all shall be peace.

HAPPINESS

"Happy is that people whose God is the Lord." Psalm 144:15

An *infidel* was once addressing a crowd of people in the open air. He was trying to persuade them that there was no God and no devil no Heaven, and no Hell, no resurrection, no judgment, and no life to come. He advised them to throw away their Bibles, and not to mind what preachers said. He recommended them to think as he did, and to be like him. He talked boldly. The crowd listened eagerly. It was "the blind leading the blind." Both were falling into the ditch! (Matthew 15:14.)

In the middle of his address, a poor old woman suddenly pushed her way through the crowd, to the place where he was standing. She stood before him. She looked him fully in the face. *"Sir,"* she said, in a loud voice, *"Are you happy?"* The infidel looked scornfully at her, and gave her no answer. "Sir," she said again, "I ask you to answer my question. Are you happy? You want us to throw away our Bibles. You tell us not to believe what preachers say about the gospel. You advise us to think as you do, and be like you. Now before we take your advice — we have a right to know what good we shall get by it. Do your fine new notions give you much comfort? Do you yourself to be really feel happy?"

The infidel stopped, and attempted to answer the old woman's question. He stammered, and shuffled, and fidgeted, and endeavored to explain his meaning. He tried hard to turn the subject. He said, he "had not come there to preach about happiness." But it was of no use. The old woman stuck to her point. She insisted on her question being answered, and the crowd took her part. She pressed him hard with her inquiry, and would take no excuse. And at last the infidel was obliged to leave the ground, and sneak off in confusion. He could not reply to the question. His conscience would not let him — he dared not say that he was happy.

The old woman showed great wisdom in asking the question that she did. The argument she used may seem very simple — but in reality it is one of the most powerful that can be employed. It is a weapon that has more effect on some minds, than the most elaborate reasoning of Butler, or Paley, or Chalmers. Whenever a man begins to take up new views of religion, and pretends to despise old Bible Christianity — thrust home at his conscience the old woman's question. Ask him whether his new views make him feel *comfortable* within. Ask him whether he can say, with honesty and sincerity, that he is *happy*. The grand test of a man's faith and religion is, *"Does it make him happy?"*

Let me now affectionately invite every reader to consider the subject of this paper. Let me warn you to remember that the salvation of your soul, and nothing less, is closely bound up with the subject. The heart cannot be right in the sight of God, which knows nothing of happiness. That man or woman cannot be in a safe state of soul, who feels nothing of peace within.

There are three things which I purpose to do, in order to clear up the subject of happiness. I ask special attention to each one of them. And I pray the Spirit of God to *apply* all to the souls of all who read this paper.

I. Let me point out some things which are *absolutely essential* to all happiness.

II. Let me expose some *common mistakes* about the way to be happy.

III. Let me show *the way to be truly happy*.

I. First of all I have to point out some things which are *absolutely essential* to all true happiness.

Happiness is what all mankind want to obtain — the desire for it is deeply planted in the human heart. All men naturally dislike pain, sorrow, and discomfort. All men naturally like ease, comfort, and gladness. All men naturally hunger and thirst after happiness. Just as the sick man longs for health, and the prisoner of war longs for liberty; just as the parched traveler in hot countries longs to see the cooling fountain, or the ice-bound polar voyager longs to see the sun rising above the horizon — just in the same way does poor mortal man long to be happy. But, alas, how few consider what they really mean, when they talk of happiness! How vague and indistinct and undefined the ideas of most men are upon the subject! They think some are happy — who in reality are miserable; they think some are gloomy and sad — who in reality are truly happy. They *dream* of a happiness which in reality would never satisfy their nature's needs. Let me try this day to throw a little light on the subject.

True happiness is not perfect freedom from sorrow and discomfort. Let that never be forgotten. If it were so, there would be no such thing as happiness in the world. Such happiness is for angels who have never fallen, and not for man. The happiness I am inquiring about, is such as a poor, dying, sinful creature may hope to attain. Our whole nature is defiled by sin. Evil abounds in the world. Sickness, and death, and change — are daily doing their sad work on every side. In such a state of things — the highest happiness man can attain to on earth must necessarily be a *mixed* thing. If we expect to find any literally perfect happiness on this side of the grave — we expect what we shall not find!

True happiness does not consist in laughter and smiles. The face is very often a *poor index* of the inward man. There are thousands who laugh loud and are merry as a grasshopper in company — but are wretched and miserable in private, and almost afraid to be alone. On the other hand, there are hundreds who are grave and serious in their demeanor — whose hearts are full of solid peace. A poet of our own has truly told us that smiles are worth but little: "A man may smile and smile — and be a villain!"

And the eternal Word of God teaches us that "even in laughter, the heart may be sorrowful." (Proverbs 14:13.) Tell me not merely of smiling and laughing faces! I want to hear of something more than that, when I ask whether a man is happy. A truly happy man no doubt will often show his happiness in his countenance; but a man may have a very merry face — and yet not be happy at all.

Of all deceptive things on earth — nothing is so deceptive as mere worldly *gaiety* and *merriment*. It is a hollow empty show, utterly devoid of substance and reality! Listen to the brilliant talker in society, and mark the applause which he receives from an admiring company; follow him to his own private room, and you will very likely find him plunged in melancholy despondency. Colonel Gardiner confessed that even when he was thought most happy — he often wished he was a dog. Look at the smiling beauty in the ball-room, and you might suppose that she knew not what it was to be unhappy; see her next day at her own home, and you may probably find her out of temper with herself and everybody else besides!

Oh, no! *Worldly merriment is not real happiness!* There is a certain pleasure about it, I do not deny. There is an animal excitement about it, I make no question. There is a temporary elevation of spirits about it, I freely concede. But do not call it by the sacred name of 'happiness'. The most beautiful cut flowers stuck into the ground, do not make a garden. When glass is called diamond, and tinsel is called gold — then, and not until then, those people who can laugh and revel will deserve to be called happy people.

Cervantes, author of Don Quixote, at a time when all Spain was laughing at his humorous work, was overwhelmed with a deep cloud of melancholy.

Moliere, the first of French *comic writers*, carried into his domestic circle a sadness which the greatest worldly prosperity could never dispel.

Samuel Foote, the noted *wit* of the last century, died of a broken heart.

Theodore Hooke, the facetious novel writer, who could set everybody laughing, says of himself in his diary, "I am suffering under a constant depression of spirits, which no one who sees me in society dreams of."

A woebegone stranger consulted a physician about his health. The physician advised him to keep up his spirits by going to hear the great comic actor of the day: "You should go and hear Matthews. He would make you well." "Alas, sir," was the reply, "I am Matthews himself!"

1. To be truly happy — *the highest needs of a man's nature must be met and satisfied.* The *requirements* of his wondrously wrought constitution must all be filled up. There must be nothing about him that cries, "Give, give," but cries in vain and gets no answer. The horse and the ox are happy — as long as they are warmed and filled. And why? It is because they are satisfied. The little infant looks happy when it is clothed, and fed, and well, and in its mother's arms. And why? Because it is satisfied. And just so it is with man. His highest needs must be met and satisfied — before he can be truly happy. All must be filled up. There must be no void, no empty places, no unsupplied cravings. Until then he is never truly happy.

And WHAT are man's principal needs? Has he a body only? No! He has something more! He has a *soul*. Has he *sensual* faculties only? Can he do nothing but hear, and see, and smell, and taste, and feel? No! He has a thinking mind and a conscience! Has he no consciousness of any world, but that in which he lives and moves? He has. There is a still small voice within him which often makes itself heard: "This life is not all! There is an unseen world! There is a life beyond the grave!" Yes! it is true. We are fearfully and wonderfully made. All men *know* it — all men *feel* it, if they would only speak the truth. It is utter nonsense to pretend that food and clothing and earthly things alone — can make men happy. There are *soul*-needs. There are *conscience*-needs. There can be no true happiness — until *these* needs are satisfied.

2. To be truly happy — *a man must have sources of gladness which are not dependent on anything in this world.* There is nothing upon earth which is not stamped with the mark of *instability* and *uncertainty*. All the good things which money can buy, are but momentary: they either leave us — or we are obliged to leave them! All the sweetest relationships in life are liable to come to an end — death may come any day and cut them off. The man whose happiness depends entirely on things here below, is like him who builds his house on sand, or leans his weight on a reed.

Tell me not of your happiness, if it daily hangs on the *uncertainties* of earth. Your home may be rich in comforts; your wife and children may be all you could desire; your means may be amply sufficient to meet all your needs. But oh, remember, if you have nothing more than this to look to — that you stand on the brink of a precipice! Your *rivers of pleasure* may any day be dried up. Your joy may be deep and earnest — but it is fearfully *short-lived!* It has no *root*. It is not true happiness.

3. To be really happy — *a man must be able to look on every side without uncomfortable feelings.* He must be able to look back to the *past* without guilty fears; he must be able to look *around* him without discontent; he must be able to look *forward* without anxious dread. He must be able to sit down and think calmly about things past, present, and to come — and feel prepared. The man who has a weak side in his condition — a side that he does not like looking at or considering — that man is not really happy.

Do not talk to me of your happiness — if you are unable to look steadily either before or behind you. Your *present* position may be easy and pleasant. You may find many sources of joy and gladness in your profession, your dwelling-place, your family, and your friends. Your health may be good, your spirits may be cheerful. But stop and think quietly over your **past** life! Can you reflect calmly on all the sins of *omission* and *commission* of by-gone years? How will they bear God's inspection? How will you answer for them at the last day?

And then look **forward**, and think on the years yet to come. Think of the *certain end* towards which you are hastening: think of death; think of judgment; think of the hour when you will meet God face to face! Are you ready for it? Are you prepared? Can you look forward to these things without alarm? Oh, be very sure if you cannot look comfortably at any season but the present — then your *boasted happiness* is a poor unreal thing! It is but a white-washed sepulcher, fair and beautiful on the outside — but bones and corruption within! It is a mere thing of a day, like Jonah's gourd. It is not real happiness.

I ask my readers to fix in their minds the account of things essential to happiness, which I have attempted to give. Dismiss from your thoughts the many *mistaken notions* which pass current on this subject, like counterfeit coin. To be truly happy — the needs of your *soul* and *conscience* must be satisfied. To be truly happy — your joy must be founded on something more than this world can give you. To be truly happy — you must be able to look on every side — above, below, behind, before — and feel that all is right. This is real, sterling, genuine happiness — this is the happiness I have in view, when I urge on your notice the subject of this paper.

II. In the next place, let me expose some *common mistakes* **about the way to be happy.**

There are several roads which are thought by many, to lead to happiness. In each of these roads, thousands and tens of thousands of men and women are continually traveling. Each imagines that if he could only attain all that he wants — that he would be happy. Each imagines, if he does not succeed — that the fault is in his lack of *luck* and *good fortune.* And all alike seem ignorant that they are *hunting shadows.* They have started in a wrong direction! They are seeking that which can never be found in the place where they seek it.

I will mention by name *some of the principal delusions about happiness.* I do it in love, and charity, and compassion to men's souls. I believe it to be a public duty to warn people against *cheats, quacks, and impostors!* Oh, how much trouble and sorrow it might save my readers, if they would only believe what I am going to say!

It is an utter mistake to suppose that **RANK** and **GREATNESS** alone can give happiness. The kings and rulers of this world are not *necessarily* happy men. They have troubles and crosses, which none know but themselves! They see a thousand evils, which they are unable to remedy! They are *slaves working in golden chains,* and have less real liberty than any in the world! They have burdens and responsibilities laid upon them, which are a *daily weight* on their hearts. The Roman Emperor Antonine often said, that "the imperial power was *an ocean of* *miseries."* Queen Elizabeth, when she heard a milk-maid singing — wished that she had been born to a lot like her's. Never did our great Poet write a truer word than when he said, *"Uneasy lies the head that wears a crown!"*

It is an utter mistake to suppose that **RICHES** alone can give happiness. They can enable a man to command and possess everything — but inward peace! They cannot buy a *cheerful spirit* and *a light heart.* There is . . .

care in the *getting* of them,
care in the *keeping* of them,
care in the *using* of them,
care in the *disposing* of them,
care in the *gathering* of them,
and care in the *scattering* of them!

He was a wise man who said that "money" was only another name for "trouble," and that the same English letters which spelled "acres" would also spell "cares."

It is an utter mistake to suppose that **LEARNING** and **SCIENCE** alone can give happiness. They may occupy a man's time and attention — but they cannot really make him happy. Those who increase knowledge — often "increase sorrow;" the more they learn — the more they discover their own ignorance. (Eccles. 1:18.) It is not in the power of earthly things — to minister to a diseased heart. The *heart* needs something — as well as the head; the *conscience* needs food — as well as the intellect. All the secular knowledge in the world will not give a man joy and gladness — when he thinks on sickness, and death, and the grave. Those who have climbed the highest — have often found themselves solitary, dissatisfied, and empty of peace The learned *Selden*, at the close of his life, confessed that all his learning did not give him such comfort as these four verses of the apostle Paul — Titus 2:11-14.)

It is an utter mistake to suppose that **IDLENESS** alone can give happiness. The laborer who gets up at five in the morning, and goes out to work all day in a cold clay ditch, often thinks, as he walks past the rich man's door, *"What a fine thing it must be to have no work to do!"* Poor fellow! he little knows what he thinks. The most miserable creature on earth — is the man who has *nothing to do.* Work for the hands or work for the head — is absolutely essential to human happiness. Without it, the *mind feeds upon itself,* and the whole inward man becomes diseased. The machinery within *will* work — and without something to work upon, will often wear itself to pieces. There was no idleness in Eden. Adam and Eve had to "dress the garden and keep it." There will be no idleness in Heaven. God's "servants shall serve Him." Oh, be very sure, that the idlest man — is the man most truly unhappy! (Genesis 2:15; Rev. 22:3.)

It is an utter mistake to suppose that **PLEASURE-SEEKING** and **AMUSEMENTS** alone can give happiness. Of all roads that men can take in order to be happy, this is the one that is most completely wrong! Of all weary, flat, dull and unprofitable ways of spending life — this exceeds all. To think of a sinful, dying creature, with an immortal soul, expecting happiness . . .

in feasting and reveling,
in dancing and singing,
in dressing and visiting,
in ball-going and card-playing,
in races and fairs,
in hunting and shooting,
in crowds, in laughter, in noise, in music, in wine!

Surely it is a sight that is enough to make the devil laugh and the angels weep! Even a *child* will not play with its toys all day long! But when grown up men and women think to find happiness in a*constant round of amusement* — they sink far below a child!

I place before every reader of this paper, these *common mistakes about the way to be happy*. I ask you to mark them well. I warn you plainly against these *pretended short cuts to happiness*, however crowded they may be. I tell you that if you imagine any one of them can lead you to true peace, that you are entirely deceived. Your *conscience* will never feel satisfied; your immortal*soul* will never feel easy; your whole inward man will feel uncomfortable and out of health. Take any one of these roads, or take all of them, and if you have nothing besides to look to — you will never find happiness. You may travel on and on and on, and the *wished-for object* will seem as far away at the end of each stage of life as when you started. You are like one *pouring water into a sieve*, or putting money into a bag with holes. *You might as well try to make an elephant happy, by feeding him with a grain of sand a day — as try to satisfy that heart of your's with rank, riches, learning, idleness, or pleasure!*

Do you doubt the truth of all I am saying? I dare say you do. Then let us turn to the *great Book of human experience*, and read over a few lines out of its solemn pages. You shall have the testimony of a few competent witnesses on the great subject I am urging on your attention.

A *King* shall be our first witness — I mean *Solomon*, King of Israel. We know that he had power, and wisdom, and wealth, far exceeding that of any ruler of his time. We know from his own confession, that he tried the *great experiment* how far the things of this world can make man happy. We know, from the record of his own hand — the result of this curious experiment. He writes it by the inspiration of the Holy Spirit, for the benefit of the whole world, in the book of Ecclesiastes. Never, surely, was the experiment tried under such favorable circumstances: never was any one so likely to succeed as the Jewish King. Yet what is Solomon's testimony? You have it in his melancholy words: "All is vanity and vexation of spirit!" (Eccles. 1:14.)

A famous French lady shall be our next witness — I mean *Madam De Pompadour*. She was the friend and favorite of Louis the Fifteenth. She had unbounded influence at the Court of France. She lacked nothing that money could procure. Yet what does she say herself? "What a situation is that of the great! They only live in the future, and are only happy in hope. There is no peace in ambition. I am always gloomy, and often unreasonably so. The kindness of the King, the regard of courtiers, the attachment of my servants, and the fidelity of a large number of friends — motives like these, which ought to make me happy, affect me no longer. I have no longer inclinations for all which once pleased me. I have caused my house at Paris to be magnificently furnished — well; it pleased for two days! My residence at Bellevue is charming — but I cannot endure it. Kind people relate to me all the news and adventures of Paris; they think I listen — but when they are done, I ask them what they said. In a word, I do not live! I am dead before my time. I have no interest in the world. Everything conspires to embitter my life. *My life is a continual death!*" To such testimony I need not add a single word. (Sinclair's Anecdotes and Aphorisms, p. 33.)

A famous German writer shall be our next witness — I mean *Goethe*. It is well known that he was almost idolized by many during his life. His works were read and admired by thousands. His name was known and honored, wherever German was read, all over the world. And yet the *praise of man*, of which he reaped such an abundant harvest, was utterly unable to make Goethe happy. "He confessed, when about eighty years old, that he could not remember being in a really happy state of mind even for a few weeks together." (See Sinclair's Anecdotes and Aphorisms, p. 280.)

An English peer and poet shall be our next witness — I mean *Lord Byron*. If ever there was one who ought to have been happy according to the standard of the world — Lord Byron was the man! He began life with all the advantages of English rank and position. He had splendid abilities and powers of mind, which the world soon discovered and was ready to honor. He had a sufficiency of means to gratify every wish, and never knew anything of real poverty. Humanly speaking, there seemed nothing to prevent him enjoying life and being happy. Yet it is a notorious fact that Byron was a miserable man. Misery stands out in his poems — misery creeps out in his letters. Weariness, satiety, disgust, and discontent appear in all his ways. He is an solemn warning that *rank, and title, and literary fame*, alone — are not sufficient to make a man happy.

A man of science shall be our next witness — I mean *Sir Humphrey Davy*. He was a man eminently successful in the line of life which he chose, and deservedly so. A distinguished philosopher — the inventor of the famous safety-lamp which bears his name, and has preserved so many poor miners from death — a Baron of the United Kingdom, and President of the Royal Society — his whole life seemed a continual career of prosperity. If *learning* alone were the road to happiness, this man at least ought to have been happy. Yet what was the true record of Davy's feelings? We have it in his own melancholy journal at the latter part of his life. He describes himself in two painful words: *"Very miserable!"*

A man of wit and pleasure shall be our next witness — I mean *Lord Chesterfield*. He shall speak for himself — his own words in a letter shall be his testimony. "I have seen the silly round of business and pleasure, and am done with it all. I have experienced all the pleasures of the world — and consequently know their *futility*, and do not regret their loss. I appraise them at their real value — which in truth is very low; whereas those who have not experience them — always overrate them. They only see their mirthful *outside*, and are dazzled with their *glare* — but I have been behind the scenes. I have seen all the coarse pulleys and dirty ropes which exhibit and move the *gaudy machine*, and I have seen and smelled the candles which illuminate the whole decoration — to the astonishment and admiration of the ignorant audience! When I reflect on what I have seen, what I have heard, and what I have done — I cannot persuade myself that all that frivolous *hurry of bustle* and *pleasure* of the world had any reality. I look on all that is past, as one of those romantic dreams which opium occasions, and I do by no means wish to repeat the *nauseous dose* for the sake of the fleeting dream!" These sentences speak for themselves. I need not add to them one single word.

The *Statesmen* and *Politicians* who have swayed the destinies of the world, ought by good right to be our last witnesses. But I forbear, in Christian charity, to bring them forward. It makes my heart ache when I run my eye over the list of names famous in English history — and think how many have worn out their lives in a breathless struggle after place and distinction! How many of our greatest men have died of broken hearts — disappointed, disgusted, and tried with constant failure! How many have left on record some humbling confession that in the plenitude of their power they were pining for rest, as the caged eagle for liberty! How many whom the world is applauding as "masters of the situation" — are in reality little better than galley-slaves, chained to the oar and unable to get free! Alas, there are many sad proofs, both among the living and the dead — that to be *great* and *powerful* is not necessarily to be happy!

I think it very likely that people do not believe what I am saying. I know something of the *deceitfulness of the heart* on the subject of happiness. There are few things which man is so slow to believe as the truths I am now putting forth about the way to be happy. Bear with me then while I say something more.

Come and stand with me some afternoon in the heart of the city of London. Let us watch the faces of most of the wealthy men whom we shall see leaving their houses of business at the close of the day. Some of them are worth hundreds of thousands — some of them are worth millions of pounds. But what is written in the countenances of these grave men whom we see swarming out from Lombard Street and Cornhill, from the Bank of England and the Stock Exchange? What do those deep lines which furrow so many a cheek and so many a brow mean? What does that air of *anxious thoughtfulness* which is worn by five out of every six we meet mean? Ah, these things tell a serious tale. They tell us that it needs something more than gold and bank notes to make men happy!

Come next and stand with me near the Houses of Parliament, in the middle of a busy session. Let us scan the faces of Nobles whose names are familiar and well-known all over the civilized world. There you may see on some fine May evening, the mightiest Statesmen in England hurrying to a debate — like eagles to the carcass. Each has a power of good or evil in his tongue, which it is fearful to contemplate. Each may say things before tomorrow's sun dawns, which may affect the peace and prosperity of nations, and convulse the world! There you may see the men who hold the *reins of power and government* already; there you may see the men who are daily watching for an opportunity of snatching those reins out of their hands, and governing in their stead. But what do their faces tell us, as they hasten to their posts? What may be learned from their care-worn countenances? What may be read in many of their wrinkled foreheads — so absent-looking and sunk in thought? They teach us a solemn lesson. They teach us that it needs something more than *political greatness* to make men happy.

Come next and stand with me in the most fashionable part of London, in the height of the season. Let us visit *Regent Street* or *Pall Mall*, *Hyde Park* or *May Fair*. How many fair faces and splendid equipages we shall see! How many we shall count up in an hour's time who seem to possess the choicest gifts of this world — beauty, wealth, rank, fashion, and troops of friends! But, alas, how few we shall see who appear happy! In how many countenances we shall read weariness, dissatisfaction, discontent, sorrow, or unhappiness — as clearly as if it was written with a pen! Yes, it is a humbling lesson to learn — but a very wholesome one. It needs something more than rank, and fashion, and beauty, to make people happy!

Come next and walk with me through some *quiet country village* in merry England. Let us visit some *secluded corner* in our beautiful old father-land, far away from great towns, and fashionable dissipation and political strife. There are not a few such to be found in the land. There are rural villages where there is neither street, nor public-house, nor beer shop — where there is work for all the laborers, and a church for all the population, and a school for all the children, and a minister of the Gospel to look after the people. Surely, you will say — we shall find happiness here! Surely such parishes must be the very abodes of peace and joy!

Go into those quiet-looking cottages, one by one, and you will soon be undeceived. Learn the inner history of each family, and you will soon alter your mind. You will soon discover that backbiting, and lying, and slandering, and envy, and jealousy, and pride, and laziness, and drinking, and extravagance, and lust, and petty quarrels — can *murder happiness* in the country, quite as much as in the city! No doubt a *rural village* sounds pretty in poetry, and looks beautiful in pictures; but in sober reality, human nature is the same evil thing everywhere! Alas, it needs something more than a residence in a quiet country village to make any child of Adam a happy man!

I know these are ancient things. They have been said a thousand times before without effect, and I suppose they will be said without effect again. I want no greater proof of the corruption of human nature, than the pertinacity with which we seek happiness where happiness cannot be found! Century after century, wise men have left on record their experience about the way to be happy. Century after century, people will have it that they know the way perfectly well, and need no teaching. They cast our warnings to the winds; they rush, every one, on his own favorite path. They walk in a vain shadow, and disquiet themselves in vain, and wake up when too late — to find that their whole life has been a grand mistake. Their eyes are blinded — they will not see that their *visions* are as *baseless* and *disappointing* as the mirage of the African desert. Like the tired traveler in those deserts, they think they are approaching a lake of cooling waters; like the same traveler, they find to their dismay that this imagined lake was a splendid *optical delusion* — and that they are still helpless in the midst of burning sands!

Are you a **young** person? I entreat you to accept the affectionate warning of a minister of the Gospel — and not to seek happiness where happiness cannot be found.

Seek it not in riches;

seek it not in power and rank;

seek it not in pleasure;

seek it not in learning.

All these are bright and splendid fountains — their waters taste sweet. A crowd is standing round them, who will not leave them; but, oh, remember that God has written over each of these fountains, "He who drinks of this water — shall thirst again!" (John 4:13.) Remember this, and be wise.

Are you **poor**? Are you tempted to imagine that if you had the rich man's place — that you would be quite happy? Resist the temptation, and cast it behind you. Do not envy your wealthy neighbors — be content with such things as you have. Happiness does not depend on houses or lands! Silks and satins cannot shut out sorrow from the heart! Castles and fine halls cannot prevent anxiety and care coming in at their doors. There is as much misery riding and driving about in splendid carriages — as there is walking about on foot! There is as much unhappiness in large mansions — as in poor cottages. Oh, remember the mistakes which are common about happiness, and be wise!

III. Let me now, in the last place — point out *the way to be really happy.*

There is a sure path which leads to happiness, if men will only take it. There never lived the person who traveled in that path, and missed the object that he sought to attain.

It is a path **open to all**. It needs neither wealth, nor rank, nor learning in order to walk in it. It is for the servant as well as for the master: it is for the poor as well as for the rich. None are excluded but those who exclude themselves.

It is the **one and only path**. All who have ever been happy, since the days of Adam, have journeyed on it. There is no *royal road* to happiness. Kings must be content to go side by side with their humblest subjects, if they would be happy.

WHERE is this path? Where is this road? Listen, and you shall hear.

The way to be happy — is to be a real, thorough-going, true-hearted Christian! Scripture declares it — experience proves it. The converted man, the believer in Christ, the child of God — he, and he alone, is the happy man.

It sounds too simple to be true — it seems at first sight so plain a receipt that it is not believed. But the *greatest* truths are often the *simplest*. The secret which many of the wisest on earth have utterly failed to discover — is revealed to the humblest believer in Christ. I repeat it deliberately, and defy the world to disprove it — the true Christian is the *only* happy man.

What do I mean when I speak of a true Christian? Do I mean everybody who goes to church or chapel? Do I mean everybody who professes an orthodox creed, and bows his head at the belief? Do I mean everybody who *professes* to love the Gospel? *No indeed!* I mean something very different. All are not Christians — who are *called* Christians. The man I have in view — is the Christian in *heart* and *life*. He who has been taught by the Spirit really to feel his sins — he who really rests all his hopes on the Lord Jesus Christ, and His atonement — he who has been born again and really lives a spiritual, holy life — he whose religion is not a mere *Sunday coat* — but a mighty constraining principle governing every day of his life — he is the man I mean, when I speak of a true Christian.

What do I mean when I say the true Christian is happy? Has he no *doubts* and no *fears?* Has he no *anxieties* and no *troubles?* Has he no *sorrows* and no *cares?* Does he never feel *pain*, and shed no *tears?* Far be it from me to say anything of the kind! He has a body weak and is frail like other men; he has affections and passions like everyone born of woman; he lives in a changeful world. But deep down in his heart, he has a mine of solid peace and substantial joy which is never exhausted! This is true happiness.

Do I say that all true Christians are *equally* happy? No, not for a moment! There are *babes* in Christ's family — as well as old men; there are *weak* members of the mystical body — as well as strong ones; there are tender lambs — as well as sheep. There are not only the cedars of Lebanon — but the *hyssop* that grows on the wall. There are *degrees* of grace and degrees of faith. Those who have most faith and grace — will have most happiness. But all, more or less, compared to the people of the world — are happy men.

Do I say that real true Christians are *equally happy at all times?* No, not for a moment! All have their *ebbs and flows* of comfort — some, like the Mediterranean sea, almost insensibly; some, like the tide at Chepstow, fifty or sixty feet at a time.

Their *bodily health* is not always the same;

their *earthly circumstances* are not always the same;

those they love fill them at seasons with special anxiety;

they themselves are sometimes overtaken by a fault, and walk in darkness.

They sometimes give way to inconsistencies and besetting sins, and lose their sense of pardon. But, as a general rule, the true Christian has a deep pool of peace within him, which even at the lowest is never entirely dry.

I use the words, "as a general rule," advisedly. When a believer falls into such a horrible sin as that of David, it would be monstrous to talk of his feeling inward peace.

The true Christian is the only happy man — because *his conscience is at peace.* That *mysterious witness for God*, which is so mercifully placed within us — is fully satisfied and at rest. It sees in the blood of Christ — a complete cleansing away of all its guilt. It sees in the priesthood and mediation of Christ — a complete answer to all its fears. It sees that through the sacrifice and death of Christ, God can now be just — and yet be the justifier of the ungodly. It no longer bites and stings, and makes its possessor afraid of himself. The Lord Jesus Christ has amply met all its requirements. *Conscience* is no longer the enemy of the true Christian — but his friend and adviser. Therefore he is happy.

The true Christian is the only happy man — because *he can sit down quietly and think about his soul.* He can look behind him and before him, he can look within him and around him, and feel, "All is well."

He can think calmly on his *past life*, and however many and great his sins, take comfort in the thought that they are all forgiven. The righteousness of Christ covers all, as Noah's flood overtopped the highest hills.

He can think calmly about *things to come* — and yet not be afraid. Sickness is painful; death is solemn; the judgment day is a solemn thing — but having Christ for him, he has nothing to fear. He can think calmly about the Holy God, whose eyes are on all his ways, and feel, "He is my Father, my reconciled Father in Christ Jesus. I am weak; I am unprofitable — yet in Christ He regards me as His dear child, and is well-pleased." Oh, what a blessed privilege it is to be able to *think* — and not be afraid! I can well understand the mournful complaint of the prisoner in solitary confinement. He had warmth, and food, and clothing, and work — but he was not happy. And why? He said, "He was obliged to *think*."

The true Christian is the only happy man, because he has *sources of happiness entirely independent of this world*. He has something which cannot be affected by sickness and by deaths, by private losses and by public calamities — the "*peace of God*, which passes all understanding." He has a *hope* laid up for him in Heaven; he has a *treasure* which moth and rust cannot corrupt; he has a *house* which can never be taken down.

His loving wife may die — and his heart feel torn in two;

his darling children may be taken from him;

he may be left alone in this cold world;

his earthly plans may be crossed;

his health may fail —

but all this time he has . . .

a *portion* which nothing can harm,

one *Friend* who never dies,

eternal *possessions* beyond the grave —

of which nothing can deprive him! His lower springs may fail — but his upper springs are never dry. This is real happiness.

The true Christian is happy, because *he is in his right position*.

His abilities are being directed to right ends.

His *affections* are not set on things below — but on things above.

His *will* is not bent on self-indulgence — but is submissive to the will of God.

His *mind* is not absorbed in wretched perishable trifles.

He *desires* useful employment — he enjoys the *luxury of doing good*.

Who does not know the *misery of disorder?* Who has not tasted the discomfort of a house where everything and everybody are in their wrong places, the last things first — and the first things last? The heart of an unconverted man is just such a house! Saving grace puts everything in that heart in its right position. The things of the *soul* come first — and the things of the world come second. Anarchy and confusion cease — unruly passions no longer run loose. Christ reigns over the whole man — and each part of him does his proper work.

The heart of the Christian is the only heart that is in *order*. He has laid aside his pride and self-will; he sits at the feet of Jesus, and is in his right mind. He loves God and loves man — and so he is happy. In Heaven all are happy — because all do God's will perfectly. The nearer a man gets to this standard — the happier he will be.

The plain truth is, that without Christ there is no happiness in this world! He alone can give the *Comforter* who abides forever.

He is the sun — without Him, men never feel warm.

He is the light — without Him, men are always in the dark.

He is the bread — without Him, men are always starving.

He is the living water — without Him, people are always athirst.

Give them what you like — place them where you please — surround them with all the comforts you can imagine — it makes no difference. Separate from Christ, the Prince of Peace — a man cannot be happy.

Give a man a sensible interest in Christ — and he will be happy in spite of **poverty**. He will tell you that he lacks nothing that is really good. He is provided for, he has all that he needs now — and riches in eternity. He has *food* to eat which the world knows nothing of. He has *friends* who never leave him nor forsake him. The Father and the Son come to him, and make their abode with him; the Lord Jesus Christ sups with him, and he with Christ. (Rev. 3:20.)

Give a man a sensible interest in Christ, and he will be happy in spite of **sickness**. His *flesh* may groan, and his *body* be worn out with pain — but his *heart* will rest and be at peace. One of the happiest people I ever saw, was a young woman who had been hopelessly ill for many years with disease of the spine. She lay in a poor garret without a fire; the straw thatch was not two feet above her face. She had not the slightest hope of recovery. But she was always rejoicing in the Lord Jesus. The spirit triumphed mightily over the flesh. She was happy, because Christ was with her.

Give a man a sensible interest in Christ, and he will be happy in spite of abounding public **calamities**.

The government of his country may be thrown into confusion;

rebellion and disorder may turn everything upside down;

laws may be trampled under foot;

justice and equity may be outraged;

liberty may be cast down to the ground;

might may prevail over *right*

— but still his heart will not fail. He will remember that the kingdom of Christ will one day be set up. He will say, like the old Scotch minister who lived unmoved throughout the turmoil of the French revolution: "It is all right! It shall be well with the righteous!"

I know well that Satan hates the doctrine which I am endeavoring to press upon you. I have no doubt he is filling your mind with objections and reasonings, and persuading you that I am wrong. I am not afraid to meet these objections face to face. Let us bring them forward and see what they are.

You may tell me that "you know many very religious people who are not happy at all." You see them diligent in attending public worship. You know that they are never missing at church. But you see in them no marks of the peace which I have been describing.

But are you sure that these people you speak of are *true* believers in Christ? Are you sure that, with all their appearance of religion, they are born again and converted to God? Is it not very likely that they have nothing — but the *name* of Christianity, without the reality; and a *form* of godliness, without the power? Alas! you have yet to learn that people may do many *religious acts* — and yet possess no saving religion! It is not a *mere formal, ceremonial Christianity* which will ever make people happy. We need something more than *going to Church* — to give us peace. There must be real, vital union with Christ. It is not the *formal* Christian — but the *true* Christian, who is the happy man.

You may tell me that "you know really spiritually-minded and converted people who do not seem happy." You have heard them frequently complaining of their own hearts, and groaning over their own corruption. They seem to you to be all doubts, and anxieties, and fears; and you want to know *where* is the happiness in these people of which I have been saying so much.

I do not deny that there *are* many saints of God such as these whom you describe, and I am sorry for it. I allow that there are many believers who *live far below their privileges*, and seem to know nothing of joy and peace in believing. But did you ever ask any of these people

300

whether they would give up their Christianity, and go back to the world? Did you ever ask them, after all their groanings, and doubtings, and fearings, whether they think they would be happier if they ceased to follow Christ? Did you ever ask those questions? I am certain if you did, that the weakest and lowest believers would all give you one answer, I am certain they would tell you that they would rather cling to their *little scrap of hope* in Christ — than possess the world! I am sure they would all answer, "Our faith is weak, if we have any; our grace is small, if we have any; our joy in Christ is next to nothing at all — but we cannot give up what we have gotten. Though the Lord slays us — we must cling to Him."

The *root* of happiness lies deep in many a poor weak believer's heart — when neither *leaves* nor *blossoms* are to be seen!

But you will tell me, in the last place, that "you cannot think that most believers are happy, because they are so grave and serious." You think that they do not really possess this happiness I have been describing — because their *countenances* do not show it. You doubt the reality of their joy — because it is so little *seen*.

I might easily repeat what I told you at the beginning of this paper — that *a merry face is no sure proof of a happy heart*. But I will not do so. I will rather ask you whether *you yourself* may not be the cause why believers look grave and serious when you meet them? If you are not converted yourself — you surely cannot expect them to look at you without sorrow! They see you on the high road to destruction, and that alone is enough to give them pain! They see thousands like you, hurrying on to weeping and wailing and endless woe! Now, is it possible that such a daily sight, should not give them grief? *Your company*, very likely, is one cause why they are grave. Wait until you are a converted man yourself, before you pass judgment on the gravity of converted people. See them in companies where all are of one heart, and all love Christ, and so far as my own experience goes — you will find no people so truly happy, as true Christians.

When the infidel Hume asked Bishop Horne why religious people always looked melancholy, the learned prelate replied, "The sight of you, Mr. Hume, would make any Christian melancholy!"

I repeat my assertion in this part of my subject. I repeat it boldly, confidently, deliberately. I say that there is no happiness among worldly people, which will at all compare with that of the true Christian. All other happiness compared with his — is moonlight compared to sunshine, and brass compared to gold. Boast, if you will, of the laughter and merriment of irreligious men; sneer, if you will, at the gravity and seriousness, which appear in the demeanor of many Christians. I have looked the whole subject in the face, and am not moved. I say that the true Christian alone is the truly happy man — and the way to be happy is to be a true Christian.

And now I am going to close this paper by a few words of plain **APPLICATION**. I have endeavored to show what is *essential to true happiness*. I have endeavored to expose the *fallacy* of many views which prevail upon the subject. I have endeavored to point out, in plain and unmistakable words, *where* true happiness alone can be found. Allow me to wind up all by *an affectionate appeal to the consciences* of all into whose hands this volume may fall.

(1) In the first place, let me entreat every reader of this paper to apply to his own heart the solemn inquiry: *Are you happy?* High or low, rich or poor, master or servant, farmer or laborer, young or old — here is a question that deserves an answer: Are you *really* happy?

Man of the world, who is caring for nothing but the things of time, neglecting the Bible, making a god of business or money, providing for everything but the day of judgment, scheming and planning about everything but eternity: Are you happy? You know you are not!

Foolish woman, who is trifling life away in levity and frivolity, spending hours after hours on that poor frail body which must soon feed the worms, making an idol of dress and fashion, and excitement, and human praise — as if this world was all: Are you happy? You know you are not!

Young man, who is bent on pleasure and self-indulgence, fluttering from one idle pastime to another, like the *moth* about the candle flame — imagining yourself clever and knowing, and too wise to be led by pastors, and ignorant that the devil is leading you captive, like the ox that is led to the slaughter: Are you happy? You know you are not!

Yes — each and all of you — you are not happy! And in your own consciences, you know it well. You may not allow it — but it is sadly true. There is a *great empty place* in each of your hearts — and nothing will fill it. Pour into it money, learning, rank, and pleasure — and it will be empty still. There is a *sore place* in each of your consciences — and nothing will heal it. Infidelity cannot; free-thinking cannot; Romanism cannot — they are all *quack medicines*. Nothing can heal it — but that which at present you have not used — the simple Gospel of Christ. Yes, you are indeed a miserable person! Take warning this day — that you never will be happy until you are converted. You might as well expect to feel the sun shine on your face when you turn your back to it, as to feel happy when you turn your back on God and on Christ.

(2) In the next place, let me warn all who are not true Christians — of the folly of living a life which cannot make them happy.

I pity you from the bottom of my heart, and would gladly persuade you to open your eyes and be wise. I stand as a watchman on the tower of the everlasting Gospel. I see you *sowing eternal misery* for yourselves, and I call upon you to stop and think, before it is too late. Oh, that God may show you your folly! You are hewing out cisterns, broken cisterns for yourselves — which can hold no water. You are spending your time, and strength, and affections on that which will give you no return for your labor, "spending your money on that which is not bread, and your labor for that which satisfies not." (Isaiah 55:2.) You are building up a *Babel* of your own contriving, and ignorant that God will pour contempt on *your schemes for procuring happiness* — because you attempt to be happy without Him.

Awake from your *dreams*, I entreat you, and show yourselves men! Think of the *uselessness* of living a life which you will be ashamed of when you die; and of having a *mere nominal religion* — which will utterly fail you when it is most needed.

Open your eyes and look round the world. Tell me who was ever really happy, without God and Christ and the Holy Spirit. Look at the road in which you are traveling. Mark the footsteps of those who have gone before you — see how many have turned away from it, and confessed they were wrong.

I warn you plainly, that if you are not a true Christian — you will miss happiness in the present world, as well as in the world to come. Oh, believe me, the way of *happiness*, and the way of *salvation* — are one and the same! He who will have his own way, and refuses to serve Christ — will never be really happy. But he who serves Christ has the promise of both lives. He is happy on earth, and will be happier still in Heaven!

If you are neither happy in this world nor the next, it will be all your own fault. Oh, think of this! Do not be guilty of such *enormous folly!* Who does not mourn over the folly of the drunkard, the opium eater, and the suicide? But there is no folly like that of the impenitent child of the world.

(3) In the next place, let me entreat all readers of this book, who are not yet happy — to seek happiness where alone it can be found.

The *keys* of the way to happiness are in the hands of the Lord Jesus Christ. He is sealed and appointed by God the Father, to give the *bread of life* to those who hunger, and to give the *water of life* to those who thirst. The *door* which riches and rank and learning have so often tried to open, and tried in vain — is now ready to open to every humble, praying believer. Oh, if you want to be happy — come to Christ! Come to Him, confessing that you are weary of your own ways, and want rest; that you find you have no power and might to make yourself holy or happy or fit for Heaven; and have no hope but in Him. Tell Him this unreservedly. This is coming to Christ.

Come to Him, imploring Him to show you His mercy, and grant you His salvation — to wash you in His own blood, and take your sins away — to speak peace to your conscience, and heal your troubled soul. Tell Him all this unreservedly. This is coming to Christ.

You have everything to *encourage* you. The Lord Jesus *Himself* invites you. He proclaims to you as well as to others, "Come unto Me, all you who labor and are heavy laden, and I will give you rest. Take my yoke upon you, and learn of Me; for I am meek and lowly in heart: and you shall find rest unto your souls. For my yoke is easy, and my burden is light." (Matthew 11. 28-30.) Wait for nothing. You may feel unworthy. You may feel as if you did not repent enough. But wait no longer. Come to Christ.

You have everything to encourage you. Thousands have walked in the way you are invited to enter, and have found it good. Once, like yourself — they served the world, and plunged deeply into folly and sin. Once, like yourself — they became weary of their wickedness, and longed for deliverance and rest. They heard of Christ, and His willingness to help and save; they came to Him by faith and prayer, after many a doubt and hesitation; they found Him a thousand times more gracious than they had expected! They rested on Him and were happy — they carried His cross and tasted peace. Oh, walk in their steps.

I beseech you, by the mercies of God, to come to Christ. As ever you would be happy, I entreat you to come to Christ. Cast off delays. Awake from your past slumber — arise, and be free! This day come to Christ.

(4) In the last place, let me offer a few hints to all true Christians for the *increase* and *promotion* of their happiness.

I offer these hints with diffidence. I desire to apply them to my own conscience as well as to your's. You have found Christ's service happy. I have no doubt that you feel such sweetness in Christ's peace that you would gladly know more of it. I am sure that these hints deserve attention.

Believers, if you would have an increase of happiness in Christ's service, labor every year to **grow in grace**. Beware of standing still. The *holiest* men are always the *happiest*. Let your aim be every year to be more holy — to know more, to feel more, to see more of the fullness of Christ !do not rest upon *old* grace — do not be content with the degree of grace whereunto you have attained.

Search the Scriptures more earnestly;

pray more fervently;

hate sin more;

mortify self-will more;

become more humble;

seek more direct personal communion with the Lord Jesus;

strive to be more like Enoch — daily walking with God;

keep your conscience clear of little sins;

do not grieve the Spirit;

avoid wranglings and disputes about the lesser matters of religion; lay more firm hold upon those great truths, without which no man can be saved.

Remember and practice these things — and you will be more happy!

Believers, if you would have an increase of happiness in Christ's service — labor every year to be more **thankful**. Pray that you may know more and more what it is to "rejoice in the Lord." (Philippians 3:1.) Learn to have a deeper sense of your own wretched sinfulness and corruption, and to be more deeply grateful, that by the grace of God you are what you are. Alas, there is too much complaining — and too little thanksgiving among the people of God! There is too much *murmuring,* and *coveting* things that we have not. There is too little praising and blessing for the many *undeserved mercies* that we have. Oh, that God would pour out upon us a great spirit of thankfulness and praise!

Believers, if you would have an increase of happiness in Christ's service, labor every year to **do more good**. Look around the circle in which your lot is cast — and lay yourself out to be useful. Strive to be of the same character with God: He is not only good — but "does good." (Psalm 119:68.) Alas, there is far too much *selfishness* among believers in the present day! There is far too much lazy sitting by the fire *nursing* our own spiritual diseases, and croaking over the state of our own hearts! Up, and be useful in your day and generation! Is there no one that you can *speak* to? Is there no one that you can *write* to? Is there literally nothing that you can *do* for the glory of God, and the benefit of your fellow-men? Oh I cannot think it! I cannot think it. There is much that you might do, if you had only the desire. For your own happiness' sake — arise and do it, without delay. The bold, outspoken, working Christians — are always the happiest!

The compromising, lingering Christian must never expect to taste perfect peace. The most decided Christian — will always be the happiest man.

THE POWER OF THE HOLY SPIRIT

There is hope in the Gospel for any man, so long as he lives. There is infinite *willingness* in Christ to pardon sin. There is infinite*power* in the Holy Spirit to change hearts. There are many diseases of the body which are incurable. The cleverest doctors cannot heal them. But, thank God! there are no incurable diseases of soul. All manner and quantity of sins can be washed away by Christ! The hardest and most wicked of hearts can be changed.

Reader, I say again, while there is life—there is hope. The oldest, the vilest, the worst of sinners may be saved. Only let him come to Christ, confess his sin, and cry to Him for pardon—only let him cast his soul on Christ, and he shall be cured. The Holy Spirit shall be sent down on his heart, according to Christ's promise, and he shall be changed by His Almighty power, into a new creature.

I never despair of anyone becoming a decided Christian, whatever he may have been in days gone by. I know how great the change is from death to life; I know the mountains of division which seem to stand between some men and heaven; I know the hardness, the prejudices, the desperate sinfulness of the natural heart. But I remember that God the Father made the glorious world out of nothing. I remember that the voice of the Lord Jesus could reach Lazarus when, four days dead, and recall him even from the grave. I remember the amazing victories the Spirit of God has won in every nation under heaven. I remember all this—and feel that I never need despair.

Yes! those very people who now seem most utterly dead in sins, may yet be raised to a new being, and walk before God in newness of life. Why should it not be so? the Holy Spirit is a mighty, merciful, and loving Spirit. He turns away from no man, because of his vileness. He passes by no one, because his sins are black and scarlet. There was nothing in the *Corinthians* that He should come down and quicken them. Paul reports of them, that they were "fornicators, idolaters, adulterers, homosexuals, thieves, covetous, drunkards, revilers, extortioners." "Such," he says, "*were* some of you!" Yet even them, the Spirit made alive. "You are *washed*," he writes, "you are *sanctified*, you are *justified* in the name of the Lord Jesus, and by the Spirit of our God" (1 Cor. 6:9-11).

There was nothing in the *Colossians* that He should visit their hearts. Paul tells us that they walked in "sexual immorality, impurity, lust, evil desire, and greed, which is idolatry." Yet these also, the Spirit quickened. He made them "put off the old man with his deeds, and put on the new man, which is renewed in knowledge after the image of Him that created him" (Col. 3:5-10).

There was nothing in *Mary Magdalene* that the Spirit should make her soul alive. Once she had been possessed with seven devils; time was, if report is true, that she had been a woman proverbial for vileness and iniquity—yet even her, the Spirit made a new creature, separated her from her sins, brought her to Christ, made her last at the cross, and first at the tomb! Never, never will the Spirit turn away from a soul, because of its corruption. He never-

has done so—He never *will*. It is His glory that He has purified the minds of the most impure, and made them temples for His own abode. He may yet take the worst of those who read this tract—and make him a vessel of grace.

Why indeed should it not be so? The Spirit is an Almighty Spirit. He can change the stony heart into a heart of flesh! He can break the strongest bad habits like wax before the fire! He can make the most difficult things seem easy, and the mightiest objections melt away like snow in spring! He can cut the bars of brass, and throw the gates of prejudice wide open! He can fill up every valley, and make every rough place smooth! He has done it often—and He can do it again,

The Spirit can take a Jew—the bitterest enemy of Christianity, the fiercest persecutor of true believers, the strongest stickler for Pharisaical notions, the most prejudiced opposer of Gospel doctrine—and turn that man into an earnest preacher of the very faith he once destroyed. He has done it already. He did it with the Apostle Paul. The Spirit can take a Roman Catholic monk, brought up in the midst of Romish superstition, trained from his infancy to believe false doctrine, and obey the Pope, steeped to the eyes in error—and make that man the clearest upholders of justification by faith the world ever saw! He has done so already. He did it with*Martin Luther.*

The Spirit can take an English tinker, without learning, patronage, or money—a man at one time notorious for blasphemy and swearing—and make that man write a pious book, which shall stand unrivaled and unequaled in its way, by any since the time of the Apostles. He has done so already—He did it with *John Bunyan*, the author of "Pilgrim's Progress."

The Spirit can take a sailor, drenched in worldliness and sin—a profligate captain of a slave ship, and make that man a most successful minister of the Gospel; a writer of letters which are a store-house of experimental religion; and of hymns which are known and sung wherever English is spoken. He has done it already. He did it with *John Newton*. All this the Spirit has done, and much more, of which I cannot speak particularly.

The arm of the Spirit is not shortened! His power is not decayed! He is like the Lord Jesus—the same yesterday, today, and forever. He is still doing wonders, and will do to the very end. I shall not be surprised to hear, even in this life, that the hardest man I know has become softened, and the proudest has taken his place at the feet of Jesus as a weaned child. I shall not be surprised to meet many on the right hand in the day of judgment, whom I shall leave, when I die, traveling in the broad way. I never despair, because I believe in the power of the Holy Spirit.

We ministers might well despair, when we look at our own performances. We are often sick of ourselves. We might well despair when we look at some who belong to our congregations; they seem as hard and insensible as the nether mill-stone! But we remember the Holy Spirit, and what He has done. We remember the Holy Spirit, and consider that He has not changed. He can come down like fire and melt the hardest hearts; He can convert the worst man or woman among our hearers, and mold their whole character into a new shape. And so we preach on. We hope, because of the Holy Spirit.

Oh, that our hearts would understand that the progress of true religion depends not on human might or power—but on the Lord's Spirit! Oh, that many of them would learn to lean less on *ministers*, and to pray more for the Holy Spirit! Oh, that all would learn to expect less from schools, and tracts, and ecclesiastical machinery; and, while using all means diligently, would seek more earnestly for the outpouring of the Spirit!

Reader, do you feel the slightest drawing towards God? Do you feel the smallest concern about your immortal soul? Does your conscience tell you this day that you have not yet felt the Spirit's power, and do you want to know what to do? Listen, and I will tell you. For one thing, you must go at once to the Lord Jesus Christ in prayer, and beseech Him to have mercy on you, and send you the Spirit. You must go direct to that open fountain of living waters, the Lord Jesus Christ, and you shall receive the Holy Spirit (John 7:39). Begin at once to pray for the Holy Spirit. To not think that you are shut up and cut off from hope—the Holy Spirit is promised to those who ask Him. His very name is the *Spirit of Promise*, and the *Spirit of Life*. Give Him no rest, until He comes down and makes you a new heart. Cry mightily unto the Lord—say unto Him, "Bless me, even me also! Quicken me, and make me alive!"

I dare not, for my part, send anxious souls to anyone but Christ. I cannot hold with those who tell men to pray for the Holy Spirit in the *first* place, in order that they may go to Christ in the *second* place. I see no warrant of Scripture for saying so. I only see that if men feel they are needy, perishing sinners, they ought to apply, first and foremost, straight and direct to Jesus Christ. I see that He himself says, "If any man thirsts—let him come unto Me and drink" (John vii. 37). I know that it is written, "He has received gifts for men, yes for the rebellious also, that the Lord God might dwell among them" (Ps.67:18). I know it is His special office to baptize with the Holy Spirit, and that "in Him all fullness dwells." I dare not pretend to be more systematic than the Bible. I believe that Christ is the meeting place between God and the soul. So my first advice to anyone who wants the Spirit, must always be, "go to Jesus, and tell your wants to Him."

For another thing, if you have not yet felt the converting power of the Spirit, you must be diligent in attending those means of grace through which the Spirit works. You must regularly hear that Word which is His sword; you must habitually attend those assemblies where His presence is promised. You must, in short, be found in the way cf the Spirit—if you want the Spirit to do you good. Blind *Bartimaeus* would never have received sight had he sat lazily at home, and not come forth to sit by the wayside. *Zaccheus* might never have seen Jesus, and become a child of God, if he had not ran before and climbed up into the sycamore tree. The Spirit is a loving and good Spirit. But he who despises means of grace, resists the Holy Spirit.

Reader, remember these two things. I firmly believe that no man ever acted honestly and perseveringly on these two pieces of advice, who did not, sooner or later, have the Spirit, and find by experience that He is "mighty to save!"

THE PRIVILEGES OF THE TRUE CHRISTIAN

"My sheep hear my voice, and I know them, and they follow me. I give eternal life to them.

They will never perish, and no one will snatch them out of my hand. My Father, who has given them to me, is greater than all. No one is able to snatch them out of my Father's hand."

(John 10:27-29)

About the first part of this text, beloved, I spoke to you this morning. I told you then that this passage contains two things—first the character of true Christians, and secondly their privileges—first what they are to their Savior, and secondly what their Savior is to them.

Let me, then, remind you what the text says of their character. "My sheep hear My voice, and I know them, and they follow Me." (John 10:27)

1. God's children, His real believing people, are compared to **sheep**, because they are gentle, quiet, harmless and inoffensive; because they are useful and do good to all around them; because they love to be together, and dislike separation; and lastly because they are very helpless and wandering and liable to stray.

2. Jesus calls them **"My sheep**," as if they were His peculiar property. "Mine," He would have us know, by election, "Mine" by purchase, and "Mine" by adoption.

3. Christ's sheep hear His voice, they listen humbly to His teaching, they take His word for their rule and guide.

4. Christ's sheep follow Him, they walk in the narrow path He has marked out, they do not refuse because it is sometimes steep and narrow--but wherever the line of duty lies they go forward without doubting.

It only remains for us now to consider the other part of my text, which respects the *blessings* and *privileges* which Jesus the Good Shepherd bestows upon His people. The Lord grant that none of you may take to yourselves promises which do not belong to you—that none may take liberty from God's exceeding mercy to continue sleeping in sin. Glorious and comfortable things are written in this passage—but remember they are given to Christ's flock only; I fence it out against all that are unbelieving and impenitent and profane. I warn you plainly, except you will hear the voice of Christ and follow Him, you have no right or portion in this blessed fountain of consolations.

Hear now what Jesus says of His believing people: "I know them. . . . I give unto them eternal life; they shall never perish, neither shall any man pluck them out of my hand."

Before we look into the meaning of these words more closely, I wish to answer two questions which may arise in the minds of some before me. **Of whom is the Lord Jesus speaking?** Are we to suppose He only has in view patriarchs and prophets and apostles—men like Abraham and David and Job and Daniel, men who through faith subdued kingdoms, wrought righteousness, stopped the mouths of lions, quenched the violence of fire, worked signs and miracles, and shed their blood for the kingdom of God's sake? Are these the sort of people who alone can take comfort from those blessed words, "I know them . . . . they shall never perish." Is everyone else to go on doubting to his life's end? God forbid that I should tell you so! it were doing Satan's work to preach such doctrine. This text may become the property of the worst of sinners—if he will only hear Christ's voice and follow Him.

Scribes and Pharisees, Sadducees and Herodians, tax collectors and harlots, drunkards and fornicators, murderers, thieves and adulterers, liars and blasphemers. Worldly-minded and covetous ones—all and each of them may lay firm hold on this text, and inherit its precious treasures—if they will only hear Christ's voice and follow Him. It is for all who repent and believe the Gospel; it is for all who mourn over their past sins with a true godly sorrow, and flee to the Lord Jesus Christ with faith and prayer as their only hope, their all-sufficient Savior, their all in all. There is not one single man or woman of whom it shall not be written in the Lamb's book of life, "This is one known of God, this is an heir of eternal life, this is a man or a woman that is never to perish, never to be plucked out of the Lord's hand," if you will only give up your sins and take Christ Jesus for your Shepherd and Redeemer. Your repentance may seem very faint, your faith may appear weak as water—but if there be so much as a grain of mustard seed, if there be enough to lead you a penitent to the foot of the cross, you shall find yourself one day numbered with the saints in glory everlasting.

The other question I wish to answer is this: **why did the Lord Jesus Christ give us this full and complete promise?** Because He knew that true Christians would always be a very doubting, fearful, faint-hearted generation, always ready to believe they shall not be saved, always afraid they shall never see the New Jerusalem, because of the inbred corruption which they find continually in their hearts. He saw they would require the strong wine of assurance like this, and so He has provided this and like texts, as a reviving cordial to cheer and enliven their hearts, whenever they feel desponding and feeble-minded and ready to halt, in their pilgrimage through this weary world.

We will now look narrowly into the parts of this promise.

I. First, says the Lord Jesus Christ of His sheep who hear His voice and follow Him, **"I know them."** I know their number, their names, their particular characters, their besetting sins, their troubles, their trials, their temptations, their doubts, their prayers, their private meditations; I know everything about everyone of them. Think what a comfortable saying that is! The *world* knows nothing about Christ's sheep; to be sure, the world remarks there are a few people, here one and there one, who live differently to others, who seem to be more serious in their deportment, who appear to be taken up with some important consideration or other—but the world only wonders they can be so particular about little sins, and when their ways run counter to the world, the world is vastly offended. But as for their fear of sin, and their carefulness about souls, the world neither knows nor understands what they are about; the secret springs of their conduct are all hidden.

Again, a Christian's *friends* do often know him not. They may possibly respect him and allow him to hold on his way unopposed—though this, alas! is not always the case—but as for his pleasures and his pains, his constant warfare with the flesh, the world and the devil, his dread of falling into temptation, his delight in all means of grace, they can neither explain nor comprehend it; there is a something hidden in his character of which they know nothing.

Be comforted, all you who are tried and buffeted with difficulties in your way towards heaven, difficulties from without and difficulties from within, difficulties abroad and difficulties at home, grief for your own sins and grief for the sins of others: the Good Shepherd Jesus knows you well, though you may not think it. You never shed a secret tear over your own corruption, you never breathed a single prayer for forgiveness and helping grace, you never made a single struggle against wickedness, which He did not remark and note down in the book of His remembrance. You need not fear His not understanding your needs, you need not be afraid your prayers are too poor and unlearned to be attended to; He knows your particular necessities far better than you do yourselves, and your humble supplications are no sooner offered up than heard. You may sometimes sigh and mourn for lack of Christian fellowship, you may sometimes lament that you have not more around you with whom you might take sweet converse about salvation—but remember there is a Good Shepherd, who is ever about your path and about your bed, His eyes are on all your movements, and no husband, brother, father, mother, sister, friend, could take more tender interest in your soul's welfare than He does. If you transgress He will grieve—but He will chasten and bring you back; if you bear good fruit, He will rejoice and give more grace; if you sorrow He will bind up your broken heart and pour in balm; He is ever watching and observing and listening; no believer is so humble and lowly, but He is acquainted with all their ways.

And does not Jesus know the men of this world, the faithless and ungodly? Unquestionably He does. He knows their proceedings; there is not a single sin they have committed but will appear written down in full in the great book—but He only knows them as His enemies—as careless, thoughtless ones, who will not take the trouble to hear His voice and follow Him—and in the last day, when all shall stand before Him, He will say, "I know you not: you would not seek to know me on earth, and I know nothing of you in heaven; depart, you cursed, into everlasting fire, prepared for the devil and his angels." No doubt there will be many a Balaam there, many a barren fig-tree, many a foolish virgin, many a fruitless vine, many a loud-talking hypocrite, who will say, "Lord, Lord, open to us! Have we not taught in Your name, and in Your name quoted many texts, and in Your name made a great profession?" but still the answer will be, "I never knew you . . . depart from Me, you who work iniquity."

Oh, what a blessed and comfortable thing to be known by Christ, known and marked as His friends, His relations, His dear children, His beloved family, His purchased possession! Here we are often cast down, often discouraged, often persecuted, often spoken against, often misunderstood—but let us take courage, our Lord and Master knows all. A day shall come when we shall no longer see through a glass darkly—but face to face—a day when we shall know even as we are now known; for the union between us and our Redeemer, which we so often feel disposed to doubt, shall then be clearly seen, and we shall no more go out to battle.

II. What is the next part of my text? The Lord Jesus says of His sheep, "**I give unto them eternal life!**" What is the portion which Jesus gives His people? "eternal life"—a perfect, never-ending happiness for that which is the most important part of a man—his immortal soul. They shall not be hurt by the second death, which alone is to be really feared. What greater things could our Lord bestow upon His people? Health and riches and honor and pleasures, houses and lands, and wives and children—what are they? how long do they last?—it is but threescore years and ten, and we must leave them all—and six feet of vile earth is room enough for us. Naked came we into the world, and naked must we return unto the dust, and carry nothing with us. What is the difference between the rich and the poor in death? They both go unto one and the same place; the worm feeds sweetly on them both; it is but a short time, and you would not be able to distinguish between their bones.

But if the poor man sleeps in Jesus, while the rich man dies in his sins, oh, what a mighty gulf then is between them! The rich will take up his abode in that fire which is never quenched; the poor will awake to find he has an everlasting treasure in heaven, even eternal life. Eternal life! compared to which this world's concerns, weighty and important as they seem, are like a drop of water. Amazing indeed that men should trouble themselves about the things of earth, and sweat and toil after a little more gold and silver, and spend their strength upon these frail, sickly bodies of ours, to get enjoyment for them, and yet remain careless and dead and frozen about the life of that precious talent the soul!

But about eternal life? "I," says the Lord Jesus Christ, "do give it to my people." Who says this? He says it who bought and paid the full price; He who has in His hands the keys of death and hell; He who opens and no man shuts, He who shuts and no man opens; He says it who is the Amen, the faithful and true Witness, who is not a man that He should lie, who never breaks His promise; He says it who has a right to say it, for He came down to do His Father's will and die in our stead to obtain redemption for us, and when He declares "I give eternal life," death and hell must be silent, none can gainsay Him.

"I give," He declares, "eternal life." He does not speak after the fashion of the world; this world is cold, and calculating and heartless; there is little giving—it is all bargaining and sell-ing and paying what is the value of things. Blessed be God, the Lord Jesus does not deal with sinners as they deal with each other. He gives eternal life *freely*, and of grace, and for nothing, without money and without price. He does not give it because we are worthy or deserving, nor yet because we shall show ourselves worthy and deserving—but He gives it as a free gift, because He loves us and has set His affection upon us.

Consider with yourselves how glorious that doctrine is; how thoroughly it takes away all excuse from the impenitent. Pardon and forgiveness are here unconditionally bestowed; we are not told that we must pay off so much every day, and then shall be saved—that would drive us to doubt and despair—but if a man will only hear Christ's voice and follow Him, "Behold "says Jesus, "I give unto him eternal life, there remains no condemnation for him."

III. The third promise in my text is as follows: Jesus says of His sheep, "**They shall nev-er perish**!" They shall never be finally cast away, if they have once been sealed and numbered in my flock. They may have many a slip and many a fall, they may experience many a short-coming and many a backsliding—but they shall never be lost eternally, they shall be kept by the power of God through faith unto salvation. Where are those fearful Christians, who think they may be Christ's sheep and yet come short at last? Behold the assurance of Him who cannot lie, "they shall never perish!"

Yes! true Christians shall never perish! Is not that great work begun within their hearts by the Holy Spirit? Has not the power of God Himself been employed in converting them from darkness to light? And shall we dare say that God will take in hand the smallest thing, and yet leave it unfinished and not bring it to perfection? Have they not been born again of incor-ruptible seed, and shall this seed be choked and bear no fruit? Have they not been made by grace new creatures, and is it possible that grace can have raised them to newness of life in vain? Where in the whole world can you find a work which the Lord has attempted, and yet been obliged to give up and leave all incomplete? Then far be it from us to suppose that a true believer can ever be cast away! If man had any share in his conversion one might reason-ably doubt—but it is not so, it is the work of God, and what He does shall always be brought to perfection. The building which the Holy Spirit has founded shall never be allowed to de-cay, it shall never be left half finished, and the top-stone shall certainly be one day laid on with shouting.

True Christians shall never perish. Are they not Christ's special property, the servants of His house, the members of His family, the children of His adoption? Then surely He will never let them be overthrown. He will watch them as tenderly as we watch over our own flesh and blood. He will guard them as we guard our valuable and precious possessions. He will cherish them as we cherish that which is most dear to our hearts. He never would have laid down His life for their sakes if He had intended to give them up.

"Never perish!" Kings of the earth and mighty men shall depart and be no more seen; thrones and dominions and principalities, rich men and honorable men shall be swept into the tomb—but the humblest Christian cottager shall never see death everlasting, and when the heavens shall pass away as a scroll, and earth shall be burned up, that man shall be found to have a house not made with hands, eternal in the heavens. That man may be poor in this world and lightly esteemed—but I see in him one who shall be a glorious saint, when those who perchance had more of this life's good things shall be in torment; I am confident that nothing shall ever separate him from the love of Christ. He may have his doubts—but I know he is provided for, he shall never be lost.

IV. There remains one thing more. Jesus adds, "**Neither shall any man pluck them out of my hand.**" There is assurance upon assurance, that none may have an excuse for doubting. There is always something plucking at Christ's sheep: the lust of the flesh, the lust of the eyes, the pride of life, the devil, and the world are ever striving hard to destroy them—but they shall not succeed! Do you think the devil will give up his kingdom without a mighty struggle? Oh no, he goes about as a roaring lion seeking whom he may devour; he wars a constant warfare with all who keep the commandments of God and have the testimony of Jesus Christ—but the word of God is pledged that he shall never prevail. Not all the powers of darkness shall avail to quench one single spark of real gospel faith.

And now, beloved, in **CONCLUSION**, let me speak a word of exhortation to all among you who hear Christ's voice and follow Him. O that the Spirit may come down among you, and add to your number a hundredfold! Are you indeed Christ's sheep? Can you feel within yourselves the working of His blessed Spirit, mortifying the works of the flesh, and drawing up your minds to heavenly things? Have you the witness in yourselves that you have gone through a real spiritual change, that you hate the sins which once you loved, and love the things which once you despised? Have you good reason to believe that you have indeed put off the old man with his deeds, and put on the new man with the lamb-like nature of your blessed Master? Then, oh, rejoice with joy unspeakable and full of glory! Pray that you may not stand still—but go on from grace to grace and strength to strength; pray that you may bear much spiritual fruit, for thus is your Father glorified, and then will you make your own calling and election sure to yourselves.

Are you indeed Christ's sheep? *Then beware of ever trusting to yourselves;* nothing offends the Good Shepherd more than to see the members of His flock, forgetting that in Him alone is all their safety, and glorying in their own attainments and performances. Think not of your weak endeavors; think not to say, "I do very little, and therefore have very little hope—by-and-by I trust I shall do much, and then I shall have much hope"; your best performances and attempts towards heaven are in themselves but broken reeds, and can bear no weight; they are precious as evidences of spiritual life—but they cannot justify. Think only of your Savior Jesus Christ, trust Him entirely, love Him affectionately, look to Him continually. As long as you lean on Him you are strong and none can touch you. Without Him and in your own might, you are weak and unstable as water.

Are you indeed Christ's sheep? *Then beware of wandering from the pasture He has provided.* The devil and the old Adam would often persuade you there is no need for this diligence in using means of grace: "Surely," they will say, "you are not such a babe but you can leave these fields for a short season; surely you need not keep so closely in your Shepherd's sight." Christian, take heed and beware of the charmer, charm he ever so wisely. Diligent private prayer, diligent Scripture searching, diligent gospel hearing—these are the pastures in which Jesus feeds His flock, and if you turn aside, if you become slack in using them, be sure your soul will soon starve for lack of its accustomed nourishment, and you will return to the fold weak and lame and lean and diseased.

Once more, and I have done. Are you indeed Christ's sheep? *then be sure you will have many a trial,*where indeed would be the value of a Savior, if there were not enemies to be saved from? Yes! you will have many a trial! **Satan** has great wrath against all who have escaped his snares, and he will bring every weapon to bear against your peace; he will start many a doubt within your mind, he will stir up many a vile and blasphemous imagination within the chambers of your heart, many a horrid thought you once would have believed impossible—but still remember those words, "never perish." Yes! you will have many a trial!

When did the ungodly **world** ever patronise and encourage a true Christian? Oh no, the world will mock and despise, and laugh and frighten, and misrepresent you, and spread false reports, and throw traps in your way, and if it dares it will persecute you.

And then there is the **flesh**, sleepy and drowsy and fond of excuses, always trying to make you believe you have more difficulties than anybody else, deceitful, treacherous, needing constant watchfulness—but still the world and the flesh can never turn you back, except you are a graceless traitor. Remember those blessed words "never perish." Christian, you may be perplexed—but you never need despair; you may be persecuted but you are not forsaken, cast down but not destroyed; you may have tribulation—but you shall not have condemnation; you shall be saved from your enemies and from the hand of all who hate you. Fear none of these things which you shall suffer; be faithful unto death, and your Good Shepherd shall give you a crown of life.

Verily He is gone before to prepare a place for those whom He knows, and where He is in glory there they shall be also. "What then shall we say about these things? If God is for us, who can be against us? He who didn't spare his own Son, but delivered him up for us all, how would he not also with him freely give us all things? Who could bring a charge against God's chosen ones? It is God who justifies. Who is he who condemns? It is Christ who died, yes rather, who was raised from the dead, who is at the right hand of God, who also makes intercession for us. Who shall separate us from the love of Christ? Could oppression, or anguish, or persecution, or famine, or nakedness, or peril, or sword? Even as it is written, "For your sake we are killed all day long. We were accounted as sheep for the slaughter." No, in all these things, we are more than conquerors through him who loved us. For I am persuaded, that neither death, nor life, nor angels, nor principalities, nor things present, nor things to come, nor powers, nor height, nor depth, nor any other created thing—will be able to separate us from the love of God, which is in Christ Jesus our Lord." (Romans 8:31-39)

GOSPEL TREASURES!

I am sure this paper will be read by some one who feels that his sins are not yet forgiven. Reader, are you that man?

My heart's desire and prayer to God is that you may seek forgiveness without delay. There is forgiveness in Jesus Christ for every one that is willing to receive it. There is every encouragement that your soul can need, to confess your sins and lay hold on this forgiveness this very day.

Reader, listen to me while I try to exhibit to you the treasure of Gospel forgiveness. I cannot describe its fullness as I ought. Its riches are indeed unsearchable (Eph. iii. 8). But if you will turn away from it you shall not be able to say in the day judgment, you did not at all know what it was.

Consider, then, for one thing, that the forgiveness set before you is **a great and broad forgiveness**. Hear what the Prince of Peace Himself declares: "All sins shall be forgiven unto the sons of men, and blasphemies with which soever they shall blaspheme" (Mark iii. 28); "Though your sins be as scarlet, they shall become as white as snow; though they be red like crimson, they shall be as wool" (Isaiah i. 18). Yes! though your trespasses be more in number than the hairs of your head, the stars in heaven, the leaves of the forest, the blades of grass, the grains of sand on the sea shore, still they can all be pardoned. As the waters of Noah's flood covered over and hid the tops of the highest hills, so can the blood of Jesus cover over and hide your mightiest sins. "His blood cleanses from all sin" (1 John i. 7). Though to you they seem written with the point of a diamond, they can all be effaced from the book of God's remembrance by that precious blood. Paul names a long list of abominations which the Corinthians had committed, and then says: "Such were some of you: but you are washed" (1 Cor. vi. 11).

Furthermore, it is **a full and complete forgiveness**. It is not like David's pardon to Absalom—a permission to return home, but not a full restoration to favor (2 Sam. xiv. 24). It is not, as some fancy, a mere letting off, and letting alone. It is a pardon so complete, that he who has it is reckoned as righteous as if he had never sinned at all. His iniquities are blotted out. They are removed from him as far as the east from the west (Psalm ciii. 12). There remains no condemnation for him. The Father sees him joined to Christ, and is well pleased. The Son beholds him clothed with His own righteousness, and says, "You are all fair, . . . there is no spot in you" (Cant. iv. 7). Blessed be God that it is so. I verily believe if the best of us all had only one blot left for himself to wipe out, he would miss eternal life. If the holiest child of Adam were in heaven all but his little finger, and to get in depended on himself, I am sure he would never enter the kingdom. If Noah, Daniel, and Job had had but one day's sin to wash away, they would never have been saved. Praised be God that in the matter of our pardon there is nothing left for man to do. Jesus does all, and man has only to hold out an empty hand and to receive.

Furthermore, it is **a free and unconditional forgiveness**. It is not burdened with an "if," like Solomon's pardon to Adonijah: "If he will show himself a worthy man (1 Kings i. 52). Nor yet are you obliged to carry a price in your hand, or bring a character with you to prove yourself deserving of mercy. Jesus requires but one character, and that is that you should feel yourself a sinful, bad man. He invites you to "buy wine and milk without money and without price," and declares, "Whoever will, let him take the water of life freely" (Isaiah lv. 1; Rev xxii. 17) Like David in the cave of Adullam, He receives everyone that feels in distress and a debtor, and rejects none (1 Sam. xxii. 2). Are you a sinner? Do you want a Savior? Then come to Jesus just as you are, and your soul shall live.

Again, it is **an offered forgiveness**. I have read of earthly kings who knew not how to show mercy—of Henry the Eighth of England, who spared neither man nor woman; of James the Fifth of Scotland, who would never show favor to a Douglas. The King of kings is not like them. He calls on man to come to Him, and be pardoned. "Unto you, O men, I call; and my voice is to the sons of men" (Prov. viii. 4). "Ho, every one that thists, come you to the waters" (Isaiah iv. 1) "If any man thirst, let him come unto Me and drink" (John vii. 37). "Come unto Me, all you that labor and are heavy laden, and I will give you rest" (Matt. xi. 28). Oh, reader, it ought to be a great comfort to you and me to hear of any pardon at all; but to hear Jesus Himself inviting us, to see Jesus Himself holding out His hand to us—the Savior seeking the sinner before the sinner seeks the Savior—this is encouragement, this is strong consolation indeed!

Again, it is **a willing forgiveness**. I have heard of pardons granted in reply to long entreaty, and wrung out by much importunity. King Edward the Third of England would not spare the citizens of Calais until they came to him with halters round their necks, and his own Queen interceded for them on her knees. But Jesus is "good and ready to forgive" (Psalm lxxxvi. 5). He delights in mercy (Micah vii.18) Judgment is His *strange* work. He is not willing that any should perish (2 Peter iii. 9). He would sincerely have all men saved, and come to the knowledge of the truth (1 Tim. ii. 4) He wept over unbelieving Jerusalem. "As I live;" He says, "I have no pleasure in the death of the wicked. Turn, turn, from your evil ways: why will you die?" (Ezek. xxxiii. 11). Ah, reader, you and I may well come boldly to the throne of grace! He who sits there is far more willing and ready to give mercy than you and I are to receive it.

Besides this, it is **a tried forgiveness**. Thousands and tens of thousands have sought for pardon at the mercy-seat of Christ, and not one has ever returned to say that he sought in vain; sinners of every name and nation—sinners of every sort and description, have knocked at the door of the fold, and none have ever been refused admission. Zaccheus the extortioner, Magdalene the harlot, Saul the persecutor, Peter the denier of his Lord, the Jews who crucified the Prince of Life, the idolatrous Athenians, the adulterous Corinthians, the ignorant Africans, the bloodthirsty New Zealanders—all have ventured their souls on Christ's promises of pardon, and none have ever found them fail. Ah, reader, if the way I set before you were a new and untraveled way, you might well feel faint-hearted! But it is not so. It is an old path. It is a path worn by the feet of many pilgrims, and a path in which the footsteps are all one way. The treasury of Christ's mercies has never been found empty. The well of living waters has never proved dry.

Beside this, it is **a present forgiveness**. All who believe in Jesus are at once justified from all things (Acts xiii. 38). The very day the younger son returned to his father's house he was clothed with the best robe, had the ring put on his hand, and shoes on his feet (Luke xv.). The very day Zaccheus received Jesus he heard these comfortable words "This day is salvation come to this house" (Luke xix. 9). The very day that David said, "I have sinned against the Lord," he was told by Nathan, "The Lord has also put away your sin" (2 Sam. xii. 13). The very day you first flee to Christ, your sins are all removed. Your pardon is not a thing far away, to be obtained only after many years. It is near at hand. It is close to you, within your reach, all ready to be bestowed. Believe, and that very moment it is your own. "He who believes is not condemned" (John iii. 18). It is not said, "he shall not be," or "will not be," but "is not." From the time of his believing, condemnation is gone. "He that believes has everlasting life" (John iii. 36). It is not said, "he shall have," or "will have," it is "has" It is his own as surely as if he was in heaven, though not so evidently so to his own eyes. Ah, reader, you must not think forgiveness will be nearer to a believer in the day of judgment than it was in the hour he first believed! His complete salvation from the power of sin is every year nearer and nearer to him; but as to his forgiveness and justification, it is a finished work from the very minute he first commits himself to Christ.

Last, and best of all, it is **an everlasting forgiveness**. It is not like Shimei's pardon, a pardon that may sometime be revoked and taken away (1 Kings ii. 9). Once justified you are justified forever. Once written down in the book of life, your name shall never be blotted out. The sins of God's children are said to be cast into the depths of the sea—to be sought for and not found—to be remembered no more—to be cast behind God's back (Mic. vii. 19; Jer. 1. 20; xxxi. 34; Isaiah xxxviii. 17). Some people fancy they may be justified one year and condemned another—children of adoption at one time and strangers by and by—heirs of the kingdom in the beginning of their days, and yet servants of the devil in their end. I cannot find this in the Bible. As the New Zealander told the Romish priest, "I do not see it in the Book." It seems to me to overturn the good news of the Gospel altogether, and to tear up its comforts by the roots. I believe the salvation Jesus offers is an everlasting salvation, and a pardon once sealed with His blood shall never be reversed.

Reader, I have set before you the nature of the forgiveness offered to you. I have told you but little of it, for my words are weaker than my will. The half of it remains untold. The greatness of it is far more than any report of mine. But I think I have said enough to show you it is worth the seeking, and I can wish you nothing better than that you may strive to make it your own.

SIMPLICITY IN PREACHING

King Solomon says, in the book of Ecclesiastes, **"Of making many books there is no end"** (12:12). There are few subjects about which that saying is more true than that of preaching. The volumes which have been written in order to show ministers how to preach are enough to make a small library. In sending forth one more little treatise, I only propose to touch one branch of the subject. I do not pretend to consider what should be the substance and matter of a sermon. I purposely leave alone such points as "gravity, unction, liveliness, warmth," and the like, or the comparative merits of written or extemporaneous sermons. I wish to confine myself to one point, which receives far less attention than it deserves. That point is **simplicity in language and style**.

I ought to be able to tell my readers something about "simplicity," if experience will give any help. I began preaching forty-five years ago, when I first took orders in a poor rural parish, and a great portion of my ministerial life has been spent in preaching to laborers and farmers. I know the enormous difficulty of preaching to such hearers, of making them understand one's meaning, and securing their attention. So far as concerns language and composition, I deliberately say that I would rather preach before the University at Oxford or Cambridge, or the Temple, or Lincoln's Inn, or the Houses of Parliament, than I would address an agricultural congregation on a fine hot afternoon in the month of August. I have heard of a laborer who enjoyed Sunday more than any other day in the week, "Because," he said, "I sit comfortably in church, put up my legs, have nothing to think about, and just go to sleep." Some of my younger friends in the ministry may some day be called to preach to such congregations as I have had, and I shall be glad if they can profit by my experience.

Before entering on the subject, I wish to clear the way by making **four prefatory remarks**.

1. For one thing, I ask all my readers to remember that **to attain simplicity in preaching is of the utmost importance to every minister who wishes to be useful to souls**. Unless you are simple in your sermons you will never be understood, and unless you are understood you cannot do good to those who hear you. It was a true saying of Quintilian, "If you do not wish to be understood, you deserve to be neglected." Of course the first object of a minister should be to preach the truth, the whole truth, and nothing but "the truth as it is in Jesus." But the next thing he ought to aim at is, that his sermon may be understood; and it will not be understood by most of his hearers if it is not simple.

2. The next thing I will say, by way of prefatory remark, is, that **to attain simplicity in preaching is by no means an easy matter**. No greater mistake can be made than to suppose this. "To make hard things seem hard," to use the substance of a saying of Archbishop Usher's, "is within the reach of all, but to make hard things seem easy and intelligible is a height attained by very few speakers." One of the wisest and best of the Puritans said two hundred years ago, "that the greater part of preachers shoot over the heads of the people." This is true also in 1837! I fear a vast proportion of what we preach is not understood by our

hearers any more than if it were Greek. When people hear a simple sermon, or read a simple tract, they are apt to say, "How true! how plain! how easy to understand!" and to suppose that any one can write in that style. Allow me to tell my readers that **it is an extremely difficult thing to write simple, clear, perspicuous, and forcible English**. Look at the sermons of Charles Bradley, of Clapham. A sermon of his reads most beautifully. It is so simple and natural, that anyone feels at once that the meaning is as clear as the sun at noonday.**Every word is the right word, and every word is in its right place.** Yet the labor those sermons cost Mr. Bradley was very great indeed. Those who have read Goldsmith's Vicar of Wakefield attentively, can hardly fail to have noticed the exquisite naturalness, ease, and simplicity of its language. And yet it is known that the pains and trouble and time bestowed upon that work were immense. Let the Vicar of Wakefield be compared with Johnson's Rasselas, which was written off in a few days, it is said, under higher pressure—and the difference is at once apparent. In fact, to use very long words, to seem very learned, to make people go away after a sermon saying, "How fine! how clever! how grand!" all this is very easy work. But to write what will strike and stick, to speak or to write that which at once pleases and is understood, and becomes assimilated with a hearer's mind and a thing never forgotten—that, we may depend upon it, is a very difficult thing and a very rare attainment.

3. Let me observe, in the next place, that when I talk of simplicity in preaching, **I would not have my readers suppose I mean childish preaching**. If we suppose the poor like that sort of sermon, we are greatly mistaken. If our hearers once imagine we consider them a parcel of ignorant folks for whom any kind of "infant's food" is good enough, our chance of doing good is lost altogether. People do not like even the appearance of 'condescending preaching'. They feel we are not treating them as equals, but inferiors. Human nature always dislikes that. They will at once put up their backs, stop their ears, and take offence—and then we might as well preach to the winds.

4. Finally, let me observe, that **it is not coarse or vulgar preaching that is needed**. It is quite possible to be simple, and yet to speak like a gentleman, and with the demeanor of a courteous and refined person. It is an utter mistake to imagine that uneducated and illiterate men and women prefer to be spoken to in an illiterate way, and by an uneducated person. To suppose that a lay-evangelist or Scripture-reader, who knows nothing of Latin or Greek, and is only familiar with his Bible, is more acceptable than an Oxford first-class man, or a Cambridge wrangler (if that first-class man knows how to preach), is a complete error. People only tolerate vulgarity and coarseness, as a rule, when they can get nothing else.

Having made these prefatory remarks in order to clear the way, I will now proceed to give my readers **five brief hints as to what seems to me the best method of attaining simplicity in preaching**.

1. My first hint is this—If you want to attain simplicity in preaching, **take care that you have a clear view of the subjectupon which you are going to preach.** I ask your special attention to this. Of all the five hints I am about to give, this is the most important. Mind, then, when your text is chosen, that you understand it and see right through it; that you know precisely what you want to prove, what you want to teach, what you want to establish, and what you want people's minds to carry away. **If you yourself begin in a fog, you may depend upon it you will leave your people in darkness.** Cicero, one of the greatest ancient orators, said long ago, "No one can possibly speak clearly and eloquently about a subject which he does not understand"—and I am satisfied that he spoke the truth. Archbishop Whately was a very shrewd observer of human nature, and he said rightly of a vast number of preachers, that "they aimed at nothing, and they hit nothing. Like men landing on an un-

known island, and setting out on a journey of exploration, they set out in ignorance, and traveled on in ignorance all the day long."

I ask all young ministers especially, to remember this first hint. I repeat most emphatically—"Take care you thoroughly understand your subject. Never choose a text of which you do not quite know what it means." Beware of taking obscure passages such as those which are to be found in unfulfilled and emblematic prophecies. If a man will continually preach to an ordinary congregation about the seals and vials and trumpets in Revelation, or about Ezekiel's temple, or about predestination, free will, and the eternal purposes of God—it will not be at all surprising to any reasonable mind if he fails to attain simplicity. I do not mean that these subjects ought not to be handled occasionally, at fit times, and before a suitable audience. All I say is, that **they are very deep subjects, about which wise Christians often disagree, and it is almost impossible to make them very simple**. We ought to see our subjects plainly, if we wish to make them simple, and there are hundreds of plain subjects to be found in God's Word.

Beware, for the same reason, of taking up what I call "fanciful subjects" and "**spiritualizing texts**"—and then dragging out of them meanings which the Holy Spirit never intended to put into them. There is no subject needful for the soul's health which is not to be found plainly taught and set forth in Scripture. This being the case, I think a preacher should never take a text and extract from it, as a dentist would a tooth from the jaw, something which, however true in itself, is not the plain literal meaning of the inspired words. The sermon may seem very glittering and ingenious, and his people may go away saying, "What a clever parson we have got!" But if, on examination, they can neither find the sermon in the text, nor the text in the sermon, their minds are perplexed, and they begin to think the Bible is a deep book which cannot be understood. If you want to attain simplicity, beware of spiritualizing texts.

When I speak of spiritualizing texts, let me explain what I mean. I remember hearing of a minister in a northern town, who was famous for preaching in this style. Once he gave out for his text, "He who is so impoverished that he has no oblation, chooses unto him a tree that will not rot" (Isa. 40:20). "Here," said he, "is man by nature impoverished and undone. He has nothing to offer, in order to make satisfaction for his soul. And what ought he to do? He ought to choose a tree which cannot rot—even the cross of our Lord Jesus Christ."

On another occasion, being anxious to preach on the doctrine of indwelling sin, he chose his text out of the history of Joseph and his brethren, and gave out the words, "The old man of whom you spoke, is he yet alive?" (Gen. 43:27). Out of this question he ingeniously twisted a discourse about the infection of nature remaining in the believer—a grand truth, no doubt, but certainly not the truth of the passage. Such instances will, I trust, be a warning to all my younger brethren. If you want to preach about the indwelling corruption of human nature, or about Christ crucified, you need not seek for such far-fetched texts as those I have named. If you want to be simple, **mind you choose plain simple texts!**

Furthermore, if you wish to see through your subjects thoroughly, and so to attain the foundation of simplicity, do not be ashamed of **dividing your sermons** and stating your divisions. I need hardly say this is a very vexed question. There is a morbid dread of "firstly, secondly, and thirdly" in many quarters. The stream of 'fashion' runs strongly against divisions, and I must frankly confess that a lively undivided sermon is much better than one divided in a dull, stupid, illogical way. Let every man be fully persuaded in his own mind. He who can preach sermons which strike and stick without divisions, by all means let him hold on his way and persevere. But let him not despise his neighbor who divides. All I say is—if we would be simple, there must be ORDER in a sermon as there is in an army. What wise general would mix up artillery, infantry, and cavalry in one confused mass in the day of battle? What giver of a banquet or dinner would dream of putting on the table the whole of the viands at once—the soup, the fish, the entrees, the meat, the salads, the sweets, the dessert, in one huge dish? Such a host would hardly be thought to serve his dinner well. Just so I say it is with sermons. By all means let there be **order**—order, whether you bring out your "firstly, secondly, or thirdly," or not—order, whether your divisions are concealed or expressed—order so carefully arranged that your points and ideas shall follow one another in beautiful regularity, like regiments marching past before the Queen on a review day in Windsor Park.

For my own part, I honestly confess that I do not think I have preached two sermons in my life without divisions. I find it of the utmost importance to make people understand, remember, and carry away what I say—and I am certain that divisions help me to do so. They are, in fact, like hooks and pegs and shelves in the mind. If you study the sermons of men who have been and are successful preachers, you will always find order, and often divisions, in their sermons. I am not a bit ashamed to say that I often read the sermons of Mr. **Spurgeon**. I like to gather hints about preaching from all quarters. David did not ask about the sword of Goliath—"Who made it? who polished it? what blacksmith forged it?" He said, "There is nothing like it"—for he had once used it to cut off its owner's head. Mr. Spurgeon can preach most ably, and he proves it by keeping his enormous congregation together. We ought always to examine and analyze sermons which draw people together. Now when you read Mr. Spurgeon's sermons, note how clearly and perspicuously he divides a sermon, and fills each division with beautiful and simple ideas. How easily you grasp his meaning! How thoroughly he brings before you certain great truths, that hang to you like hooks of steel, and which, once planted in your memory, you never forget!

My first point, then, if you would be simple in your preaching, is, that you must thoroughly understand your subject, and if you want to know whether you understand it, try to divide and arrange it. I can only say for myself; that I have done this ever since I have been a minister. For forty-five years I have kept note books in which I write down texts and heads of sermons for use when require. Whenever I get hold of a text, and see my way through it, I put it down and make a note of it. If I do not see my way through a text, I cannot preach on it, because I know I cannot be simple; and if I cannot be simple, I know I had better not preach at all

2. The second hint I would give is this—**Try to use in all your sermons, as far as you can—simple WORDS.** In saying this, however, I must explain myself. When I talk of simple words, I do not mean words of only one syllable, or words which are purely Saxon. I cannot in this matter agree with Archbishop Whately. I think he goes too far in his recommendation of Saxon, though there is much truth in what he says about it. I rather prefer the saying of that wise old heathen Cicero, when he said, that orators should try to use words which are "in daily common use" among the people. Whether the words are Saxon or not—or of two or three syllables. It does not matter so long as they are words commonly used and understood by the people. Only, whatever you do, beware of what the poor shrewdly call "dictionary" words, that is, of words which are abstract, or scientific, or pedantic, or complicated, or vague, or very long. They may seem very fine, and sound very grand, but they are rarely of any use. **The most powerful and forcible words, as a rule, are very short.**

Let me say one word more to confirm what I have stated about that common fallacy of the desirableness of always using Saxon English. I would remind you that a vast number of words of other than Saxon origin are used by writers of notorious simplicity. Take, for instance, the famous work of John Bunyan, and look at the very title of it—The Pilgrim's Progress. Neither of the leading words in that title is Saxon. Would he have improved matters if he had called it "The Wayfarer's Walk"? In saying this I admit freely that words of French and Latin origin are generally inferior to Saxon; and, as a rule, I would say—use strong pure Saxon words—if you can. All I mean to say is, that you must not think it a matter of course that words cannot be good and simple if they are not of Saxon origin. In any case, beware of long words.

Dr. Gee, in his excellent book, 'Our Sermons', very ably points out**the uselessness of using long words and expressions not in common use**. For example, he says, "Talk of happiness rather than of felicity; talk of almighty rather than omnipotent; forbidden rather than proscribed; hateful rather than noxious; afterwards rather than subsequently; call out and draw forth instead of evoke and educe." We all need to be pulled up sharply on these points. It is very well to use fine words at Oxford and Cambridge, before classical hearers, and in preaching before educated audiences. But depend upon it, when you preach to ordinary congregations, the sooner you throw overboard this sort of English, and use plain common words, the better. One thing, at all events, is quite certain,**without simple words you will never attain simplicity in preaching**.

3. The third hint I would offer, if you wish to attain simplicity in preaching, is this—**Take care to aim at a SIMPLE style of composition.** I will try to illustrate what I mean. If you take up the sermons preached by that great and wonderful man Dr. Chalmers, you can hardly fail to see what an enormous number of lines you meet with without coming to a full stop. This I regard as a great mistake. It may suit Scotland, but it will never do for England. If you would attain a simple style of composition, beware of writing many lines without coming to a pause, and so **allowing the minds of your hearers to take breath**. Beware of colons and semicolons. Stick to commas and full stops, and take care to write as if you were asthmatical or short of breath. Never write or speak very long sentences or long paragraphs. Use stops frequently, and start again—and the oftener you do this, the more likely you are to attain a simple style of composition. Enormous sentences full of colons, semicolons, and parentheses, with paragraphs of two or three pages' length, are utterly fatal to simplicity. We should bear in mind that preachers have to do with hearers and not readers, and that what will "read" well will not always "speak" well. A reader of English can always help himself by looking back a few lines and refreshing his mind. A hearer of English hears once for all, and if he loses the thread of your sermon in a long involved sentence, he very likely never finds it again.

Again, simplicity in your style of composition depends very much upon **the proper use of proverbs and pointed sentences**. This is of vast importance. Here, I think, is the value of much that you find in Matthew Henry's commentary, and Bishop Hall's Contemplations. There are some good sayings of this sort in a book not known so well as it should be, called 'Papers on Preaching'. Take a few examples of what I mean: "What we weave in time—we wear in eternity." "Hell is paved with good intentions." "Sin forsaken, is one of the best evidences of sin forgiven." "It matters little how we die—but it matters much how we live." "Meddle with no man's person—but spare no man's sin." "The street is soon clean when every one sweeps before his own door." "Lying rides on debt's back—it is hard for an empty bag to stand upright." "He who begins with prayer—will end with praise" "All is not gold that glitters." "In religion, as in business—there are no gains without pains." "In the Bible there are shallows where a lamb can wade—and depths where an elephant must swim." "One thief on the cross was saved, that none should despair—and only one, that none should presume."

Proverbial, pointed, and antithetical sayings of this kind give wonderful perspicuousness and force to a sermon. Labor to store your minds with them. Use them judiciously, and especially at the end of paragraphs, and you will find them an immense help to the attainment of a simple style of composition. But of long, involved, complicated sentences—always beware!

4. The fourth hint I will give is this: **If you wish to preach simply—use a DIRECT style.** What do I mean by this? I mean the practice and custom of saying "I" and "you." When a man takes up this style of preaching, he is often told that he is conceited and egotistical. The result is that many preachers are never direct—and always think it very humble and modest and becoming to say "we." But I remember good Bishop Villiers saying that "we" was a word kings and corporations should use, and they alone—but that parish clergymen should always talk of "I" and "you." I endorse that saying with all my heart. I declare I never can understand what the famous pulpit "we" means. Does the preacher who all through his sermon keeps saying "we" mean himself and the bishop? or himself and the Church? or himself and the congregation? or himself and the early Fathers? or himself and the Reformers? or himself and all the wise men in the world? or, after all, does he only mean myself, plain "John Smith" or "Thomas Jones"? If he only means himself, what earthly reason can he give for using the plural number, and not saying simply and plainly "I"? When he visits his parishioners, or sits by a sick-bed, or catechises his school, or orders bread at the baker's, or meat at the butcher's—he does not say "we," but "I." Why, then, I should like to know, can he not say "I" in the pulpit? What right has he, as a modest man, to speak for anyone but himself? Why not stand up on Sunday and say, "Reading in the Word of God, **I** have found a text containing such things as these, and I come to set them before you"?

Many people, I am sure, do not understand what the preacher's "we" means. The expression leaves them in a kind of fog. If you say, "**I**, the pastor of the parish, come here to talk of something that concerns your soul, something you should believe, something you should do"—you are at any rate understood. But if you begin to talk in the vague plural number of what" we" ought to do, many of your hearers do not know what you are driving at, and whether you are speaking to yourself or them. I charge and entreat my younger brethren in the ministry not to forget this point. **Do try to be as direct as possible.** Never mind what people say of you. In this particular do not imitate Chalmers, or Melville, or certain other living pulpit celebrities. Never say "we" when you mean "I." The more you get into the habit of talking plainly to the people, in the first person singular, as old Bishop Latimer did—the simpler will your sermon be, and the more easily understood. The glory of Whitefield's sermons is their directness. But unhappily they were so badly reported, that we cannot now appreciate them.

5. The fifth and last hint I wish to give you is this: **If you would attain simplicity in preaching, you must use plenty of anecdotes and illustrations.** You must regard illustrations as windows through which light is let in upon your subject. Upon this point a great deal might be said, but the limits of a small treatise oblige me to touch it very briefly. I need hardly remind you of the example of Him who "spoke as never any man spoke"—our Lord and Savior Jesus Christ. Study the four Gospels attentively, and mark what a wealth of illustrations His sermons generally contain. How often you find figure upon figure, parable upon parable, in His discourses! There was nothing under His eyes apparently from which He did not draw lessons. The birds of the air, and the fish in the sea, the sheep, the goats, the cornfield, the vineyard, the ploughman, the sower, the reaper, the fisherman, the shepherd, the

vinedresser, the woman kneading meal, the flowers, the grass, the bank, the wedding feast, the sepulcher—all were made vehicles for conveying thoughts to the minds of hearers. What are such parables as the prodigal son, the good Samaritan, the ten virgins, the king who made a marriage for his son, the rich man and Lazarus, the laborers of the vineyard, and others— what are all these but **stirring stories** that our Lord tells in order to convey some great truth to the souls of His hearers? Try to walk in His footsteps and follow His example.

If you pause in your sermon, and say, "Now I will tell you a story"—I pledge that all who are not too fast asleep will pick up their ears and listen. People like similes, illustrations, and well-told stories—and will listen to them when they will attend to nothing else. And from what countless sources we can get illustrations! Take all the book of **nature** around us. Look at the sky above and the world beneath. Look at history. Look at all the branches of**science**, at geology, at botany, at chemistry, at astronomy. What is there in heaven above or earth below from which you may not bring illustrations to throw light on the message of the gospel? Read Bishop Latimer's sermons, the most popular, perhaps, that were ever preached. Read the works of Brooks, and Watson, and Swinnock, the Puritans. How full they are of illustrations, figures, metaphors, and stories! Look at Mr. Moody's sermons. What is one secret of his popularity? He fills his sermons with pleasing stories.**He is the best speaker**, says an Arabian proverb, **who can turn the ear into an eye!**

For my part, I not only try to tell stories, but in country parishes I have sometimes put before people familiar **illustrations** which they can see. For instance—Do I want to show them that there must have been a first great cause or Being who made this world? I have sometimes taken out my watch, and have said, "Look at this watch. How well it is made! Do any of you suppose for a moment that all the screws, all the wheels, all the pins of that watch came together by accident? Would not any one say there must have been a watchmaker? And if so, it follows most surely that there must have been a Maker of the world, whose handiwork we see engraved on the face of every one of those glorious planets going their yearly rounds and keeping time to a single second. Look at the world in which you live, and the wonderful things which it contains. Will you tell me that there is no God, and that creation is the result of chance?" Or sometimes I have taken out a bunch of keys and shaken them. The whole congregation, when they hear the keys, look up. Then I say, "Would there be need of any keys if all men were perfect and honest? What does this bunch of keys show? Why, they show that the heart of man is deceitful above all things, and desperately wicked." **Illustration**, I confidently assert, is one of the best receipts for making a sermon simple, clear, perspicuous, and easily understood. Lay yourselves out for it. Pick up illustrations wherever you can. Keep your eyes open, and use them well. Happy is that preacher who has an eye for **similitudes**, and a memory stored with well-chosen stories and **illustrations**. If he is a real man of God, and knows how to deliver a sermon, he will never preach to bare walls and empty benches.

But I must add a word of caution. There is a proper way of telling stories. If a man cannot tell stories naturally—he had better **not** tell them at all. Illustration, again, after all I have said in its favor, may be carried too far. I remember a notable instance of this in the case of the great Welsh preacher, Christmas Evans. There is in print a sermon of his about the wonderful miracle that took place in Gadara, when devils took possession of the swine, and the whole herd ran down violently into the sea. He paints it so minutely that it really becomes ludicrous by reason of the words put in the mouth of the swine-herders who told their master of the loss he had sustained. "Oh! sir," says one, "the pigs have all gone!" "But," says the master, "where have they gone?" "They have run down into the sea." "But who drove them down?" "Oh! sir, that wonderful man." "Well, what sort of a man was he? What did he do?" "Why, sir, he came and talked such strange things, and the whole herd ran suddenly down the steep place into the sea." "What, the old black boar and all?" "Yes, sir, the old black boar has gone too; for as we looked round, we just saw the end of his tail going over the cliff." Now that is going to an extreme. So, again, Dr. Guthrie's admirable sermons are occasionally so overlaid with illustrations as to remind one of cake made almost entirely of plums and containing hardly any flour. Put plenty of color and picture into your sermon by all means. Draw sweetness and light from all sources and from all creatures—from the heavens and the earth, from history, from science. But after all there is a limit. You must be careful how you use color—lest you do as much harm as good. Do not put on color by **spoonfuls**, but with a **brush**. This caution remembered, you will find color an immense aid in the attainment of simplicity and perspicuousness in preaching.

And now bear in mind that my five points are these—

1. If you want to attain simplicity in preaching, you must **have a clear knowledge of what you are going to preach**.

2. If you would attain simplicity in preaching, you must **use simple words**.

3. If you would attain simplicity in preaching, you must **seek to acquire a simple style of composition**, with short sentences and as few colons and semicolons as possible.

4. If you would attain simplicity in preaching, **aim at directness**.

5. If you would attain simplicity in preaching, **make abundant use of illustration and anecdote**.

Let me add to all this one plain word of **APPLICATION**. You will never attain simplicity in preaching without **plenty of work**—pains and trouble, I say emphatically, pains and trouble. When Turner, the great painter, was asked by some one how it was he mixed his colors so well, and what it was that made them so different from those of other artists—"Mix them? mix them? mix them? Why, with brains, sir." I am persuaded that, in preaching,**little can be done except by trouble and by pains.**

I have heard that a young and careless clergyman once said to Richard Cecil, "I think I need more faith." "No," said the wise old man—"you need more work. You need more pains. You must not think that God will do work for you—though He is ready to do it by you." I entreat my younger brethren to remember this. I beg them to make time for their composition of sermons, to take trouble and to exercise their brains by reading. Only mind that you read what is useful.

I would not have you spend your time in reading the early church Fathers in order to help your preaching. They are very useful in their way, but there are many things more useful in modern writers, if you choose them discreetly.

Read good models, and become familiar with good specimens of simplicity in preaching. As your best model, take the English Bible. If you speak the language in which that is written, you will speak well. Read John Bunyan's immortal work, the Pilgrim's progress. Read it again and again, if you wish to attain simplicity in preaching. Do not be above reading the Puritans. Some of them no doubt are heavy. Goodwin and Owen are very heavy, though excellent artillery in position. Read such books as Baxter, and Watson, and Traill, and Flavel, and Charnock, and Hall, and Henry. They are, to my mind, models of the best simple English spoken in old times. Remember, however, that language alters with years. They spoke English, and so do we, but their style was different from ours. Read beside them the best models of modern English that you can get at. I believe the best English writer for the last hundred years was William Cobbett, the political Radical. I think he wrote the finest simple Saxon-

English the world has ever seen. In the present day I do not know a greater master of tersely spoken Saxon-English than John Bright. Among old political orators, the speeches of Lord Chatham and Patrick Henry, the American, are models of good English. Last, but not least, never forget that, next to the Bible, there is nothing in the English language which, for combined simplicity, perspicuousness, eloquence, and power, can be compared with some of the great speeches in Shakespeare. Models of this sort must really be studied, and studied "with brains," too, if you wish to attain a good style of composition in preaching. On the other hand, do not be above talking to the poor, and visiting your people from house to house. Sit down with your people by the fireside, and exchange thoughts with them on all subjects. Find out how they think and how they express themselves, if you want them to understand your sermons. By so doing you will insensibly learn much. You will be continually picking up modes of thought, and get notions as to what you should say in your pulpit.

A humble country clergyman was once asked "whether he studied the fathers." The worthy man replied, that he had little opportunity of studying the fathers, as they were generally out in the fields when he called. But he studied the mothers more, because he often found them at home—and he could talk to them.

Wittingly or unwittingly, the good man hit a nail right on the head. We must talk to our people when we are out of church—if we would understand how to preach to them in the church.

1. I will only say, in CONCLUSION, that whatever we preach, or whatever pulpit we occupy, whether we preach simply or not, whether we preach written or extempore, we ought to aim not merely at letting off fireworks, but at **preaching that which will do lasting good to souls!** Let us beware of fireworks in our preaching. "Beautiful" sermons, "brilliant" sermons, "clever" sermons, "popular" sermons, are often sermons which have no effect on the congregation, and do not draw men to Jesus Christ. Let us aim so to preach, that what we say may really come home to men's minds and consciences and hearts, and make them think and consider.

2. All the simplicity in the world can do no good, unless you **preach the simple gospel of Jesus Christ so fully and clearly that everybody can understand it.** If 'Christ crucified' has not His rightful place in your sermons, and 'sin' is not exposed as it should be, and your people are not plainly told what they ought to believe, and be, and do—**your preaching is of no use!**

3. All the simplicity in the world, again, is useless without **a good lively delivery**. If you bury your head in your bosom, and mumble over your manuscript in a dull, monotonous, droning way, like a bee in a bottle, so that people cannot understand what you are speaking about—your preaching will be in vain. Depend upon it, delivery is not sufficiently attended to in our Church. In this, as in everything else connected with the science of preaching, I consider the Church of England is sadly deficient. I know that I began preaching alone in the New Forest, and nobody ever told me what was right or wrong in the pulpit. The result was that the first year of my preaching was a series of experiments. We get no help in these matters at Oxford and Cambridge. The utter lack of any proper training for the pulpit is one great blot and defect in the system of the Church of England.

4. Above all, let us never forget that all the simplicity in the world is useless without **prayer for the outpouring of the Holy Spirit**, and the grant of God's blessing, and a life corresponding in some measure to what we preach. Be it ours to have an earnest desire for the souls of men, while we seek for simplicity in preaching the gospel of Jesus Christ, and let us never forget to accompany our sermons by holy living and fervent prayer!

Also from Benediction Books ...
Wandering Between Two Worlds: Essays on Faith and Art
Anita Mathias
Benediction Books, 2007
152 pages
ISBN: 0955373700

Available from www.amazon.com, www.amazon.co.uk

In these wide-ranging lyrical essays, Anita Mathias writes, in lush, lovely prose, of her naughty Catholic childhood in Jamshedpur, India; her large, eccentric family in Mangalore, a sea-coast town converted by the Portuguese in the sixteenth century; her rebellion and atheism as a teenager in her Himalayan boarding school, run by German missionary nuns, St. Mary's Convent, Nainital; and her abrupt religious conversion after which she entered Mother Teresa's convent in Calcutta as a novice. Later rich, elegant essays explore the dualities of her life as a writer, mother, and Christian in the United States-- Domesticity and Art, Writing and Prayer, and the experience of being "an alien and stranger" as an immigrant in America, sensing the need for roots.

About the Author

Anita Mathias is the author of *Wandering Between Two Worlds: Essays on Faith and Art.* She has a B.A. and M.A. in English from Somerville College, Oxford University, and an M.A. in Creative Writing from the Ohio State University, USA. Anita won a National Endowment of the Arts fellowship in Creative Nonfiction in 1997. She lives in Oxford, England with her husband, Roy, and her daughters, Zoe and Irene.

Visit Anita at http://www.anitamathias.com.

The Church Thad Had Too Much
Anita Mathias
Benediction Books, 2010
52 pages
ISBN: 9781849026567

Available from www.amazon.com, www.amazon.co.uk

The Church That Had Too Much was very well-intentioned. She wanted to love God, she wanted to love people, but she was both hampered by her muchness and the abundance of her possessions, and beset by ambition, power struggles and snobbery. Read about the surprising way The Church That Had Too Much began to resolve her problems in this deceptively simple and enchanting fable.

About the Author

Anita Mathias is the author of *Wandering Between Two Worlds: Essays on Faith and Art.* She has a B.A. and M.A. in English from Somerville College, Oxford University, and an M.A. in Creative Writing from the Ohio State University, USA. Anita won a National Endowment of the Arts fellowship in Creative Nonfiction in 1997. She lives in Oxford, England with her husband, Roy, and her daughters, Zoe and Irene.

Visit Anita at http://www.anitamathias.com

Francesco, Artist of Florence: The Man Who Gave Too Much
Anita Mathias
Benediction Books, 2014
52 pages (full colour)
ISBN: 978-1781394175

In this lavishly illustrated book by Anita Mathias, Francesco, artist of Florence, creates magic in pietre dure, inlaying precious stones in marble in life-like "paintings." While he works, placing lapis lazuli birds on clocks, and jade dragonflies on vases, he is purely happy. However, he must sell his art to support his family. Francesco, who is incorrigibly soft-hearted, cannot stand up to his haggling customers. He ends up almost giving away an exquisite jewellery box to Signora Farnese's bambina, who stands, captivated, gazing at a jade parrot nibbling a cherry. Signora Stallardi uses her daughter's wedding to cajole him into discounting his rainbowed marriage chest. His old friend Girolamo bullies him into letting him have the opulent table he hoped to sell to the Medici almost at cost. Carrara is raising the price of marble; the price of gems keeps rising. His wife is in despair. Francesco fears ruin.

* * *

Sitting in the church of Santa Maria Novella at Mass, very worried, Francesco hears the words of Christ. The lilies of the field and the birds of the air do not worry, yet their Heavenly Father looks after them. As He will look after us. He resolves not to worry. And as he repeats the prayer the Saviour taught us, Francesco resolves to forgive the friends and neighbours who repeatedly put their own interests above his. But can he forgive himself for his own weakness, as he waits for the eternal city of gold whose walls are made of jasper, whose gates are made of pearls, and whose foundations are sapphire, emerald, ruby and amethyst? There time and money shall be no more, the lion shall live with the lamb, and we shall dwell trustfully together. Francesco leaves Santa Maria Novella, resolving to trust the One who told him to live like the lilies and the birds, deciding to forgive those who haggled him into bad bargains--while making a little resolution for the future